1959 The first psychotherapy benefit in a pre-paid insurance plan appears.

1965 Chicago Training Conference.

1968 Psy.D. training program begins at the University of Illinois, Urbana-Champaign.

Second edition of *Diagnostic and Statistical Manual (DSM–II)* published.

Committee on Health Insurance begins campaign to allow payment of clinical psychologists' services by health insurance plans without requiring medical supervision.

1969 California School of Professional Psychology founded.

APA begins publication of journal, *Professional Psychology*.

1970 Department of Defense health insurance program authorizes payment of clinical psychologists' services without medical referral.

Classes begin at California School of Professional Psychology, the first independent clinical psychology training program in the U.S.

1971 Council for the Advancement of Psycological Professions and Sciences, a political advocacy group for clinical psychology, is organized.

Journal of Child Clinical Psychology published.

1972 Menninger Conference on Postdoctoral Education in Clinical Psychology.

1973 Vail, Colorado, Training Conference.

1974 National Register of Health Service Providers in Psychology established.

Federal government allows payment for clinical psychologists' services to its empoyees without medical supervision or referral.

APA establishes *Standards for Providers of Psychological Services*.

First Interamerican Congress of Clinical Psychology held in Porto Alegre, Brazil.

1977 All fifty U.S. states have certification or licensing laws for clinical psychologists.

1980 Third edition of *Diagnostic and Statistical Manual (DSM–III)* published.

Smith, Glass, and Miller publish *The Benefits of Psychotherapy*.

Blue Shield health insurance companies in Virginia successfuly sued for refusing to pay for clinical psychologists' services to people covered by their plans.

1981 APA publishes its revised *Ethical Principles of Psychologists*.

1983 Joint Commission for the Accreditation of Hospitals allows clinical psychologists to become members of hospital medical staffs.

1987 *DSM–III–R* published.

Conference on graduate education in psychology, Salt Lake City, Utah.

1988 American Psychological Society formed.

1990 California Supreme Court affirms right of clinical psychologists to independently admit, diagnose, treat, and release mental patients without medical supervision.

1993 Commander John L. Sexton and Lt. Commander Morgan T. Sammons complete psychopharmacology program at Walter Reed Army Medical Center, becoming first psychologists legally permitted to perscribe psychoactive drugs.

1994 *DSM–IV* published.

Amendment to Social Security Act guarantees psychologists the right to independent practice and payment for hospital services under Medicare.

1995 APA task force of clinical psychologists publishes list of empirically validated psychological therapies and calls for students to be trained to use them.

1995 APA establishes new guidelines for the accreditation of programs in professional psychology, including clinical psychology. These guidelines reflect Shakow's original desire for flexible accreditation criteria.

1996 Dorothy W. Cantor becomes first president of APA to hold the Psy.D. degree rather than the Ph.D.

2000 *DSM–IV–TR* published.

2002 New Mexico grants prescription privileges to specially trained clinical psychologists.

Introduction to Clinical Psychology

SIXTH EDITION

MICHAEL T. NIETZEL

University of Kentucky

DOUGLAS A. BERNSTEIN

University of Illinois

GEOFFREY P. KRAMER

Grand Valley State University
West Shore Community College

RICHARD MILICH

University of Kentucky

Prentice
Hall

Upper Saddle River, NJ 07458

Library of Congress Cataloging-in-Publication Data

Nietzel, Michael T.

    Introduction to clinical psychology / Michael T. Nietzel, Douglas A. Bernstein, Geoffrey P. Kramer, Richard Milich. — 6th ed.

      p. cm.

    Includes bibliographical references and index.

    ISBN 0-13-098082-X

    1. Clinical psychology.   I. Bernstein, Douglas A.   II. Milich, Richard.

   III. Title.

RC467.N54 2002

616.89—dc21

                         2002005832

Editor-in-Chief: Leah Jewell
Managing Editor (editorial): Sharon Rheinhardt
Production Liaison: Joanne Hakim
Project Manager: Karen Berry/Pine Tree Composition
Prepress and Manufacturing Buyer: Tricia Kenny
Cover Director: Jayne Conte
Cover Designer: Kiwi Design
Cover Art: Stavros/Stock Illustration Source
Image Coordinator: Charles Morris
Director of Marketing: Beth Gillett Mejia
Marketing Manager: Sheryl Adams

This book was set in 10/12 Garamond Book by Pine Tree Composition, Inc., and was printed and bound by R.R. Donnelley & Sons Company. The cover was printed by Phoenix Color Corp.

© 2003, 1998, 1994, 1991, 1987 by Prentice-Hall, Inc.
Upper Saddle River, New Jersey 07458

Printed in the United States of America
10 9 8 7 6 5 4 3 2 1

ISBN: 0-13-098082-X

Pearson Education Ltd., *London*
Pearson Education Australia PTY. Limited, *Sydney*
Pearson Education Singapore, Pte. Ltd
Pearson Education North Asia Ltd, *Hong Kong*
Pearson Education Canada, Ltd., *Toronto*
Pearson Educación de Mexico, S.A. de C.V.
Pearson Education—Japan, *Tokyo*
Pearson Education Malaysia, Pte. Ltd
Pearson Education, *Upper Saddle River, New Jersey*

Contents

CHAPTER 5
Testing in Clinical Psychology　171

CHAPTER 6
Clinical Interventions: An Overview　211

CHAPTER 7
Clinical Intervention: Methods
of Psychotherapy　230

CHAPTER 12
Clinical Neuropsychology   398

CHAPTER 13
Forensic Psychology   425

CHAPTER 14
Professional Issues in Clinical Psychology   452

Preface

In the five previous editions of this book, we tried to accomplish three goals. First, we wanted a book that, while appropriate for graduate students, was written especially with sophisticated undergraduates in mind. Many undergraduate psychology majors express an interest in clinical psychology without having a clear understanding of what the field involves and requires. An even larger number of nonmajors also wish to know more about clinical psychology. We felt that both groups of undergraduates would benefit from a thorough survey of the field which does not go into all the details typically found in "graduate study only" texts.

Second, we wanted to present a scholarly portrayal of the history of clinical psychology, its scope, functions, and future that reviewed a full range of theoretical perspectives. For this reason, we have not allowed our preference for cognitive-behavioral theories to limit our presentation. Instead, we present psychodynamic, phenomenological/experiential, interpersonal, and biological perspectives as well, and we have sought to do so in as neutral a manner as possible. We do champion the empirical research tradition of clinical psychology throughout the book because we believe it is a necessary and useful perspective for all clinicians to follow, regardless of their theoretical orientation.

Third, we wanted our book to be interesting and enjoyable to read. Because we like being clinical psychologists and because we enjoy teaching courses in the field, we tried to create a book that communicates our enthusiasm for its content.

Our goals for this sixth edition remain the same. However, in addition to the comprehensive updating of the content of all chapters, we have introduced some new material and reorganized our coverage of existing material somewhat. For example, we have expanded the coverage of clinical interventions to four chapters by adding a new chapter on alternative modes of intervention: group therapy, couples therapy, family therapy, psychosocial rehabilitation, prevention, community psychology, and self-help. We have also combined the presentation of interviewing and observation into one chapter to reflect the complementary nature of these activities. In our updating of the major theoretical orientations and psychotherapeutic approaches, we have added new information on the movement toward theoretical integration and eclecticism. Sociocultural diversity affects psychological assessment, psychotherapy, and clinical research, so we have included new information on this topic throughout the book. Since our last edition, numerous changes have occurred in the health care delivery system, both in the United States and in other countries. Accordingly, we have addressed how managed care has continued to influence research and practice in clinical psychology since our last edition. Rapid changes have also occurred in psychotherapy research, so we have expanded our presentation of empirically supported treatments and of research on nonspecific treatment factors (i.e., therapist, client, and therapeutic relationship variables). Finally, we have expanded our discussions of the growing employment arenas for clinical psychologists in the fields of neuropsychology, health psychology, clinical child psychology, and forensic psychology.

ACKNOWLEDGMENTS

We want to thank several people for their valuable contributions to this book. Our colleagues, Debra A. Hope, University of Nebraska–Lincoln, Martin Zelin, Tufts University, Lyn Friedman, Carnegie Mellon University, and Edward J. Yelinek, Wilson College, carefully read parts of the manuscript and offered many valuable suggestions for improving it. We also wish to express our appreciation to Professor Wendy Heller for her careful updating of the chapter on neuropsychology, and to Elaine Cassel for her expertise in updating the chapter on forensic psychology.

Countless undergraduate and graduate students asked the questions, raised the issues, and argued the opposing positions that have found their way into the text; they are really the people who stimulated the creation of this book, and who continue to make us want to revise and update its content. We thank them all. We also want to thank Sharon Rheinhardt, our editor at Prentice Hall for her help and patience in guiding the creation of this latest edition, and Karen Berry from Pine Tree Composition, who coordinated production of the manuscript.

MICHAEL T. NIETZEL

DOUGLAS A. BERNSTEIN

GEOFFREY P. KRAMER

RICHARD MILICH

Chapter 1

Clinical Psychology: Definitions and History

Psychology has consistently been one of the most popular undergraduate majors at colleges and universities in the United States, and it will likely maintain this status for a long time to come. By 1997, for instance, more than 74,000 bachelor's degrees were being awarded annually to psychology majors, a figure reflecting annual increase of nearly 5% per year, and a total increase of approximately 85% since 1985. The number of master's and doctor's degrees has also increased. Even though enrollment to graduate programs in psychology has leveled off in recent years (Kyle & Williams, 2000), the number of doctoral degrees awarded in 1997 (4,053) still surpassed the number from any previous year (National Center for Education Statistics, 2000).

Much of psychology's popularity can be attributed to its largest subfield: clinical psychology. As one of psychology's *health service provider professions*, clinical psychology attracts far more graduate school applications than any other area in psychology.[1] The particular appeal of clinical psychology is also reflected in the composition of the American Psychological Association (APA), the largest organization of psychologists in the United States. APA has over 155,000 members, and more than four times as many of them list clinical psychology as their specialty as list any other area (American Psychological Association, 2000). It is no wonder, then, that of the 48 divisions within APA, the Division of Clinical Psychology is by far the largest.

---

[1]APA-accredited colleges and universities offering a clinical PhD accept approximately 7% of the applications they receive (Pate, 2001). The acceptance rate is higher—up to 36%—if one includes all doctoral-level clinical programs (i.e., APA-accredited; non-APA accredited; PhD, PsyD and EdD granting programs).

The prominence of clinical psychology is all the more remarkable when you consider that it is barely 100 years old and did not begin to grow rapidly until about 50 years ago. What defines the field of clinical psychology, and what is it that clinical psychologists do that makes so many people want to become one? There are no simple answers to these questions, but in this book we attempt to describe the field in a way that will allow you to draw your own conclusions. In the process, we examine the history, current status, and future of clinical psychology; its uniqueness and its overlap with other fields; the training and activities of its members; the factors that unite it; and the issues that threaten to divide it.

WHAT IS CLINICAL PSYCHOLOGY?

It is difficult to capture in a sentence or two the ever-expanding scope and ever-changing directions of clinical psychology. Thus, before offering any official definitions of the field, we will describe some of the characteristics that, taken together, roughly define the essential nature of clinical psychology.

First, as its name implies, clinical psychology is a subfield of the larger discipline of psychology. This means that, like all psychologists, clinical psychologists are interested in *behavior and mental processes.* Unlike some of their colleagues in other psychological subfields, however, clinicians are concerned almost entirely with human—rather than animal—behavior and mental processes.

Second, clinical psychologists conduct *research* on behavior and mental processes. Given their focus on humans, clinicians mainly study people, though they may do research on animals when practical or ethical concerns rule out working with people, and when they believe that studying animal behavior can lead to a better understanding of humans. Of course, psychologists in many other subfields also conduct research on human behavior and mental processes, so clinical psychologists' research activities do not make their subfield unique. Neither does the fact that clinicians seek to apply the knowledge gained from research to improve human welfare. Other specialties—such as educational, social, industrial/organizational, health, and engineering psychology—are also noted for their applied orientation.

A third important aspect of clinical psychology is its involvement in the *assessment or measurement* of the abilities and characteristics of individual human beings. Clinicians collect information that will be analyzed and interpreted to support conclusions about the person observed. While such information might be collected from many people as part of a clinical research project, it is more frequently employed by the clinician to understand one particular person. These assessment activities, however, do not set clinicians entirely apart, because other psychologists—especially those in the personality and industrial/organizational areas—administer and score various kinds of individual assessments.

A fourth characteristic of clinical psychology is the effort to *help* people who are psychologically distressed. Indeed, when members of the general public are asked what clinical psychologists do, they usually mention the treatment of mental disorders as a prominent activity. Still, providing therapy is not unique to clinical psychology:

Psychiatrists, family physicians, social workers, counselors, nurses, educators, and the clergy also intervene to alleviate psychological problems.

In summary, clinical psychology is a subarea of psychology whose members, like some other psychologists, generate research about human behavior, seek to apply the results of that research, and engage in individual assessment. And like the members of some other professions, clinical psychologists provide assistance to those who need help with psychological problems. So what distinguishes clinical psychology from the other branches of psychology? The most notable distinguishing feature has been called the *clinical attitude* or the *clinical approach* (Korchin, 1976), the tendency to combine knowledge from research on human behavior and mental processes with efforts at individual assessment in order to understand and help a particular person.

The clinical attitude sets clinicians apart from other psychologists who search for general principles that apply to human behavior problems in general. Clinical psychologists are interested in research of this kind, but they also want to know how general principles shape lives, problems, and treatments on an individual level. The clinical attitude is distinctive with respect to the helping professions outside psychology. The psychiatrists, social workers, and others who assist people in psychological distress work in fields that are not traditionally noted for research on—or systematic assessment of—the problems they seek to alleviate.

The clinical attitude can be most clearly seen when contrasted with the approach taken by psychologists in other subfields—and by professionals outside of psychology—in relation to a particular case. Suppose, for example, that upon admission to a mental hospital, a disheveled and confused man reports that space aliens are stealing his thoughts. In reading notes about this person, an experimental psychopathologist would probably be most interested in whether there are psychological and biological factors in the man's background that might support a certain theory about the cause of schizophrenia. Reading the same notes, a psychiatrist (a physician who specializes in psychological problems) might wonder whether the man should be given psychological, medical, or combined treatments. A clinical psychologist, however, would probably plan a strategy for further assessing the nature of the man's problem and, depending upon the outcome of the assessment process, develop an intervention for reducing his distress. Much of the research evidence that guides the clinical psychologist in these pursuits (and also aids other helping professions) may have come from the work of fellow clinical psychologists.

In other words, it is not the research, or the assessment, or the treatment, or any of the other activities described so far that makes clinical psychology unique. Rather, it is the clinical attitude which leads clinical psychologists to not only learn about behavior (particularly problematic behavior) but also to do something about it that is indigenous to clinical psychology (Wyatt, 1968). This emphasis on combining several functions within a single field is consistent with the "official" definition of clinical psychology adopted in 1991 by APA's Division of Clinical Psychology: "The field of Clinical Psychology involves research, teaching, and services relevant to the applications of principles, methods, and procedures for understanding, predicting, and alleviating intellectual, emotional, biological, psychological, social and behavioral maladjustment, disability and discomfort, applied to a wide range of client populations"

(Resnick, 1991). A similar definition has been adopted by the Section on Clinical Psychology of the Canadian Psychological Association (Vallis & Howes, 1995). Thus, no single activity defines clinical psychology. Its uniqueness stems from the use of science and theory to guide specific interventions for persons experiencing adjustment problems or mental disorders.

CLINICAL PSYCHOLOGISTS AT WORK

Having outlined the nature of clinical psychology, let's consider in a little more detail some of the activities that clinical psychologists pursue, the variety of places in which they are employed, and the array of clients and problems on which they focus their attention. Not all clinicians are equally involved with all the functions, locations, clients, and problems we will describe, but our review should provide a better understanding of the wide range of options open to those who enter clinical psychology and, thus, of why the field remains so attractive to so many students.

The Activities of Clinical Psychologists

It is probably fair to say that 95% of all clinical psychologists spend their working lives engaged in some combination of six activities: assessment, treatment, research, teaching, consultation, and administration.

Assessment. Assessment involves collecting information about people: their behavior, problems, unique characteristics, abilities, and their intellectual functioning. This information may be used to diagnose problematic behavior, to guide a client toward an optimal vocational choice, to facilitate selection of job candidates, to describe a client's personality characteristics, to select treatment techniques, to guide legal decisions regarding the commitment of individuals to institutions, to provide a more complete picture of a client's problems, to screen potential participants in psychological research projects, to establish pretreatment baseline levels of behavior against which to measure posttreatment improvement, and for literally hundreds of other purposes. Most clinical assessment devices fall into one of three categories: tests, interviews, and observations.

Tests, interviews, and observations are not always distinct means of assessment. For example, a clinician might observe the nonverbal behavior of a client during a testing session or an interview to estimate the client's level of discomfort in social situations. Further, a test may be embedded in an interview, as when the client is asked to provide specific information whose accuracy provides clues to reality contact.

Various modes of assessment are combined in assessment batteries and multiple assessment strategies. Here, information necessary for the clinician's work is collected through a series of procedures, sometimes including a variety of tests. Often, a more elaborate combination of tests, interviews, and observations focuses not only on the client, but also on family, friends, and others in the client's life who can provide additional information.

Treatment.   Clinical psychologists offer treatments designed to help people better understand and solve distressing psychological problems. These interventions may be called psychotherapy, behavior modification, psychological counseling, or other names, depending upon the theoretical orientation of the clinician, and may involve an enormous range of specific treatment methods. As many as 400 "brand name" therapies have been identified (Feltham, 2000), and they literally run the gamut from A (Aikido) to Z (Zaraleya psychoenergetic technique) (Herink, 1980). Individual psychotherapy has long been the single most frequent activity of clinicians (e.g., Phelps, Eisman, & Kohout, 1998; Norcross, Prochaska, & Gallagher, 1989a,b), but psychologists may also treat two or more clients together in couple, family, or group therapy. Sometimes, two or more clinicians work in therapy teams to help their clients.

Treatment by a clinical psychologist may be conducted on an outpatient basis (i.e., the client lives in the community) or as one of the services offered to residents (inpatients) of mental health institutions. It may be as brief as one session or extend over several years. Treatment sessions may include client or therapist monologues, painstaking construction of new behavioral skills, episodes of intense emotional drama, or many other activities that range from the highly structured to the utterly spontaneous.

Treatment goals can range widely as well. They may be as limited as finding a specific solution to a particular problem, as ambitious as a complete analysis and reconstruction of a client's personality, or may fall somewhere between these extremes. And while most clinical psychologists design their treatments to reduce existing problems, we will see in Chapter 8 that some focus instead on preventing psychological problems by altering the institutions, environmental stressors, or behavioral skills of people "at risk" for disorder (e.g., teenage parents) or of an entire community.

Therapy can be offered free of charge, for a fixed fee, as part of a pre-paid health care plan, or on a sliding scale that is adjusted in light of the client's ability to pay. The results of treatment are usually positive, though in some cases the change may be small, nonexistent, or even negative.

Research.   By training and by tradition, clinical psychologists are research oriented. This research activity makes clinicians stand out among other helping professions, and we believe that it is in this area that they make their greatest contribution. In the realm of psychotherapy, for example, theory and practice were once based mainly upon case study evidence, subjective impressions of treatment efficacy, and rather poorly designed research. This "prescientific" era (Paul, 1969a) in the history of psychotherapy research has now evolved into an "experimental" era in which the quality of research has improved greatly and the conclusions we can draw about the effects of therapy are much stronger (Lambert & Bergin, 1994). This development is due in large measure to the research of clinical psychologists.

The areas investigated by clinicians range widely, from neuropsychology, psychopharmacology and health psychology, to the causes of mental disorders in children and adults; from the diagnosis of those disorders to community interventions designed to prevent them, and from the evaluation of professional psychotherapy to the impact of nonprofessional helpers. A glance at a journal called *Psychological Abstracts*, which contains brief summaries of research in psychology, will document the diversity and intensity of clinical psychologists' involvement in research. Another journal, *Clinical Psychology Review*, includes longer reviews of topics germane to clinical psychology, while the *Journal of Consulting and Clinical Psychology, Psychological Assessment*, and the *Journal of Abnormal Psychology* publish many of the most influential research studies in clinical psychology.

Clinical research varies greatly with respect to its setting and scope. Some studies are conducted in the confines of a research laboratory, while others are conducted in the more natural, but less controllable, conditions prevailing in the world beyond the lab. Some projects are supported by governmental or private grants which pay for research assistants, clerical staff and other costs, but a great deal of clinical research is performed by investigators whose budgets are limited and who depend on volunteer help and their own ability to obtain space, equipment, and subjects.

Clinical psychology's tradition of research is reflected in graduate school admission criteria, which often emphasize applicants' grades in statistics or research methods over grades in abnormal psychology or personality theory, and which weigh applicants' research experience and publications at least as heavily as their clinical experiences. Graduate departments in psychology in the United States typically regard research experience as among the three most important criteria for admission (Pate, 2001). And even though most clinical psychologists do not end up pursuing a research career—many never publish a single piece of research—most graduate programs in clinical psychology still devote a significant amount of time to training in empirical research. Why?

There are at least four reasons. First, it is important that all clinicians be able to critically evaluate published research so that they can determine which assessment procedures and therapeutic interventions are likely to be effective for their clients and which have not been empirically validated (Chambless et al., 1995). Second, research training can help clinicians objectively evaluate the effectiveness of their own clinical work. This aspect of clinical research—systematically evaluating one's treatment outcomes—has become tremendously important in recent years, and it will probably become more important as time goes on (see Cone, 2000). Third, when psychologists who work in community mental health centers or other service agencies are asked to assist administrators in evaluating the effectiveness of the agency's programs, their research training can be very valuable. Finally, clinicians who work in academia must often supervise and evaluate research projects conducted by their students. In other words, the majority of clinical psychologists can assume that their research skills will be called upon sometime in their professional careers.

Teaching.   A considerable portion of many clinical psychologists' time is spent in educational activities. Clinicians who hold full- or part-time academic positions teach graduate and undergraduate courses in areas such as personality, abnormal psychology, introductory clinical psychology, psychotherapy, behavior modification, interviewing, psychological testing, research design, and clinical assessment. They conduct specialized graduate seminars on advanced topics, and they supervise the work of graduate students who are learning assessment and therapy skills in practicum courses.

Supervising practica is a special kind of teaching which relies partly on empirical research evidence and partly on the instructor's clinical experience to enhance students' assessment and treatment skills. In most practica, each student sees one or more clients on a regular basis and, between sessions, meets with the supervisor to discuss the case (the client is aware of this arrangement, of course). Supervision may occur on an individual basis or may be part of a meeting with a small group of practicum students, all of whom keep what they hear strictly confidential.

A good deal of clinical psychologists' teaching takes the form of research supervision. This kind of teaching begins when a student comes to the supervisor with a research topic and asks for advice and a list of relevant readings. In addition to providing the reading list, most research supervisors help the student frame appropriate research questions, apply basic principles of research design to address those questions, and introduce the student to the research skills relevant to the problem at hand.

Clinical psychologists also do a lot of teaching in the context of in-service (i.e., on-the-job) training of psychological, medical, or other interns, as well as social workers, nurses, institutional aides, ministers, police officers, suicide prevention personnel, prison guards, teachers, administrators, business executives, day-care workers, lawyers, probation officers, dentists, and many other groups whose vocational skills might be enhanced by increased psychological sophistication. Clinicians even teach while doing therapy—particularly if they adopt a behavioral approach in which treatment includes helping people learn more adaptive ways of behaving (see Chapter 7). Finally, many clinicians teach part-time in colleges, universities, and professional schools. Working as an adjunct faculty member provides another source of income, but clinicians often teach because it offers an enjoyable way to share their professional expertise and to remain abreast of new developments in their field.

Consultation. Clinical psychologists often provide advice to organizations about a variety of problems. This activity, known as consultation, combines aspects of research, assessment, treatment, and teaching. Perhaps this is why some clinicians find consultation satisfying and lucrative enough that they engage in it full time. Organizations that benefit from consultants' expertise range in size and scope from one-person medical or law practices to huge government agencies and multinational corporations. The consultant may also work with neighborhood associations, walk-in treatment centers, and many other community-based organizations. Consultants perform many kinds of tasks, including education (e.g., familiarizing staff with research relevant to their work), advice (e.g., about cases or programs), direct service (e.g., assessment, treatment, and evaluation), and reduction of intraorganizational conflict (e.g., eliminating sources of trouble by altering personnel assignments).

When consulting is *case* oriented, the clinician focuses attention on a particular client or organizational problem and either deals with it directly or offers advice on how it might best be handled. When consultation is *program* or *administration* oriented, the focus is on those aspects of organizational function or structure that are causing trouble. For example, the consultant may suggest and develop new procedures for screening candidates for various jobs within an organization, set up criteria for identifying promotable personnel, or reduce staff turnover rates by increasing administrators' awareness of the psychological impact of their decisions on employees.

In some cases, responsibility for the solution to an organization's problem is transferred to the consultant, as when a mental health clinic signs a contract with a clinician who then conducts neuropsychological tests when new clients are suspected of having brain damage. More commonly, however, the responsibility for problem resolution remains with the organization served. A clinician may participate in decisions about which treatment would most benefit a client, but if the client gets worse instead of better, the responsibility lies with the clinic, not the consultant.

Administration.   Many clinical psychologists find themselves engaged in the management or day-to-day running of organizations. Examples of the administrative posts held by clinical psychologists include: head of a college or university psychology department, director of a graduate training program in clinical psychology, director of a student counseling center, head of a consulting firm or testing center, superintendent of a school system, chief psychologist at a hospital or clinic, director of a mental hospital, director of a community mental health center, manager of a government agency, and director of the psychology service at a Veterans Administration (VA) hospital.

Administration has become an increasingly popular professional activity for psychologists. Indeed, it may be the third most important job market for clinical psychologists, after direct clinical service and academic jobs. In one survey (Norcross, Prochaska & Gallagher, 1989a), clinicians reported spending an average of 16% of their time on administrative work.

Distribution of Clinical Activities

Though some clinical psychologists spend all of their time at one of the six activities we have described, most engage in two or more, and some perform all six. To many clinicians, the potential for distributing their time among several functions is one of the most attractive aspects of their field. Table 1.1 shows how licensed psychologists responded to questions about their allocation of time (Phelps, Eisman, & Kohout, 1998). The survey, commissioned by the American Psychological Association's Committee for the Advancement of Professional Practice (CAPP), included 15,918 responses from practicing psychologists, making it one of the largest surveys of its kind. Because the survey was directed at only practicing clinicians, some clinical psychologists who do not practice or hold licenses may not have been included, making the results somewhat skewed toward treatment and away from research. Nevertheless, the results are informative about clinical functions.

Table 1.1 shows clearly that the distribution of clinical functions varies considerably across practice setting. For instance, psychologists in academic settings spend more professional time teaching than anything else, while those in private practice spend most of their time doing psychotherapy. Much of this is expected, but problems can arise when practitioners are insufficiently involved in research or when researchers (usually in academic settings) become isolated from clinical realities because they no longer treat clients (Himelein & Putnam, 2001). Ideally, practice and research should inform each other.

TABLE 1.1 Percentage of Time Licensed Psychologists Spend in Activities in Different Work Setting

Activity	Primary Work Setting				
	Independent practice (*N* = 7,749)	Academic (*N* = 1,625)	Government (*N* = 1,104)	Medical (*N* = 1,949)	Total (*N* = 15,918)
Assessment	15[a]	5	19	23	16
Treatment	61	18	28	30	44
Research	1	15	4	9	4
Teaching[b]	5	40	12	13	11
Consulting	5	5	7	5	6
Administration	4	15	20	12	9
Other	8	3	9	7	7

[a]All numbers within the table are percent.
[b]Includes supervision.

SOURCE: Phelps, R., Eisman, E. J., & Kohout, J. (1998). Psychological practice and managed care: Results of the CAPP practitioner survey. *Professional Psychology: Research and Practice, 29,* 31–36. Online version accessed via the American Psychological Association's website: http://www.apa. org/practice/cappsurvey.html. Accessed December 13, 2001.

Table 1.2 presents data from several surveys conducted over the last 35 years and provides another view of functions and work settings for psychologists. These surveys in Table 1.2 often asked about clinical functions in different ways, making direct comparisons across them difficult, but some obvious trends appear. For one thing, clinicians spend more time in various service activities than they do in research, and the majority of clinicians identify themselves primarily as practitioners rather than as researchers or academicians. Also, the percentage of clinicians engaged in full-time private practice doubled between 1964 and 1989; if we add to the private practice figure the 30% of clinicians employed in some kind of direct service agency, we see that by 1990 two-thirds of clinicians were working primarily in a health service provider role.

In the 1990s, however, the shape of clinical practice began to change, mainly as a result of health care reform and shifts in the payment methods for clinical services. We discuss these changes in more detail in Chapter 14, but it is relevant to highlight here the impact of managed care, an increasingly popular system of health care which has made it so difficult for clinical psychologists to function as solo private practitioners that, for the first time in the history of their field, the percentage of clinicians employed in traditional private practice settings has declined. Managed care systems have had this effect mainly because they use business principles, not just clinicians' judgments, to determine how much mental health treatment clients enrolled in the system may receive, and they place limits on the kinds of services for which they will pay. These systems also authorize payment only to their "approved providers," clinicians who are paid lower fees for their services than would be the case under clinician-controlled plans.

As clinical psychologists find it more difficult to make a living as solo practitioners with clients whose health care is paid for by managed care systems, more of them are joining the staffs of hospitals, medical clinics, rehabilitation centers, nursing homes, and other general health care facilities (Groth-Marnat & Edkins, 1996), consulting with or joining the private practice of primary care physicians (Belar, 1995; Bray & Rogers, 1995), or offering clinical services through health maintenance organizations (HMOs), group practices, and specialty clinics. Too, the services that clinical psychologists offer are changing to better match those for which managed care systems will pay. Clinicians are doing less long-term therapy and testing and more brief psychotherapy and specialized treatment of childhood disorders, substance abuse problems, and difficulties associated with chronic medical illnesses (Johnstone et al., 1995; Nickelson, 1995; Norcross, Prochaska, & Gallagher, 1989a; Wiggins, 1994).

Clients and Their Problems

Within the limits imposed by their areas of expertise, clinical psychologists work on almost any kind of human behavioral problem. According to one survey of more than 6,500 clinicians, the most commonly treated problems are, in order of frequency: anxiety and depression, difficulties in interpersonal relationships, marital problems, school difficulties, psychosomatic and physical symptoms, job-related difficulties, alcoholism or other forms of drug abuse, psychoses, and mental retardation (VandenBos & Stapp, 1983). The types of problems for which people seek help have remained much the same over the years.

TABLE 1.2 Percentage of Clinicians Employed in Various Work Settings

	Kelly (1964) (*N* = 1,024)	Goldschmid et al. (1969) (*N* = 241)	Garfield & Kurtz (1976) (*N* = 855)	Stapp & Fulcher (1983) (*N* = 2,436)	Norcross, Prochaska & Gallagher (1989b) (*N* = 579)	Kohout & Wicherski (1999)[e] (*N* = 1,296)
Academic	20	17	29	17.9	21	30.6
Direct service[a]	50	44	35	39.8	30	37.1[f]
Schools	3	[d]	[b]	1.3	[d]	5.4
Private practice	17	28	23.3	31.1	35	5.9
Other[c]	8	11	12.7	8.6	10	20.2

[a]Includes hospitals, clinics, medical schools, mental health centers, community agencies, etc.

[b]Included in "other."

[c]Includes government, business, industry, military, etc.

[d]Not included.

[e]It is important to note that figures for private practice are likely depressed in this study because the survey was of recent (1997) graduates of doctoral programs. Because of supervision and licensing requirements, the financial burdens of establishing a private practice, and other reasons, few persons starting out their careers begin in independent private practice.

[f]After removing 5.9% in private practice from 43% in the direct human service sector

11

Requests for assessment and treatment services may come from the clients themselves, from the client's family, from a court or other legal agency, or from a hospital, school, or community service center. Because client complaints are often complex and frequently stem from a combination of biological, psychological, and social factors, the clinical psychologist—even the private practitioner—may not work alone. In many cases, clients are referred to another clinical psychologist, a psychiatrist, or a social worker for specialized testing, medication, or other services and, in some cases, clients may be served by an assessment and treatment team composed of experts from several helping professions.

Employment Settings and Salaries for Clinical Psychologists

At one time, most clinical psychologists worked in a single type of facility: child clinics or guidance centers. Today, however, the settings in which clinicians function are much more diverse. You will find clinical psychologists in college and university psychology departments, law schools, public and private medical and psychiatric hospitals, in city, county, and private mental health clinics, community mental health centers, student health and counseling centers, medical schools, the military, university psychological clinics, child treatment centers, public and private schools, institutions for the mentally retarded, police departments, prisons, juvenile offender facilities, business and industrial firms, probation departments, rehabilitation centers for the handicapped, nursing homes and other geriatric facilities, orphanages, alcoholism treatment centers, health maintenance organizations (HMOs), and many other places. Further, as already noted, many clinicians are employed in full- or part-time private-practice positions, but, increasingly, as members of a group practice or behavioral health care network.

The dramatic growth of private practice in the 1980s (see Table 1.2) was caused in part by the satisfaction that private practitioners draw from independent work (Norcross & Prochaska, 1983) and also by the lower level of perceived stress compared to academic or mental health agency jobs (Boice & Myers, 1987; Raquepaw & Miller, 1989). The financial rewards were significant, too. According to an APA survey, the median 1999 salary of doctoral-level psychologists in individual independent practice ranged from $64,000 to $80,000. Those in group psychological practices earned from $60,000 to $85,000. Compare these with the range of $49,00 to $55,000 for doctoral levels working in community mental health settings, or $50,500 to $58,500 for those working in public psychiatric hospitals (Williams, Wicherski, & Kohout, 2000).

As managed care systems have grown, however, the financial advantages for independent practice have tended to erode. In one survey of independent practitioners, over half reported a decrease in salary from 1998 to 1999 and attributed it to the health care system (Williams, Kohout, & Wicherski, 2000). As a result, the salary discrepancy between private practice and other areas of clinical work is now smaller than it used to be. For instance, faculty salaries at university departments of psychology, range from near a median of $41,000 for assistant professors to $72,000 for full professors. The median salary for full professors at university-affiliated professional schools of psychology is $57,500. When adjusted for the 9- to 10-month academic year, these academic salaries are now closer to the salaries earned by private-practice clinicians.

The American Psychological Association periodically surveys its members concerning salaries, demographics, practice concerns, and many other topics, then makes the results available. Much of that information is readily accessed at APA's website: http://www.apa.org (though some information is available only to APA members).

Sociocultural Diversity Among Clinical Psychologists

The gender distribution within psychology has changed considerably over the past half century. In 1950, women earned 15% of the doctoral degrees awarded in psychology; in 1997, they earned about 67% of them (National Center for Education Statistics, 2000). Figures for 1999 to 2000 show a continuation of this trend, with women making up at least two-thirds of psychology graduate students (Pate, 2001). Because clinical psychology represents the largest portion of psychology graduate students, the 2 to 1 ratio of women to men has begun to appear in clinical degree programs as well. Of course, there is a lag of several years between enrollment in a degree program and the attainment of senior status within a profession. Because of this, the are still more men among senior faculty in colleges and universities, and more men among the higher-salary private practitioners. But at all levels, the clear trend is toward greater representation of women.[2]

Ethnic minorities currently make up about 18% of the students accepted into clinical psychology doctoral programs and about 25% of those in counseling psychology doctoral programs (Norcross et al., 1998). African-Americans represent the highest percentage of minorities in all psychology graduate programs, followed closely by persons of Hispanic and Asian origin; Native Americans represent about 1% (Pate, 2001). Minority representation at the graduate school level is currently greater than minority representation at higher-status levels of the profession, a situation parallel to that with women, but as minority students successfully work through the training pipeline, this traditional imbalance in the profession should begin to moderate.

It is noteworthy that the proportion of minorities in *all* doctoral psychology programs has edged up from below 7% in 1985 to its current level (Kohout & Wicherski, 1999), partly because of efforts to recruit minority students. A recent survey of graduate departments of psychology showed that approximately half were in institutions that had specific recruitment plans for targeting persons of color, and many departments had their own department-level strategies for recruiting minorities (Kyle & Williams, 2000). Examples of such efforts include outreach programs to "feeder" schools, financial assistance to persons of color, brochures or other materials geared toward persons

---

[2]There are some indications that the trend toward women in higher-status positions within clinical psychology is changing at a slower rate than the trend toward greater representation of women in graduate clinical programs. One possible reason for this is lingering gender bias. Another is that women are much more likely than men to leave full-time employment at some point in their careers and work part time, often to devote time to their families (see Kohout & Wicherski, 1999). These career decisions can make it more difficult for women clinicians to attain higher-status positions when those positions are based on longevity, experience, or similar criteria.

of color, and involvement of more persons of color in the recruitment and screening process.

At Work with Three Clinical Psychologists

Having described clinical psychologists' functions, clients, and work settings, let's consider a few specific examples of how and where clinicians actually spend their time. Remember, though, that these examples are just the tip of the iceberg: As scientific discoveries continue, particularly in the areas of childhood psychopathology and treatment (Chapter 10), health psychology (Chapter 11), and neuropsychology (Chapter 12), clinicians will continue to expand the scope of their assessment and intervention techniques and the range of settings in which they perform their academic and service work (DeSantis & Walker, 1991). As we enter the 21st century, expect to see clinical psychologists devoting more of their expertise to ever more specialized services for substance abuse programs, forensic agencies, and medical facilities and to traditionally underserved groups such as the elderly, the poor, and members of ethnic minority groups. Clinicians will also find themselves increasingly called upon to guide policy decisions in the areas of health care, child care, education, and social services.

Dr. Sandy D'Angelo. I work in a hospital pediatrics department, where my clinical activities include: (1) delivering outpatient assessment and treatment services to children with behavioral and learning problems; (2) consulting with staff who serve children with craniofacial abnormalities, limb amputation, cerebral palsy, or other disabilities; (3) counseling teen parents and their children; (4) providing clinical assessments in an infant-toddler evaluation center; and (5) helping parents learn to manage infants and toddlers with behavior problems. In these roles, I often work with general pediatricians and with pulmonologists, cardiologists, nephrologists, surgeons, and other medical specialists.

My job is different every day. In the morning, I might assess the cognitive development of children displaying autism, violent temper tantrums, brain damage, or visual and hearing impairments. In the afternoon, I might assess suicide risk in a homeless 17-year-old, counsel an unwed teenage mother, and assist in hospitalizing a teen displaying severe mental disorder. On other days, I might help educate medical students and residents by leading a discussion, delivering a lecture, or conducting a case conference. I also devote a small portion of my time to working with other faculty on a research project on how children and their families cope with chronic illnesses.

The most appealing aspects of my position are the variety of services I am called on to perform, the wide range of childhood problems I see, the opportunity to work with professionals who view children's problems from different perspectives, and the chance to continue learning about childhood disorders and development.

Dr. Hector Machabanski. Practically all facets of clinical psychology are represented in my work, including direct clinical and community services, teaching, administration, and consultation. I am a faculty member at a school of professional psychology, where I teach courses in family therapy and culture and mental health. I also advise and mentor clinical graduate students and sit on various academic committees. In addition, I do accreditation site visits for the American Psychological Association, and I have served on the executive committee of national professional organizations. Finally, I offer workshops and presentations to hospital, mental health, and other professional groups, usually on topics related to culture and mental health. Other aspects of my teaching include speaking to community groups—including those in the Spanish-speaking community—on topics such as parenting, stress management, conflict resolution, and self-improvement.

My private practice focuses on delivering assessment and treatment services to culturally diverse clients—including children, adults, and families who are Spanish-speaking, bilingual, and who are immigrants—with a wide range of psychological concerns. I receive referrals from insurance companies, managed care organizations, private physicians, attorneys, and mental health professionals. Because I am a certified school psychologist as well as a clinical psychologist, my consulting activities involve schools as well as hospitals. I spend one day a week in the schools, meeting with parents, teachers, and administrators, observing and assessing children, and providing recommendations pertaining to individual children and group situations. Through employees under my supervision, I also provide psychological services to local Head Start programs. In addition, I offer pro bono services at an international center for torture survivors, providing psychotherapy for victims of torture from Latin America, working with attorneys on political asylum cases, and giving technical support to the administration.

The most appealing aspect of my work is my involvement in a broad range of services that constitute what clinical psychology is today. The diverse settings, populations, and problems that constitute my professional life are brought together by my interest in providing services to what have been underserved client populations.

Dr. Geoffrey Thorpe. I am a professor of psychology at a state university. My teaching, research, and service activities are quite diverse, and vary from day to day. I teach an undergraduate class in abnormal psychology three times a week, and I spend considerable time preparing lectures, study guides, and other course materials for use in class. My graduate teaching involves leading weekly three-hour seminars in which six graduate students and I discuss advanced topics covered in assigned readings. I also conduct live or videotaped observations of clinical psychology graduate students as they practice assessment and therapy methods in our training clinic, and then conduct weekly individual and group supervisory sessions with them.

My research activities involve exploring various aspects of behavior therapy. I meet for two hours each week with my staff of graduate and undergraduate research assistants to discuss current progress, plan new studies, and, sometimes, work on grant proposals.

Because I am the director of clinical training, I have significant administrative responsibilities. In this administrative role, I coordinate our doctoral program in clinical psychology, which includes chairing meetings of the clinical faculty, supervising the admissions process, establishing and overseeing off-campus practicum placements, organizing the doctoral qualifying exams, preparing students for their clinical internships, and insuring that our program meets APA accreditation standards. I perform service in the form of paid and unpaid consulting to community agencies, and as a reviewer for editors at scholarly journals and textbook publishing companies. I also maintain a part-time private practice in clinical psychology.

I find being a clinical psychologist in an academic setting rewarding because, first, it offers me a variety of challenging roles that helps me avoid monotony and "burnout." In addition, the daily contact with colleagues and students creates a professional environment that inspires me to keep up with the latest developments in the exciting field of clinical psychology.

The way clinical psychologists spend their time is determined partly by their individual interests and expertise, partly by the demands of the work settings they choose, and partly by larger social factors. For example, a clinician could not work in a Veterans Administration hospital today if federal legislation had not been passed in the 1940s creating such hospitals. Similarly, much of the research conducted by clinical psychologists depends on grants from governmental agencies such as the National Institute of Mental Health, whose existence depends on continued congressional appropriations. Further, the clinical functions we have described are possible only because they are perceived by other professions—and the general public—as legitimate. If no one saw the clinician as capable of doing effective therapy, that function would soon disappear from the field.

In short, what clinicians do and where they do it has always depended—and always will depend—on the cultural values, prevailing attitudes, political climate, and pressing needs of the society in which they function. A look at the history of clinical psychology clearly shows the role played by these sociocultural factors in the development of the discipline.

THE ROOTS OF CLINICAL PSYCHOLOGY

Anyone born in the United States after World War II might assume that the field of clinical psychology has always existed. However, clinical psychology did not emerge as a discipline until the beginning of the 20th century, and did not really begin to develop until World War II ended. Now, more than 50 years later, this child of the postwar era is experiencing a "midlife crisis" centering on several of the same issues that occupied its adolescence: How should clinical psychologists be trained? What is the role of science in the field? What are the best ways to ensure that clinicians offer high-quality services to the public?

The roots of clinical psychology extend back to periods before the field was ever named and to prewar years when it appeared only in embryonic form (Reisman, 1976; Resnick, 1997; Routh, 1994). Three sets of social and historical factors initially shaped the field and continue to influence it. These factors include (1) the use of scientific research methods in psychology, (2) the study of human individual differences, and (3) changes in how behavior disorders have been viewed and treated over the years.

The Research Tradition in Psychology

From its 19th-century beginnings in the psychophysics of Weber and Fechner, the experimental physiology of Helmholtz, and the work of the first "official" psychologist, Wilhelm Wundt, psychology sought to establish itself as a science that—like biology, physics, and other sciences—seeks knowledge through the application of empirical research methods. Even though the roots of psychology were partly in philosophy, and though many early psychologists were preoccupied with philosophical questions, the discipline was determined to study human behavior by conducting research that employed the two most powerful tools of science, observation and experimentation. Thus, the early history of psychology, which began in Wundt's psychological laboratory at the University at Leipzig in 1879, is primarily the history of experimental psychology (Boring, 1950).

By the time clinical psychology began to emerge, 17 years after the founding of Wundt's laboratory, the experimental research tradition in psychology was well established. Psychology laboratories had been set up at major universities in Europe and the United States, and early psychologists were experimenting on human behavior. The first clinicians had been trained as scientists in these laboratories, and thus tended to think about clinical problems in scientific terms and to use laboratory research methods in dealing with them. The research tradition they brought to their work took root and grew in the new field until clinical psychologists attained special recognition among the helping professions as experts in research.

The scientific orientation and the skills that form the basis of clinicians' continuing reputation for research expertise also form the strongest link between clinical psychology and the larger discipline of psychology from which it grew. The question of whether this link should be maintained, intensified, or deemphasized in the training and daily activities of clinical psychologists continues to be one of the liveliest issues in the field. Nevertheless, the research tradition of experimental psychology undeniably shaped the development of clinical psychology. It provided a methodology for approaching clinical subject matter, engendered empirical evaluation of clinical functions, and, as a point of contention, keeps clinicians engaged in the healthy process of self-examination.

Attention to Individual Differences

Because clinical psychology deals with the individual, it could not appear as a discipline until differences among human beings began to be recognized and measured. There would be little impetus for learning about individuals in a world where everyone is thought to be about the same.

Differences among people have always been noticed and assessed. In his Republic, Plato pointed out that people should do work for which they are best suited; he suggested specifically that prospective soldiers be tested for military ability prior to their acceptance in the army. In the sixth century B.C., Pythagoras selected members of his brotherhood on the basis of facial characteristics, intelligence, and emotionality, and—4,000 years ago—prospective government employees in China were given individual ability tests prior to hiring (DuBois, 1970; McReynolds, 1975). It was not until the early 1800s, however, that the idea of paying systematic attention to subtle psychological differences really caught on. Until then, people were thought of as falling into a few categories such as male–female, good–evil, noble–commoner, sane–insane, wise–foolish.

The earliest developments in the scientific measurement of individual differences came in the fields of astronomy and anatomy. The astronomical story began in 1796, when Nevil Maskelyne was Astronomer Royal at the Greenwich (England) Observatory. He had an assistant named Kinnebrook, whose recordings of the moment at which various stars and planets crossed a certain point in the sky consistently differed from those of his boss by five- to eight-tenths of a second. Maskelyne assumed that his readings were correct and that Kinnebrook was in error. As a result, Kinnebrook lost his job.

This incident drew the attention of F. W. Bessel, an astronomer at the University of Konigsberg (Germany) observatory. Bessel wondered whether Kinnebrook's "error" might reflect something about the characteristics of various observers, and, over the next several years, he compared his own observations with those of other experienced astronomers. Bessel found that discrepancies appeared regularly and that the size of the differences depended upon the person with whom he compared notes. The differences associated with each observer became known as the "personal equation," because they allowed calculations to be corrected for personal characteristics. Bessel's work led to later research by psychologists on the speed of, and individual differences in, reaction time.

A second source of interest in individual differences stemmed from the early nineteenth-century work of anatomist Franz Gall and his pupil, Johann Spurzheim. As a child in Germany, Gall thought he saw a relationship between his schoolmates' mental characteristics and the shapes of their heads. This notion later led Gall to espouse phrenology, an alleged science based on the assumptions that (1) each area of the brain is associated with a different faculty or function (e.g., self-esteem, language, or reverence); (2) the better developed each of these areas is, the more strongly that faculty or function is manifested in behavior; and (3) the pattern of over- or underdevelopment of each faculty is reflected in corresponding bumps or depressions in the skull. Although the brain does play a major role in controlling behavior, and though some of its areas are associated with certain functions such as vision, movement, and language, Gall's specific claims were recognized—even by the scientists of his day—as spectacularly wrong.

Undeterred, Gall traveled throughout Europe measuring the bumps on people's heads. He began with prisoners and mental patients whose behavioral characteristics seemed well established (he thought the "acquisitiveness" bump was especially strong among pickpockets). Later, under Spurzheim's influence, a map of the brain's 37 "powers" or "organs" was drawn, and phrenological measurements were made on more respectable segments of society. Many people actually paid to "have their head examined," after which they received a profile allegedly describing their mental makeup. Other efforts to relate people's physical characteristics to their mental or behavioral traits appeared in the late 19th-century work of Cesare Lombroso, an Italian psychiatrist whose theory of physiognomy correlated facial features with personality (Pettijohn, 1991).

Though World Wide Web sites dealing with phrenology and physiognomy exist, the two are no longer influential in scientific circles. Still, their orientation toward systematically measuring individuals' characteristics—and then drawing conclusions about those individuals—presaged the assessment function seen in clinical psychology today. The methods ultimately used in clinical assessment were quite different, however. They came not from measuring physical dimensions, but from systematically collecting samples of behavior from large groups of people as they responded to standard sets of stimuli. Such behavior samples were first used to make general statements about individual mental characteristics, but as statistical analyses became more sophisticated in the nineteenth century, they were used to establish group norms against which a person could be evaluated quantitatively. These behavior sampling procedures came to be called mental tests by 1890, but their story began some 30 years earlier.

In 1859, Charles Darwin published his momentous work, *Origin of Species*, in which he proposed two important ideas: that (1) variation of individual characteristics occurs within and between species (including humans), and (2) natural selection takes place in part on the basis of those characteristics. Darwin's cousin, Sir Francis Galton, was fascinated by these ideas, and he quickly applied Darwin's notions to the inheritance of individual differences—especially in mental abilities.

Galton designed tests aimed at measuring the relatively fixed capacities, structures, and functions he thought comprised the mind. Many of these tests focused on sensorimotor capacity. For example, Galton (1883) tried to distinguish high from low intelligence on the basis of individuals' ability to make fine discriminations between objects of differing weight and between varying intensities of heat, cold, and pain. He sought to measure individual differences in vividness of mental imagery; for this purpose, he invented the questionnaire. Galton's interests also extended to associative processes, so he developed the word association test to explore this phenomenon. Eventually, Galton set up a laboratory in London where, for a small fee, anyone could take a battery of tests and receive a copy of the results. This facility, the world's first mental testing center, was included in the health exhibition in the 1884 International Exhibition (an early World's Fair).

Galton's work began nearly 20 years before the official founding of psychology, but by the late 1880s, psychologists, too, were interested in measuring individual differences in mental functioning. The person usually credited with merging individual mental measurement with the new science of psychology is James McKeen Cattell, an American who completed his doctorate in Wundt's laboratory in Leipzig in 1886. Cattell's interest in applying psychological methods to the study of individual differences, already evident in his doctoral dissertation on individual variation in reaction time, was intensified when he met Galton while lecturing at Cambridge University in 1887. In 1888, Cattell founded the third psychological laboratory in the United States (the first lab was set up by William James at Harvard in 1879; the second was established by G. Stanley Hall at Johns Hopkins in 1883). Cattell was one of the first psychologists to appreciate the practical uses of tests in the selection and diagnosis of people. This recognition of the applied potential of mental tests foreshadowed the emergence of clinical psychology.

Cattell's experience in Wundt's laboratory taught him that "psychology cannot attain the certainty and exactness of the physical sciences unless it rests on a foundation of experiment and measurement" (Dennis, 1948, p. 347). Consequently, one of his first tasks was to construct a standard battery of mental tests for use by researchers interested in individual differences. He chose ten tests that reflected the then-prevalent tendency to use sensorimotor functioning as an index of mental capacity, and he tested people's performance under varying conditions. He also collected less systematic information about people's dreams, diseases, preferences, recreational activities, and future plans (Shaffer & Lazarus, 1952).

Sensorimotor mental tests were adopted at universities, including Wisconsin, Clark, and Yale, but they were also criticized because of their low correlations with most other mental ability criteria (Reisman, 1976). By this time, however, an alternative approach to testing began to appear in several quarters. In 1891, Hugo Munsterberg, a psychologist at the University of Freiburg (Germany) who later came to Harvard, constructed a set of 14 tests to assess children's mental abilities. These tests went beyond the Galton-Cattell tasks to measure more complex functions such as reading, classifying objects, and performing mathematical operations. The German psychiatrist Emil Kraepelin (originator of an early system for classifying mental disorders) also designed tests of complex mental functions such as memory and attention.

Finally, and most importantly, in 1895, Alfred Binet—the French lawyer and scientist who founded the first French psychology lab with Henri Beaunis—began to develop measures of complex mental ability in normal and defective children. Binet's involvement in this testing grew out of the recognition that retarded children (who had been distinguished as a diagnostic group only as late as 1838) might be helped if they could be identified and given special educational attention. In 1896, Binet and his colleague Victor Henri described a battery of tests that measured not just "simple part processes" such as space judgment, motor skills, muscular effort, and memory, but also comprehension, attention, suggestibility, aesthetic appreciation, and moral values.

Thus, by 1896 psychology was involved in measuring individual differences in mental functioning, and it hosted two overlapping approaches to the task: (1) the Galton-Cattell sensorimotor tests, aimed at assessing inherited, relatively fixed mental *structures*, and (2) the instruments of Binet and others, which emphasized complex mental *functions* which could be taught to some degree. Each of these approaches was important to the development of clinical psychology, the former because it fostered the appearance of the first psychological clinic and the latter because it provided a mental test which was to give the new field its first clear identity. Although early American psychologists came to rely on Binet's test, they embraced Galton's belief that intelligence was largely inherited.

The rest of this story must wait, however, until we examine a third major influence on clinical psychology: changing views of behavior disorder and its treatment.

Changing Conceptions of Behavior Disorder

From the beginning of recorded history, human beings have tried to explain behavior that is bizarre or apparently irrational. As the popularity of various theories has waxed and waned over the centuries, so too has the influence of various helping professions, including clinical psychology.

The earliest explanations of disordered behavior involved magical forces and supernatural agents. Persons who acted "crazy" were said to be possessed by demons or spirits, and treatment involved various forms of exorcism (including *trephining*, or boring small holes in the skull to provide evil spirits with an exit). In Greece before Hippocrates, these ideas appeared in revised form: Disordered behavior was attributed to the influence of one or more of the gods. Even in early monotheistic cultures, God was seen as a possible source of behavior problems. In the Old Testament, for example, we are told that "the Lord shall smite thee with madness, and blindness, and astonishment of heart" (Deuteronomy 28:28). Where supernatural approaches to behavior disorders were prevalent, philosophy and religion were dominant in explaining and dealing with them. (Though they are not prominent in Western cultures today, supernatural—and especially demonological—explanations remain influential in other cultures around the world and in some ethnic and religious subcultures in North America, too.)

Supernatural explanations of behavior disorders were still highly influential when, in about the 4th century B.C., the Greek physician Hippocrates suggested that these aberrations stem from natural causes. Hippocrates argued that behavior disorders, like other behaviors, are a function of the distribution of four bodily fluids, or humors: blood, black bile, yellow bile, and phlegm. This theory, generally acknowledged as the first medical model of disordered behavior, paved the way for the concept of *mental illness* and legitimized the involvement of the medical profession in its treatment. From Hippocrates until the fall of Rome in 476 A.D., physicians supported and reinforced a physical, or medical, model of behavior disorder.

In the Middle Ages, however, the medical model was swept away. The church became the primary social and legal institution in Europe, demonological explanations of behavior disorders regained prominence, and religious personnel again took over responsibility for dealing with all cases of deviance. Ever resourceful, many physicians soon became priests. The church began treating the "insane" by exorcising the spirits presumed to possess them.

Gradually, the treatment of deviant individuals took the form of confinement in newly established hospitals and asylums, such as London's St. Mary of Bethlehem (organized in 1547 and referred to by locals as "bedlam"). The hospital movement saved many lives, but it did not necessarily make them worth living. Even though many 18th-century scholars agreed that the insane were suffering from mental illness (not possession), the medical profession, which was now back in charge of the problem, had little to offer in the way of treatment. Feared and misunderstood by the general public—many undoubtedly still believed them to be possessed—the insane were little more than prisoners who lived under abominable conditions and received grossly inadequate care. Their doctors saw their mental illness as resulting from brain damage or—harking back to Hippocrates—an overabundance of blood.

Thanks to the efforts of European and North American reformers of the 18th and early-19th centuries (Philippe Pinel, William Tuke, Benjamin Rush, and Eli Todd), more humane living conditions and treatments began to appear in mental institutions. Pinel ushered in this era of moral treatment with the following comment: "It is my conviction that these mentally ill are intractable only because they are deprived of fresh air and liberty" (quoted in Ullmann & Krasner, 1975, p. 135). Thus began a new awareness of the possibility that mental patients could be helped, rather than simply hidden, and physicians retained the responsibility for helping them emerge from their confinement. The role of physicians in treating mental disorders was further solidified when, later in the 19th century, syphilis was identified as the cause of general paresis, a deteriorative brain syndrome that had once been treated as a form of insanity. Finding an organic cause for this mental disorder bolstered the view that all behavior disorders are organically based and that other disease entities awaited discovery. The notion that there could be "no twisted thought without a twisted molecule" (Abood, 1960) hastened the decline of the moral treatment approach and triggered a "psychiatric revolution" in which doctors searched feverishly for organic causes of—and physical treatments for—all forms of mental illness (Zilboorg & Henry, 1941).

Ironically, this revolution also led to the idea that mental disorders might have *psychological* causes, too. In the mid-1800s a few French physicians, including Jean-Martin Charcot, Hippolyte Bernheim, and Pierre Janet, began studying what Franz Anton Mesmer had called "animal magnetism" and what James Braid, an English surgeon, later termed "hypnotism." They found that hypnosis could alleviate certain behavior disorders, particularly hysteria (now known as conversion disorder) and speculated that, if mental illness is at least partly psychological, then psychological rather than medical treatment might be effective in dealing with it. Their work struck a responsive chord in a young Viennese neurologist named Sigmund Freud, who, by 1896, had already proposed the first stage of a theory in which behavior disorders were seen not as the result of organic problems, but as a consequence of the dynamic struggle of the human mind to satisfy instinctual (mainly sexual) desires while also coping with the rules and restrictions of the outside world. Freud's theory brought a less-than-ethusiastic reaction from his medical colleagues. One doctor called Freud's idea "a scientific fairy tale" (Krafft-Ebing, quoted in Reisman, 1976, p. 41). Nevertheless, the idea grew to become a comprehensive theory of the dynamic nature of behavior and behavior disorder, and it ultimately redirected the entire course of the mental health professions, including clinical psychology.

Freud's influence on clinical psychology was slight at first, partly because his theory was so controversial and partly because it dealt with mental illness, which was—in the late-19th century—wholly within the province of the medical profession. Psychologists laid no claim to a treatment function at that time, but we shall see that the dynamic approaches to behavior pioneered by Freud and his followers shaped the activities of clinical psychologists in other areas and ultimately provided the foundation for their involvement in therapy.

THE BIRTH OF CLINICAL PSYCHOLOGY: 1896–1917

Our examination of the three main roots of clinical psychology shows that, by the end of the 19th century, the ground had been prepared for its appearance as a discipline. Psychology had emerged as a science, psychologists had started applying scientific methods to the study of individual differences, and Freud's dynamic approach to behavior disorder was about to open vast new areas of inquiry for psychologists interested in understanding deviance.

In this historical context, the first clinical psychologist appeared, an American named Lightner Witmer. Following his graduation from the University of Pennsylvania in 1888, Witmer worked on his PhD in psychology with Wundt at the University of Leipzig. After completing his doctorate in 1892, Witmer was appointed director of the University of Pennsylvania psychology laboratory.

In March of 1896, a local schoolteacher named Margaret Maguire asked Witmer to help one of her students, "Charles Gilman," whom she described as a "chronic bad speller." Once a schoolteacher himself, Witmer "took the case," thus becoming the first clinical psychologist and simultaneously beginning an enterprise that became the world's first psychological clinic (Routh, 1996). The willingness of a psychologist to work with a child's scholastic problems may not now seem significant enough to mark the founding of a profession, but remember that, until this point, psychology had dealt with people only to study their behavior in general, not to become concerned about them as individuals. Witmer's decision was as unusual then as would be an attempt by a modern astronomer to determine the "best" orbit for the moon in order to alter its path.

Witmer's approach was to assess Charles's problem and then arrange for appropriate remedial procedures. His assessment showed that Charles had a visual impairment, as well as reading and memory problems that Witmer termed "visual verbal amnesia." Today, these difficulties would probably be diagnosed as dyslexia, a learning disability. Witmer recommended intensive tutoring to help the boy recognize words without having to spell them first. This procedure successfully brought "Charles" to the point where he could read normally (McReynolds, 1987).

Lightner Witmer (1867–1956).
(Courtesy of George Eastman House. Reproduced by permission.)

Not everything Witmer did was to be equally influential, but several aspects of his new clinic came to characterize subsequent clinical work for some time:

1. Most of his clients were children, a natural development since Witmer had been offering a course on child psychology, had published his first papers in the journal *Pediatrics*, and had attracted the attention of teachers concerned about their students.
2. His recommendations for helping clients were preceded by diagnostic assessment.
3. He did not work alone, but in a team approach which saw members of various professions consulting and collaborating on cases.
4. He emphasized prevention of future problems through early diagnosis and remediation.
5. He emphasized that clinical psychology should be built on the principles being discovered in scientific psychology as a whole.

In a talk at the 1896 meeting of the 4-year-old American Psychological Association, Witmer described his new brand of psychology. His friend Joseph Collins recounted the scene as follows:

> [Witmer said] that clinical psychology is derived from the results of an examination of many human beings, one at a time, and that the analytic method of discriminating mental abilities and defects develops an ordered classification of observed behavior, by means of postanalytic generalizations. He put forth the claim that the psychological clinic is an institution for social and public service, for original research, and for the instruction of students in psychological orthogenics which includes vocational, educational, correctional, hygienic, industrial, and social guidance. The only reaction he got from his audience was a slight elevation of the eyebrows on the part of a few of the older members. (Quoted in Brotemarkle, 1947, p. 65)

This lead-balloon reception is understandable given the following four facts prevalent at the time:

> *One*, the majority of psychologists considered themselves scientists and probably did not regard the role described by Witmer as appropriate for them. *Two*, even if they had considered his suggestions admirable, few psychologists were prepared by training or experience to perform the functions he proposed. *Three*, they were not about to jeopardize their identification as scientists, which was tenuous enough in those early years, by plunging their profession into what they felt were premature applications. *Four*, aside from any prevalent skeptical and conservative attitude, Witmer had an unfortunate talent for antagonizing his colleagues. (Reisman, 1976, p. 46)

The responses to Witmer's talk provided the first clues that conflicts would arise between psychology as a science and psychology as an applied profession. As noted earlier, some of these conflicts are at least as active today as they were in 1896.

In spite of his colleagues' objections, Witmer continued his clinical work and expanded his clinic facility in order to handle the increasing caseload. At first, the clientele consisted mainly of "slow" or retarded children, but later, the clinic accepted children with speech disorders, sensory problems, and learning disabilities. Consistent with his orthogenic (preventive guidance) orientation, Witmer also worked with "normal" and intellectually superior children and provided guidance and advice to their parents and teachers.

In 1897, the new clinic began offering a four-week summer course in child psychology consisting of case presentations, instruction in diagnostic testing, and demonstrations of remedial techniques. By 1900, three children a day were being served by a clinic staff that had grown to eleven members and, in 1907, Witmer set up a residential school for training retarded children. That same year, he founded and edited the first clinical journal, *The Psychological Clinic*. By 1909, over 450 cases had been seen in Witmer's facilities. Under Witmer's influence, the University of Pennsylvania began offering formal courses in clinical psychology during the 1904 to 1905 academic year. Clinical psychology was on its way.

However, the influence of Witmer's clinic, school, journal, and training courses was limited. Witmer got clinical psychology rolling but he had little to do with steering it, mainly because he ignored most of the developments that would later become prominent in clinical psychology. For example, Witmer ignored Alfred Binet's new intelligence test, the Binet-Simon scale, when it was introduced in the United States. Like Binet's earlier tests, this instrument was designed to measure complex mental processes, not the fixed mental structures with which Witmer was concerned. In spite of Binet's warning that it did not provide a wholly objective measure of intelligence, the Binet-Simon test gained wide attention. Henry H. Goddard of the Vineland (New Jersey) Training School heard about it while in Europe in 1908 and brought the Binet-Simon scale to the United States for assessing the intelligence of "feebleminded" children in the clinic he had set up 2 years earlier. The popularity of Goddard's translation of the Binet-Simon scale and Lewis Terman's 1916 revision of it (known as the Stanford-Binet) grew so rapidly in the United States that they overshadowed all other tests of intelligence, including those used by Witmer. The Binet scales provided a focus for clinical psychology's assessment function which, until 1910, had been rather disorganized. All over the United States, new university psychological clinics (more than 20 of them by 1914) and institutions for the retarded began adopting the Binet approach while deemphasizing Witmer's "old-fashioned" methods.

Witmer also ignored the clinical assessment of adults, a service that other clinicians began to perform to help psychiatrists diagnose and plan treatment for brain damage and other problems. Indeed, after 1907, psychological examination of mental patients in some hospitals became routine. Similar assessments were done in prisons to assist staff members to identify disturbed convicts or plan rehabilitation programs.

Finally, Witmer did not join other clinicians in practicing psychotherapy or in adopting the Freudian approach to behavior disorder. Freud's approach became known to clinical psychology through association with psychiatry in mental hospitals and also through child-guidance clinics which, though often run by psychiatrists, routinely employed psychologists. The child-guidance movement in the United States was stimulated by the National Committee for Mental Hygiene, a group founded by a former mental patient, Clifford Beers, and supported by William James, a Harvard psychologist, and Adolf Meyer, the country's most prominent psychiatrist. With funds from philanthropist Henry Phipps, the committee (which ultimately became the National Association for Mental Health) worked to improve treatment of the mentally ill and to prevent psychological disorders.

The first child-guidance clinic was founded in Chicago in 1909 by an English-born psychiatrist named William Healy. Like Witmer, Healy worked with children, employed a team approach, and emphasized prevention, but otherwise his orientation was quite different. For one thing, instead of dealing mainly with learning disabilities or other educational difficulties, Healy focused on cases of child misbehavior that drew the attention of school authorities, the police, or the courts. Healy's clinic operated on the assumption that juvenile offenders suffered from mental illness that should be dealt with before it caused more serious problems. Second, the approach taken by the staff at Healy's Chicago clinic (first called the Juvenile Psychopathic Institute and later the Institute for Juvenile Research) was heavily influenced by Freud's psychodynamic theories.

This dynamic approach received a huge boost in popularity when, in the same year Healy opened his clinic, G. Stanley Hall, a psychologist, arranged for Sigmund Freud and two of his followers, Carl Jung and Sandor Ferenczi, to speak at the twentieth-anniversary celebration of Clark University in Worcester, Massachusetts. This event and the lectures associated with it "sold" psychoanalysis to American psychologists (though not to Witmer, who did not attend; Routh, 1996). Freud's theory was compatible with the psychologists' interest in the way the mind deals with its environment (the functionalism of William James and G. Stanley Hall), as opposed to what it is made of (the structuralism of Wundt). It also appealed to the emphasis on pragmatism in the United States.

As a result of this excitement over Freud, psychological and child-guidance clinics began to follow Healy's model, not Witmer's. This fact, coupled with the spreading use of Binet intelligence tests, left Witmer in the background of the clinical psychology he founded. He remained active, of course, but mainly with functions and clients that have since become more strongly associated with school psychology, vocational counseling, speech therapy, and remedial education than with clinical psychology (Fagan, 1996).

Once clinical psychology adopted the Binet-Simon scales, it became identified primarily with the testing of problematic children in clinics and guidance centers. This image led critics to argue that clinicians spent too much time diagnosing hopeless cases and that they were not sufficiently psychoanalytic in orientation. These criticisms had relatively little effect, however, because schools and other institutions that dealt with children were searching for clinical psychologists to do the testing which was fast becoming fashionable. As the need for clinicians' services slowly grew, so too did the field of clinical psychology during the years from 1910 to 1917. Clinicians gave established tests, constructed new ones, and conducted research on the reliability and validity of them all. Most of the new instruments were aimed at measuring intelligence, but a few focused on the assessment of personality through word associations or questionnaire items.

However, people who sought training in clinical psychology faced some real problems during this period. A few internships were available at places such as the Vineland Training School, and a few courses in intelligence testing and related subjects were taught here and there, but there were no formalized clinical training programs. Virtually anyone could claim the title of "clinical psychologist." The APA offered little help in addressing clinical training needs because of its preoccupation with the scientific aspects of psychology. Indeed, its only official recognition of the problems of the new field was to pass a resolution in 1915 discouraging the use of mental tests by unqualified persons.

In December 1917, a group of disgruntled clinicians agreed that they could best advance the interests of their new profession by forming a separate organization, called the American Association of Clinical Psychologists (AACP). Their strategy was not successful, however, and, after the APA promised to give more consideration to professional issues and problems, the AACP rejoined the APA as its clinical section in 1919.

BETWEEN THE WARS: 1918–1941

When the United States entered World War I, large numbers of military recruits had to be classified in terms of intellectual prowess and psychological stability. No techniques existed to do this, so the Army asked Robert Yerkes (then APA president) to head a committee of assessment-oriented experimental psychologists who were to develop appropriate measures. To measure mental abilities, the committee produced the Army Alpha and Army Beta intelligence tests (for group administration to literate or nonliterate adults, respectively), and to help detect behavior disorders, it recommended Robert Woodworth's Psychoneurotic Inventory (discreetly retitled "personal data sheet"; Yerkes, 1921, in Dennis, 1948). By 1918, psychologists had conducted evaluations of nearly 2 million men.

The role of clinical psychology in wartime assessment did not change some clinicians' focus on assessing children, but many began to find growing employment opportunities as testers in adult-oriented facilities as well. Clinicians were also using a wider variety of intelligence tests for children and adults and adding new measures of personality, interests, specific abilities, emotions, and traits. They developed many of these tests themselves, while adopting others from the psychoanalytically oriented psychiatrists of Europe. Some of the more familiar instruments of this period include Jung's Word Association Test (1919), the Rorschach Inkblot Test (1921), the Miller Analogies Test (1926), the Goodenough Draw-A-Man Test (1926), the Strong Vocational Interest Test (1927), the Thematic Apperception Test (TAT) (1935), the Bender-Gestalt Test (1938), and the Wechsler-Bellevue Intelligence Scale (1939).

In fact, so many psychological tests appeared (over 500 by 1940) that a Mental Measurements Yearbook was needed to catalog them (Buros, 1938). The development, administration, and evaluation of these instruments continued to stimulate clinicians' assessment and research functions. In 1921, Cattell formed the Psychological Corporation to sell tests and provide consultation and research services to business and industry. Clinical psychologists of this period also developed theories and conducted research on such topics as the nature of personality, the source of human intelligence (i.e., heredity or environment), the causes of behavior disorders, the uses of hypnosis, and the relationship between learning principles and deviance.

By the mid-1930s, there were fifty psychological clinics and at least a dozen child-guidance clinics in the United States. Clinical psychologists in these settings "perceived themselves as dealing with educational, not psychiatric problems. But this distinction was growing increasingly difficult to maintain" (Reisman, 1976, pp. 176–177). Slowly, clinicians added a treatment function to their assessment, training, and research roles. By the late-1930s, a few had even gone into private practice. For most clinicians of the day, this treatment function was a natural outgrowth of the diagnostic and remedial services they were already providing to children. It stemmed also from clinicians' growing use of personality tests—such as the Rorschach and the TAT. Discussing the results of these tests with therapists (psychiatrists) in a common clinical language brought clinical psychologists that much closer to the treatment role. They were motivated to enter that role because it expanded their professional identity beyond that of testing, allowed them to become involved with the "whole patient," and opened the door to better-paying, more responsible jobs.

Even though its settings, clients, and functions were expanding throughout the 1930s, clinical psychology was not yet a recognized profession. At the beginning of World War II, there were still no official training programs for clinicians. A few held PhDs, some had MAs, most had BAs or less. To get a job as a clinical psychologist, all a person needed was a few courses in testing, abnormal psychology, and child development, along with an "interest in people." University psychology departments were reluctant to develop graduate programs in clinical psychology because their faculties tended to question the appropriateness of "applied" psychology and to worry about the cost of clinical training. Nor was much help forthcoming from the APA. It had appointed committees on clinical training at various times during the 1920s and 1930s (and had even set up a short-lived clinical certification program), but its involvement was half-hearted. For example, in 1935 the APA Committee on Standards of Training in Clinical Psychology suggested that a PhD plus 1 year of supervised experience was necessary to become a clinical psychologist, but after issuing its report the committee disbanded and little came of its efforts.

The discontent of clinical and other nonacademic psychologists erupted in 1937, and they again broke away from APA to form a separate organization, this time called the American Association of Applied Psychology (AAAP). It contained divisions of consulting, clinical, educational, and industrial psychology and remained independent for 6 years before rejoining APA.

By the end of the 1930s, all the ingredients for the modern field of clinical psychology had been assembled: Its six functions (assessment, treatment, research, teaching, consultation, and administration) had appeared. Clinical psychology had expanded beyond its original clinics into hospitals, prisons, and other settings. Its practitioners worked with adults as well as children, and were motivated to stand on their own as a profession. Only the support of clinical psychology's parent discipline and the society it served was still needed. This support came as a result of World War II.

THE POSTWAR EXPLOSION

When the United States entered World War II, mass testing of the intelligence, ability, and personality of military personnel was again necessary and, as in World War I, a committee of psychologists was formed to help with the task. Because psychometric and clinical sophistication had increased greatly since the time of the Yerkes committee, this new group of psychologists produced a wider range of military-oriented tests, including the Army General Classification Test (a group intelligence instrument), a psychiatric screening questionnaire called the Personal Inventory, brief measures of intelligence, short forms of the Rorschach and the TAT, and several ability tests for selection of officers, pilots, and the like.

The involvement of psychology in World War II was also far deeper than it had been in World War I. For example, about 1,500 psychologists (nearly 25% of those available) served in World War II. They were commissioned officers, just like physicians, and in 1944 alone, they gave over 60 million psychological tests to 20 million soldiers and civilians (Reisman, 1976). In addition to giving tests, psychologists conducted interviews, wrote psychological reports, and, because of the overwhelming caseload of psychological casualties, performed psychoanalytically oriented therapy. For those who had been clinicians before the war, military life meant an opportunity to consolidate and expand their clinical functions, but such individuals were in the minority. Most wartime psychologists came from academic settings. For them, the army's desperate need for applied psychological services meant taking on clinical responsibilities for the first time. These converted clinicians found they were able to handle their new jobs remarkably well.

By the end of the war, many clinicians were "hooked" on doing therapy with adults, and many former experimentalists became enamored of clinical functions. Military and civilian authorities, too, were impressed with psychologists' clinical skills, which brought psychologists increasing public attention and prestige. This awakening of interest in psychologists' clinical work might have come to nothing if there had not been so much of it to do. The war left over 40,000 people in Veterans Administration (VA) neuropsychiatric hospitals, and there were nowhere near enough clinical psychologists and psychiatrists to serve these patients adequately.

Where the APA and university psychology departments had vacillated over the education and roles of clinicians, the needs of the federal government prompted immediate action. A 1946 VA circular defined clinical psychology as a profession that engaged in diagnosis, treatment, and research relating to adult disorders; it described clinicians as holders of the PhD. More important, the VA said it needed 4,700 of these individuals to fill lucrative, high-prestige jobs and that it would help pay for clinical training. "This document, more than any other single thing, has served to guide the development of clinical psychology" (Hathaway (1958, p. 107). Here was the support clinical psychology had been waiting for. Early in 1946, the chief medical director of the VA met with representatives of major universities to ask them to start formal clinical training programs; by that fall, 200 graduate students became VA clinical trainees at twenty-two institutions (Peck & Ash, 1964). By 1951, the VA had become the largest single employer of psychologists in the United States.

Given their earlier misgivings, not all psychology departments that began clinical training programs after the war were enthusiastic about doing so. Faculty members sympathetic to clinical work saw government support as a boon, but those devoted to keeping psychology a "pure" science objected to professional training as an intrusion that was being performed only because the government (first through the VA and then the United States Public Health Service, USPHS) was willing to pay for it. David Shakow (1965) characterized this conflict as pitting the "virgins" against the "prostitutes." Whatever one calls it, the debate centered on the same "science versus profession" controversy that first appeared in 1896 and which continues today.

In any case, the VA and USPHS went ahead with their funding plans and turned to the APA for guidance about which university clinical programs merited federal support. In 1947, APA's Committee on Graduate and Professional Training provided a preliminary report on existing programs (Kelly, 1961). Later that year, a more extensive report came from David Shakow's Committee on Training in Clinical Psychology, which had been appointed by the APA to (1) recommend the content of clinical programs, (2) set up training standards to be followed by universities and internship facilities, and (3) report on current programs (Shakow, 1978). This "Shakow Report" was meant only to provide training guidelines, but since it was so intimately tied to the dispensation of federal money to individual students and whole departments, the "guidelines" were adopted as policy "and soon became the 'bible' of all departments of psychology desirous of having their programs evaluated and reported on favorably by the APA" (Kelly, 1961, p. 110). Shakow felt that this reaction prematurely froze the nature of clinical training, and that, if the guidelines had been less rigidly interpreted, the resulting programs might have been better.

Indeed, the Shakow Report laid the groundwork for later controversy over how clinicians should be trained, an issue that related directly to the science-profession problem. The recommendations in the report that have the greatest contemporary importance are these:

1. Clinical psychologists should be trained first as psychologists (i.e., as scientists) and second as practicing professionals.
2. Clinical training should be as rigorous as that given to nonclinicians and thus should consist of a four-year doctorate, including a year of supervised clinical internship experience.
3. Clinical training should focus on the "holy trinity" (assessment, research, and treatment) by offering courses in general psychology, psychodynamics, assessment techniques, research methods, and therapy (APA, 1947; Shakow, 1978).

Thus began "what later came to be recognized as something of an educational experiment: the training of persons both as scientists and as practitioners, not in a separate professional school [as is the case in medicine or law], but in the graduate schools of our universities" (Kelly, 1961, p. 112). This experiment continued with the support of the APA, the federal government, internship facilities, and universities. Two years after the Shakow report appeared, participants in a national conference on clinical training at Boulder, Colorado, formally adopted its recommendations. In addition, the APA created an Education and Training Board to evaluate and publish lists of accredited doctoral-level clinical programs and internship settings.

The scientist-professional training package described in the Shakow Report and adopted at the Boulder Conference in 1949 came to be known as the "Boulder model"; it set the pattern for clinical training for the next 25 years. Nevertheless, not everyone in the field was enthusiastic about it, and though its official APA status was reaffirmed at subsequent training conferences in 1955, 1958, 1962, 1965, and 1973, discontent remained. In Chapter 14, we consider the details of these conferences and the modifications of the Boulder model that have ensued. Suffice it to say here that psychologists committed to professional practice felt that the model emphasized research training at the expense of preparation for applied work, while more research-oriented psychologists failed to see the need for so much emphasis on application.

As debate continued over the appropriateness of the Boulder model, government support of its use in university-based clinical training programs fueled explosive growth in clinical psychology. In 1948, there were 22 APA-approved clinical training programs; there were 60 by 1962, 83 by 1973, more than 150 by 1993, and 187 exist today. Personality and intelligence assessment mushroomed following the introduction of tests like the Minnesota Multiphasic Personality Inventory (MMPI), new scoring procedures for projectives like the Rorschach, and new adult intelligence scales. Clinical psychologists' treatment roles, now recognized by the government and by the public, blossomed as well. Three times as many clinical psychologists engaged in therapy after the war as before it, and though many still treated children, the emphasis began to swing toward adult clients. As shown in Table 1.1, the clinician in private practice became more common as practitioners sought to pattern themselves after physicians.

Legal recognition of clinical psychology as a profession was growing as well. In the postwar years, states began passing laws providing for licensure or certification of qualified clinicians, and the APA set up an independent certification group to identify individuals who had attained particularly high levels of clinical experience and expertise. The APA also developed a code of ethics governing the behavior of all its members, but focusing on those engaged in applied activities. These and other aspects of clinical psychology as a profession are discussed more fully in Chapter 14.

Clinical research also expanded after World War II and produced some disturbingly negative conclusions on the usefulness of some personality tests (e.g., Magaret, 1952), the value of clinicians' diagnostic judgments when compared to statistically based decisions (Meehl, 1954), and the effectiveness of traditional (mainly Freudian) psychotherapy (Eysenck, 1952). This research created discontent with standard clinical assessment methods and motivated the development of many new approaches to treatment, including humanistic and behavioral varieties.

By the 1980s, almost everything that could have been said about clinical psychology before World War II had changed. The clinical psychologist before the war was primarily a diagnostician whose clients were children. After 1945, the functions, settings, and clients of clinical psychology expanded dramatically. Today's clinician enjoys a wider range of theoretical approaches and practical tools for assessing and altering human behavior.

CLINICAL PSYCHOLOGY IN THE 21ST CENTURY

The chronology on the inside front cover of this book shows that clinical psychology has advanced in spectacular fashion over the last 100 years, but neither its development nor its self-examination is complete. As clinical psychology enters the 21st century, it faces an unprecedented number of issues and challenges that promise to change almost every aspect of the field, including the way clinical students are trained, the services clinicians provide, the settings where they provide them, the manner by which they are paid, and the theories that guide their explanations and treatment of psychological disorders (Clarke-Kudless, 1996). Some of these issues and challenges—such as the scientist-practitioner distinction, the value of assessment and therapy, how to prevent psychological problems, and how best to serve the poor and other underserved populations—have been around for decades. Issues and challenges of more recent origin include whether clinicians should have the right to prescribe psychoactive drugs, the impact of health care reforms on private practice and the quality of clinical services, and the increasingly interdisciplinary and specialized nature of clinical work. We discuss all these factors in later chapters; here we highlight just a few.

The Challenges of Health Care Reform

For many decades, clinical psychology operated on a fee-for-service basis. That is, clients or their insurance companies reimbursed clinicians for whatever assessment or therapy services were provided. However, the last 15 years have seen dramatic changes in the financing of the services provided by all health care professions, including clinical psychology. By far, the most important of these changes has been the introduction by insurance companies of *managed care*, a general strategy which, as mentioned earlier, controls health care costs by paying only for certain treatments, offered by specifically approved providers, for limited periods of time. In many managed care plans, the consumer pays a fixed annual fee, which is passed on to health care providers. If, in a given year, these providers offer fewer services than the prepaid plan anticipated, they stand to make a profit; if they must offer more services, they suffer a loss.

Fundamental changes in the practice of clinical psychology have already occurred as a result of these economic forces, and we expect further changes during the 21st century, including (1) a continuation of the post-1990 decline in the solo private practice of psychology as more clinicians join group practices in order to cut costs, (2) an increase in the use of brief therapies that emphasize problem-solving skills and rapid symptom reduction, (3) an emphasis on prevention, so that fewer clients will need extensive (and expensive) individual therapy, (4) a demand that clinicians employ only those treatment methods that have been empirically demonstrated to be effective, whether or not they are the ones the clinicians normally use, (5) a larger role for clinicians trained at BA or MA levels, because they tend to be paid less than doctoral personnel, (6) more involvement of clinicians with clients suffering from cancer, cardiovascular diseases, head and spinal cord injuries, diabetes, and other health problems associated with or complicated by psychological factors, and (7) more intense pressure for clinical psychologists to obtain privileges to prescribe cost-effective psychoactive drugs (Cullen & Newman, 1997; Cummings, 1995; Murray, 1996; VandenBos & Williams, 2000).

Trends Toward Integrated Theories and Interdisciplinary Work

In the next chapter, we will see that clinicians are influenced by several specific psychological theories of personality and psychopathology, but it is also the case that many of these theories are becoming increasingly multidisciplinary. That is, clinicians are becoming increasingly aware that mental disorders can often best be understood and treated by focusing on a combination of biological, sociocultural, and psychological factors. In particular, the increasing prominence of biological factors in these theories is rapidly changing how clinical psychologists are trained and how they think about mental disorders. As scientists continue making new discoveries in behavioral genetics, as neuroimaging studies of the living brain become more sophisticated, and as the biochemistry of behavior becomes better understood, we suspect that assessments, explanations, and treatments of many mental disorders will take a pronounced biological turn. Indeed, almost every major mental disorder has now been linked to interactions of various biological vulnerabilities and psychological processes, and these diathesis-stress theories are generally proving much more powerful than the single-variable explanations of the past. Clinicians of the 21st century need training in, and an appreciation of, the neurosciences if clinical psychology is to continue as a psychological science.

At the same time, fewer psychologists maintain strict adherence to traditional theoretical approaches (see Chapter 2). Increasing numbers of clinicians refer to themselves as *eclectic*—meaning that they borrow from various approaches. Even those who ascribe to one theoretical model in theory are not likely to stick with only that model's techniques in practice (see McWilliams, 1999). The existence of the *Journal of Psychotherapy Integration* also attests to the interest in bridging the gaps among psychological theories.

Just as strict boundaries among psychological theories are fading, so are boundaries between psychological and other conceptions of human behavior. For instance, psychologists have traditionally treated "mental illness" while physicians have treated "medical illness." But physical and psychological disturbances co-occur in a great many illnesses, and changes in psychological functioning can often have dramatic effects in physical functioning (and vice versa). Recognition of this has led to clinical psychologists' increasing levels of employment in medical settings. Indeed, integration with the more biologically-oriented professions has been one of the most pronounced trends in clinical psychology.

Specialization of Clinical Activity

In the past, the ideal training for clinical psychologists included a core of knowledge about scientific methods and psychopathology, along with courses in and practical experience with valid assessment and treatment strategies. This "core curriculum" model has come under increasing challenge, mainly because clinical psychologists are now working in many specialized areas that demand specialized training not included in traditional graduate programs. Increasingly, this training is provided through post-doctoral traineeships in which clinicians work under expert supervision for a year or two in a designated specialty area. Several of these specializations are described in later chapters; in fact, most of the revisions we have made to this book over the past two decades have been designed to keep up with this "specializing" of clinical psychology. Consistent with trends in psychology in general, many of the developing clinical specialties reflect a biological orientation; neuropsychology, health psychology or behavioral medicine, and pediatric psychology are prominent examples. Forensic psychology is another specialization that will expand the definition of clinical psychology in the 21st century. In short, it is unclear today whether clinical psychology will best be understood as one large field or several smaller ones. There are currents in both directions—the movement toward integration and interdisciplinary collaboration pulls the field together while the movement toward intense specialization threatens to segment the field.

The Challenge of Cultural Diversity

The proportion of ethnic minorities in the United States, particularly Hispanic minorities, is growing, and it is expected to continue growing at a faster pace than the white population, resulting in an increasingly diverse population. For instance, over half of public school students in the state of California are people of color (Sue & Sue, 1999). But diversity refers not only to racial and ethnic variations, but also to variations in sexual orientation, religious orientations, or other dimensions that create psychological experiences that are significantly different from experiences of persons in other cultures or groups.

As the population becomes increasingly diverse, clinical psychologists need to be more aware of how diversity affects clinical practice. For instance, psychological disorders sometimes manifest themselves very differently across cultural groups (Lopez & Guarnaccia, 2000). As a result, traditional diagnostic categories may not fit the symptoms of certain culturally-bounded dysfunctions, and clinician who are not aware of the specific symptoms and cultural contexts can make inaccurate diagnoses and assessments. They might also alienate clients, thus failing to provide effective therapy. It is no coincidence that more than half of ethnic minority clients terminate therapy prematurely (often after only one visit), whereas the figure for European-Americans is less than 30% (Sue & Sue, 1999).

To respond to such problems, clinical psychology is becoming more culturally sensitive. Evidence for this increased sensitivity can be seen in the appearance of large numbers of journal articles on the effects of sociocultural factors on clinical practice, and in the publication of books and guidelines for working with clients who represent a different sociocultural background (e.g., APA's 2001 Guidelines for Psychotherapy with Lesbian, Gay, and Bisexual Clients; McGoldrick, Giordano, & Pearce, 1996; Sue & Sue, 1999). These sources discuss the problems therapists might encounter when working with persons from different cultures, and some also provide background information on cultural differences in world views and identity-formation processes (Sue & Sue, 1999). We address such cultural considerations in several places throughout this book.

The Scientist-Practitioner Issue

In contemporary clinical psychology, there are—to use William James's famous distinction—"tough-minded" clinicians who insist that clinical work should be based on scientifically verified findings and that clinical training should be grounded in basic psychological theory and rigorous research. There are also "tender-minded" clinicians who believe that wisdom can be distilled from many sources, including research, clinical experience, and personal intuitions, and that scientific methods may not capture the subtleties of human behavior and are therefore an insufficient base for clinical practice. Although many clinicians try to stake out a middle ground that allows them to be both empirical and intuitive, the fact is that the gulf between tender- and tough-minded clinicians is often wide and reflects fundamental differences in the way they are trained, the types of clinical services they provide, and the sort of evidence they consider convincing. In fact, the extent to which clinicians endorse tough- or tender-minded beliefs predicts their positions on many of the major controversies facing clinicians today—such as whether memories of childhood trauma can be repressed and then accurately recalled years later, whether specific types of psychotherapy are effective, and even whether certain mental disorders are real (Hasemann, Nietzel, & Golding, 1996).

Can clinicians be tough-minded without being cold-hearted? Can they be critical enough to scrutinize faddish ideas and fuzzy thinking without being so skeptical that they reject all new ideas whose worth is simply hard to prove? Finding just the right balance between close-minded skepticism and uncritical acceptance of anything that "feels" right is an elusive goal, not only in clinical training, but also in the daily activities of clinicians already in the field. These clinicians continue to ask how they can be scientifically-minded psychologists who wait for carefully validated evidence before diagnosing a condition or proceeding with a treatment and, at the same time, function as "front-line" practitioners who try to help distressed people with complex problems about which little knowledge may be available.

Some observers feel that the scientific and professional roles are basically incompatible, and that a psychologist must choose one or the other. Accordingly, some clinical students become intuitive practitioners to whom data is a nasty word, while others work as full-time researchers in hopes of generating empirical findings that will someday make all clinical practice scientific. Another indication of the conflict between academic psychologists and practitioners is seen in their preferences for the type of professional organization that best represents their respective views. In 1988, the American Psychological Society (APS) was formed by a group of psychologists who wanted an organization that is more scientifically-oriented than what, in their eyes, the APA had become. Although some research-oriented clinicians belong to both APA and APS, most full-time practitioners appear to prefer APA over APS as their professional "home."

If the past is any indication of the future, the scientist-professional debate will continue well into the 21st century. Unfortunately, the debate has polarized clinical psychology. It threatens to isolate practitioners from research that may be useful in applied work, and it may keep researchers in laboratory settings that are so artificial that their results apply only to other laboratories or to situations where the most interesting and important clinical problems may not appear. The cumulative result of this polarization could be a reduction in the mutual stimulation between clinic and laboratory that we, and many others in the field, consider vital to the future of clinical psychology (Bootzin, 1996; Strupp, 1989).

In our view, clinical psychology will advance and prosper as a profession and a scholarly field only to the degree that it remains firmly grounded in the foundations of science. We recognize that science can be defined in several ways (Gergen, 1985; 2001), but for our purposes in this book the essential feature of a scientific clinical psychology is that clinicians evaluate the validity of their theories, the effectiveness of their techniques, and the impact of their practice with public, replicable, and well-controlled empirical research methods. The clearest call for building a scientific clinical psychology has been sounded in Richard McFall's (1991) "Manifesto for a Science of Clinical Psychology." McFall's manifesto has been echoed by other clinical psychologists (Chambless et al., 1995; Sechrest, 1992) and consists of the following three principles:

1. Scientific clinical psychology is the only legitimate and acceptable form of clinical psychology.
2. Psychological services should not be delivered to the public (except under strict experimental control) until they meet four criteria: the service is described clearly, its claimed benefits are stated explicitly, its effects are validated scientifically, and its positive effects are shown to outweigh its possible negative effects.
3. The primary and overriding objective of doctoral training programs in clinical psychology must be to produce the most competent clinical scientists possible.

As the size and stature of clinical psychology have grown, the field has become more tolerant of divergent ideas about clinical training, professional roles, and basic issues like the development of human problems and the means through which they can best be alleviated. Throughout this book we review the most important of these contrasting ideas and illustrate their importance for clinical psychologists. We have tried to describe the various models and methods of clinical psychology fairly, but we also intend the book to reflect our conviction that these models and methods are best judged against the scientific standards suggested by McFall's manifesto.

CHAPTER SUMMARY

Clinical psychology, the largest single subfield within the larger discipline of psychology, involves six main functions: assessment, treatment, research, teaching, consultation, and administration. In carrying out these functions, clinicians are distinguished from other psychologists, and other helping professions, by their clinical attitude: the tendency to use the results of research on human behavior in general to assess, understand, and assist particular individuals. They deal with a wide range of clients from all age groups and focus on an even wider range of behavior problems, from anxiety, depression, and psychoses, to occupational stress, mental retardation, and difficulties at school. Clinical psychologists are employed in many different settings, from university psychology departments and medical clinics to community mental health centers and prisons. Many are self-employed private practitioners.

Clinical psychology began in 1896, when Lightner Witmer agreed to assess and treat a child with problems at school. His efforts in this regard, and his establishment of the world's first psychological clinic, were not supported by most other psychologists (who saw these professional activities as falling outside the realm of scientific psychology), but the assessment and treatment functions of clinical psychology grew over the next 100 years, spurred by the need for psychological testing and treatment services in schools, military recruitment centers, and hospitals that cared for veterans, especially the psychological casualties of World War II. After that war, the prestige, activities, and training programs for clinical psychologists experienced explosive growth. Today, clinical psychology is a well-established field whose members engage in an ever-expanding range of research and services while continuing to address a number of persistent issues (such as the scientist-practitioner distinction) and to face challenges posed by health care reform and other social changes.

Chapter 2

Approaches to Clinical Psychology

The field of clinical psychology can be most fully understood when examined from several different perspectives, each of which emphasizes some of its aspects over others. Each of these perspectives, or approaches, tries to explain how behavior develops and becomes problematic, and each influences the assessment, treatment, and research activities of those who adopt a particular approach. For example, suppose there were an approach to clinical psychology which sees behavior as caused by what people eat. Clinicians taking this approach would probably make predictions about how diet affects human development (e.g., "Mushy foods produce mushy thinking and uncoordinated behavior."). They would also generate hypotheses about how diet is related to mental disorder (e.g., excess carbohydrate intake causes anxiety; too little fiber creates obsessive rituals). They would develop specialized measurement procedures to assess clients' eating patterns and to monitor the nutritional components of each meal. Their treatments would probably focus on changing clients' eating habits; merely talking about a client's problems would be regarded as a waste of time. Finally, their research would probably evaluate procedures for measuring and altering food intake, as well as test the validity of causal links between diet and disorder.

Though diet is important in many aspects of life, the thinking and activities of most clinicians today are influenced mainly by some combination of the *psychodynamic, behavioral, humanistic,* and *interpersonal* approaches to clinical psychology. In this chapter, we review the assumptions and implications of these approaches.

THE PROS AND CONS OF TAKING A SPECIFIC APPROACH

Human behavior can be examined on several levels, from the interactions among brain cells to the interactions among people, or even among nations or cultures. Clinicians must decide which aspects of behavior deserve special attention, which kinds of assessment data will be of greatest value for a given purpose, which treatment techniques merit exploration, and which research targets are likely to be most fruitful. A clinician's approach guides these decisions. The various approaches to clinical psychology help clinicians organize their thinking about behavior, thereby imposing order on, and suggesting relationships among, vast amounts of complex material. To be of greatest value to clinical psychologists, an approach should include a complete and testable account of the development, maintenance, and alteration of both problematic and nonproblematic human behavior.

Ironically, a specific approach to clinical psychology can act not only as a compass and guide, but also as a set of blinders. Each specific approach tends to attract followers whose commitment to it ranges from healthy skepticism to fanatic zeal. Some clinicians allow their favorite approach to so completely organize their thinking about behavior that they become rigid and closed to new and potentially valuable ideas associated with other approaches. In short, their views become not just organized, but fossilized in a way that makes objective evaluation and subsequent modification of professional practices unlikely. Clinicians who become overly dependent on a specific approach may continue to perform in strict accordance with its tenets even when empirical evidence suggests that change is in order. In other words, taking a consistent perspective can evolve from an asset to a liability if it produces such a narrow focus that other points of view are overlooked.

An approach is also like a region of the world that develops its own dialect. That dialect eases communication among those who share it; terms become a professional shorthand, making communication more efficient. But for those who do not share it, the dialect can obstruct discussions. Often, the exchange of ideas between persons espousing different approaches to clinical psychology is hampered by this kind of language barrier. Both parties think they are speaking clearly and comprehensibly when, in fact, their specialized terms and meanings keep them from fully understanding each other.

Fortunately, most problems associated with taking a specific approach to clinical psychology can be reduced by (1) avoiding the overzealous commitment to it that fosters conceptual rigidity, behavioral inflexibility, and semantic narrowness, and (2) evaluating that approach according to rigorous scientific methods, and revising the approach when the data demand it. This is not to say that systematic use of a particular approach is not important; quite the opposite. However, understanding and appreciating other points of view can act as insurance against a narrow-mindedness that could be detrimental to clinicians and clients alike.

We hope that the material in this chapter will help you remain open-minded. If you are already acquainted with psychodynamic, behavioral, humanistic, and interpersonal theories of personality, some of the chapter may be familiar, but we also go beyond abstract theory to outline the assessment and treatment implications that flow from each approach and how they are likely to be applied to individual cases. In subsequent chapters, we will consider in more detail the specific tactics that translate these strategies into action.

One final point: Each of the models discussed in this chapter is made up of variations on a basic theme; thus, to characterize adequately each model, we must describe several of these variations.

THE PSYCHODYNAMIC APPROACH

The psychodynamic model is rooted in the writings of Sigmund Freud, but it has broadened to include the ideas of those who revised and challenged many of Freud's concepts. The model is based upon the following assumptions:

1. Human behavior is determined by impulses, desires, motives, and conflicts that are intrapsychic (within the mind) and often out of awareness.
2. Intrapsychic factors cause both normal and abnormal behaviors. Thus, just as disabling anxiety might be attributed to unresolved conflicts or unmet needs, a person's outgoing style might be seen as reflecting inner fears of worthlessness or a hidden desire to be more popular than a sibling.
3. The foundations for behavior are set down in childhood through satisfaction or frustration of basic needs and impulses. Because of their central role in these needs, early relationships with family, peers, and authority figures are given special attention.
4. Clinical assessment, treatment, and research should emphasize the aspects of intrapsychic activity which, though often hidden from direct observation, must be uncovered if behavior is to be understood and behavior problems are to be alleviated.

Freudian Psychoanalysis

Freud's psychodynamic theory, known as *psychoanalysis*, was founded on a few basic principles. One of these is *psychic determinism*, the notion that behavior can be caused by psychological factors that are hidden from outside observers and from the behaving individual as well (Funder, 2001). From this perspective, almost all behaviors (even "accidents") are seen as meaningful because they provide clues to hidden conflicts and motivations (Freud, 1901). Thus, reading the word *breast* when the text says *beast,* forgetting a relative's name, or losing a borrowed book might all be interpreted as expressing feelings or impulses that may not appear in awareness. Freud called *unconscious* the part of mental functioning that is out of awareness and not readily accessible to it.

Another of Freud's basic postulates was that human behavior is derived from the constant struggle between the individual's desire to satisfy inborn sexual and aggressive instincts and the need to respect the rules and realities imposed by the outside world. He saw each individual facing a lifelong search for ways of expressing instinctual urges without incurring punishment or other negative consequences. To Freud, then, the human mind is an arena where what the person *wants* to do (instinct) must be reconciled with the controlling requirements of what can or *should* be done (reason and morality).

Mental Structure. In Freud's system, unconscious instincts make up the *id*, which is present at birth and contains all the psychic energy—or *libido*—available to motivate behavior. Id seeks to gratify its desires without delay, and therefore it is said to operate on the *pleasure principle* (i.e., "If it feels good, do it!"). As the newborn grows and the outside world imposes more limitations on direct id gratification, the *ego* begins to organize as an outgrowth of id around the age of 1 year and begins to find safe outlets for expression of instincts. Since ego adjusts to external demands, it operates on the *reality principle* (i.e., "If you are going to do it, at least do it quietly."). A third mental agency, *superego*, is another result of the socializing influence of reality. It contains all the teachings of family and culture regarding ethics, morals, and values, and according to Freud, these teachings are internalized to become the "ego ideal," or how one would like to be. Superego also contains the conscience, which seeks to promote perfect, conforming, and socially acceptable behavior usually opposed by id.

Mechanisms of Defense. Freud's three-part mental structure is constantly embroiled in anxiety-provoking internal conflicts. The ego's primary function is to protect against the anxiety that we would feel if we became aware of socially unacceptable id impulses or if we thought about violating the superego's rules (Funder, 2001). The ego attempts to keep these conflicts and their discomfort from reaching consciousness by employing a variety of *defense mechanisms*, usually at an unconscious level. One of the most common—and for Freud, the most prototypic of these mechanisms—is *repression,* where ego simply holds an unacceptable thought, feeling, or impulse out of consciousness. Repression has also been called motivated forgetting. For example, an individual whose hatred toward a parent is not consciously experienced may repress that hatred (when a person is aware of an impulse and consciously denies its existence, the process is called *suppression*).

In spite of constant efforts at repression, undesirable urges—much like an inflated balloon held under water—may sometimes threaten to surface. To guard against this, the ego employs additional unconscious defenses, such as *reaction formation*, in which the person thinks and acts exactly opposite to the unconscious impulse. Thus, a son who hates his father may express unbounded love and concern for him. If the defense mechanism called projection is used, the son may attribute negative feelings to others and accuse them of mistreating their fathers. A defense mechanism called *displacement* allows some expression of id impulses, but it aims them at safer targets, such as co-workers or others who may be father figures. Thus, the son may harshly criticize an older colleague instead of his father.

Though they may be at least temporarily successful, defense mechanisms waste a lot of psychic energy, and, under stress, they may fail, thus forcing the troubled person to fall back, or *regress*, to levels of behavior characteristic of earlier, less mature stages of development. The depth of regression in a given case is partly a function of the individual's history of psychosexual development.

   Developmental Stages.   Freud postulated that children pass through several psychosexual stages of development, each named for the part of the body most associated with pleasure at the time. The first year or so is called the *oral* stage, because eating, sucking, biting, and other oral activities are the predominant sources of pleasure. If, because of premature or delayed weaning, oral needs are frustrated or overindulged, the child may fail to pass through the oral stage without clinging to, or becoming *fixated* on, behavioral patterns associated with it. Adults who depend inordinately upon oral behavioral patterns such as smoking or overeating may be seen as orally fixated. Freud felt that the stronger an individual's fixation at a given psychosexual stage, the more behaviors typical of that stage would be shown at a later point and the more likely it would be that regression to that level would occur under stress. A person who becomes excessively dependent or depressed when dependency needs are not met are sometimes viewed by Freudians as having regressed to the oral stage.

   The second year or so is called the *anal* stage, because Freud saw the anus and the stimuli associated with eliminating and withholding feces as the important sources of pleasure at that point. The significant feature of this period is toilet training, in which there is a clash of wills between parents and children. Anal fixation is thought to result from overly strict or overly permissive practices in this area. Adults who are either stingy, obstinate, highly organized, and overconcerned with cleanliness, or who are sloppy, disorganized, and especially generous with money might be seen as fixated at the anal stage.

   The child enters Freud's *phallic* stage at about age 3 or 4, as the genitals become the primary source of pleasure. He theorized that during the phallic stage young boys begin to have sexual desires for their mothers and to want to do away with their fathers' competition. This situation was labeled *Oedipal* because it recapitulates the plot of the Greek tragedy *Oedipus Rex*. Because the boy fears punishment for his incestuous and murderous desires, Oedipal conflicts are normally resolved by repressing sexual desires toward the mother, *identifying* with the father, and ultimately finding an appropriate female sex partner.

   Although Freud emphasized male psychosexual development, he did discuss a female Oedipus complex—he rejected the term *Electra complex*, used by some of his students—in which a little girl suffers penis envy and a sense of inferiority because she believes she has already been "castrated" for desiring her father. She ultimately sublimates these feelings by substituting a desire to have a baby for a desire to have a penis, thus identifying with her mother. (As you might imagine, these views have not made Freud a popular figure among feminists.) Freud believed that successfully resolving conflicts in the phallic stage was crucial to healthy psychological development and that fixation at the phallic stage is responsible for many adult interpersonal behaviors, including rebellion, aggression, and problematic sexual practices such as exhibitionism and fetishism.

   Freud believed a dormant or *latency* period follows the phallic stage. During latency, id impulses recede and the reality principle becomes a stronger force in the child's life, allowing the child to focus on developing social and academic skills. The latency period extends until adolescence, when the individual's physical maturity ushers in the genital period. In this final stage—which lasts throughout the adult years—pleasure is again focused on the genital area, but if all has gone well in earlier stages, sexual interest is directed not just toward the self-satisfaction characteristic of the phallic period, but toward establishment of a stable, long-term relationship in which the needs of another are valued and considered.

Other Psychodynamic Approaches

Some of Freud's followers created variations on his psychodynamic approach, and later psychodynamic theorists maintained certain key elements but modified their theories to place greater emphasis on ego functioning, development of the self, and interpersonal relationships. These variations were stimulated by several factors, including (a) dissatisfaction with the central role Freud gave to unconscious instincts in motivation, (b) increased recognition of the influence of social and cultural variables on human behavior, (c) recognition of the role of conscious aspects of personality, and (d) belief that personality development does not end in childhood (see Schultz & Schultz, 2001).

An important revision of psychoanalysis was presented by Erik H. Erikson, an American psychologist who emphasized social factors in human development. Erikson (1959, 1963) outlined a sequence of eight psychosocial stages that is oriented toward people's social, rather than intrapsychic, activities. As shown in Table 2.1, a social crisis is either successfully handled or left partly unresolved at each stage.

Other psychodynamic theorists rejected rather than revised certain aspects of psychoanalysis. For example, Alfred Adler, one of Freud's original followers, developed a brand of psychoanalysis known as *individual psychology*, in which the most impor-

TABLE 2.1   Erikson's Eight Stages or Crises and Associated Emerging Traits

Stage	Age	Successful Resolution Leads to:	Unsuccessful Resolution Leads to:
I. Trust vs. Mistrust (Oral)*	Birth–1 yr.	Hope	Fear
II. Autonomy vs. Shame and Doubt (Anal)*	1–3 yr.	Willpower	Self-doubt
III. Initiative vs. Guilt (Phallic)*	4–5 yr.	Purpose	Unworthiness
IV. Industry vs. Inferiority (Latency)*	6–11 yr.	Competency	Incompetency
V. Ego Identity vs. Role Confusion	12–20 yr.	Fidelity	Uncertainty
VI. Intimacy vs. Isolation	20–24 yr.	Love	Promiscuity
VII. Generativity vs. Stagnation	25–65 yr.	Care	Selfishness
VIII. Ego Integrity vs. Despair	65 yr.–death	Wisdom	Meaninglessness and despair

*Roughly corresponding Freudian stage.

SOURCE: E. J. Phares. *Introduction to Personality*, 2nd ed. Glenview, IL: Scott, Foresman and Company, 1988, p. 123.

tant psychological factor in human behavior and development is inferiority, not instinct. Adler also emphasized the family as a whole, not just the Oedipal situation. He proposed a theory about the effects of birth order on personality which is still debated today (Sulloway, 1996). Noting that each person begins life in a helpless and inferior position, Adler suggested that subsequent behavior represents a compensatory "striving for superiority" (first within the family, then in the larger social world). The particular ways each individual seeks superiority comprise a style of life. Adaptive lifestyles are characterized by cooperation, social interest, courage, and common sense. Maladaptive styles are reflected in extreme competitiveness or dependency, lack of concern for others, and distortion of reality. Revisions and reformulations of Freud's ideas by other theorists such as Carl Jung, Karen Horney, Erich Fromm, and Harry Stack Sullivan also contributed to the psychodynamic approach to clinical psychology (see Munroe, 1955).

Psychoanalysis and its early variations continue as important forces, but most of today's psychodynamically-oriented clinicians practice more recent variations rather than classical Freudian analysis (see Gabbard, 2000; Prochaska & Norcross, 1999). For instance, Heinz Hartmann (1958), David Rapaport (1951), and others developed *ego psychology*, which places a greater emphasis on adaptive ego functioning. These theorists see ego as a positive, creative, coping mechanism, not just the "referee" in intrapsychic conflicts. Viewed this way, defense mechanisms need not always be unconscious mechanisms for hiding the truth from one's conscious self; they can sometimes be adaptive. Psychologists such as George Vaillant have explored how various defense mechanisms can facilitate more or less adaptive functioning over the life span (see Vaillant, 1977; 2000).

Donald Winnicott (1965), W. R. D. Fairbairn (1952), Margaret Mahler (Mahler, Pine, & Bergman, 1975), and others developed *object relations theory*. The special focus of object relations theory is on how early relationships influence psychological development and later adult relationships. Infant-caregiver interactions in particular act as prototypes, and the nature of early child-parent attachments affects self-image, identity, security, and social relationships later in life (Simpson & Rholes, 2000). Closely aligned with object relations theory are the views of Otto Kernberg (1976) and Heinz Kohut (1977), both of whom stressed that adult personality is based on the nature of very early interactions between infants and their caregivers. We discuss object relations theories further in Chapter 7.

Evaluation of the Psychodynamic Approach

Sigmund Freud presented the most comprehensive and revolutionary theory of behavior ever articulated. The intensive study of a single individual, the one-to-one assessment or treatment session, the view that overt behavior is systematically related to identifiable psychological causes, the possibility that individuals' behavior may be influenced by factors of which they are unaware, the effects of childhood experience on adult behavior, the symbolic significance of overt behavior, the importance of conflict and anxiety, and other factors emphasized by many types of clinicians are directly traceable to Freud. These elements have been retained by most contemporary variations of psychodynamic theory.

Still, the psychodynamic approaches have generated harsh criticism on several grounds:

1. Basic psychodynamic concepts—such as projection, unconscious motivation, and repression—are seen as too vague to be measured and tested scientifically (e.g., Crews, 1996). Indeed, attempts to empirically investigate psychoanalytic constructs (e.g., Epstein, 1994; Silverman & Weinberger, 1985) have been faulted for methodological and conceptual problems (e.g, Brand, 1995). A related critique is that the psychoanalytic view is not easily influenced by contradictory data. For example, hostile behavior can be evidence for unconscious feelings of hostility, but so too can friendly behavior—if it is seen as a reaction formation.

2. Freud's approach did not evolve out of systematic research but out of his clinical experiences with a small number of upper-class patients living in Vienna in the late 1800s. Questions have been raised about whether these case reports might have been biased, or, in some instances, even falsified, to suit Freud's pet theories (e.g., Esterson, 1993; MacMillan, 1991) and about how well Freud's ideas apply to people from other socioeconomic and cultural backgrounds (Feist & Feist, 2001; Landrine & Klonoff, 1992). Freud's biased views about women have also caused many male and female feminists to reject his account of human development (Chesler, 1972).

3. The reliability and validity of techniques designed to measure Freudian personality constructs appear weak (Smith & Dumont, 1995; Wood, Nezworski, & Stejskal, 1996; see Chapter 5), and the effectiveness of psychoanalytic treatment has been questioned (see Chapter 9).

4. Classical psychoanalytic explanations of behavior place too much emphasis on sexual and aggressive instincts and not enough on people's inherent growth potential, learning experiences, and sociocultural background. This criticism applies less to more contemporary psychodynamic approaches.

5. The emphasis on childhood causes of adult behavior in psychoanalytic theory and in many psychodynamic variations neglects the role of more immediate situational influences on behavior. Indeed little support exists for predictions about how experiences in various developmental stages (e.g., anal, Oedipal) lead to personality traits later in life. This aspect of psychoanalysis led some neo-Freudians (e.g., Erikson) to stress the importance of factors that stretch across the life span, an emphasis that the other approaches to clinical psychology share.

THE BEHAVIORAL APPROACH

Instead of emphasizing intrapsychic conflicts, instincts, or unconscious motivation in the development and alteration of human behavior, the behavioral approach focuses directly on that behavior and its relationship to the environmental and personal conditions that affect it. The basic assumption of this approach is that behavior is primarily influenced by *learning*, which takes place in a *social context*.

Clinicians who take a behavioral approach tend to attribute individual differences in behavior to people's unique learning histories, not to traits, personality characteristics, or "mental illness." Thus, a student who benefitted in the past from cheating may cheat again to earn a high grade, while an individual rewarded in the past for diligent study may be less likely to behave dishonestly. More general cultural factors are also seen as a part of people's learning histories. Upon receiving a failing grade on a vital exam, some students' cultural values may prompt so much shame as to engender a suicide attempt; for others, the failure may evoke a culturally traditional desire for revenge.

The behavioral approach sees similarities among people as resulting from the commonalities in rules, values, and learning histories shared by most people in the same culture. Thus, students' attentiveness during a lecture would not be seen as a collective manifestation of some intrapsychic process, but rather as a group fulfillment of the socially learned student role, which appears in certain academic situations for specified periods of time.

The same principles of learning that account for behavioral differences and similarities *among* individuals are also employed to explain consistencies and discrepancies *within* individuals. Behaviorists view behavioral consistency (which other approaches refer to as "personality") as stemming from generalized learning, stable cognitive abilities, and/or similarities across stimulus situations. For example, a person may appear calm under most circumstances if calmness has been rewarded over a period of years in a wide range of social situations. The behavioral approach explains *inconsistencies* and other unpredictable human phenomena in terms of *behavioral specificity*. Walter Mischel (1971, p. 86) summarized this point as follows:

> Consider a woman who seems hostile and fiercely independent some of the time but passive, dependent, and feminine on other occasions. . . . Which one of these two patterns reflects the woman that she really is? Is one pattern in the service of the other, or might both be in the service of a third motive? . . . Social behavior theory suggests that it is possible for the lady to be *all* of these—a hostile, fiercely independent, passive, dependent, feminine, aggressive, warm, castrating person all in one. . . . Of course which of these she is at any particular moment would not be random and capricious; it would depend on discriminative stimuli—who she is with, when, how, and much, much more. But each of these aspects of her self may be a quite genuine and real aspect of her total being.

The three main versions of the behavioral approach—operant learning, respondent learning, and cognitive-behavioral—differ on certain specifics, but share a common set of assumptions:

1. Measurable behavior is seen as the subject matter of clinical psychology. *Measurable* does not always mean "overt." The behaviorally oriented clinician may be interested in behaviors ranging from the objective and obvious (amount of time spent in conversation) to the subtle and covert (clarity of visualization, content of thoughts). Almost any behavior can be the target of the behavioral approach as long as it can be reliably measured.

2. While genetic and biological factors provide the foundation from which behavior develops, environmental factors are especially important influences. Thus, it is assumed that genes influence a person's general behavioral tendencies, which learning experiences then shape into more specific patterns.

3. Empirical research methods are the best way to learn about the assessment, development, and modification of behavior. The behavioral approach to clinical psychology has led the way in operationalizing and experimentally investigating psychopathology and psychotherapy.

4. Clinical assessment and treatment should be guided by the results of empirical research. The behavioral approach encourages practitioners to scrutinize the empirical evidence about an assessment or treatment procedure before deciding to adopt it and to proceed with caution in areas where little empirical evidence is available.

5. The same principles of learning determine both problematic and nonproblematic behaviors. Therefore, clinical assessment should be designed to determine how a client's current difficulties were learned and how they are being maintained so that more adaptive, individually tailored learning can be arranged. In working with a kindergarten child's fear of school, for example, the behaviorally oriented clinician's treatment would not be based on "standard procedures" for dealing with children diagnosed as phobic, but would depend instead on what the assessment data have to say about what is causing the problem. In other words, treatment and assessment should be integrated.

Three versions of the behavioral approach differ primarily in terms of whether they emphasize operant conditioning, classical conditioning, or social/cognitive factors in learning.

Operant Learning

The operant version of the behavioral approach reflects the ideas of B. F. Skinner. Skinner argued that learned relationships between environmental stimuli and overt behavior—especially the relationships between behavior and its antecedents and consequences—can fully explain the development, maintenance, and alteration of human behavior. Skinner's methods are called *functional analysis* because they focus on describing and explaining functional relationships among stimuli, responses, and consequences.

Thus, rather than assuming that human behavior reflects various motives or needs (e.g., aggressive behavior indicates needs for dominance), the Skinnerian clinician looks at the relationship between aggressive behavior and its consequences. If a client's aggressive behavior has been rewarded, at least part of the time, no further explanation in terms of internal need is necessary; the client has simply learned to behave aggressively. Similarly, a mental hospital resident who spends the day staring into space and is incontinent need not be considered "mentally ill." Instead, these behaviors can be thought of as learned responses prompted by environmental factors and maintained by the reinforcement of "crazy" behavior provided by society and especially by the hospital (Ullmann & Krasner, 1975).

Classical Conditioning

Another version of the behavioral approach is exemplified by the writings of Joseph Wolpe (1958, 1982) and Hans Eysenck (1982). They focus on the applications of *classical*, or *respondent* conditioning principles (Hull, 1943; Pavlov, 1927) to understanding and eliminating human distress, particularly anxiety. While not denying the importance of operant reinforcement and punishment in shaping behavior, behaviorists who emphasize classical conditioning emphasize the association of conditioned and unconditioned stimuli. For example, a man who fearfully avoids social events may do so not only because of past humiliations or other negative experiences (i.e., operant conditioning), but also because the discomfort from those experiences has, through classical conditioning, become so *associated* with parties that he may experience anxiety upon receiving a party invitation.

Social-Cognitive (Cognitive-Behavioral) Theories

The views of Skinner, Wolpe, Eysenck, and others who focus on overt behaviors as the targets of clinical assessment and treatment have been quite influential, but some behaviorists see these views as incomplete. Accordingly, *social-cognitive* and *cognitive-behavioral* theorists have added an emphasis on the role of cognitive (i.e., thought) processes in the development, maintenance, and modification of behavior. Two of the most prominent representatives of the social-cognitive point of view are Albert Bandura and Walter Mischel, who have studied and described how social influence and cognitive activity contribute to learning (Bandura, 1986; Mischel, 1993).

A major feature of Bandura's theory is its attention to *observational learning* or *vicarious cognitive processes*. In his view, behavior develops not only directly through operant and classical conditioning, but also *indirectly* (vicariously) through observation and cognitive representations of the world. For example, Bandura highlighted the fact that humans can acquire new behaviors without obvious reinforcement or practice, but rather by observing another individual, or *model*, engage in the behavior. In one illustrative experiment, preschoolers who had observed a model behaving aggressively toward an inflatable "Bobo" doll later tended to match the models' behavior, while those who had seen a passive model tended to be nonaggressive (Bandura, Ross & Ross, 1963). According to Bandura, the effects of vicarious processes can be as substantial as the effects of direct learning.

Bandura also sees cognitive variables playing a role in behavior disorders. Consider the man mentioned earlier who feared social situations. Bandura would point out that his discomfort stems not only from negative social experiences and environmental stimuli associated with them, but also from anxiety-provoking thoughts about social situations (e.g., "I will make a fool of myself" or "I'm no good at making friends") that serve to support continued avoidance. Cognitive experiences can lead to anxiety and avoidance, as they can in psychodynamic theory, but social-cognitive theorists look to *conscious* thoughts and emotions, rather than unconscious ones, for clues to behavior

(Bandura, 2001). Bandura believes that people's expectancies about what they can and cannot do in given situations—their sense of *self-efficacy* (Bandura, 1986)—exerts an enormous influence over how they actually behave. The higher the level of self-efficacy, he says, the better their performance will be.

Bandura (1982) proposes that people's emotional life is largely determined by the combined influence of their self-efficacy and outcome judgments. For example, people who are low in self-efficacy are likely to feel apathy if they also believe that no one can control any life events, anxiety if they feel unable to control life's dangers, and depression if they believe that other people's actions, but not theirs, bring about desired outcomes. People who have high self-efficacy are likely to be resentful if they also see the world as unresponsive to their efforts, but self-assured if they see their efforts as bringing good outcomes.

Table 2.2 summarizes five cognitive factors, or *person variables*, that Mischel (1986) sees as important to understanding human behavior from a social-cognitive point of view. Other cognitive-behavioral theorists have drawn attention to several additional factors, including how people evaluate and explain their own behavior and how they believe that events in the world should unfold (Abramson, Seligman & Teasdale, 1978; Beck, 1976; Ellis, 1962). These additional factors have proven especially useful in dealing with depression and anxiety disorders.

For example, according to Aaron Beck (1976), people's cognitive evaluations, or *appraisals*, of their own behavior precede and influence their emotional reactions to events. Thus, individuals who continually evaluate their performance as inadequate are likely to interpret compliments as evidence that others are merely being polite. Thus, they gain no pleasure from positive reinforcement, may tend to see themselves as worthless and inadequate and are thus predisposed to depressive thoughts. According to Beck, these thoughts can eventually become so automatic that they influence future emotional reactions without conscious awareness. The goal of Beck's cognitive-behavioral therapy is to make these automatic thoughts conscious, so the individual can logically appraise their merit (see Chapter 7).

TABLE 2.2   Summary of Cognitive Social Learning Person Variables

1. *Competencies*: Ability to construct (generate) particular cognitions and behaviors. Related to measures of IQ, social and cognitive (mental) maturity and competence, ego development, social-intellectual achievements and skills. Refers to what the person knows and can do.

2. *Encoding Strategies and Personal Constructs*: Units for categorizing events, people, and the self.

3. *Expectancies*: Behavior-outcome and stimulus-outcome relations in particular situations; self-efficacy or confidence that one can perform the necessary behavior.

4. *Subjective Values*: Motivating and arousing stimuli, incentives, and aversions.

5. *Self-Regulatory Systems and Plans*: Rules and self-reactions for performance and for the organization of complex behavior sequences.

SOURCE: Mischel, W. *Introduction to Personality*, 4th ed. © 1986 Holt, Rinehart & Winston.

Habitual explanations, or *attributions*, about the causes of events—including one's own behavior—can also have important emotional consequences. These attributions tend to vary along three dimensions: *internality*—whether people see the cause of an event as due to something about themselves or something about the environment; *stability*—whether they see the cause as persisting or temporary; and *globalness*—whether they see the cause as specific to a given situation or as operating in all situations. For example, explaining poor performance on a test by blaming it on test difficulty exemplifies an external, unstable, and specific attribution. Saying "I am just plain stupid" would reflect an internal, stable, and global attribution. Individuals who make internal, stable, and global attributions for failure experiences are especially likely to experience depressive symptoms (Seligman et al., 1979, 1984).

Albert Ellis's (1962, 1993) cognitive-behavioral theory focuses not only on the role of people's expectancies, appraisals, and attributions, but also on how specific irrational and self-defeating long-term beliefs can produce psychological distress. These irrational beliefs often include "should" statements ("Everyone should like me.") and unrealistically high standards ("I must be perfect.") that doom people to failure or disappointment. Ellis's *rational-emotive behavior therapy* attacks such beliefs until the client realizes they are counterproductive and abandons them (see Chapter 7).

Evaluation of the Behavioral Approach

Since its beginnings in the late 1950s, the behavioral approach has enjoyed enthusiastic support from an increasing number of adherents who value its scientific view of human behavior, its operationally defined concepts, its application of laboratory-based learning principles to clinical problems, and its commitment to empirical evaluation of assessment and treatment. In short, the behavioral approach is seen as the best approach to applying psychology *as a science of behavior* in the clinical field. Nevertheless, critics fault this approach on several counts:

1. It is seen by some as reducing humans to a set of acquired responses derived from a mechanistic relationship with the environment. Even its cognitive-behavioral versions appear to pay less attention than other approaches do to subjective experiences and to genetic, physiological, and other non-learning-based influences on behavior.

2. Learning principles might explain phobias and other relatively simple stimulus-response relationships, but may not adequately deal with more complex, internal processes. In short, behavioral approaches lack coherent organizing constructs (such as the self or ego) that describe how collections of learned responses are related into a view of a whole person. "Likening human to animal behavior, and focusing on visible behavior rather than inner states, minimizes precisely those values, feelings, fantasies, and motives which most distinguish and trouble human life" (Korchin, 1976, p. 349).

3. The learning principles on which the behavioral approach is based are still a matter of debate among learning theorists and, even if all these principles were

agreed upon, there is the question of whether their animal-laboratory origins allow them to be applied meaningfully to human beings.

4. The behavioral approach is not as uniquely scientific or as clearly validated as its proponents might wish. Many of its assessment and treatment procedures are based more on clinical experience than experimental research, and where research evidence is available, it is often not unequivocally supportive of learning-based techniques (see Chapter 9).

THE HUMANISTIC APPROACH

So far we have considered approaches to clinical psychology in which human behavior is viewed as primarily influenced by (a) instincts and intrapsychic conflicts, or (b) the environment and cognitive factors. The humanistic approach—also called the phenomenological approach—rejects many assumptions of both psychodynamic and behavioral clinicians, asserting instead that the behavior of each human being at any given moment is determined primarily by that person's unique *perception of the world*.

Consider two college students on the first day of class. While one of them is enthralled by the professor, the other stomps out and drops the course. Humanistic psychologists attribute such divergent reactions as reflecting different perceptions of the same professor. Clinicians who take a humanistic approach tend to share the following assumptions:

1. Human beings are active, thinking people who are individually responsible for what they do and fully capable of making choices about their behavior. In fairness, it should be pointed out that psychodynamic and cognitive-behavioral clinicians also see people in this way, but their approaches tend to look at the *processes and causal determinants* underlying self-discipline, decision making, and other uniquely human characteristics rather than to focus on those characteristics themselves.

2. No one can understand another person's behavior without perceiving the world through that person's eyes. In line with this notion, the humanistic approach assumes that all human activity is comprehensible *when viewed within the social context, and from the point of view, of the person being observed.* Thus, a violent woman would not be seen as expressing id impulses or displaying reinforced behavior, but as behaving in line with her perception of those around her at the time.

The humanistic approach evolved partly as a reaction against Freud that began when Adler rejected instincts as the basis of behavior and emphasized people's perceptions and growth potential. Emphasis on individual perceptions of reality was also prompted by Heidegger, Kierkegaard, Sartre, and other existentialist philosophers who asserted that the meaning and value of life are not intrinsic, but are constructed by the perceiver. Thus, people are not attractive or ugly; these qualities are assigned when someone else reacts to them, and there is a different "reality" in the eye of each beholder. This focus on individual views of reality was sharpened by a group of German psychologists—known as the *Gestalt school* (e.g., Koffka, 1935; Köhler, 1925)—who noted there are many cases in which a person's subjective perception goes beyond the stimuli that are "objectively" there and in which the "same" object may be interpreted in different ways (see Figure 2.1).

In North America, clinicians who adopt a humanistic approach tend to assume that each person possesses a potential for growth that gives impetus to most behavior. They see people as basically good and as striving naturally toward creativity, love, and other positive goals (for this reason, their approach is often called *humanistic*). In their clinical work, the emphasis is not on gathering assessment data about a client's past or trying to solve specific behavioral problems, but on facilitating clients' personal growth and choice in the "here and now."[1]

Kelly's Personal Construct Theory

George Kelly (1955) developed a theory based on the fundamental assumption that human behavior is determined by *personal constructs*, or ways of anticipating the world. Kelly believed individuals act in accord with their unique set of expectations

FIGURE 2.1 What is "Reality"? Your shifting perceptions of this fixed stimulus allow you to see it as either a young woman in a feathered hat or an old woman in a shawl.

---

[1]Another humanistic approach popular in Europe has been called "philosophically grounded phenomenology" (Fischer, 1989). Based on the writings of Edmund Husserl (1969), Martin Heidegger (1968), and other European philosophers, this approach is devoted to the qualitative study of human knowledge and human consciousness. While philosophically grounded phenomenologists may adopt a humanistic perspective as practicing therapists, their theoretical approach to psychology differs from the humanistic wing of phenomenology in several ways. Unlike humanistic traditionalists, they do not concentrate on conscious experience alone, do not deny the importance of exploring the past, and do not assume that all behavior is rational or that all human beings are basically good.

about the consequences of behavior (note the similarity to Bandura) and that people's constructs about life comprise their reality and guide their behavior. For example, a person who sees knives as potentially dangerous would exercise caution when handling them. Because caution reflects an accurate anticipation of the consequences of carelessness and does avoid accidents, the construct "sharp knives are dangerous" is validated. In Kelly's view, the major goal of human beings is not to satisfy their instincts or maximize their rewards but to validate their personal constructs, and thus to make sense of the world as they perceive it. Like scientists who revel in discovering why and when a phenomenon occurs, people seek to understand and predict the phenomena in their lives.

Kelly's theory says that disordered behavior results when a person develops inaccurate, oversimplified, or otherwise faulty constructs about social experiences. Much as a scientist will make incorrect predictions from faulty constructs, people are likely to behave inappropriately if their personal constructs do not allow them to anticipate and comprehend daily events. Thus, a man who construes everything in life as either "good" or "bad" is going to have problems, because not all events and people can be classified this way without distorting them. He may decide that all college students, political activists, and foreigners are bad, and that all children, doctors, and clergy are good, but he will be wrong—at least part of the time. He will also be seen by others as close-minded, prejudiced, and a poor judge of character. His interpersonal relationships are likely to be stormy.

Rogers's Self Theory

The prolific writings of Carl Rogers (1942, 1951, 1961, 1970) have made his name practically synonymous with the humanistic approach to clinical psychology in North America. Rogers assumed that people have an innate motive toward growth, which he called *the actualizing tendency*: "the directional trend which is evident in all organic and human life—the urge to expand, extend, develop, mature—the tendency to express and activate all the capacities of the organism" (Rogers, 1961, p. 351). Rogers saw all human behavior—from basic food-seeking to artistic creativity, from normal conversation to bizarre delusions—as a reflection of the individual's efforts at *self-actualization* in a uniquely perceived world.

In Rogers's view, these efforts begin at birth. As the developing child begins to differentiate between the self and the rest of the world, there is a growing awareness of this self—a recognition of the "I" or "me." According to Rogers, all of a person's experiences, including "self" experiences, are evaluated as positive or negative, depending on whether they are consistent or inconsistent with the child's self-actualizing tendency. However, these evaluations are not made on the basis of direct or *organismic* feelings alone, as when a child evaluates the taste of candy as positive. They are also influenced by the judgments of other people. Thus, a young boy may end up negatively evaluating the experience of fondling his genitals (even though the direct feelings are positive) because his parents tell him that he is a bad boy to do so.

These socializing influences help integrate the developing individual into society, especially when the judgments of others coincide with organismic feelings. For example, if a child practices reading and experiences both positive direct feelings upon gaining competence and positive regard from a parent for doing so, the result will be a positively evaluated self-experience ("I like to read"). Here, the self-experience is congruent with the organismic experience and the child is able to reconcile behavior ("I read a lot") and its evaluation ("I enjoy reading").

Rogers noted, however, that most people value the positive regard of others so highly that they will seek it even if it means thinking and acting in ways that are *incongruent* with organismic experience and the self-actualizing motive. This tendency is encouraged by what Rogers called *conditions of worth*—circumstances in which a person receives positive regard from others (and, ultimately, from the self) only for certain approved behaviors, attitudes, and beliefs. Conditions of worth are usually first created by parents, family, and other societal agents, but they are later maintained internally by the individual (note the similarity to Freud's concept of superego). People who face extreme or excessive conditions of worth are likely to be uncomfortable. If they behave primarily to please others, it may be at the expense of personal growth, as in the case of a woman who tries to fulfill the culturally encouraged role of working mother despite genuine desires to be a full-time homemaker. On the other hand, people who display authentic feelings and behaviors that are discrepant with conditions of worth risk loss of the positive regard of others and the self.

Rogers believed that to reduce discomfort stemming from such incongruity, individuals may distort reality in problematic ways. For example, a man whose parents set up conditions of worth in which crying was discouraged and stoic "masculinity" was praised may assert that "anyone who cries is weak." This statement may represent a distortion of his true feelings, however. Rogers believed that the greater the discrepancy between the individual's real feelings and the individual's socially influenced self-concept, the more severe will be the problematic behavior that results. Thus, if admitting failure in social dating would be somewhat discrepant with a young man's self-concept, he might simply become "too busy" to ask anyone for a date. But suppose the discrepancy is more extreme, as in a man whose self-concept casts him as self-sufficient and career-oriented when he really wants to enjoy quiet mediocrity. If this man were passed over for promotion or got a poor performance rating, his responses might be quite inappropriate. Instead of recognizing that his lack of success stems from lack of genuine interest in his work, he may claim that others are out to get him. Concerns over persecution may grow to the point that he trusts no one and sees conspiracies on every side. Ultimately, his behavior may become so troublesome as to require hospitalization.

Rogers believed that these problems can be avoided. "If an individual should experience only unconditional positive regard, then no conditions of worth would develop, self-regard would never be at variance with organismic evaluation, and the individual would continue to be psychologically adjusted, and would be fully functioning" (Rogers, 1959, p. 224). Even if these optimal conditions have not existed in the past, they may help in the present. Accordingly, Rogers developed a therapeutic approach that employs unconditional positive regard and other factors to help troubled people reduce incongruity without having to distort reality (see Chapter 7).

Maslow and Humanistic Psychology

Abraham Maslow's (1954, 1962, 1971) version of the humanistic approach has also been influential in North America. In founding the movement known as humanistic psychology, Maslow emphasized that which is positive and creative about human beings. Like Rogers, Maslow saw people as capable of (and needing) self-actualization, but he suggested that failure to realize one's full potential is caused not by incongruity between self-experience and organismic experience, but by the presence of unmet needs.

Maslow believed that those needs form a hierarchy starting with basic requirements (like food and water) and moving to higher-level requisites like safety, security, love, belonging, self-esteem, and, finally, self-actualization. Satisfaction of needs at one level, he said, is unlikely until needs at lower levels have been met. Thus, a person will not be concerned with the need for love and belonging when there is uncertainty over where that person's next meal is coming from. Maslow pointed out that most people in Western cultures seek to meet needs below the self-actualization level, and are thus oriented toward what they lack—usually things relating to security, love, belonging, and self-esteem. These *deficiency-motivated* people's incompletely satisfied needs often lead them to engage in mindless buying, vicious competitiveness, and other problematic need-seeking behaviors. Only in rare cases, said Maslow, are all lower-order needs satisfied, thus freeing the person to seek full self-actualization. These fortunate few have what Maslow called *growth motivation*, which allows them to focus on what they can be, not on what they do not have. Momentary experiential high points, or *peak experiences*, at which full self-actualization is reached, are common in these individuals and represent the best that is within all of us. Maslow's approach to therapy focused on helping people overcome the obstacles blocking their natural growth, happiness, and fulfillment.

Perls and Gestalt Psychology

Yet another humanistic view was provided by Frederich S. (Fritz) Perls, a European psychiatrist who first expressed dissatisfaction with traditional Freudian theory in a 1947 book, *Ego, Hunger and Aggression: A Revision of Freud's Theory and Method*. Perls, working with his wife, Laura, felt that Freud overemphasized sexual instincts and ignored what he called hunger: an instinct or tendency toward self-preservation and self-actualization. Like Freud, Perls saw the ego as facilitating people's growth and self-preservation by mediating conflicts between internal needs and environmental pressures. However, he thought of ego not as a psychic structure, but as a process whose goal is the reduction of tension between the person and the environment.

As this process takes place, the person grows psychologically, finding new ways to take environmental demands into account while meeting internal needs. Perls said that this growth depends on the person remaining acutely *aware* of these internal needs and environmental demands. However, if people organize their attention and perceptions so as to avoid focusing on unpleasant demands, unmet needs, or distressing conflicts, their awareness can become fragmented or distorted. When this happens, growth stops and problems start. For example, a person with strong sexual desires who grows up in a family where such feelings are considered "immoral" may find certain distortions of awareness to be temporarily helpful, but ultimately problematic. These distortions may involve denying sexual feelings or perceptions that exaggerate peer pressures for sexual promiscuity. More severe distortions can result in more serious problems. If a person is unable to consciously acknowledge hostile feelings toward others, for example, the result might be a perception of other people as hostile (a form of projection) and intense anxiety about being away from home. This person may selectively attend to the ordinary risks that surround us all and, "because the world is so dangerous," refuse to leave home. Perls's treatment approach, called *Gestalt therapy*, aims at restarting growth by reestablishing aware processes (see Chapter 7).

Evaluation of the Humanistic Approach

The humanistic approach to clinical psychology has a strong intrinsic appeal. It gives a central role to each person's experience, it emphasizes each person's uniqueness, and it celebrates those human characteristics that make our species special. Finally, humanistic psychologists' optimistic approach focuses on the potential of human life and on each individual's capability to grow toward maximum personal fulfillment.

Still, the humanistic approach seen in North American clinical psychology has its share of detractors. Critics say that:

1. Humanistic phenomenology is too concerned with immediate conscious experience and does not pay sufficient attention to unconscious motivation, reinforcement contingencies, situational influences, and biological factors.

2. The approach does not deal adequately with the *development* of human behavior. Postulating an innate tendency toward actualization can account for development, but does not explain its processes. Saying that a child develops because of an actualizing tendency is like saying that a person eats because of hunger; this may be true, but it says little about what hunger is or how it influences behavior. More generally, though humanistic theories provide excellent descriptions of human behavior, they are not focused on the scientific exploration of its causes. To suggest that people act as they do because of their unique perceptions of reality may be personally satisfying, but not very informative in terms of understanding the variables that promote, maintain, and alter human behavior.

3. Humanistic concepts are vague and difficult to comprehend, let alone investigate. Although humanistic psychologists have been chided for being unscientific, it may be more accurate to describe them as pursuing an approach to science that violates Western traditions. Their research methods are more qualitative than quantitative, and they approach psychology as a human science, not as a natural science.

4. The clinical applicability of the humanistic approach is limited to those segments of the population whose intellectual and cultural background is compatible with its introspective nature. Further, the range of problems addressed by the approach is limited. Humanistic notions may be of great subjective value to the

person struggling with a crisis of identity or values, but these notions (like the tenets of most other approaches) may not be very useful in situations where human distress results from unmet needs near the bottom of Maslow's hierarchy—needs for food, decent housing, and a job, for example.

5. Finally, humanists' tendency to define ideal personality development in terms of personal growth, independence, and self-actualization fits closely with certain value systems prevalent in North America and in some Western cultures, but it may not apply to cultural traditions that emphasize interrelatedness and community (Heine et al., 1999).

INTERPERSONAL PERSPECTIVES

There are several interpersonal theories of human behavior, though most textbooks on personality theory, abnormal psychology, psychopathology, and clinical psychology pay scant attention to them. This neglect stems partly from the fact that the major approaches to clinical psychology, especially the behavioral and psychoanalytic, have absorbed so many principles from interpersonal theories that there is no single, distinctly interpersonal approach to psychological assessment, disorder, and treatment. Further, most early interpersonal theorists, such as Harry Stack Sullivan, were not prolific writers, and did not try to popularize their views, attract followers, or build a clinical movement. Finally, unlike the three dominant approaches to clinical psychology we have reviewed, interpersonal theories have not traditionally been associated with explaining or treating specific forms of psychopathology, such as hysterical symptoms, phobias, or existential crises.

Nevertheless, we believe that interpersonal theories offer a perspective whose influence on clinical psychology now matches that of the approaches emphasized in most textbooks. In this section, we summarize two major interpersonal theories and consider their implications for clinical psychology. [More detailed coverage of this material is provided by Anchin and Kiesler (1982), Carson (1969), Kiesler (1983), and Wiggins (1982).]

Harry Stack Sullivan's Interpersonal Theory

Although he is often described as a neo-Freudian, American psychiatrist Harry Stack Sullivan (1892–1949) developed a personality theory and treatment approach that was much different from other revisionists of Freud. Believing that personality consists of "the relatively enduring pattern of recurrent interpersonal situations which characterize a human life" (Sullivan, 1953, pp. 110–111), he sought to understand personality as it was revealed in the pattern of what a person did with others, said to others, and believed about others. Sullivan also saw psychological disorders as stemming from interpersonal relationships that have become so taxing, cumbersome, or frustrating that constructive, or "normal" interactions with others are not possible. Sullivan believed that individuals overcome these problems by becoming aware of their interpersonal relations and understanding them in a way that is consistent with the views of others.

In Sullivan's view, the development of personality begins with biological and acquired needs that require infants to interact repeatedly with caregivers, especially the mother. Out of these interactions, the infant experiences the caregiver's moods through what Sullivan called "empathy." An infant feels fear or joy, for example, through empathy with mother's anxious or happy moods. Similarly, through a primitive form of understanding that Sullivan called the "prototaxic" mode of experience, the infant comes to associate the caregiver's approval or disapproval with two different "personifications" (a personification is our mental image, or organized understanding, of a person which—even if inaccurate—guides our subsequent behavior toward that person). A "good mother" personification grows from satisfying, pleasurable experiences the infant has in mother's presence; the "bad mother" image develops from experiencing anxiety in her presence. Gradually, the infant also develops a personification of "me," which is the beginning of the self. This personification is based on what Sullivan called "reflected appraisals"; infants gain an early sense of self based on the way significant others in their world behave toward them. It is as if others' reactions to us provide a kind of mirror in which we see ourselves. The major aspects of the self that are established in these early years consists of (1) a "good me," the result of reflected appraisals conveying tenderness and acceptance of positive feelings, (2) a "bad me," the outcome of anxiety and reflected disapproval from others, and (3) the "not me," the result of such intense anxiety or panic that the person feels that the associated experience is not really happening.

The self develops to preserve the child's feelings of security in an interpersonal world where feelings of anxiety are the major threat. The self functions like a benevolent authority figure who guides the development of personality, tries to maintain security with other people, seeks prestige, and protects against anxiety and threats to self-esteem. This is accomplished by several psychological processes, including selective inattention (ignoring upsetting information about oneself), dissociation (a more extreme form of denial in which information is banished from awareness), sublimation (substituting an acceptable activity for one less socially approved), and obsessionalism (a preoccupation with details that distract oneself and others from sources of anxiety). If anxiety becomes too severe, these maneuvers can become so extreme or so rigid that disturbed interpersonal relationships result.

Like Freud, Sullivan saw personality developing in a series of stages. However, where Freud emphasized the psychosexual qualities of these developmental periods, Sullivan concentrated on the major interpersonal issues typical of each stage (in this sense, his theory is similar to Erikson's). Sullivan's first stage is *infancy*, extending from birth to the development of meaningful speech at around the age of fifteen to eighteen months. During this period, babies gradually shift from primitive prototaxic understandings to "parataxic" thought which allows them to associate events that occur close together in time. While more sophisticated than the prototaxic mode, parataxic thought is impulsive, highly idiosyncratic, and based on hunches; it is not much more advanced than superstitious or stereotyped thinking.

In *childhood*, an era extending from the end of infancy to about the age of 4, thought and language develop further. The child begins to engage in greater amounts of "syntaxic" thinking, which requires the use of consensually understood language and other symbols. These skills are essential for communicating effectively with other people. Children also begin to experience punishment more frequently in this stage, as their parents attempt to train them to behave in certain ways. At the same time, the child begins to learn how to use language to manipulate parents. What parent hasn't been dissuaded from following through on a threatened punishment by their child's plaintive "I'm sorry," followed by the promise that "I'll never do it again"? Language also makes it possible for children to play "pretend," acting as if they were a grown-up and imitating adult behaviors.

In the *juvenile* era, lasting from about 4 to 10 years of age, people learn to cooperate and compete with peers. Rejection is a painful experience of the juvenile era, and juveniles will go to great lengths to avoid it. Strong identification with a close-knit group of schoolmates is commonly observed.

The *preadolescent* era, which lasts from about the age of 10 until puberty, is important because its main interpersonal task is learning how to be psychologically intimate with another person. Such relationships usually involve a friend, whom Sullivan termed a "chum." A chum is central to a later capacity for closeness because he or she serves as the first peer to whom we divulge our secrets and disclose our fears. And, through the chum's self-disclosure, we realize that other people also have fears, fantasies, doubts, preoccupations, and other characteristics that we once thought were ours alone.

In *early adolescence*, ushered in by the onset of puberty, the person becomes more driven by lustful urges. Ideally, the adolescent will be able to integrate lustful needs with a desire for psychological intimacy with a partner. By *late adolescence*, the person uses increasing syntaxic understanding to enter into a range of satisfying sexual and nonsexual interpersonal relationships.

To the extent that people's behavioral options are restricted during development because of inaccurate personifications or extensive anxiety, they will be unable to participate fully in satisfying interpersonal relationships.

Timothy Leary's Interpersonal Circle

A major system for organizing interpersonal behavior was developed by Timothy Leary and his associates at the Kaiser Foundation in Oakland, California. As described in his 1957 book, *Interpersonal Diagnosis of Personality*, Leary's system organizes different styles of interpersonal behavior around a circle, called a circumplex. As shown in Figure 2.2, the vertical axis of the circumplex runs along a dimension from dominance to submission, while the horizontal axis connects the polar opposites of love and hate. Each of eight sections, or octants, described around the perimeter of the circle represents differing blends of power (dominance-submission) and affiliation (love-hate) in interpersonal behavior. The first word of each octant's label (e.g., aggressive) describes a mild form of the interpersonal behavior represented in that slice of the circle; the second word (e.g., sadistic) refers to an extreme form of the behavior. In addition, the intensity of interpersonal behavior increases as one moves from the center of the circle to the perimeter. For example, "manage, direct, lead" becomes, in its extreme form, "dominate, boss, order."

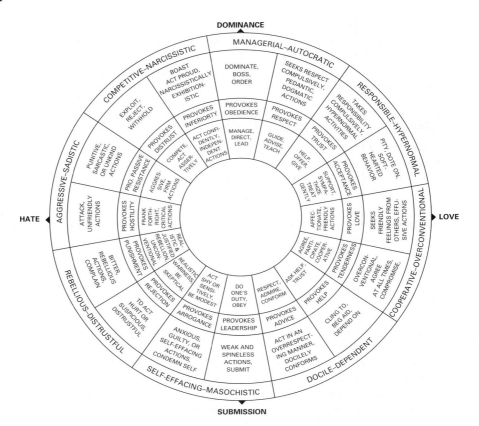

FIGURE 2.2 The Interpersonal Behavior Circle (Source: Timothy Leary. *Interpersonal Diagnosis of Personality—A Functional Theory and Methodology for Personality Evaluation*, copyright © 1957 John Wiley & Sons, New York.)

The sectors of the circumplex that are closer to each other are assumed to be more positively correlated with each other. Thus, cooperative-overconventional behavior should correlate more highly with docile-dependent behavior than it would with self-effacing-masochistic behavior. Further, sectors lying directly opposite each other on the circle (e.g., aggressive-sadistic and cooperative-overconventional) should be strongly negatively correlated. Empirical research conducted on Leary's system and others similar to it (Wiggins, 1982) has supported this circular ordering of interpersonal styles, although certain octants are not as well understood or described as others.

Leary's system and other circular models suggest that a person can "pull" certain behaviors from others by deploying a typical interpersonal style. Robert Carson (1969) observed that this "pull" is Leary's way of describing Sullivan's idea that people develop unique interpersonal styles to protect security and prevent anxiety in their interactions.

Are certain "pulls" or combinations of interpersonal actions and reactions more common than others? In general, the *rule of complementarity* predicts the following interpersonal matches: Along the dominance-submission axis, dominant behavior is reciprocated by submissiveness and vice versa; along the love-hate dimension, there is correspondence—with love inviting love and hate evoking hate.

Using Interpersonal Theory in Clinical Psychology

A number of clinical psychologists have argued that mental disorders can be conceived of as rigid and extreme patterns of interpersonal behaviors (e.g., Kiesler, 1986a). Interpersonal theories seem especially useful for explaining *personality disorders*, which are lifelong patterns of inflexible and maladaptive behavior and thought that cause substantial difficulties in a person's social or occupational life and may lead to unhappiness and distress (American Psychiatric Association 1994). Examples include antisocial personality disorder (which involves irresponsible, often repetitively unlawful, behavior about which the person feels no remorse), dependent personality disorder (characterized by inability to make even simple decisions without lots of advice and reassurance from others), and schizoid personality disorder (typified by indifference to social relationships and a constricted range of emotional feeling and expression).

As these examples illustrate, many personality disorders involve interpersonal behaviors that are extreme versions of various octants around Leary's interpersonal circle (Kiesler, 1986a; Widiger & Frances, 1985; Wiggins & Pincus, 1989). Antisocial personality disorder, for example, can be seen as pathologically intense displays of the hateful and dominant behaviors found in the upper left section of the circle. Dependent personalities appear to "live" in the docile-dependent octant, where they show extremely clingy submissiveness. In schizoid personality disorder, the introverted aloofness found in the lower left portion of the circle is extended (Soldz et al., 1993).

Interpersonal theories have also influenced clinicians' thinking about other mental disorders, including depression. As depressed people develop feelings of inferiority and powerlessness, they often look to others for help and support. Others typically respond to these requests with suggestions and advice which inadvertantly reinforce the depressed person's feelings of inadequacy and lead to even more demanding dependence. Irritated and frustrated, these well-intentioned advisors begin to avoid or berate the depressed person, thus deepening the depression (Coyne, 1976; Horowitz & Vitkus, 1986). This analysis fits nicely with cognitive-behavioral views of depression. Indeed, some authors are so convinced of the value of interpersonal theories for understanding abnormal behavior, that they have recommended abandoning the traditional diagnostic methods described in Chapter 3 in favor of a system in which behavioral disorders would be described almost exclusively in interpersonal terms (Benjamin, 1980; 1993).

Interpersonal theories have also led to suggestions about how therapists should respond to their clients' habitual interpersonal maneuvers. Interpersonal theory suggests, for example, that clients continue malaladaptive behavior because they "pull" behaviors from others that justify and reinforce those maladaptive behaviors. If this is the case, it might be a good idea for therapists to adopt a stance that defeats their clients' usual interpersonal gambits and promotes different, and more adaptive alternatives. For example, the hostile dominance of an antisocial client typically "pulls" hostile submissiveness from others. However, if the therapist acts in a friendly, dominant manner, this might swing the client around the interpersonal circle toward friendly submissiveness. Psychodynamic, behavioral, and humanistic therapists have all incorporated various interpersonal strategies into their treatment methods (see Chapter 7).

BIOLOGICAL INFLUENCES ON CLINICAL PSYCHOLOGY

Various approaches to clinical psychology traditionally emphasize psychological variables such as unconscious conflicts, learned associations, and self-actualizing tendencies, but research in neuroscience, experimental psychopathology, behavioral genetics, and related areas has made today's clinicians increasingly aware that the behavioral and mental processes they study and treat rest on a foundation provided by each person's biological makeup. This makeup includes genetically inherited characteristics as well as the activity of the brain and other organs and systems that underlie all kinds of behavior, both normal and abnormal (Bernstein et al., 2002). Some researchers and practitioners in clinical psychology pay more attention to biological influences than others, but few would disagree that disordered behavior can be most fully understood by taking biological as well as psychological factors into account. In fact, the growing recognition of biological factors in shaping human behavior suggests that there may eventually be a full-fledged biological approach to clinical psychology.

To take but one example, the role of genetics in personality is being explored in research like the Minnesota Study of Twins Reared Apart (Bouchard, 1984; Tellegan et al., 1988). This study and others have compared the personality similarities of identical versus nonidentical twin pairs and show that an average of about 50% of the differences in most personality characteristics is caused by genetic influence (McCartney, Harris & Bernieri, 1990; Tellegen et al., 1988).

Clinical psychologists' growing appreciation and acceptance of biological factors in psychopathology stem in part from the results of research showing clear genetic, anatomical, or neurochemical contributions to certain mental disorders (Nietzel et al., 1998). Investigators have attempted to identify not only the relative contributions of genetics on behavior and behavior disorders, but also the specific genes involved (Plomin & Crabbe, 2000). Now that the Human Genome Project has, as of 2001, identified all of the approximately 30,000 genes in the human genome, it should be easier to begin identifying which genes affect which psychological processes, and how they do so.

Clinicians also recognize that finding biological contributions to disorders does not automatically negate the value of psychological treatments. Thus, even if a child's hyperactivity is traced to a neurological defect, a solution might be provided by cognitive-behavioral therapy instead of, or in addition to, drugs. Clinicians are also becoming more interested in biological causes of mental disorders because it appears that those factors can sometimes be modified by psychological interventions. You will see in Chapter 11, for example, that researchers in health psychology are finding that the mind and body affect each other in ways that we are just beginning to understand. In short, recognizing the importance of biological variables in psychopathology does not render traditional approaches to clinical psychology irrelevant; indeed, it deepens and expands their range of inquiry.

The Role of Biological Factors in Psychopathology

Biological factors can influence mental disorders in various ways. Sometimes, the influence is direct, as when alcohol or other drugs cause intoxication, when degeneration of neurons in certain areas of the brain causes Alzheimer's disease, and when genetic abnormalities cause particular forms of mental retardation. Other disorders can result from more than one cause, only some of which involve biological factors. Such multiple pathways to disorder are suspected in the appearance of various subtypes of depressive disorders, anxiety disorders, schizophrenia, and personality disorders. However, clinical researchers today are focusing special attention on the diathesis-stress view of psychopathology, in which biological factors are seen as one of three causal components.

The first, known as a *diathesis,* is the presence of some kind of biological defect—usually a biochemical or anatomical problem in the brain, the autonomic nervous system, or the endocrine system. This defect or set of defects is often inherited, but can also result from physical trauma, infection, or other disease processes.

Second, the diathesis may create a *vulnerability* to developing a psychological disorder. People who carry certain diatheses are said to be "at risk" or "predisposed" to developing the disorders with which those diatheses have been associated.

The third causal component is the presence of *pathogenic (disease-causing) stressors.* If at-risk persons are exposed to such stressors, their predisposition for disorder may actually evolve into disorder. However, if those same at-risk individuals encounter less stressful environmental experiences, their predisposition may never express itself as a clinically significant disturbance.

The diathesis-stress view has been employed in the construction of a vulnerability model of schizophrenia which includes and integrates biological, psychological, and environmental causes (Cornblatt & Erlenmeyer-Kimling, 1985; Zubin & Spring, 1977). This model suggests that (1) vulnerability to schizophrenia is mainly biological, (2) different people have differing degrees of vulnerability, (3) vulnerability is transmitted partly through genetics and partly through neurodevelopmental abnormalities associated with prenatal risk factors, birth complications, and other problems (Barr, Mednick & Munk-Jorgensen, 1990; DiLalla & Gottesman, 1995; Susser & Lin, 1992; Tyrka et al., 1995), and (4) psychological components, such as exposure to poor parenting or inadequate coping skills, may play a role in whether schizophrenia appears—and in how severe it will be (Wearden et al., 2000).

As shown in Figure 2.3, many different blendings of vulnerability and stress can lead to schizophrenia. And, in accordance with the diathesis-stress perspective, people vulnerable to schizophrenia will be especially likely to actually display it if they are exposed to environmental demands, family conflicts, and other stressors that elicit and maintain schizophrenic patterns of thought and action. Those same stressors would not be expected to lead to schizophrenia in people who are less vulnerable to it.

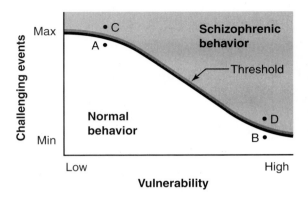

FIGURE 2.3 The Vulnerability Model of Schizophrenia. According to this model, a strong predisposition for schizophrenia and little environmental stress (point D), a weak predisposition and a lot of stress (point C), or any other sufficiently potent combination can lead a person to cross the threshold into schizophrenia.

Numerous textbooks on abnormal psychology provide more detailed coverage of biological factors in mental disorders, and of the use of diathesis-stress perspectives in explanatory theories (e.g., Nietzel et al., 1998).

CLINICAL APPROACHES IN ACTION

Having described the main approaches to clinical psychology, and the interpersonal and biological theories that have influenced them, it is time to examine how they affect the day-to-day assessment, treatment, and research activities of clinical pschologists.

Perhaps the best way to do this is to consider the clinical strategies that would be employed by adherents of each approach in relation to a hypothetical case. Reading real clinicians' descriptions of their strategies will give you an idea of how the principles and assumptions of each general approach act as a guide to dealing with the problems of a specific troubled person. In addition, reading discussions of the same person by clinicians who take different approaches will highlight an important point about those approaches: Human behavior does not have to appear in any particular form in order to be dealt with by a particular approach, nor does any particular approach have a monopoly on describing and explaining certain kinds of behavior. Any pattern of behavior can be dealt with by any approach.

We asked several clinicians to read a case report on "Mr. B." and to describe (1) their initial reaction, (2) the assessment strategy they would use to learn more about the client, (3) their hypotheses about the cause of his problems, (4) the potential impact of further assessment data, and (5) an outline of their plan for treating the client. Most of these clinicians represent the psychodynamic, behavioral, or humanistic approaches, but one takes the interpersonal perspective described earlier as being related to all three. Here is the case they read, and the responses they gave.

The Case of Mr. B.

Mr. B. is a 58-year-old business executive at a national computer company. He grew up in a working-class family, the oldest of three brothers. He was an average student throughout his school years, and though he never gave his parents any trouble, he also remembers "never having much fun." As a child, he was pampered by his parents and teased by his peers for being a "momma's boy." He was somewhat overweight as a teenager and always felt slighted by other boys who were more interested in and successful at sports. Mr. B. married his high-school girlfriend while both were attending the same college. They have been married for 35 years and have two grown children. In addition to his salary of about $150,000 per year, Mr. B. has reaped large profits from rental properties and other business ventures.

Mr. B. tends to judge himself and others in terms of material wealth and physical appearance. He is always fishing for compliments, sometimes to the point of annoying people, and while he is hypersensitive to criticism by others, he is also hypercritical of others. Mr. B. has always tried to win his children's affection with money and other gifts, but his relationship with them remains rather distant. He feels he has "bought" a say in how they live their lives, but they tend to reject his advice as unwelcome interference. His constant lament is "I work my butt off, and nobody seems to notice."

Mr. B. has felt restless and unhappy for the past 2 years, and has been "constantly nervous" for the last year or so. His stomach is "always upset," and he often "can't catch my breath." A medical examination revealed that Mr. B. has Crohn's disease, a potentially dangerous intestinal disorder. Some of the numerous physicians he has consulted have prescribed anti-anxiety or antidepressant medications, but the side effects always cause Mr. B. to stop taking them. At the moment, he feels so agitated that he can't sit still, can't concentrate at work, and has trouble remembering things. Recently, he drove home from work and left his briefcase on the ground in the office parking lot. The quality of his work has also begun to decline. He doesn't fall asleep until 3:00 A.M. most nights because his mind is "spinning" with worry about work and marital problems.

He describes his marriage as "extremely tense and uncomfortable"; he and his wife avoid each other as much as possible. Though he reports being sexually "impotent" with his wife—a problem that caused them to "just give up" trying to have sex—he has maintained a sexual affair with a co-worker for over a year. He feels that the deceptions involved in hiding this relationship from everyone are beginning to take a toll on him. Mr. B. is also worried because his company is "downsizing" its work force. Other mid-level executives have been fired recently, and Mr. B. is sure it is just a matter of time before he gets his pink slip. He is convinced that, at his age, no one else will hire him. Increasingly, when he thinks about the future, Mr. B. feels depressed and desperate. In fact, he becomes so obsessed that he will die an early death that he sometimes wonders if he just shouldn't kill himself and put an end to his insecurity and fear.

A Psychoanalytic Approach to Mr. B.: Dr. Thomas A. Widiger[2]

1. Initial Reaction.   My initial impression is that Mr. B. is suffering from a generalized anxiety disorder with clinically significant narcissistic personality traits. A

---

[2]Professor, Department of Psychology, University of Kentucky

careful, systematic assessment might indicate the presence of a mood disorder, but what is most significant is that Mr. B.'s anxiety and dysphoria are due in part to, and are occurring in the context of, quite significant narcissistic pathology.

There are a number of overt indicators of a narcissistic personality disorder, including Mr. B.'s excessive need for admiration (e.g., "always fishing for compliments"), preoccupation with success and status (e.g., judging himself and others by superficial indicators of value, such as wealth, occupational success, and physical appearance), hypersensitivity to criticism, derogatory and disdainful attitude toward others (hypercritical), and lack of empathy (e.g., distant relationship with children and wife). Dysphoria is in fact not uncommon during this period of life in persons with narcissistic conflicts. It is not unusual for persons with narcissistic personality disorder to avoid its complications, pain, and suffering for substantial periods, as long as their narcissistic insecurity continues to be fed (or avoided) by occupational success or social popularity. However, the illusions are often crushed in middle age by accumulating effects of occupational stagnation, failed relationships, and declining physical health. Mr. B. appears to have been hit on all three fronts. His facade of what he has valued or worked for in life is now crumbling, and he lacks sufficient personal security and social support to overcome the injuries.

2. Assessment Strategy.   I would first obtain a more detailed life history, with particular attention to his experiences in childhood and the course of his relationships and symptoms over time. I would like to hear Mr. B. describe his life in his own words, and assess his motivation for treatment, particularly his capacity for and receptivity to self-criticism, change, and insight.

I might also administer psychological tests to alert me to areas of conflict, symptomatology, and dysfunction that I have missed, as well as to provide a possible confirmation of the formulation that I have proposed. The Thematic Apperception Test (TAT) (see Chapter 5) would be particularly useful to assess interpersonal dynamic issues. His responses to the TAT stimuli might also indicate his disposition toward and receptivity to self-reflection.

Mr. B.'s overt suggestion of suicidal ideation should be carefully assessed and closely monitored. I do not currently consider Mr. B. to be a serious suicide risk. However, I am concerned about the future potential for suicide, particularly if he were in fact to lose his job, marriage, and health.

3. Causal Hypotheses.   Feelings of self-esteem and security are due in large part to the experience of having been loved, valued, encouraged, and supported by the significant persons of one's life. How one feels about oneself is, for the most part, a reflection of how one was appreciated, valued, or loved by one's parents. In more technical terms, persons introject their parents' view of them as their own self-concept.

Narcissistic conflicts are usually a reflection of a conflicted or contingent parental love. Ideally, parents would provide an unconditional positive regard. Children would be valued for their own sake, developing thereby a strong, confident, and resilient self-image and self-esteem. However, the love provided by many parents is ambivalent, conflicted, or inconsistent. As a result, children become comparably uncertain, ambivalent, or insecure in how they feel about themselves.

Mr. B. does not describe his parents as being indifferent, ambivalent, or inconsistent in their affection and love for him. However, we also know very little about his childhood. We do know that it was a time of "never having much fun" and this does suggest that it was not a normal, happy, or satisfying childhood. What is childhood to a child other than a time for having fun? It is quite revealing that Mr. B. characterizes it otherwise. In addition, Mr. B. indicates that "he never gave his parents any trouble." This was not a child who felt comfortable simply being himself.

Mr. B. suggests that he was "pampered" by his parents, to the point that others characterized him as a "momma's boy." This does not suggest an indifferent or ambivalent attachment, but it does suggest a pathological relationship, one in which they, or perhaps especially she, related to him more for their (or her) own needs than for his best interests or personal development. He probably did receive substantial attention and overt affection, at least from his mother, but apparently at the cost of not being any trouble and never having any fun. It was a love contingent on something; it was not an unconditional positive regard. We also know that he felt inadequate as a male, and was apparently unsuccessful in traditional masculine activities. This does suggest that he did not spend a significant amount of time bonding with his father (or his father also felt comparable inadequacies).

Life as an adult for a narcissistic person is often a continued search for symbolic representations of a sense of worth, value, and meaning. This preoccupation with superficial symbols is usually unfulfilling, as it is only symbolic of what one really wants but cannot obtain. As Mr. B. states in "his constant lament, 'I work my butt off, and nobody seems to notice.'" "Nobody" is his parents. They never really did "notice" and never will.

Narcissistic persons will often extend and exacerbate their conflicts by re-creating the pathology within their adult relationships. They will seek others who will value and admire them primarily for their achievements and will fail to obtain any truly intimate or meaningful relationships. They are usually impaired in their ability to value, appreciate, or love others. Acknowledging the worth or meaning of others would only make them susceptible to acknowledging the absence of such a relationship with the persons who, for the longest and most significant period of time, meant the most to them.

Mr. B. married his high-school girlfriend, and has been married for 35 years, but it does not appear to have been a mutually satisfying relationship. He has had at least one extramarital affair, he has been sexually impotent with his wife, and they "avoid each other as much as possible." His relationship with his children does not appear to be much better. "Mr. B. has always tried to win his children's affection with money and other gifts." He is unable, or is at least substantially impaired, in his ability to obtain their affection through his own affection for them. "His relationship with them remains rather distant." They probably recognize, at least to some extent, that any effort to relate to him in a meaningful way, to need him as a sincerely intimate and involved father, would be disappointing. "He feels he has 'bought' a say in how they live their lives, but they tend to reject his advice as unwelcome interference." Emotionally, they have left him behind, in a manner perhaps comparable to his wife.

Many narcissistic persons could simply abandon their spouses, children, and friends, as long as they continue to be successful at work. As long as there are achievements to be made, and other persons who will admire them, they are able to avoid the emptiness of their personal lives. However, at some point the achievements may wane, and the emptiness can become apparent. Mr. B. has apparently placed considerable importance on his occupational success for his sense of self-worth, but he is now "sure it is just a matter of time before he gets his pink slip." He is failing at that by which he believes he is valued by others. He could not hope to win back his wife, his children, or his mistress, if he is a failure at work. Mr. B. laments that others have failed to notice how hard he has tried and despairs at how inadequate he has become in the effort. A person who had developed substantively meaningful attachments to others could weather the storm of an occupational setback. His wife and children would still love him. Mr. B, however, has failed to establish their emotional investment and support, and he will be left with nothing if his career and health fail him.

The impending sense of loss has become so severe that he is unable to evaluate accurately his chances of occupational and physical survival. "He is convinced that, at his age, no one else will hire him" and that he may even "die an early death." Hypochondriacal concerns are common in persons with a narcissistic personality disorder. Narcissistic persons often have difficulty downplaying the meaning of minor ailments. What is only a minor symptom to others is of major importance to them. Their worth is that which is superficial, as beneath the surface there really is very little. If the surface wealth and health are peeled away, they will have little left to sustain them.

Crohn's disease is not, of course, trivial or insignificant. It is a potentially dangerous intestinal disorder. However, it need not be lethal. It does not mean that life is over. Mr. B., however, has become "so obsessed that he will die an early death that he sometimes wonders if he just shouldn't kill himself and put an end to his insecurity and fear."

4. Potential Influence of Further Assessment Data. We currently know very little about Mr. B.'s childhood. My psychodynamic speculations could be entirely wrong, although I am confident that the roots of his current difficulties in his marriage, in his relationships with his children, and in his inability to withstand the stress of the setbacks to his health and career, can be traced to issues and conflicts that developed over time within his relationship with his parents.

I would be particularly interested in learning more about his relationship with his father. There are allusions to conflicts regarding an inadequate masculine identity, but we know very little about how this father and son related to one another. Some theorists suggest that narcissism is derived in part through an overevaluation of the child by one or both parents. There is a reference to pampering, but I believe this was an infantalization conveying a low self-esteem rather than an idealization contributing to feelings of excessive self-importance and arrogance. Nowhere in the description of Mr. B. are there indications of a cocky, self-assured arrogance, although I suspect that Mr. B. was very self-assured, self-absorbed, and perhaps even arrogant when the narcissistic illusion was being maintained by his occupational success, his mistress, and the facade of a successful family life.

5. General Treatment Plan. Personality disorders are among the most difficult to treat, as many of the problematic traits, beliefs, values, and attitudes are ego-syntonic (i.e., feel normal). Narcissistic persons can be especially difficult to treat because the need for psychotherapy is itself an injury to self-esteem. To be in treatment is to acknowledge a character flaw, an inadequacy, a failure. They often feel terribly ashamed and embarrassed at being so apparently inadequate and needing the help of others.

The treatment of Mr. B. should initially be supportive and nonthreatening. He might convey the impression that he needs to be considered as a particularly special, unique, or important client, and this defensive, face-saving illusion would not be questioned in the early stages of treatment. He will also need to be reassured that he will once again become "captain of his universe," although his ultimate success in life will come when he no longer wants to be.

It is unlikely that Mr. B. would stay in treatment if he did not experience immediate improvement. However, psychodynamic treatment would ultimately require Mr. B.'s willingness to uncover, acknowledge, and address additional stressors from his past, and he does not currently appear to have the emotional strength or resilience to do this work. Uncovering therapy might also have to wait until his concentration, sleep, and mood returned to a more normal level. Cognitive-behavioral techniques and pharmacologic interventions would be particularly helpful in this respect. Mr. B. has currently refused pharmacotherapy because of his experience of its side effects, but the basis for this refusal is likely to be irrational and could itself be an early focus of treatment. It is possible that he perceives medication as a further sign of personal inadequacy, or he has an exaggerated fear of the meaning of the side effects.

Ironically, it is possible that once Mr. B. experienced sufficient relief from his dysphoria he would lose the motivation for a more thorough, exploratory psychodynamic treatment. Ideally, he would recognize that a patching of his feelings of self-confidence and self-control would provide only a temporary solution. He needs to discover the true extent and source of his insecurities if he is to overcome his vulnerabilities and make a lasting and meaningful change in his life with his wife, his children, and his friends.

I would be nondirective within the sessions, allowing Mr. B. to govern the focus and pace. This does not imply a passive acceptance of resistance to change, but a respect for the limits on his readiness and receptivity to change. I would encourage Mr. B. to discuss and reflect on his problems, attempting to discover how they developed, how they are being maintained, and what needs to change. He would be instructed to say whatever came to his mind, freely associating to his thoughts and fantasies. I would respond by reflecting and clarifying his thoughts, feelings, and associations to highlight what I believe are the most important issues upon which to focus his attention. Interpretations would focus on the thematic relationships among Mr. B.'s associations, dreams, clinical symptoms, current relationships, and childhood history. Interpretations would be offered in a nonthreatening and suggesting manner, always encouraging him to offer his own insights and interpretations, as the most compelling insights will be the ones he reaches himself.

A good prognostic sign is the apparent guilt Mr. B. experienced over his affair. "The deceptions involved in hiding this relationship from everyone are beginning to take a toll." Mr. B. was not empathic enough to avoid deceiving his wife and children for a significant period of time, but he does, at least to some extent, recognize cognitively and appreciate emotionally that there is something wrong in what he has been doing within his marriage. In more severe forms of narcissistic pathology, the person would fail to have any feelings of empathy, doubt, or guilt, providing instead some form of rationalization to justify deceit, exploitation, and/or mistreatment. Mr. B. has opened the door to some extent for questioning himself; perhaps he would be willing and able to reflect more broadly on his life and his relationships.

A Behavioral Approach to Mr. B.: Dr. Edward Craighead and Dr. Linda Wilcoxon Craighead[3]

1. Initial Reaction.   During the first 4 weeks the therapist would meet twice each week with Mr. B.; thereafter, he would be seen once per week until he is substantially improved, which usually takes 12 to 16 weeks for individuals with problems similar to his. The initial sessions would focus on gathering additional information from Mr. B. about the nature of his various problems. In addition, the first two sessions would be used to begin to establish an alliance with Mr. B. The first session would begin with a discussion of confidentiality and a few brief statements about the therapist's background and experience, and a brief overview of the model of therapy (i.e., that cognitive-behavior therapy focuses on identifying current problems and working with the client to arrive at possible solutions to those problems). Mr. B. would then be asked to describe his problems as he sees them, beginning with the most urgent. If the discussion does not include Mr. B.'s suicidal ideation, this topic would be brought up near the end of the first session in order to allow the therapist to determine if any specific precautions or contracts regarding self-harm are warranted.

2. Assessment Strategy.   The second session would continue the discussion of problems as Mr. B. sees them. Because Mr. B. has been diagnosed with Crohn's disease, he would be referred to a gastroenterologist to determine the seriousness of the disorder and how much it is interacting with his psychological problems.

During the second week of therapy, the therapist would conduct the relevant portions (e.g., anxiety and mood disorders) of the Structured Clinical Interview for DSM-IV Axis I Disorders (SCID) [see Chapter 4]. Based on the information in the case report of Mr. B., the preliminary diagnosis is generalized anxiety disorder, major depression, and dysthymia. Mr. B. may very well meet criteria for one or more Axis II disorders (narcissistic personality disorder and obsessive-compulsive personality disorder are most likely), but a formal interview such as the International Personality Disorders Examination will be administered only if the patterns of behavior associated with Axis II type problems interfere with therapy. Although cognitive-behavioral therapists

---

[3]Professor and Associate Professor, respectively, Department of Psychology, University of Colorado

avoided making formal diagnoses during the 1960s and 1970s, we have come to realize there may be considerable clinical value to conducting such a formal overview of clients' problems. In addition, the current system of mental health services delivery necessitates obtaining diagnostic information to allow for a diagnosis in DSM-IV terms.

In addition to the interviews and the SCID, the therapist would rate the client after each session on a clinical rating scale for the symptoms of anxiety and depression (e.g., the Hamilton Anxiety Rating Scale, the Hamilton Depression Rating Scale, or the Montgomery-Asburg Depression Rating Scale). In an effort to conduct efficient assessment and minimize Mr. B.'s expenses, the therapist would ask him to complete the following self-report scales: Beck Depression Inventory-II; Attributional Style Questionnaire (assesses client's view of causality for positive and negative events); Dysfunctional Attitudes Scale (measures perfectionism and need for social approval); and Dyadic Adjustment Scale (measures marital satisfaction), which would also be completed by his wife if she would be willing to do so. The BDI-II, ASQ, DAS (cognitive), and DAS (marital) would be given to Mr. B. after the first session, and he would be asked to return them at the second session; his wife would be asked to mail her completed copy of the DAS (marital) to the therapist.

The BDI-II would also be administered to Mr. B once each week for weeks one to six and once every other week for the remainder of the therapy sessions; this instrument gives the therapist a quick overview of Mr. B's level of depression, and it serves as a measure of change over time. One of the cardinal features of cognitive-behavior therapy is that the therapist evaluates the effectiveness of the therapy on an ongoing basis. The other scales provide information to the therapist and client about how his cognitive styles compare to those of other individuals his age, and they give the therapist a good idea of which cognitive patterns are most clearly associated with Mr. B.'s anxiety and depression. Although it is obvious that Mr. B. is not very happily married, the information on the Dyadic Adjustment Scale will provide detailed information about the level of discord in his marriage as well as his wife's view of their problems.

After the first three to five assessment sessions (assuming there are no immediate crises), the therapist would offer a summary of Mr. B.'s clinical problems, along with formal diagnoses and a treatment plan. The treatment plan would include the rationale for each component of the proposed treatment and how each therapeutic intervention will address Mr. B.'s problems. (For present purposes, it is assumed that Mr. B. is not imminently suicidal and that, while his stress may be aggravating his Crohn's disease, and vice versa, the treatment of the Crohn's disease and his mental health problems will not have a major impact on each other.)

3. Causal Hypotheses. Mr. B. meets the criteria for Generalized Anxiety Disorder (GAD): He worries on a regular basis, and he finds it difficult to control the worrying; he worries about several aspects of his life; he is distressed by his level of anxiety and worry; and he is restless, has difficulty concentrating, is forgetful, tense, and has difficulty getting to sleep. He also suffers from Major Depressive Disorder (MDD), which has been present for several months and is causing him great distress. Indicators of depression include his being "down" almost every day, a loss of pleasure in many aspects of his life, his initial insomnia, problems concentrating, poor memory, and suicidal ideation. Because of the chronicity of several symptoms, Mr. B. also meets criteria for dysthymia: His dysphoric symptoms have persisted for two years, and his depressed mood is present for more days than not; he also experiences initial insomnia, low self-esteem, poor concentration, and a sense of hopelessness. Although Mr. B. meets criteria for Axis II Personality Disorders of narcissistic and obsessive-compulsive types, the problems associated with these disorders overlap substantially with the problems associated with the Axis I diagnoses, so Axis II diagnoses will not be discussed here except to point out the persistence of some of his interpersonal difficulties. Finally, Mr. B. also suffers from both parent-child and from partner relational problems. In DSM parlance, these disorders will initially be diagnosed on Axis IV, but if they become the major focus of treatment (marital discord is likely to need treatment), then each may be considered as a major Axis I problem.

Based on what is known from the case report, it appears that Mr. B.'s various disorders have been brought about by independent causes which interact in certain ways.

Mr. B.'s high need for approval appears to stem from lack of acceptance as a child, both within the context of his family and with his peers. He seldom received positive social feedback as a child and adolescent, and, although not much is known about his college experiences, it seems likely that the absence of social approval continued during that period of his life. Also, his parents were not good role models for the expression of affection and approval. Consequently, it seems that he has never developed the ability to understand and express the feelings that are essential to long-standing and meaningful relationships. There are several indications of his poor social functioning in that he constantly seeks approval from others, is lonely and close to no one, and has difficulty communicating, which has taken its toll on his 35-year marriage (e.g., the lack of positive feeling and affection—"distance"—is probably fundamental to the lack of a satisfying sexual relationship with his wife). The social issues likely also play a role in the development of his ongoing affair. For example, the lack of interpersonal and sexual satisfaction in the marital relationship may have contributed to his search outside the marriage for approval both socially and sexually. The affair helps to meet his high need for approval (the sexual gratification in addition to being immediately reinforcing also serves to support a self-view that he is okay). Even though the affair has been ongoing for a year it seems that it is happening in the context of a fairly comfortable but superficial (distant?) relationship. His excessive need for approval stems from both the lack of good social skills and a fundamental belief (schema) that he is a good person only if other individuals approve of him. Undoubtedly, his almost continuous worry about the possibility of his ongoing affair's being discovered and the anticipated resulting social disapproval contribute to his stress.

In the work area, Mr. B. also has excessively high standards regarding his performance and financial success. He tends to evaluate everyone, including himself, on the level of material success. This seems to be important in a symbolic as well as literal way. For example, he tries to "buy" the approval and affection of his children, even though they are adults, and his view of his own adequacy appears to be connected to his attainment of financial success. His view of himself as successful is now being threatened by the possibility of his being given a "pink slip." Even though the firing of his colleagues resulted from "downsizing," Mr. B can only think about his own firing as a sign of failure.

Mr. B's early life experiences probably began a process in which he developed and maintained a "schema" or belief of inadequacy that is being activated by the stress of impending job loss and the stress of his thought patterns associated with that possibility. In other words, his "self-talk" is creating a crisis about the work situation.

4. Potential Influence of Further Assessment Data.   It is important to sort out Mr. B.'s presenting problems, fit them into their proper domains, and try to determine their causes. It is important to determine causes because there are alternative solutions to the various problems, and the intervention strategy chosen will be partially determined by the clinician's conceptualization of those causes. For example, there are effective sex therapy strategies for treating Mr. B.'s ineffective sexual behavior with his wife, but it would be inappropriate to implement those strategies in the context of his poor marital relationship. In other words, his inability to perform sexually with his wife would be viewed as being caused by the relationship rather than Mr. B.'s physical inability to perform sexually. (Also, he is able to perform in the context of his affair.) This does not mean that a therapist must always figure out exactly what caused a problem in order to help the client change, but the more valid the clinician's understanding of the cause, the more effective the treatment is likely to be. For this reason, the therapist would continue to collect assessment data and revise the treatment plan in ways the data indicate are necessary.

5. General Treatment Plan.   The relative urgency of Mr. B.'s problems will be a major factor determining the sequencing of the treatment plan, and that information will be obtained from the assessments conducted during the first three to five sessions. The following treatment plan is based on what is known of Mr. B. at this point in time; the order of treatment strategies and the use of possible alternatives would depend on additional assessment information.

The absence of most of the major biological symptoms of GAD or MDD, as well as Mr. B.'s prior failure to respond to anti-anxiety or antidepressant medications, suggests that cognitive-behavioral therapy (CBT) should begin without an initial referral to a psychiatrist for possible drug treatment. The main environmental problem that is a candidate for change is his marital discord (he has not yet been fired, so his worry about the "pink slip" may be a cognitive distortion). His cognitive problems appear related mainly to his distorted negative self-statements regarding social situations and work as well as his fundamental schemata regarding his inadequacy as a person. His behavioral problems include poor communication skills, lack of positive assertion, and general lack of social skills. Within a CBT model, change of emotions is achieved indirectly, in other words, through change in other domains such as cognitive restructuring, biological change (e.g., relaxation), and behavioral change. It will be important for Mr. B. to adopt this view—that his emotional states are a function of his behavioral and cognitive patterns.

The therapist would begin treatment by teaching Mr. B. progressive muscle relaxation. The reason for beginning with relaxation training (or a comparable procedure such as biofeedback or a form of meditation), is that it should help reduce his stress during the day, and most importantly, he can use the relaxation to prevent his insomnia. Clients also often become more expressive about their problems during therapy as they become more relaxed.

Cognitive restructuring would be undertaken so Mr. B. can learn to talk differently to himself and, ultimately, to change his fundamental views of himself as inadequate. His negative cognitive style, particularly in regard to work, is viewed as a major aspect of his stress. Mr. B. would first be taught to monitor his strong feelings (both good and bad), to record the situations in which they occur, and then to record the thoughts he had in those situations. The major purpose of this type of three-column (situations-thoughts-feelings) monitoring is to allow Mr. B. to see that his feelings are caused by his thoughts both at work and socially. Since Mr. B. is catastrophizing about the work situation and, in particular, distorting the situation regarding his being fired (he is talking to himself as if it had already happened), the first attempts at cognitive change would focus on work. A particular area of emphasis will be to get Mr. B. to see how his high standards for social approval result in his feeling negative toward himself, even when he receives a "normal" level of positive feedback from others. Once Mr. B. develops a clear understanding of the role of thoughts in relation to feelings, he will be taught to substitute alternative thoughts for the self-defeating thoughts characteristic of GAD and MDD. Then, he would continue monitoring using five columns (situations-thoughts-feelings-alternative thoughts-new feelings). It typically takes four to six sessions of monitoring for clients to become proficient at developing alternative adaptive thoughts in stressful situations. (Since clients need to have firsthand experience with this method of changing feelings in order to believe that this process works, do not be surprised if, at about this point, you are saying to yourself, "that would never work for me, my feelings are too strong, and they are independent of my thought processes." Monitoring and changing cognitions are not easy to learn, even with the help of a good clinician, but it does seem to work for most people.)

The next step in CBT would focus on helping Mr. B. develop an understanding of how his automatic thoughts are related to his fundamental beliefs or schemata of inadequacy and social rejection. This would be accomplished through a variety of hypothesis testing and cognitive challenging procedures. Mr. B. would come to see that the stressors he is currently facing are activating fundamental questions about his self-sufficiency and self-efficacy, and he would learn new ways of thinking about himself (both at the level of self-statements and at the more fundamental beliefs level).

CBT would then focus on helping Mr. B. change several of his behaviors, particularly in the social area. Many of Mr. B.'s problems are due to his lack of skill in adaptively interacting with others. Behavioral change therapy would include teaching him positive assertions skills—such as how to give and receive compliments and how to express positive feelings toward others. Improving specific communication skills with co-workers would be addressed (communications skills would also be a major component of marital therapy). General social skills training including such matters as over-self-disclosure, appropriate approval-seeking behavior, tone of voice, smiling, etc., would also be a part of therapy.

Two other major issues would still need to be addressed—the extramarital affair (a behavioral problem) and the marital discord (an environmental problem). These may have already been touched on during assessment or therapy sessions, but once cognitive and behavioral procedures have reduced Mr. B.'s anxiety and depression (it usually takes about 6 to 8 weeks until clients with GAD and MDD start to feel considerably better), the therapist would initiate discussion of the affair and the marital relationship. Regarding the affair, Mr. B. first would have to decide if he wants to continue it, knowing that it may be discovered. This issue would be discussed within the context of his value system, since the guilt associated with the affair appears to be coming from his behaving inconsistently with that value system. The discord in the marriage would also be discussed, and alternative ways of addressing it would be developed. Mr. B. has to make some very difficult decisions, which he has probably avoided; individuals with MDD typically have a difficult time making decisions. In Mr. B.'s case this difficulty may have been complicated by fear regarding his career.

If Mr. B. decided he wants to stay in the marriage, and if his wife were willing to participate, they would be referred to a cognitive-behavioral marital therapist. Since there are many individual problems which Mr. B. must address, including the loss associated with terminating the affair or the difficulty in dealing with two relationships (depending on his choice), he would be continued in individual CBT until these stresses are relieved and his GAD and MDD have improved. If Mr. B. stayed in his marriage, and if he and his wife and adult children were interested in doing so, it could also be valuable for them to have a few sessions of family therapy. This intervention would focus on the new ways of living that Mr. B. has developed over the course of therapy and how the family members could develop more positive and meaningful relationships with one another.

The therapist would consider termination of individual therapy at the point that Mr. B. reports significant reduction of his presenting problems (i.e., falling asleep within 30 minutes most nights, few somatic complaints other than those associated with the Crohn's disease, substantially less anxiety and dysphoria, and improved performance at work). At that time, Mr. B. should also understand how his longstanding family and marital difficulties and his affair contributed to his depression, and he would have made some decisions about how to resolve those ongoing concerns. Therapy would be likely to have helped him clarify how he contributed to his problems and the necessity of taking an active role in creating a life that will be more satisfying for him. Within the CBT approach, the goal is to help the client resolve the presenting problems and learn skills so that he is better equipped to deal with new problems in living as they arise. It is likely that Mr. B. would demonstrate significant changes in the specific interpersonal behaviors that were contributing to distress and unhappiness in his relationships (through increased assertion and better communication), but he should also be more aware of his cognitive patterns and the ways in which he is most vulnerable to new stressors.

Therapy would be decreased from once a week, to every other week, to monthly in order to ease the transition as Mr. B. takes more responsibility for making changes. This tapering of therapy sessions is likely to increase his confidence that he can handle any new problems that might arise. The therapist would express confidence that Mr. B. will be able to handle new problems, but will also remain available as a consultant if he needs future assistance, either for a few sessions just to get back on track or to restart therapy should there be a significant return of symptoms.

An Existential-Humanistic Approach to Mr. B.:
Dr. Constance T. Fischer[4]

1. Initial Reaction.   My initial impressions took form as the case reverberated with my experience of prior clients, with other aspects of my own life, with theoretical writings, with traditional and qualitative research, and with diagnostic literature. These perspectives sensitized me to Mr. B.'s situation, but I did not impose any of them as a single best explanation. In terms of the prevailing diagnostic system (DSM IV), Mr. B.'s current state meets the criteria for dysthymic disorder and for generalized anxiety disorder. His longstanding efforts to be beyond criticism probably meet criteria for narcissistic personality disorder. These classifications coalesce much of Mr. B.'s reported struggles, and they remind us of additional features that may turn out to pertain to Mr. B. My point of departure into such classifications and my point of return from that framework is Mr. B.'s life. I ask myself how the "disorders" point back to a disordering of his life—a disruption of a personal world that used to make sense and used to support his goals, values, and actions. What has changed for Mr. B.? Who was he trying to be? Where was he going? What were his assumptions about life? What purpose does his behavior now serve?

The following initial impressions will serve as a useful starting point for exploration with Mr. B., but they might be modified through use of tests and through discussions with him and his family. It seems likely that Mr. B. grew up extraordinarily attuned to the danger of being criticized. I wonder if his reports of never giving his parents any trouble, and of never having had much fun reflect a lonely life, one in which he worried about sustaining what pampering he received, and in which he tried to solidify his place within his family. He must have been keenly sensitive to being teased by his peers for his chubbiness, for being a mama's boy, for being only an average student, and for not quite fitting in. Marrying a high school girlfriend while in college may have served to avoid risking himself with other women. By his late-50s however, through "working his butt off," he had built a stronghold of income, business position, and investments that announced to himself and others that he was indeed accomplished and worthy, and safe from criticism. In getting there, with his central concern being his own safety, he likely did not develop much empathy in relation to his children or to other people. Perhaps his bastion is barren. The case example does not report satisfying interpersonal involvement. And now, suddenly, he is under siege: He is acutely anxious and despairing at the prospect of being "downsized."

2. Assessment Strategy.   Before meeting with Mr. B., I would review my initial impressions and conjectures so that I could revise them as I came to know Mr. B. more directly. I would not be looking for proof of my impression nor for causes of his condition, but rather for a revised, refined, and deepened understanding of what that condition is, especially in terms of how Mr. B. participated in bringing it about and how he is living it now. In my meeting with him, I would try to assess how viable his prior life course might still be, and how I and others might help him revise his assumptions, goals, and ways of going about being the person he has strived to be.

---

[4]Professor, Department of Psychology, Duquesne University

Our starting point would be Mr. B.'s own story, which would be our common ground for collaborative exploration. We would try to make sense of his life in its own terms, using his language and themes. Perhaps I would affirm that he must feel terribly disoriented, as though the ground had shifted under him, leaving him and his accomplishments to crumble. I would ask if I was on track in assuming that he must be wondering whether he had overreached, whether he was only average after all. We would try to make sense of when and how he had begun to fall apart, as well as of what options he could now conceive.

The purpose of assessment, beyond understanding the person's circumstance, is to identify viable interventions and points at which he or she might opt for alternative, more satisfying routes. I would hope that during the assessment process, Mr. B. would rediscover that he does participate in directing his life. In this way, transformation is initiated prior to, and sometimes instead of, counseling or psychotherapy. To underline his responsibility and possibilities, I speak in past and in future tense, and in verbs and adverbs rather than constructs, and I ask for instances when the person has made other choices. For example, if Mr. B. says, "I've been told that I have this tendency toward self-aggrandizement," I might reply, "It does seem that up to now you have often thought more about looking good than about the other person's well-being. But you also told me that you have tried to make arrangements for your secretary to be transferred if your unit is closed. Tell me what you already know about the circumstances in which you have empathized with another person's situation and have helped out even though you didn't get any credit." We might then go on to look at instances of what may have been meant by self-aggrandizement, and at how Mr. B. now imagines he could bypass such excesses and still feel good about himself.

I would want to conduct part of the assessment in Mr. B.'s home, where I could see more of his life, observe him interacting with his wife, and perhaps engage her in the assessment. More of his actual life would therefore be available to both of us. I might use psychological tests, for three main purposes. First, patterns and specific responses might surprise me and allow me to consider additional perspectives. For example, the MMPI-2 [see Chapter 5] might suggest that Mr. B. has been much more outgoing than I had imagined. Second, Mr. B. would make discoveries of his own, perhaps realizing as he tells a story for a TAT card, that just as he wants to have control over the characters, so he has wanted to direct his family's ways of relating to him. Third, test data would provide concrete instances of our general discussions, which we could then explore collaboratively as we developed understandings of Mr. B.'s life journey, crisis, and options.

3. Causal Hypotheses.   In my effort to understand Mr. B.'s disordered life situation, I would not look for "the cause of his problem," but rather try to appreciate how he has his own "life journey" and how he engages that situation now. By "situation," I include interpersonal, biological, physical, cultural, historical features. Once we have understood this development holistically, and in ways that promote viable change, we have successfully accounted for Mr. B.'s situation. The existential aspect of this approach is its attention to Mr. B.'s co-authoring of his life—his purposes, choices, and responsibility for the meaning of his life across his life course, even though none of us can ever clearly foresee all options and consequences. Moreover, neurophysiology, culture, developmental events, and so on, also co-author our lives.

In order to explore Mr. B.'s journey from his parental home to his present crisis, I might remark that he must feel betrayed by life, which suddenly no longer honored his hard work, production, and control. I also might say that he must feel that events had left him with no way to continue his past into the future. Depending on his responses, I might pursue with him the idea that his acute anxiety, depression, and resulting memory problems were all parts of an understandable life crisis.

We probably would meet several times, affording Mr. B. time to experience and reflect on the issues we raised. As we went further, I might suggest that even without the likelihood of being fired, he had probably already been wondering what all his work and control had been for if it not only did not buy him a say in his children's lives but resulted in their distancing themselves from him. I might mention that the name "introjective depression" is sometimes given to the experience of failure in having been work-oriented rather than person-oriented as one pursed one's parents' values. I would also say that (humanistic) research has indicated that sometimes depression is largely despair—holding one's self accountable for not living up to one's core values, perhaps for example, his not having let his children know that they were as special to him as he was to his parents, and perhaps that his office affair had betrayed his wife.

I would ask whether he had discovered that he could be a different person with the woman at work, and whether he had discovered new personal potential. If this seemed to be at least partially the case, we would explore whether he now felt guilty, and how that played into his current emotional state and his impotence at home. If instead he replied in essence that his lover provided him with adoration and unconditional sympathy, and if his concerns about deceiving his wife were not evidence of growth beyond self-centeredness but were only fears of being caught, then I would be less hopeful that his crisis might serve as a developmental transformation point.

In any case, we would wonder together about the extent to which his pain and anguish at least served to gain family sympathy, and perhaps as an excuse for the affair.

4. Potential Influence of Further Assessment Data. While developing the preceding understandings, I would have assessed the following, each of which is important for advising Mr. B. and his family: (a) danger of suicide; (b) whether Mr. B. experienced full-fledged panic attacks; (c) appropriateness of a referral to a psychiatrist for evaluation for possible reinstatement of medication for depression and anxiety/panic; (d) whether the memory problems were related to neurological conditions beyond anxiety or panic; (e) whether his "obsession" with death is an instance of a general obsessive coping style; and (f) how his siblings and children are faring, how they and his wife relate to Mr. B. A Rorschach test and Wechsler subtest [see Chapter 5] would help me estimate how far Mr. B. has fallen from his earlier levels of functioning and what his current strengths are.

Perspectives offered by Mrs. B. and the children, including descriptions of the influence of the B.'s parents on their lives and marriage, would affect my understandings and suggestions. Upon receiving legal releases, I might check with Mr. B.'s superiors for their views of his performance and future.

5. General Treatment Plan. Our assessment sessions were meant to lead to change: We assessed Mr. B.'s current situation and his readiness to understand it in revised ways and to consider moving on in modified ways and directions. We already would have made some sense together of how his controlling style in conjunction with circumstances beyond his control contributed to specific features of his Crohn's disease, anxiety, and depression. We also would have assessed his employment and retirement options. Further sessions would continue this process, inviting Mr. B. to comprehend his interpersonal world still more fully, to own his missteps and losses even while recovering the useful aspects of his style, values, and accomplishments, and to expand them into a less restrictive existence. As he reported his efforts to try himself out in slightly revised ways, he would discover that although his old ways were an appropriate solution early in his life, they were by now no longer useful or necessary. Concurrently, Mr. B. would rediscover lost desires and would dare to pursue them.

I would repeatedly affirm Mr. B.'s experience of being personally "downsized," and of having experienced multiple criticisms and losses. His legitimate worth, past productivity, and personal ambitions would be affirmed even as his interpersonal shortcomings were also acknowledged. A therapist would do well to gently and honestly apprise Mr. B. of moments when he or she felt dismissed or affirmed by him, and of what that was like. He would be reminded that no one can always control outcomes, that we must all plan and accommodate. In the context of his life stage and crisis, Mr. B. likely would gradually acknowledge that he, as all of us, is both special and not so special, and yet no more at risk than most of us. Nevertheless, I would guess that Mr. B. for the rest of his life would remain in many instances more self-centered than others would wish.

Working with Mr. B. in the company of any willing family members would enhance recovery and growth through building shared understandings. In addition, Mr. B. would discover that his worth is not just in being right and materially productive, but also in the quality of his relationships. He would come to appreciate more consistently the inevitability of diverse viewpoints and the wisdom of respecting both diversity and ambiguity.

Along the way I would no doubt witness episodes of angry blame toward myself and others as Mr. B. protested breaches of his (unilateral) contract with the world: that if he produced material evidence of his worth and rightness, he would be respected by everyone. The course of recovery and growth would at first appear chaotic, and would require many difficult decisions on Mr. B.'s part. Nevertheless, he would find that he is not helpless, that he can pick up and continue on a modified course, engaging in productive activities. Indeed he would find that his crisis, for all its pain, has occasioned new possibilities.

An Interpersonal Perspective on Mr. B.: Dr. Todd F. Van Denburg[5]

1. Initial Reaction. Interpersonal treatment of Mr. B. would focus on the apparent lack of security and intimacy he experiences in his relationships. The symptoms

---

[5]Associate Professor, Department of Psychology, Transylvania University.

associated with the ostensible diagnosis of generalized anxiety disorder would not be targeted initially in treatment. Instead, their significance within the client's central interpersonal maladaptive patterns and his maladaptive sense of self would be assessed throughout the course of therapy. I expect that treatment of his basic interpersonal problems will begin to relieve Mr. B.'s emotional and cognitive symptoms. However, an immediate and continuing priority would be the close monitoring of Mr. B.'s suicidal thoughts.

The data suggest that Mr. B. has significant features of a narcissistic personality disorder which, in turn, suggests a preliminary baseline profile translation onto a version of the interpersonal circle at the competitive, dominant, and assured categories (see Figure 2.4). However, this hypothesized preferred interpersonal profile of Mr. B. would require validation through further interpersonal assessment.

2. Assessment Strategy.   A basic assumption of interpersonal therapy is that the client's central problems reside in maladaptive transaction cycles (MTC) with significant others, including the therapist. The therapist must identify the specific components of this repetitious, self-defeating maladaptive pattern: the client's covert experience (e.g., "I work my butt off, and nobody seems to notice"), overt actions (e.g., his attempts to elicit compliments while criticizing others), the covert experience of others in reaction to the client (e.g., Mr. B.'s children experience him as controlling and interfering), and the overt reactions of significant others (e.g., his family's rejection of him) which in turn, confirm the client's maladaptive covert experience of himself and others. The client's specific MTC needs to be the central target of psychotherapy; the therapist attempts to help the client understand and disrupt the maladaptive vicious cycle at any or all of these four MTC components (Kiesler, 1996; Van Denburg & Kiesler, 1996).

The interpersonal circle helps the therapist identify the specific content present in the four causally linked components of the client's MTC. The circle both guides interpersonal diagnosis and permits formulation of interpersonal interventions with a particular client. A repertoire of interpersonal measures, with multiple applications, is available to locate and describe a client's interpersonal behavior at specific segments of the circle.

FIGURE 2.4   Kiesler's Version of Leary's Interpersonal Circle. Donald Kiesler (1983) revised the original arrangement shown in Figure 2.2, using somewhat different labels. We include the newer version here so that Dr. Van Denburg's clinical conception of Mr. B. can be more easily visualized.

I would concentrate on determining Mr. B.'s predominant interactional patterns with significant others in his life. I would use the Check List of Interpersonal Transactions-Revised (CLOIT-R) (Kiesler, 1987a), the Impact Message Inventory (IMI) (Kiesler, 1987b; Kiesler et al., 1985), and the Inventory of Interpersonal Problems (IIP) (Horowitz et al., 1988). I would use three sources of assessment: (a) Mr. B. himself (who would be asked to describe his own typical, desired, and dreaded interpersonal behavior on three separate CLOIT-Rs, and to characterize his interpersonal problems on the IIP); (b) Mr. B.'s wife and children (who would rate Mr. B.'s interpersonal behavior on the CLOIT-R and report their covert experiences of him on the IMI); and (c) my own CLOIT-R ratings of Mr. B.'s actions with me and my report—via the IMI—of the impacts I experience with him. The results would be circle profiles of Mr. B.'s interpersonal behavior with his spouse, his children, and his therapist—as well as his perceptions of his own typical, dreaded, and desired interpersonal behavior patterns and of his interpersonal problems.

As his interpersonal behavior appears rigid across relationships, it is likely that his significant others' ratings of Mr. B.'s interpersonal functioning would show a high degree of consistency and generality. Since clients are often unaware of the negative impacts their interpersonal styles have on others, I would also expect that there would be important discrepancies between Mr. B.'s characterizations of himself and those coming from others. For example, Mr. B.'s significant others may view his enacting of behaviors from the competitive, dominant, and assured segments of the interpersonal circle as shrewd, dictatorial, and egotistical, while Mr. B. may see them as industrious, decisive, and self-reliant. Others are also more likely than Mr. B. himself to see him behaving in a hostile-dominant manner.

3. Causal Hypotheses. Mr. B.'s most prototypical self-definition (Sullivan's "self-personification") seems to be that he is hard-working, ambitious, in control, fiscally successful, and generally knows what is best. In general, in interpersonal therapy, it is assumed that individuals' sense of self and interactional tendencies develop in order to gain acceptance and security and to avoid anxiety in relationships. Although there is not enough detailed information about his developmental history to speculate specifically about how his sense of self and interactional tendencies were formed, some tentative hypotheses may be made concerning the formulation of his self-system.

The contradiction between being described as "pampered" by his parents and remembering "never having much fun" as a child points to his having internalized a stance of entitlement, yet not believing others will readily and easily provide him what he wants. In other words, Mr. B. is not comfortable experiencing, acknowledging, or expressing dependency needs. Several manifestations of this conflict include attempting to elicit compliments, being sensitive to criticisms, possessing empathic deficits, and in general, maintaining a superficial stance in his relationships—as illustrated by judging himself and others by physical appearances and financial status. The outcome of this internalization process likely currently operates outside of awareness. When significant others behave toward him in unassured, submissive, and deferent ways that complement his preferred interpersonal baseline, Mr. B.'s psychological equilibrium is maintained. When this is not the case, however, his personification (schema) of others seems to be that they are being hostile (resisting advice), detached (not initiating contact), and inhibited (not expressing positive emotions for him). At these times, Mr. B. reacts by being hostile, cold, and mistrusting.

His physical problems, his estrangement from his family, and his perceived tenuous job status seem to be challenging Mr. B.'s lifelong self-definition. His recent behavior is producing major dissonance in relation to his self-conception and, in turn, lowering his self-esteem. Anxious, depressed, and desperate, he has lost the success of his job performance. Instead of being in control and receiving accolades for his performance, he feels impotent; instead of thanking him for the money and gifts he has provided, his children become more distant; instead of experiencing intimacy with his wife, he has engaged in an affair—probably in an attempt to bolster his flagging self-esteem. However, Mr. B. is blind to the automatic process through which his own rigid and extreme controlling stance with significant others eventually actually evoke and reinforce these behaviors. Unsuccessful in changing other people's reactions, he intensifies his maladaptive pattern ("transactional escalation"), becomes increasingly disparaging of others, and develops symptoms of an anxiety disorder.

4. Potential Influence of Further Assessment Data.   In assisting Mr. B. to tell and explore the story of his life and problems I would be especially attentive to those interpersonal situations I hypothesize to be problematic. First, I would explore more fully his relationships with his parents, siblings, and peers during his childhood and adolescence to help him, and me, to understand the roots of his maladaptive transactional cycle. Also, I would want to understand how he and his wife have become so distant from one another and try to understand the functions that his affair is serving. Further, I would want to assess the nature of Mr. B.'s relationships with his co-workers and friends. Finally, I would carefully monitor his suicidal thinking, especially during periods of heightened stress, both within and outside of therapy sessions.

5. General Treatment Plan.   Because of the apparent intensification of Mr. B.'s symptoms, I would initially arrange to see him twice a week. The goal of therapy would be to help Mr. B. increase the experience, frequency, and intensity of interpersonal actions that represent segments on the interpersonal circle opposite to those that currently underlie his rigid and extreme maladaptive interpersonal behavior. Those opposite segments are unassured (relies on others for support, humble, etc.), submissive (accepts advice, agrees to others' wishes, etc.), and deferential (compliments others, content, etc.).

Especially in early therapy sessions, I would expect that Mr. B.'s interpersonal behavior will evoke or "pull" from me covert and overt responses that are complementary to his behavior. Thus, I would be likely to enact unassured, submissive, and deferential behaviors, and in the process inadvertently reinforce and confirm his maladaptive interpersonal approach to living. For example, I might find myself letting him dominate our conversations, tacitly agreeing that his wife and children are ungrateful, and complimenting him on his financial success. And I would soon experience the negative impacts reported by others who interact with Mr. B.

To disengage myself from the responses Mr. B. pulls from me, and to help him become aware of what he is doing, I would begin to detect and label the complementary engagements (thoughts, feelings, action tendencies, images, etc.) being evoked during our sessions. This disengagement process would permit me to discontinue my complementary responses and to begin applying interventions (clarifications, reflection of feelings surrounding areas of conflict). My goal would be to help Mr. B. experience the cognitive and emotional ambiguity that results when his preferred maladaptive style does not produce its expected effects.

During the middle and later stages of therapy, I would emphasize interpersonal feedback in the form of "therapeutic metacommunication" (Kiesler, 1996; Kiesler & Van Denburg, 1993) in which I would disclose to Mr. B. my perceptions of and reactions to his interpersonal actions. My disclosures would focus on the four components of the maladaptive transaction cycle: my covert experiences (impacts), my overt reactions and any discrepancies or incongruities I notice, Mr. B.'s covert experience (as I infer them to be), and Mr. B.'s overt maladaptive pattern as it occurs in our sessions, and elsewhere. For example, I might say to Mr. B., "I'm trying to figure out why it is that at those times you seem most upset, you are the least willing to allow me to try to help you. It is as if you expect me to somehow humiliate you for feeling vulnerable," or "When I would not join you in criticizing your children for being ungrateful brats, you looked like you felt resentful and angry at me. This made me feel that if I don't agree with you one hundred percent of the time, that I am of no use to you. I wonder if your children ever have a similar reaction?" Together, we would continue to validate these components until the regularity of their appearance with me, and with his family, are indisputably obvious.

As a crucial first step in discovering more adaptive interpersonal alternatives—in this case, unassured, submissive, deferent behaviors—Mr. B. and I would seek to "etch in marble" the vicious MTC that represents his central problem in living with his significant others. In the pretermination stage of therapy, we would focus on helping Mr. B. display alternative interpersonal behaviors with me. Ideally, he will see that his fears about expressing his dependency needs are unfounded and he will experience relief and a heightened security and intimacy in our relationship. We would then explore ways for Mr. B. to interact with his family that are more likely to create intimacy than the heavyhanded strategies he had been using. Finally, we would assess the status of his anxiety symptoms, discuss what future interpersonal situations are likely to trigger anxiety, and design strategies for coping adaptively with these circumstances.

There are similarities among the conceptualizations of Mr. B.'s case offered by these clinicians. They all note Mr. B.'s interpersonal difficulties, his rigid personality style, and his depressive mood. However, it is also evident that the type of therapeutic experience Mr. B. would have depends on whose office door he enters. These therapists reveal dramatic differences in the ways they conceptualize Mr. B.'s difficulties, the types of assessment data they would gather, the issues they would focus on in therapy, and the way they would conduct the interventions. For example, the behavioral approach focuses on the present-day nature of Mr. B.'s depression and interpersonal problems, whereas the psychodynamic approach downplays these symptoms and attempts to uncover unresolved conflicts from childhood. Similarly, the various therapeutic descriptions differ in how directive, confrontive, or nondirective the therapist would be with Mr. B. The diversity of these four presentations demonstrates that the approach to clinical psychology that clinicians take influences all aspects of their work.

CHOOSING AN APPROACH TO CLINICAL PSYCHOLOGY

How do clinicians choose their approach to clinical psychology? There are no universally agreed-upon criteria available to guide the choice; even the advice offered at the beginning of this chapter about the value of scientifically testable approaches is based on the authors' personal biases, which, though shared by many, are biases nonetheless. Freudians might suggest that unconscious motivation influences clinicians' choices, behaviorists might argue that we tend to choose the approach modeled for us by our mentors, while humanistic psychologists might seek the answer in the perceived congruity between a particular approach and the self-concepts of its adherents. Perhaps the choice is made on the basis of "cognitive style" (Kaplan, 1964), emotional and personality characteristics (L'Abate, 1969), world view (Andrews, 1989), or just plain "personal preference" (Zubin, 1969).

The truth is that no one really knows exactly why particular clinicians choose particular approaches, but we do know what approaches they choose. Among clinicians expressing a specific choice, cognitive and cognitive-behavioral approaches are selected most often. By the mid-1990s, close to one quarter of clinicians identified cognitive as their preferred theoretical orientation (Norcross, Karg, & Prochaska, 1997). This represents a change over the last 40 years because virtually no adherents selected cognitive prior to the 1970s, when this approach to clinical psychology was in its infancy. The percent of clinicians identifying themselves as behavioral has remained relatively steady (just under 15%), as has the number of persons selecting humanistic approaches (2% to 6%). The behavioral and cognitive-behavioral models appear to be especially attractive to scientist-practitioners (Zook & Walton, 1989). Psychodynamic approaches, on the other hand, have lost popularity. Though nearly one-fifth of persons currently describe themselves as having this orientation, that is approximately half the proportion that did 40 years ago (Norcross et al., 1997). There are several other orientations (e.g., systems theory) that claim a small percentage of adherents.

However, we have not yet mentioned the choice made by the largest single group of clinical psychologists. When asked about their theoretical orientation, more clinicians say that they have not made a clear choice among the various approaches, or they do not confine themselves to only one of the above (Milan, Montgomery & Rogers, 1994; Norcross et al., 1997). They tend, instead, to adopt those aspects of two or more approaches that they find valuable and personally satisfying (Zook & Walton, 1989).

To those who value openmindedness, flexibility, and moderation above systematic consistency, this approach—called *eclecticism*—is a reasonable one. To those who emphasize the value of an integrated and unitary point of view, eclectics are merely confused individuals destined to spin their intellectual wheels for lack of theoretical traction. Whatever the case, the ranks of the eclectic have grown in clinical psychology. Estimates of clinicians identifying themselves as eclectic range from near one third (Norcross, Karg, & Prochaska, 1997) to two thirds (Slife & Reber, 2001). Indeed, the spirit of current times seems to favor a search for commonalities among various approaches, not evidence of their differences (Callaghan, 1996; Kimble, 1989; Staats, 1991).

CHAPTER SUMMARY

Each of several theoretical approaches to clinical psychology emphasizes different explanations of how behavior develops and becomes problematic, and each influences the assessment, treatment, and research activities of clinicians who adopt a particular approach.

The psychodynamic approach is based on Sigmund Freud's psychoanalysis, which sees both normal and abnormal behavior as determined by intrapsychic processes—and conflicts among id, ego, and superego—that have roots in childhood. These conflicts revolve around the expression of sexual and aggressive instincts while heeding society's rules. Defense mechanisms employed by the ego keep us largely unaware of these conflicts, but their nature, severity, and outcome are seen in overt behavior. Revisions of Freud's theories tend to de-emphasize instincts and the unconscious and focus instead on the adaptive role of the ego, and on the importance of sociocultural rather than intrapsychic processes in shaping behavior and behavior disorders.

The behavioral approach focuses on measurable behavior, not inferred personality constructs, and assumes that that behavior is primarily influenced by learning experiences, especially those occuring in a social context. This approach emphasizes the principles of operant learning, classical conditioning, and the processes related to observation, expectations, and other similar "person variables." In recent years, the behavioral approach has tended to blend with cognitive theories, which focus on habitual, learned ways of thinking about events. The combination—cognitive-behavioral—has become one of the most popular approaches in clinical psychology, perhaps the most popular among those favoring a specific theoretical orientation.

The humanistic approach sees behavior as determined primarily by unique perceptions of the world, as experienced by humans who are responsible for themselves and capable of changing themselves. Kelly, Rogers, Maslow, Perls, and other clinicians taking this approach try to see the world through their clients' eyes and help them reach self-actualization by encouraging their awareness of genuine feelings, wishes, and goals.

From the interpersonal perspective of Sullivan, personality is revealed in the recurrent patterns of social interactions that develop in infancy, childhood, and adolescence as people work to protect their security and self-esteem. Sullivan said that psychological disorders occur when these interpersonal relationships become dysfunctional and that becoming aware of problematic interpersonal patterns is the first step to changing them. Leary developed a system for organizing various styles of interpersonal behavior around a circle, or circumplex.

Research in neuroscience and other areas has made clinicians from all approaches aware of the important role played by genetics, the nervous system, and other biological factors in behavior and behavior disorders. The value of integrating psychological and biological factors can be seen in diathesis-stress explanations of various forms of mental disorder and in the growth of fields such as health psychology and neuropsychology.

Though some approaches to clinical psychology are more popular than others, none has a monopoly on describing and explaining behavior; many clinicians adopt elements of more than one of them in their daily work.

Chapter 3

Assessment in Clinical Psychology

Dictionaries define assessment as an estimate of value or worth. A real estate assessor, for example, looks at a house and estimates its value. Assessment does not take place in isolation, however; it is a process leading to a goal. The value assigned to a house will be used to establish its market value or the property tax to be paid on it. For our purposes, then, assessment can be defined as the process of collecting information to be used as the basis for informed decisions by the assessor or by those to whom results are communicated.

Almost everyone engages in some type of assessment at one time or another. For example, whether we realize it or not, we collect, process, and interpret information about the background, attitudes, behaviors, and characteristics of the people we meet. Then, in light of our experiences, expectations, and sociocultural frame of reference, we form impressions that guide social decisions that prompt us to seek out some people and avoid others. When accurate social assessment data are processed efficiently and without too much bias, our decisions are likely to be good ones. Thus, our ability to see beyond someone's tough talk to appreciate the sensitive person behind it can mark us as a good judge of character and a source of good advice about people.

However, our social judgments and decisions are prone to errors caused by problems in data collection, data processing, or both. For example, it is easy to jump to false conclusions about another person on the basis of inadequate information ("As soon as he said he hated ballet, I knew I wasn't going to like him."), unrepresentative behavior (someone in a foul mood seldom leaves a good impression), stereotypes ("Her accent really turned me off."), and personal biases ("I love people who wear sweaters like that!").

Clinical psychologists collect and process assessment information that is more formal and systematic than that available to nonprofessionals, but because they are still human beings, the quality of their judgments and decisions about clients can be threatened by the same sources of bias and error that affect everyone else. This fact is of special concern because, unlike most people, the consequences of bias or error in clinical assessment can be more dramatic and enduring than merely spending time with a boring companion. In this chapter, we consider what clinical psychologists—as fallible humans possessed of no unique powers of perception or judgment—have learned about the challenge of clinical assessment and how they have attempted to meet that challenge.

We will discuss assessment techniques throughout this and the next two chapters, but first we should address a fundamental question about assessment: Can we really measure human behavior and mental processes? If we take the position that the variables most important to clients and clinicians can never be quantified, much of assessment becomes a sideline exercise that has little to do with "real" psychology. But it is important to think carefully about psychological assessment.

Whether they recognize it or not, psychologists and their clients deal with quantities. A client seeking psychotherapy wants, at the very least, to experience *less* suffering, to feel *better*. A humanistically oriented therapist wants to help a depressed client develop *greater* self-acceptance, just as behaviorally oriented therapist wants to help an obsessive-compulsive client *reduce* incidence of compulsive hair pulling.

So the question usually is not *whether* psychological variables can be measured, but rather *how* any variable of interest should best be measured. When we consider assessment, we need to ask: What observations best reflect the variables interest? How should we record those observations? What types of measurement scales should we use? What time frame should we adopt? How can we determine whether our measures are reliable and valid? It is around such questions that psychological assessment is developed.

THE CLINICAL ASSESSMENT PROCESS

Clinical assessment has been described in various ways (Tallent, 1992), but all of them portray it as a process of gathering information to solve a problem and recognize that, to be most effective, assessment activities should be organized in a sequence of systematic, logically related steps (see Figure 3.1).

At each step, clinicians are confronted by important questions and daunting challenges. With respect to planning and data collection, for example, how much information about a person is "enough"? Which kinds of data will be most valuable? How can inaccurate information be detected and eliminated? Where should information be sought? The data-processing step raises questions such as: How should assessment data be combined? How can the assessor minimize bias when interpreting data? Might a

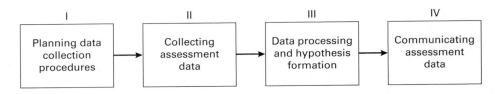

FIGURE 3.1   A schematic view of the clinical assessment process.

computer process assessment data more competently than a human being? And with respect to communicating assessment data: Who should be given access to assessment results, and for what purposes? How will assessment affect those who are assessed? How can people be protected from misuse or abuse of assessment information? We will examine these and many other clinical assessment issues in the following sections.

Planning for Assessment

Two related questions must be answered before clinical assessment can begin (McReynolds, 1975): What do we want to know, and how should we find out about it? Replies to both questions tend to be dictated by what factors clinicians see as most important in shaping human behavior and mental processes. As we saw in Chapter 2, different sets of factors are emphasized by different theoretical approaches to clinical psychology. So, depending on the approach or approaches adopted, a clinician's assessment efforts might focus on a client's personality dynamics and traits, learning history and current environmental factors, interpersonal interaction patterns, perceptions of self and reality, or genetic background and physiology.

Even with guidance from one's theoretical approach, the particulars of exactly what to look for, and how, can still vary enormously in each case, making it a challenge to plan, organize, and implement an efficient and useful assessment strategy. To illustrate the problem, consider the sheer number of things that can be asked about a person at several interrelated levels, from biological functioning to relationships with other people (see Table 3.1). The enormous diversity of possible assessment data means that we can never learn all there is to know about a client. Even if total knowledge were possible, it would not be a practical goal. Fully exploring every assessment level for a given client would be extremely expensive and time-consuming, and though it would surely turn up a lot of important information, the process would also reveal much that is trivial, redundant, outdated, or irrelevant to the goals of the assessment.

The Case Study Guide

The clinician's plans for exploring particular levels form a rough outline of the assessment task. Ideally, this outline, or case study guide, will be broad enough to provide a general overview of the client, yet focused enough to allow coverage of all the more specific questions that the clinician wishes to address. Table 3.2 presents a comprehensive and theoretically neutral example of a case study guide. Notice that it is sufficiently problem-oriented to be used with clients seeking help, while also reminding the assessor to consider broader and less problematic aspects of a person's life.

TABLE 3.1   Levels of Assessment and Some Representative Data From Each

Assessment Level	Type of Data
1. Somatic	Blood type, RH factor, autonomic stress response pattern, kidney and liver function, genetic characteristics, basal metabolism, visual acuity, diseases
2. Physical	Height, weight, sex, eye color, hair color, body type
3. Demographic	Name, age, address, telephone number, occupation, education, income, marital status, number of children
4. Overt behavioral	Reading speed, eye-hand coordination, frequency of arguments with other people, conversational skill, interpersonal assertiveness, occupational competence, smoking habits
5. Cognitive/intellectual	Response to intelligence test items, reports on thoughts, performance on tests of information processing or cognitive complexity, response to tests of reality perception and structuring
6. Emotional/affective	Reports of feelings, responses to tests measuring mood states, physiological responsiveness
7. Environmental	Location and characteristics of housing; number and description of cohabitants; job requirements and characteristics; physical and behavioral characteristics of family, friends, and co-workers; nature of specific cultural or subcultural standards and traditions; general economic conditions; geographical location

Case study guides tied to a particular theoretical approach to clinical psychology encourage the clinician to pursue questions and levels emphasized by that approach. Thus, psychodynamically oriented outlines (e.g., Gabbard, 2000) tend to include questions about unconscious motives and fantasies, ego functions, early developmental periods, object relations, and character structure. Cognitive-behavioral case study outlines (e.g., Kanfer & Saslow, 1969) focus on clients' skills, habitual thought patterns, and the stimuli that precede and follow problematic behaviors. Humanistically oriented clinicians are less likely to follow a set assessment outline; indeed, they are likely to see assessment as a collaborative process in which they seek to understand with each client how that client perceives the world (Fischer, 2001).

Factors Guiding Assessment Choices

Clinicians' choices about how much attention should be devoted to each assessment level, what questions to ask at each level, and what assessment techniques to employ are guided not only by their theoretical approach, but also by research on the reliability and validity of the interviews, tests, observations, and life records that serve as the main sources of assessment data in clinical psychology. Indeed, reliability and validity are the primary criteria by which any assessment instrument should be judged.

TABLE 3.2   A Case Study Guide

1. *Identifying data*, including name, sex, occupation, income (of self or family), marital status, address, date and place of birth, religion, education, cultural identity.

2. *Reason for coming* to the agency, expectations for service.

3. *Present and recent situation*, including dwelling place, principal settings, daily round of activities, number and kind of life changes over several months, impending changes.

4. *Family constellation* (family of orientation) including descriptions of parents, siblings, other significant family figures, and respondent's role growing up.

5. *Early recollections*, descriptions of earliest clear happenings and the situation surrounding them.

6. *Birth and development*, including age of walking and talking, problems compared with other children, view of effects of early experiences.

7. *Health and physical condition*, including childhood and later diseases and injuries, current prescribed medications, current use of unprescribed drugs, cigarettes, or alcohol, comparison of own body with others, habits of eating and exercising.

8. *Education and training*, including subjects of special interest and achievement, out-of-school learning, areas of difficulty and pride, any cultural problems.

9. *Work record*, including reasons for changing jobs, attitudes toward work.

10. *Recreation, interests, and pleasures*, including volunteer work, reading, respondent's view of adequacy of self-expression and pleasures.

11. *Sexual development*, covering first awareness, kinds of sexual activities, and a view of adequacy of current sexual expressions.

12. *Marital and family data*, covering major events and what led to them, and comparison of present family with family of origin, ethnic or cultural factors.

13. *Social supports, communication network, and social interests*, including people talked with most frequently, people available for various kinds of help, amount and quality of interactions, sense of contribution to others and interest in community.

14. *Self-description*, including strengths, weaknesses, ability to use imagery, creativity, values, and ideas.

15. *Choices and turning points in life*, a review of the respondent's most important decisions and changes, including the single most important happening.

16. *Personal goals and view of the future*, including what the subject would like to see happen next year and in 5 or 10 years, and what is necessary for these events to happen, realism in time orientation, ability to set priorities.

17. Any further material the respondent may see as omitted from the history.

(From N. D. Sundberg, 1977, *Assessment of Persons*, pp. 97–98, Reprinted by permission of Prentice-Hall, Inc.)

Reliability.   *Reliability* refers to consistency in or agreement among assessment data. It can be evaluated in several ways. If the results of repeated measurements of the same client are very similar, the assessment procedures are said to have high *test-retest* reliability, analogous to a bathroom scale that shows the same weight when someone steps off and back on again. Another way to evaluate reliability is to examine internal consistency. If data from one part of an assessment—such as odd-numbered test items—are similar to other parts—such as the even-numbered items—that assessment is said to be *internally consistent*. This dimension has sometimes been called split-half reliability. Finally, *interrater* reliability is measured by comparing the conclusions drawn by different clinicians using a particular assessment system to diagnose, rate, or observe the same client. The more they agree, the higher the interrater reliability.

    Validity. The *validity* of an assessment method reflects the degree to which it measures what it is supposed to measure. Like reliability, validity can be evaluated in several ways. The *content* validity of an assessment method is determined by how well it taps all the relevant dimensions of its target. An interview-based assessment of depression that includes questions about sad feelings, but not about their duration or cause would have low content validity. *Predictive* validity is measured by evaluating how well an assessment forecasts events—violent behavior or suicide attempts, for example. When two assessment devices agree about the measurement of the same quality, they are said to have *concurrent* validity. Predictive and concurrent validity are subtypes of *criterion* validity, which measures how strongly an assessment result correlates with important independent criteria of interest.

    Finally, there is *construct* validity (Cronbach & Meehl, 1955). To oversimplify somewhat, an assessment device has good construct validity when its results are shown to be systematically related to the construct it is supposed to be measuring. Psychologists evaluate construct validity by determining whether a test or other assessment method yields results that make sense in light of some theory about human behavior and mental processes. For example, scores on a measure of anxiety should increase under circumstances thought to increase anxiety (e.g., facing major surgery). If no change occurs, the measure's construct validity is suspect. Fully evaluating construct validity requires numerous studies and an elaborate set of statistical analyses (Campbell & Fiske, 1959).

    After reviewing these separate aspects of validity, Samuel Messick (1995) has suggested that construct validity can and should be viewed in a way that incorporates all of them, and more. To him, the *unified validity* of any assessment method should be evaluated not only in terms of content, predictive, and concurrent validity, but also in terms of how well the method taps into the mental characteristics and processes of interest, whether the construct to be measured has guided the development and scoring of the method, and whether using the method results in decisions about people that are unbiased and beneficial to them in the short-run and the long-run.

    While validity is related to reliability—an assessment device cannot be any more valid than it is reliable—high reliability is no guarantee of high validity. Consider a situation in which 50 people use their eyes to assess the gender of a man skilled in female impersonation. All 50 observers might agree on their judgment that the man is a female, but they would all be wrong. Here is a case in which visual assessment had high interrater reliability but very poor criterion validity.

    It is important to remember two other points about reliability and validity. First, reliability and validity are matters of degree, not all-or-none propositions. Imprecision occurs with all measurement, psychological measurements included. The question is always how much imprecision is tolerable in an assessment. For instance, if a bathroom scale varied by only a few ounces in test-retest procedures, we would likely consider the instrument reliable for our purposes, but if a letter scale varied by this much, we would consider it unreliable. How much error one tolerates depends on the goals and potential uses of the assessment, on the availability of alternative measurement instruments, and on practical constraints such as time and resources. The second point is that the validity of an instrument must always be viewed in relation to the purposes for which the assessment instrument is to be used. For example, a test might be a valid measure of typing skill, but an invalid measure of aggressiveness. Test validity can only reasonably be assessed when tests are used for the purposes for which they were designed.

Clinician-Specific Factors.   Clinicians' assessment choices are also influenced by personal experiences and preferences. Clinical psychologists may tend to use, or avoid, particular assessment methods simply because those methods were either emphasized or criticized by faculty in their graduate training program. Similarly, those who find certain measurement tactics tedious or unrewarding tend to seek answers to assessment questions through other procedures with which they are more comfortable. These personal factors help explain why some assessment methods continue to be used by some clinicians even when research evidence fails to support their reliability or validity.

Bandwidth-Fidelity Issues.   Clinicians' assessment choices are further guided by their attempts to resolve the "bandwidth-fidelity" dilemma (Shannon & Weaver, 1949). Just as greater bandwidth is associated with lower fidelity in broadcasting, clinicians have found that—given limited time and resources—the more extensively they explore a client's behavior, the less intensive each aspect of that exploration becomes (and vice versa). The breadth of an assessment device is thus referred to as its *bandwidth* and the depth or exhaustiveness of the device as its *fidelity* (Cronbach & Gleser, 1965). If, during a 2-hour interview, for example, a clinician tries to cover a long list of questions, the result would be superficial information about a wide range of topics (broad bandwidth, low fidelity). If the time is spent exploring the client's early childhood memories, the result would be a lot of detailed information about only one part of the client's life (narrow bandwidth, high fidelity).

Accordingly, clinicians must seek assessment strategies and measurement tools that result in an optimum balance of bandwidth and fidelity. The choices they make are dictated not only by the time and resources available, but by the goals of their assessment enterprise. The questions, levels of inquiry, and assessment techniques that will be useful in identifying stress-resistant executives differ substantially from those that will help detect brain damage in a 4-year-old child.

THE GOALS OF CLINICAL ASSESSMENT

The major goals of clinical assessment fall into three general categories: *diagnostic classification, description,* and *prediction.* Each of these goals may be sought in relation to one client or as part of clinical research projects in which assessment is conducted with groups of people.

Diagnostic Classification

Once clinical psychologists began working with adult clients during and after World War I, they came under the influence of medical personnel, particularly psychiatrists. As a result, they were often asked to perform clinical assessments for the purpose of diagnosing mental disorders in psychiatric patients—a process variously referred to as diagnostic classification, psychodiagnosis, differential diagnosis, or diagnostic labeling. Today, diagnostic classification remains a significant part of clinical research and practice, especially among clinicians who work in psychiatric or other medically oriented settings.

Accurate psychodiagnosis is important for several reasons. First, proper treatment decisions often depend on knowing what, exactly, is wrong with a client (Vermande, van den Bercken, & De Bruyn, 1996). Second, research into the causes of psychological disorders requires reliable and valid identification of disorders and accurate differentiation of one disorder from another. Finally, classification allows clinicians to efficiently communicate with one another about disorders in a professional "shorthand" (Sartorius et al., 1996).

Diagnostic Systems: DSM-IV.   Though various systems for classifying mental disorders had been used since the early 1900s, classification of mental disorders became more formalized in 1952 when the American Psychiatric Association published its first official classification system, the *Diagnostic and Statistical Manual of Mental Disorders.* This system, known as DSM-I, remained in use until 1968, when—to make the DSM more similar to the World Health Organization's (WHO) *International Classification of Diseases* (ICD)—it was replaced by DSM-II.

DSM-I and DSM-II provided a uniform terminology for describing and diagnosing abnormal behavior, but they offered no clear rules to guide mental health professionals' diagnostic decisions. Accordingly, DSM-III appeared in 1980, followed in 1987 by a revised version called DSM-III-R. DSM-III gave clinicians a set of operational criteria for assigning each diagnostic label. These criteria—which referred mainly to specific symptoms and symptom durations, not inferred causes—were increased in number and specificity in DSM-III-R. Clients were now to be diagnosed with a particular disorder only if they met a preestablished number of criteria from the full list of criteria associated with that disorder. Because a client need not meet every criterion for a disorder to be diagnosed with it, clients with similar, but not identical, sets of symptoms may receive the same label—much as physical resemblance among relatives identifies them as members of the same family. There is evidence that the introduction of operational criteria improved the reliability of psychiatric diagnoses (APA, 1980; Grove, 1987).

DSM-III and DSM-III-R allowed clinicians to describe clients along five different dimensions or *axes*, providing a more complete picture of clients' problems and the factors affecting them. Any of sixteen major mental disorders displayed could be listed on Axis I, while various developmental problems and personality disorders could appear on Axis II. Placing these latter difficulties on a separate axis was designed to ensure that they are not overlooked when an Axis I disorder is present. Axis III provided a place to list physical disorders or conditions that might be related to a person's mental disorder, while Axis IV provided a six-point scale for rating the severity of recent psychosocial stressors that may have contributed to an Axis I or II disorder. Axis V listed the clinician's rating of the person's psychological, social, and occupational functioning during the past year.

In spite of the improvements they contained, DSM-III and DSM-III-R were criticized because some of their diagnostic criteria were still too vague and open to biased use, because Axes II, IV, and V had measurement deficiencies, and because too little emphasis was placed on the construct validity of diagnoses (Bellack & Hersen, 1988; Kaplan, 1983; Millon & Klerman, 1986; Nathan, 1987; Vaillant, 1984). DSM-III and DSM-III-R were to have reflected the latest research on diagnoses, but this goal was not fully realized, partly because too few adequate diagnostic studies were available and because no specific guidelines had been established for translating research findings into specific diagnostic criteria. As a result, final decisions about diagnostic criteria often reflected experts' best clinical judgments rather than available empirical findings (Widiger et al., 1991). Because neither DSM-III nor DSM-III-R documented the rationale or empirical support for the diagnostic criteria they established, it was difficult to critically evaluate the validity of these classification systems. So in 1988, only a year after DSM-III-R appeared, the American Psychiatric Association established a task force to begin work on DSM-IV. The rush to develop a new edition of DSM was also spurred by the World Health Organization (WHO)'s plan to publish the 10th edition of its ICD in 1993.[1]

Further impetus for DSM-IV came from a desire to increase the empirical foundation of diagnostic practices. To do this, DSM IV planners organized numerous experts into 13 work groups, each of which followed a three-step procedure for studying a different set of disorders and how best to diagnose them (Widiger et al., 1991). Each group first reviewed all the clinical and empirical literature relevant to a given disorder and used their findings to guide initial suggestions for changes in diagnostic criteria for that disorder. When literature reviews failed to resolve issues, the work groups sought to conduct analyses on existing patient data sets. A total of 40 analyses were ultimately carried out. The third step involved asking clinicians to use diagnostic criteria in clinical settings with real clients. Conducted at more than 70 sites worldwide, these focused field trials examined issues such as how alternate wordings or alternate thresholds (cutoffs) affected reliability, prevalence rates, or concordance with the parallel diagnoses from ICD-10 (Nathan & Langenbucher, 1999). The DSM-IV, with its revised diagnostic criteria, was published in 1994.

Since the publication of DSM-IV, research on psychodiagnosis has expanded considerably. Results from many of the field trials have becomes available, and other investigations have been conducted. In order to accommodate the rapidly growing body of knowledge, the text of DSM-IV was revised in 2000. The *DSM-IV-Text Revision* (DSM-IV-TR) did *not* change the diagnostic criteria contained in DSM-IV, rather, it updated information about prevalence rates, onset, course, familial patterns, cultural, age, gender, and other related features (APA, 2000). As before, Axis I disorders are assigned only if

---

[1]Treaty obligations require the United States to maintain classification systems consistent with those of WHO. DSM-IV was coordinated with ICD-10, but in spite of efforts being made to develop international guidelines for their use (Sartorius et al., 1996), several differences in the two systems persist, both in terms of specific diagnostic criteria and overall orientations (Frances, Pincus, & Widiger, 1996).

the person meets a preset minimum number of criteria from a longer list of symptoms. The DSM-IV-TR also retains the multiaxial structure of DSM-III-R and DSM-IV.

The DSM-IV/DSM-IV-TR criteria continue to be the standard diagnostic classification system used by clinical psychologists and other mental health professionals in North America (see Table 3.3). To be diagnosed with schizophrenia, for example, a person must display two of the following five symptoms for at least one month: delusions, hallucinations, disorganized speech, grossly disorganized or catatonic behavior,

---

TABLE 3.3   Classification of Mental Disorders Using DSM-IV-TR

DSM-IV-TR retains the multiaxial system of classification and diagnosis first introduced in DSM-III, with some modifications in the earlier terminology and rating schemes used on the various axes.

Axis I: Major Mental Disorders

1. Disorders Usually First Diagnosed in Infancy, Childhood, or Adolescence (e.g., hyperactivity, severe conduct problems)
2. Delirium, Dementia, Amnestic and Other Cognitive Disorders (problems caused by deterioration of the brain due to aging, drugs, or disease)
3. Mental Disorders Due to a General Medical Condition Not Elsewhere Classified
4. Substance-Related Disorders (problems caused by alcohol, cocaine, or other drugs)
5. Schizophrenia and Other Psychotic Disorders (severe abnormalities in thinking, perception, emotion, motivation, or movement; often accompanied by hallucinations and/or delusions)
6. Mood Disorders (disturbances in mood, especially severe depression, overexcitement, or alternating periods of both)
7. Anxiety Disorders (e.g., specific or general fears, panic attacks, physical or mental rituals to control anxiety)
8. Somatoform Disorders (e.g., blindness, deafness, or paralysis that have no physical cause; preoccupation with physical health or illness)
9. Factitious Disorders (faking disorder for psychological reasons)
10. Dissociative Disorders (e.g., memory loss or identity fragmentation caused by psychological factors)
11. Sexual and Gender Identity Disorders (unsatisfactory sexual interactions, arousal prompted by problematic stimuli, or identification with the opposite gender)
12. Eating Disorders (self-starvation or binge eating followed by self-induced vomiting)
13. Sleep Disorders (severe problems caused by sleeping too little or too much)
14. Impulse Control Disorders Not Elsewhere Classified (e.g., compulsive gambling, stealing, or fire-setting)
15. Adjustment Disorders (failure to adjust to divorce or other stressors)
16. Other Disorders That May Be a Focus of Clinical Attention (e.g., noncompliance with treatment, problems caused by medication, or effects of physical or sexual abuse)

Axis II: Here, the diagnostician can list various forms of mental retardation and various personality disorders, such as paranoid, antisocial, narcissistic, avoidant, and dependent.

and lack of emotion or extreme apathy. In addition, the person must show marked deterioration in a major area of functioning such as work, interpersonal relations, or self-care. There must also be continuous signs of disturbance for at least 6 months, including 1 month during which symptoms from the first list of five are present. Finally, other conditions that might account for all these problems must be ruled out. And, as before, DSM-IV would place clients into one of five schizophrenia subtypes (paranoid, disorganized, catatonic, undifferentiated, or residual), depending upon their current condition and which symptoms are most prominent. The diagnosis would be further embellished by indications of whether the disorder is continuous or occurs in episodes, and by information on Axes II, III, IV, and V.

The DSM-IV diagnosis of Mr. B, whose case was addressed in detail in Chapter 2, might look like this:

Axis I: Generalized Anxiety Disorder

Axis II: Narcissistic Personality Disorder

Axis III: Crohn's Disease

Axis IV: Occupational problems (note that the six-point severity scale used in DSM-III-R is replaced in DSM-IV with named stressors)

Axis V: Global assessment of functioning: 45 [on a scale from 100 (superior functioning) down to 1 (indicating very poor functioning)]

The developers of DSM-IV and DSM-IV-TR sought to establish a classification system with a strong empirical base. They hoped to extend the improvements in reliability begun with DSM-III-R's use of observable criteria and to develop categories that might relate well to specific outcomes (predictive validity) or specific underlying neurological or genetic constellations (construct validity). The efforts to improve psychological diagnoses have been extensively reviewed (Mineka, Watson, & Clark, 1998; Nathan & Langenbucher, 1999; Widiger & Sankis, 2000). How successful were they? Nathan & Langenbucher (1999) report that "DSM-IV's strong empirical base has yielded an instrument with good to excellent reliability and improved validity"(p. 79).

Despite its empirical foundations, the DSM-IV diagnostic system has drawn criticisms. While many Axis I disorders show good to excellent reliability, disorders within the schizophrenic spectrum and some childhood and adolescence disorders do not. Axis II disorders, particularly antisocial, narcissistic, and paranoid personality disorders, continue to show unacceptably low interrater reliability and test-retest reliability (Zanarini et al., 2000).

Critics also question whether the either-or categorizations imposed by DSM-IV criteria are the best way to understand psychopathology. If individuals meet a certain number of criteria, they are said to "have" a disorder, while if they do not reach the cutoff they do not "have" it. Critics argue that psychological disorders can be present in varying degrees, but the current scheme fails to take this into account. They also note that current diagnoses fail to make clear distinctions between "normal" states and psychopathology, such as between bereavement and depression (Prigerson, et al., 1999) or between physical disorders and psychological disorders (Widiger & Sankis, 2000).

Critics also dislike modeling psychological diagnoses after medical diagnoses. A medical model views disorders as distinct types, each disorder with its own identifying physiological or genetic markers. Much of the validation work on DSM-IV has been geared toward finding genetic-familial or neurophysiological markers for psychological disorders. However, neurobiological validators are unclear because, as Widiger and Sankis (2000) point out, neurochemical states can be the result of a disorder or the cause. And genetics alone seldom identify who will and who will not get a disorder. Even with disorders such as schizophrenia, genetic markers show vulnerabilities that may or may not be expressed depending on other factors (Andreasen, 1997).

Behaviorally oriented clinicians are particularly concerned that DSM-IV classification ignores the context in which "symptoms" occur, thus providing no basis for understanding the meaning or purpose that the same behavior might have in different social circumstances (Follette, 1996). By failing to promote such an understanding, they argue, DSM-IV has done little to promote progress in discovering the psychological and social causes of many kinds of behavioral problems (Follette & Houts, 1996). So although DSM-IV pays more attention to overt behavior than earlier versions did, behavioral theorists see its failure to analyze behavior in relation to antecedents and consequences as one of its biggest failings (Wulfert, Greenway, & Dougher, 1996).

Alternative Diagnostic Proposals. Clinicians and researchers concerned about these shortcommings in the DSM-IV are increasingly interested in alternate diagnostic systems (Widiger & Sankis, 2000). One alternative, called the *dimensional approach*, avoids the either-or dichotomy by measuring people on a select number of personality dimensions. Those dimensions might include extroversion, openness to experience, conscientiousness, emotional stability, and agreeableness (the "big five") or other traits measured by modern personality tests. Efforts to employ the dimensional approach have focused especially on personality disorders, where symptom overlap is greatest, but mood disorders, anxiety disorders, and schizophrenia have also received attention (Brown, Chorpita, & Barlow, 1998; Grube, Bilder, & Goldman, 1998).

One advantage of the dimensional approach is that it reflects how normality shades into psychopathology rather than imposing an arbitrary boundary between the two. Another is that it allows persons to be described in terms of strengths and weaknesses, correcting what many see as an overemphasis on pathology in current diagnostic procedures. These features are appealing, but the dimensional approach is still hampered by the fact that theorists have been unable to agree on the nature or number of dimensions necessary to adequately describe psychopathology (Millon, 1991). In addition, much more work is needed to establish the reliability, validity, and clinical utility of dimensional approaches (Nathan & Langenbucher, 1999; Widiger & Sankis, 2000).

Other diagnostic proposals call for describing psychopathology in terms of specific theories or contextual principles. For instance, Wulfert, Greenway, and Dougher (1996) offered a diagnostic approach consistent with behavioral principles. Barron (1998) explored how diagnoses can be made more meaningful from point of view of psychodynamic theory. Sarbin (1997) advocated an approach that examines how disorders are affected by people's use of strategic self-narratives. Of course, the difficulty with these *contextual* or *theoretically coherent* approaches is deciding which theory to favor in developing a diagnostic system. Until an integrated theoretical approach is accepted in the field, it seems unlikely that a theoretically coherent approach would gain broad appeal. DSM-IV was purposely atheoretical, favoring diagnoses based on observable symptoms rather than on criteria congenial to any one theory, and that was considered one of its strengths.

It is no wonder that the diagnostic classification enterprise continues to be a hotbed of controversy. After all, it attempts to reliably differentiate a wide variety of complex, socioculturally defined disorders caused by multiple (often unknown) factors using a relatively small set of shorthand labels organized in a way that will help clinicians' make the best possible decisions about their clients. No diagnostic system is likely to ever accomplish all these goals. Though the alternate approaches have advantages, it is unlikely the categorical classification system will be eliminated because it is consistent with the medical model that dominates the health-care industry, and it offers an efficient shorthand for clinicians communicating with each other. Alternate dimensional models could be unwieldy for clinicians and for insurance companies trying to make fair and uniform decisions about what level of coverage applies to what disorders.

Of course, diagnostic classification is not the only goal of assessment, and perhaps we should not expect a classification system to convey all that is meaningful or useful about a person suffering from a psychological disorder. At a minimum, classification should be reliable and valid and serve as an efficient shorthand for communication among clinicians and researchers. The trick for future diagnostic schemes will be to continue to improve reliability and validity while still maintaining an efficient system.

Description

The desire to go beyond diagnostic classification intensified after World War II as clinical psychology developed an identity independent of psychiatry (see Watson, 1951). Encouraged by burgeoning self-confidence, psychologists sought to conduct broader assessments that produced a fuller understanding of persons. They especially wanted to understand the social, cultural, and physical context of behavior. The result was a movement toward assessments that went beyond diagnosis to describe people's personalities and person–environment interactions.

For many clinicians today, descriptive assessment is more important than diagnostic classification. Assessment by a cognitive-behavioral therapist, for instance, might focus on describing factors such as antecedent conditions, environmental incentives and disincentives, alternate sources of reward, cognitive complexity, and attributional style. A psychodynamic therapist might focus on describing ego strengths and weaknesses, defense mechanisms, quality of family and other relationships, and characteristics of the self (Gabbard, 2000). Of course, diagnostic classification and descriptive assessment can go hand-in-hand. Bertelsen (1999), for instance, suggests that clinical assessment should work at two separate levels—one concerned with diagnostic classification, the other concerned with evaluating multiple factors that influence the course of treatment.

Description-oriented assessment makes it easier for clinicians to pay attention to clients' assets and adaptive functions, not just to their weaknesses and problems. Accordingly, descriptive assessment data are used to provide pretreatment measures of clients' behavior, to guide treatment planning, and to evaluate changes in behavior after treatment. They also are valuable in clinical research. For example, in an investigation of the relative value of two treatments for depression, assessments that describe clients' post-treatment behaviors (e.g., absenteeism, self-reported sadness, and depression test scores) are of greater value than diagnostic labels (e.g., depressive versus nondepressive).

Unfortunately, the movement toward broad description of persons is unlikely to dominate clinical assessment, especially in inpatient psychiatric settings and other managed-care facilities. As skyrocketing health-care costs have increased economic pressures to limit hospital stays and to concentrate on short-term treatments, comprehensive battery-based patient evaluations are becoming too time-consuming and expensive. Further, they are not sufficiently focused on reaching a discrete diagnosis that can be associated with a particular treatment plan (which in turn can be associated with a particular cost). The managed-care industry increasingly demands evidence-based assessments that are closely tied to treatment planning and outcome (Groth-Marnat, 2000). Today, many clinicians are asked to limit their assessments to initial screening of patients, rapid measurement of symptoms, differential diagnosis of disorders, and recommendations for treatment (Fox, 1995; Miller, 1996). In response to these demands, more clinicians than ever before are using the structured interviews and computerized testing services described in Chapters 4 and 5. At the same time, clinicians are stepping up their efforts to demonstrate empirically that specific assessment procedures have both validity and clinical utility in health care settings (Kubiszyn et al., 2000).

Prediction

The third goal of clinical assessment is to make predictions about human behavior. For example, clinicians are sometimes asked by businesses, government agencies, police and fire departments, and the military to help them select people who are most likely to perform well in certain jobs. In such cases, the clinician must first collect or examine descriptive assessment data on which to base predictions and selections.

A classic example of how descriptive and predictive assessment can overlap was provided by Henry Murray's use of specialized tests, interviews, and observations to select soldiers who would be the most successful spies, saboteurs, and other behind-enemy-lines operatives during World War II (Office of Strategic Services, 1948). Murray's assessment program was so comprehensive that it took several days to complete and measured everything from intelligence to ability at planning murder.

Similar, though less extensive, prediction-oriented clinical assessment programs also appeared in large-scale postwar screening programs designed to select civilian and military employees (Institute of Personality Assessment and Research, 1970), graduate students in clinical psychology and psychiatry (Holt & Luborsky, 1958; Kelly & Fiske, 1951), and Peace Corps volunteers (Colmen, Kaplan, & Boulger, 1964). Because such assessment programs influence decisions affecting large numbers of people, they must be evaluated not only for their predictive validity, but also for their impact on the people being assessed and on the organizations that utilize them. One must be concerned with the number of correct and incorrect selections, and with the benefits and costs associated with them.

Predicting Dangerousness. These concerns become especially harrowing when clinical predictions involve life and death situations, such as "Will Client X attempt suicide?" or "Is Client Y going to hurt someone if released from a mental hospital?" How accurate are such predictions?

In fact, clinical psychologists find it difficult to predict dangerousness accurately (Monahan, 1988; Borum, 1996). One reason for this problem is that the *base rate*, or frequency with which dangerous acts are committed in any group of people, is usually very low. The following example shows why this is important. Assume that a clinician is 80% accurate in predicting homicidal behavior. Assume also that the base rate for homicide in the population the clinician examines is 10 murders per 10,000 people. The accuracy of predictions can be evaluated in terms of the pattern of four possible outcomes. If the clinician predicts dangerousness and the person indeed behaves dangerously, the outcome is called a *true positive*. If the clinician predicts that there is no danger, and the person does not behave dangerously, we have a *true negative* outcome. If the clinician predicts no danger, but the person does act dangerously, a *false negative* outcome occurs. Finally, when the clinician predicts dangerous behavior but dangerous acts do not occur, we call it a *false positive*. As indicated in Table 3.4, the clinician would correctly predict who 8 of the 10 murderers would be. However, if the clinician is 80% accurate, he would incorrectly categorize 20% of the 9,990 persons who would not commit violence. The 8 true positives must be viewed in light of 1,998 false positive cases in which the clinician predicted homicides that did not occur.

In this example, then, the clinician's *positive predictive power* to identify murderers would be woefully low (less than 1% of predicted murderers would actually kill someone), while the accuracy of predicting nondangerousness, called *negative predictive power*, would be greater than 99.9%. To maximize true positives, then, the clinician could predict that no one will commit a murder, a prediction that would be correct 99.9% of the time. However, all the errors would be false negatives, and society

TABLE 3.4 Measuring the Accuracy of Clinical Predictions of Dangerousness

	Ultimate Outcome	
Clinician's Prediction	**Homicide**	**No Homicide**
Homicide	8 (True positives)	1,998 (False positives)
No homicide	2 (False negatives)	7,992 (True negatives)

usually believes that such mistakes (i.e., predicting that dangerous people are safe) are more serious than false positives.

To err on the side of caution, clinicians tend to overpredict dangerousness. Of course, if there are no serious consequences to false positive errors, overprediction is not a problem. But typically, there are consequences to errors in either direction. Imagine, for instance, trying to predict which teenagers are likely to engage in school violence. Recent school shootings in Columbine, Colorado, and Paducah, Kentucky, have heightened concerns about the possibility of such violence, and several school systems have undertaken measures to make their schools safer. But school shootings are extremely low-base-rate events, so trying to identify at-risk individuals will inevitably result in many false positive errors. For every correctly identified killer youth, dozens or hundreds of others will likely be incorrectly stigmatized with the same label (Mulvey & Cauffman, 2001).

It is tempting to dismiss the effects of low base rates on prediction—after all, they are only statistics—and cling to the belief that, when push comes to shove, the "experts" will be able to predict accurately. But the experts—those who try to predict school violence, suicide, or other violent criminal acts—do not cling to such beliefs. They know that these statistics reflect how difficult it is for clinicians (and others) to predict dangerousness accurately. The American Psychiatric Association has taken the position that psychiatrists have no special knowledge or ability which allows them to accurately predict dangerous behavior (1983).

Those who attempt to predict dangerousness try to minimize false positives by following certain guidelines. For example, Cassel and Bernstein (2001) report that researchers seeking to improve prediction increasingly focus on combining assessment evidence from four domains: 1) the defendant's dispositional tendencies, such as anger or impulsiveness, 2) clinical factors, such as evidence of mental or personality disorders, 3) historical factors, especially a record of violence, and 4) contextual factors such as the strength of social support from family and friends (see also Gardner et al., 1996; Monahan & Steadman, 1994; Zabow & Cohen, 1993).

COLLECTING ASSESSMENT DATA

So far we have looked at ways clinicians answer the first question about assessment: "What do we want to know?" Now it is time to answer the second question: "How should we find out about it?"

Sources of Assessment Data

As noted earlier, clinical psychologists collect assessment data from four main sources: interviews, tests, observations, and life records. The first three of these sources are so central to clinical assessment that we offer detailed coverage of them in the next two chapters. In this chapter, we merely touch on their strengths and weaknesses and consider how the data arising from them are integrated into assessment reports.

Interviews. George Kelly (1958, p. 330) said, "If you don't know what is going on in a person's mind, ask him; he may tell you." The simple truth of this statement is one reason why the interview is the most basic and widely employed source of clinical assessment data. It is popular for other reasons as well. For one thing, interviews mimic ordinary social interaction, thus providing a way of collecting simultaneous samples of a person's verbal and nonverbal behavior. Second, interviews require no special equipment and can take place almost anywhere. Third, the interview is highly flexible. Except when research purposes prescribe interview content, the clinician is free to direct the inquiry to whatever topics and issues might help the assessment process.

What about the quality of interview data? Donald Peterson (1968, p. 13) noted that the interview is ". . . another form of data whose reliability, validity, and decisional utility must be subjected to the same kinds of scrutiny required for other modes of data collection." As we will see in the next chapter, interview data can be distorted by interviewer characteristics and questions, by client characteristics, including memory skills and frankness, and by the circumstances under which the interview takes place.

Observations. The old adage that "actions speak louder than words" supports many clinicians' desire to supplement interviews or tests with direct observation of clients' behavior in situations of interest. The goal of observation is to go beyond what clients say to find out what they do.

Indeed, many consider observation the most valid form of clinical assessment because it is so direct and capable of circumventing problems of memory, motivation, response style, and situational bias that can reduce the value of interviews and tests. Teachers' self-reports about the amount of attention paid to male and female students, for example, might be affected by self-perceptions, memory retrieval errors, or a desire to avoid appearing sexist. Analysis of a videotapes of actual classroom behavior, however, would get around these biasing factors.

A second advantage of observation is its relevance to behaviors of greatest clinical interest. A child's aggressiveness, for example, can be observed as it occurs on the playground, where the problem has been most acute. A related advantage is that observation can assess behavior in its social context. Knowing that a mental hospital patient appears most depressed following a visit from family members may be more valuable to a therapist than an affirmative response to the query, "Are you ever depressed?" Finally, observations allow for description of behavior in specific terms and in great detail. For example, a person's sexual arousal in response to particular stimuli might be defined in terms of penile volume or vaginal blood flow, both of which can be objectively measured with special monitoring equipment. Observations can also quantify psychotic behavior by recording the frequency of explicitly defined actions (e.g., Paul & Lentz, 1977).

In spite of its advantages, observational assessment is not problem free. As described in Chapter 4, the reliability and validity of observational data can be threatened by observer error or bias, inadvertent observer influences on behavior under observation, and specific situational factors.

Tests. Like interviews, tests provide a sample of behavior, but the stimuli to which the client responds on a test are more standardized than in most interviews. A test exposes each client to the same stimuli under the same circumstances. Tests can be easy, economical, and conveniently administered (in some cases, a mental health professional need not be present). Further, the test's standardized form helps eliminate bias that might otherwise influence an assessor's inquiries. Responses to most tests can be translated into scores, thus making quantitative summaries of a client's behavior possible.[2] In this way, test data facilitate communication between professionals about a client. Finally, test data allow the clinician to compare a client's behavior with that of thousands of others who have taken the same test.

The use of these reference scores, or norms, allows the clinician to establish a frame of reference for interpreting the meaning of a given client's test score. Assume, for instance, that during a word-association test, the first thing that pops into a client's mind when the tester says "house" is "pantyhose." If the clinician had never heard this association before, she might interpret it as unusual, perhaps even indicative of a psychological problem. But if the tester has access to a book containing the associations of 12,000 subjects to the word "house," she might discover that "pantyhose" is a popular response and thus not worthy of concern. (This is not what she would discover, by the way.)

However, tests are not magical devices that always reveal the "truth" about people. Like interviews, they must be evaluated in terms of reliability and validity and, like other assessment techniques, they are sometimes found wanting. As described in Chapter 5, anything that is not standard about test stimuli, including the tester, the client, or the testing situation, can threaten the value of test data.

Life Records.   As they pass through life, people leave a paper trail consisting of school, work, police, medical, and financial records, letters and diaries, photographs, awards, and the like. Much can be learned about a person through these life records, and because this approach to assessment does not require the client to make any further responses (as do interviews, tests, and observations), there is little chance that memory, motivation, response style, or situational factors can distort the data obtained. Thus, a 10-minute review of a person's high school transcript may provide more specific and accurate academic information than a 1-hour interview focused on questions such as "How did you do in school?" Similarly, diaries written during significant periods in a client's life can reveal feelings, wishes, actions, and situational details that might be lost or distorted by imperfect recall during an interview.

By summarizing a lot of information about a client's thinking and behavior over a long period of time and across a range of situations, life records provide an inexpensive way for clinicians to understand their clients better. They act like a wide-angle camera lens that brings into view material that might otherwise be missed. Wide-angle lenses produce distortion, however, and life records can do the same. For one thing, they tend to be superficial and often incomplete. Records may show that a person was divorced in 1995, but they may say nothing about why, or how the person felt about it.

---

[2]Certain aspects of interview and observational data can be handled in this way, as well, but may involve more cumbersome procedures.

The Value of Multiple Assessment Sources

Clinical psychologists seldom rely on a single source of assessment data as they create a working image of a client. Instead, they use multiple assessment channels to cross-validate information. Thus, hospital records may reveal that a patient has been there for 20 years, thus correcting the patient's self-reported estimate of 6 months. Indeed, the whole story of a client's problems is seldom clear until multiple assessment sources are tapped. One study showed, for example, that college students who described themselves as socially unassertive were observed to be capable of assertiveness, given the right conditions (Nietzel & Bernstein, 1976). It often takes multiple sources of assessment to separate those who cannot engage in certain behaviors from those who do not engage in them.

Another benefit of using multiple assessment sources appears when the clinician evaluates the effects of treatment. Suppose a couple enters therapy because they are considering divorce and then, 3 months later, they do divorce. If the only outcome assessment employed in this case were "marital happiness," as expressed during interviews, the treatment might be seen as having worsened marital distress. However, observations, third-person reports, and life records might show that one or both partners find their newly divorced status liberating and that they are developing new interests and abilities. These changes might not be obvious in an interview if the clients feel guilty about divorce, or if they fear appearing callous. Similarly, a young man whose therapy has helped him stand up for his rights may report improved self-esteem and comfort in social situations, but he might fail to mention that he has become too pushy and aggressive. Observational assessment might reveal this potentially problematic situation.

PROCESSING ASSESSMENT DATA

After assessment goals are established and data are collected, the clinician must determine what those data mean. If the information is to be useful in reaching the clinician's assessment goals, it will have to be transformed from raw form into interpretations and conclusions. For example, it is important to know that a young child cries at high intensities for certain lengths of time each evening when placed in its crib. It is also important to know that after the crying continues for varying periods, someone enters the baby's room to provide comfort. However, these data mean little in psychological terms until the clinician translates them into meaningful statements about the infant's behavior and interprets what psychological processes are involved. This crucial part of assessment is often referred to as data processing or clinical judgment.

The processing task is formidable because a degree of inference is involved, and inference requires a mental leap from known data to what is assumed to be true on the basis of those data. In general, as the leap from data to assumption gets longer, inference becomes more vulnerable to error.

Consider this: A young boy is sitting on a lawn cutting an earthworm in half. It would be easy to infer from this observational data that the child is cruel and aggressive and that he might become dangerous later in life. These inferences would be off the mark, however, for "what the observer could not see . . . was what the boy—who happened to have few friends—thought as he cut the worm in half: 'There! Now you will have someone to play with'" (Goldfried & Sprafkin, 1974, p. 305). In short, elaborate inference—especially when based on minimal data—can be dangerous. Processing assessment data is difficult also because few empirical guidelines exist for how to combine data from interviews, tests, observations, and other sources into an integrated assessment.

The only way to eliminate inference error is to eliminate inference, but doing so would also eliminate the meaning of most assessment data. Indeed, the main questions about clinicians' processing of assessment data do not revolve about whether inferences will be drawn, but about what kinds of inferences to draw, how clinicians go about drawing them, how accurate they are, and how inference error can be minimized.

Levels of Clinical Inference

Clinicians' judgments or inferences can be characterized in terms of their goal, their level of abstraction, or their underlying theoretical approach to clinical psychology. As we have suggested above, an inference might serve the goal of classification ("the client suffers from an anxiety disorder"), description ("his symptoms worsen in the presence of women"), or prediction ("he will benefit from cognitive-behavioral therapy").

Inferences can vary widely in their level of abstraction, from cautious, low-level inferences that do not stray far from the original data to bolder statements that go well beyond the data on the basis of the assessor's theoretical approach, personal experience, or even intuitive hunch. At the lowest inference level, assessment data are taken at face value, as when a test score determines whether a student is admitted to graduate school. At higher inference levels, statements go somewhat beyond what assessment data actually say. For example, behavior revealed through tests, interviews, observations, and records might be interpreted as characteristic of the person and then used to justify trait labels such as anxious, depressed, hostile, or agreeable. At the highest level of abstraction, assessment data are processed more elaborately to form an overall picture of the client. Ideally, the person's "whole story" is reconstructed, and any mental disorders are viewed in light of this panorama. It is at this level, where clinical judgment ventures furthest from the original data, that clinicians depend most on their theories and experience to guide their inferences. The examples above reflect the three main ways that clinicians tend to view assessment information: as samples, correlates, or signs (Goodenough, 1949; Wiggins, 1973).

Samples.   Consider the following raw assessment data: A person took 16 sleeping pills before going to bed at a hotel last night, but was saved after being discovered by a housekeeper and rushed to a hospital.

If this incident is seen as a *sample* of the client's behavior, the following judgments might result:

1. The client has access to potentially lethal medication.
2. The client did not wish to be saved because no one knew about the suicide attempt before it occurred.
3. Under similar circumstances, the client may attempt suicide again.

Notice that viewing the client's behavior as a sample results in low-level inferences. The suicide attempt is seen as an example of what the client is capable of doing under certain circumstances. No effort is made to infer why the individual tried suicide; more assessment would be required before specific causal statements would be justified.

Correlates. The same incident could be viewed as a *correlate* of other aspects of the client's life. Even though no further information is available about the client, knowledge of similar cases might guide the following inferences:

1. The client is likely to be an elderly male who is single, divorced, or widowed and lives alone with some physical illness.
2. The client is, or has recently been, depressed.
3. The client has little emotional support from family or friends.

Here, higher-level inferences are based on a combination of (1) facts about the client's behavior, and (2) the clinician's knowledge of what tends to correlate with that behavior. These inferences go beyond the original data with the support of empirically demonstrated relationships among variables such as suicide, age, gender, marital status, social support, and depression. In general, the stronger the known relationships between variables, the more accurate the inferences will be.

This correlate-oriented, or psychometric, approach is not tied to any theoretical approach. Any kind of quantifiable assessment data—tests of ego strength, reinforcer preferences, personality traits, perceptions of others—can be dealt with as correlates. Accordingly, the psychometric view of assessment data processing links individual-oriented clinical psychology to the broader field of research on general personality theory.

Signs. Finally, the suicide attempt might be viewed as a *sign* of other, less obvious client characteristics. A sign-oriented view might result in inferences like these:

1. The client's aggressive impulses have been turned against the self.
2. The client's behavior reflects intrapsychic conflicts.
3. The pill-taking represents an unconscious cry for help.

These inferences go well beyond the information at hand, using assessment data as signs that can be interpreted by a particular theory of behavior—in this case, psychodynamic theory. Indeed, the relationship between sign and inference may stem solely from theoretical speculation.

Levels of Inference and Theoretical Approach

A clinician's theoretical approach often influences the types of inferences he or she favors.

When assessment information is viewed primarily as a behavior sample, inference is likely to be minimal and the guiding theory will probably be behavioral. Viewing assessment data as signs usually results in higher levels of inference often guided by a psychodynamic or humanistic approach. Using our example of a client's suicide attempt, a psychodynamic assessor might see it as stemming from conflicted identification with a parent who had abandoned the client at an early age. To a humanistic clinician, the attempt might be seen as reflecting the client's perception that there was no other way to deal with the world.

In between, where assessment data are viewed as correlates, inferences tend to be at low to moderate levels, and there is more emphasis on statistical analyses of relationships among variables representing a range of theories. A cognitive-behavioral clinician might infer that the attempt reflected a habitual pattern of pessimistic thinking about a lost reinforcer. In the next section, we examine the ways clinicians have followed different traditions as they draw inferences about assessment data.

The Process of Clinical Inference

The mass media have long cast clinical psychologists as experts who can astutely translate obscure signs into accurate statements about a person's past, present, or future.

Clinical Intuition.   A few such long-shot inferences have been known to hit the mark, but empirical research does not support the idea that clinicians have special inferential capabilities. Donald Peterson made this point forcefully 30 years ago: "The idea that clinicians have or can develop some special kinds of antennae with which they can detect otherwise subliminal interpersonal stimuli and read from these the intrapsychic condition of another person is a myth which ought to be demolished" (Peterson, 1968, p. 105).

In fact, when clinical psychologists use an informal approach to assessment data processing (i.e., one based on subjective and sign-oriented judgments about the meaning of assessment data), they are not significantly better than nonclinicians at making judgments, and do not make more accurate judgments than could be obtained through formal, statistical procedures. Let's first review research comparing the inference abilities of clinicians and others and then look at data comparing the quality of inferences based on formal versus informal procedures.

The Clinician as Inference Expert.   A classic example of research on the clinician's alleged special inference abilities is provided by a study in which people were asked to infer the presence of brain damage on the basis of clients' responses to a psychological test widely used for such purposes (Goldberg, 1959). Half of the 30 clients actually had organic damage; the other half did not. The test results were judged by 4 PhD clinical psychologists with 4 to 9 years of experience with the test, 10 master's-level psychology trainees who had used the test for 1 to 4 years, and 8 secretaries with no psychology background or experience with the test. The inference to be drawn in this study was simply "organic" or "not organic," so the probability of being correct by chance in any given case was 50%. However, only 1 of the 4 Ph.D. clinicians did better than chance. Indeed, they were no better than their students or their secretaries. More recent studies have obtained similar results (e.g., Gardner et al., 1996).

Other research shows that clinical psychologists also have no special memory capacity or other information-processing abilities. For example, numerous studies suggest that having larger amounts of assessment information may increase clinicians' confidence about their inferences, but it does not necessarily improve the accuracy of those inferences (Einhorn & Hogarth, 1978; Garb, 1984; Kleinmuntz, 1984; Rock et al., 1987). Some studies do show that trained clinicians can be more accurate judges than laypersons when they use well-validated psychological tests (Garb, 1992), but this advantage is neither large nor frequent, and many other studies find no superiority for trained clinicians' judgments. Why don't clinicians make better clinical judgments than other people, even after years of training and experience?

The *ecological* argument says that clinicians underperform because researchers set up situations that do not reflect the way clinicians actually practice, putting clinicians at an unfair disadvantage (e.g., Rock et al., 1987). For example, researchers might ask clinicians to make predictions about criteria such as school grades, which are not part of the clinician's normal practice or training. Research protocols sometimes require clinicians to use assessment devices that they may not normally use in their day-to-day work. While this "stacking the deck" ecological objection may occasionally be true, studies in which judges are familiar with the instruments and decisions alternatives still find clinical judgment less than impressive.

A more substantive explanation of inaccuracies in clinical judgments is that clinicians are prone to the same cognitive habits and biases that can lead to error in anyone's information processing (MacDonald, 1996). For example, there are limits on how much data any human can perceive, hold in memory, and mentally combine, so people develop cognitive habits, called *heuristics*, that serve as shortcuts in drawing conclusions and making judgments (Garb, 1996; Tversky & Kahneman, 1974). These mental rules of thumb save time, but they can also cause errors, including errors in inferences based on clinical assessment data (Faust & Ziskin, 1988).

Clinicians' judgments may rely too heavily on experiences that are recent enough or remarkable enough to make them especially available to recall. This *availability bias* can lead to judgment errors if what one recalls from highly memorable cases does not apply in the current case, and if it causes potentially important, but less memorable, information to be neglected (Garb, 1996). Availability bias can even create *illusory correlations* (Chapman & Chapman, 1967). Memorable clinical "folklore" can influence clinicians to draw false inferences from assessment data (Krol, DeBruyn, & van den Bercken, 1995; Lewis, 1991). Thus, some clinicians see paranoid tendencies in clients who draw large eyes on figure-drawing tests—even though there is no firm empirical evidence to support this association (Golding & Rorer, 1972).

Like the first impressions all people form, clinicians also tend to display an *anchoring bias* in which they establish their views of a client more on the basis of the first few pieces of assessment information than on any subsequent information (Tutin, 1993). Anchoring bias can also influence clinicians to let assessment information coming from certain sources (e.g., a parent's report of a child's behavior) outweigh any other information they receive (McCoy, 1976). If anchoring bias combines with *confirmation bias*—the tendency to interpret new information in line with existing beliefs—the clinician may ignore contradictory evidence or even distort it to fit initial impressions (Strohmer & Shivy, 1994).

Clinicians may be prone to error because they misremember information or do not get important information. Like other people, clinicians tend to remember their successes more clearly than their failures and so may remain wedded to incorrect inference tendencies (or invalid assessment methods) simply because they think of them as valid (Garb, 1989). Alternately, clinicians may not get enough *accurate feedback* about their successes and failures. Contrast a clinician who predicts dangerousness or infers that a person has homosexual tendencies based on unresolved Oedipal issues with a meteorologist who predicts the weather. The meteorologist receives regular, timely, and unambiguous feedback about his inferences; the psychologist seldom does.

Various personal biases can also distort inferences (Rabinowitz, 1993). For example, clinicians' theoretical approach to clinical psychology can give them specific preconceptions about what behaviors to expect from clients and what those behaviors mean (Shoham-Salomon, 1985, Yoav, 2000). Further, some clinicians may more readily infer the presence of disorder, or certain kinds of disorder, in males versus females, or in people of a particular age, health status, or ethnic group (Atkinson et al., 1996; Coontz, Lidz, & Mulvey, 1994; Hickling, McKenzie, Mullen, & Murray, 1999; Hatala & Case, 2000; James & Haley, 1995). In one study of gender bias (Ford & Widiger, 1989), for example, psychologists were asked to diagnose a case report with clear signs of either antisocial personality disorder (APD; usually seen in males) or histrionic personality disorder (HPD; usually seen in females). Some of the psychologists in each group were told that the client was female, others were told the client was male. The inference errors made by both male and female psychologists showed gender bias in that they were significantly more likely to miss the APD diagnosis if they thought the client was female and significantly more likely to miss the HPD diagnosis if they thought the client was male. Though other studies have failed to find a robust overall bias in clinical judgments based on gender (e.g., Lopez, Smith, & Wolkenstein, 1993; Tomlinson-Clarke & Camilli, 1995), socioeconomic class, or ethnic minority status (Atkinson, et al., 1996; Tomlinson-Clarke & Cheatham, 1993), individual clinicians must always guard against such bias (Lopez, 1989; Malgady, 1996).

Finally, as mentioned earlier, the accuracy of clinical judgments will suffer if clinicians ignore the base rates of events they are trying to predict (Faust & Ziskin, 1988). Unfortunately, clinicians seldom have accurate knowledge of these base rates or do not pay sufficient attention to them.

In short, there is "little empirical evidence that justifies the granting of 'expert' status to the clinician on the basis of . . . training, experience, or information processing ability" (Wiggins, 1981). As we shall see later, however, proposals have been made to make clinical reasoning a more explicit, rather than implicit, part of training in the hopes of teaching health professions to avoid the more common sources of inference errors (Round, 1999). Further, there are clinicians whose inference accuracy appears superior to that of their colleagues and intelligent lay persons. Does this superiority reflect a stable ability, or is it more sporadic, depending on the client, situation, and judgment task involved? The answer is not yet clear; a person's inference ability may be a joint function of general skill as it interacts with situational variables (Bieri et al., 1966).

Inference by Formal Versus Informal Procedures. The sobering body of research that tarnished the image of clinicians as experts who consistently draw accurate inferences from assessment signs was prompted by research on another question about their inference ability. Many investigators had wondered whether clinicians' informal, subjective inferences were any more accurate than inferences based upon formal, statistical data processing. Clinicians have traditionally been divided on this question. Those who favor the informal, "clinical" approach see it as meaningful, organized, rich, deep, and genuine, and they see the formal "statistical" approach as artificial, trivial, superficial, and rigid. Proponents of formal, "statistical" inference praise it as objective, reliable, precise, and empirical, and they label the informal clinical approach as mystical, vague, unscientific, sloppy, and muddleheaded.

When clinicians interpret assessment data informally, make recommendations based on these interpretations, and do research on such activities, it is usually because they believe that they, and perhaps most members of their profession, are good at these things. Thus it came as a shock when Paul Meehl's 1954 review of 20 studies comparing formal versus informal inference methods found that, in all but one case, the accuracy of the statistical approach equaled or surpassed that of the clinical approach. Later, even the sole exception to this surprising conclusion was called a tie, and, as additional research became available, the superiority of the statistical method of prediction was more firmly established (Dawes, Faust, & Meehl, 1989; Meehl, 1957, 1965; see Table 3.5).

In the years since Meehl's review, numerous published responses appeared, many of which pointed out methodological defects in some of the studies that could have biased results in favor of statistical procedures. The ecological validity of the research was also questioned; many felt that the variables being predicted (e.g., grades) were not like those typically dealt with by practicing clinicians, while others suggested that the clinicians in several studies were handicapped by inadequate or unfamiliar information about clients and about what they were supposed to predict (Holt, 1958, 1978). Frederick C. Thorne (1972, p. 44) put it this way: "The question must not be what naive judges do with inappropriate tasks under questionable conditions of comparability with actual clinical situations, but what the most sophisticated judges can do with appropriate methods under ideal conditions." Still, the furor over Meehl's conclusions could not negate the fact that inference based on subjective, clinical methods is not as accurate as it was assumed to be (Dawes, 1994).

A recent meta-analysis comparing clinical versus mechanical prediction supports this conclusion. William Grove and colleagues (Grove, Zald, Lebow, Snitz & Nelson, 2000) conducted a meta-analysis of 136 studies comparing clinical versus mechanical prediction. The studies included ones in which psychologists predicted outcomes within their areas of expertise, including psychotherapy outcome, future criminal behavior, fitness for military service, marital satisfaction, diagnoses, success on psychology internship, and several other issues. Other studies included in the meta-analysis

TABLE 3.5 Summary of Outcomes of Studies Comparing Clinical vs. Statistical Prediction

Source	Number of Studies Reviewed	Variables Predicted	Outcome		
			Clinical Better	Statistical Better	Tie
Meehl (1954)	20	Success in school or military; recidivism or parole violation; recovery from psychosis	1[a]	11	8
Meehl (1957)	27	Same as above, plus personality description; therapy outcome	0	17	10
Meehl (1965)	51	Same as above, plus response to shock treatment; diagnosis label; job success and satisfaction; medical diagnosis	1[b]	33	17
Grove et al. (2000)	136	Same as above, plus marital satisfaction; success on psychology internship; performance in medical school; and others.	8	63	65

[a]Later called a tie.

[b]Later called a tie by Goldberg (1968).

SOURCE: Wiggins, J. S. (1973). *Personality and Prediction: Principals of Personality Assessment.* Reading, MA: Addison-Wesley.

examined counselor's judgments within their area of expertise (e.g., college academic performance, job performance) and physicians' judgments within theirs (e.g., diagnosis of cardiac disease, cerebral lesions, students' performance in medical school). The results were consistent with previous studies: mechanical prediction outperformed clinical prediction overall, regardless of the type of judges, judges' experience, type of data being combined, or the design of the study. The advantage for statistical prediction was not large—roughly 10% on average—and in many studies mechanical and statistical prediction were essentially the same. But when one method outperformed the other, it was almost always mechanical prediction that did better (see Table 3.5). In the small percentage of studies (6 to 16%) where clinical prediction outperformed mechanical prediction, the authors found no pattern of variables that reliably distinguished when or why clinical prediction outperformed. Interestingly, clinical prediction tended to fare less well when interview data was one of the predictors.

Clinicians may find it discouraging to hear that their inferences are often inferior to mechanical ones that can be implemented by anyone who has the relevant input data and a high school reading level. Yet, if one takes a broader view, the general superior performance of actuarial models need not be seen as a sign of professional failure. A great deal of clinical experience and research typically goes into the development of useful actuarial models. Further, we seldom denigrate meteorologists or stock brokers when they rely on statistical models and computer-generated forecasting, nor do we distrust physicians who access large computer databases to help them diagnose illnesses.

Meehl's reviews, along with other reports focusing on limitations on clinicians' information-processing capabilities, stimulated research into what factors can improve both formal and informal inference (Kleinmuntz, 1984; Ruscio, 2000; Wiggins, 1981). Finally, as Tony Ward (1999) and Howard Garb (2000) point out, in the course of treating persons there still exists many less-structured assessment tasks for which no statistical decision rules have been developed, tasks such as describing symptoms, personality, or behavior, making causal inferences or treatment decisions. These require clinical judgment, so clinicians need to possess a wide range of cognitive skills and be able to apply various types of judgments appropriately.

Improving Informal Inference. Thorne suggested that "clinicians must become much more critical of the types of judgments they attempt to make, the selection of cues upon which judgments are based, and their modes of collecting and combining data" (1972, p. 44). Work in these areas began in the 1960s as researchers attempted to analyze the logic of inference (Sarbin, Taft, & Bailey, 1960), relate it to social and physical judgment processes and errors (Bieri et al., 1966; Hunt & Jones, 1962), analyze the nature and influence of specific cues used by clinicians (Goldberg, 1968; Hoffman, 1960), optimize the amount of assessment data to be processed (Bartlett & Green, 1966), and identify the conditions under which inference can be most reliable and valid (Watley, 1968). These efforts continue today (e.g., Garb & Lutz, 2001; Garb & Schramke, 1996; Sleek, 1996; Todd, 1996).

Unfortunately, the results of most efforts to help clinicians avoid the common pitfalls that beset informal clinical judgment have been disappointing. Experienced clinicians still tend to do no better at personality assessment than inexperienced clinicians or graduate students (Garb, 1989). Clinicians with training in specific assessment areas perform better than laypersons, but the size of their advantage is surprisingly small. Informing clinicians about their biases is also not very helpful, although there may be benefits from having clinicians keep a written record of the biases they show and the mistakes they make (Dawes, 1986). Accurate feedback data can help reduce bias.

Even though the accuracy of clinical inference can be improved over levels previously reported (Kahneman & Tversky, 1979), it is not clear that the amount of improvement justifies the extra effort. Even the most superior human judges operating under optimal conditions are variable enough in their accuracy to raise questions about their suitability for the data-processing task. Consider, for example, a study which tried to specify the rules by which the very best clinical judges draw inferences from a particular personality test. In this study, a recognized expert at drawing inferences from the test was asked to "think aloud" while interpreting the test scores of 126 people (Kleinmuntz, 1963). The decision rules that emerged for designating these people as "adjusted" or "maladjusted" were then used to write a computer program that would formalize the process of interpreting the test. The study showed that an expert clinician's inference rules can be objectified and taught, but that the best "student" may not be a human. The computer used the rules so perfectly and consistently with each new set of test scores that—in line with earlier data on formal versus informal inference—it did better at interpreting subsequent test scores than the clinician who had "taught" it (Kleinmuntz, 1969).

   Improving Formal Inference.   The success of formal inference procedures has stimulated clinicians to improve them. One approach has been to map out the assessment tasks at which clinicians can be most effective.

   Meehl (1954) and other researchers (e.g., Sawyer, 1966) have distinguished between the clinical psychologist's role in *data processing* versus *data collection*. They highlighted the fact that, just as data processing can be formal or informal, collection of assessment data can be done mechanically (with objective tests and life records) or subjectively (through unstructured interviews and informal observations). Thus, as shown in Table 3.6, many combinations of formal and informal procedures are possible in a given assessment enterprise. When the studies reviewed by Meehl are reexamined with the collection-processing distinction in mind, it becomes clear that while clinicians' subjective methods may be inferior to statistical methods for processing assessment data, their uniquely human abilities at collecting data and reporting judgments

TABLE 3.6   Some Combinations of Formal and Informal Procedures for the Collection and Processing of Assessment Data

Data-Collection Procedure	Data-Processing Procedure	Example
1. Formal	Formal	Psychological test scores processed by computer according to a statistical formula which predicts potential for behavior problems
2. Formal	Informal	Psychological test scores interpreted by clinician based on experience, theory, and hunches to establish psychiatric diagnosis
3. Informal	Formal	Clinician's subjective judgments (based on an interview) converted into quantitative ratings, which are then processed by a computer or statistical formula to describe client's personality
4. Informal	Informal	Subjective impressions and judgments (from interviews, projective tests, etc.) interpreted subjectively to decide whether client needs to be hospitalized
5. Formal and Informal	Formal	Psychological test scores and clinician's subjective impressions and judgments all fed into computer, which used complex formula to describe client or make predictions about behavior
6. Formal and Informal	Informal	Psychological test scores and clinician's subjective impressions and judgments all scanned and interpreted by clinician to decide whether client is capable of standing trial for a crime.

can make vital contributions to the assessment process (Sawyer, 1966). Indeed, the most accurate clinical inferences are likely to be based on the formal, statistical processing of data collected by both mechanical and subjective techniques—for example, by objective tests and clinical interviews (Sawyer, 1966). "... The clinician may be able to contribute most not by direct prediction, but rather by providing, in objective form, judgments to be combined mechanically" (Sawyer, 1966, p. 193).

This research confirms a role for clinicians in the assessment process. They may not be very accurate combiners of assessment data, but they can be an unsurpassed source of data (Anastasi, 1988). Guided by their theoretical approach, they can develop hypotheses about what aspects of clients' lives warrant further exploration, and they provide a stimulus that elicits a sample of how clients respond in a social situation. Though disagreement remains over exactly what assessment questions and roles clinicians should handle, the following conclusion still seems to apply: "Clinicians need not view themselves as second-rate IBM machines unless they choose to engage in activities that are more appropriately performed by such machines. In the realm of clinical observation and hypothesis formation, the IBM machine will never be more than a second-rate clinician" (Wiggins, 1973).

With this conclusion in mind, many clinicians and researchers now tend to focus on upgrading observational and other data-collection skills to optimize their value in the clinical assessment process. For example, clinical "intuition" has been recast as skill in observing a client's verbal and nonverbal behavior. Viewed this way, "intuition" can be developed, practiced, and improved (see Arkes, 1981; Dawes, 1986).

At the same time, other investigators are studying the accuracy of statistical, usually computer-based, data-processing methods. Some of these methods are thoroughly mechanical and empirical, as when a client's test scores are interpreted according to formulae derived from statistical relationships between other clients' test scores and behavior (see example 1 in Table 3.6). Here, the computer takes the client's test profile and "looks up" the characteristics of other people with similar profiles. Developing this type of purely actuarial program is expensive because it requires a storehouse of data from thousands of clients.

When, as is usually the case, there are too few data on the relationship between assessment results and client characteristics to create a good statistical formula for drawing inferences, hybrid systems of formal data processing have evolved. As in the Kleinmuntz (1963) study, such systems use a computer to interpret assessment data, not through an empirically derived formula, but through decision rules distilled from clinicians' experiences and beliefs. This process of "automating clinical lore" (Wiggins, 1973) has resulted in systems that can generate computerized narrative interpretations of the results of more than 100 psychological tests. As shown in Table 3.7, these interpretations can be remarkably detailed, but the programs that generate them vary considerably in sophistication and quality. Many have been developed with the logic pioneered by Benjamin Kleinmuntz (1963), but their usefulness remains questionable because they are based on information that has not been demonstrated to make valid predictions, and because they are sometimes based on information that is readily available through other means such as history or observation (Garb, 2000).

TABLE 3.7 A Computerized Narrative Interpretation of the Marital Satisfaction Inventory

A carefully developed computerized interpretation system is available for use with the 280-item, 11-scale Marital Satisfaction Inventory (MSI; Snyder, 1981). Here are excerpts from a computer's report on Mr. and Mrs. D., a couple who had just entered marital therapy (Snyder, Lachar, & Wills, 1988). Each spouse took the MSI independently, but the report combines their results.

Global Marital Affect

Both spouses openly acknowledge serious difficulties in their marriage and dissatisfaction with their spouse; they may have a tendency to emphasize marital conflict to the exclusion of acknowledging more positive aspects of their relationship. Relationship problems are likely to be of long duration and generalized across different areas of the marriage. Persons with similar profiles describe their marriage as a major source of disappointment. Determination of specific steps either spouse has taken toward separation or divorce would be prudent.

Spousal Communication

Both spouses express dissatisfaction with the amount of affection shown by their partner, although the wife reports somewhat less distress in this regard. Women with similar scores often feel emotionally distant from their husbands, and may feel unappreciated or misunderstood. In comparison, the husband describes extensive dissatisfaction with the quality of affective communication in the marriage. Men with similar scores typically describe their wives as emotionally distant and uncaring. Both the husband and wife describe difficulties in resolving disagreements although the husband's dissatisfaction in this regard is somewhat less than his wife's. When differences arise, there may be a notable shift toward more negative forms of interaction including reciprocity of negative affect, failure to acknowledge each other's view, or attribution of negative intentions to the partner's behavior. There may exist a long accumulation of unresolved differences, such that even minor disagreements precipitate major arguments. Each partner is likely to regard the other as being entrenched in their own position and unresponsive to legitimate concerns or complaints.

Specific Areas of Interaction

Overall, the husband and wife have evaluated specific dimensions of spousal interaction in a somewhat different manner. This divergence in spouses' views of the marriage may hinder their collaboration in rank-ordering relationship concerns and identifying therapeutic goals. Both respondents indicate dissatisfaction with their sexual relationship, although the wife reports somewhat less distress in this area. Disagreements regarding the frequency or variety of sexual behaviors may be frequent; it is somewhat unlikely that sexual difficulties evolve exclusively from more general marital distress, and specific interventions in this area may be warranted.

Concerns Regarding Children

The husband and wife both indicate significant conflict rearing childrearing issues, although the husband reports somewhat less distress in this respect. Conflicts around division of child care responsibilities are likely, and spouses may experience frequent disagreements regarding discipline and their children's privileges and responsibilities. The couple could likely benefit from interventions aimed at clarifying their respective expectations for their children's behavior and identifying each spouse's responsibilities for various childrearing tasks. Given the respondents' somewhat different perceptions in this area, a careful assessment should be conducted of possible alliances of one or more children with one parent against the other; an in-depth evaluation of one or more children may be warranted.

TABLE 3.7   A Computerized Narrative Interpretation of the Marital Satisfaction Inventory (*Continued*)

Role Orientation and Family History

The husband and wife differ sharply in their role orientations, with the husband expressing a more traditional view toward marital and parental roles. The husband may prefer a traditional division of household and childrearing responsibilities, with his assuming the role as primary wage-earner and the wife investing herself more fully in her role as wife and mother at home. In contrast, the wife describes a fairly nontraditional view of marital and parental roles. She is likely to prefer a more flexible division of household and child-rearing tasks, with both spouses pursuing independent careers and sharing equally in decision making and in housework and child care responsibilities at home. Given their different attitudes in this domain, the potential for marital role conflict merits further examination. Finally, both respondents report a history of moderate distress within their families of origin. Maladaptive relationship patterns in both families of origin should be carefully examined to determine the extent to which they generalize to the couple's own marriage.

SOURCE: Reprinted from Volume 14, Number 4, of the *Journal of Marital and Family Therapy*, Copyright © 1988, American Association for Marriage and Family Therapy. Reprinted with permission.

Critics have also noted the following additional limitations and problems associated with computerized assessment:

1. Actuarial techniques can be applied only where adequately developed, fully standardized assessment devices, inference norms, and formulae are available. Although the number of actuarial assessment systems is increasing, many clinicians still do not use them, preferring instead to rely on their personal judgments and predictions.

2. New discoveries about behavior are less likely to occur if clinicians become less involved in assessment data processing.

3. Relegation of clinicians to a data-collection role decreases the chances of future improvement of human data-processing skills (Matarazzo, 1986).

4. Excluding the clinician from the data-processing role reduces the probability that rare behavioral events and relationships will be noticed, because actuarial tables and statistical formulae may not be sensitive to them.

5. Certain kinds of assessment may be more appropriately dealt with by informal means. For example, specific, "bounded" questions (Will this person be likely to abuse children?) may most adequately be answered by formal data processing, while more general "unbounded" concerns (What is this person like?) seem best handled through informal means (Levy, 1963).

6. Computerized testing may make it easier for poorly trained testers to provide impressive-sounding assessment reports that they may not fully understand and are not prepared to use in the most appropriate way.

7. Computerized narratives usually focus on only one plausible interpretation of test results rather than considering and evaluating the merits of the several possible interpretations that a more complete assessment battery almost always suggests (Matarazzo, 1986).

As criticisms like these focused attention on crucial computerized assessment issues, several steps were taken to improve and regulate computer-based testing and interpretation. There is now a special set of guidelines pertaining to computer testing (APA, 1986), the APA's *Standards for Educational and Psychological Testing* (APA, 1985) includes several provisions about computerized testing, the journal called *Computers in Human Behavior* includes a section on computer software used to interpret psychological tests, and numerous journal articles on the pros and cons of computerized psychological assessment have appeared (e.g., Fowler, 1985). Despite these concerns, computer-assisted assessment has grown rapidly over the past decade, and that growth is expected to accelerate as more normative data are collected, as reliability and validity concerns are addressed, and as administration of computerized tests become more flexible and interactive (Groth-Marnat, 2000).

One point that some critics of computer-based test interpretation appear to miss is that many of their criticisms apply at least as well to the assessment reports of human clinicians. A core problem in clinical assessment is the lack of validation research on all kinds of assessment reports, whether computer generated or prepared by people (Ben-Porath & Butcher, 1991).

The Behavioral Approach to Assessment

Clinical psychologists have traditionally been concerned with formal and informal processing of assessment data that are viewed as signs or correlates. In that tradition, assessment information is interpreted in terms of psychological traits or intrapsychic dynamics, and the clinician's goal is to predict something about the client or to describe the client's personality. Clinical psychologists who adopt a behavioral approach tend not to adopt these guidelines. Their main criticisms and alternative formulations can be summarized as follows:

1. The use of assessment data as signs of personality traits involves too much inference. Behaviorists do not see personality traits, psychological dispositions, or personality dynamics as the most useful concepts for learning about people. In their view, dispositional constructs have limited utility for describing people, predicting their behavior, or evaluating behavior change programs.

   Many behaviorists argue that part of the reason for clinicians' poor data-processing skills is that they use vague trait concepts to reach inferences that stray too far from initial assessment information. When clinicians do not share common definitions for terms like anxiety, aggression, and ego, the reliability and validity of clinical judgments are likely to be low (Goldfried, 1995). Trait concepts are seen by behavioral assessors as adding confusing and ultimately superfluous labels to behavior that does not need them. As noted earlier, the behavioral approach treats assessment data as samples of client capabilities, not evidence for personality traits or dynamic states.

2. Trait concepts often isolate people's behavior from the environment in which it occurs. Since behavior is learned in a social context, one cannot describe or predict that behavior accurately unless situational factors are taken into account: A person who displays dominance on a psychological test may behave quite differently toward a supervisor at work.

   Accordingly, behavioral assessment includes collecting information about (a) client capabilities, (b) characteristics of the physical and social environment in which behavior occurs, and (c) the nature of client–environment interactions. The person–situation orientation in the behavioral view of assessment has emphasized interactionism or the reciprocal relationship between people and the situations which they create and to which they respond (Bandura, 1978; Mischel, 1984).

3. Traditional clinical assessment practices promote separation between data collection and data use. Too often, assessment information is processed into descriptions or predictions that are sufficiently irrelevant to planning or evaluating treatment that they may actually be ignored (Dailey, 1953; Meehl, 1960).

From the behavioral perspective, clinical assessment must be tied to efforts at modifying behavior (Haynes, 1993). Toward this end, clients, situations, and client–situation interactions are described along dimensions that are as precise and data-based as possible, have direct implications for treatment planning, and can be monitored during and after treatment. Rather than merely describing a child's problem in trait-oriented terms such as aggressiveness or hyperactivity, behavioral assessment would focus on the frequencies, durations, or intensities with which specific acts (e.g., striking others) occur, the settings in which they occur, and the environmental factors that appear to elicit and reinforce them. The acronym SORC, for Stimulus-Organism-Response-Consequence, captures the variables that a thorough behavioral assessment must consider (Goldfried & Sprafkin, 1974). The spirit of interactionism is suggested by this system's attention to environmental (the C and S components) and organismic (the O component) control of important responses (R). Behaviorists also study extended sequences, or chains, of interaction in an attempt to understand the nature of, and problems in, the complex and reciprocal influences that occur as people interact in couples or other social situations (Gottman & Roy, 1990).

In general, questions asked during behavioral assessment are not oriented toward why people behave in a particular way, but what they do, and when, where, and under what circumstances they do it. When behavior is described in this fashion, tactics for changing behavior tend to follow directly from assessment. If assessment suggests that Sam's high-frequency whining in the classroom is reinforced by teacher attention, a program to terminate reward of the maladaptive behavior and plan reinforcement of more appropriate behaviors might be instituted. As that program begins, its effect on the variables identified in the initial assessment would be observed and used as a guide for continuing, altering, or terminating the intervention.

In recent years, behavioral and more traditional approaches to assessment have begun to recognize each other's strengths (Groth-Marnat, 1999; Haynes & Uchigakiuchi, 1993). For their part, behaviorists increasingly stress the need to demonstrate rather than presume that their assessment methods meet the classic psychometric criteria of reliability and validity. And where they once avoided considering client personality characteristics, behaviorists are now more willing to recognize the importance of internal "person variables" and aspects of cognition that give stability and unity to behavior across situations (Fernandez-Ballesteros & Staats, 1992; Mischel, 1986, 1993). At the same time, those engaged in trait assessment and psychiatric diagnosis have embraced some behavioral recommendations. One example of the influence of behavioral assessment principles on traditional diagnostic practices is seen in the specific, criterion-based decision-making structure used in DSM-IV.

The behavioral approach to assessment is not without its critics, however. Many clinicians see objective assessment of overt behaviors in relation to specific environmental situations as too narrow and inadequate for tapping the various personality dimensions stressed in their own approaches. Other critiques center on the fact that, compared to traditional personality tests, for example, many behavioral assessment instruments are still in a rather primitive stage of development in terms of standardization norms. Still others note that, like other clinicians, those using behavioral assessments usually do so without benefit of statistical inference formulae and thus depend on their own subjective judgments in interpreting the data they collect. Also, though behavioral assessment provides excellent descriptions of behavior that can be used to guide treatment planning, it has not resolved the question of what behaviors constitute a problem and who sets up the definitions (Morganstern, 1988). Finally, behavioral assessment has not yet reached a level of sophistication that allows for a reliable, empirically determined choice of specific treatment techniques, especially in complex cases. (For more on the theory, practice, and problems of behavioral assessment, see Bellack & Hersen, 1988; Ciminero, Calhoun, & Adams, 1986).

Humanistic Psychology and Assessment

Many objections raised by behavioral theorists to traditional assessment procedures relate to the belief that people should not be examined apart from their physical and social environment and burdened with labels that focus on problems and weaknesses to the exclusion of assets and strengths. In this respect, the behavioral and humanistic approaches to assessment are in accord. However, humanistically oriented clinicians have suggested assessment alternatives that differ substantially from those of the behavioral approach (e.g., Fischer, 2001; Fischer & Fischer, 1983). Some of them have argued against assessment on the grounds that such procedures are dehumanizing, take responsibility away from clients, and threaten the quality of clinician–client relations (Rogers, 1951). Advocates of this position may be unwilling even to review existing assessment data and inferences made about a client by others because they assume that all the information necessary will emerge during interviews with the client (see Chapters 4 and 7).

Other humanistic psychologists raise the possibility that assessment data collected through traditional means can be useful if they are processed in line with humanistic principles (Fischer, 1989). For example, test results can be viewed as clues to how a client looks at the world, and conducting those tests can provide opportunities for the clinician and client to build their relationship (Dana & Leech, 1974). Constance T. Fischer, for instance, argues that assessments using standardized empirically-validated instruments can be both scientific and therapeutic when assessments are conducted interactively between therapist and client. She gives examples of discussing DSM-IV criteria and possible interpretations of MMPI-2 profiles with clients, arguing that such collaboration not only provide additional data for assessments, but avoid objectifying the client (Fischer, 2001; see also Finn, 1996). Humanistic psychologists who feel that traditional assessment devices do not facilitate the growth of clinician–client relationships have also developed specialized instruments that they believe do the job better. These tests include the Personal Orientation Inventory (Shostrom, 1968) and the Purpose-in-Life Test (Crumbaugh, 1968).

COMMUNICATING ASSESSMENT DATA

The organized presentation of assessment results is called an assessment report. If assessment results are to have maximal value, they must be presented in reports that are clear, relevant to assessment goals, and useful to the intended consumer. Accordingly, clinicians must guard against problems that can make reports vague, irrelevant, and useless.

Report Clarity

The first criterion for an assessment report is clarity. Without this basic attribute, relevance and usefulness cannot even be evaluated. Lack of clarity in psychological reports is troublesome because misinterpretation of a report can lead to misguided decisions. Here is a case in point:

> A young girl, mentally defective, was seen for testing by the psychologist, who reported to the social agency that the girl's test performance indicated moderate success and happiness for her in "doing things with her hands." Three months later, however, the social agency reported to the psychologist that the girl was not responding well. Although the social agency had followed the psychologist's recommendation, the girl was neither happy nor successful "doing things with her hands." When the psychologist inquired what kinds of things, specifically, the girl had been given to do he was told "We gave her music lessons—on the saxophone." (Hammond & Allen, 1953, p. v)

A related problem exists when the assessor uses jargon that may be meaningless to the reader. Consider the following excerpt from a report on a 36-year-old man:

> Test results emphasize a basically characterological problem with currently hysteroid defenses. Impairment of his ability to make adequate use of independent and creative fantasy,

associated with emotional lability and naivete, are characteristic of him. . . . Due to markedly passive-aggressive character make-up, in which the infantile dependency needs are continually warring with his hostile tendencies, it is not difficult to understand this current conflict over sexual expression. (Mischel, 1968, p. 105)

The writer may understand the client, but will the reader understand the writer? Anyone not well versed in psychoanalytic terminology would find such a report mystifying. Professionals may not even agree on the meaning of the terms employed. Factors such as excessive length (or cryptic brevity), excessively technical information (statistics or esoteric test scores), and lack of coherent organization also contribute to lack of clarity in assessment reports (Olive, 1972; Tallent & Reiss, 1959).

Relevance to Goals

The second requirement of a valuable assessment report is that it be relevant to the goal that prompted the assessment in the first place. If that goal was to classify the client's behavior, information relevant to classification should be highlighted. If description of the client's current psychological assets and liabilities was the purpose, the report should contain those descriptions. If predictions about a client are requested, these should appear, unless the clinician believes that no sound basis exists for making them.

These simple, self-evident prescriptions are sometimes lost, especially when explicit assessment goals are never stated. Although far less common today than in the past, clinicians may still be asked for "psychologicals" (usually a standard test battery and interview) without being told why assessment is being done. Under such circumstances, the chances of writing a relevant report are minimal. Unfortunately, there are other cases in which a report's lack of relevance is due mainly to the clinician's failure to keep established objectives in mind.

Usefulness of Reports

Finally, one must ask if an assessment report is useful. Does the information it contains add anything important to what we already know about the client? Reports that present clear, relevant information that is already available through other sources may appear useful, but have little real value. Such reports tend to be written when the assessor has either failed to collect new information or has not made useful statements about new data. In the former case, the clinician may have employed techniques that have low incremental validity (Sechrest, 1963). For example, a clinician may use psychological tests to conclude that a client has strong hostile tendencies, but if police records show that the client repeatedly has been arrested for assault, this conclusion doesn't add much to the clinical picture. In other instances, the assessor's report may have limited usefulness because it says nothing beyond what would be expected on the basis of base rate information, past experience, and common sense.

Consider the following edited version of a report written entirely on the basis of two pieces of information: (1) The client is a new admission to a Veterans Administration (VA) hospital, and (2) the case was to be discussed at a convention session entitled "A Case Study of Schizophrenia." The report said:

> This veteran approached the testing situation with some reluctance. He was cooperative with the clinician, but mildly evasive on some of the material. Both the tests and the past history suggest considerable inadequacy in interpersonal relations, particularly with members of his family. It is doubtful whether he has ever had very many close relationships with anyone.... He has never been able to sink his roots deeply. He is immature, egocentric, and irritable, and often he misperceives the good intentions of the people around him.... He tends to be basically passive and dependent, though there are occasional periods of resistance and rebellion against others.... Vocationally, his adjustment has been very poor. Mostly he has drifted from one job to another. His interests are shallow and he tends to have poor motivation for his work. Also he has had a hard time keeping his jobs because of difficulty in getting along with fellow employees. Although he has had some relations with women, his sex life has been unsatisfactory to him. At present, he is mildly depressed.... His intelligence is close to average, but he is functioning below his potential.... Test results and case history ... suggest the diagnosis of schizophrenic reaction, chronic undifferentiated type. Prognosis for response to treatment appears to be poor. (Sundberg, Tyler, & Taplin, 1973, pp. 577–579)

In generating this impressive but utterly generic report, the clinician relied heavily on knowledge of VA hospital residents and familiarity with hospital procedures. For example, since the case was to be discussed at a meeting on schizophrenia, and since schizophrenic diagnoses are common for VA residents, it was easy to surmise the correct diagnosis. Also, because it fits the "average" VA resident, the report was likely to be at least partially accurate. This bogus document exemplifies a feature of assessment reports that reduces their usefulness: overgenerality, or the tendency to write in terms that are so ambiguous they can be true of almost anyone. Documents laden with overly general statements have been dubbed "Barnum Reports" (in honor of P. T. Barnum's maxim that there is a sucker born every minute), "Aunt Fanny Reports" (because the statements could be true of "my aunt Fanny"), or "Madison Avenue Reports" (given that they "sell" well) (Klopfer, 1983; Meehl, 1956; Tallent, 1992). Such overly general material has the dual disadvantages of spuriously increasing a report's impressiveness while actually decreasing its usefulness.

Organizing Assessment Data

While there is no universally "right" way to organize assessment data, several guidelines are worth noting. First, the criteria of clarity, relevance, and usefulness may be more easily achieved by using an outline organized around the issues that the clinician's theoretical approach suggests are most important to the goals of assessment. Here we present sample outlines representing three approaches to clinical psychology. [For more detailed discussions of the techniques and problems associated with writing clinical assessment reports, see Sattler (1988) and Tallent (1976, 1992).]

A Psychodynamic Outline.   This outline is one suggested as a general guideline for clinical psychodynamic assessments (Gabbard, 2000, p. 86):

I. Historical data
   A. Present illness with attention to associative linkages and Axis-IV stressors
   B. Past history with emphasis on how the past is repeating itself in the present
      1. Developmental history
      2. Family history
      3. Cultural/religious background
II. Mental status examination
   A. Orientation and perception
   B. Cognition
   C. Affect
   D. Action
III. Projective psychological testing (if necessary)
IV. Physical and neurological examination
V. The psychodynamic diagnosis
   A. Descriptive DSM-IV diagnosis
   B. Interactions among Axes I-V
   C. Characteristics of the ego
      1. Strengths and weaknesses
      2. Defense mechanisms and conflicts
      3. Relationship to superego
   D. Quality of object relations
      1. Family relationships
      2. Transference-countertransference patterns
      3. Inferences about internal object relations
   E. Characteristics of the self
      1. Self-esteem and self-cohesivenes
      2. Self-continuity
      3. Self-boundaries
      4. Mind-body relationships
   F. Postmodern considerations (biases introduced by gender, culture, religion, etc.)
   G. Explanatory formulation using above data

*A **Humanistically-Oriented Report.*** In line with their subjective approach and tendency to avoid formal assessment, humanisticly oriented clinicians are more likely to follow general frameworks rather than detailed outlines:

I. Client from own point of view
II. Client as reflected in tests
III. Client as seen by assessor

*A **Cognitive-Behavioral Outline.*** Here is an assessment outline representative of the cognitive-behavioral approach (Pomeranz & Goldfried, 1970):

I. Description of client's physical appearance and behavior during assessment
II. Presenting problems

    A. Nature of problems
    B. Historical background of problems
    C. Current situational determinants of problems
    D. Relevant organismic variables
       1. Physiological states
       2. Effects of medication
       3. Cognitive determinants of problems
    E. Dimensions of problems
       1. Duration
       2. Pervasiveness
       3. Frequency
       4. Magnitude
    F. Consequences of problems
       1. Positive
       2. Negative
III. Other problems (observed by assessor but not stated by client)
IV. Personal assets
V. Targets for change
VI. Recommended treatments
VII. Client motivation for treatment
VIII. Prognosis
IX. Priority for treatment
X. Client expectancies
    A. About solving specific problems
    B. About treatment enterprise in general
XI. Other comments

Table 3.8 illustrates how an assessment outline—in this case, a cognitive-behavioral outline—is translated into an assessment report.

A Note on Ethics

The collection, processing, and communication of assessment data require that clinicians have access to sensitive information that the client might not ordinarily reveal. This places a heavy responsibility on the assessor to use and report this privileged information in a fashion that safeguards the client's welfare and dignity and shows concern for (1) how psychological assessment data are being used, (2) who may have access to confidential material, and (3) the possibility that improper or irresponsible interpretation of assessment information will have negative consequences for clients.

With these concerns in mind, clinicians must first be sure their inquiries do not comprise an unauthorized invasion of a client's privacy (see Bongar, 1988, for suggestions on how to maintain privacy when using computers in assessment). Next, care should be taken to assure that assessment goals are not socially or culturally biased so that certain clients (e.g., members of ethnic or racial minorities) are placed at a

TABLE 3.8   An Assessment Report Based on a Cognitive-Behavioral Outline

Behavior During Interview and Physical Description

James is a clean-shaven, long-haired young man who appeared for the intake interview in well-coordinated college garb: jeans, wide belt, open shirt, and sandals. He came across as shy and soft-spoken, with occasional minor speech blocks. Although uneasy during most of the session, he nonetheless spoke freely and candidly.

Presenting Problem:

A. *Nature of problem*: Anxiety in public speaking situations, and other situations in which he is being evaluated by others.

B. *Historical setting events:* James was born in France, and arrived in this country seven years ago, at which time he experienced both a social and language problem. His social contacts had been minimal until he entered college, at which time a socially aggressive friend of his helped him to break out of his shell. James describes his father as being an overly critical and perfectionistic person who would, on occasion, rip up his homework if it fell short of the mark. The client's mother is pictured as a controlling, overly affectionate person who was always showing concern about his welfare. His younger brother, who has always been a good student, was continually thrown up to James by his parents as being far better than he.

C. *Current situational determinants:* Interaction with his parents, examinations, family gatherings, participation in classes, initial social contact.

D. *Relevant organismic variables:* The client appears to be approaching a number of situations with certain irrational expectations, primarily unrealistic strivings of perfection and an overwhelming desire to receive approval from others. He is not taking any medication at this time.

E. *Dimensions of problem:* The client's social and evaluative anxiety are long-standing and occur in a wide variety of day-to-day situations.

F. *Consequences of problem:* His chronic level of anxiety resulted in an ulcer operation at the age of 15. In addition, he has developed a skin rash on his hands and arms, apparently from excessive perspiration. He reports that his nervousness at one time caused him to stutter, but this appears to be less a problem in more recent years. His anxiety in examination situations has typically interfered with his ability to perform well.

Other Problems:

A. *Assertiveness:* Although obviously a shy and timid individual, James said that lack of assertiveness is no longer a problem with him. At one time in the past, his friends would take advantage of him, but he claims that this is no longer the case. This should be followed up further, as it is unclear what he means by assertiveness.

B. *Forgetfulness:* The client reports that he frequently misses appointments, misplaces items, locks himself out of his room, and generally is absent-minded.

Personal Assets:

The client is fairly bright and comes across as a warm, friendly, and sensitive individual.

Targets for Modification:

Unrealistic self-statements in social-evaluative situations; possibly behavioral deficits associated with unassertiveness; and forgetfulness.

Recommended Treatment:

It appears that relaxation training would be a good way to begin, especially in light of the client's high level of anxiety. Following this, the treatment should move along the lines of rational restructuring, and possibly behavior rehearsal. It is unclear as yet what would be the best strategy for dealing with forgetfulness.

TABLE 3.8   An Assessment Report Based on a Cognitive-Behavioral Outline
(Continued)

Motivation for Treatment:
High.

Prognosis:
Very good.

Priority for Treatment:
High.

Expectancies:
On occasion, especially when going out on a date with a female, James would take half a sleeping pill to calm himself down. He wants

to get away from this, and feels what he needs is to learn to cope with his anxieties by himself. It would appear that he will be very receptive to whatever treatment plan we finally decide on, especially if the emphasis is on self-control of anxiety.

Other Comments:
Considering the brief time available between now and the end of the semester, between-session homework assignments should be emphasized as playing a particularly important role in the behavior change process.

From *Clinical Behavior Therapy* by M. R. Goldfried and G. C. Davison, pp. 52–53. Copyright © 1976 by Holt, Rinehart and Winston. Reprinted by permission of Holt, Rinehart and Winston.

disadvantage (Malgady, 1996). For example, some psychological tests are alleged to be inappropriate for use with minority groups, leading to court decisions prohibiting their use for educational placement and other purposes (see Lambert, 1981, for discussion of the landmark *Larry P. v. Wilson Riles* case in California). When conducting assessments on clients from different cultures, clinicians need to be knowledgeable about how culture can affect diagnosis, assessment, and treatment (Lopez & Guarnaccia, 2000). Finally, clinicians must wrestle with the problem of who may have access to assessment data if they do not maintain sole control over them. When test scores, conclusions, predictions, and other information are communicated in a report, they may be misused by persons who see the report but are not qualified to interpret it. In such cases, not only is the client's privacy invaded, but the assessment may harm the client. Minimizing these problems is a major concern of public officials, government agencies, citizens groups, and private individuals. Some of them advocate elimination of all psychological assessment (especially testing), while others urge safeguards to protect clients from assessment abuses. The latter option has been adopted by the American Psychological Association, whose *Ethical Principles of Psychologists and Code of Conduct* (APA, 1992), *General Guidelines for Providers of Psychological Services* (APA, 1987), and *Standards for Educational and Psychological Testing* (APA, 1985) contain extensive guidelines for assessors to follow as they go about the sensitive task of learning about their clients. These guidelines reflect federal legislation, including the Equal Employment Opportunity Act (part of the Civil Rights Act of 1964), which prohibits discriminatory use of tests that have "adverse impact" on the selection of minority group job candidates, and the Civil Rights Act of 1991 which bans adjustment of test scores on the basis of race, color, religion, sex, or national origin (Sackett & Wilk,

1994). The guidelines must also be implemented in accordance with the regulations of the Individuals with Disabilities Education Act and the Americans with Disabilities Act. Ethical problems and standards associated with clinical psychology will be considered in greater detail in Chapter 14.

CHAPTER SUMMARY

Clinical assessment is the process of collecting information to be used as the basis for informed decisions by the assessor or by those to whom results are communicated. A combination of interviews, tests, observations, and life records serves as the main sources of assessment data in clinical psychology. The clinical assessment process includes four stages: planning, collecting, processing, and communicating assessment data. The methods and levels of inquiry in assessment tend to follow a case study guide that is shaped by the clinician's goals, theoretical approach, personal preferences, and time constraints. Selection of assessment methods is also guided by research on their reliability (consistency) and validity (ability to measure what they are supposed to measure).

The goals of clinical assessment tend to involve diagnostic classification, description, and prediction. Diagnostic classification normally employs DSM-IV-TR. Description involves broader assessments of clients' personalities by looking at person–environment interactions. Predictions often involve personnel selection but sometimes focus on a client's potential for violence or suicide.

Unfortunately, clinicians have no unique intuitive power or special information-processing capacity, so the quality of their judgments and decisions about clients can be threatened by the same cognitive biases and errors that affect all human beings. Indeed, research on clinical judgment suggests that, in many situations, clinicians can make their greatest contribution to assessment as collectors of information that is then processed by computer-based statistical formulae.

Instead of using assessment data as signs or correlates, behaviorally oriented clinicians see them as samples of the specific stimuli, skills, consequences, and cognitive tendencies that account for a client's behavior. Advocates of the humanistic approach view assessment data as clues to how a client looks at the world, and they use the assessment process as an opportunity to build a relationship with the client.

The results of clinical assessment are presented in an organized assessment report which should be clear, relevant to assessment goals, and useful to the intended consumer. These reports usually reflect the theoretical approach taken by each clinician.

Chapter 4

Interviewing and Observation in Clinical Psychology

Interviews and observations are the most widely employed tools in clinical psychology. They are central to clinical assessment and also play prominent roles in psychological treatment. Indeed, much of what we have to say in this chapter about assessment interviews and observations also applies to treatment because treatment usually begins in—and is based on—the relationship established through the assessment process.

In this chapter, we describe a variety of interview and observation techniques. The chapter does not attempt to teach you how to conduct specific types of interviews or observations; it offers instead an introduction to interviewing and observation as assessment data sources. For both interview and observation, we also evaluate reliability and validity and describe current trends in the field.

CLINICAL INTERVIEW SITUATIONS

In simplest terms, an interview is a conversation with a purpose or goal (Matarazzo, 1965). Good interviewing techniques are described in a number of sources (e.g., Cormier & Cormier, 1991; Fine & Glasser, 1996; Othmer & Othmer, 2002; Pedersen & Ivey, 1993; Rogers, 2001; Shea, 1998; Shipley & Wood, 1996), but learning how to use these techniques effectively takes more than reading (Bogels, 1994). Clinicians must also engage in carefully supervised practice as part of their professional training.

The fact that interviews resemble other forms of conversation makes them a natural source of clinical information about clients, an easy means of communicating with them, and a convenient context for attempting to help them. Interviews are flexible, relatively inexpensive, and, perhaps most important, provide the clinician with simultaneous samples of clients' verbal and nonverbal behavior. These advantages make the interview useful in a variety of clinical situations.

Intake Interviews

The most common type of clinical interview occurs when a client first comes to the clinician because of some problem in living. These *intake interviews* are designed mainly to establish the nature of the problem. Information gathered in this situation may also help the clinician decide whether the client has come to the right place. The interviewer must answer questions such as, Can I work with this person? Is this problem within my area of expertise? and Will this person likely benefit from treatment? (e.g., Couch, 1995; Safran et al., 1993). If, on the basis of one or more intake interviews, the answer to such questions is no, the clinician will refer the client to another professional or agency for alternative services. If further contact is seen as desirable, assessment or treatment sessions are scheduled. Most clinicians conduct their own intake interviews, but in some agencies and group practices, social workers or other personnel perform this function.

Often, the intake interviewer is asked for a classification or diagnosis of the problem in the form of a DSM-IV Axis I label (e.g., Major Depressive Disorder), along with associated descriptions on the other four axes. If not required to provide diagnostic labels, behaviorally and humanistically oriented clinicians may use intake interviews to develop broader descriptions of clients and the environmental context in which their behavior occurs (see Chapter 3).

Some intake interviews are structured according to a sequence of important topics suggested by the case study outlines described in Chapter 3. Originally patterned after the question-and-answer format of medical history taking, many psychiatric interviews also include a mental status examination, a planned sequence of questions designed to assess a client's mental functioning in a number of important areas (see Table 4.1). The mental status examination is analogous to the physical exam that makes up part of the assessment of medical problems.

Intake interviews may also lay the groundwork for subsequent therapy efforts by establishing a productive working relationship and organizing the clinician's hypotheses about the origins and development of the client's problems (Siassi, 1984). The intake interview is often critically important to successful treatment because almost half the clients who attend an intake interview fail to return for scheduled treatment (Baekeland & Lundwall, 1975; Morton, 1995). The clients' initial perception of their intake interviewer appears to affect this pattern. Clients are more likely to return for subsequent treatment after talking to an interviewer who they feel treated them with warm friendliness as opposed to businesslike professionalism (Kokotovic & Tracey, 1987; Patterson, 1989; Tryon, 1990). Clients also rate interviews more positively when interviewers express correct understandings of the clients' partially or indirectly expressed concerns and emotions (Dimatteo & Taranta, 1976).

TABLE 4.1   The Mental Status Examination (MSE)

Here is a typical MSE topic outline (Siassi, 1984), followed by a short excerpt from an MSE interview:

I. General appearance and behavior—client's level of activity, reaction to interviewer, grooming and clothing are assessed.

II. Speech and thought—Is client's speech coherent and understandable? Are delusions present?

III. Consciousness—Is the sensorium clear or clouded?

IV. Mood and affect—Is client depressed, anxious, restless? Is affect appropriate to situation?

V. Perception—Does client experience hallucinations, depersonalization?

VI. Obsessions and compulsions—amount and quality of these behaviors are noted.

VII. Orientation—Is client aware of correct time, place, and personal identity?

VIII. Memory—What is condition of short- and long-term memory?

IX. Attention and concentration—Asking client to count backwards by 7's is a common strategy.

X. Fund of general information—Questions like "Who is the President?" or "What are some big cities in the U.S.?" are asked.

XI. Intelligence—estimated from educational achievement, reasoning ability, and fund of information.

XII. Insight and judgment—Does patient understand probable outcomes of behavior?

XIII. Higher intellectual functioning—What is the quality of patient's form of thinking? Is patient able to deal with abstraction?

CLINICIAN: Good morning. What is your name?

CLIENT: Randolph S.

CLINICIAN: Well, Mr. S, I would like to ask you some questions this morning. Is that all right?

CLIENT: Fine.

CLINICIAN: How long have you been here?

CLIENT: Since yesterday morning.

CLINICIAN: Why are you here?

CLIENT: I don't know. I think my wife called the police and here I am.

CLINICIAN: Well, what did you do to make her call the police?

CLIENT: I don't know.

CLINICIAN: What day is today?

CLIENT: Tuesday, the twelfth.

CLINICIAN: What year is it?

CLIENT: 1997.

CLINICIAN: What city are we in?

CLIENT: Chicago.

CLINICIAN: Who is the mayor of Chicago?

Problem-Referral Interviews

Clinicians sometimes serve as diagnostic consultants to psychiatrists, courts, schools, employers, social service agencies, or others. In these circumstances, the client is often referred, not necessarily for treatment, which usually prompts an intake interview, but to answer a specific question such as, Is Mr. P. competent to stand trial?, Is Mrs. L. psychotic?, Is Jimmy G. mentally retarded? Will such-and-such a custody arrangement with Ms. M. be in the best interest of this child?

In these circumstances, clinicians might gather information similar to that in an intake interview. They might also advance a diagnosis, but the central goal of the interview is to address the referral question. For this reason, it is important that the referral question be stated clearly. Questions such as "give me a profile on Mr. Q." or "Will Ms. Y. make a good parent or is she disturbed?" are too general or vague. The interviewer must also decide whether the answer to the referral question falls within his or her scope of expertise and is appropriate. Referrals such as "Please test my child's IQ so I can prove to the schools that he should be in the gifted class" should raise red flags about the appropriateness of conducting the assessment without further clarification and consultation.

Orientation Interviews

People receiving psychological assessment or treatment often do not know what to expect, let alone what is expected of them. This is especially true if they have had no previous contact with mental health professionals. To make these new experiences less mysterious and more comfortable, many clinicians conduct special interviews (or reserve segments of interviews) to acquaint the client with the assessment, treatment, or research procedures to come (Prochaska & Norcross, 1994).

Such *orientation interviews* are beneficial in at least two ways. First, because the client is encouraged to ask questions and make comments, misconceptions that might obstruct subsequent treatment progress can be discussed and corrected. Thus, clients are more likely to speak freely once an orientation interview assures them that the clinician will hold the content of their sessions in confidence. Orientation interviews can also help clients understand upcoming assessment and treatment procedures and what their roles in these procedures will be (Couch, 1995). Thus, the clinician might point out that the clients who benefit most from treatment are those who are candid, cooperative, serious, and willing to work to solve their problems. Good orientation interviews, then, can help focus clinicians' efforts on those clients who are most willing to be full partners in the assessment or treatment enterprise.

Orientation interviews are also important for research participants. Though a clinician or researcher might not reveal every detail of their clinical research (for obvious reasons), he or she is ethically required to make sure that each participant understands the nature of the tasks the participant will perform and any risks associated with them. Such interviews satisfy the rule of "informed consent," but they also help insure motivated cooperation from the participants, something especially important in long-term clinical trials and longitudinal research.

Termination and Debriefing Interviews

A different kind of orienting interview occurs when it is time to terminate a clinical relationship. For example, people who have just completed a series of assessment sessions involving extensive interviews, tests, and observations are understandably anxious to know "what the doctor found," how the information will be used, and who will have access to it. These concerns are particularly acute when the assessor has acted as consultant to a school or a court. A *termination interview* can help alleviate clients' anxiety about the assessment enterprise by explaining the procedures and protections involved in transmission of privileged information, and by providing a summary and interpretation of the assessment results.

Termination interviews following clinical research are called *debriefing*, and include an explanation of the project in which the person has participated and a discussion of the procedures employed in it. Debriefings permit participants to ask questions and make comments about their research experiences. In accordance with the standards for ethical research established by the APA and other organizations, debriefing of participants is aimed at assuring that the research experience has done no harm and that the participant feels comfortable about it (APA, 1992; see Chapter 14). Debriefing interviews can also benefit the clinical researcher by helping to clarify how participants perceived the experiment and whether factors outside the experimenter's control affected participants' behavior (Orne, 1962).

Termination interviews also occur when psychological treatment is completed. Many loose ends need to be tied up: There is gratitude to be expressed and accepted, reminders to be given about the handling of future problems, plans to be made for follow-up contacts, and reassurance given to clients about their ability to go it alone. Treatment termination interviews help make the transition from treatment to posttreatment as smooth and productive as possible.

Crisis Interviews

When a person's problems are intense and pressing, and when normal problem-solving skills prove inadequate to deal with the situation, that person is said to be in a crisis. When people in crisis appear at clinical facilities or call a hotline, suicide prevention center, or other agency, interviewers do not have the luxury of scheduling a series of assessment and treatment sessions. Instead, they conduct *crisis interviews* in which they attempt to provide support, collect assessment data, and provide help, all in a very short time (Somers-Flanagan & Somers-Flanagan, 1995).

The interviewer must deal with the client in a calm and accepting fashion, ask relevant questions ("Have you ever tried to kill yourself?" "What kinds of pills do you have in the house?"), and work on the immediate problem directly or by putting the client in touch with other services. One or two well-handled interviews during a crisis may be the beginning and the end of contact with a client whose need for assistance was temporary and situation-specific. For others, the crisis interview leads to subsequent assessment and treatment sessions.

Observational Interviews

As already noted, interviews provide an opportunity to observe particular client behaviors, such as how the person deals with stressful, ambiguous, or conflict-laden situations. We discuss observational procedures later in this chapter.

INTERVIEW STRUCTURE

The most fundamental feature of clinical interviews is their structure: the degree to which the interviewer determines the content and course of the conversation. At one end of the structure continuum are *nondirective interviews*, in which the clinician does as little as possible to interfere with the natural flow of the client's speech and choice of topics. At the other end are *structured interviews*, which involve a carefully planned question-and-answer format (see Table 4.1). In between are many blends, usually referred to as guided or *semi-structured interviews*.

Several factors influence the degree of structure in an interview, among them the theoretical orientation and personal preferences of the interviewer. In general, humanistic clinicians tend to establish the least interview structure. Psychodynamically oriented clinicians usually provide more, while cognitive-behavioral clinicians are likely to be the most verbally active and directive. While some clinicians consistently adopt a structured or nondirective approach, most adjust interview structure in light of circumstances and assessment goals. Structure may also change during an interview—many interviewers begin in a nondirective way and become more structured as the interview continues. The interview situation also strongly affects the degree of structure. For instance, by their nature, crises demand more structure than might be desirable during a routine intake interview.

Nondirective Interviews

Consider first this segment from a nondirective intake interview.

CLINICIAN: [Your relative] didn't go into much detail about what you wanted to talk about, so I wonder if you'd just start in at whatever you want to start in with, and tell me what kind of nervousness you have.

CLIENT: Well, it's, uh, I think if I were to put it in, in a few words, it seems to be a, a, a complete lack of self-confidence in, and an extreme degree of self-consciousness. Now, I have always been a very self-conscious person. I mean every, just about, since I was probably 14 years old the first I remember of it. But for a long time I've realized that I was sort of using people as crutches. I mean I, a lot of things I felt I couldn't do myself I did all right if someone was along.

CLINICIAN: Um-hm.

CLIENT: And it's just progressed to the point where I'm actually using the four walls of the house as an escape from reality. I mean I don't, I don't care to go out. I, I certainly can't go out alone. . . . It's sort of a vicious circle. I find out I can't do it, and then I'm sure the next time I can't do it.

CLINICIAN: Um-hm.

CLIENT: And it just gets progressively worse. I think the first that I ever noticed it . . . (Wallen, 1956, p. 146)

The client continued a narrative about the onset and duration of her problems, her occupation and marriage, her father's death, and other topics. Notice that the clinician hardly says a word, although as we shall see below, there are things he could have done to nondirectively encourage the client to talk had it been necessary. The nondirective interviewer uses direct questions sparingly and relies instead on responses designed to facilitate the client's talking about his or her concerns.

Semi-structured Interviews

Compare this nondirective approach to the following semi-structured interview, in which an organized set of topics is explored in a way that gives the interviewer flexibility in wording questions, interpreting answers, and guiding decisions about what to address next.

> CLINICIAN: You say that you are very jealous a lot of the time and this upsets you a great deal.
>
> CLIENT: Well, I know it's stupid for me to feel that way, but I am hurt when I even think of Mike with another woman.
>
> CLINICIAN: You don't want to feel jealous but you do.
>
> CLIENT: I know that's not the way a "liberated" woman should be.
>
> CLINICIAN: What is your idea of how a liberated woman should feel?
>
> CLIENT: I don't know. In many ways I feel I have changed so much in the last year. I really don't believe you have the right to own another person—and yet, when it happens to me, I feel really hurt. I'm such a hypocrite.
>
> CLINICIAN: You're unhappy because you are not responding the way you really would like to?
>
> CLIENT: I'm not the person I want to be.
>
> CLINICIAN: So there's really "double jeopardy." When Mike is with someone else, it really hurts you. And, when you feel jealous, you get down on yourself for being that way.
>
> CLIENT: Yes, I guess I lose both ways. (Morganstern & Tevlin, 1981, p. 86)

Notice the nondirective features in this excerpt—the clinician's responses conveyed an understanding of the client's experience and encouraged further talk, but did not dictate what the client talked about by requesting specific information. However, the interviewer also placed limits on the topic by asking a specific question. The more specific questions the interviewer asks, the more structure he or she imposes on the interview.

Structured Interviews

In structured interviews, the interviewer asks a series of specific questions phrased in a standardized fashion and presented in a pre-established order. Consistent rules are also provided for scoring the clients' answers or for using additional probes to elicit scorable responses. Thus, while structured interviews do not outlaw open-ended questions or prohibit interviewers from formulating their own questions to clarify ambiguous responses, they do provide detailed rules (sometimes called "decision trees" or "branching rules") that tell the interviewer what to do in certain situations (e.g., "if the respondent answers 'no' skip to question 32; if the respondent answers 'yes' inquire as to how many times it happened and continue to the next question"). Many structured interviews were designed to help clinicians arrive at psychiatric diagnoses by asking questions relevant to specific DSM diagnostic criteria. This can be seen in Table 4.2, which lists some of today's most widely-used structured and semi-structured interviews.

Structured interviews continue to be developed for tasks other than DSM diagnoses, such as planning and evaluating rehabilitation treatments (Ownsworth, McFarland, & Young, 2000; Rogers, Ustad, & Salekin, 1998). For more detailed coverage of structured interviews, see Rogers (2001).

Trends Toward Structure

In recent years, new structured and semi-structured interviews have proliferated for use in a variety of situations (Rogers, 1995; 2001). The popularity of these new interview formats stems partly from the fact that they provide a systematic way of reliably measuring many of the specific criteria used in making psychiatric diagnoses via DSM-IV or international classification systems (Robins, 1995). Structured interviews have also proven valuable in clinical research, where they help select participants who have the specific characteristics or problems the researcher is seeking (e.g., Kendler & Roy, 1995). In addition, structured interviews have become almost indispensable in epidemiology, the study of how disorders and other behavior patterns are distributed in the population and of the factors that affect this distribution (Wittchen, 1994; Loranger, 1992).

Structured interviews offer several major advantages, including improved reliability of assessment, a standard format that allows interviews to be conducted systematically by professional clinicians, trained nonprofessionals, or even computers (Groth-Marnat, 1999; Pilkonis et al., 1995; Reich et al., 1995; Wittchen et al., 1995), and assurance that the interview will be long enough and comprehensive enough to reach assessment goals.

The increasing use of structured interviews parallels other trends in the history of clinical assessment. We saw in Chapter 3, for example, that using formal, statistical rules for combining assessment data is more effective than clinicians' subjective judgments. Structured interviews are designed to make the data collection process more consistent by replacing or at least controlling clinicians' judgment via formal decision rules.

At the same time, however, clinicians who depend too much on structured interviews run the risk of becoming so "protocol bound" that they miss important information that the interview protocol did not explore. Further, the routine nature of structured interviews can alienate clients if the clinician fails to establish rapport, the harmonious and comfortable working relationship that helps ensure clients' motivation and cooperation (Rosenthal, 1989). Finally, structured interviews—like all other

TABLE 4.2   Structured Interviews Frequently Used in Clinical Psychology

Name of Interview	Reference	Purpose
Interviews for Axis I Disorders		
The Schedule for Affective Disorders & Schizophrenia (SADS)	Endicott & Spitzer (1978)	Semi-structured interview for differential diagnosis of more than twenty categories of mental disorder.
Diagnostic Interview Schedule (DIS-IV)	Robins et al. (1995)	Extensive structured interview with several modules used in large-scale epidemiological studies; Chinese and Spanish versions available.
Structured Clinical Interview for DSM-IV (SCID)	Spitzer et al. (1990)	Broad-scale differential diagnoses tied to DSM-IV criteria.
Diagnostic Interview Schedule for Children, Revised (DISC-R)	Shaffer et al. (1993)	Parallel formats for children and parents for making differential diagnoses of childhood disorders.
Composite International Diagnostic Interview (CIDI-2)	World Health Organization—Alcohol, Drug, and Mental Health Administration (1997)	Many of the same items as the DIS, but with modifications to improve cross-cultural use.
Interviews for Axis-II Disorders		
Internationan Personality Disorder Examination (IPDE)	Loranger (1999)	Differential diagnoses among DSM-III personality disorders; module available for DSM-IV.
Structured Clinical Interview	First et al. (1997)	Semi-structured interview for DSM-IV personality disorders; combined SCID and SCID-II are designed to provide a comprehensive diagnostic assessment interview.
Specialized Interviews		
Psychopathy Checklist (PCL-R)	Hare (1980; 1991)	Semi-structured interview consisting of structured questions and optional probes for evaluating antisocial functioning.
Rogers Criminal Responsibility Assessment Scale (RCRAS)	Rogers, Wasyliw, & Cavanaugh (1984)	Assess criminal responsibility against specific legal criteria.
Structured Interview of Reported Symptoms (SIRS)	Rogers et al. (1991)	Assess malingering in clinical populations.
Schedules for Clinical Assessment in Neuropsychiatry (SCAN)	World Health Organization (1994)	Used in national and international studies of the epidemiology of mental disorders; also in individual diagnoses.
Cambridge Cognitive Examination (CAMDEX)	Roth et al. (1986)	Assess cognitive dysfunctions such as memory loss and language problems.

interviews—depend heavily on the memory, candor, and descriptive abilities of respondents. So while the reliability of clients' reports (or of different clinicians' inferences from those reports) might be excellent, the validity or meaning of structured interview data can be threatened if the client misunderstands questions, is not motivated to answer truthfully, or can't recall relevant information. We will return to issues of interview reliability and validity later.

Structured interviews blur the line between interviewing and testing. When clinicians follow a standard protocol, ask questions, record responses in a structured sequence, and then use well-developed inference rules to determine the significance of those responses, interviewing and testing are hardly distinguishable. This may not be a bad thing, especially if reliability and validity are improved. But clinicians must use interactions outside the structured interview (and possibly during it) to enhance rapport.

Because both the questions and the inference rules of structured interviews are scripted, they might not require highly-trained clinicians to administer them. Researchers have investigated administering structured and semi-structured interviews using a) experienced interviewers with no formal clinical training (Brugha, Nienhuis, Bagchi, Smith, & Meltzer, 1999), b) computers (Peters, Clark, & Carroll, 1998), c) the telephone (Cacciola, Alterman, Rutheford, McKay, & May, 1999), and d) self-administered questionnaires rather than face-to-face contact (Erickson & Kaplan, 2000). As yet, no statement about the general effectiveness of these techniques seems warranted. It will take considerable research to establish the conditions under which these variations are preferable to more traditional ways of conducting interviews.

As noted earlier, structured interviews are most easily developed for clinical decision tasks that have well-defined decision criteria. They have become widely used for forming diagnoses, for gathering epidemiological data on the prevalence of various mental disorders, and for identifying research participants who display particular forms of disorder (e.g., Kendler & Roy, 1995; Lewis et al., 1992; Robins & Regier, 1991). But though their use is still expanding, it is important to remember that structured interviews do not exist for the majority of face-to-face clinical contact hours (e.g., therapy interviews). Because of this, clinical interviewing remains a complex social interaction requiring training and skill. Despite recent trends toward increasing the structure of many clinical interactions, clinicians still need to have a broad base of interviewing skills. They must also know what valid structured and semi-structured interviews are available and when to use them appropriately.

STAGES IN THE INTERVIEW

No one has developed a single "right" way to conduct an interview, but certain strategies have proven valuable in practice and have thus been adopted by skilled clinicians representing every theoretical approach (Goldfried, 1980). In the following sections, we examine the interview techniques commonly employed by clinical psychologists.

Interviews can be characterized as having a beginning (Stage 1), a middle (Stage 2), and an end (Stage 3). These three stages are most obvious in intake or problem-referral interviews, which usually begin with efforts at making the client comfortable and ready to speak freely (Stage 1), continue into a central information-gathering stage (Stage 2), and end with summary statements, client questions, and, if appropriate, plans for additional assessment sessions (Stage 3). If more than one assessment interview occurs, Stage 1 tends to grow shorter while Stage 2 grows longer. Similarly, Stage 3 may be brief until the final assessment interview, when it may take up most of the time available.

Treatment interviews follow a different three-stage format. A session may begin with the client's report on thoughts and events since the last meeting, continue with whatever treatment procedures are being employed, then conclude with a summary of current progress, plans for the next meeting, and/or "homework" assignments.

Though not all interviews are organized around a beginning–middle–end framework, the three-stage model offers a convenient guide for our discussion of "typical" clinical interviews.

Stage 1: Beginning the Interview

In one sense, the interview begins with the clinician's preparation. Certain settings are especially conducive to building rapport for most clients. Except for clients whose cultural background might cause such surroundings to be threatening, interviews are best conducted in a comfortable, private office. This is because most people find it easier to relax when they can be physically comfortable. Also, privacy makes it easier to assure the client of the interview's confidential nature.

Several other office characteristics can aid rapport. A reassuring equality is established when two people sit a few feet apart on similar chairs of equal height. If the clinician sits in a massive, high-backed chair behind a huge desk placed 6 feet from the client's smaller, lower seat, rapport may be impaired. A desk cleared of other work, along with precautions to hold phone calls and prevent other intrusions, makes it clear that the clinician is fully attentive and sincerely interested in what the client has to say. The list of rapport-building techniques could be extended almost indefinitely; the point is that from the beginning, the clinician should try to create a warm, comfortable environment that encourages the client to speak freely and honestly about whatever topics are relevant to the interview.

The clinician's preparation should also include becoming familiar with any available referral information. Sometimes the clinician will have only a client's general complaint, perhaps voiced to a secretary at the time of a self-referral. Other times, medical, school, court, or other mental health records may be available. Such information can help the clinician to decide whether specific interviewing or testing materials might be needed.

It is important that clinicians handle the first few minutes of initial interviews carefully. This early stage is important because clients may not be ready to talk candidly about personal matters yet, preferring instead to take a wait-and-see approach in which they carefully control what they say and don't say. If this reserved attitude prevails throughout the interview, the clinician is unlikely to gather very much valuable assessment information.

Accordingly, most clinicians see establishing rapport as their main task during the first part of initial interviews. Rapport can be built in several ways, many of which involve common sense and courtesy. A client's anxiety and uncertainty can be eased by demystifying the interview. A warm smile, a friendly greeting, and a handshake are excellent beginnings to an interview. "Small talk" about the weather or difficulty in finding the office also ease the client's transition into the interview. This should not go on so long that the interview loses its distinctive quality, or that the client begins to suspect that the interviewer might wish to avoid the topics that prompted the interview. The skilled interviewer relaxes the client by appearing warm and approachable, but gets down to business, thereby communicating that the client's time and suffering are important. Skilled clinicians can establish remarkable rapport during the first stage of an initial interview, but even for them, the process continues into the second and third stages and into subsequent sessions as well.

Stage 2: The Middle of the Interview

Transition to the middle of an initial interview should be as smooth as possible. The ways in which the clinician accomplishes this transition illustrate a number of important interview tactics.

    Nondirective Techniques.   In most cases, interviewers begin the second stage with nondirective, *open-ended* questions. Common examples are: "So what brings you here today?" or "Would you like to tell me something about the problems you referred to on the phone?" A major advantage of this approach is that it allows a client to begin in his or her own way. An open-ended invitation to talk allows the client to ease into painful or embarrassing topics without feeling coerced.[1] This relatively nonstressful way of beginning can also aid rapport because it lets clients know that the clinician is willing to listen to whatever they have to say.

Contrast the open-ended questions just mentioned with more "binding" questions like: "You said on the phone there is a sex problem in your marriage. Is it yours or your wife's?" Openings of this type focus the conversation on topics that may be too threatening to address for the moment. An interview whose second stage employs binding questions can degenerate into a question-and-answer session in which the client may feel put-upon, misunderstood, and frustrated. As noted earlier, clinicians using structured interview formats must guard against this situation.

Open-ended questions are used whenever the clinician wishes to prompt clients to speak while exerting as little influence as possible over what they say. Classic remarks like "Tell me a bit more about that" and "How did you feel about that?" exemplify a nondirective strategy. This strategy is supplemented by tactics designed to help clients express themselves fully and to enhance rapport by communicating the clinician's understanding and acceptance. The most general of these tactics is called *active listening*, which involves responding to the client's speech in ways that indicate

---

[1]Clients often begin with a "ticket of admission" problem which may not be one of the greatest concerns to them. The real reason for the visit may appear only after they have "tested the water" with varying amounts of diversionary conversation.

understanding and encourage further elaboration. Active listening was represented in the clinician's "mm-hmms" in the nondirective interview excerpt presented earlier. Other signs of active listening include comments such as "I see," "I'm with you," "Right," or even nodding of the head.

A related nondirective strategy is called *paraphrasing*, in which clinicians restate what their clients say in order to (1) show that they are listening closely, and (2) give the client a chance to correct the remark if it was misinterpreted. Carl Rogers called this strategy *reflection* and emphasized the importance of not only restating content, but also highlighting client feelings. Consider these examples.

Example A:

CLIENT: Sometimes I get so mad at my husband, I could kill him.

CLINICIAN: You would just like to get rid of him altogether.

Example B:

CLIENT: Sometimes I get so mad at my husband, I could kill him.

CLINICIAN: He really upsets you sometimes.

Notice that, in example A, the clinician merely reworded the client's remark. In example B, the feeling contained in the remark was reflected. Most clients respond to paraphrasing by continuing to talk, usually along the same lines as before, often in greater detail. Paraphrasing often is preferable to direct questioning because such questioning tends to change or restrict the conversation, as illustrated in the following interactions.

Example A:

CLIENT: What it comes down to is that life just doesn't seem worth living sometimes.

CLINICIAN: Sometimes it all just seems to be too much.

CLIENT: Yeah, and I don't know what to do when I feel that way. I don't really think I want to die, not really. But I also dread the thought of another day starting. For example . . .

Example B:

CLIENT: What it comes down to is that life just doesn't seem worth living sometimes.

CLINICIAN: How often do you feel that way?

CLIENT: Oh, off and on.

There is a place for questions like the one in example B, but unless the clinician knows enough about the general scope of a problem to start pinpointing specifics, interrupting with such questions is likely to limit, and even distort, the assessment picture. Clients who are immediately hit with direct queries may conclude that they should wait for the next question rather than spontaneously tell their story. For many clients, this experience can be frustrating and damaging to rapport.

Paraphrasing can also be helpful when the clinician is confused about what a client has said. Consider the following:

> CLIENT: I told my husband that I didn't want to live with him anymore so he said "fine" and left. Well, when I got back, I found out that the son of a bitch kept all our furniture!

Most clinicians would have a hard time deciphering the sequence of events described here, but if they say "What?", the client might be put off or assume that the clinician is a dunce. Instead, a combination of paraphrase and request for clarification serves nicely:

> CLINICIAN: OK, let's see if I've got this straight. You told your husband you didn't want to live with him, so he left. You later came back to your house from somewhere else and found he had taken the furniture?

Ideally, the client will either confirm this interpretation or fill in the missing pieces. If not, the clinician may wish to use more direct questioning.

Directive Techniques. Most interviewers supplement nondirective tactics with more directive questions whose form, wording, and content are often the result of careful (though often on-the-spot) planning. Consider the following illustrative questions:

A. Do you feel better or worse when your husband is out of town?

B. How do you feel when your husband is out of town?

Example A offers a clear, but possibly irrelevant, two-choice situation. This is a "Do you walk to work or carry your lunch?" question, for which the most valid answer may be "Neither." Some clients are not assertive enough in an interview to ignore the choice, so they settle for one unsatisfactory response or the other. Unless there is a special reason for offering clients only a few response alternatives, skilled interviewers ask direct questions in a form—such as in example B, above—that gets at specific information, but also leaves clients free to choose their own words.

Experienced clinicians also avoid asking questions that suggest their own answers. Notice the implications contained in this query: "You've suffered with this problem a long time?" Such questions communicate what the interviewer expects to hear, and some clients will oblige by biasing their response. "How long have you had this problem?" is a better alternative. Similarly, inquiries based on unwarranted assumptions should be avoided. Notice the hidden assumption in the example: "How bad is your insomnia when you are depressed?" If the client tends to oversleep when feeling low, this question cannot be answered without contradicting the clinician. A careful interviewer might explore the sleep topic with the following question: "You said you are often depressed. What changes in yourself do you notice during those times?"

Combining Interview Tactics. Because interviews can be flexible, clinicians are usually free to combine the tactics we have described. They may facilitate the client's speech with open-ended requests, paraphrasing, prompts, and other active listening techniques, and then use more directive questions to "zoom in" on topics of special importance. However, directive procedures do not take over completely as interviews progress. They continue to be mixed with less directive tactics. An example of this blending is provided by the concept of *repeated scanning and focusing*, in which interviewers first scan a topic nondirectively, then focus on it in more directive fashion:

> CLINICIAN: You mentioned that your family is back East. Could you tell me something about them?
>
> CLIENT: There's not much to tell. There's Dad, Mom, and the twins. They all seem to like it back there so I guess they'll stay forever.
>
> CLINICIAN: What else can you say about them?
>
> CLIENT: Well, Dad is a retired high school principal. Mom used to be strictly a housewife but, since us kids have grown, she's been working part-time.
>
> CLINICIAN: How did you get along with your folks when you lived at home?
>
> CLIENT: Really fine. I've always thought they were great people and that's probably why they had so little trouble with me. Of course, now and then there would be a problem, but not often.
>
> CLINICIAN: What kinds of problems were there?

The interviewer might go on to explore several specific issues about the client's relationship with both parents, then move on to another topic, again beginning with scanning procedures and later moving on to more direct questions.

Stage 3: Closing the Interview

The last stage of an interview can provide valuable assessment data as well as an opportunity to enhance rapport. The interviewer may initiate the third stage with a statement like this:

> We have been covering some very valuable information here and I appreciate your willingness to tell me about it. I know our session hasn't been easy for you. Since we're running out of time for today, I thought we could look back over what we've covered and then give you a chance to ask *me* some questions.

The clinician accomplishes several things here. First, the impending conclusion of the interview is signaled. Second, the client is praised for cooperativeness and reassured that the clinician recognized how stressful the interview has been. Third, the suggested plan for the final minutes invites the client to ask questions or make comments that may be important, but had not been put into words.

The clinician's recap of the session summarizes interview content and checks that nothing important was misunderstood. Comments from the client during this stage can be enlightening, especially when they disclose misconceptions or information gaps. This part of the interview (especially when it ends a first contact) becomes a miniature version of the termination interview described earlier. It usually concludes with leave-taking rituals ("It was good of you to come") and, when appropriate, confirmation of plans for future contact with the interviewer or another professional.

Sometimes, the last stage of an interview evokes clinically significant behavior or information. For example: "Oh gosh, look at the time. I have to hurry to my lawyer's office or I won't be able to find out until Monday whether I get custody of my son." Some clients wait until the end of the interview to reveal this kind of information because they want the clinician to know about it, but they had not yet been ready to discuss it. Others might just let such information slip out because the interview "feels" over and they let down the defenses they had been using earlier. Some simply don't want the interview to end. For these reasons, the clinician attaches as much importance to the final stage of the interview as to the stages that precede it.

Note-taking and Recording

Notes help clinicians capture more information, and they reduce the chance that important information will be forgotten or distorted when it comes time to record therapy case notes, write reports, or otherwise document a contact. But taking notes can also divert the clinician's attention away from the client, potentially jeopardizing rapport or causing the clinician to miss other information. There is also the risk that note-taking will raise clients' concerns about confidentiality. Most clinicians recommend a middle ground that involves occasional note-taking, usually jotting key words or phrases (Groth-Marnat, 1999). Clients rarely have a problem with this, particularly if the interviewer has discussed confidentiality beforehand (as they are ethically bound to) and matter-of-factly explained the reasons for note-taking, such as by saying, "I plan to take a few notes to help me remember the things we've talked about."

Note-taking may not be necessary if audiotaping or videotaping is used. With today's technology, it is simple to record an entire session, though this should never be done without the client's prior informed consent. Most clients forget about being recorded as the interview progresses. Recorded interviews are especially useful for training, supervision, and research purposes, but they might not otherwise be superior to occasional note-taking unless the clinician plans to review the entire recording for important information that he or she failed to recall.

COMMUNICATION IN THE INTERVIEW

The fundamental problem in interview communication—as in all human communication—is to accurately encode, transmit, and decode messages. Speakers must encode what they want to convey into transmittable messages made up of words and gestures which listeners must receive and decode (interpret) within their personal and cultural frame of reference. Lapses in both verbal and nonverbal communication can occur at many points in this process. To take just the simplest of examples, giving the "thumbs up" sign signals approval to people in the United States, but it says "up yours" in Australia.

Clinicians attempt to avoid the much more subtle communication problems that can plague interviews by maximizing the clarity of the messages they send to their clients and by clarifying the meaning of the messages received from them. Let's consider an example of poor clinical communication and then look at some ways to reduce the likelihood of such communication breakdowns. In the following hypothetical exchange, the speakers' thoughts are in parentheses:

> CLINICIAN: (I wonder what his teenage social life was like.) Tell me a little about the friends you had in high school.
>
> CLIENT: (I had dozens of social acquaintances but only one person who was a really close friend.) There was just one, a guy named Mike.
>
> CLINICIAN: (So he was pretty much of a loner.) How did you feel about that?
>
> CLIENT: (It was fine. I had a great time, went to lots of parties, had lots of dates, but knew I could always depend on Mike to talk with about really personal things.) I enjoyed it. Mike and I got along really well.
>
> CLINICIAN: (Not only was he a social isolate, he claims to have liked it that way. I wonder if he is being honest with himself about that.) Did you ever wish you had more friends?
>
> CLIENT: (For crying out loud, he makes it sound like it's a crime to have one really close friend. I think we've talked enough about this.) No.

Verbal Communication

In the preceding illustration, the clinician used *friend* to refer to casual as well as intimate acquaintances. Because this word had a different meaning for the client, it led to misunderstanding. The conversation could have gone on in this fruitless way for quite a while before the interviewer and the client straightened out their communication problem.

Although the client and clinician may technically be speaking the same language and thus assume they understand one another, the interviewer must be aware that educational, social, ethnic, cultural, economic, and religious factors can impair communication (Yutrzenka, 1995). For instance, what constitutes problem behavior in children can be quite different among different ethnic and cultural groups (Lopez & Guarnaccia, 2000). A complaint issued by a mother from one cultural group (e.g., "He is very often bad.") might easily be misunderstood by an interviewer from another. Unless the clinician takes the client's background and frame of reference into account, and asks for clarification (e.g., "How many times per week does he behave this way?") when verbal referents are unclear, the interview will suffer. Consider this example:

> CLIENT: When I'm in such heavy situations, I just get real uptight.
>
> CLINICIAN: What makes you uptight?
>
> CLIENT: Well, the whole thing. Everybody kind of hanging out and running around. I can't seem to get it together with anybody, so I guess I freak out.
>
> CLINICIAN: And then what happens?
>
> CLIENT: I usually go home and go to sleep. But I'm usually pretty bummed out.
>
> CLINICIAN: Are you saying that you don't fit in with these people and that's what makes you feel bummed out?

CLIENT: Well, I don't know. These are my friends, I guess—but it never seems to work out. (Morganstern & Tevlin, 1981, p. 91)

Do these two people understand each other? We do not know for sure, and as long as the interview goes on this way, neither will they. Obviously, the clinician needs to ask the client to clarify some terms:

CLIENT: When I'm in such heavy situations, I just get real uptight. . . .

CLINICIAN: When you say that you're uptight in these situations, what does that mean to you?

CLIENT: Well, uptight, you know. Tense.

CLINICIAN: You mean your muscles get tense?

CLIENT: My neck gets very sore—and I get a headache lots of times.

CLINICIAN: What else happens?

CLIENT: Well, either because of my neck or my headache, I start sweating a lot.

CLINICIAN: When you say you're uptight you are really experiencing it physically. What are you thinking when this happens?

CLIENT: I'm thinking, man you are really paranoid. You just can't relax in any situation. You really are a loser. And then I want to get out of there fast. . . . (Morganstern & Tevlin, 1981, p. 91)

Clients can become as confused as clinicians, but if they are reluctant to appear stupid or to question a person in authority they may not reveal their dilemma. Some evidence on this point comes from a study conducted in a medical setting by Korsch and Negrete (1972). Their data showed that communication from doctors to patients' mothers in a pediatric clinic was obstructed by the use of medical terms and that client confusion and dissatisfaction often resulted. For example, a "lumbar puncture" (spinal tap) was sometimes assumed to be an operation for draining the child's lungs; "incubation period" was interpreted by one mother as the time during which her child had to be kept in bed.

Circumventing such problems in clinical interviews can be facilitated by attention to certain guidelines. Skilled interviewers avoid jargon, ask questions in a straightforward way ("What experiences have you had with masturbation?" not "Do you ever touch yourself?"), and request feedback from their client ("Is all this making sense to you?" or "Did I understand you correctly that . . ."). They also try to assure that their verbal behavior conveys patience, concern, and acceptance. Expressing impatience or being judgmental are not usually desirable.

Nonverbal Communication

As in all human communication, a constant stream of nonverbal behavior accompanies the clients' and interviewers' verbal behavior. Indeed, the nonverbal communication channel usually remains open even when the verbal channel shuts down. Since both members of an interview dyad are sending and receiving nonverbal messages, clinicians must not only be sensitive to incoming signals but also to those they transmit.

Here are some aspects of clients' nonverbal communication that tend to be of greatest interest to clinicians during interviews:

1. Physical appearance—height, weight, grooming, style and condition of clothing, unusual characteristics, muscular development, hairstyle
2. Movements—gestures; repetitive arm, hand, head, leg, or foot motions; tics or other apparently involuntary movements; pacing; handling of cigarettes, matches, or other objects
3. Posture—slouching, rigidity, crossed or uncrossed arms or legs, head in hands
4. Eye contact—constant, fleeting, none
5. Facial expressions—smiles, frowns, grimaces, raised eyebrows
6. Emotional arousal—tears, wet eyes, sweating, dryness of lips, frequent swallowing, blushing or paling, voice or hand tremor, rapid respiration, frequent shifts in body position, startle reactions, inappropriate laughter
7. Speech variables—tone of voice, speed, slurring, lisp, stuttering, blocking, accent, clarity, style, sudden shifts or omissions

In addition to noting nonverbal client behaviors, clinicians also look for inconsistencies between the verbal and nonverbal channels. The statement "I feel pretty good today" will be viewed differently if the client is on the verge of tears than if a happy smile is evident.

Interviewers also try to coordinate their own verbal and nonverbal behavior so as to convey unambiguous messages to their clients. A client will perceive the message to "take your time" in talking about a sensitive topic as more genuine if the clinician says it slowly and quietly than if it is blurted out after glancing at the clock. Similarly, friendly eye contact, some head nodding, an occasional smile, and an attentive posture lets the client know that the interviewer is listening closely. Overdoing it may backfire, however. A plastered-on smile, a continuously knitted brow, sidelong glances, and other theatrics are more likely to convey interviewer anxiety or inexperience than concern.

Observation of nonverbal behavior begins when the client and clinician meet and continues until they part. Clinicians differ, however, as to what their clients' nonverbal behavior means. Interviewers committed to a sign-oriented approach draw higher-level inferences from nonverbal behaviors than those adopting a sample-oriented stance. For example, a behaviorist's interpretation of increased respiration, perspiration, and fidgeting while a client talks about sex would probably be that emotional arousal is associated with that topic. Psychodynamic interviewers may infer more, postulating perhaps that nonverbal behaviors (e.g., twirling a ring on a finger) are symbolic representations of sexual activity. Gestalt therapists might suspect that the client is avoiding awareness of unpleasant feelings associated with the belief that he or she is just "going round in circles." Alfred Adler interpreted where a client chose to sit: "One moves toward the desk; that is favorable. Another moves away; that is unfavorable" (Adler, 1933). Whatever they might infer from it, most clinicians believe that nonverbal behavior serves as a powerful communication channel and a valuable source of interview data.

In addition to concerns about nonverbal communication and the other aspects of interviewing that we have covered in this chapter, clinicians face many other interview-related challenges. Dealing with silences, how to address the client, handling personal questions from clients, and confronting a client's inconsistencies are just a few of these. (If you are interested in a more detailed exploration of interviewing issues and techniques, consult the interviewing textbooks listed at the beginning of this chapter.)

RESEARCH ON THE INTERVIEW

Clinicians must also remain aware of empirical research on the value of interviews as a source of assessment data and a format for therapy. Such awareness can point clinicians to areas where their own interviewing could be improved.

Social Interaction and Influence in the Interview

Until 1942, when Carl Rogers published the first transcripts from phonographic recordings of therapy interviews, the exact nature of clinical interactions had been unknown.[2] Research on the clinical interview grew rapidly thereafter. At first it focused on such issues as the effects of audio recording and the accuracy of clinicians' summaries versus electrical recordings of the same interview (Covner, 1942; Snyder, 1945). After it was established that recording devices were not disruptive and provided the most complete account of an interview, research expanded in several new directions.

One of these new directions involved efforts to describe relationships between interview characteristics—such as warmth and empathy—and outcome variables such as rapport-building and therapy effectiveness. Some studies focused on differences in interview tactics used by Rogerians and non-Rogerians (Porter, 1943; Seeman, 1949; Strupp, 1960), while others tried to define interview variables such as client resistance (Snyder, 1953). Still other investigators performed detailed analyses of the content of conversations as a means of better understanding the interview process (Auld & Murray, 1955). One team of researchers devoted years to the content analysis of the first five minutes of a single interview (Pittenger, Hockett, & Danehy, 1960).

Other research found that clinicians could systematically influence noncontent variables in the interview. For example, the duration of interviewees' speech tends to increase when interviewers nod their heads or say "mm-hmm" while listening (Kanfer & McBrearty, 1962; Matarazzo, 1965). When interviewers first increased, then decreased, the duration of their own utterances over three parts of a conversation, interviewees did the same. When the interviewer's speech duration first decreased, then increased, interviewees again followed suit (Matarazzo et al., 1963). However, this synchrony phenomenon does not always appear (Matarazzo et al., 1968). And in therapy situations, the synchrony-producing influence of clinician upon client may be moder-

---

[2]Rogers's recordings were considered scandalous at the time because tradition ruled out all but narrative case reports. The fact that he was a psychologist (not a psychiatrist) doing therapy with adults made Rogers's revelations even more distasteful to those not yet accustomed to the expanding roles of postwar clinicians.

ated, or even reversed, by the client's influence on the clinician. Thus, the duration of a therapist's utterances may increase with quiet clients and decrease with those who are more talkative (Lennard & Bernstein, 1960). Social status can also affect interview interactions. In one laboratory study, synchrony occurred when students were interviewed by fellow students, but it disappeared when they were interviewed by high-status professionals (Pope et al., 1974).

The accuracy of interview responses can be affected by a number of factors. The phrasing of questions is one such factor. A client's responses to "Tell me something about your marital problems" will probably be more accurate and less distorted by defensiveness than if the interviewer asked "Why can't you get along with your spouse?" (e.g., Thomas, 1973). The client's comfort with the interviewer is another factor. Kaiser & Priebe (1999) found, for instance, that schizophrenic patients rated the quality of their lives more favorably if questions were asked by their case manager than if the same questions were asked by an external researcher. Responses to clinical and survey research interviews may be more accurate when people feel comfortable with the interviewer, a factor that may be enhanced when the two of them share the same gender, ethnicity, and native language (Axin, 1991; Grantham, 1973; Kane & Macauley, 1993; Sue et al., 1991; Webster, 1996; Ying, 1989). Other aspects of a person's emotional state can also affect response accuracy. For example, mothers' reports about their children's behavior are significantly influenced by the mothers' emotional adjustment, in particular by feelings of depression (Webster-Stratton, 1988).

In short, investigations into social and interpersonal aspects of interviews reveal that they are not only data-gathering contexts, but complex influence situations as well. Several client and situational variables can influence the content and form an interview takes.

Reliability and Validity of Interview Data

Reliability refers to the degree to which clients give the same information on different occasions or to different interviewers, while validity is concerned with the degree to which interview data or conclusions are accurate. The impact of these factors is of special interest to researchers trying to establish the value and understand the limits of interview data.

Reliability.   To study the reliability of interview data, researchers examine the consistency of clients' responses across repeated interview occasions by the same or different interviewers. Some researchers have studied interview reliability by looking at the degree to which different judges agree on the inferences (ratings, diagnoses, or personality trait descriptions) they draw from conversations with the same client (DiNardo et al., 1993; Ferro et al., 1995). However, this approach confounds the reliability of what the client said with the quality of the interviewer's inference system. If a client tells two clinicians the same thing and they draw different conclusions from it, it may be the interviewers' inference system, not the interview, that is unreliable. One strategy for isolating the reliability of interviewers' judgments is to have several clinicians view videotaped interviews and then make ratings or draw other inferences from the tapes. This approach has been widely used to establish the reliability of clinicians' judgments about DSM-IV diagnoses (Widiger et al., 1991), clients' progress in therapy (Goins, Strauss, & Martin, 1995), the severity of Alzheimer's disease (Boothby, Mann, & Barker, 1995), the credibility of children's reports of sexual abuse (Anson, Golding, & Gully, 1993), and the like (Derksen, Hummelen, & Bouwens, 1994).

As you might expect, test-retest reliability tends to be highest when adult clients are asked for innocuous information such as age and other demographic data and when the interval between interviews is short (e.g., Ross et al., 1995). Lower reliability coefficients tend to appear when test-retest intervals are long, when clients are young children, and when interviewers explore sensitive topics such as illegal drug use, sexual practices, or traumatic experiences (Fallon & Schwab-Stone, 1994; Schwab-Stone, Fallon, & Briggs, 1994; Weiss et al., 1995). Conclusions about sensitive information tend to be less reliable in unstructured interviews (e.g., Rogers, 1995; 2001; Ruegg et al., 1990; Steiner et al., 1995).

Of course, sensitive information, rather than innocuous demographic information, is often of greatest interest to clinicians. For this reason, structured interviews have attracted a great deal of recent attention. Overall, the test-retest reliability of structured interviews tends to be +.70 or higher, even when the most sensitive information is requested for diagnostic or other purposes (e.g., Cohen & Vinson, 1995; Grant et al., 1995; Segal, Hersen, & Van Hasselt, 1994).[3]

Validity.　In 1968, Walter Mischel cited evidence that what people say they will do is a better predictor of future behavior than test scores are. Mischel's data reflect a view held by many clinicians today, namely that the validity, or accuracy, of interview data is superior to that of any other assessment source. Faith in the validity of interviews is also evident in employment practices; few employers hire without first drawing on impressions they formed during hiring interviews.

The most obvious threats to interview validity occur if clients misremember or purposely distort information. The probability of error or distortion increases when clients are mentally retarded (e.g., Heal & Sigelman, 1995), suffer from various brain disorders (e.g., West, Bondy, & Hutchinson, 1991), or would prefer not to reveal the truth about their behavior problems, drug use, sexual behavior, criminal activity, or previous hospitalizations (e.g., Morrison et al., 1995; Williams, 1994). At the other extreme, clients motivated to appear mentally disturbed may give inaccurate interview responses aimed at creating the appearance of a mental disorder. Concern about such *malingering* led to the creation of special interview methods aimed at detecting it (Rogers, Gillis, Dickens, & Bagby, 1991; see Table 4.2). In short, the desire to present oneself in a particular light to a mental health professional—called "impression-management" (Braginsky, Braginsky, & Ring, 1969)—can undermine the validity of interview data.

---

[3]Interrater reliability is often calculated by determining the overall agreement between raters. However, if a disorder occurs at a very low base rate, reliability can sometimes be artificially inflated. For instance, when one rater *never* judges a disorder as present and another rater, who is more discriminating, *infrequently* judges it present, the similarity in their ratings would be high *by chance alone*. To correct for this, researchers sometimes calculate *kappa*, a chance-corrected index of agreement that is usually lower than overall agreement.

As stated in Chapter 3, validity can be established in several ways, such as by including all of the relevant aspects of a target domain (content validity), by comparing interview results with other valid measures of the same concept (concurrent validity), or by an interview's ability to predict expected future outcomes (predictive validity). When clinicians select an external criterion as the standard against which an assessment tool is measured, that criterion is sometimes referred to as the *gold standard* (Komiti, Jackson, Judd, Cockram, Kyrios, Yeatman, et al., 2001). An odd situation sometimes occurs with decisions about the "gold standard." When structured diagnostic interviews are first developed, they are often validated against the gold standard of clinical judgment (e.g., Zetin & Glenn, 1999). Imagine, for instance, the development of a new structured interview to diagnose hypochondriasis. Developers decide to compare the results of their interview with diagnoses of hypochondriasis made by experienced clinicians. If the new structured interview agrees with clinical judgments, the interview's claim to validity is strengthened. Sometimes, however, it works the other way around—structured interviews become the "gold standard" against which clinical judgments are compared (e.g., Komiti et al., 2001). How can we evaluate structured interviews if they are first validated against clinical judgment and then later used as a standard for clinical judgment?

Greater confidence in validity of any assessment tool is warranted when it has been cross-validated with several indices. When an assessment tool correlates with several conceptually similar indices, it is said to have *convergent validity*. Validity is also strengthened by showing that a tool does not correlate with measures of conceptually different phenomena, known as *discriminant validity* (e.g., a structured interview for hypochondriasis should not correlate highly with measures of antisocial personality disorder unless there is a strong theoretical reason to do so). In general, structured interviews that have the highest validity, such as those in Table 4.2, have been cross-validated using multiple indices. Clinicians' faith in the validity of structured interviews, once developed, is reflected in the fact that the results of such interviews are often used as the standard for evaluating psychological tests. Thus, the validity of a test for depression, for example, will be seen as supported if clients' scores on the test correlate strongly with what they say about depression during a structured interview (Rogers, 1995, 2001).

Interviewer Error and Bias

Clinicians must also consider the ways in which they could introduce error into the assessment by biased processing of what the client has said or how the client behaved. Some errors are accidental, as when the volume of incoming information overwhelms the interviewer's memory capacity and results in the loss or distortion of information. This problem can be minimized by the use of note-taking or audio- or videotaping.

More worrisome is the possibility that personal biases might affect interviewers' perceptions and color their inferences and conclusions about what clients say during interviews. The role of such biases was noted nearly 70 years ago in a study showing that social workers' judgments of why "skid row bums" had become destitute were related to the interviewers' personal agendas, not just to what respondents said (Rice,

1929). Thus, an anti-alcohol interviewer saw drinking as the cause of poverty, while a socialist interviewer concluded that interviewees' plights stemmed from capitalist-generated economic conditions. Similarly, as discussed in Chapter 2, psychoanalysts and behavior therapists tend to draw different causal conclusions about the behavior problems clients describe during interviews (Plous & Zimbardo, 1986). Indeed, interview-based psychodiagnoses, job interview decisions, and the outcome of medical school admissions interviews may all be prejudiced by information that interviewers receive about interviewees prior to the interview (Dipboye, Stramler, & Fontenelle, 1984; Shaw et al., 1995; Temerlin, 1968).

Other biases or preconceptions about client characteristics can also affect interviewers' interpretations of interview data. In one large-scale study, for example, medical and mental health professionals were more likely to diagnose depression in female rather than male clients, whether or not these clients' interview responses met standard criteria for defining depressive disorders (Potts, Burnam, & Wells, 1991). Other studies conducted in mental health, employment, and other settings have shown that interviewers' judgments, evaluations, and conclusions can also be affected by clients' ethnicity (Singer & Eder, 1989; Tomlinson & Cheatham, 1989). These effects are not always large or significant, however (e.g., Garb, 1995; Williams, 1988; Williams & Heikes, 1993), and they can be further reduced through the use of structured interviews that provide clear rules about what to infer from particular interview responses. Computer-based interviewing can also help reduce the impact of interviewer preconceptions (Rodgers, 1987), as can training programs that sensitize interviewers to the potential effects of personal biases (Brown, 1990; Sinacore-Guinn, 1995).

To sum up, research on the interview as an assessment tool does not justify a single, all-encompassing conclusion. As one distinguished researcher put it, "The interview has been used in so many different ways for various purposes, by individuals with varying skills, that it is a difficult matter to make a final judgment concerning its values" (Garfield, 1974, p. 90). The skill of the interviewer is very important, but the exact nature of what "skill" means is still not clear. Although the interview will continue to occupy a primary assessment role in clinical psychology, it must also remain the object of research. Any tendency to view interviews as primarily an art form practiced by gifted clinicians and therefore exempt from scientifically rigorous examinations of reliability and validity will ultimately result in the loss of the interview's utility as an important assessment tool.

GOALS AND BENEFITS OF OBSERVATIONAL ASSESSMENT

Interviews provide not only verbal and nonverbal communication, but also opportunities to observe clients in a specific situation. Clinicians are often interested in observing client responses in other situations as well.

The goals of observational assessment systems are to (1) collect information that is not available in any other way, and/or (2) supplement other data as part of a multiple-assessment approach. For example, if a teacher and a pupil give different reports of why they fail to get along ("He's a brat." "She's mean."), a less-biased picture of the relationship will probably emerge from observations by neutral parties of relevant classroom interactions. In other instances, knowing what a person can or will do is so important that only observation can suffice. Thus, knowing that a mentally disturbed person feels better and wishes to leave the hospital may be less valuable than observing that person's ability to hold a job, use the bus system, and meet other demands of everyday life.

The more importance clinicians attach to observational data, the more systematic they are likely to be in gathering and analyzing those data. At one end of the spectrum are informal, anecdotal accounts of client behaviors occurring during tests or interviews. Clinicians who place greater emphasis on overt behavior improved on casual observation methods in at least two ways. First, they developed more accurate and systematic methods for observing and quantifying behavior. Second, they demonstrated the feasibility of collecting observational data in situations beyond the testing or interview room. Together, these developments make it possible for clinicians and researchers to observe scientifically a wide range of human behavior in a multitude of settings.

Collecting observational data can be a difficult, time-consuming, and expensive procedure, and the problems associated with this type of assessment discourage many clinicians from attempting to do it (Mash & Foster, 2001). Despite these obstacles, proponents of observational assessment argue that its benefits more than outweigh its difficulties, and they offer several reasons why observation is necessary if clinicians are to obtain a complete picture of their clients' functioning.

Supplementing Self-Reports

Self-reports gathered via interviews and some tests may be inaccurate. It is very difficult for most people to provide objective and dispassionate reports on their own behavior, especially in relation to highly charged emotional events. It is questionable, for example, whether a distressed couple can accurately and objectively describe their own behavior, especially behavior that occurs during arguments. Other clients, such as those with dementia, are sometimes unable to give accurate self-reports despite their best intentions to do so. Observational data are likely to provide much more valid information in these situations (Gottman & Levenson, 1992; Smallwood, Irvine, Coulter, & Connery, 2001).

In some cases, clients purposely distort their self-reports, usually by offering an overly positive portrayal of their behavior. Such distortions are particularly common in the self-reports of participants in smoking, drug, or alcohol treatment programs, which is the main reason why such reports are often supplemented by family members' observations or by biological measures that can detect target substances. Intentional distortions on personality tests such as the MMPI-2 are so widely recognized that special indicators have been devised to detect it when clients do not respond honestly (Berry, Baer, & Harris, 1991; Storm & Graham, 2000; see Chapter 5).

Even when clients try to give accurate reports, perceptual biases and expectations can easily cause them to misinterpret or misremember events (Dawes, 1986). Thus, parents who report that their child engages in "constant" temper tantrums are often surprised to learn that such tantrums actually occur an average of twice a day. If the tantrums are intense and upsetting enough to color the parents' perceptions, a clinician who gathers no observational data might get a distorted view of the target problem.

Highlighting Situational Determinants of Behavior

Much of traditional assessment is guided by the assumption that responses to interviews and tests are adequate for understanding clients' personalities and problems because these responses reflect traits that control behavior across differing situations and relatively long time periods. For clinicians adopting this view, observations are seen as *signs* of more fundamental, unobservable constructs. In contrast, clinicians who take a behavioral or cognitive-behavioral view tend to regard observational data as *samples* of behavior that help them understand important *person-situation interactions* rather than draw inferences about hypothesized personality characteristics or problems. Though all clinicians rely on observation, more systematic observational methods are usually associated with clinicians favoring a behavioral orientation.

These clinicians do not necessarily deny that traits or person variables help account for behavior (Mischel, 1993), but they argue that clinical assessment must also explore the role played by the larger context in which behavior occurs (Follette, 1996). Observational assessments allow the clinician to determine the circumstances under which problematic behaviors are most likely to occur, what situational stimuli tend to trigger the behaviors, and what reinforcing consequences in the situation serve to maintain the unwanted actions (Patterson, 1982). Traditional tests and interviews are not designed to accomplish this kind of functional analysis (Cairns & Green, 1979).

Minimizing Inference

Conducting observation-driven functional analyses allows clinicians to avoid the relatively high levels of inference associated with sign-oriented testing and interviewing approaches. Of course, some degree of inference is found in virtually any kind of clinical assessment. Even clinicians who employ systematic observational assessments realize that it is difficult, if not impossible, to eliminate all clinical inference, and they also know that a certain amount of inference may be justified, even desirable, at times. However, in the tradition of Sergeant Friday on the old "Dragnet" television series, observational procedures are designed to collect "just the facts," thereby minimizing the likelihood of drawing incorrect inferences about clients. Using observational data, clinicians can develop hypotheses about the causes or maintenance factors in behavior problems by looking at the specific antecedents and consequences surrounding those problems; they do not have to infer what the problems mean about the client.

Enhancing Ecological Validity

Advocates of observational assessment argue that it can provide the clearest possible picture of people and their problems because observations can occur in the physical and social environments where clients actually live their lives. Not only are these observations likely to be *ecologically valid*, they often provide situational details that help clinicians design treatment programs that can be most easily implemented in the home, school, or work environments where clients function every day. This custom-tailoring of interventions may increase the chances for treatment success. We will return to the issue of ecological validity later in the chapter.

Approaches to Observational Assessment

The appeal of observational assessment is that it provides a first-hand look at behaviors of clinical interest and yields many clues about the causes and treatment of those behaviors. What, exactly, does it entail?

Observational methods have been defined as "the *selection, provocation, recording,* and *encoding* of . . . behaviors" (Weick, 1968; italics added). This definition highlights the fundamental elements of nearly every type of observational system. The observer first *selects* people, classes of behavior, events, situations, or time periods to be the focus of attention. Second, a decision is made about whether to *provoke* (i.e., artificially bring about) behaviors and situations of interest or to wait for them to happen on their own. Third, plans are made to *record* observations using observer memory, record sheets, audio- or videotape, physiological monitoring systems, timers, counters, or other means. Finally, a system for *encoding* raw observations into usable form must be developed. Encoding is often the most difficult aspect of any observational procedure.

Differing assessment goals, unique client populations, specific environmental limitations, and other factors result in many approaches to clinical observation. The clearest way to organize this array is in terms of the observational *settings* employed. At one extreme is *naturalistic observation*, where the assessor looks at behavior as it occurs in its natural context (e.g., at home or school). *Controlled* observation lies at the other extreme, as the clinician or researcher sets up a special situation in which to observe behavior. Between these extremes are approaches that blend elements of both to handle specific assessment needs, thus creating many subtypes of both naturalistic and controlled observation. In some assessment situations, observers may be *participants* who are visible to the clients being watched and who may even interact with them (as when parents record their child's behavior). *Nonparticipant* observers are not visible, although in most cases the clients are aware that observation is taking place.

To present a reasonably complete picture of clinical observation, we describe naturalistic and controlled observational systems that focus on several kinds of behavior. The examples we have chosen will illustrate the use of (1) participant and nonparticipant observers; (2) human, mechanical/electronic, and combined recording procedures; and (3) informal and formal encoding systems that deal with behavior as samples and signs. More comprehensive coverage of this material is available in a number of sources (e.g., Bellack & Hersen, 1998; Ciminero, Calhoun, & Adams, 1986; Haynes & O'Brien, 2000; Repp & Horner, 2000).

NATURALISTIC OBSERVATION

Watching clients behave spontaneously in a natural setting such as their homes has several obvious advantages. Natural settings provide a background that is realistic and relevant for understanding the client's behavior and the factors influencing that behavior. Additionally, naturalistic observation can be done in ways that are subtle enough to provide a picture of behavior that is not distorted by client self-consciousness or motivation to convey a particular impression.

Naturalistic observation has been used to infer personality characteristics (Santostefano, 1962), intelligence (Lambert, Cox, & Hartsough, 1970), social goals (Brown, Odom, & Holcombe, 1996), and cognitive development (Schweinhart et al., 1993), but its primary focus has been on assessing the nature of, and changes in, problems that clinicians are asked to solve—everything from eating disorders, intrusive thoughts, maladaptive social interactions, and psychotic behavior to community problems such as classroom violence and littering (Haynes, 1990).

The classic case of naturalistic observation is the anthropological field study in which a scientist joins a tribe, subculture, or other social organization to observe its characteristics and the behavior of its members (e.g., Mead, 1928; Williams, 1967). In such cases, the observer is a participant in every sense of the term, and observations are usually recorded in anecdotal notes which later appear as a detailed account called an *ethnography*.

In its early forms, naturalistic clinical observation required observers to make decisions and draw inferences about what certain behaviors mean and which behaviors should or should not be recorded. As a result, the interobserver reliability of naturalistic observation suffered. Lee Cronbach (1960, p. 535) summarized the problem well: "Observers interpret what they see. When they make an interpretation, they tend to overlook facts which do not fit the interpretation, and they may even invent facts needed to complete the event as interpreted." Figure 4.1 shows how observations of the same client can differ. Attempts to improve anecdotal accounts in naturalistic clinical observation have taken many forms. To reduce unsystematic reporting of client behaviors, most modern observation schemes focus the observer's attention on specific behaviors. The frequency and intensity of these behaviors are then recorded on a checklist or rating scale. The observers are also trained to use these methods consistently so that interobserver reliability is as high as possible.

Another approach to naturalistic observation is to inspect the by-products of behavior. For example, school grades, arrest records, and court files have been used to evaluate the treatment of delinquent youth and adult offenders (Davidson et al., 1987; Rice, 1997); changes in academic grade point averages have served as indices of improvement in test anxiety (Allen, 1971). Life records, also called *institutional* or *product-of-behavior* measures (Haynes, 1990; Maisto & Maisto, 1983), are actually part of a broader observational approach, called *nonreactive* or *unobtrusive* measurement, that clinical psychologists and other behavioral scientists use to learn about people's behavior without altering it in the process (see Webb et al., 1966).

In clinical research, unobtrusive measures may be used to test theories about the causes of behavior problems. One research team, for example, was interested in the hypothesis that social isolation early in life, and particularly during adolescence, was related to a later diagnosis of schizophrenia (Barthell & Holmes, 1968). As a partial test of this hypothesis, they inspected the high school yearbooks of people labeled "schizophrenic" or "neurotic" and compared the activities listed for these individuals with nonlabeled students from the same schools. A similar use of life records is illustrated by research that relates factors such as age, marital status, employment history, and education to the development of schizophrenia and to chances for its improvement. Another creative use of unobtrusive measures in identifying the precursors of schizophrenia is

Observer A: (2) Robert reads word by word, using finger to follow place. (4) Observes girl in box with much preoccupation. (5) During singing, he in general doesn't participate too actively. Interest is part of time centered elsewhere. Appears to respond most actively to sections of song involving action. Has tendency for seemingly meaningless movement. Twitching of fingers, aimless thrusts of arms.

Observer B: (2) Looked at camera upon entering (seemed perplexed and interested). Smiled at camera. (2) Reads (with apparent interest and with a fair degree of facility). (3) Active in roughhouse play with girls. (4) Upon being kicked (unintentionally) by one girl he responded (angrily). (5) Talked with girl sitting next to him between singing periods. Participated in singing. (At times appeared enthusiastic.) Didn't always sing with others. (6) Participated in a dispute in a game with others (appeared to stand up for his own rights). Aggressive behavior toward another boy. Turned pockets inside out while talking to teacher and other students. (7) Put on overshoes without assistance. Climbed to top of ladder rungs. Tried to get rung which was occupied by a girl but since she didn't give in, contented himself with another place.

Observer C: (1) Smiles into camera (curious). When group break up, he makes nervous gestures, throws arm out into air. (2) Attention to reading lesson. Reads with serious look on his face, has to use line marker. (3) Chases girls, teases. (4) Girl kicks when he puts hand on her leg. Robert makes face at her. (5) Singing. Sits with mouth open, knocks knees together, scratches leg, puts fingers in mouth (seems to have several nervous habits, though not emotionally overwrought or self-conscious). (6) In a dispute over parchesi, he stands up for his rights. (7) Short dispute because he wants rung on jungle gym.

Observer D: (2) Uses guide to follow words, reads slowly, fairly forced and with careful formation of sounds (perhaps unsure of self and fearful of mistakes). (3) Perhaps slightly aggressive as evidenced by pushing younger child to side when moving from a position to another. Plays with other children with obvious enjoyment, smiles, runs, seems especially associated with girls. This is noticeable in games and in seating in singing. (5) Takes little interest in singing, fidgets, moves hands and legs (perhaps shy and nervous). Seems in song to be unfamiliar with words of main part, and shows disinterest by fidgeting and twisting around. Not until chorus is reached does he pick up interest. His special friend seems to be a particular girl, as he is always seated by her.

FIGURE 4.1 Four observations of the same client. Notice the differing images and inferences generated by four observers who watched a ten-minute film, *This is Robert*, which showed a boy in classroom and playground situations. (The observers were told to use parentheses to indicate inferences or interpretation. The numbers used refer to scenes in the film and were inserted to aid comparison.) SOURCE: Excerpts from pages 534–535 from *Essentials of Psychological Testing* 5th Ed. by Lee J. Cronbach. Copyright 1949. © 1984 by Harper and Row, Publishers, Inc. Copyright © 1960, 1970, 1990 by Lee J. Cronbach.

seen in a study which took advantage of the fact that many families today make video-tapes of their children as they grow (Walker et al., 1993). In this study, trained observers analyzed childhood videotapes of individuals who later became schizophrenic, as well as of their same-sex siblings who did not. The results revealed that, long before they were diagnosed, the schizophrenics-to-be showed significantly more negative facial expressions than the other children (some of the differences appeared before the children were 4 years old).

In the following sections, we consider a set of naturalistic observation systems that, while not entirely unobtrusive, do allow for recording the frequency, intensity, duration, or form of specific categories of behaviors by persons who are both familiar to clients and in a position to observe them in a minimally intrusive way.

Hospital Observations

Observations of hospitalized patients is an important component of their assessment. The Inpatient Multidimensional Psychiatric Scales, or IMPS (Lorr, McNair, & Klett, 1966), is an excellent example of a hospital observation system that can be used by ward staff. The IMPS contains 75 items, which are either rated by the observer on 5- or 9-point scales or responded to with a yes or no. These data are translated into scores on dimensions such as excitement, hostile belligerence, paranoid projection, grandiose expansiveness, disorientation, and conceptual disorganization. The scores can then be plotted as a profile describing the observed client. A more recent example of such systems include the Routine Assessment of Patient Progress, or RAPP (Ehmann et al., 1995).

Other hospital observation systems not only specify the targets to be recorded, but also reduce the observer/coder inferences required by having observers record a client's behavior as it occurs. When such observations are made at regular intervals (e.g., once per hour), the process is called *time sampling*. When only certain activities are observed and recorded (e.g., social interactions or aggressive episodes), the method is called *event sampling*. These techniques are often combined, as when observations are made once per minute during meals or on other occasions. One example of the former is the Time-Sample Behavioral Checklist (TSBC) (Paul & Lentz, 1977; Paul & Licht, 1987), which was developed to allow trained observers to assess a large number of behaviors displayed by psychiatric inpatients.

School Observations

The desire to observe children's behavior for clinical purposes has spawned a number of systems for use in schools, playgrounds, and similar settings (Ollendick & Greene, 1990). In the tradition of early experimental sociologists (e.g., Dawe, 1934), recording and coding systems designed by Sidney Bijou (Bijou, Peterson, & Ault, 1968) and Daniel O'Leary (O'Leary & Becker, 1967) use symbols to represent the behavior of children and the adults around them during time-sample observations. Like other observation systems of this type, the data gathered can be summarized in quantitative form. In this case, percentages can be calculated to summarize how much time a child spends on-task, out-of-seat, or talking to other children. Classroom observation may focus on a single child and those with whom the child interacts, or an observer can sequentially attend to and assess the behavior of several target children or even of a whole class (Milich & Fitzgerald, 1985).

Home Observations

Observational assessment procedures are also available to measure clinically relevant behaviors in clients' homes. As was the case in other areas, early home-based clinical observations allowed much inference and rather unsystematic target selection (e.g., Ackerman, 1958). More reliable home observation systems have now evolved. One of the first of these was designed by Gerald Patterson (Patterson et al., 1969) for use in the homes of conduct-disordered children. After obtaining consent to do so, Patterson places trained observers in the client's living area for an hour or two on each of several days, usually just before dinner. The observers avoid interacting with the family and concentrate on using Patterson's Family Interaction Coding System to record the behavior of one member at a time as well as the family member with whom the person interacted. It is thus possible to record the target child's inappropriate behavior as well as the antecedents and consequences of this behavior (Patterson, 1982). Other home observation systems are available as well (see McIntyre et al., 1983), some of which have been used not only to assess individual clients but to gather data on how certain parental behaviors contribute to children's maladjustment (e.g., Forehand et al., 1986). Recently, structural equation modeling and other complex mathematical procedures have been applied to the analysis of data flowing from these systems (e.g., Melby et al., 1995).

More complex recording and encoding systems are usually needed when the goal is to observe adult interactions at home. For example, in a study of social skills in depressed clients (Lewinsohn & Shaffer, 1971), the system used to encode time-sampled observations of family interactions at mealtimes categorized verbal behavior as self-initiated *actions* (questions, comments, requests for information, complaints) or positive and negative *reactions* to the behavior of others (approval, laughter, criticism, disagreement). These dimensions were then used to examine differences between depressed and nondepressed persons (e.g., Johnson & Jacob, 1997; Libet & Lewinsohn, 1973), as well as changes in depressed behavior as a function of treatment.

Observations by Insiders

The naturalistic observation systems we have described so far employ specially trained personnel as participant or nonparticipant observers. Because some researchers question whether these outsiders can do their job without inadvertently influencing the behavior they are to watch, some observations are conducted by persons who are part of the client's day-to-day world. The IMPS data collected by nurses or other ward staff is an example of such a system.

Another example is the Child Behavior Checklist (Achenbach, 1994). The CBCL is one of several instrument gaining popularity among those interested in assessing behavior problems in children and adolescents. In addition to an overall score, it yields scores on eight factors: withdrawn, somatic complaints, anxious/depressed, social problems, thought problems, attention problems, delinquent behavior, and aggressive behavior. As with all instruments, the CBCL faces challenges to its validity and its cross-cultural generality. Such challenges must be resolved by ongoing evaluation efforts such as a recent study by Heubeck (2000) which found that approximately 90% of the items on the

CBCL showed convergent validity across samples from Holland, Australia, and the USA. It takes considerable time and effort to examine whether results from any instrument hold across different populations, but the effort is critical if we are to learn the limitations of an assessment instrument such as the CBCL.

The use of insiders as observers of adult behavior for clinical purposes is less common, but not unknown. For example, in helping clients quit smoking, a clinician may ask for corroborative reports of success or failure from family members or friends (e.g., Mermelstein, Lichtenstein, & McIntyre, 1983). Such reports may also be solicited as part of the assessment of alcoholism (e.g., Foy, Nunn, & Rychtarik, 1984), sexual activity (e.g., Rosen & Kopel, 1977), marital violence (Jouriles & O'Leary, 1985), and other adult behaviors (Margolin, Michelli, & Jacobson, 1988).

Self-Observation

Although insiders usually have a less-obstructed view of a client's behavior than an outside observer would, no one spends as much time with the client as the client. In many clinical and research settings, therefore, clients are asked to observe and record their own behavior using a procedure called *self-monitoring*. Though usually done by adults, self-monitoring can be done successfully by children as well.

Self-monitoring requires clients to record the frequency, location, duration or intensity of events such as exercise, headaches, pleasant thoughts, hair pulling, giving or receiving praise, pain, and so on. Self-monitoring diaries might also be used for recording smoking behavior, eating habits, stress, sleep disorders, anxiety disorders, health-promoting behaviors, or many other concerns. Unfortunately, self-monitoring can be *reactive*, meaning that the mere act of self-observation might alter the observed behavior. Further, the effects of reactivity are difficult to predict; self-monitoring sometimes increases and sometimes decreases the rate of observed behavior (Kanfer & Gaelick, 1986; Nelson, 1977).

CONTROLLED OBSERVATION

The major appeal of naturalistic observation is that it yields large samples of spontaneous client behavior occurring under circumstances of greatest relevance and interest to the clinician. The assets of naturalistic observation can become liabilities, however, especially when observation targets occur infrequently. Suppose, for example, that the clinician wants to observe a client's response to stress. Using naturalistic procedures, the client's behavior would have to be continuously monitored in all settings where stressful events might occur. However, there is no guarantee that the client will actually encounter clinically relevant stress in a given situation, so much time and effort could be wasted.

Further, as its name implies, naturalistic observation usually takes place in an uncontrolled environment, so even if a stressor occurs, unanticipated events can interfere with the assessment: The client may move out of the observer's line of vision or might get help from someone else in dealing with the stressor. How would the client have reacted without help? The assessor would not know unless the same situation recurs when the client is alone and under observation. The fact that the situation of interest may not soon recur points to another limitation of naturalistic observation: Repeated assessment of a client's reaction to low-probability events is difficult. This problem is important because comparison of the behavior of many people under identical conditions is a cornerstone of many experimental designs and assessment approaches.

One way of getting around some of the difficulties associated with naturalistic observation is to set up special circumstances under which clients can be observed as they react to planned, standardized events. This approach is usually called *controlled observation* because it allows clinicians to maintain control over the assessment stimuli in much the same way as they do when giving the psychological tests described in Chapter 5. Controlled observations are also referred to as *analogue behavior observation* (ABO), *situation tests*, and *contrived observations*.

During World War II, military psychologists devised controlled observations for assessing personality traits as well as behavioral capabilities. In the Operational Stress Test, for example, would-be pilots were asked to manipulate the controls of an aircraft flight simulator. The candidates did not know that the tester was purposely trying to frustrate them by giving increasingly complicated instructions accompanied by negative feedback (e.g., "You're making too many errors"; Melton, 1947). During the test, the assessor rated the candidate's reaction to criticism and stress, and these ratings supplemented objective data on skill with the simulator.

Traits of initiative, dominance, cooperation, and group leadership were inferred from observational assessments developed by the staff of the Office of Strategic Services (OSS; later to become the CIA) to help select espionage agents and other special personnel. One example was a construction test, in which a candidate was assigned to build a 5-foot cube-shaped frame out of large wooden poles and blocks resembling a giant Tinker Toy® set. Because the test was supposed to measure the candidate's organizational and leadership ability, he was given two "assistants" (actually, psychologists) who called themselves Buster and Kippy.

> Kippy acted in a passive, sluggish manner. He did nothing at all unless specifically ordered to, but stood around, often getting in the way. . . . Buster, on the other hand, . . . was aggressive, forward in offering impractical suggestions, ready to express dissatisfaction, and quick to criticize what he suspected were the candidate's weakest points. . . . It was their function to present the candidate with as many obstructions and annoyances as possible in ten minutes. As it turned out, they succeeded in frustrating the candidates so thoroughly that the construction was never . . . completed in the allotted time. (OSS, 1948, p. 103)

Since World War II, milder versions of the OSS situational tests have been used for personnel selection. In current clinical and research settings, controlled observations take many forms. In some cases, the "control" consists of asking clients (usually couples, families, or parent–child pairs) to come to a clinic or laboratory and have a discussion, attempt to solve a problem, or just talk while under observation by TV cameras, tape recorders, or human coders (e.g., Hahlweg, Revenstorf, & Schindler, 1984; Johnson & Jacob, 1997). In other instances, clients are presented with a structured task or situation designed to elicit behaviors of relevance to clinical assessment (e.g., Humphrey, Apple, & Kirschenbaum, 1986).

Role-Playing Tests

Psychologists sometimes create make-believe situations in which the client is asked to *role-play* his or her typical behavior. Role-playing has been advocated by clinicians for many years (e.g., Borgatta, 1955) and serves as the cornerstone for several group, psychodynamic, and humanistic treatments (e.g., Moreno, 1946; Perls, 1969). However, it was not until the late 1960s that role playing became part of systematic clinical assessment. Its most common use in controlled observation has been in the assessment of social competency, self-expression, and assertiveness.

Role-playing tests have become a standard ingredient in the observational assessment of children's social and safety skills (Harbeck, Peterson, & Starr, 1992), parent–child interactions (Jouriles & Farris, 1992), depressive behavior (Bellack, Hersen, & Himmelhoch, 1983), and the social competence and conversational skills of socially anxious or chronically mentally ill persons (Bellack et al., 1990; Dilk & Bond, 1996; Norton & Hope, 2001). In most role-plays, the clients' responses are videotaped and then rated by observers on any of dozens of criteria such as appropriateness of content, level of positive and refusal assertiveness, anxiety, latency to respond, response duration, speech dysfluencies, posture, eye contact, gaze, hand gestures, head movements, and voice volume.

A number of variables influence the way people respond to role-playing assessments. Instructions to behave as one naturally would versus instructions to behave as an assertive person would have been shown to produce very different behavior (Kazdin, Esveldt-Dawson, & Matson, 1983; Rodriguez, Nietzel, & Berzins, 1980; Wallace et al., 1992). The content of the scenes used in role plays (Nelson et al., 1985), their level of difficulty (Kolotkin, 1980), the responses of the experimenter to the client (Kirchner & Draguns, 1979), and the social impact of role-played behavior (Kern, Cavell, & Beck, 1985) also influence performance. As investigators have learned about the impact of these and other variables, they have modified role-playing methods to make them more realistic and more diagnostic of the specific problems of individual clients. For example, the Extended Interaction Test assesses the generality and robustness of clients' assertiveness skills by presenting a tape-recorded antagonist who makes a series of gradually escalating unreasonable requests and demands (McFall & Lillesand, 1971). Here is an excerpt from the Extended Interaction Test:

> Narrator: You are feeling really pressed for study time because you have an exam on Friday afternoon. Now, you are studying at your desk, when a close friend comes in and says, "Hi, Guess what. My parents just called and offered to pay for a plane ticket so I can fly home this weekend. Great, huh!? The only problem is, I'll have to skip my Friday morning class, and I hate to miss out on those notes; I'm barely making it in there as it is. Look, I know you aren't in that class, but it'd really be a big help if you'd go to the class Friday and take notes for me so I could go home. Would you do that for me?"

> If subject refuses, the tape continues:

> "I guess it is kinda crazy to expect you to do it, but, gee, I've got so many things to do if I'm gonna get ready to leave, and I don't want to waste the time asking around. Come on, will you do it for me this once?"

If subject refuses, the tape continues:

"Look, what're friends for if they don't help each other out of a bind? I'd do it for you if you asked. What do you say, will you?"

If subject refuses, the tape continues:

"But I was counting on you to do it. I'd hate to have to call my folks back and tell them I'm not coming. Can't you spare just one hour to help me out?"

If subject refuses, the tape continues (sarcastically):

"Now look, I don't want to impose on your precious time. Just tell me. Will you do it or do I have to call my folks back?"

Presumably, a person who withstands repeated requests is more assertive than one who gives in after an initial refusal. The Extended Interaction Test provides but one example of assessing the generality of client behavior through controlled observation. Some administer various role-play items to measure the range of situations in which a client is skilled or assertive (e.g., Edelstein & Eisler, 1976), while others attempt to observe the client in naturalistic settings (e.g., Kazdin, Matson, & Esveldt-Dawson, 1984). Because the first strategy may not be realistic and because the second is difficult to arrange, a third approach, called the *staged naturalistic event* is sometimes used. The idea here is to look at behavior in a controlled setting that appears naturalistic to the client (Gottman & Markman, 1978). For example, unobtrusive role-playing tests have been used to measure social skills in psychiatric inpatients (Goldsmith & McFall, 1975). In these tests, the client is asked to meet and carry on a conversation with a stranger (actually an assistant to the clinician) who has been instructed to confront the client with three "critical moments": not catching the client's name, responding to a lunch invitation with an excuse that left open the possibility of lunch at another time, and saying "Tell me about yourself" at the first convenient pause in the conversation. Similar contrived situations have been used in other psychiatric settings (Holmes, Hansen, & St. Lawrence, 1984), with children (Saywitz & Snyder, 1996), and with college students (Kern, 1982).

Of course, observations involving deception and possible invasion of privacy must be set up with care and with regard for clients' welfare and dignity. Proponents of unobtrusive controlled observation try to avoid its potential dangers and point out that its value may be limited to measuring specific behaviors (such as refusal) rather than more complex interactive social skills.

Performance Measures

In most of the controlled observations described in the previous section, the client is asked to act as if an event were taking place. In other controlled observational assessments, however, clients actually face a clinically relevant situation. Controlled observations of performance have focused on behaviors such as eating, drinking, or smoking. For example, the eating style (amount, speed, preferences) of normal or obese individuals has been recorded during a meal or snack in a controlled setting (Spiegel, Wadden, & Foster, 1991). Alcoholic and nonalcoholic drinkers have been observed in specially constructed cocktail lounges or living rooms located in hospitals (Collins, Parks, & Marlatt, 1985). The details of cigarette use (puff rate, depth of inhalation, number of puffs) have been scrutinized in volunteers smoking in simulated social settings (Ossip-Klein et al., 1983).

Physiological Measures. Other performance tests measure physiological activity—such as heart rate, respiration, blood pressure, galvanic skin response, muscle tension, and brain waves—that appears in relation to various stimuli. An early example was provided by a study of forehead muscle tension in a headache patient as she watched a film about headaches (Malmo, Shagass, & Davis, 1950). In recent years, clinical psychologists have increased their use of such physiological measures because (1) they have become much more involved in studying insomnia, headache, chronic pain, sexual dysfunctions, gastrointestinal disorders, diabetes, and other disorders that have clear physiological components; and (2) assessment of physiological responses becomes crucial in evaluating treatments for several of these disorders.

Physiological measures are also important in the assessment of sexual arousal, particularly arousal in response to socially inappropriate stimuli. In one such performance assessment system, male subjects listen to or watch tapes that present various types of erotic behavior involving appropriate and inappropriate sexual stimuli. While the tape is playing, a strain gauge attached to the subject's penis records changes in its circumference. Greater erectile responses to the taped material are assumed to signal higher levels of sexual arousal. Several studies have shown rapists have equal or greater arousal to rape stimuli than to scenes of consenting sexual activity (Hall, 1990). In contrast, nonrapists usually show less sexual excitation in response to rape scenes. Similar procedures have been used in the diagnosis of pedophilia (Freund & Watson, 1991) and in the identification of child molesters (Haywood, Grossman, & Cavanaugh, 1990). Unfortunately, the expected patterns of arousal are not found consistently enough to ensure that physiological measures are valid measures of deviant sexual arousal.

Assessment of the physiology of fear in controlled settings has also occupied many clinical researchers. A classic example was Gordon Paul's (1966) use of measures of heart rate and sweating taken just before giving a talk to help identify speech-anxious clients. These measures were repeated following various anxiety-reduction treatments to aid in the evaluation of their effects (see also Nietzel, Bernstein, & Russell, 1988). With increased interest in the role of psychological factors in health and illness (see Chapter 11), the use of physiological recording devices in clinical assessment probably will continue to increase as well. This is especially likely now that many companies are able to market relatively inexpensive, portable recording devices.

Having ever more precise measurements of the physiological responses that occur while clients experience fear, anger, or other intense emotions is helping psychologists to better understand emotional behavior and emotional disorders (Lang, 1995). For example, better physiological measures have led to new theories of and treatments for such serious problems as posttraumatic stress disorder.

Behavioral Avoidance Tests (BATs). Another popular performance measure in controlled observation is the behavioral avoidance test, or BAT, which is designed to assess overt anxiety in relation to specific objects and situations. In BATs, clients are confronted with a stimulus they fear while observers record the type and degree of avoidance displayed. Informal BATs were conducted with children as early as the 1920s (e.g., Jones, 1924a, b), but it was not until the early 1960s that systematic avoidance-testing procedures became a common form of controlled observational assessment.

In a study of systematic desensitization (see Chapter 7) for snake phobia, Peter Lang and David Lazovik (1963) asked clients to enter a room containing a harmless caged snake and to approach, touch, and pick up the animal. Observers gave the clients avoidance scores based on whether they were able to look at, touch, or hold the snake. Many other fear stimuli, including rats, spiders, cockroaches, and dogs have been used in other versions of the BAT, and the "look–touch–hold" coding system for scoring responses has been replaced by more sophisticated measures. These include recording how close the client is able to come to the fear target, maximum amount of interaction achieved, length of time between entering the test room and making physical contact with the target, overt anxiety behaviors during the test, and changes in physiological arousal (heart rate, respiration, galvanic skin response). Usually, clients are asked to approach the feared target, but occasionally BATs are set up to measure how long clients can look at a frightening stimulus or how close they will allow that stimulus to approach them.

A recent development in performance-based observational assessment is made possible by computer technology. With sophisticated computer equipment, it is now possible to produce simulated environments to which clients react. Thus, *virtual reality assessment and treatment* has begun to appear on the horizon. For example, researchers at the Department of Biomedical Engineering Graduate School in Korea exposed clients suffering from agoraphobia to a virtual environment tunnel scene of a traffic jam. They measured the clients' blood pressure, respiration, and heart rate. They also collected subjective measures of fear and anxiety. Unfortunately, though some of the patients showed elevated levels, most reported that they were unable to become immersed in the virtual environment, so the therapy treatment was not conducted. The authors recommended improving the simulation (Jang, Ku, Shin, Choi, Kim, 2000). At this point, it is unclear to what extent virtual reality assessment procedures will be developed, but the use of virtual reality in both assessment and treatment is receiving attention (see Rothbaum, Hodges, Smith, Lee, & Price, 2000). Clinicians may some day be able to assess and treat persons with phobias more effectively by using computer-generated phobia scenario simulators.

RESEARCH ON OBSERVATIONAL ASSESSMENT

As noted in Chapter 3, direct observation of behavior can help avoid many inference problems that reduce the reliability and validity of some interview and test procedures. Behaviorally oriented clinicians, the most enthusiastic proponents of observational assessment, have argued that this approach provides the most accurate and relevant source of clinical assessment data. Observations have even been likened to photographs in that they are thought to provide a clear and dispassionate view of human behavior. But just as a photograph is the combined product of the content of the scene, the equipment used, the photographer's techniques, and the developing process, data from observational procedures are influenced by factors other than the behavior of clients. Some of these factors can distort observational assessment, meaning that observations are not automatically reliable and valid.

To illustrate, consider a situation in which a clinician decides to include observational procedures as part of an assessment battery for a distressed couple. A controlled situation is set up in which the couple is videotaped as they talk about one of their problems and attempt to resolve it. Later, the videotape is scored by trained observers using a coding system. A summary of the couple's behavior would result, and it might be inferred that the tape conveyed a representative sample of how the members of the pair relate to one another. This observational procedure is direct and apparently objective, but is it reliable and valid?

Reliability of Observational Assessment

To what extent do observers arrive at the same ratings or conclusions about the behavior they see? Fortunately, the interobserver reliability of modern clinical observation systems that use trained observers is usually very high; coefficients in excess of .80 and .90 are not uncommon (Paul & Lentz, 1977; Ward & Naster, 1991; Zuardi, Loureiro, & Rodrigues, 1995). When clients observe their own behavior through self-monitoring, agreement between their data and those of external observers is sometimes in the .90s (Kazdin, 1974). Reliability figures may be inflated by certain calculations, such as including every instance of when two recorders agree that a low base rate event did *not* occur, so it is important to know whether mathematical procedures to correct such problems have been used (see footnote 3 on page 149). When such procedures are used and high reliabilities are still found, it is usually because the clinical assessor has avoided some of the pitfalls, caused by the following factors, that can threaten the reliability of observational data (see Cone & Foster, 1982).

If observers must make many difficult discriminations in recording, coding, or rating behavior, reliability will probably be lower than if fewer, easier judgments are required (Mash & McElwee, 1974). Reducing *task complexity* often increases reliability (e.g., the observer uses a fifteen-category rather than a one-hundred-category coding system). *Observer training* can also affect reliability. Whether a clinician or assistants observe, if they intend to record laughter, for instance, but are not given a definition of laughter, one observer might count belly laughs but not giggles, while another might include everything from smiles to violent guffaws. Finally, when people are first trained to use an observation system, they usually work hard during practice sessions and pay close attention to the task, partly because they are being evaluated. Later, when "real" data are being collected, the observers may become careless if they think no one is checking their reliability (Taplin & Reid, 1973). Accordingly, supervision of persons doing observation and coding is sometimes necessary.

Validity of Observational Assessment

Are observational procedures measuring what they are supposed to measure, and how well are they doing it? At first glance, observation of behavior would appear to rank highest in validity among all clinical assessment approaches. Instead of hearing about behavior in interviews or speculating about behavior through tests, the clinician using observation can watch the "real thing."

To a certain extent, however, the directness or face validity of clinical observation has led to a deemphasis on measuring its validity in traditional terms (Cone, 1988). After all, if we observe aggression in our married couple, are we not assessing aggression, and is that not enough to establish the validity of our technique? The answer is yes only if we can show that (1) the behaviors coded (e.g., raised voices) constitute a satisfactory definition of aggression, (2) the data faithfully reflect the nature and degree of aggression occurring during observation, and (3) the clients' behaviors while under observation accurately represent their behavior in related, but unobserved, situations.

When numerous nonparticipant observers repeatedly report that a child engages in violent, unprovoked attacks on siblings and peers at home and in school, and when these data agree in detail with the reports of parents and teachers, the validity of the observational data seems well-established. Still, there are a number of factors that can threaten the validity of observation.

Defining Observation Targets. A fundamental requirement for establishing the validity of observational assessment is clarifying the target to be measured. Thus, instructions to observers about what aspects of behavior to look for and code, and how these targets are defined, reflect the assessor's view of what constitutes assertiveness. One clinician might assess assertiveness by observing clients' ability to refuse unreasonable requests, while another might focus on the direct expression of positive affect. This problem of definition may never be resolved to everyone's satisfaction, but evaluating the validity of an observational system begins with questions about what behavioral features are being coded.

Another way to assess the validity of observation is to ask to what extent the resulting data correlate as expected with other criteria. For example, does the ability to refuse unreasonable requests occur more often in people judged to be assertive by their peers? If the observation system is targeting an important part of a phenomenon of interest, meaningful relationships of this type should emerge (Foster et al., 1988). Clinicians who assume that such relationships exist, but don't measure them, run the risk of collecting samples of behavior whose validity is minimal beyond the confines of the clinicians' idiosyncratic target definitions.

Observer Effects. Clinicians and researchers must attend to several issues relating to observer accuracy. Just as interviewers sometimes remember certain client responses more accurately than others, observers can also make mistakes. The quality of observational data can be compromised by observer bias (Harris & Lahey, 1982). The effects of bias are stronger when observers are asked to make broad, general ratings about behavior after getting information about what to expect (e.g., Martell & Willis,

1993). In one study of this phenomenon, psychiatrists, psychologists, and graduate students listened to a taped interview in which an actor portrayed a well-adjusted man (Temerlin, 1968). When they listened under neutral conditions, 57% of the observers rated the man as "healthy," while 43% called him "neurotic." No one thought he was psychotic. However, ratings were biased if the tape was described as either that of a "perfectly healthy man" or a person who "looks neurotic but actually is psychotic." In the healthy-bias condition, 100% of the listeners rated the man as "healthy," but in the psychotic-bias condition, an average of nearly 30% diagnosed the man "psychotic," and over 60% called him "neurotic."

Representativeness of Observed Behavior.   In addition to worrying about observer bias, clinicians using observational assessment must be concerned about clients under observation intentionally or unintentionally altering the behaviors that are of greatest clinical interest. Awareness of the *reactivity* of clinical observation has a long history (Covner, 1942), but the magnitude of the problem is still unclear.

To be on the safe side, it would appear that clinicians should observe clients as unobtrusively as possible (using two-way mirrors and hidden video cameras), or at least schedule assessment sessions that are long enough to give clients ample time to become used to being observed (Haynes & Horn, 1982).

Even after reactive effects have disappeared, observed behavior may not provide a representative or ecologically valid (Brunswick, 1947) picture of the client. There is a certain irony to this criticism, because it implies that observations fail to meet the main goal for which they were designed. However, the problem arises because the high cost of observations often limits the number of occasions on which they are made. Therefore, any idiosyncratic events that may arise on those occasions can undermine the validity of the observation. For example, the client might have a hangover on the day of an observation, or there may have been a recent death in the family. Any number of factors can result in temporary patterns of depressed, euphoric, or hyperactive behavior that are atypical of the client.

Further, the observation situation itself can exert an influence on client behavior through social cues, or *demand characteristics* (Orne, 1962), that suggest what actions are, or are not, appropriate and expected. Thus, if a clinician observes a couple in a setting that contains strong social cues about how the clients should behave (e.g., "We would like to measure just how much fighting you two actually do."), the observation may reveal a degree of conflict that is unusually high for that couple. For example, in a study designed to measure assertiveness, college students were asked to respond to tape-recorded social situations similar to those described earlier (Nietzel & Bernstein, 1976). The assertiveness of their responses was scored on a five-point scale. All subjects heard the tape twice, under either the same or differing demand situations. The "low-demand" situation asked subjects for their "natural reactions," but in the "high-demand" situation they were told to be "as assertive as you think the most assertive and forceful person could be." The results are summarized in Figure 4.2. Obviously, these instructions not only had an initial effect, but were capable of significantly altering subjects' behavior from test to test. Other research on observational anxiety assessment has shown that the instructions given, the presence or absence of an experimenter, the

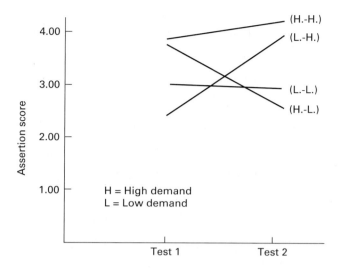

FIGURE 4.2 Situational effects on observed assertiveness. (Nietzel & Bern-

characteristics of the physical setting, and other situational variables influence the amount of fear clients display during BATs (e.g., Bernstein, 1973; Bernstein & Nietzel, 1977). Demand characteristics may also influence the symptoms of mental disorder observed in psychotherapy. Some researchers believe, for example, that the dramatic changes in clients' behavior and emotion seen in cases of dissociative identity disorder (formerly multiple personality disorder) may be a response to cues coming from therapists during treatment sessions (Spanos, 1994).

Various strategies have been suggested to minimize situational bias in observational assessment (Bernstein & Nietzel, 1977; Borkovec & O'Brien, 1976), but the problem cannot be entirely eliminated. As long as the stimuli present when the client's behavior is being observed differ from those present when the client is not being observed, we cannot be sure that the behavior displayed during formal observation will generalize to other situations. The best clinicians can do is minimize any cues that might influence client behavior. Utterly naturalistic or unobtrusive observation is theoretically possible, but often not practical. Accordingly, clinicians will continue to rely on contrived, analogue observations to assess some behavioral targets.

Trends in the Use of Observations Methods

Behaviorally-oriented clinicians were at the forefront of developing observational assessment. Over the past two decades, however, behavioral and cognitive approaches to assessment have tended to merge. This trend has affected observational assessment as well, primarily by including client cognitions as targets during behavioral observations. Cognitions are inherently unobservable, so their inclusion in behaviorally-oriented observations seems to violate the spirit of traditional behaviorism. However, the practice is increasingly accepted because 1) evidence about the role of cognition in mental health and illness has been convincing, and 2) some clinicians have become discouraged that years of atheoretical, sample-oriented behavioral observations have not led to theories that guide clinical practice (see Fincham, 1999). Recent examples of including cognitions include asking clients to *think aloud* at particular points during an observation. Sometimes this *thought sampling* is prompted by a beeper or other device (Groth-Marnat, 1999). Clients might also be asked to report their thoughts at particular points in a videotape as a clinician replays it for them (Sanders & Dadds, 1992).

Naturalistic and informal observation remains a fundamental source of data for most clinicians, but the same cannot be said for many controlled observation. In 1984, only 20% of the American Association of Behavior Therapists recommended the clinical use of controlled observational methods (Piotrowski & Keller, 1984), and more recent surveys continue to show that controlled or analog behavioral observations receive little attention in clinical practice and in graduate training programs (Mash & Foster, 2001). Researchers remain interested in developing and extending the use of systematic observational methods, but clinicians have not made these methods a staple of their practice.

Several reasons are offered for the underutilization. The most prominent reasons relate to pragmatic concerns such as time and money. It takes considerable time and resources to undertake some of the observations we have described. There are situations to construct, coding systems to learn, observers to hire and train, data to compile and encode. While these activities are standard fare for research clinicians in university-based clinics and training hospitals, they exceed the resources of most practicing clinicians. Some practitioners are also concerned that the content and presentation of controlled observational methods are not standardized in ways that, for example, the MMPI-2 or WAIS-III are (Norton & Hope, 2001). Combine these concerns with the limited accessibility to, and lack of detailed information for, all but a few of the most popular observational techniques and it becomes clear why clinicians have not adopted them the way they have adopted more available and cost-effective psychological tests or structured interviews (which are like tests in many respects). Mash and Foster (2001, p. 13) conclude that "ABO [analog behavioral observation] has what may generously be described as a promising but disappointing track record as a method of clinical assessment."

It may be fair to say instead that controlled behavioral observation has had an indirect influence on clinical practice. Indeed, psychological assessment has moved toward trying to identify specific behaviors and cognitions associated with specific contexts, a direction entirely compatible with the goals of behavioral observation assessment (and, it seems, a direction favored by managed care providers).

Perhaps the biggest challenge still facing clinicians is to translate often cumbersome, expensive, and time-consuming procedures into a practical approach for collecting observational data that has clear utility in practice. In addition, the clinician or researcher must observe in a way that minimizes the influence of the various distorting factors we have discussed, so that the data generated can have maximum value in an overall assessment plan.

CHAPTER SUMMARY

Interviews are defined as conversations with a purpose, and, in clinical situations, these purposes include client intake, problem-referral, orientation, termination, crisis intervention, and observation. In nondirective interviews, the clinician interferes as little as possible with the client's speech, while structured interviews present planned inquiries in a fixed sequence. Semistructured interviews fall between these extremes.

Most interviews have a beginning, a middle, and an end. Intake and problem-identification interviews, for example, usually begin with efforts at making the client comfortable, enter an information-gathering middle stage, and end with a summary and discussion. Conducting each phase of an interview and moving smoothly from one to the next requires a combination of common sense, active listening skills, well-phrased questions, and tact. If interviews are to have maximum value, communication between client and interviewer must be as clear as possible in both verbal and nonverbal channels.

While the reliability of interviews, especially structured interviews, is generally good, it can depend on several variables, including how questions are phrased, the client's comfort with the interviewer, emotional state, memory skills, and motivation. Reliability and validity can both be threatened by interviewer errors or biases, especially those relating to preconceived views of clients with particular characteristics. Eliminating such errors and biases is a major challenge for clinicians.

Observational assessment systems are designed to collect information about clients that is not available in other ways or that corrects for biases inherent in other assessment methods (e.g., biases in self-reports from interviews). Observation can be conducted in naturalistic or controlled settings (or some blend of the two) by participant or nonparticipant observers. Sometimes, clients are asked to observe and record their own behavior, a procedure called self-monitoring.

Naturalistic observation systems have been developed for use in hospitals, schools, and homes. These systems have the advantage of realism and relevance, but they are expensive and time-consuming, and may be affected by uncontrollable situational factors. To minimize these problems, clinicians often use controlled observations—special circumstances under which clients can be observed as they react to standardized events—including role-played social interactions and performance tests of smoking, eating, drinking, or dealing with a feared object or situation. During controlled observation, clinicians may monitor clients' physiological as well as overt responses.

While observation gets around some of the inference problems that reduce the reliability and validity of many interview and test procedures, it is not a perfect assessment tool. For one thing, data from observational assessments can be influenced by factors other than the behavior of clients. The reliability and validity of observational data depend on the careful training and constant monitoring of observers, precise definition of observation targets, and efforts to guard against the effects of observer bias, reactivity in the observation process, and situational influences such as demand characteristics that might create unrepresentative samples of client behaviors.

Chapter 5

Testing in Clinical Psychology

As described in Chapter 1, the history of clinical psychology is intimately related to the development and use of psychological tests. And though clinicians now perform many functions in addition to testing, tests remain an important part of clinical research and practice. In this chapter, we consider the nature of psychological tests, how they are constructed, and the research on their value as assessment tools.

WHAT IS A TEST?

A test is a systematic procedure for observing and describing a person's behavior in a standard situation (Cronbach, 1970). Tests present a set of planned stimuli (inkblots or true–false questions, for example) and ask the client to respond to them in some way. The client's reactions become the test's results or scores, to be used as samples, signs, or correlates in the clinician's assessment strategy. Test data may lead to conservative, situation-specific statements ("The client appeared disoriented during testing and was correct on 15 out of 60 items.") or to sweeping, high-level inferences ("The client's ego boundaries are so ill-defined as to make adequate functioning outside an institution very unlikely."). Most commonly, test results guide inferences that are between these extremes.

Tests are like highly structured interviews in that they ask clients to respond to specific assessment stimuli presented in a predetermined sequence. They also share characteristics with observational assessments by providing an opportunity for the clinician to watch the client in the test situation. In some ways, however, tests are distinct from all other assessment techniques. For example:

1. A test can be administered in a nonsocial context in which observational assessment does not supplement test data.

2. Usually, a client's test responses can be quantitatively compared to statistical norms established by the responses of hundreds or thousands of other people who have taken the same test under standardized conditions. Standardization—in which all respondents take the test under similar physical circumstances and all scoring is done using uniform methods—is designed to insure that differences in testing methods do not influence test results.

3. Tests can be administered in groups as well as individually. The SAT and other college entrance examinations provide examples of how tests are used to assess large numbers of people at the same time.[1]

WHAT DO TESTS MEASURE?

The thousands of psychological tests used today are administered to infants, children, adolescents, adults, senior citizens, students, soldiers, mental patients, office workers, prisoners, and every other imaginable group (Impara & Plake, 2001). Some of these tests pose direct, specific questions ("Do you ever feel discouraged?"), while others ask for general reactions to less distinct stimuli ("Tell me what you see in this drawing."). Some have correct answers ("What is a chicken?"), while others probe for opinions or preferences ("I enjoy looking at flowers—True or False"). Some are presented in paper-and-pencil form, some are given orally. Some require verbal skill ("What does 'analogy' mean?"), some ask the client to perform various tasks ("Please trace the correct path through this puzzle maze."), and still others combine verbal, numerical, and performance items.

Despite their enormous variety, many tests have similar purposes and can be grouped into four general categories based on whether they seek to measure (1) *intellectual functioning*, (2) *personality characteristics*, (3) *attitudes, interests, preferences, and values*, or (4) *ability*. The tests most commonly used by clinical psychologists in the United States and elsewhere are those of intellectual functioning and personality (Archer et al., 1991; Chan & Lee, 1995; Miller, 1991; Piotrowski & Keller, 1989). This pattern results not only because these variables are especially relevant to most clinicians' treatment and research activities, but also because other people expect clinicians to offer advice on such things.

One reason for the proliferation of tests is that testers are forever hoping to measure clinical constructs in ever more reliable, valid, and sophisticated ways. For exam-

---

[1]The SAT has received some recent criticism. The University of California system, the largest public university system in the United States, recently decided to discontinue using SAT scores as one criterion for college admission. They did so partly on the basis of a U. C. study showing that the SAT was a poor predictor of college grades (Gladwell, 2001).

ple, one clinician may feel that a popular anxiety test does not really "get at" anxiety very well, and so the clinician creates a new, improved instrument. Other psychologists might be dissatisfied with both tests and soon come up with yet other devices. This sequence is especially noticeable in personality testing, but it is evident in other test categories as well. Another factor responsible for the increasing array of tests is that testers' interests are becoming more specific, thus prompting the development of special-purpose tests. In intelligence testing, for example, instruments are available for use with infants, the physically handicapped, and persons not fluent in English or from specific cultural backgrounds. Similarly, surveys of general preferences or interests can now be followed up with special-purpose tests aimed at assessing the way adolescents spend leisure time or the things children find rewarding.

There are so many psychological tests available that it takes special publications to list them all and review their reliability, validity, and utility. The best known and most authoritative of these is the *Mental Measurements Yearbook*, first published in 1938 (Buros, 1938), and updated frequently; the latest edition appeared in 2001 (Impara & Plake, 2001).

TEST CONSTRUCTION PROCEDURES

The seemingly odd items on some psychological tests, especially on certain personality tests, lead many people to ask "How do psychologists come up with these things?" The answer is that they usually construct their tests using *analytic* or *empirical* approaches, though they sometimes use a *sequential system* approach, which combines the two (Burisch, 1984).

Psychologists using the analytic approach, sometimes called the rational approach, begin by asking, "What are the qualities I want to measure?", "How do I define these qualities?", and "What kind of test and test items would make sense for assessing these qualities?" They then proceed to build a test that answers the last question. In short, the *analytic approach* is a deductive approach to test construction. In its simplest form, it relies on creating content validity by designing tests that include items tapping all aspects of some domain. A more comprehensive analytic approach involves deriving test items from a theory of the characteristics to be measured.

To illustrate the simplest analytic approach, suppose a clinician wants to use it to develop a test for reliably and accurately identifying adult humans as male or female. The first step would be to ask what kinds of test items are likely to be answered differently by members of the two sexes. The choice of items, then, will be shaped by what the clinician's knowledge, experience, and favorite theories say is different about males and females. If the clinician chooses to focus on variations in physical characteristics, and prefers a true–false format, the test might contain items such as:

1. I was born with a prostate gland.
2. I was born with a uterus.
3. I was born with a penis.
4. I was born with a vagina.

Suppose, however, that the clinician believes that physical characteristics are only surface indicators of sex and that to get at "real" sex differences, a test should tap unconscious processes associated with masculinity and femininity. Such a test might search for unconscious themes by asking clients to fill in incomplete sentences such as:

1. A dependent person is _____.
2. Strength is _____.
3. The trouble with most men is _____.
4. Most women are _____.

This example also illustrates the importance of clearly defining the concept to be measured—a tester interested in gender is likely to construct very different instruments depending on whether he or she wants to measure biological sex, gender identity, or gender-role stereotypes. In any case, items on an analytically constructed test will strongly reflect the tester's theory of what aspects of some concepts should be tested, and how.

The main alternative to analytic test construction is the *empirical approach*. Here, instead of deciding ahead of time what test content should be used to measure a particular target, the tester lets the content "choose itself." Thus, in building a sex test, the clinician would amass a large number of self-report test items, performance tasks, or inkblots, and then administer all of them to a large group of people *who have already been identified* as males or females using a criterion such as chromosome analysis or other biological measure. The clinician would then examine the entire group's responses to all these testing materials to see which items, tasks, or other stimuli were consistently answered differently by men and women.

Any test stimuli that differentiated the sexes would be used to create the initial version of the sex test, *regardless of whether they have any obvious relationship to sex differences*. Thus, if only males answered "true" to items like "Coffee makes me sleepy" or "My shoes are too tight," those items would be made part of the developing test. The reasons why such items separate males from females might become the subject of further theoretical research, but for practical purposes testers are usually willing to employ an empirically constructed test in spite of the fact that the conceptual relevance of its individual items cannot be explained clearly. *This* is why some tests contain such apparently odd items.

Several factors affect test developers' choice between analytic and empirical procedures. The analytic approach can be faster and less expensive because it does not require initial administration of many items to many people in order to settle on those that will comprise the test. These features make analytic procedures attractive to clinicians who do not have access to a large pool of test material and willing subjects or who are forced by circumstances to develop a test on short notice. Analytic procedures also tend to be favored by clinicians evaluating a particular theory. Suppose that theory suggests that people differ in terms of "geekiness," but that no test is available to measure it. To explore the geekiness dimension of personality, the researcher will need a test that taps what the theory says geekiness is and that uses methods consistent with what the theory says about how it should be measured. Development of a Geek Test would thus likely proceed on analytic grounds.

Clinicians who have time and other resources available often find the empirical approach more desirable, especially when attempting to make specific predictions about people. If the tester's task is to identify individuals likely to graduate from law school, for example, it makes sense to find out if students who graduate respond to any test items in a way that is reliably different from those who fail or drop out.

The *sequential system approach* to test construction combines aspects of the analytic and empirical techniques. For example, testers who choose initial test items analytically may then examine results statistically to determine which item responses are, and are not, correlated with one another, which items are too easy or too difficult, which items do and do not discriminate. Groups of correlated items are then identified as *scales*, which are thought to be relatively pure measures of certain dimensions of personality, mental ability, or the like (Maloney & Ward, 1976). The sequential system approach is also valuable to those wishing to construct a test using empirical procedures, but who don't want to include hundreds or thousands of items in the initial research trial. The decision about which items to try is usually made on analytic grounds; some items are selected from existing tests, while others are those the clinician believes "ought" to be evaluated.

Regardless of how a test is constructed initially, its value as an assessment instrument ultimately must be established through empirical research on its reliability and validity (see Chapter 3). Later we shall look at how various tests have fared when scrutinized by such research. For now, let's consider prominent examples of tests designed to assess (1) intellectual functioning, (2) ability, (3) attitudes, interests, preferences, and values, and (4) personality. We begin our exploration of psychological tests with measures of intelligence, because, as noted in Chapter 1, the early history of clinical psychology is essentially the early history of intelligence tests.

TESTS OF INTELLECTUAL FUNCTIONING

While everyone would agree that intelligence is a good thing to have, there is far less consensus about what intelligence actually *is* (Furnham, 2000; Sternberg & Detterman, 1986). This state of affairs has generated the half-joking suggestion among clinicians that "intelligence is whatever intelligence tests measure." Indeed, the developers of most intelligence tests have initially proceeded on analytical grounds; each of the more than 200 assessment instruments they have produced reflects its creator's theoretical views about the essential nature of intelligence and about how best to measure intellectual functioning.

A description of those theories is beyond the scope of this chapter (see Neisser et al., 1996 for a succinct review), but it is worth noting that various researchers employing a mental testing, or *psychometric* approach to intelligence have described it as a *general* characteristic (called g), as a set of up to 150 *specific* intellectual functions (called s's) such as word fluency, reasoning, and memory, or as some hierarchical combination of the two (Carroll, 1993). The practical relevance of whether intelligence is g, a set of s's, or something else is limited by the fact that none of the major intelligence tests in wide use today reflects the g or s approach clearly enough to provide definitive validation of one theory or another (Kaufman & Harrison, 1991). Nor do those tests measure all aspects of what might be considered intelligence (Neisser et al., 1996). They are, however, the main methods clinicians have available for assessing certain kinds of mental abilities.

The Binet Scales

Alfred Binet was not the first person to develop a measure of intelligence, but his original test and the revisions based on it have been among the most influential means of assessing the mental ability of children. In its earliest form (1905), Binet's test consisted of 30 questions and tasks, including things like unwrapping a piece of candy, following a moving object with the eyes, comparing objects of differing weights, repeating numbers or sentences from memory, and recognizing familiar objects. The child's test score was simply the number of items passed.

Beginning with a 1908 revision, the tasks in Binet's test were *age graded*, which means that the items were arranged so that younger children were expected to pass the earlier ones, while older children were expected to pass later ones. Binet and his collaborator, Theodore Simon, observed the test behavior of about 200 children and suggested, for example, that 3-year-olds ought to be able to identify their eyes, nose, and mouth, repeat a 2-digit number and a 6-syllable sentence, and give their last name. At 7 years, success at finding missing parts of drawings, copying simple geometric figures, and identifying denominations of coins was expected.

The 1908 scale was brought to the United States by Henry Goddard and revised in 1916 by Lewis Terman, a Stanford University psychologist. Terman adopted an idea suggested in 1912 by German psychologist William Stern for representing numerically the relationship between mental and chronological age: *Stanford-Binet* results were expressed as the intelligence quotient (or IQ) that results when mental age (MA) is divided by chronological age (CA) and multiplied by 100. Thus, a 6-year-old whose score on the Stanford-Binet yielded a mental age of 8 would have an IQ of 133 [(8/6 × 100]. He also suggested that various IQ ranges be given labels such as "average," "feeble-minded," and "genius." Today, the following categories are used: "very superior," "superior," "high average," "average," "low average," "borderline," and "mentally retarded." Similar systems are used to classify persons at the lower end of the IQ scale as "mildly," "moderately," "severely," or "profoundly" retarded. The original intent of such labels was to provide a shorthand summary of a person's score relative to others of the same age. However, IQ scores and the labels associated with them are often overemphasized and misused, especially by those unfamiliar with their meaning. This unfortunate tendency is one reason why, as we shall see later, the use of IQ data for diagnostic, academic, or occupational decision-making is so controversial.

The Stanfort-Binet became the most popular intelligence test among clinical psychologists in the United States. Terman and his colleague, Maud Merrill, revised the test in 1937, 1960, and again in 1973. The 1960 edition changed the way IQ was derived. Rather than computing, clinicians used IQ tables in which the formula's results were corrected in light of mean and variance IQs at each age level. The 1973 edition used a larger and more diverse sample to establish norms.

In spite of its widespread use with children, the Stanford-Binet continued to be criticized for its emphasis upon verbal aspects of intelligence, its outdated item content, and its reliance on one score rather than a pattern of different cognitive strengths and weaknesses.

The fourth edition of the Stanford-Binet, published in 1986, addressed many of these concerns (Thorndike, Hagen, & Sattler, 1986). The fourth edition is still an individually administered test, and it retains many of the same kinds of items as in earlier editions, but the organization and content have dramatically changed. Unlike previous editions, which grouped items according to age levels, items in the fourth edition are grouped into 15 subtests (some examples are described in Table 5.1). Within each subtest, the items are arranged in increasing order of difficulty and their results are organized to assess four major areas of intellectual functioning: verbal reasoning, abstract/visual reasoning, quantitative reasoning, and short-term memory.

Because the 15 subtests can be given in varying combinations, the latest edition of the Stanford-Binet is more flexible than previous versions, and it is more useful as a diagnostic tool for the assessment of cognitive strengths and weaknesses in individuals aged two to adult. The choice of which tests to give and at what level of difficulty to begin each depends on the purpose of the evaluation, the client's age (not all of the tests are appropriate for children of certain ages), and initial test results that help guide the examiner to the correct entry level for individual tests. Typically, examiners administer between 8 and 13 subtests, although a quick screening battery of 4 tests (vocabulary, bead memory, quantitative, and pattern analysis) is recommended when testing must be completed in less than 40 minutes.

A *Standard Age Score*, or *SAS*, is determined for each subtest by using tables that convert raw scores to normalized standard scores with a mean of 50 and a standard

---

TABLE 5.1 A Sampling of Subtest Items Similar to Those Included in the Fourth Edition of the Stanford-Binet

Vocabulary: Define words like train, wrench, letter, error, and encourage.

Comprehension: Answer questions like, "Why should people brush their teeth?" "Why should people be quiet in a library?" "What is one advantage and one disadvantage of living in a small town instead of a big city?"

Absurdities: Identify the mistakes or "silly" aspects of pictures in which, for example, a man is shown using the wrong end of a rake or a girl is shown putting a piece of clothing on incorrectly.

Copying: Arrange a set of blocks to match different designs; draw designs like those shown in pictures.

Memory for Objects: Choose the right order in which a series of pictures were presented.

Number Series: Determine which numbers come next in a series of numbers such as the following—32, 26, 20, 14, ____, ____.

Verbal Relations: Indicate how three objects or words are alike but different from a fourth. For example, how are dog, cat, horse alike but different from boy.

Bead Memory: Arrange different colored and shaped beads to match pictures of the beads organized in different layouts.

deviation of 8 for each age group. For example, an SAS of 58 would be one standard deviation above the mean for children of a given age and would place a child at the 84th percentile—meaning that 58 is better than 84% of the child's age mates obtained. The tables can also be used to calculate composite SAS scores for each of the four content areas and for any combination of them. These area and composite scores are also normalized standard scores, and because their means are 100 and their standard deviations are 16, they can be expressed in the same units as the deviation IQ scores used in earlier versions of the test.

Research on the fourth edition of the Stanford-Binet suggests that it has very high internal consistency and test–retest reliability (generally, above .90). In addition, its scores correlate highly with other measures of intelligence and discriminate among samples of gifted, retarded, and learning-disabled children (Anastasi & Urbina, 1997; Barrett & Depinet, 1991). However, though the fourth edition of the Stanford-Binet was designed to yield separate scores for four different cognitive abilities, the extent to which it does this is unclear. The test's *Technical Manual* indicates support for three of the four factors, while other factor-analytic studies find fewer factors (Reynolds, Kamphaus, & Rosenthal, 1988) or components of intelligence that might be more important at different ages (Laurent, Swerdlik, & Ryburn, 1992). Despite concerns about its factor structure, the Stanford-Binet remains a highly reliable test widely used for testing of children, diagnosing mental retardation, and predicting and explaining academic achievement (Walsh & Betz, 2001).

The Wechsler Scales

In the 1930s, David Wechsler, chief psychologist at New York's Bellevue Psychiatric Hospital, began developing an intelligence test specifically for adults. The result of his efforts, the *Wechsler-Bellevue* (W-B) *Intelligence Scale,* was published in 1939. This test differed in several ways from the Stanford-Binet, even though some W-B tasks were borrowed or adapted from it. First, the W-B was aimed at adults, aged 17 and older. Second, the W-B was a *point* scale in which the client receives credit for each correct answer. With this method, IQ does not reflect the relationship between mental age and chronological age, but a comparison of points earned by the client to those earned by persons of equal age in the standardization sample.

Like the latest version of the Stanford-Binet, Wechsler-Bellevue items were arranged in groups or *subtests* based on similarity. Each subtest contained increasingly difficult items. For example, on the digit-span subtest, the client was asked to repeat numbers, starting with three digits and progressing to nine digits. The score on this subtest was determined by the maximum number of digits the client could repeat without error. The W-B contained six *verbal* subtests (information, comprehension, arithmetic, similarities, digit span, and vocabulary) and five *performance* subtests (digit symbol, picture completion, block design, picture arrangement, and object assembly).

In 1955 Wechsler revised his test and restandardized it on a more ethnically diverse and representative sample of more than 2,000 individuals (aged 16 to 74) living in all parts of the United States. This revision was called the *Wechsler Adult Intelligence Scale*, or WAIS, and it soon became the most popular adult intelligence test in the

United States. Like the W-B, the WAIS contained six verbal and five performance sub-tests, allowing computation of a client's Verbal IQ, Performance IQ, and Full-Scale IQ (which combines the other two). The test was revised again in 1981 and restandardized on a sample of 1,880 U.S. adults whose age, ethnicity, and other demographic characteristics reflected 1970 census data (Wechsler, 1981). The most recent revision of the test, the WAIS-III, occurred in 1997.

As with previous versions of the test, items on the WAIS-III are still arranged and presented in order of increasing difficulty within subtests. The clinician discontinues each subtest after a predetermined number of failures and then begins the next subtest. When the test is completed, the clinician can compute Full Scale, Verbal, and Performance IQs by converting the client's point totals to standardized IQ scores with a mean of 100 and standard deviation of 15. Some examples of the types of items included on the WAIS-III are presented in Table 5.2.

TABLE 5.2   Items of the Type Included in the Wechsler Adult Intelligence Scale-Revised (WAIS-III)

	(WAIS-III)
Information:	What does bread come from?
	What did Shakespeare do?
	What is the capital of France?
	What is the malleus malleficarum?
Comprehension:	What should you do with a wallet found in the street?
	Why do foreign cars cost more than domestic cars?
	What does "the squeaky wheel gets the grease" mean?
Arithmetic:	If you have four apples and give two away, how many do you have left?
	If four people can finish a job in six days, how many people would it take to do the job in two days?
Similarities:	Identify similar aspects of pairs like: hammer-screwdriver, portrait-short story, dog-flower.
Digit Symbol/Coding:	Copy designs that are associated with different numbers as quickly as possible.
Digit Span:	Repeat in forward and reverse order: two- to nine-digit numbers.
Vocabulary:	Define: chair, dime, lunch, paragraph, valley, asylum, modal, cutaneous.
Picture Completion:	Find missing objects in increasingly complex pictures.
Block Design:	Arrange blocks to match increasingly complex standard patterns.
Picture Arrangement:	Place increasing numbers of pictures together to make increasingly complex stories.
Symbol Search:	Visually scan and recognize a series of symbols.

The WAIS-III differs in some ways from its predecessors. It has an extended age range that allows computation of IQ scores through age 89. This was made possible by the addition of new items more appropriate for older adults and by norming the test on a sample of 2,450 persons, aged 16 to 89. The sample was also stratified according to age, gender, education, and geographic region. The test also has a lower "floor," which refers to the lowest scores that can be measured by the test. The test measures Full Scale, Verbal, and Performance IQs into the 40s.

One of the biggest changes on WAIS-III has been the addition of four new "Index" Scores: Verbal Comprehension, Working Memory, Perceptual Organization, and Processing Speed. Each Index Score is obtained by combining scores on selected subtests. For instance, a score on Perceptual Organization is derived from subtest scores on Picture Completion, Block Design, and Object Assembly. These four index scores are compatible with recent theories of what intelligence is, and factor analytic studies support the measurement of these factors by the test (Saklofske, Hildebrand, & Gorsuch, 2000).

With WAIS-III, clinicians can obtain a multifaceted description of a person's cognitive strengths and weaknesses. Some clinicians use WAIS subtest variability, or "scatter," to help them reach clinical diagnoses, to assess the possibility of brain damage, or to describe impulsivity or other personality characteristics (e.g., Ryan, Paolo, & Smith, 1992). Though unequivocal diagnoses of brain damage, Alzheimer's, or other neurological conditions can rarely be made using the WAIS-III alone—the test was not designed for neuropsychological assessment—hypotheses that lead to further assessment can be obtained from patterns of subtest scores (see Groth-Marnat, 1999).

After publication of the W-B, Wechsler's interest in extending the point-scale test format to children resulted in the *Wechsler Intelligence Scale for Children* (WISC). Appearing in 1949, the WISC was made up of 12 subtests (6 verbal, 6 performance) of which only 10 were usually administered. The subtests were similar to those of the W-B, but easier. The WISC was standardized on 2,200 European-American children from all parts of the United States, but because they ranged in age from 5 to 15, the WISC was not useful for the very young. The *Wechsler Preschool and Primary Scale of Intelligence* (WPPSI) was developed later, but still only reached the 4-year-old level (Wechsler, 1967). A revision of this test (WPPSI-R) lowers the age limit to 3 years. In 1974, a new version of the WISC was published. Called the WISC-R, it included 6 verbal and 6 performance subtests; again, only 5 of each are usually administered. The content of the WISC-R items was changed to make it more representative of current social and cultural values, and the entire test was standardized on a new sample of 2,200 ethnically diverse children from varying socioeconomic levels and geographical locations.

The latest version of the WISC, the WISC-III, was published in 1991 (Wechsler, 1991). Although it retains the basic structure and format of its predecessors, scoring of the WISC-III is based on new norms collected on 2,200 children, ranging in age from six to sixteen and representative of 1988 U.S. census data. New items were added to replace WISC-R items that were outdated, culturally unfair, too easy, or too difficult. In addition, a new subtest called Symbol Search was added as a supplementary test that can be substituted for the Coding subtest. In addition to Full Scale, Verbal, and Performance IQ scores, the WISC-III can be interpreted in terms of four other factors: Verbal

Comprehension and Perceptual Organization (which are similar, but not identical to, Verbal and Performance IQ, respectively), Freedom from Distractibility (emphasizing memory and attention), and Processing Speed.

Both the WAIS-III and the WISC-III have strong psychometric properties. The split-half reliabilities for Full Scale, Verbal, and Performance IQ Scores on the WAIS-III are .93 or above across all age ranges, and reliabilities for the Index Scores are nearly as high. The test correlates well with the Stanford-Binet Fourth Edition and with school grades. This information, as well as an extensive discussion of content, criterion, and construct validity are provided by the test's *Technical Manual*, published by the Psychological Corporation (Wechsler, 1997). The WISC-III Manual (Wechsler, 1991) presents similarly thorough data about the test's reliability and validity. WISC-III scores are extremely stable over time and show very high correlations with the WISC-R, as well as appropriately strong correlations with criteria such as school grades, achievement test scores, and neuropsychological performance (Braden, 1995).

Other Intelligence Tests

Another intelligence test that has gained popularity in recent years is the *Kaufman Assessment Battery for Children* (K-ABC) (Kaufman & Kaufman, 1983). Suitable for children 2½ to 12½ years of age, the K-ABC was based on research and theory in cognitive psychology and neuropsychology. It defines intelligence as the ability to solve new problems (an ability sometimes referred to as *fluid intelligence*) rather than knowledge of facts (which has been termed *crystallized intelligence*). The standardization sample for the K-ABC was closely matched to the U.S. census on several demographic factors, and its psychometric qualities are excellent. In addition, several studies show that the K-ABC can be used to assess and study neuropsychological problems in children (Kaufman & Harrison, 1991). A brief version called the *Kaufman Brief Intelligence Test* (K-BIT) (Kaufman & Kaufman, 1991) and an adult version, the *Kaufman Adolescent and Adult Intelligence Test* (KAIT), are also available (Kaufman & Kaufman, 1993). Recent evidence suggests that the KAIT does indeed measure factors of fluid and crystalized intelligence in young adolescents (Caruso & Jacob-Timm, 2001).

Another relatively new intelligence test is the 1989 revision of the *Woodcock-Johnson Psycho-Educational Battery* (Woodcock & Johnson, 1977, 1989). Although usually administered to children, this test can also be used with adults. A special feature of the Woodcock-Johnson is that its 27 subtests cover cognitive ability, academic achievement, and individual interests. Scoring is more complex than for most other intelligence tests, and there is some evidence that the separate ability and achievement subtests are not as clearly differentiated as intended (Kaufman & Harrison, 1991).

Several other intelligence tests in use today assess intelligence without emphasis on verbal or vocalization skills. *The Peabody Picture Vocabulary Test-Revised*, the *Porteus Maze Test*, the *Leiter International Performance Scale*, and the *Raven's Progressive Matrices*, for example, allow clinicians to assess intellectual functioning in clients who are very young or have other characteristics that impair their ability at verbal tasks. These tests also provide a backup in cases where the clinician suspects that a client's performance on a standard IQ test may have been hampered by anxiety, verbal deficits, cultural disadvantages, or other situational factors.

Further information about these and other intelligence tests for individual and group administration to adults and children is available from numerous sources (e.g., Anastasi & Urbina, 1997; Goldstein & Hersen, 1990; Groth-Marnat, 1999; Kaufman, 1994; Impara & Plake, 2001; Vane & Motta, 1990).

ABILITY TESTS

Intelligence is one aspect of mental ability, and intelligence tests can be viewed as general mental ability instruments. However, there are a number of other tests designed to measure more specific mental abilities. These include aptitude and achievement tests. Aptitude tests are designed to predict success in an occupation or an educational program. They measure the accumulated effects of many different educational and living experiences and attempt to forecast future performance on the basis of these effects. The *Scholastic Aptitude Test* (SAT), used to predict high school students' potential for college-level work, is an example familiar to most undergraduates.

Achievement tests measure proficiency at certain tasks; that is, they measure how much people know or how well they can perform. The *Wide Range Achievement Test* (WRAT-3) is a well-known example (Wilkinson, 1993). Though achievement tests measure the effects of a more uniform set of learning or training experiences than do aptitude tests, many psychologists argue that intelligence, aptitude, and achievement tests are more alike than they are different in that they all attempt to measure "developed abilities" (Reschly, 1990). While the Wide Range Achievement Test remains the most popular of these achievement tests, three more sophisticated alternatives have now been developed and may find increased use by clinicians: the achievement subtests of the Woodcock-Johnson test mentioned earlier, the *Kaufman Test of Educational Achievement* (K-TEA) (Kaufman & Kaufman, 1985), and the *Wechsler Individual Achievement Test* (WIAT), which was introduced in 1992. The more specific the ability or aptitude tested, the less familiar the test is likely to be. If you have never heard of the *Seashore Measures of Musical Talents* or the *Crawford Small Parts Dexterity Test*, it is probably because you have never had occasion to be tested on these very specialized abilities. Such ability testing is more often done by personnel officers and educational, vocational, and guidance counselors than by clinical psychologists.

Clinicians' interest in ability testing is usually related to assessment of specific cognitive capabilities or deficits. Though clinicians may draw inferences about specific cognitive abilities, deficits, or even brain damage from the pattern of subtest scores on the WAIS-III or the WISC-III, they may also utilize a variety of special-purpose tests, some of which emphasize perception and memory. For example, the *Benton Visual Retention Test* (Benton, 1974), the *Bender Visual Motor Gestalt* (or Bender-Gestalt), (Bender, 1938) and the *Memory-for-Designs Test* (Graham & Kendall, 1960) ask the client to copy or draw from memory geometric figures or other designs. Other tests in this category assess the client's ability to form concepts and engage in other types of abstract thinking. The use of tests to detect brain damage or deterioration is known as neuropsychological assessment and is described in more detail in Chapter 12.

TESTS OF ATTITUDES, INTERESTS, PREFERENCES, AND VALUES

Clinical psychologists often find it useful to assess a person's attitudes, interests, preferences, and values. For example, before beginning to work with a distressed couple, the clinician may wish to get some idea about each spouse's attitudes about marriage. Similarly, it may be instructive for the clinician to know that the interests of a client who is in severe conflict about entering the medical profession are utterly unlike those of successful physicians. Finally, assessment of attitudes, interests, preferences, and values can encourage clients to engage in their own self-exploration with respect to career decisions (Holland, 1996). We do not have room to describe all the many tests available to assess these dimensions (see Anastasi & Urbina, 1997 for a review), but some of the more commonly used tests in this category include the *Strong-Campbell Interest Inventory* (Hansen & Campbell, 1985), the *Kuder Occupational Interest Survey* (Zytowski, 1985), the *Career Assessment Inventory* (Johansson, 1982), the *Self-Directed Search* (Holland, 1994), and the *Career Attitudes and Strategies Inventory* (Holland & Gottfredson, 1994). These are paper-and-pencil tests designed to assess clients' preferences for various pursuits, occupations, academic subjects, recreational activities, and people. Many of these tests result in an interest profile that can be compared with composite profiles gathered from members of occupational groups such as biologists, engineers, army officers, carpenters, police, ministers, accountants, salespeople, lawyers, etc. The Self-Directed Search is notable for attempting to predict job satisfaction, stability, and productivity by looking at how well clients' scores on six personality-related dimensions (realistic, investigative, artistic, social, enterprising, and conventional) match up with the demands and opportunities associated with various job environments (Gottfredson & Holland, 1989; Holland, 1996).

Generalized life orientations can be assessed via the *Allport-Vernon-Lindzey Study of Values* (Allport, Vernon, & Lindzey, 1970), a paper-and-pencil test that asks the client to choose among alternatives about things like use of leisure time, interest in various news items, and the importance of various activities. The resulting profile of values shows the relative strength of six basic interests: theoretical ("intellectual"), economic, aesthetic, social, political, and religious. More humanistically oriented general value assessments include the *Purpose-in-Life Test* (Crumbaugh, 1968) and the *Personal Orientation Inventory* (Knapp, 1976; Shostrom, 1968).

There are many tests designed to assess more specific interests and preferences (Hansen, 1984). For example, the behavioral model of clinical psychology has generated several tests aimed at illuminating client preferences and attitudes as a prelude to treatment. Among the most prominent of these is the *Reinforcement Survey Schedule* (Cautela & Kastenbaum, 1967), a list of situations and activities that the client rates in terms of their desirability. *The Pleasant Events Schedule* (MacPhillamy & Lewinsohn, 1976) provides an example of a behaviorally oriented preference assessment.

PERSONALITY TESTS

People's attitudes, interests, preferences, and values can be seen as one aspect of their personalities, but the tests described in the previous section are not meant to be personality tests. In this section, we consider prominent examples of psychological tests that *have* been designed specifically to assess various aspects of personality.

Personality can be defined as the pattern of behavioral and psychological characteristics by which a person can be compared and contrasted with other people. When studying personality, then, clinicians seek ways to describe and understand consistencies and inconsistencies in a given person, and also how people in general tend to resemble and differ from one another. Guided by their theoretical approaches, some clinicians see personality as an organized collection of traits, while others see it in terms of dynamic relationships among intrapsychic forces, recurring patterns of learned behavior, or perceptions of the world. This theory-driven variation in how clinicians think about personality is reflected in a wide range of methods through which they have attempted to assess it. Indeed, more psychological tests are devoted to personality assessment than to any other clinical target.

There are two major types of personality tests: *objective* and *projective*. Objective tests present relatively clear, specific stimuli such as questions ("Have you ever wanted to run away from home?"), statements ("I am never depressed.") or concepts ("Myself" or "Large dogs") to which the client responds with direct answers, choices, or ratings. Most objective personality tests are of the paper-and-pencil variety and can be scored arithmetically, often by computers, much like the multiple-choice or true-false tests used in many college classes. Some objective tests focus on one aspect of personality such as anxiety, dependency, or ego strength, while others provide a comprehensive overview of many personality dimensions.

Projective tests grew out of the psychodynamic approach to clinical psychology, especially from the idea that people use unconscious defense mechanisms to protect themselves from anxiety or guilt arising from unacceptable impulses and wishes. Broadening Freud's notion that people "project," or attribute to others, the unacceptable aspects of their own personality, it was suggested that there is a "tendency of people to be influenced in the cognitive mediation of perceptual inputs by their needs, interests, and overall psychological organization" (Frank, 1939, quoted in Exner, 1976, p. 61). In other words, the *projective hypothesis* states that each individual's personality will determine, in part at least, the way she or he interprets things. Tests that encourage clients to display this tendency are called "projective methods" (Frank, 1939). Clients taking these tests are usually asked to respond to ambiguous or unstructured stimuli (such as inkblots, drawings, or incomplete sentences), and their responses are interpreted as a reflection of both conscious and unconscious aspects of their personality structure and dynamics.

Objective Personality Tests

The first objective personality test developed by a psychologist was the *Personal Data Sheet* used during World War I to screen soldiers with psychological problems (Woodworth, 1920). It asked for yes or no answers to questions such as "Did you have a happy childhood?" "Does it make you uneasy to cross a bridge?" These items were selected because they reflected problems and symptoms reported at least twice as often by previously diagnosed "neurotics" as by "normals." No item was retained in the test if more than 25% of a normal sample answered it in an unfavorable manner. Item selection procedures such as these were a prelude to later, more sophisticated empirical test construction procedures (Butcher & Keller, 1984).

The MMPI.   Among the hundreds of objective personality measures that have appeared since the Personal Data Sheet, the most influential and widely used is the *Minnesota Multiphasic Personality Inventory* (MMPI). This test was developed during the late 1930s at the University of Minnesota by Starke Hathaway (a psychologist) and J. C. McKinley (a psychiatrist) as an aid to psychiatric diagnosis of clinical patients. The MMPI was one of the first personality tests to be constructed empirically. Hathaway and McKinley took about 1,000 items from older personality tests and other sources and converted them into statements to which clients could respond "true," "false," or "cannot say." More than half of these items were then presented to thousands of normal people as well as to people already diagnosed with psychiatric disorders.

Certain response patterns appeared. When compared to normals, members of various diagnostic groups showed statistically different responses to many items. For example, a particular group of items tended to be answered in the same way by depressed persons, while another group of items was answered in a particular way by persons diagnosed as schizophrenic. Eight of these item groups, or scales, were identified as being associated with a certain diagnostic category and as discriminating between normal and abnormal individuals. Later, two additional scales were identified as being responded to differently by males and females and by shy, introverted college students. Thus, there are 10 clinical scales on the MMPI; their titles and a sample item[2] from each are presented in Table 5.3.

Also included in the MMPI are four *validity scales*. These are groups of items designed to help detect various test-taking attitudes or response distortions. The *cannot say*, or *?*, scale is the number of items that the respondent does not answer. An elevated ? scale can be attributed to reading problems, uncooperativeness, failure to understand items, or defensiveness. The *L*, or *lie*, scale consists of statements which, if answered honestly, reveal mildly negative characteristics (such as the fact that the respondent does not keep up with world news every day). The assumption behind the *L* scale is that clients who deny trivial negative behaviors or thoughts will probably not be honest about more serious problems covered by other items. The *F*, or *frequency*, scale contains items rarely endorsed by normal people, but which are not associated with any particular diagnosed group. A high *F* score is interpreted as indicating carelessness in responding, a purposeful attempt to exaggerate symptoms, a very severe disorder, or some related factor. The *K*, or *correction*, scale is designed to detect a client's tendency to be overly defensive or overly disclosing about problems. A high

---

[2]To avoid biasing the responses of readers who might take the MMPI-2 at some point, only items of the type found on the test are presented here. The MMPI has been widely parodied in "tests" such as the "Maryland Malpractice and Pandering Inventory," whose items include: "I used to tease vegetables" and "The sight of blood no longer excites me."

TABLE 5.3 MMPI Scales and Simulated Items

Validity (or Test-Taking Attitude) Scales

? (Cannot Say) Number of items left unanswered.

L (Lie) Fifteen items of overly good self-report, such as "I smile at everyone I meet." (answered True)

F (Frequency or Infrequency) Sixty items answered in the scored direction by 10% or less of normals, such as "There is an international plot against me." (True)

K (Correction) Thirty items reflecting defensiveness in admitting to problems, such as "I feel bad when others criticize me." (False)

Clinical Scales

1 or Hs (Hypochondriasis). Thirty-two items derived from patients showing abnormal concern with bodily functions, such as "I have chest pains several times a week." (True)

2 or D (Depression) Fifty-seven items derived from patients showing extreme pessimism, feelings of hopelessness, and slowing of thought and action, such as "I usually feel that life is interesting and worthwhile." (False)

3 or Hy (Conversion Hysteria) Sixty items from neurotic patients using physical or mental symptoms as a way of unconsciously avoiding difficult conflicts and responsibilities, such as "My heart frequently pounds so hard I can feel it." (True)

4 or Pd (Psychopathic Deviate) Fifty items from patients who show a repeated and flagrant disregard for social customs, an emotional shallowness, and an inability to learn from punishing experiences, such as "My activities and interests are often criticized by others." (True)

5 or Mf (Masculinity-Femininity) Fifty-six items from patients showing homoeroticism and items differentiating between men and woman, such as "I like to arrange flowers." (True, scored for femininity)

6 or Pa (Paranoia) Forty items from patients showing abnormal suspiciousness and delusions of grandeur or persecution, such as "There are evil people trying to influence my mind. (True)

7 or Pt (Psychasthenia) Forty-eight items based on neurotic patients showing obsessions, compulsions, abnormal fears, and guilt and indecisiveness, such as "I save nearly everything I buy, even after I have no use for it." (True)

8 or Sc (Schizophrenia) Seventy-eight items from patients showing bizarre or unusual thoughts or behavior, who are often withdrawn and experiencing delusions and hallucinations, such as "Things around me do not seem real" (True) and "It makes me uncomfortable to have people close to me." (True)

9 or Ma (Hypomania) Forty-six items from patients characterized by emotional excitement, overactivity, and flight of ideas, such as "At times I feel very 'high' or very 'low' for no apparent reason." (True)

0 or Si (Social Introversion) Sixty-nine items from persons showing shyness, little interest in people, and insecurity, such as "I have the time of my life at parties." (False)

Source: Adapted from Norman Sundberg, *Assessment of Persons*, © 1977, p. 183. (Reprinted by permission of Prentice-Hall, Inc.)

K score is taken as evidence that the client is downplaying the severity of his or her problems; a low *K* score suggests that problems are being overstated. In either case, the *K* scale is used as a guide for "correcting" scores on five of the clinical scales.

People's responses to the 567 items on the MMPI are converted into clinical and validity scale scores. Originally, scores on the clinical scales were taken literally; people with high depression or schizophrenia scores, for example, were diagnosed as depressive or schizophrenic. It soon became obvious, however, that elevation of a particular scale did not always mean that the individual belongs in the associated diagnostic category. Recognition of this problem led to the practice of calling the clinical scales by number (1 to 10) rather than by name, and also to plotting all scale scores on a graph and analyzing the resulting profile, not just the highest score.

Clinicians conduct these profile analyses by comparing a client's MMPI scores with those of other clients. This can be done *clinically* by recalling previous clients' patterns, or *statistically* by reference to books containing sample profiles and the characteristics of the people who produced them (e.g., Butcher & Williams, 1992; Dahlstrom, Lachar, & Dahlstrom, 1986; Dahlstrom, Welsh, & Dahlstrom, 1972; Graham, 1990). The MMPI can also be scored by computers using either statistical formulae or automated clinical lore (Butcher, 1987; see Chapter 3) to match a current client's profile with those in large databases.

Though widely used (it has even been translated into American Sign Language; Brauer, 1993), the original MMPI was eventually widely criticized for its outdated and unrepresentative standardization sample, for deficiencies in its coverage of some aspects of mental disorders, for its antiquated items, and for the unreliability of some of its scales (Dahlstrom, 1992). Accordingly, an extensive revision of the MMPI began in 1982. Those revising the test wanted to correct the test's deficiencies but preserve the basic MMPI format so that the extensive research base would still be relevant. The revision effort focused on gathering new normative data from randomly selected samples of normal adults and adolescents in seven U.S. states, as well as from several clinical populations. The 2,600 people included in the restandardization sample represented the 1980 U.S. census figures in terms of age, marital status, and ethnic group membership. Also, 154 items were evaluated for possible addition to the test. Some were reworded examples of existing items, but most were new items intended to provide better coverage of topics and problems not covered in the original item pool.

The revised test, called the MMPI-2 (Butcher et al., 1989) was made available for general clinical use in 1989. Among the major new developments contained in the MMPI-2, three are especially important:

1. There are fifteen new content scales which allow supplementary assessment of personality factors not previously measurable with the basic clinical scales (see Table 5.4).

2. Some new validity scales have been added to supplement the *?, L, F,* and *K* scales. Two of these new scales, abbreviated VRIN and TRIN, are designed to identify people whose test responses were inconsistent or careless.

TABLE 5.4   The MMPI-2 Content Scales

Among the changes appearing in the MMPI-2 are 15 new content scales. The developers of these new scales began by defining clinically relevant areas of personality that were not measured specifically enough by the MMPI. They then used sequential test construction procedures to create groups of items that clinical judgment and statistical analyses suggested would tap these areas. The names and targets of these new scales are as follows:

Scale Name	Description of Content
Anxiety	Measures symptoms of anxiety, including tension, physical complaints, sleep problems, worry, and/or concentration.
Fears	Assesses the presence of many specific fears such as fear of the dark, fire, leaving home, etc.
Obsessiveness	High scores on this scale indicate people who have trouble making decisions and ruminate excessively. They may also show some compulsive behaviors.
Depression	Measures symptoms of depression including sad mood, hopelessness, suicidal concerns, and despair.
Health Concerns	Measures frequent complaints about health, covering several different body systems. High scorers worry a lot about their health.
Bizarre Mentation	Persons who score high on this scale may show psychotic thinking. They may recognize that their thoughts are strange and peculiar.
Anger	Measures problems with controlling anger. High scorers on this scale report being irritable, grouchy, impatient, hotheaded, and stubborn.
Cynicism	High scorers on this scale see hidden, negative motives behind the acts of others. They are frequently distrustful of people.
Antisocial Practices	Measures a tendency toward mistrust as well as a pattern of such problem behaviors and antisocial practices as being in trouble with the law, stealing, or shoplifting.
Type A	High scorers on this scale are hard-driving, fast-moving individuals who are absorbed in their work and frequently become impatient, irritable, and annoyed.
Low Self-Esteem	Persons who score high on this scale hold low opinions of themselves. They feel that they are not liked by others and that they are not important.
Social Discomfort	Measures a tendency to be very uneasy around others and to prefer to be alone. High scorers feel shy and dislike group activities.
Family Problems	Assesses family discord. High scorers describe their families as quarrelsome, unpleasant, and lacking in love.
Work Interference	A high score on this scale indicates behaviors and attitudes likely to lead to poor work performance. The problems include low self-confidence, concentration problems, and difficulties in making decisions.
Negative Treatment	Measures the tendency to hold negative attitudes toward doctors and mental-health treatment. Persons scoring high on this scale are not comfortable discussing their problems with others.

3. Scoring has been changed to equalize the clinical significance of similar scores on different scales. In the original MMPI, similar scores on different scales signified different levels of disturbance (Tellegen & Ben-Porath, 1992). In addition, the definition of a clinically significant score elevation has been lowered from 70 or higher on the MMPI to 65 or higher on the MMPI-2.

Interpretation of the MMPI-2 is similar to that of the original version, although changes in the wording and ordering of the items, along with the addition of new items, is designed to allow better assessment in areas such as substance abuse and certain personality patterns. A sample MMPI-2 profile is presented in Figure 5.1.

According to Walsh and Betz (2001), "There is little question that the Minnesota Multiphasic Personality Inventory (MMPI) . . . is the most useful psychological test available in clinical and counseling settings for assessing the degree and nature of emotional upset" (p. 112). The test has spawned thousands of research reports, more than any other test. Hundreds of experimental scales have been constructed from its items, many of which go beyond the test's original diagnostic purposes. For example, MMPI items have been grouped into scales designed to measure such specific areas as ego strength, anxiety, dependency, dominance, cynicism, family problems, work interference, social status, and prejudice. These new scales have been used in conjunction with the full MMPI-2, or as separate tests. Shortened versions of the MMPI have also been developed. Called the "Mini-Mult" or "Midi-Mult," these abbreviated editions are less comprehensive and designed for quick classification and screening purposes (Stevens & Reilly, 1980). A shorter form developed for adolescents, the MMPI-A, consists of 478 items, but it is still long enough to correlate highly with the MMPI and MMPI-2.

The MMPI or restandardized MMPI-2 is sometimes administered and scored by computer, as are many other booklet-type objective personality tests. Some clinicians have expressed concern that computer-administered versions of the test will yield results different from those obtained by clinician-administration versions, but this concern appears unwarranted. Finger and Ones (1999) conducted a meta-analysis of studies comparing computer versus standard administrations and found negligible to no differences between scores obtained by the two formats. It appears that this and similar tests can be administered by computer without compromising results. We will have more to say about interpreting test results and generating narrative reports via computer in a later section.

The CPI. *The California Psychological Inventory* is another prominent example of a broad-range, empirically constructed, objective personality test. It was introduced in 1957 and revised in 1987 with updated content and reworded items (Gough, 1987). In contrast to the MMPI, the CPI was developed specifically for assessing personality in the "normal" population. About half of its 462 true–false items come from the MMPI, but CPI items are grouped into more diverse and positively oriented scales including sociability, self-acceptance, responsibility, dominance, self-control, and others. There are also three validity scales that serve essentially the same purpose as those on the MMPI. The CPI's strengths include the representativeness of its standardization sample (13,000 males and females from all socioeconomic categories and all

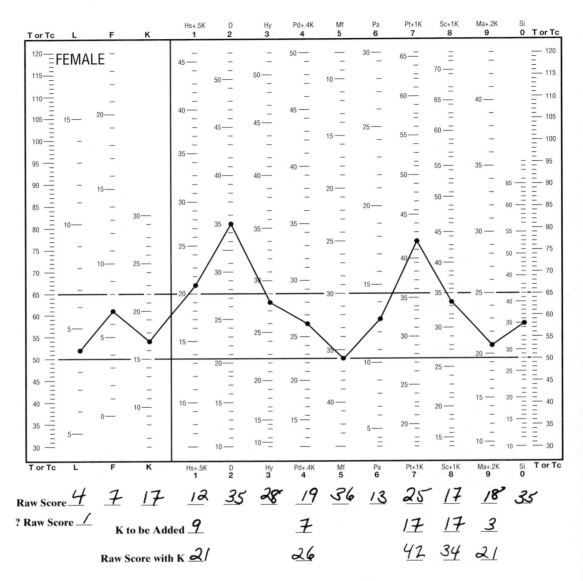

FIGURE 5.1 An MMPI-2 profile. (Minnesota Multiphasic Personality Inventory-2. Copyright © by THE REGENTS OF THE UNIVERSITY OF MINNESOTA 1942, 1943 [renewed 1970], 1989. This Profile Form 1989.)

parts of the United States) and its relatively high reliability. The test has been used to predict delinquency, parole outcome, academic grades, and the likelihood of dropping out of high school (Anastasi & Urbina, 1997). Computerized scoring and interpretation services are available.

The PRF, MCMI-II, and MBTI.   Other objective personality inventories that deserve mention here are the *Personality Research Form* (PRF), the *Millon Clinical Multiaxial Inventory* (MCMI-II), and the *Myers-Briggs Type Indicator* (MBTI). The PRF (Jackson, 1984) is one of the best examples of the sequential system approach to test construction. Its items were selected on theoretical grounds (using Henry Murray's 1938 book, *Explorations in Personality*, as a guide), combined into scales on empirical grounds, and then empirically validated against external criteria. In addition, the PRF was constructed to minimize response biases that can distort test results. It comes in 5 different forms, the most comprehensive of which contains 440 true–false items combined into 22 independent scales, and is generally used with normal rather than clinical populations (MacLennan, 1992).

The MCMI-III, a 175-item test first published in 1982, was revised 5 years later and again in 1997 (Millon, Millon, & Davis, 1997). It reflects Millon's unique theory of personality (Millon, 1981) and was designed to coordinate its interpretations with the diagnostic criteria of the DSM (Craig, 1993).

The Myers-Briggs Type Indicator (Myers & Briggs, 1943), an analytically derived test based on Jung's personality-type classification system, has become quite popular in nonclinical settings for describing and matching people who work together (Bayne, 1995).

Objective Tests Based on Factor Analysis.   For much of the 20th century, psychologists have tried to determine the minimum number of traits or characteristics necessary for an adequate description of human personality. One approach to this problem has been to examine how much different traits overlap with one another. *Factor analysis* is a mathematical procedure that helps reduce the complexity of many different traits by grouping them into clusters or factors based on the pattern of correlations between the different traits.

For example, Raymond B. Cattell used factor analysis to identify sixteen basic factors in personality, and created the *Sixteen Personality Factors Questionnaire*, or 16PF, to measure them in particular individuals (Cattell, Eber, & Tatsuoka, 1970, 1992). Hans Eysenck's factor-analytic methods led him to three basic personality factors—Psychoticism, Introversion–Extraversion, and Emotionality–Stability—and to develop the *Eysenck Personality Questionnaire* (Eysenck & Eysenck, 1975) to measure them. Factor-analytic methods also guided Auge Tellegen (1982) in the development of the *Multidimensional Personality Questionnaire* (MPQ), a 300-item personality inventory that measures three factors called Positive Emotionality, Negative Emotionality, and Constraint.

Many factor analyses have resulted in a five-factor system for describing and assessing personality. These "big five" factors include (1) *neuroticism* (a tendency to feel anxious, angry, and depressed in many situations), (2) *extraversion* (a tendency to be assertive, active, and to prefer to be with other people), (3) *openness* (a quality indicating active imagination, curiosity, and receptiveness to many experiences), (4) *agree-*

ableness (an orientation toward positive, sympathetic, helpful interactions with others), and (5) *conscientiousness* (a tendency to be reliable and persistent in pursuing goals). The *NEO Personality Inventory* (NEO-PI; Costa & McCrae, 1985) was designed to assess these five factors (NEO refers to Neuroticism, Extraversion, and Openness). Its latest revision, called the NEO-PI-R (Costa & McCrae, 1992a) consists of 243 items that measure the "big five" dimensions as well as six specific facets of each. The NEO-PI-R was developed as a comprehensive measure of normal adult personality, but its authors suggest that it can also be used to diagnose psychological disorders, predict progress in psychotherapy, and select optimal forms of treatment for some clients (Costa & McCrae, 1992b). This suggestion has been challenged by clinicians who are not convinced that instruments like the NEO-PI-R add any clinically useful information beyond that provided by tests like the MMPI-2 (Ben-Porath & Waller, 1992).

Behavioral Tests. In accordance with their view of personality as a pattern of learned behavior, proponents of the behavioral approach to clinical psychology have constructed objective tests which, unlike those described so far, gather behavior samples from which only minimal inferences are drawn. These tests tend to be short and analytically constructed.

One of the earliest and most frequently employed behavioral "personality tests" is the *Fear Survey Schedule* (FSS). It is simply a list of objects, persons, and situations that the client rates in terms of fearsomeness. Differing versions of this test contain from 50 to 122 items and use 1-to-5 or 1-to-7 scales for the fear ratings (e.g., Geer, 1965; Lawlis, 1971; Wolpe & Lang, 1969). The current version, FSS-III, is used to assess the prevalence of various fears in the general population, to identify persons with specific fears, and to measure progress in fear-reduction treatment. The FSS-III has been translated into several languages (Abdel, 1994; Johnsen & Hugdahl, 1990) and there are special written and illustrated versions available for use with normal and retarded children (Fleisig, 1993; Gullone & King, 1992; Ramirez & Kratchowill, 1990).

Other behavioral tests of anxiety include the *State-Trait Anxiety Inventory* (Spielberger et al., 1983), the *Social Avoidance and Distress Scale* (Watson & Friend, 1969), the *Social Phobia and Anxiety Inventory* (SPAI) (Turner et al., 1989), and the *PTSD Symptom Scale—Self-Report* (PSS-SR) (Foa et al., 1993). Behaviorally oriented clinicians have also developed tests that assess other clinical targets (Ciminero, Calhoun, & Adams, 1986; Mash and Terdal, 1988). These tests include the *Beck Depression Inventory* (Beck et al., 1961), the *Multiple Affect Adjective Checklist* (Zuckerman & Lubin, 1965), the *Bulimia Test-Revised* (BULIT-R) (Thelen et al., 1991), the *Expanded Attributional Style Questionnaire* (Peterson & Villanova, 1988), and the *Maudsley Obsessional-Compulsive Inventory* (Hodgson & Rachman, 1977).

Projective Personality Tests

Projective assessment goes back to the 1400s, when Leonardo da Vinci is said to have selected his pupils partly on the basis of the creativity they displayed while attempting to find shapes and patterns in ambiguous forms (Piotrowski, 1972). In the late 1800s, Binet adapted a parlor game called "Blotto" to assess "passive imagination" by asking children to tell what they saw in inkblots (Exner, 1976). Sir Frances Galton constructed a word association test in 1879, and Carl Jung was using a similar test for clinical assessment by 1910. These informal projective techniques evolved into projective tests when their content was standardized such that each client was exposed to the same stimuli in the same way.

We have space here to consider only a few of the most prominent projective personality tests, but much more detailed coverage of the full range of such tests is available in standard references (e.g., Exner, 1993; Groth-Marnat, 1999; Impara & Plake, 2001).

The Rorschach Inkblot Test.   One of the most widely known and frequently employed projective tests of personality is the *Rorschach Inkblot Test*, a set of 10 colored and black-and-white inkblots created by Swiss psychiatrist Hermann Rorschach between 1911 and 1921. At that time, many researchers in Europe and North America already employed inkblots to assess fantasy, imagination, and perception, but it was Rorschach who first attempted to use such stimuli for diagnosis and personality assessment.

Rorschach began with geometric figures cut from colored paper and later switched to inkblots, partly as a result of having read about an inkblot test of fantasy developed by a Polish medical student named Hens. The book in which Rorschach described his test and its interpretation was rejected by seven publishers; an eighth agreed to print it only if he would cut five of his original fifteen inkblots. When the book finally appeared (Rorschach, 1921), the few copies sold were not well received. European test experts such as William Stern "denounced it as faulty, arbitrary, artificial, and incapable . . . of understanding human personality. . . ." (Reisman, 1976).

The Rorschach would have had an early demise if David Levy, an American psychiatrist studying in Switzerland in 1921, had not brought a copy of the test back to the United States and, in 1927, instructed a psychology trainee named Samuel Beck in its use. Beck published the first North American report involving the Rorschach, and, in 1937, he provided a standardized procedure for administering and scoring the test. Another scoring manual appeared that same year (Klopfer & Kelley, 1937), and the Rorschach was on its way to popularity among North American psychologists who, until then, had no global test of personality available to them. The growing clinical use of the test was paralleled by an explosion of research on its reliability, validity, scoring, and interpretation.

The test itself is simple. The client is shown ten cards, one at a time. Each presents an inkblot similar to that shown in Figure 5.2 and the client is asked what she or he sees or what the blot could be. The tester records all responses verbatim and takes notes about response times, how the card was held (e.g., upside down, sideways) as responses occurred, noticeable emotional reactions, and other behaviors. After the last card is presented, the tester goes back through the set of cards and conducts an *inquiry* or systematic questioning of the client about the characteristics of each blot that prompted the responses.

Initial reactions to the blots and the comments made during the inquiry are coded, using a special scoring system. Scoring involves the location, determinants, content, and popularity of the responses. *Location* refers to the area of the blot to which the client responds: the whole blot, a common detail, an unusual detail, white space, or some combi-

FIGURE 5.2 Inkblot similar to those used in the Rorschach. (From Norman D. Sundberg. *Assessment of Persons,* © 1977, p. 207. Reprinted by permission of Prentice-Hall, Inc., Englewood Cliffs, New Jersey.)

nation of these are location responses. The *determinants* of the response refer to the characteristic of the blot that influenced a response; they include form, color, shading, and "movement." While there is no movement in the blot itself, the respondent's perception of the blot as a moving object is scored in this category. *Content* refers to the subject matter perceived in the blot. Content might include human figures, parts of human figures, animal figures, animal details, anatomical features, inanimate objects, art, clothing, clouds, blood, X-rays, sexual objects, and symbols. *Popularity* is scored on the basis of how often various responses have been made by previous respondents.

Assume that a client responded to Figure 5.2 by saying, "It looks like a bat" and during subsequent inquiry noted that "I saw the whole blot as a bat because it is black and is just sort of bat shaped." Using one of the available scoring systems, these responses would probably be coded as "WFC9 + AP," where W indicates that the whole blot was used (location); F means that the blot's form (F) was the main determinant of the response; and C9 means that achromatic color was also involved. The + shows that the form described corresponded well to the actual form of the blot; A means that there was animal content in the response; and P indicates that "bat" is a popular response to this particular card.

The fact that responses could be coded somewhat differently by different scoring systems, and that each system tends to be used somewhat differently by individual clinicians, led John Exner (1974, 1993) to propose what he called a Comprehensive System for scoring and interpreting the Rorschach via seven coding categories. Though now quite popular, the Comprehensive System has not eliminated variance in coding Rorschach responses (Wood, Nezworski, & Stejskal, 1996). Nor has it eliminated clinician subjectivity in drawing inferences about Rorschach results. Those inferences can be based on normative data about the popularity of particular responses, and even on computer-based systems for interpreting clinician-coded responses (Cohen, Swerdlik, & Smith, 1992; Fowler, 1985), but for the most part, clinicians tend to rely on subjective judgments based on their personal experience with the test and on general interpretive guidelines.

Using the Comprehensive System, the clinician looks for recurring patterns of responses across cards, and certain test statistics contained in a "structural summary" are interpreted. The overall number of responses (called *productivity*), the frequency of responses in certain categories, and more than twenty response percentages, ratios, and relationships between and among categories are seen as significant (Exner, 1993). For example, because most people tend to use form more often than color in determining their responses, a high proportion of color-dominated determinants may be taken as evidence of weak emotional control. The client's overt behavior while responding to Rorschach cards is also interpreted by the clinician. Evidence of tension, enjoyment, or confusion; attempts to impress the examiner; and other behavioral cues are an important part of Rorschach interpretation (e.g., Goldfried, Stricker, & Weiner, 1971).

There are a number of variants on the Rorschach, the most notable of which are mainly new sets of blots. With the possible exception of the *Holtzman Inkblot Test* (Holtzman et al., 1961), none of these procedures has approached the popularity of the Rorschach.

The Thematic Apperception Test.   The *Thematic Apperception Test* (TAT) consists of 30 drawings of people, objects, and landscapes (see Figure 5.3). In most clinical applications, about ten of these cards (one of them blank) are administered; the subset chosen is determined by the client's age and sex and by the clinician's interests. A separate set of cards depicting African-Americans is also available. The examiner shows each picture and asks the client to make up a story about it, including what led up to the scene, what is now happening, and what is going to happen. The client is encouraged to say what the people in the drawings are thinking and feeling. For the blank card, the respondent is asked to imagine a drawing, describe it, and then construct a story about it. The TAT was designed in 1935 by Christiana D. Morgan and Henry Murray at the Harvard Psychological Clinic (Murray, 1938, 1943). It was based on the projective hypothesis and the assumption that, in telling a story, the client's needs and conflicts will be reflected in one of the story's characters (Lindzey, 1952).

Analysis of the TAT can focus upon both the *content* and the *structure* of TAT stories. Content refers to what clients describe: the people, the feelings, the events, the outcomes. Structure refers to how clients tell their stories: their logic, organization, and use of language, the appearance of speech dysfluencies, the misunderstanding of instructions or stimuli in the drawings, and obvious emotional arousal. The original interpretive scheme (Morgan & Murray, 1935) takes a "hero-oriented" approach in which responses are seen as reflecting the needs (e.g., for achievement, aggression, affiliation) and presses (perceived environmental influences such as criticism, affection, or physical danger) associated with the story's main character (with whom the client often identifies). The frequency and intensity of each need and press are scored on a 1-to-5 scale, and the themes and outcomes of each story are noted as well.

FIGURE 5.3 Drawing of the type included in the TAT. (Reprinted by permission of the publisher from Henry A. Murray, *Thematic Apperception Test*, Cambridge, MA: Harvard University Press, copyright © 1943 by the president and fellows of Harvard College. © 1971 by Henry A. Murray.)

As with the Rorschach, however, there is more than one way to score and interpret clients' TAT responses. In fact, there are at least twenty systems available (Harrison, 1965). Those that use elaborate quantitative procedures for scoring TAT stories helped create TAT response norms to which clinicians can compare their clients' responses (Vane, 1981). Others make little use of formal scoring procedures (Henry,

1956), while still others combine preliminary quantitative analysis with subjective interpretation of the resulting numbers (Bellak, 1986).

Most clinicians seem to prefer TAT scoring systems that are relatively unstructured. As with the Rorschach, they tend to employ TAT response norms and formal scoring criteria only as general guides as they develop an idiosyncratic combination of principles derived from psychodynamic theory and their own clinical experience. This tendency is illustrated by a TAT user's working notes about the following story told by a 25-year-old single man in response to a TAT card showing a young boy looking at a violin resting on a table in front of him:

> This child is sick in bed. He has been given sheet music to study, but instead of the music, he has come across a novel that interests him more than the music. It is probably an adventure story. He evidently does not fear the chance that his parents will find him thusly occupied as he seems quite at ease. He seems to be quite a studious type and perhaps regrets missing school, but he seems quite occupied with the adventure in the story. Adventure has something to do with ocean or water. He is not too happy, though not too sad. His eyes are somewhat blank—coincidence of reading a book without any eyes or knowing what is in the book without reading it. He disregards the music and falls asleep reading the book.

Here are some of the clinician's notes: "On the basis of this story alone, I feel certain that there is a schizophrenic process present, even though not necessarily a pure schizophrenia. Slightly pretentious, facade tone, helped along with basic fact of perverse refusal to acknowledge presence of violin, strongly suggests that he *does* see violin but consciously thinks that he's being "clever" or "original," or is out-tricking the examiner (whom he might see as trying to trick him) by ignoring it or seeing it as a book. That he is aware of it on some level is suggested by the fact that the basic theme, *p* Parental Imposed Task → *n* Auto Resis, passive Aggression, comes through. Consistent also is statement at the end: he *disregards* the music. Not a psychopath trying to act smart—too schizzy.

"*Sick in bed as a child* may be an autobiographical theme. He's almost certainly 'sick' (that is, psychotic) now, and so that may be enough explanation for it. But most psychotics don't [see the card this way]; therefore it becomes plausible that he may have had long illnesses as a child, cutting him off from other kids, and → to fantasy escape—dreams of travel and adventure. Sentence 3 may also describe his overt behavior: nonchalant, seemingly 'at ease,' really frightened underneath. Above are almost all hypotheses, to be confirmed or excluded by later stories. *Strong passivity* throughout—especially in outcome. Also suggestion of *flight* and *avoidance* of very passive sort—drastic enough to include denial of threatening aspects of reality. *Nothing holds* his interest long—not even adventure novel. Hero soon withdraws into his own fantasy, to conviction of knowing what's in book without reading it even though 'took a chance' to read it, and finally withdraws into sleep" (Holt, 1978, pp. 166–167).

Other projective tests similar to the TAT include the *Rosenzweig Picture-Frustration Study* (Rosenzweig, 1949, 1977), which presents 24 cartoons showing one person frustrating another in some way (e.g., "I'm not going to invite you to my party."). The client's task is to say what the frustrated person's response would be. The cards of the *Children's Apperception Test* (CAT) (Bellak, 1992) depict animal characters rather than human beings; those of the *Roberts Apperception Test for Children* (RATC) (McArthur & Roberts, 1982) show children interacting with adults and other children. Scores on several RATC scales are derived by comparing children's responses to norms collected on 200 well-adjusted children.

Incomplete Sentence Tests.   As their name implies, these tests ask clients to complete incomplete sentences. The projective assumption is that how the client finishes the sentences reflect important personality characteristics. Originally used as a measure of intellect in the nineteenth century (Reisman, 1976), incomplete sentences began to be widely employed as projective stimuli in the 1940s; they are now among the most frequently used of all projective tests (Watkins et al., 1995).

The most popular version of sentence completion tests is the *Rotter Incomplete Sentences Blank* (Rotter & Rafferty, 1950). It contains forty sentence stems such as "I like . . . ," "My father . . . ," "I secretly . . ." The client's response to each stem is compared to norms provided in the test manual and is then rated on a seven-point scale of adjustment–maladjustment based on how much they deviate from those norms. Finally, ratings for all the sentences are summed to provide an overall adjustment score. These relatively objective scoring procedures are primarily associated with Rotter's test and a few other research-oriented sentence-completion instruments aimed at assessing specific aspects of personality (Lanyon & Lanyon, 1980).

Projective Drawings.   Another projective test whose name describes its nature is the *Draw-a-Person Test*, or DAP (Machover, 1949). The client's drawings of a person—and sometimes also of a family, a mother, the self, and so on—serve as the basis for the clinician's inferences about various aspects of the client's personality. These inferences are guided by projective assumptions that the inclusion, exclusion, and characteristics of each body part, along with the placement, symmetry, organization, size, and other features of the drawing, are indicative of the client's self-image, conflicts, and perceptions of the world (Machover, 1949).

Other projective drawing tests include the *House-Tree-Person Test* (HTP), which asks clients to draw each of those objects and then discuss them in an extended interview (Buck, 1948), and the *Bender-Gestalt Test.* The latter is a figure-copying test described earlier as measuring certain aspects of mental ability, but some clinicians see errors and distortions in the copied figures as indicators of a client's personality.

THE STATUS OF TESTING IN CLINICAL PSYCHOLOGY

The role of testing as an activity in clinical psychology has undergone large shifts in popularity. Beginning in the 1930s and continuing through the mid-1960s, tests were touted as semi-magical pathways to the "truth" about intelligence, personality, and ability (Reisman, 1976). During those years, clinical psychology students were trained intensively in the use of tests. One prominent clinician noted that "it is hard to conceive . . . of anyone in the field of clinical psychology reaching the postdoctoral level without being thoroughly well-versed in the Rorschach" (Harrower, 1965, p. 398).

From the late 1960s through the 1970s, however, testing lost much of its appeal and was deemphasized as a training goal and professional activity for clinicians. The decline of testing during this time was brought about by several factors. For one thing, as behavioral approaches gained influence in clinical psychology, there was a corresponding shift away from traditional diagnostic assessment, including the tests used for that purpose. Further, many clinicians did not like the "tester" role, which they saw as subservient to psychiatry and potentially damaging to relationships with clients. Finally, clinical psychologists, the public, the government, and clients were becoming increasingly critical of the whole testing enterprise. These concerns stemmed from (1) unflattering results from research on the reliability and validity of many tests; (2) awareness of the susceptibility of tests to various biases; (3) recognition that tests, particularly those assessing intelligence, may place members of certain minority groups at a disadvantage; (4) fear that the testing process may invade respondents' privacy; and (5) worry that tests are too easily misused or misinterpreted. These issues, and the responses to them, are discussed in more detail below.

The Psychometric Properties of Tests

In this section we address the fundamental criticism that psychological tests, in general, do not do their job very well; that is, they are unreliable, invalid, or both. While it is unfair to say that this is true about all tests under all circumstances, research on their psychometric properties has often been unfavorable. Yet if one compares psychological tests with assessment instruments used in other areas of health care, psychological assessment does not fare so badly.

Reliability. In general, the reliability of psychological tests tends to be adequate, but not uniformly so. Test–retest reliability coefficients for the MMPI and MMPI-2 scales range from .60 to .90, for example (Pope, Butcher, & Seelen, 1993). Parallel form, test–retest, and split-half reliabilities are commonly .80 to .96 for major intelligence tests. Similarly, aptitude and ability tests such as the GRE, the Miller Analogies Test (MAT), the Medical College Admission Test (MCAT), and the Law School Admission Test (LSAT) display reliability coefficients ranging from .71 to .97. Tests of interests and values have produced reliabilities from the .70s to the low .90s.

Determining reliability of projective tests is problematic because split-half, parallel form, and test–retest coefficients often do not make sense with such instruments (see Atkinson, 1981). This is partly because, compared to the true–false choices or ratings flowing from objective tests, projective test responses are more difficult to translate into numerical scores. Further, the scoring of projective tests has traditionally been far more subjective than for objective tests. Guidelines came from experts, who, after administering hundreds of projective tests, summarized their experience into numerous rules of thumb for scoring and interpreting various responses. Interrater reliabilities for the Rorschach, the TAT, and other projective tests have tended to be low (Anastasi & Urbina, 1997; Vane, 1981), but did that reflect unreliable tests or inconsistent scoring methods?

To help answer this question, clinicians developed more objective scoring systems for some of the most popular projective tests, such as the Rorschach (Exner, 1986, 1993). Projective test advocates now point to the relatively high levels of agreement shown by different clinicians using similar scoring systems. Interrater and intrarater reliability coefficients for the Rorschach, for example, have been found to average above .80 (Exner, 1996; Parker, Hanson, & Hunsley, 1988). While these figures are comparable to those for the WAIS and MMPI, critics note that the way they are calculated gives an overestimate of the Rorschach's reliability (Wood, Nezworski, & Stejskal, 1996), and interrater reliabilities continue to be low when clinicians use different scoring methods.

Validity. Overall, the validity of psychological tests has been less impressive than their reliability. To a certain extent, this must be the case because the principles of mathematics dictate that no test's validity can be higher than its reliability. Still, for most tests the size of the discrepancy between reliability and validity is too great. In general, the closer a test's content or tasks are to the content or tasks being assessed (i.e., the criterion), the higher the validity will be.

For example, aptitude and ability tests that ask respondents to provide information or perform tasks directly related to academic skills are consistently among the most valid tests available. The major intelligence tests are next in terms of relative validity. These tests, especially their verbal sections, correlate with academic performance, specific skills (such as reading and arithmetic), and teacher ratings in the .17 to .75 range. When intelligence tests are used to draw inferences about a client's psychiatric disorder or personality characteristics, however, validity has been disappointing (Boone, 1993; Williams, Voelker, & Ricciardi, 1995), just as it has when IQ tests are used to predict job performance, socioeconomic status, or other important social outcomes (Neisser et al., 1996). True, IQ scores are correlated with such measures, but not as strongly as has sometimes been claimed. Personality tests have been among the less valid assessment instruments, with the validity of objective personality tests superior to that of projective tests (Anastasi & Urbina, 1997).

Concerns about the validity of projective tests have focused on what the tests actually measure and what can be done with those measurements. For many years, clinicians have used the Rorschach to help them make DSM diagnoses, but with the exception of diagnoses for schizophrenia, bipolar disorder and one or two of the personality disorders, diagnoses based on the Rorschach have made a poor showing. Even clinicians with more training and expertise in projective testing are unable to make Rorschach-based diagnoses with acceptable levels of validity (Wood, Lilenfeld, Garb, & Nezworski, 2000). Empirical support has also failed to materialize for other traditional uses of projective tests, such as to predict dangerousness, predict response to treatment, or detect child sexual abuse. Many of the indices derived from projective tests also lack evidence of validity (Lilienfeld, Wood, & Garb, 2000).

Advocates of projective tests have generally backed away from claims that projective tests are valuable for predictive or diagnostic purposes. Weiner (2000), for instance, says that the Rorschach is an instrument designed to measure personality dynamics, and that it makes little sense to use the test to classify someone according to a diagnostic system that changes from one revision to the next.

Though projective tests have fared poorly in empirical studies as a rule, the scales derived from them are not uniformly inferior. In their meta-analysis of projective techniques, Lilienfeld et al. (2000) identified a few indices that evidence validity (e.g., Thought Disorder Index from the Rorschach, the Overall Quality measure for projective drawings). A recent large-scale study of psychological validity shows that, despite perceptions to the contrary, comparisons of validity coefficients for the Rorschach and TAT are not *consistently* lower than for other personality tests (Meyer, Finn, Eyde, Kay, Moreland, Dies et al., 2001). The problem is that too few of the many scales and indices from projective tests have such support.

Lilienfeld et al. (2000) suggest that projective tests may underperform because of design flaws. Most projective tests were developed before psychometrics were well understood, yet despite advances in the field, the stimulus materials for these tests have remained largely unchanged. Poor validity might also result because many of the indices are based on small samples of behavior, or because they attempt to measure poorly defined or unusual criteria. This idea receives support from the observation that the empirically supported projective indices usually measure straightforward criteria and are based on aggregation of multiple responses.

In the face of mounting criticism, the burden of proof has fallen to the advocates of projective tests to show that such measures add useful, valid, and reliable information to clinical practice beyond that obtainable by less time-consuming methods. Though projective instruments have remained among the most popular tests, the trend is moving away from them. The Division of Clinical Psychology of the American Psychological Association recently excluded, for the first time, the Rorschach from its recommendations for a model curriculum in assessment, and a recent survey of training directors of APA-approved doctoral programs found a decline in emphasis on projective techniques, a trend first noted a few years prior (Belter & Piotrowski, 2001).

The Validity of Psychological Versus Medical Testing.   When we evaluate the reliability or validity of psychological tests, describing them as good, average, or poor, we imply comparison against a standard. However, it is important to specify what standard is being used. If psychological tests are compared against perfection, all tests fare poorly. If tests are compared against some statistical cut-off (e.g., .80 reliability; 70% accuracy in identifying a criterion), some do well and others poorly. But what is the best standard by which we should judge psychological tests?

In a recent report, Greg Meyer and colleagues provided a revealing look at the adequacy of psychological assessment (Meyer et al., 2001). Their report summarized results from a large and systematic study comparing the validity of psychological assessments with the validity of medical assessments. The study was commissioned by the Psychological Assessment Work Group (PAWG), a group formed by the American Psychological Association's Board of Professional Affairs in 1996. Most people, psychologists included, have generally assumed that, when it comes to accuracy, psychological tests lag well behind medical tests. Yet Meyer and his colleagues found otherwise. Combining data from more than 125 meta-analyses examining test validity, they found that over a wide range of assessment procedures, the validity of psychological testing is indistinguishable from that of medical testing. Both disciplines have tests ranging from those that are basically uninformative for identifying a criterion to those that are highly informative. Figure 5.4 presents a few illustrative comparisons between medical and psychological test procedures.

Obviously there is room for improvement in assessment validity in both fields, but if the standard by which we judge the adequacy of psychological tests is the validity of medical tests, psychological tests fare reasonably well.

Distortion of Test Scores

Tests are designed to collect assessment data under standard conditions. When those conditions are not standard, test scores may be distorted in ways that can mislead clinicians. A multitude of factors can alter the outcome of all types of tests. A classic exam-

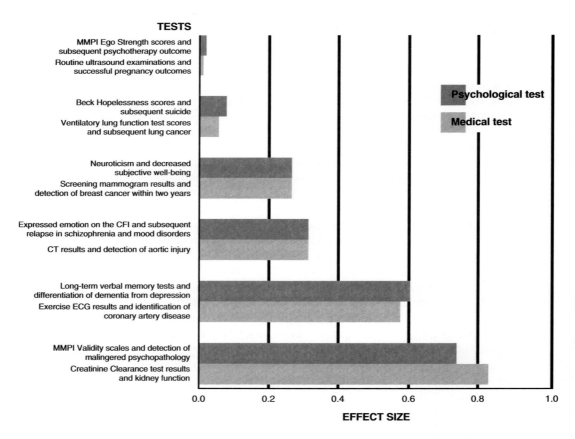

FIGURE 5.4 Sample effect sizes for psychological and medical tests. (SOURCE: Psychological Testing and Psychological Assessment, *American Psychologist*, Feb. 2001, pp. 136–143, Table 2.)

ple is provided by a study in which college men who had just seen photographs of nude females gave more sex-related responses to the TAT when it was administered by a young, informally dressed male graduate student than when given by a man who was older and more formal (Mussen & Scodel, 1955).

Clients' motivation can also influence their test responses. In one study, for example, mental hospital residents took a true-false psychological test after hearing either that it was an index of mental illness on which "true" responses indicated pathology or that it measured self-insight and that "true" responses were associated with readiness to leave the hospital (Braginsky, Grosse, & Ring, 1966). Scores on the "mental-illness" test were higher for those who wished to stay in the hospital than for those who wanted to leave. The "self-insight" description was associated with the opposite pattern: Patients wishing to leave scored higher than those wanting to stay. Motivational effects have also appeared on employee integrity tests (Alliger, Lillienfeld, & Mitchell 1996), IQ tests (Englemann, 1974), and objective and projective personality tests (Barrick & Mount, 1996; Stewart & Patterson, 1973).

On some tests, the structure of the items and response alternatives may influence results. Suppose a tester wants to know how parents feel about allowing their children to display aggression toward them. The tester may write an item that says "No child should be permitted to strike a parent" and ask the client to agree or disagree. In order to decide whether to agree or disagree, however, the client must mentally construct the item's opposite, such as, "A child should be encouraged to strike a parent." Because each respondent is likely to construct different mental opposites the psychological content of the test may vary from client to client.

The circumstances under which a test is given—anything from temperature extremes and outside noise to crowding and the presence of a stranger—can also affect its results if they act as stressors (Plante, Goldfarb, & Wadley, 1993). In one case, for example, a child's scores on repeated IQ tests went from 68 to 120 and back to 79 depending on whether or not a particular adult was in the testing room (Handler, 1974). Establishing trust can thus become an important element maximizing the validity of certain kinds of tests (e.g., Grossarth, Eysenck, & Boyle, 1995).

Another source of distortion in test results is the fact that some clients tend to respond in particular ways to most items, regardless of what the items are. This tendency has been called *response set* (Cronbach, 1946), *response style* (Jackson & Messick, 1958), and *response bias* (Berg, 1955). For example, clients exhibiting a *social desirability bias* will respond to test items in ways that are most socially acceptable, whether or not those responses reflect their true feelings or impulses (Edwards, 1957; Rychtarik, Tarnowski, & St. Lawrence, 1989). Clients have also been suspected of *acquiescent response styles* (Jackson & Messick, 1961), in which they tend to agree with virtually any self-descriptive test item. Defensive, deviant, and exaggerated styles have also been postulated (e.g., Isenhart & Silversmith, 1996). The significance of response styles in determining test scores has been hotly debated, partly because it is unclear whether response tendencies represent stable client characteristics (McCrae & Costa, 1983) or temporary behaviors dictated and reinforced by the testing circumstances (Linehan & Nielsen, 1983). Whatever the case, the client's point of view while taking a test cannot be ignored when evaluating a test.

Other client variables may also be important determinants of test responses. For example, clients whose cultural background leaves them unfamiliar with the concepts and vocabulary of middle-class America may perform poorly on psychological tests whose items reflect those concepts and words (Herrnstein & Murray, 1994). The influence of one's cultural and ethnic background on intelligence test scores is of particular concern, especially to members of certain minority groups in the United States (Laosa, 1996). As noted earlier, one approach to this problem has been to develop intelligence tests that are not strongly influenced by culture-specific experiences or particular verbal skills. Unfortunately, "culture-fair" tests may be influenced just as much as, or more than, standard tests by cultural and environmental factors (Samuda, 1975), and their validity tends to be lower (Humphreys, 1988). Another approach has been to "correct" for ethnic differences in test scores by adjusting those scores on the basis of norms associated with various ethnic groups. This practice, known as *subgroup norming*, enjoys some popularity among social scientists, but it was banned by the Civil Rights Act of 1991 (Gottfredson, 1994; Sackett & Wilk, 1994).

It has been suggested that instead of trying to *remove* all cultural effects from IQ tests, we should *examine* the differential performance of various groups in order to identify those who are most in need of corrective educational programs (Krull & Pierce, 1995). As Anne Anastasi (1988) put it:

> Tests are designed to show what an individual can do at a given point in time. They cannot tell us *why* he performs as he does. To answer that question, we need to investigate his background, motivations, and other pertinent circumstances. Nor can tests tell how able a culturally or educationally disadvantaged child might have been if she had been reared in a more favorable environment. Moreover, tests cannot compensate for cultural deprivation by eliminating its effect from their scores. On the contrary, tests should reveal such effects, so that appropriate remedial steps can be taken. To conceal the effects of cultural disadvantages by rejecting tests or by trying to devise tests that are insensitive to such effects can only retard progress toward a genuine solution of social problems. Such reactions toward tests are equivalent to breaking a thermometer because it registers a body temperature of 101°. Test scores should be used constructively: by the individual in enhancing self-understanding and personal development and in educational and vocational planning; by teachers in improving instruction and in adjusting instructional content to individual needs; and by employers in achieving a better match between persons and jobs, recognizing that persons can be trained and jobs can be redesigned. (p. 66)

Others have made a related suggestion for reducing irrelevant cultural effects: When specific predictions are desired, use instruments that sample as directly as possible the particular behaviors and skills of interest. When this is done, the opportunity for extraneous characteristics to distort performance is greatly reduced. The sources of test-score bias discussed here barely scratch the surface of the problem, which is discussed at far greater length in numerous sources (e.g., Anastasi & Urbina, 1997).

Abuse of Tests

Like all assessment procedures, tests involve entry by the clinician into the privacy of clients' thoughts and behaviors. The extent to which such entry is desirable or even legal is a matter of debate and litigation. Many observers contend that there are too many tests and too much testing. They argue that testing is irrelevant, inaccurate, and too easily misused. Overdependence on IQ scores by ill-informed test consumers and misinterpretation of personality tests by clinicians provide two examples (Anastasi, 1992; Clark & Abeles, 1994).

During the mid-1960s, the U.S. Congress conducted hearings on psychological testing, particularly as it was being used in educational and vocational selection. These inquiries were prompted in part by serious, knowledgeable test critics and also by the appearance of nonexpert books with sensational titles like *The Brain Watchers* (Gross, 1962), *The Tyranny of Testing* (Hoffman, 1962), and *They've Got Your Number* (Wernick, 1956). The concern over privacy and other issues produced restrictions on testing in certain settings (Cohen et al., 1992; Reschly, 1984). For example, personality tests have been eliminated from routine selection procedures for federal employees. IQ tests are restricted in some school systems, and the Civil Rights Act of 1991 prohibits their use in hiring decisions if they result in bias against minorities.

The American Psychological Association is sensitive to these issues and has urged its members to reduce the possibility of abuse in the testing field by adhering to its *Standards for Educational and Psychological Tests* (APA, 1985), which were recently supplemented by a *Statement on Test-Taker Rights and Responsibilities* (Roberts, 1996) and by the APA's *Guidelines for Test User Qualifications*. In addition, the *Uniform Guidelines on Employee Selection Procedure* was developed by the Equal Employment Opportunity Commission (EEOC) to regulate the use of tests and other methods as selection techniques. These documents reflect the argument that, when developed, evaluated, administered, interpreted, and published with due regard for scientific principles and the rights and welfare of clients, psychological tests can positively contribute to society (Robertson & Eyde, 1993). More extensive discussions of the pros and cons of testing are available in a variety of sources (e.g., Anastasi & Urbina, 1997; Kaplan & Saccuzzo, 1993; Neisser et al., 1996).

Testing Today

One might anticipate that the many problems associated with testing would make clinicians wary of using tests as a source of assessment data. This does not appear to be the case, however. Testing is still an active enterprise in North America and elsewhere (Chan & Lee, 1995; Belter & Piotrowski, 2001), in spite of the fact that (1) many managed health care plans provide limited support for the pretreatment psychological testing that was once routine for clinicians, and (2) structured interviews are becoming a popular alternative diagnostic tool (see Chapter 4). Though clinicians spend considerably less time engaged in testing and other methods of assessment compared with 50 years ago (Groth-Marnat, 1999; 2000), learning to use traditional test instruments is still considered an essential part of clinical training (Belter & Piotrowski, 2001).

New psychological tests are introduced every year (see Anastasi & Urbina, 1997; Impara & Plake, 2001; Goldstein & Hersen, 1990; and the *Journal of Personality Assessment*), but more established tests continue to attract attention from practitioners and researchers. Overall preferences for psychological tests—in North America and elsewhere—have remained surprisingly stable over the past fifty years. As shown in Table 5.5, the most popular tests are "the old reliables": the MMPI, the Wechsler Scales, the Rorschach, and the TAT (Borum & Grisso, 1995; Chan & Lee, 1995; Piotrowski & Keller, 1992; Sharpley & Pain, 1988; Watkins et al., 1995).

Why has psychological testing remained so much a part of clinical psychology despite a general deemphasis of formal assessment?

For one thing, focusing attention on the shortcomings of tests and the testing process provided the impetus for efforts to improve both (Glaser & Bond, 1981). There is more careful theorizing about the nature and structure of intelligence, mental abili-

TABLE 5.5   Testing's Top Ten

Test	Sundberg (1961)[a]	Lubin, Wallis, & Paine (1971)[b]	Lubin, Larsen, & Matarazzo (1984)[c]	Sweeney, Clarkin, & Fitzgibbon (1987)[d]	Watkins et al. (1995)[e]	Camara, Nathan, & Puente (2000)
WAIS	6	1	1	4[f]	1	1
MMPI	7.5	6	2	2	2	2
Bender-Gestalt Visual Motor Test	4	3.5	3	5	6	5
Rorschach	1	2	4	1	5	4
TAT	2.5	3.5	5	3	4	6
WISC	10	7	6	4[f]	9	3
Peabody Picture Vocabulary Test	—	13	7.5	—	12	20
Sentence Completion Tests (All Kinds)	13.5	8.5	7.5	7	3	15
House-Tree-Person Test	12	9	9	6	7	8
Draw-A-Person Test	2.5	5	10	6	7	[not included]

[a]Ranking of 185 respondents mentioning some use of test.

[b]Ranking of 251 respondents mentioning some use of test.

[c]Ranking of 221 respondents mentioning some use of test.

[d]Ranking of 107 Directors of Association of Psychology Internship Centers.

[e]Ranking of 410 to 412 respondents mentioning some use of test.

[f]Reported for WAIS and WISC combined.

ties, attitudes, and personality, leading in turn to broader conceptualizations of the construct validity of psychological tests. As noted in Chapter 3, construct validity refers to the ability of an instrument to measure a psychological quality in ways related to a theory of the quality in question. Construct validation of a test never stops; it is a continuing process of elaborating and testing theories about what a construct actually means (Messick, 1995). An unwavering commitment to construct validation not only enhances test development, it also promotes a better understanding of fundamental psychological phenomena such as intelligence and personality.

Testing has remained viable also because there is increasing interest in developing well-constructed tests for the assessment of specific clinical targets such as marital distress (Jones et al., 1995; Snyder, 1981), eating disorders (Thelen, Mintz, & Boman, 1996), and social support and coping resources (Cohen et al., 1985; Folkman & Lazarus, 1988). Greater attention is also being given to psychometrically sound evaluation of children and adolescents. Prominent examples include the MMPI-A, a special form of the MMPI for adolescents (Butcher et al., 1992) and the Child Behavior Problem Checklist (CBCL) (Achenbach & Edelbrock, 1991). Current assessment procedures now more specifically relate to the criteria they attempt to describe or predict.

While some areas of testing are being deemphasized (e.g., projective tests, use of SAT scores for college admission), other areas are seeing greater emphasis. One such area is neuropsychological assessment. Today, psychological expertise is needed in the field of health psychology, where clinical psychologists, often working teams with doctors and other health professionals, are often called upon to assess brain-injured clients' cognitive strengths and weaknesses, to integrate that with information about clients' emotional adjustment, and to answer specific, practical questions. Such questions might be "Which combination of physical and psychological therapies might be most beneficial for this patient?" or "Is this client employable in such-and-such a capacity?" Because clinical psychologists today are expected to be familiar with the rapidly growing field of neuropsychology, Chapter 12 will be devoted to a more detailed coverage of the area.

The use of computers in testing is another area of expanding interest. Clinicians have used computers to score psychological tests for decades, but there has been a recent increase in computer-based administration and interpretation of tests. This raises the question of whether results from computer-given tests are comparable to results from human-given tests. The answer is: sometimes. Clients who are uncomfortable with computers can feel awkward and give responses different from those they might give to a clinician. On the other hand, clients who are comfortable with computers sometimes even prefer computer administration over a face-to-face interactions and may also be more willing to admit to sensitive issues, making test results more valid (Hile & Adkins, 1997). The type of test also affects whether computer-given tests and clinician-given tests are comparable. In a review of the literature, James N. Butcher and colleagues concluded that some personality assessment instruments, such as the MMPI, show promising results, while others, such as neuropsychological tests and psychiatric screening instruments should be viewed with caution. They emphasize the need to evaluate computer-administration of tests on a case-by-case basis (Butcher, Perry, & Atlis, 2000).

While it might not be too difficult to write computer programs that administer or score a test, particularly when the test items are simple and clearly-written and when response options are few and unambiguous (such as the MMPI's "true," "false," or "cannot say"), it can be very difficult to write programs that combine scores into a good narrative report. That is why, so far, the results from most computer-generated report-writing programs are less promising. Older programs simply generate a collection of sentences based on test scores—the "look-up and list" method—resulting in reports that fall short of being an integrated description of a person. With advances in technology and in psychological research, automated programs have improved, but many remain unvalidated and therefore of questionable value (Garb, 2000). This, however, is likely to change. Assessment experts foresee computer-based test interpretation making large advances in the not-too-distant future (see Groth-Marnat, 2000), particularly in the areas where human judgment is most suspect, such as those discussed in Chapter 3.

Another reason for clinicians' continued involvement in testing is that the availability of improved tests sustains a demand for it, especially in educational, industrial, and medical settings. Clinicians' testing activities can be profitable, especially with computers making administration, scoring, and interpretation of tests easier and more efficient. Tests that purport to measure conditions or populations in the most time-efficient manner are on the rise (Corcoran & Fischer, 2000). These tests, sometimes called *rapid assessment instruments* (RAIs), have both advantages and disadvantages, but they appear to be gaining popularity both among clinicians and among managed care institutions that oversee administration of psychotherapeutic services. Indeed, most clinicians' strong personal interest in at least one specific type of testing has prompted many of them to develop a testing specialty within their professional practice.

Finally, as ordinary mortals, clinical psychologists tend to form habits that are hard to break. Graduate training tends to set patterns of assessment practices to which clinical psychologists become personally attached. In other words, clinicians tend to do what they were taught to do and tend to continue doing so because it is what they have always done.

Fair enough, but why don't they at least abandon tests such as the DAP and the TAT, whose validity appears weakest (Boyle, 1995; Keiser & Prather, 1990; Smith & Dumont, 1995)? Part of the answer is that many clinicians pay more attention to data that supports these tests than to damaging evidence about their validity. Indeed, they may view negative research findings about a test as irrelevant to that test's clinical value (Masling, 1992). One observer put it this way: "Published indexes of validity . . . are but rough guides, for the psychologist must reach his own judgments of clinical validity and meaningfulness in each particular case" (Tallent, 1976, p. 14).

Indeed, certain clinicians are, for reasons not clearly understood, able to draw remarkably accurate inferences from test data. Almost every practitioner knows of at least one MMPI or Rorschach "ace" whose reputation shores up general confidence in particular tests. Most clinical psychologists are themselves reinforced for using even the least scientifically-supported tests by the fact that, now and then, they make their own insightful inferences on the basis of test data. Clinicians remain loyal to projective tests, in particular, because they believe that—regardless of what research results show—these measures offer special information about clients. They may also find them useful for building rapport with clients (especially children) and for confirming what they might already suspect about a client on the basis of other assessment data.

These cognitive and practical factors, in combination with the traditional view of clinical psychologists as test experts and the societal demand for testing services, make the continued popularity of psychological testing more comprehensible. And after all, when important decisions about people must be made, a psychological test with even modest proof of validity will usually be accepted for use because it promises at least some increase in the accuracy of those decisions. Thus, though more stringent standards and limitations regarding the use of tests in many spheres appear likely, testing will probably continue to be a major activity of clinical psychologists.

CHAPTER SUMMARY

Psychological testing is an important part of clinical assessment research and practice. A test is a systematic procedure for observing and describing behavior in a standard situation. Test responses can be used as samples, signs, or correlates in drawing inferences about clients.

Most psychological tests are designed to measure intellectual functioning; ability; attitudes, interests, preferences, and values; or personality. They are usually constructed either analytically (on the basis of what a theory says they should contain) or empirically (on the basis of research on which items tap dimensions of interest). The sequential system approach combines aspects of both methods. Regardless of how a test is constructed, it must be evaluated in terms of its reliability and validity.

Prominent tests of intellectual functioning (whose results are usually expressed as IQ scores) include the Stanford-Binet (4th edition), and the Wechsler Scales (e.g., WAIS-III, WISC-III). The Scholastic Aptitude Test (SAT) and the Wide Range Achievement Test (WRAT) exemplify general ability tests in use today; others, such as the Bender-Gestalt, test more specific abilities. Attitudes, interests, preferences, and values are typically measured through tests such as the Strong-Campbell Interest Inventory, the Self-Directed Search, the Allport-Vernon-Lindzey Study of Values, and the Reinforcement Survey Schedule. Tests of personality can be objective or projective. The Minnesota Multiphasic Personality Inventory (MMPI-2), the California Psychological Inventory (CPI), the Personality Research Form (PRF), the Sixteen Personality Factor Questionnaire (16PF), and the NEO Personality Inventory (NEO-PI-R) are examples of widely-used objective tests. The Rorschach, the Thematic Apperception Test (TAT), sentence completion tests, and the Draw-a-Person (DAP) test are projective instruments.

Although the tests listed above have remained very popular around the world over the past 50 years, testing itself came under heavy criticism during the 1970s because of concerns about the reliability and validity of tests, about factors that distort their results and interpretation, and about their potential for misuse. Today, the reliability of many tests, especially those of intellectual functioning, is adequate or better, and while the validity of some tests (particularly projective personality tests) remains marginal, the validity of others is satisfactory. The testing enterprise continues because tests can be useful and because clinical traditions and societal demands make it difficult to abandon this activity. Standards published by the APA and the federal government are designed to assure that tests are used with due regard for scientific principles and the rights and welfare of clients.

Chapter 6

Clinical Interventions: An Overview

When a clinician acts in a professional capacity to influence clients, the activity is called clinical intervention because it constitutes a deliberate attempt to change behavior or social circumstances in a desirable direction. Clinical intervention can take many forms, including psychotherapy, psychosocial rehabilitation, and prevention. Our description of clinical intervention spans four chapters, beginning here with an overview of psychotherapy, the form of intervention most traditionally associated with clinical psychology. In this chapter, we pay special attention to the common features of most therapeutic interactions, core assumptions shared by most psychotherapists, and goals of most therapeutic interventions. Chapter 7 then focuses on the approaches to psychotherapy, particularly individual psychotherapy, that grow from dominant theoretical orientations (i.e., psychodynamic, behavioral and cognitive-behavioral, humanistic, and eclectic). In Chapter 8, we discuss various alternatives to individual psychotherapy, such as group therapy, couples therapy, family therapy, psychosocial rehabilitation, community psychology, and self-help. Chapter 9 then examines research methods and findings on the effectiveness of the various modes of psychotherapy.

WHAT IS PSYCHOTHERAPY?

In a nutshell, psychotherapy is a treatment offered within the bounds of a professional relationship by trained therapists to help clients in distress. While no definition of psychotherapy satisfies everyone, this one identifies psychotherapy's participants (clients and therapists), the basic framework (professional relationship), and the general goal (reduction of emotional distress).

THE PARTICIPANTS

The participants in psychotherapy, clients and therapists, can vary in many ways: gender, age, racial or ethnic background, belief systems, personal strengths and weaknesses, communication styles, and so on. Psychotherapy can involve more than one client at a time (e.g., couples therapy, group therapy), or more than one therapist at a time (e.g., co-therapists, therapeutic teams). Below we examine the therapist and client variables that clinicians have suspected play important roles in psychotherapy.

Therapists

By special training and experience, the therapist is prepared to help clients overcome the disturbances that require treatment. Which therapist characteristics are essential and which are supplementary for successful therapy? This has been debated for many years, but most agree that a therapist should possess skills that enable them to understand clients' problems and then to interact with clients in a way that helps them alleviate, or at least cope more effectively with, those with problems. Those skills are either developed or improved during *advanced training.*

Clinical Psychologists.   A fully licensed clinical psychologist has completed a PhD or PsyD in an APA-approved graduate training program. In most instances, this involves a minimum of 4 years of graduate study, during which the student takes several courses designed to develop expertise in assessment, treatment, and research. A supervised internship follows the course work and, in some programs, so does a doctoral dissertation (a detailed report of one's own original research and the state of the art in that particular area). Many clinicians begin employment, usually working part-time as they complete school, as early as the first or second year of graduate training. That employment might involve assisting with or conducting research or working with clients in circumscribed capacity such as an intake worker, case manager, or psychodiagnostician. After earning the advanced degree, doctoral-level clinicians obtain supervision for an initial period of practice (e.g., 2 years or 2,000 hours), and once this is completed, they are eligible to take a national licensing exam, which, if passed, allows them to practice independently. Licensing requirements in the United States vary, but most states have transfer agreements that allow clinicians licensed in one state to be licensed in another. The road to fully independent clinical psychology practice often takes 6, 7, 8, or even more years, though most persons work in the field during much of this time. In practice, many clinicians combine psychotherapy practice with assessment, teaching, research, supervision, or consultation (Norcross, Karg, & Prochaska, 1997; also see Chapter 1).

Master's level clinical psychology programs typically take 2 years to complete. They include some of the same course work as is required for a PhD. Persons who graduate with a master's degree in clinical psychology can provide psychotherapy and do psychological assessments, but most states require that they practice under supervision of a licensed psychologist or psychiatrist. MA-level clinicians sometimes face restrictions on their practice, such as third-party reimbursers (i.e., insurance companies) refusing to pay for certain services or state-regulating agencies imposing prohibitions against setting up private practices. Persons who complete bachelor's degrees in psychology provide some forms of therapy or supportive interventions appropriate to their level of training. Pay scales for the different types of clinical work are, as one would expect, generally commensurate with the level of training.

Related Core Mental Health Professions.

Clinical psychologists are among the professionals considered the *core mental health professions*. Others include counseling psychology, social work, psychiatry, psychiatric nursing, and marriage and family therapy. These professionals are recognized by governmental agencies and insurance providers as critical providers of mental health services, providers whose level of training and professional affiliation insures quality treatment. Each of these professions has national or international organizations, a network of accredited training programs, well-established research traditions, and specific licensing or certification requirements. Each group has its own unique history and traditions, but practitioners from each group offer psychotherapeutic services in one form or another.

Counseling psychologists are generally the most similar to clinical psychologists in their training and in the types of services they offer. Counseling psychology programs are sometimes housed in psychology departments, but they are often offered through education departments or other departments or divisions. Counseling psychologists earn a PhD, PsyD, or EdD degree, and they are generally eligible for the same licensure, insurance reimbursement, and professional benefits as clinical psychologists (Norcross et al., 1998). Much of their course work and supervised training also overlaps with that of clinical psychologists—they are trained in psychopathology, interviewing, counseling and psychotherapy theories, research, etc. Differences between the professions are largely a matter of emphasis. Both professions are concerned with treatment and prevention of psychological disorders, but counseling psychologists deal also with normal transitions and adjustments people may face. Besides doing psychotherapy, counseling psychologists might, for instance, do career counseling or other forms of counseling related to life change or developmental issues (Division 17 Counseling Psychology, 2001). Clinical psychologists, on the other hand, focus more specifically on prevention, diagnosis, and treatment of psychological problems and on research related to these issues, and they generally deal with more severe pathology. Despite these general differences however, there is considerable overlap between the professions.

As the nation's largest group of mental health services providers, *social workers* are employed in a variety of settings, including hospitals, businesses, community mental health centers, courts, prisons, and family services agencies. About half of the National Association of Social Workers are engaged in direct clinical services, including various forms of therapy; the rest work in areas such as administration, public policy, research, and community organizing. Social workers also earn bachelor's, master's, or doctoral degrees in their profession (National Association of Social Workers, 2001).

Psychiatry is a specialty within the medical profession, just as pediatrics (children), ophthalmology (eyes), or neurology (brain and nervous system) are. Psychiatrists are doctors who go beyond their MD degree to specialize in treating psychological disorders. After completing requirements to be a physician, persons training to be psychiatrists typically complete a psychiatric residency, where they take course work in psychology and undergo supervision by psychiatrists in their work with patients. This often occurs in a hospital setting, but it may also occur in outpatient settings. In addition to doing therapy, psychiatrists can prescribe medication and conduct or order other medical tests. In general, though psychiatrists have more medical training, clinical psychologists have more formal training in psychological assessment and a variety of approaches to psychology.

Psychiatric nursing is a specialty within the nursing profession. Its practitioners are trained in the care and treatment of persons with psychiatric disorders. They usually work in hospital settings and operate as part of a treatment team, often headed by a psychiatrist.

Marriage and family therapists (MFTs) are trained to treat psychological disorders as they occur within the context of marriage, couples, and families. MFTs earn master's or doctoral degrees within their profession and also have supervised clinical experience. Their training often emphasizes family systems models (discussed in Chapter 8) and psychotherapy techniques applicable to the populations they treat.

A number of other applied specialties within psychology overlap with clinical psychology. Some of these, such as health psychology and rehabilitation psychology, can be specialties adopted by persons trained within clinical psychology programs. Alternately, persons who adopt certain specialties can attend graduate program specifically devoted to that specialty. For instance, many school psychologists graduate from school psychology programs, though some clinically trained psychologists end up working as school psychologists as well.

Paraprofessionals.   Persons trained to assist in or supplement mental health services are called *paraprofessionals*. They generally work as part of a treatment team, and their activities are supervised by professionals. Paraprofessionals are usually bachelor's-level or associate-level personnel trained to administer a specific form of treatment to a specific population. Examples include occupational therapists, rehabilitation counselors, and music therapists. Other examples are case workers trained to conduct group sessions with teen drug users in a residential facility or volunteers at telephone hot lines or other crisis intervention centers.

The number and types of paraprofessionals has expanded considerably in recent years because research has shown they can be quite effective. In fact, some studies have found that paraprofessionals achieved outcomes equal or superior to those obtained by more extensively-trained professionals (Atkins & Christensen, 2001; Durlak, 1981; Hattie, Sharpley, & Rogers, 1984; Holland, 1998). Some have criticized that research for having methodological limitations (Nietzel & Fisher, 1981), and other research has found that professional training leads to better outcomes in specific areas, such as greater client retention, briefer therapy, and better overall well-being for clients (see Atkins & Christensen, 2001).

As you might expect, findings like this caused a stir among the professional community and among managed care providers interested in lowering costs. The effectiveness of paraprofessionals relative to professionals remains controversial, but it is clear that well-trained paraprofessionals can perform valuable roles in the delivery of mental health services.

Other Specialists and Caregivers.   Mental health services are also offered by a variety of other *specialists* and *caregivers*. Pastoral counselors typically get training in counseling from a faith-based perspective. For clients whose religious faith is central to their identity and outlook on life, the availability of a counselor who affirms this faith is important. Indeed, for many persons, a rabbi, priest, minister, or other religious leader is the first person to consider when they need to talk about a distressing personal problem.

Some specialists, such as art therapists, recreation therapists, or music therapists are considered paraprofessionals because they work closely with professionals and come from disciplines that have that have some or all of the following indicators of professional quality: well-articulated standards of practice, national organizations that promote and oversee the profession, course offerings in colleges or universities, empirical research traditions and peer-reviewed journals (e.g., see Field's 1998 article in the *American Psychologist* for a review of research on the effects of massage therapy).

Others specialties, such as aromatherapy, reflexology, acupuncture, homeopathy, or spiritual healing techniques have few or none of these indicators and might be described as further from the mainstream of mental health treatment. Often classified as *alternative treatments* or *alternative medicine*, many of these further-from-the-mainstream treatments combine somatic or sensual experiences with variants of psychological, social, or spiritual intervention. Some practices derive from ancient traditions; some are new inventions. Persons who practice alternative treatments often describe their work falling within a "holistic" tradition that emphasizes the integration of mind, body, and spirit (Feltham, 2000). The popularity of such interventions has grown considerably in the last several years (see Ernst, 2000; Unutzer, Klap, Strum, Young, & Marmon et al., 2000).

While it is easy to dismiss all alternative therapies as quackery—and some surely are—it is noteworthy that within the last several years an increasing number of health professionals have recommended conducting careful investigations into the effectiveness of selected alternative therapies. Careful study is necessary because when clients report improvement, it is important to know whether they got better because a) the practitioner used some unique alternative technique or b) the practitioners, in the course of applying their alternative treatments, simply did what most effective therapists do: express warmth and concern, listen nonjudgmentally, reflect accurately the clients' partially-expressed thoughts and emotions, suggest alternatives, etc. In short, alternative treatments should be held to the same standards as other treatments: Claims of effectiveness first need independent verification, then the treatments need to be studied to rule out *placebo effects* or other alternative explanations as the causes for effectiveness.

Finally, there are a variety of *nonprofessional caregivers*, including friends, physicians, ministers, teachers, police officers, lawyers, family members, and neighbors. When people have psychological difficulties, they are likely first to consult one of these. Emory Cowen (1982) studied four groups of these "natural caregivers"—hairdressers, divorce lawyers, bartenders, and industrial supervisors—and found that some of the helping strategies they used resembled professionals' techniques (e.g., proposing alternative solutions). Just as psychotherapy is not the exclusive province of clinical psychologists, efforts to help people change are not restricted to the mental health professions alone.

Therapist Characteristics. Therapists differ in their formal training, level of experience, personality, age, sex, ethnicity, and so on. Which of these, if any, are most important in psychotherapy?

As a general rule, broad demographic variables such as the therapist age, sex, ethnicity, or socioeconomic status play relatively insignificant roles in the overall effectiveness of therapy (Beulter, Machado, & Neufeldt, 1994). In particular cases, one or more of these variables might be important, such as when an elderly female client finds it hard to confide in a male therapist, but as a general rule, they do not exert strong effects on therapy outcome. More important are therapist training and certain interpersonal skills that the therapist brings to the therapy.

Hardly anyone doubts the claim that therapists need advanced training, and research supports the claim. For instance, Machado, Beulter, and Greenberg (1999) found that trained therapists could recognize others' emotions better than untrained novices could. Because emotion recognition is necessary for understanding another person and for expressing empathy with them, it is a critical psychotherapy skill. Therapists with more training and experience also have lower client drop-out rates (Lubrosky, 1989).

Though advanced training is necessary, it is not clear exactly what kind of training or what level of experience are best. Among the core mental health professions, for instance, none can claim convincing evidence that they produce superior results. As we suggested in our discussion of paraprofessionals, persons with brief, narrowly focused training sometimes produce results equal to those obtained by persons who have had long-term professional training. Still, most people would prefer to go to a therapist with greater training and experience, just as they would prefer a physician with more training and experience. We will discuss training and its effects more in Chapter 9 (Research on Clinical Interventions) and in Chapter 14 (Professional Issues in Clinical Psychology).

In addition to advanced training, psychotherapists are expected to possess certain interpersonal skills that contribute to therapy. These include communication skills, relationship-building skills, and self-monitoring skills (Inskipp, 2000).

At a minimum, effective therapy requires the ability to listen well and to convey a sense of understanding, both of which depend on *communication skills*. All methods of psychotherapy teach therapists ways of verbally capturing human experience and behavior. Therapists then help their clients make behavioral, cognitive, and emotional changes by using those concepts. In many instances, therapists teach clients a new vocabulary, new ways of understanding their experience. Verbal communications skills are central to this process.

As we will discuss shortly, the relationship that develops between therapist and client strongly affects therapy outcome. For this reason, *relationship-building skills* are critical. Therapists need to communicate sincerity, the presentation of oneself free from pretense or affectation. They must also have an ability to warmly support troubled clients without judging them, while, at the same time, reminding them of their capacity and responsibility for making beneficial changes in their lives. Clinicians often summarize these relationship qualities as *genuineness, empathy*, and *unconditional positive regard*. These are called *Rogerian* qualities because Carl Rogers claimed that they are the necessary and sufficient conditions for bringing about therapeutic change.

Finally, therapists need skills in self-awareness or self-management. As in any other line of work, the ability to monitor factors that interfere with performance is important. It is especially important for therapists, who often need to stay focused as clients experience intense emotions. *Self-monitoring skills* are seldom directly taught in a therapist's training, but much of training and supervision in psychotherapy is indirectly aimed at developing it. Psychoanalytically oriented therapists typically undergo analysis as the way to achieve self-monitoring skills. Cognitive or behaviorally oriented therapists are more likely to take an empirical approach, evaluating whether personal issues might be interfering when their interventions seem ineffective (see Burns, 1980 for an interesting discussion of how a cognitive therapist self-monitors reactions that interfere with therapy). Whatever the approach, a therapist needs some way to monitor his or her contributions to the therapy.

These broad skills—communication, relationship building, and self-monitoring—can be considered *macro skills*. They are needed regardless of the theoretical orientation of the therapist. These contrast with *micro skills*, those relating to specific techniques of psychotherapy, which we discuss in the next chapter.

Clients

People seek psychotherapy for a variety of reasons. An unhappy marriage, a lack of self-confidence, a nagging fear, an identity crisis, depression, sexual problems, and insomnia are just a few of the problems that motivate people to enter psychotherapy. In some clients, the disturbance is so great that day-to-day functioning is impaired, there is a risk of suicide or harm to others, and hospitalization may be necessary. In others, the disturbance may be less extreme, but still very upsetting. The common essential feature is that the person's usual coping strategies—such as utilizing the support of friends and family or taking a vacation—are no longer sufficient to deal with the problems.

Because they are in distress, the vast majority of clients voluntarily seek psychotherapy. Occasionally, however, clients enter therapy because someone else becomes distressed. A parent, judge, employer, spouse, or other family member may be disturbed by the client's behavior and compel the individual to seek help. Therapy can be difficult when clients are referred by others because the clients might be unmotivated and emotionally uninvolved in the process, or they might terminate early.

Client Characteristics

Conventional wisdom holds that client motivation is directly related to therapeutic outcome, and at one level, this is certainly true—clients who terminate therapy prematurely do not benefit. Though clients who are more invested and try harder tend to do better, some studies have found little or no relationship between client motivation and therapeutic outcomes (Garfield, 1994). This might occur because only some minimal amount of motivation is actually needed for successful therapy, or because motivation is inherently difficult to measure (it could change from session to session, or even within sessions). To get around the latter issue, investigators have sometimes used indirect measures of motivation. One proxy for motivation is client's compliance with homework assignments. A large percentage of therapists assign homework (Kazantzis & Deane, 1999). Do clients who complete homework fare better than those who do not? Apparently they do; Burns and Spangler (2000) found that homework compliance had a strong causal effect on changes in depressed clients. From the available studies, it appears that client motivation affects therapy, but initial motivation might not be the most important client factor.

Clinicians and researchers have investigated many other client characteristics, usually with an eye toward finding whether those characteristics affect treatment outcomes. Sex, age, ethnicity, intelligence, type and severity of disorder, religious attitudes, and dozens of other personality and demographic variables have been considered. Of these, only a few show modest relationships with therapy outcome, while most appear to have little or no relationship to outcome. For example, there is no strong evidence that the sex of the client is related to psychotherapy outcome (Garfield, 1994). Women seek psychotherapy more often than men, but the gender distribution for psychotherapy clients varies mostly as a function of specific disorders (e.g., major depression is more common among women, alcoholism is more common among men, and an equal number of men and women suffer from bipolar disorder). Clients' ages are similarly influenced by the typical age of onset for various disorders, but age alone seems to have a negligible effect on therapeutic outcome.

Perhaps it is not so surprising that client demographic variables generally have little influence on therapy. Yet it seems obvious that the strengths a client brings to the therapy would have considerable influence on outcome. Therapists intuitively assume that a client's openness and certain cognitive or emotional variables should matter. Orlinsky, Grawe, and Parks (1994) offer support for this, reporting that in psychotherapy research, two client variables consistently show up as important: cooperation versus resistence and openness versus defensiveness.

An interesting pattern appears in the studies of client (and therapist) characteristics: Few client characteristics, examined in isolation, appear to affect therapy, and those that do often have lesser effects than anticipated. Researchers continue to search for how various client characteristics affect therapy. Knox, Goldberg, Woodhouse, and Hill (1999), for instance, studied clients' "internal representations" of their therapists, which they defined as how clients brought to awareness the image of their therapist (including the therapist's physical appearance, verbalizations, emotional tone, etc.) and found that these related to benefits in therapy. Others (e.g., Beutler & Harwood, 2000;

Beutler, Mohr, Grawe, Engle, & McDonald, 1991) have examined how client characteristics might interact with treatment factors. For instance, some evidence suggests that clients who begin therapy as more resistant benefit more from nondirective interventions, while more cooperative clients benefit more from directive interventions. If client characteristics interact with treatment variables, it is not surprising that when researchers study client variables in isolation, such variables show limited effects. What is probably more important is how client, therapist, and treatment variables interact.

THE THERAPEUTIC RELATIONSHIP

What makes professional psychotherapy unique is not its cast of characters, but the special relationship that develops between therapist and client. That relationship is shaped partly by professional and legal standards that guide the conduct of therapists and partly by how the unique characteristics of the therapist and client combine in their interpersonal relationship.

Professional Guidelines for the Therapeutic Relationship

The practice of psychotherapy imposes commitments on the therapist's part. Those commitments protect the client and insulate the relationship from the influence of outside forces. *Confidentiality* is the most essential of these commitments. The therapist protects the client's privacy and, except in specific circumstances, does not reveal information that the client shares in therapy. In addition, therapists are obligated to regard the welfare of their clients as their main priority. With very few exceptions, the therapist's commitment must be directed by a singular concern: What is best for my client?

Informed consent is also very important. Therapists are obliged to let clients know what limits might be placed on confidentiality. For instance, if a therapist has clear evidence that a client intends to commit suicide or homicide, the therapist is ethically bound to break confidentiality. Therapists conducting marital therapy typically inform clients that one possible outcome of the therapy is the couple could decide to divorce. We discuss several of these professional guidelines on the therapeutic relationship in Chapter 14.

Psychotherapy often begins with a therapeutic contract that specifies the goals of treatment, the procedures to be employed, the potential risks, and the rights and responsibilities of client and therapist. In many instances the contract is negotiated informally, with both parties providing information about what they expect therapy to accomplish. In other instances, the contract takes the form of a signed document. In either case, contracts are designed to help the therapeutic relationship become one in which clients are active decision makers, not passive recipients of help (Blau, 1988).

Rules about the therapeutic relationships and the conduct of therapists within those relationships are published in the American Psychological Association's *Ethical Principles of Psychologists and Code of Conduct*, often referred to as the Ethics Code (APA Ethics Committee, 1992). This publication, which is updated periodically (along with a casebook discussing ethical considerations in specific cases) provides guidelines for many issues that come up in therapy. We discuss these in detail in Chapter 14.

Therapist Objectivity and Self-disclosure

Although the therapist may be friendly and sympathetic, the therapeutic relationship involves more than compassion. Therapy sometimes requires the clinician to be an objective assessor of clients' problems and at other times to be an insistent coach who helps clients overcome their reluctance to look at and deal with those problems. Therapists give psychological support even as they challenge clients to give up old ways of thinking and behaving in exchange for new, more adaptive alternatives. Thus, the therapeutic relationship requires a "balance of attachment and detachment" (Korchin, 1976). With some clients, a therapeutic relationship develops easily; with others, the "capacity for collaboration" is lacking and therapy suffers as a result (Strupp & Hadley, 1979).

The intensity of the therapeutic relationship may tempt the therapist to discard a professional orientation toward clients in favor of more spontaneous reactions, including pity, frustration, hostility, boredom, or sexual attraction. Most therapists try to stay alert to the way in which their personal needs intrude upon therapy (i.e., through self-monitoring). Still, there are many instances in which therapists must decide whether to share personal reactions or incidents from their own lives. Such sharing is called *therapist self-disclosure*. Clients are expected to self-disclose (indeed, therapy would be impossible without it), but what about therapists? Should a therapist reveal to a client feelings of irritation or boredom, bereavement, a former addiction, or experiences related to when the therapist was in therapy?

There are potential benefits and risks in both directions. Therapists who never self-disclose risk being perceived as aloof or more impersonal, which might damage the therapeutic relationship. Therapists who frequently self-disclose risk being perceived as impulsive, self-focused, or compromising the professional nature of the client-therapist relationship.

There is no firm rule on this, and practices vary depending on theoretical orientation. Psychoanalytic therapists advocate abstinence—therapists should not disclose—while some humanistically oriented therapists favor considerable therapist disclosure. Therapists from other orientations fall in between.

The Therapeutic Alliance

The therapeutic relationship has many dimensions, some more important to therapy outcome than others. Two dimensions that are especially important are 1) the emotional bonds that develop between the therapist and client (liking, trust, etc.), and 2) the shared understanding of what is to be done (tasks) and what is to be achieved (goals). Together, these two dimensions of the relationship are often called the *therapeutic alliance* (see Bordin, 1979; Martin, Garske, & Davis, 2000).

Varying Views of the Therapeutic Alliance. No one deserves more credit than Carl Rogers, the founder of client-centered therapy, for drawing attention to the therapeutic alliance. Rogers took the position that the client–therapist relationship is the crucible in which all the necessary and sufficient ingredients for therapeutic change were generated. In a departure from traditional views of therapy, Rogers emphasized that relationship itself, rather than the techniques employed by the therapist, were the curative factors in psychotherapy. According to Rogers (1951, pp. 172–173), "the words—of either client or [therapist]—are seen as having minimal importance compared with the present emotional relationship which exists between the two."

Rogers believed that a positive therapeutic relationship develops because the therapist offers certain conditions: acceptance, genuineness, unconditional positive regard. Rogers did not stress the client's role in creating the therapeutic alliance; it was assumed that if the therapist offered the proper conditions, the relationship would typically develop and clients would benefit (Hovarth, 2000). *Humanistically oriented* therapists since Rogers have continued to share a similar view the therapeutic relationship. In their view, the alliance is not merely the context for treatment, it *is* the treatment.

In *classical psychoanalysis*, the relationship only presents the conditions for therapy; it is not seen as curative in itself. Psychoanalysts see the therapeutic relationship as an arena in which clients begin to see how their present behavior is determined by experiences in earlier periods of life. Psychoanalysts speak of the *transference relationship*, or simply *transference* to refer to the fact that, after a period of therapy, the client begins to attach to the therapist the friendly, hostile, or ambivalent attitudes and feelings the client formerly felt in relation to parents or other significant figures from the past. To encourage transference, the analyst remains detached and far less spontaneous than is the case in Rogerian therapy, for example. One way the therapist does this is by avoiding therapist self-disclosure. By carefully guarding against intrusion of his or her own personality, the analyst makes it easier for patients to project their historically based perceptions onto the analyst, as if they were projecting onto an opaque screen. The analyst then helps the client recognize these projections through various analytic techniques.

Contemporary psychodynamic therapists stress that, in addition to the transference relationship, there is also a reality-based relationship between client and therapist. This reality-based relationship is based on accurate perceptions, on liking, and on shared commitment. The therapist's job is still to help the client understand and work through the transference (i.e., how the past inappropriately intrudes on the present relationships), but the reality-based alliance between the therapist and client provides the secure base from which to do this. Even with this more humanized view of the therapeutic relationship however, the therapist's techniques are still considered critical for effective psychotherapy, and the relationship is seen as the vehicle.

Most *behavioral* and *cognitive-behavioral* therapists tend to view the therapy relationship as an important but not sufficient condition of therapy (Sweet, 1984). Early behaviorists even went so far as to reverse the usual formula. Rather than viewing effective therapy as something that occurs after a good relationship develops, they said a good relationship develops after initial therapeutic efforts have been effective (Hovarth, 2000). Few behavioral and cognitive-behavioral therapists hold this position today. Rather, most see the therapeutic alliance as a useful context in which more specific behavior-change techniques are introduced. In this sense, they are similar to psychoanalytic theorists—both view the relationship as the context for techniques—and different from the humanistically oriented therapists who view the relationship as a treatment in itself.

Other behavioral therapists believe that the therapeutic relationship plays a larger role; they see it as the crucial element in bringing about beneficial change because it gives the therapist the opportunity to model new skills and reinforce specific changes in the client's behavior (Follette, Naugle, & Callaghan, 1996). In their view, providing contingent reinforcement of clients' appropriate behavior as it occurs in the therapeutic relationship is one of the most powerful intervention tools therapists have (Kohlenberg & Tsai, 1991).

Research on the Therapeutic Alliance

Good psychological research depends on careful measurement, and careful measurement depends on specific definitions of terms. Fortunately, this has happened with the concept of therapeutic alliance. Landmark articles by Bordin (1979) and Luborsky (1976) were instrumental in operationally defining the term. This, in turn, stimulated researchers to develop measurement scales. Several now exist, including the *Working Alliance Inventory* (Hovarth & Greenberg, 1989), the *California Psychotherapy Alliance Scales* (Marmar, Gaston, Gallagher, & Thompson, 1989), the *Vanderbilt Psychotherapy Process Scale* (Suh, Strupp, & O'Malley, 1986), and the *Therapeutic Bond Scales* (Saunders, Howard, & Orlinsky, 1989). Some of the scales were designed with specific theoretical views of the alliance in mind (e.g., psychodynamic), while others were designed to measure the alliance generally. Yet, despite their different intents, most scales are highly intercorrelated, which suggests that they measure essentially the same thing. The scales also have acceptable internal consistency and interrater reliability (Cecero, Fenton, Frankforter, Nich, & Carroll, 2001; Martin et al., 2000).

In general, therapeutic relationships flourish when both parties are capable of bringing three elements to the situation (Orlinsky & Howard, 1986): role investment (the personal effort both parties commit to therapy), empathic resonance (the degree to which both parties are "on the same wavelength"), and mutual affirmation (the extent to which both parties care for each other's well-being). Still, questions about the therapeutic relationship remain: Does it matter more for some disorders or therapies more than others? Can it be predicted ahead of time? How can therapists be trained to improve their relationships with clients? Questions such as these are under investigation.

THE SETTINGS OF PSYCHOTHERAPY

The settings of psychotherapy are most easily divided into two categories: *outpatient settings* and *inpatient settings*. The former includes therapists' offices, rented spaces in community centers or church basements, or anywhere else clients and therapists agree to meet. The latter includes facilities such as hospitals, prisons, or residential treatments centers where patients reside for days, months, or years.

Outpatient Settings

Therapists' offices are by far the most common setting for psychotherapy. The requirements for a therapist's office are minimal, but certain features are important. The first is privacy. Because of the emotional nature of therapy, clients have a right to expect that their communications remain between themselves and their therapists. For this reason, most therapists expect soundproof rooms, or something very close to them. It is advisable for offices to be private, but not too far removed from other people. Unfortunately, litigation, for actual or fabricated malpractice, is a threat in this society (and one of the causes of skyrocketing malpractice insurance costs). Some therapists also treat potentially aggressive clients, and for them it makes sense to have other persons not too far away from the office setting. Comfortable places to sit are also essential. If the therapist is working with children, the therapy space should have toys and furniture appropriate to the clients' ages. In short, office accommodations should be designed to maximize the treatment goals for the population with which a therapist works.

Not all therapy takes place in an office. Groups are often conducted in rented or donated space, such as in community centers, senior centers, or church basements. As with offices, therapists should try to structure the environment in way that maximize therapeutic goals.

Many therapists accompany clients into the community as part of a treatment plan. Indeed, some types of intervention are specifically designed for the community rather than the office. For instance, a therapist treating a client with panic disorder (an anxiety disorder characterized by intense episodes of panic and the fear of panic, especially in public places) might accompany the client to a mall where he or she can practice anxiety-management techniques learned in therapy. Therapists sometimes take client groups on outings where they can practice skills first learned in an office setting (also see Chapter 8).

Inpatient Settings

Inpatient settings include public, private, and VA hospitals, residential rehabilitation and treatment centers, prisons, jails, etc. Any group setting where clients reside can be considered an inpatient setting. The requirements for therapy here are similar to those for inpatient settings—clients have a right to expect privacy and professional treatment. But there are important differences as well.

Hospitals, the most common inpatient setting, are usually involved in treating patients who have more severe psychological disorders such as schizophrenia, bipolar disorder, major depression, brain injuries, dissociative identity disorder, borderline or antisocial personality disorder, or anorexia nervosa. Clinicians working within hospitals are often part of a treatment team that includes physicians, psychiatrists, social workers, and other personnel. This means that psychotherapists try to coordinate psychotherapy with other treatments such as medication, physical therapy, or psychosocial rehabilitation. As with outpatient psychotherapy, clinicians who treat hospitalized or residential treatment clients may also arrange treatments outside the facility.

THE PROCESS AND GOALS OF PSYCHOTHERAPY

There are dozens of psychotherapeutic techniques. Every system of psychotherapy has its preferred procedures, and every therapist has a unique style of employing those procedures. The therapist's methods are usually based on some formal theory of personality and psychopathology in general and the client's problem in particular (see Chapter 2). Although therapists remain flexible, their therapeutic methods are also usually guided by personal preferences and the general principles which they believe underlie effective treatment. These general principles should be grounded in empirical research, though many therapists do employ methods whose effectiveness is not well-supported (see Chapter 9).

Psychotherapeutic approaches differ in the extent to which their underlying theories of personality and disorder are related to specific techniques. For example, complex psychoanalytic theories of personality are not very specific about what procedures should be used in applying them to a given case, while many behavioral and cognitive-behavioral theories specify in great detail the procedures to employ in treatment.

Treatment approaches also vary in terms of the changes they are designed to produce (Andrews, 1989; Messer & Winokur, 1980). (Refer again to the case of Mr. B. in Chapter 2.) Behavioral therapists are likely to deal directly with the problem as the client initially presents it (along with other difficulties that might contribute to the primary complaint). For example, a mother who reports depression and fears that she will kill her children might be assigned a variety of "homework assignments" involving her relationship with her husband, disciplinary methods for her children, or the development of new, out-of-the-house activities for herself. By contrast, a psychoanalyst would explore the presumed underlying causes of the mother's depression; therapy might be aimed at helping the woman understand how her current symptoms relate to feelings of inadequacy as a mother because of failure to meet her own mother's rigid and unrealistic standards. Finally, a humanistic therapist might deal with the problem by helping the mother discover her potential for creating alternatives that would free her from the one-dimensional life in which she now feels trapped.

These theory-driven differences notwithstanding, several common factors are found in most therapeutic approaches. One of these, as already noted, is the use of the therapeutic relationship in the client's best interests. The others are described in the following sections.

Fostering Insight

Insight into psychological problems was a chief objective for Freud, who described it as "re-education in overcoming internal resistances" (Freud, 1904, p. 73). While Freud was interested in a particular type of insight—analysis of unconscious influences—most therapists aim for insight in the general sense of greater self-knowledge. Clients are expected to benefit from learning why they behave in certain ways, because such knowledge is presumed to contribute to the development of new behavior. The psychotherapist's rationale for fostering a client's insight is like the well-known justification for studying history: to know the errors of the past in order to avoid repeating them.

Therapists of all theoretical persuasions seek to promote self-examination and self-knowledge in their clients, though they may go about it in differing ways. Some clinicians focus on a specific type of content; dream analysis would be an example. Others try promoting insight by asking their clients to examine the implications of certain behaviors (e.g., "What relationship do you see between your troubles with your boss and the dislike you express for your father?"). Behavioral therapists stress the importance of helping the client understand how behavior is functionally related to past learning and current environmental factors.

A common technique for developing insight is for the therapist to *interpret* the client's behavior. The purpose of interpretation is not to convince clients that the therapist is right about the significance of some event but to motivate clients to carefully examine their own behavior and draw new conclusions about its meaning. Although interpretation remains a main technique for many psychotherapists, some clinicians caution against the dangers of interpretations that are too confrontive or challenging (Strupp, 1989). Particularly when working with very disturbed clients, therapists who minimize their use of interpretation in favor of being actively supportive, emotionally soothing, and directly reassuring tend to achieve the best outcomes. Conversely, less-disturbed clients benefit more from therapy experiences in which the therapist interprets connections between their behavior in therapy and their relationships outside of therapy (Jones, Cumming, & Horowitz, 1988).

Reducing Emotional Discomfort

Clients sometimes come to a therapist in such emotional anguish that it is difficult for them to participate actively in therapy. In such instances, the therapist will try to reduce the client's distress enough to allow the person to begin working on the problem. Therapists do not strive to eliminate all discomfort; in so doing, they might also eliminate the client's motivation for working toward more lasting change. The challenge is to diminish extreme distress without sapping the client's desire to deal with enduring problems.

A common method for reducing client discomfort is to use the therapeutic relationship to boost the client's emotional strength. Clients gain emotional stability and renewed confidence by knowing that the therapist is a personal ally, a buffer against the onslaughts of a hostile world. Some therapists offer direct reassurances such as "I know things seem hopeless right now, but I think you will be able to make some important changes in your life."

Encouraging Catharsis

Clients are usually encouraged to express emotions freely in the protective presence of the therapist. This technique is known as *catharsis*, and it involves the release of pent-up emotions that the client has not acknowledged for a long time, if ever. The therapist encourages the client to give voice to those emotions, believing that through their release they will be eased. At the least, catharsis may help the client become less frightened of certain emotions.

Although therapists have always been concerned with their clients' emotional experiences, empirical research on the value of emotion-focused techniques has been slow to accumulate. Recent research points to the value of emotion-focused interventions in at least five areas (Greenberg & Safran, 1989): (1) synthesizing or getting in touch with emotions so they can be understood and expressed in acceptable, even constructive ways; (2) intensifying certain emotions, often through nonverbal, expressive methods, so they can instigate useful behavior; (3) restructuring emotions by giving new information that allows emotions to be modified in desired directions; (4) evoking emotions so that thoughts and behaviors strongly and specifically bound up with these emotions can be reexamined; and (5) directly modifying those emotions that have become so maladaptive that the client's functioning is impaired.

Providing New Information

Psychotherapy is often educational. The therapist provides new information to correct gaps or distortions in a client's knowledge. Certain areas of adjustment are plagued by misinformation, sexual functioning being a notable example. Some therapists offer direct advice to their clients, adopting a teacher-like role. Others suggest reading material about a topic, a process known as *bibliotherapy* (Marx et al., 1992). Still others rely on less direct methods—a shrug of the shoulder or a skeptical facial expression—to suggest to clients that there are other ways of perceiving the world. New information gives clients an added perspective on their problems that makes them seem less unusual as well as more solvable.

Assigning Extratherapy Tasks

Therapists often ask clients to perform tasks outside of therapy for the purpose of encouraging the transfer of positive changes to the "real world." Behavioral and cognitive-behavioral therapists are enthusiastic advocates of homework assignments, believing them to be an effective way to promote the generalization of new skills learned in the therapist's office (Nietzel, Guthrie, & Susman, 1991).

Developing Faith, Hope, and Expectations for Change

Of all the procedures common to all systems of therapy, raising clients' faith, hope, and expectations for change is the ingredient most frequently mentioned as a crucial contributor to therapeutic improvement. The curative power of faith is not restricted to psychotherapy. It has been said, for example, that the history of medical treatment is largely the history of the placebo effect (Shapiro, 1971). Some therapy techniques may be particularly potent in raising expectations and creating placebo effects because they appear dramatic or high-tech or because they tap into ingrained cultural norms associated with the best ways to achieve personal change.

Clinicians are so accustomed to thinking about placebo effects in psychotherapy that many attribute much of the success of psychotherapy not to specific techniques, but to the ability of those techniques to generate clients' expectancy for improvement. Recognizing placebo effects in psychotherapy does not eliminate the importance of the specific techniques that distinguish one therapeutic approach from another. It does mean, however, that one important element (some might say the most important element) of any effective therapy is that it causes clients to believe that positive changes are attainable (Orlinsky, Grawe, & Parks, 1994).

Part art and part science, psychotherapy profits from the mystique that surrounds both fields. Clients often begin psychotherapy with the belief that they are about to engage in a unique, powerful experience conducted by an expert who can work miracles. The perceived potency of psychotherapy is further enhanced by the fact that clients usually enter it after having fretted for a long time about whether they really need treatment. By the time this internal debate is resolved, the client has a large emotional investment in making the most of a treatment that is regarded with a mixture of fear, hope, and relief.

For their part, therapists encourage clients' faith in the power of psychotherapy by providing assurance that they understand the problem and that, with hard work and commitment by both partners in the therapy relationship, desired changes are possible. The client's perception that "I have been heard and understood and can be helped" can be as important as the soothing effect that physicians create by displaying calm confidence in the face of a patient's mysterious physical symptoms. Most therapists bolster this perception by offering a theory-based *rationale* for why psychotherapy will be effective.

Having structured therapy to increase the client's motivation and expectations for success, the therapist attempts to ensure that the client actually does experience some success as soon as possible. This success might be minor at first—a limited insight after a simple interpretation by the therapist or the successful completion of a not-too-difficult homework assignment. Whatever the means, the objective is to bring about the kind of change the client expects. The cumulative impact of many small changes in the initial stages of therapy helps reinforce clients' confidence that they can control their lives and that their problems are understandable and solvable. As more positive expectancies are confirmed, they grow and, as clients believe that more meaningful changes can be attained, they pursue them with even greater determination which, in turn, makes further success more likely (Howard et al., 1993). All the while, the therapist enhances the client's self-esteem by pointing out that the changes are the result of the client's own efforts (Bandura, 1982).

Some Conclusions

Our discussion reveals that the answer to the question "What is psychotherapy?" must emphasize the following attributes:

1. Psychotherapy consists of a relationship between at least two participants, one of whom has special training and expertise in handling psychological problems and one of whom is experiencing a problem in adjustment and has entered the relationship to alleviate this problem.

2. The psychotherapeutic relationship is a nurturant but purposeful alliance in which varying methods are employed to bring about the changes desired by the client.

3. These methods are based on some theory regarding psychological problems in general and the specific complaint of the client in particular.

4. Regardless of theoretical preferences, most therapists employ several of the following techniques: development of a productive therapeutic relationship, fostering insight, reducing emotional discomfort, encouraging catharsis, providing new information, assigning extra-therapy tasks, and raising clients' expectancy for change.

ALTERNATIVE MODES OF CLINICAL INTERVENTION

So far, we have focused primarily on the best-known and most widely used mode of clinical intervention: individual, or one-to-one, psychotherapy. In the next chapter, we expand our discussion of individual psychotherapy by describing the psychotherapeutic techniques that grow from the major "schools" of psychotherapy (psychodynamic, behavioral, cognitive, etc.). These schools differ in how they understand the causes of and cures for disorders. Historically, the differences among major approaches have been emphasized, but while there are real differences among approaches, effective therapists from different orientations probably behave more similarly than differently. Accordingly, we also discuss in the next chapter the movement toward *psychotherapy integration*.

Sometimes the client is not an individual, but two or more individuals, and the therapist's focus is on the *relationships* rather than on individuals per se. Among these relationship-oriented modes of therapy are group therapy, marital or couples therapy, and family therapy. Clinicians who work with groups and families often use techniques similar to those in individual psychotherapy, but they also have techniques specifically adapted to multi-person clients. Other alternative modes of intervention—such as psychosocial rehabilitation and primary prevention—bear almost no resemblance to individual psychotherapy. They rely on different techniques, embrace different assumptions about mental disorders, and may pursue different goals. Each of these alternative intervention modes tend to be more social- than psychotherapy in the sense that they seek, in varying degrees, to deal with how other people contribute to or are affected by disturbed behavior. In Chapter 8, we discuss these social-psychological modes of clinical intervention.

THE EFFECTS OF PSYCHOTHERAPY

An enormous amount of research has been devoted to measuring the outcome of psychotherapy and to understanding the process through which therapy works. We discuss this research in more detail in Chapter 9, but the short version of the story is that (1) most forms of therapy usually help most clients (Lambert & Bergin, 1994; Smith,

Glass, & Miller, 1980), and (2) the benefits of all forms of treatment probably depend on a few core elements (Orlinsky, Grawe, & Parks, 1994). The most important of these elements appears to be the establishment of a strong therapeutic alliance or relationship in which clients feel supported, accepted, and therefore more capable of changing for the better. When therapists can form a good therapeutic relationship with such clients, the therapeutic techniques described in the next two chapters have the greatest chance of being successful.

CHAPTER SUMMARY

Clinical intervention involves a deliberate attempt to make desirable changes in clients' behavior or social circumstances. Treatment is initiated when a client in need of help is seen by a therapist with special training. Our special interest is training in clinical psychology, but therapists can also include persons trained in counseling psychology, psychiatry, psychiatric social work, psychiatric nursing, family counseling, or a variety of other paraprofessional and specialty areas.

The participants in psychotherapy—the therapists and clients—bring individual strengths and weaknesses to the situation. Most clinicians agree that effective therapy is facilitated by the development of a supportive, yet objective, relationship which, in turn, is fostered by certain therapist and client contributions. Effective therapists need advanced training and interpersonal skills in communication, relationship building, and self-monitoring. Characteristics described by Carl Rogers as genuineness, empathy, and unconditional positive regard are especially important in developing a strong therapeutic relationship. Client characteristics such as motivation and openness also contribute to the effectiveness of therapy, but the therapeutic alliance—the emotional bond between therapist and client and their agreement on tasks and goals—remains one of the best predictors of therapeutic outcome.

Psychotherapy is most often conducted in an individual format in an outpatient setting. However, it is also conducted in inpatient settings. Each setting constitutes part of the environment or situation in which therapy takes place.

Therapists who take differing theoretical approaches tend to use differing treatment methods, but there are some common features, too, including efforts to foster insight, reduce emotional discomfort, encourage catharsis, provide new information, assign extratherapy tasks, and promote clients' faith, hope, and expectations for change.

Chapter 7

Clinical Intervention: Methods of Psychotherapy

In the previous chapter, we provided an overview of clinical intervention, focusing on the features common to the various approaches. In this chapter, we focus more specifically on psychotherapy, the most common form of clinical intervention. By some estimates, there are as many as 400 kinds of psychotherapy (Feltham, 2000), but it is doubtful that all the distinctions made among these approaches are significant. Accordingly, our review discusses psychotherapy within a broad classification of psychotherapy orientations: psychodynamic, behavioral/cognitive-behavioral, and humanistic (also called phenomenological or experiential). We also introduce integrative approaches, which seek to combine or blend techniques from the various schools.

PSYCHODYNAMIC THERAPIES

Sigmund Freud was the founder of psychotherapy as we know it today. In developing psychoanalysis, he pioneered psychotherapy as a one-on-one treatment involving frank discussion of a client's thoughts and feelings. His emphasis on searching for relationships between a person's developmental history and current problems, conflicts, thoughts, and emotions, as well as his emphasis on the special nature of the therapist–patient relationship, pervade all modern treatment methods.

Though Freud's theories attracted a broad following, some of his contemporaries disagreed with certain aspects of psychoanalytic theory and developed alternative theories. Later theorists also sought to preserve certain ideas and techniques from psychoanalytic theory, while modifying the rest. Collectively, the therapies that share basic assumptions first advanced by Freud are called psychodynamic psychotherapies.

As discussed in Chapter 2, psychodynamic approaches are based on the assumption that mental life is best understood as the interaction among powerful competing forces within the person (the word *dynamic* refers to this tension-filled interaction). Both sources of conflicts and one's habitual ways of coping with them are presumed to be largely *unconscious* and rooted in *early experiences*.

During therapy, psychodynamic therapists try to understand each client's personal ways of coping with conflict. The therapist's job is essentially to help make the client's unconscious processes conscious. Because unconscious conflicts produce anxiety, clients are inclined to employ *defense mechanisms* of various sorts. Clinical work in this tradition therefore requires considerable inference on the part of the clinician—indirect *sign-oriented* methods of assessment and intervention predominate—and an emphasis on specific techniques such as timing and judicious use of interpretation. A key goal of psychodynamic psychotherapy is *insight*, when a client recognizes how the past inappropriately distorts and intrudes upon current thoughts and actions.

Our review of psychodynamic approaches begins with classical psychoanalysis, which placed considerable emphasis on id drives and intrapsychic conflicts. More recent psychodynamic approaches have shifted the emphasis from drives to ego functioning and to relationship formation. All psychodynamic therapies, however, stress the importance of understanding a client's unique set of compromises to their largely unconscious conflicts, and of working through these conflicts within the therapist-client relationship.

The Beginnings of Classical Psychoanalysis

In 1886, with the help of a senior colleague, Joseph Breuer, Freud began the private practice of medicine in Vienna. Like Breuer, Freud often saw patients with neurological symptoms for which no organic cause could be found. Some, for example, complained of paralysis that affected their entire hand, but not their arm. Others suffered paralysis of the legs during the day, but walked in their sleep. These patients were called *neurotics*, and Freud dealt with the most common type: those displaying hysterical (i.e., nonorganic) paralyses, amnesia, anesthesia, blindness, and speech loss. In Freud's day, treatment for hysteria included "wet packs" and baths or electrically generated heat. Freud believed that whatever success these methods had were caused by suggestion, so he began experimenting with techniques that maximized the benefits of suggestion, foremost among which was *hypnosis*.

Freud's use of hypnotic suggestion produced temporary results, and around 1890 he began to combine hypnosis with a new technique called the *cathartic method*, which he learned from Breuer.

Breuer had stumbled on this technique while attempting to relieve the hysterical symptoms of a patient known as Anna O. The symptoms—which included headaches, a severe cough, neck and arm paralyses, and other problems—began during her father's illness and intensified following his death. She began to display extremes of mood which went from agitation and hallucinations during the day to calm, trancelike states in the evenings. Breuer was struck by the fact that these "trances" resembled hypnosis.

> Breuer discovered that if Anna were permitted while in the hypnotic state to recite the contents of all her hallucinations from the day, then she invariably would leave the trance state and enjoy a period of almost normal tranquility and lucidity during the following late night hours. . . . Anna came to refer to the exercise of reciting her hallucinations as the "talking cure," or . . . "chimney sweeping." (Fancher, 1973, p. 48)

This "talking cure" did not eliminate Anna's daytime disorders, however, and new symptoms began to appear. In attempting to cure one of these, an inability to drink liquids, Breuer made the discovery that would later start Freud on the road to psychoanalysis:

> During one of Anna's hypnotic states . . . she began describing to Breuer an Englishwoman whom she knew but did not especially like. The woman had a dog that Anna particularly despised. Anna described how on one occasion she entered the woman's room and observed the dog drinking water from a glass. When the event occurred, Anna was filled with strong feelings of disgust and loathing, but out of politeness she was unable to express them. As she recited this account to Breuer, she for the first time permitted herself the luxury of expressing fully and animatedly her negative feelings about the dog's drinking. When she emerged from the trance she immediately asked for a glass of water, which she . . . drank without the slightest difficulty. (Fancher, 1973, p. 49)

Sigmund Freud (1856–1939). (Courtesy of Historical Pictures Service, Inc., Chicago, Illinois. Reprinted by permission.)

Removal of Anna's fear of drinking was apparently brought about by her vivid recollection of a forgotten event while in a trance. It occurred to Breuer that other hysterical symptoms might be caused by forgotten memories and that their recall might cure them. He began hypnotizing Anna and asking her to remember everything she could about her symptoms.

> (H)e discovered that every symptom could be traced to a traumatic or unpleasant situation for which all memory was absent in the waking state. Breuer found that whenever he could induce Anna to recall those unpleasant scenes and, more importantly, to *express the emotions* they had caused her to feel, the symptoms would disappear. (Fancher, 1973, pp. 49–50; italics added)

Freud also found the cathartic method successful, but not all his patients could be hypnotized. In addition, Freud found that recalling memories and expressing emotions associated with them is most beneficial when patients remember these experiences after their hypnotic sessions, which some did not. To facilitate *conscious* recognition of emotional memories, Freud began asking his patients to relax with their eyes closed and to report whatever thoughts, feelings, or memories came to mind. Recall was often helped by having the patient lie on a couch. This procedure later became known as free association, a mainstay among the psychoanalytic techniques to be described later.

At first, Freud's nonhypnotic treatment of neurotic patients focused mainly on helping them remember important, usually unpleasant, memories and emotions that had been protected from recall by various *defense mechanisms* (see Chapter 2). For example, Freud saw evidence that many of his patients had suffered early sexual trauma, usually molestation by a parent or other relative, and he assumed that such events were the basis for most hysterical symptoms. By the turn of the century, however, he was convinced that this "seduction theory" was incorrect and that there were more important causal factors to be considered. For one thing, he found it hard to believe that the sexual abuse of children was as widespread as was suggested by his cases.

Second, Freud began to pay attention to dreams (his patients' and his own) and concluded that they represented the fulfillment of fantasies and wishes, many of which are socially unacceptable and thus appear—often in disguised form—only when defenses are relaxed during sleep. He suggested that, like dreams, hysterical symptoms could be based on unconscious wishes and fantasies, not just on memories of real events. Thus, a patient's "memory" of childhood seduction by a parent might actually be a *fantasy* or *wish* about such an encounter. The implications of this new theory altered Freud's approach to therapy as well. His *psychoanalytic* treatment of neurosis shifted from the recovery of memories to the illumination of the unconscious.

Goals of Psychoanalysis

According to Freud, when patients understand the real, often unconscious, reasons why they act in maladaptive ways and see that those reasons are no longer valid, they will not have to continue behaving in those ways. However, it is not enough for the therapist simply to describe the unconscious material that appears to be at the root of clients' problems; with the therapist's guidance, clients must make these discoveries for themselves. The process of self-understanding includes *intellectual* recognition of one's innermost wishes and conflicts, *emotional* involvement in discoveries about one-self, and the *systematic tracing* of how unconscious factors have determined past and present behaviors and affected relations with other people.

Thus, the main goals of psychoanalytic treatment are (1) intellectual and emotional *insight* into the underlying causes of the client's problems, (2) *working through* or fully exploring the implications of those insights, and (3) strengthening the ego's control over the id and the superego (see Chapter 2). Freud saw working through as particularly important because clients need to understand how pervasive their unconscious conflicts and defenses are if they are to be prevented from returning. Thus, it would do little good for a patient to know that she has unconscious feelings of anger toward her mother if she did not also see that she deals with women in the present as if they were her mother, and that her problems in relation to these women are based on unconscious hostility and/or attempts to defend against it. Insight provides the outline of a patient's story; working through fills in the details.

Reaching the ambitious goals set by classical psychoanalysis involves dissecting and gradually reconstructing the patient's personality. This process requires a lot of time (3 to 5 sessions each week for 2 to 15 years), a lot of money (fees exceed $100 per hour), and, presumably, a great deal of therapist skill.

Psychoanalytic Treatment Techniques

Classical psychoanalysts assume that the client's most important unconscious feelings and conflicts are protected by psychological defenses. They seek to show their clients how and where to look for important material and to help them understand what emerges. To accomplish these tasks, most analysts depend on a few basic techniques. Many of these techniques are also used in other psychodynamic approaches.

Free Association.   As noted earlier, free association evolved from Freud's search for a nonhypnotic way to help his patients recover memories. It requires the client to follow a single fundamental rule: to say everything that comes to mind without editing or censorship. It is assumed that, by removing the constraints of logic, social amenities, and other rules, unconscious material will surface more easily.

Still, because of defenses, the unconscious bases for clients' current problems are seldom clearly revealed in the memories, feelings, and wishes arising through free association. It is the therapist's task to try to make sense of the bits and pieces that emerge. *Patterns of association* are often important in doing so:

> CLIENT: My dad called last night. It was nice to hear from him, but I never quite feel comfortable when we talk. Once we get through the usual "hello; how are you" part, there just doesn't seem to be anything to say. (long silence) I almost fell asleep there for a minute. I used to do that a lot in college. I must have

slept through half my classes. Once I woke up and saw the professor standing over me, shaking me, and the whole class was laughing.

The fact that thoughts about his father led to memories about a threatening authority figure could have significance, especially if this pattern is repeated in other sessions. It could mean that the client still has unresolved feelings of fear and hatred toward his father, feelings that need to be clarified and dealt with.

What the client says during free association may be defensive in nature. The client whose mind goes blank or who comes up with only trivial details of the day is seen as erecting barriers to self-exploration. According to psychoanalytic theory, these defenses must be recognized by the therapist and made clear to the client if they are to be overcome.

The Use of Dreams.   Because unconscious material is believed to be closer to the surface in dreams than during waking consciousness, great importance is attached to them in psychoanalysis. The client's description of a dream—in which, say, she is running through the woods and suddenly falls into a lake—reveals its *manifest content* or obvious features. Manifest content often contains features associated with the dreamer's recent activities that day (called "day residue").

For psychoanalytic purposes, the most interesting aspect of dreams is their *latent content:* the unconscious ideas and impulses that appear in the form of a safe compromise between repression and expression. The process of transforming unacceptable material into acceptable manifest content is called *dream work* (Freud, 1900), so most manifest dream content is viewed as being symbolic of something else—the specifics of which differ from person to person and from dream to dream. In spite of the popular belief that certain dream symbols (e.g., a snake) always mean the same thing (e.g., a penis), Freud believed dreams must be interpreted more flexibly (he is said to have pointed out that "sometimes a cigar is just a cigar").

Dream work can take many forms. For example, an unconscious desire to have extramarital sex might be *displaced* to a position of minor importance in the dream, appearing as an adult bookstore glimpsed from a moving car. Or an apparently innocuous dreamed event—such as one's brother leaving for a vacation—may *substitute* for taboo wishes (e.g., the brother's death). Dream work may also devalue significant material. Ruth Munroe (1955) tells of a prudish woman who often dreamed of being unashamedly naked in public. Presumably, the woman defended against unconscious sexual wishes by making them seem unimportant. Unconscious material often appears in *condensed* form, including *alogical sequences* (e.g., in which there is a sudden shift of time or place) or *dramatizations* (as when two people fighting might represent conflicting tendencies within the dreamer).

A common analytic procedure is to ask the client to free associate to a dream's manifest content. In the process, unconscious material may be revealed.

Frequently, a series of dreams is explored in analysis as a way of finding patterns of latent content and of not overemphasizing the importance of a single dream. In other words, dreams provide ideas for further probing more often than they provide final answers.

Analysis of Everyday Behavior. In line with his notion of psychic determinism, Freud believed that unconscious wishes, fantasies, and defenses shape all behavior, including apparently meaningless everyday acts. Accordingly, psychoanalysts are as attentive to clients' reports of activities outside of treatment as they are to what happens during treatment sessions. The analyst tries to maintain an "evenly divided" or "free-floating" attention to trivial as well as momentous events, to purposeful acts and accidental happenings, to body language as well as spoken language. Mistakes in speaking or writing (so-called "Freudian slips"), accidents, memory losses, and humor are seen as especially important sources of unconscious material.

Analysis of Resistance. Any client behavior that interferes with the analytic process is considered a sign of resistance against achieving insight. To overcome resistance, psychoanalysts try to help clients recognize its presence in obstructed free associations, distorted dream reports, missed appointments, lateness for treatment sessions,[1] avoidance of certain topics, or failure to pay the therapist's bill (Fine, 1971). Even clients' desire to address troubling symptoms rather than intrapsychic conflicts, or their request for evidence of the value of treatment is likely to be identified by psychoanalysts as an effort to divert attention from the unconscious causes of their problems.

Analysis of the Transference. The client's feelings toward and relationship with the therapist are called the *transference*. Some of these feelings are determined by the therapist's characteristics and behavior, but others are seen as influenced by unconscious conflicts about authority figures from childhood which lie at the root of the client's current problems. To facilitate the transference, many analysts maintain an "analytic incognito," revealing so little about themselves that the client can be free to *project* onto them the attributes and motives that are unconsciously associated with parents and other important people in their lives. So at various times, the client may see the therapist as a loving caregiver, a vengeful father, a seductive mother, a jealous lover, or the like.

When the patient–therapist relationship creates a miniature version of the causes of the client's problems, it is referred to as the *transference neurosis* and becomes the central focus of analytic work. This reproduction of early unconscious conflicts allows the analyst to deal with important problems from the past as they occur in the present. Transference and transference neuroses must be handled with care as analysts try to decode the meaning of their clients' feelings toward them. If an analyst responded "normally" to a client's loving or hostile comments, the client would not learn much about what those comments reflect. Instead, the goal is to focus on and work through the meaning of the client's feelings for the therapist. If this can be done, the transference neurosis will be resolved and, with it, the client's main unconscious conflicts. Because

---

[1]Some have jokingly suggested that you cannot win in analysis because you are dependent if you show up early, resistant if you show up late, and compulsive if you are right on time.

sensitive handling of the transference is thought so crucial to psychoanalysis, analysts are trained to be keenly alert to their own unconscious feelings toward clients—known as the *countertransference*—so that these feelings do not distort the analytic process. Psychoanalysts typically learn to guard against intrusions of their own problems by undergoing analysis themselves. Training, supervision, and peer consultation are also used, as they are in other forms of therapy, to insure that the therapist consistently responds in ways helpful to the client.

Making Analytic Interpretations.

Making Analytic Interpretations.   Analysts want clients to gain insight into unconscious conflicts, but they don't want to overwhelm them with potentially frightening material before they are ready to handle it. This is where analytic interpretation comes in. Through questions and comments about the client's behavior, free associations, dreams, and the like, the analyst guides the process of self-exploration. Thus, if the client shows resistance to seeing the potential meaning of some event, the therapist not only points this out, but offers an interpretation of what is going on.

The interpretive process is tentative and continuous, a constant encouragement of clients to consider alternative views, to reject obvious explanations, to search for deeper meanings. However, the analyst does not interpret everything of unconscious significance as soon as it is detected. An interpretation is best delivered when the client is nearly aware of something important but has not yet been able to verbalize it. Interpretations can be blunt or subtle, depending on what the therapist thinks the client can handle. Here is one that falls somewhere in between:

> You know, it's very interesting that whenever you say something that is a little bit nasty to anyone you smile. After you've been a little bit aggressive, you become very agreeable and nice, and I notice it here. I wonder if when you were with your father you discovered that the only way to keep him from attacking you was to become more sociable, amiable, in this kind of smiling, passive way. . . . (Barton, 1974, p. 33)

As interpretations help clients understand and work through the transference, the therapeutic relationship changes. Clients not only see how defenses and unconscious conflicts caused problems, they learn to deal differently with the world, beginning with the therapist. They also learn that forces from their past no longer need dictate their behavior in the present. Ideally, this emotional understanding will liberate the patient to deal with life in a more realistic and satisfying manner than before.

Our brief account of classic psychoanalytic techniques has left out many details and oversimplified others. More complete coverage of the approach is contained in numerous standard references (e.g., Freud, 1949; Gabbard, 2000; Menninger, 1958; Kernberg, 1976).

Variations on Classical Psychoanalysis

Freud attracted many followers. Some sought to preserve his ideas and techniques in their original form; others advocated changes ranging from minor alterations to wholesale rejection of fundamental principles. Early variations were proposed by Freud's contemporaries, such as Alfred Adler and Carl Jung. Major contemporary variations include psychoanalytically-oriented psychotherapy, ego psychology, object relations theory, self psychology, short-term dynamic therapy, and postmodern dynamic approaches (Gabbard, 2000; Prochaska & Norcross, 1999). Though psychoanalysis continues as an important force, most of today's psychodynamically oriented clinicians practice one or more variations rather than classical Freudian analysis. In this section, we describe a few of these treatment variations (also see Table 7.1).

Alfred Adler's Individual Psychology. Alfred Adler was an early follower of Freud who was the first to defect from the ranks of orthodox psychoanalysis. As described in Chapter 2, he retained a psychodynamic orientation, but he deemphasized

TABLE 7.1 Variations on Freudian Psychoanalysis

Approach	Theorists	Emphasis
Early Alternatives to Freudian Psychoanalysis		
Individual psychology	Alfred Adler	Striving to overcome feelings of inferiority; importance of social motives and social behavior
Analytical psychology	Carl Jung	Reconciliation of opposites (e.g., anima, animus) in personality, personality orientations of introversion and extroversion, personal and collective unconscious
Will therapy	Otto Rank	Client choice; therapist humanity rather than technical skill
Interpersonal relations school	Harry Stack Sullivan	Interpersonal contexts of disorders and treatment
Contemporary Psychodynamic Approaches		
Ego psychology	Anna Freud, Heinz Hartman, David Rappaport	Focus on adaptive ego functioning and establishment of firm identity and intimacy
Object relations theory	Melanie Klein, Otto Kernberg David Winnicott, W. R. D. Fairbairn, and the "British school"	Modifying mental representations of interpersonal relationships that come from early attachments
Self psychology	Heinz Kohut	Closely related to object relations theory, but stresses development of autonomous self
Short-term psychodynamic approaches	Wilhelm Stekel, Hans Strupp	Coping strategies stressed over historical interpretation
Postmodern approaches	Robert Stolorow, George Atwood	Exploration of the "intersubjective space" created jointly by client and therapist.

SOURCES: Adapted from Gabbard, 2000; Kutash, 1976; Hergenhahn, 1994; Prochaska and Norcross, 1999.

Freud's theory of instincts, infantile sexuality, and the role of the unconscious in determining behavior. Because Adler believed that people's problems (or maladaptive lifestyles, as he called them) were based largely on the misconceptions they held, his treatment methods focused on exploring and altering those misconceptions.

So where a strict Freudian might see a teenage boy's vomiting before school each morning as a defense of some kind, the Adlerian analyst would view the problem as reflecting tension brought about by a misconception such as "I must do better than everyone else." And while the vomiting might be explored in Freudian analysis through free association, a therapist using Adler's individual analysis would discuss the symptom with the client as an illustration of a style of life driven by misconceptions which function to protect the client from perceived weaknesses. The youngster would then be helped to form more appropriate attitudes and given encouragement to change his style in a more adaptive direction.

In Adlerian analysis, client and therapist sit face to face in similar chairs. The feelings and reactions expressed toward the therapist (transference) are interpreted not as reflecting unconscious childhood conflicts, but as the client's habitual style of dealing with people like the therapist. Similarly, Adlerians view resistance as a sample of how the client usually avoids unpleasant material, and dreams are interpreted—not as symbolic wish fulfillment—but as a "rehearsal" of how the client might deal with problems in the future. And where Freudians offer interpretations designed to promote insight into past causes of current problems, Adler interpreted in order to promote insight into the patient's current lifestyle. He often phrased his interpretations as questions, such as, "Could it be that your unhappiness with your work is related to your insistence that everything must go perfectly for you?" This style of interpretation emphasizes the purpose of the client's behavior rather than its cause, and it encourages the client to be an active collaborator in the search for this purpose. Once clients see what it is they are doing, it becomes harder to maintain maladaptive ideas and behaviors.

Adlerian therapists are more involved than Freudians are in advising and encouraging their clients to change. For example, once a client realizes that her dependence on her husband is part of her overall style of seeking protection (and thus controlling others), the therapist might point out several alternative ways she might start to change. Adlerians also use modeling, homework assignments, and other techniques to help patients become aware of their lifestyle and to prompt them to change. Many of these methods are similar to tactics employed in the behavioral and humanistic therapies described later.

Psychoanalytically Oriented Psychotherapy.

Therapists whose psychoanalytic procedures depart only slightly from the guidelines set down by Freud are said to employ psychoanalytically oriented psychotherapy. For example, during the 1930s and 1940s, Franz Alexander and his colleagues at the Chicago Psychoanalytic Institute questioned the belief that treatment must be intense, extended, and fundamentally similar in all cases (Alexander & French, 1946). They also sought to apply psychoanalysis to "nontraditional" clients such as the young and the severely disturbed.

In psychoanalytically oriented psychotherapy, not every patient is seen for the standard five sessions per week because daily sessions may foster too much dependence on the analyst or may become so routine that the patient pays too little attention to them. The frequency of sessions varies as circumstances dictate. Early in treatment the patient may be seen every day; later, sessions may take place less often. Alexander even suggested that temporary interruptions in treatment could be beneficial by testing the patient's ability to live without therapy and reducing reliance on the therapist. He noted as well that, while some clients need lengthy psychoanalysis in order to fully explore and work through resistance, insights, and the transference, others—especially those whose problems are either relatively mild or especially severe—are candidates for less extensive treatment aimed at support rather than at the uncovering and reconstructing associated with classical analysis (for a more recent example of this approach, see Davanloo, 1994).

Practitioners of psychodynamically oriented therapy (e.g., Strupp, 1989; Strupp & Blinder, 1984) try to create an empathic and supportive atmosphere in which the client feels cared for and understood, a key outcome known as *corrective emotional experiences*. In this context, the patient begins to reenact conflicts from the past with the therapist (the transference). In response to these reenactments, psychodynamically oriented therapists are likely to be more emotionally supportive and less prone to interpretation than are classic psychoanalysts. They also tend to be more active. For example, while Freudian analysts discouraged clients from making major life decisions during treatment (in order to prevent errors born of maladaptive impulses, false insights, or neurotic defenses) the analytically oriented therapist may encourage such decisions. The idea is that the therapeutic relationship provides a stable context in which to form plans for progress that can be tested in real life. Thus, a client who is unhappy about an unsatisfying job might be encouraged to look for a better position.

Psychoanalytically oriented therapists use a number of other unorthodox techniques, including the following:

1. The patient may sit up and face the analyst rather than lie on a couch.
2. Normal conversation may be substituted for free association.
3. Hypnosis may be used to promote self-exploration.
4. The nature of current problems and their solution is emphasized.
5. The patient's family may be consulted (or even offered treatment) as part of a broad-based effort at helping the patient.

Ego Psychology.   While psychoanalytically oriented psychotherapists mainly revised Freud's procedures, another group of therapists known as ego analysts, challenged some of his basic principles. They argued, for example, that Freud's preoccupation with sexual and aggressive instincts (the id) as the basis for behavior and behavior disorder is too narrow. Behavior, they said is determined to a large extent by the ego, which can function not just to combat id impulses, but also to promote learning and creativity.

These ideas led analysts such as Heinz Hartmann (1958), David Rapaport (1951), Erik Erikson (1946), and even Freud's daughter, Anna Freud (1946), to use psychoanalytic techniques to explore patients' adaptive ego functions as well as their id instincts. Ego-analytic techniques differ from classical analytic techniques in that therapists focus less on working through early childhood experiences and more on working through current problems. Therapists assess and attempt to bolster the client's *ego strengths*, which includes reality testing, impulse control, judgment, and the use of more "mature" defense mechanisms such as sublimation (as opposed to denial or repression, which are less mature; see Vaillant, 1977; also Chapter 2). The therapeutic relationship remains important, but less so for its distorting transferences and more for its supportive and trusting functions in helping the client explore. Ego-analytic therapists view therapy as more than a means of treating disorders by exploring and working through early childhood experiences; it is a relationship experience that can lead to client self-actualization. As such, ego analysis has much in common with the humanistic approach to therapy described later. Several excellent references provide more detailed coverage of the theory and practice of ego analysis (Eagle, 1984; Guntrip, 1973; Slipp, 1981).

Object Relations and Self Psychology.

Object Relations and Self Psychology. One of the most important developments in modern variations on psychoanalysis has been the emergence of object relations theory, a movement associated with a group of influential British analysts including W. R. D. Fairbairn (1952), Donald Winnicott (1965), Melanie Klein (1975), and Margaret Mahler (Mahler, Pine, & Bergman, 1975), as well as Otto Kernberg (1976) and Heinz Kohut (1971, 1977, 1983). While ego psychology expanded the role of the ego, object relations theory expanded the role of relationships, especially early relationships, in psychodynamic thought.

Object relations theories, and the therapies based on them, focus on the nature of interpersonal relationships that are built from very early infant–mother interactions and on the nature of the personality characteristics—especially the self—that result from these interactions (Blatt & Lerner, 1983; Eagle, 1984). Because these early relationships act as prototypes for later relationships, disruptions at this stage can have profound consequences later in life. Object relations theorists have focused especially on how disruptions in the prototypical relationship can produce certain primitive defenses in severely disturbed persons. An example of this is *splitting*, in which another person is regarded as either all good or all bad. Therapists working with psychotic or personality-disordered clients, for instance, might find that their client idealizes them at one point and demonizes them at another. With such clients, working through relationship concerns is expected to be difficult and time-consuming.

In Kohut's *self-psychology,* the analyst's task is to provide the type of empathic responding and nurturing that the client is assumed to have missed as an infant. Thus, in contrast to classical psychoanalysts, object relations theorists view the therapeutic relationship not as transference to be analyzed, but as a "second chance" for the client to obtain in a close relationship the gratification that was absent during infancy. This emphasis on ego support, acceptance, and psychological "holding" of damaged selves has made object relations therapies among the most popular versions of psychoanalysis, largely because they allow a friendly, naturally human stance toward the therapeutic relationship which many therapists prefer to traditional Freudian neutrality. It is a stance that is similar to that taken in some of the humanistic/phenomenological therapies discussed later (Kahn, 1985).

Short-term Psychodynamic Psychotherapy. Until recently, few people associated short-term treatments with the psychodynamic approach, even though several of Freud's early treatments were brief (Levison & Strupp, 1999). *Short-term dynamic psychotherapy* approaches emphasize pragmatic goals that can be obtained in few meetings, typically 20 sessions or less. Therapists focus on helping the client cope with a current crisis or problem rather than on working through of early relationships or reconstructing the personality.

Short-term dynamic therapists stress forming a working therapeutic alliance as quickly as possible and then helping clients adopt coping strategies within specific domains. They might focus on anxiety management or coping with a problem relationship at work. Because the pace of therapy is accelerated, therapists are more active than in other forms of psychodynamic therapy. They may use traditional techniques of psychoanalysis, but they also might assign homework, refer clients to self-help groups, or adopt other techniques not typically associated with psychodynamic treatment. There are several models for short-term dynamic therapy, some with manuals for treating specific disorders (Levenson & Strupp, 1999). Interpersonal psychotherapy (IPT), a treatment typically used for persons with depressive disorders, is an example of a short-term dynamic treatment that has shown promising results (Klerman, Weissman, Rounsaville & Chevron, 1984).

By limiting the number of sessions they are willing to pay a provider for treating a specific disorder, insurance companies and managed care payers have stimulated competition to develop shorter, more circumscribed treatments among all schools of psychotherapy. But market forces are not the only reason short-term dynamic therapies have grown. As distinctions among the major schools of psychotherapy have been breaking down, the borrowing of techniques across theoretical lines has increased. Short-term psychodynamic psychotherapy reflects this movement toward eclecticism and integration, which we discuss below and later in this chapter.

Other Variants of Psychodynamic Therapy. Some variants of psychoanalysis are related to the humanistic/phenomenological/experiential treatments described later. For example, when Otto Rank, another early follower of Freud, left the fold, he developed a therapeutic approach that emphasized the client's innate *will to health* as a vehicle for promoting mature independence. He saw the therapist mainly as a *facilitator* of the patient's inherent potential for growth, not as a relentless explorer of the unconscious. We shall see that Carl Rogers's client-centered therapy was built partly on these concepts.

Similarly, Harry Stack Sullivan, discussed in Chapter 2 as the father of the interpersonal perspective, employed therapy methods that anticipated the cognitive-behavioral approaches described in the next section (Wachtel, 1977). Sullivan believed that the therapist should carefully observe interpersonal relationships and then use these observations to clarify for clients how their typical cognitions and behaviors interfere with successful living. Clients would then be able to use this information to stop perpetuating interpersonal conflicts and to develop more adaptive ways of living.

Finally, there are *postmodern* psychodynamic approaches. Also called *intersubjectivism, constructivism,* or *relational theory,* these approaches stress the subjective nature of the therapist-client relationship. The post-modern approaches share many features with the humanistic school, but some psychodynamically oriented clinicians also adopt the approach. Therapists advocating postmodern positions believe that the client and the therapist both work from subjective points of view, but that neither is the objectively "correct" view. In therapy, this joint reality is viewed as a psychological system in its own right, worthy of analysis (Stolorow, 1993). For this reason, postmodern therapies are sometimes called "two-person theories" (Gabbard, 2000). (We discuss the post-modern approaches in more detail in the humanistic psychotherapy section.)

Our review of variations on psychodynamic psychotherapy has barely scratched the surface of the methods available (see Table 7.1). Far more detailed coverage is available in several excellent texts on psychotherapy (e.g., Gabbard, 2000, Corsini & Wedding, 2000).

BEHAVIORAL AND COGNITIVE-BEHAVIORAL THERAPIES

Behavioral and cognitive-behavioral therapies are based on the principles and assumptions of the behavioral approach to clinical psychology (see Chapter 2). This means that:

1. Behavior disorders are seen as developing through the same laws of learning as any other behaviors.

2. Therapy methods should be guided by the results of research on learning. When behavioral treatments first emerged, they relied mainly on the principles of classical and operant conditioning of overt behavior, but today they have expanded to encompass the latest about what psychologists in cognitive, social, and biological psychology have learned about how people think and feel (Viken & McFall, 1994).

3. Therapy should be aimed at modifying overt, maladaptive behaviors, as well as the cognitions, physical changes, and emotions that accompany overt behavior. The covert aspects of clients' problems should be dealt with as directly as possible.

4. Treatment should address clients' current problems by dealing with the contemporary environmental forces, learned habits, and cognitive factors that maintain them. Treatment can proceed without exploring early childhood experiences, unconscious processes, inner conflicts, or the like.

5. There is a commitment to the experimental evaluation of treatment. Behavioral therapists are particularly likely to employ techniques whose efficacy has been established by the results of controlled research.

This learning-oriented, empirical, here-and-now approach to treatment is not impersonal, however. Like other clinicians, behavioral therapists believe that treatment proceeds best when offered in the context of a supportive and productive therapeutic relationship. Indeed, some behavioral therapists believe that the therapeutic relationship serves as the ideal context for modeling, then reinforcing, adaptive client behaviors.

The Beginnings of Behavior Therapy

The term *behavior therapy* first appeared in a 1953 paper that described the use of operant conditioning to improve the functioning of chronic schizophrenics (Lindsley, Skinner, & Solomon, 1953). Today, behavior therapy has become one of the most popular approaches to treating all sorts of behavior disorders in adults and children (Wilson, 1995).

Groundwork for the emergence of behavior therapy occurred in the 1920s, when psychologists became interested in studying the role of conditioning and learning in the development of anxiety. For example, Ivan Pavlov observed *experimental neuroses* in his dogs after exposing them to electric shock or requiring them to make difficult sensory discriminations. The dogs' symptoms included agitation, barking, biting the equipment, and forgetting things they had previously learned. In the 1940s, Jules Masserman of Northwestern University studied the conditioning and deconditioning of experimental neuroses in cats.

The discovery of experimental neuroses in animals led to research on similar problems in humans. The most famous of these studies was a classic experiment in 1920 by John B. Watson and his graduate student, Rosalie Rayner. A 9-month-old infant, Albert B., was presented with several stimuli such as a white rat, a dog, a rabbit, a monkey, masks, and a burning newspaper. He showed no fear toward any of these objects, but he did become upset when a loud noise was sounded by striking a steel bar with a hammer. To see whether Albert's fear could be conditioned to a harmless object, Watson and Rayner associated the loud noise with a tame white rat. Albert was shown the rat and, as soon as he began to reach for it, the noise was sounded. After several pairings, the rat alone elicited a strong emotional reaction in the child. This conditioned fear also generalized to some extent to other, previously neutral, furry objects including a rabbit, a fur coat, Watson's own hair, and even a Santa Claus mask. Albert's fear persisted in less extreme form during assessments conducted over a 1-month period.

A few years later, Mary Cover Jones, another of Watson's students, investigated several techniques for *reducing* children's fears (Jones, 1924a, b). For example, she used *social imitation* to help a 3-year-old named Peter conquer his fear of rabbits. "Each day Peter and three other children were brought to the laboratory for a play period. The other children were selected carefully because of their entirely fearless attitude toward the rabbit. . . ." (Jones, 1924b, p. 310). The fearless examples set by the other children helped Peter become more comfortable with the rabbit, but his treatment was interrupted by a bout of scarlet fever, and his progress was jeopardized by a frightening encounter with a big dog. When treatment resumed, it included *direct conditioning*, a procedure in which Peter was fed his favorite food in a room with a caged rabbit. At each session—some of which were attended by Peter's fearless friends—the bunny was placed a little closer to him. This procedure eliminated Peter's fear of rabbits; Peter summed up the results of the treatment by announcing, "I like the rabbit."

The cases of Albert and Peter encouraged the application of conditioning principles to the treatment of fear and many other disorders; the 1920s and 1930s saw learning-based treatments for sexual disorders, substance abuse, and various anxiety-related conditions. However, it was not until the late 1950s and early 1960s that behavior therapy began to achieve its status as a major treatment approach. It was then that treatment research in South Africa, England, and the United States by Joseph Wolpe, Stanley Rachman, Arnold Lazarus, Hans Eysenck, Knight Dunlap, Andrew Salter, and others began to attract widespread attention among clinicians. Their work, which laid the foundation for the behavioral treatment methods described in the following sections, was described in several influential books, including *Psychotherapy by Reciprocal Inhibition* (Wolpe, 1958), *Conditioning Techniques in Clinical Practice and Research* (Franks, 1964); *Case Studies in Behavior Modification* (Ullmann & Krasner, 1965); *Research in Behavior Modification* (Krasner & Ullmann, 1965); and *Behavior Therapy Techniques: A Guide to the Treatment of Neuroses* (Wolpe & Lazarus, 1966). B.F. Skinner's (1953) *Science and Human Behavior* provided a blueprint for the therapeutic use of operant conditioning.

Systematic Desensitization

The anti-anxiety treatment known as *systematic desensitization* (SD) was developed in 1958 by Joseph Wolpe, a South African psychiatrist, as a result of his efforts to help cats overcome laboratory-induced experimental neuroses. The animals had been repeatedly shocked in a special cage, so they resisted being put in that cage and refused to eat while there. Wolpe reasoned that if conditioned anxiety could inhibit eating, perhaps eating might inhibit conditioned anxiety through the principle of *reciprocal inhibition*. According to Wolpe (1958): "If a response antagonistic to anxiety can be made to occur in the presence of anxiety-evoking stimuli so that it is accompanied by a complete or partial suppression of the anxiety responses, the bond between these stimuli and the anxiety responses will be weakened" (p. 71). In fact, when he "counterconditioned" the cats' fear by hand-feeding them in cages that were closer and closer to where their anxiety had been learned, most animals showed greatly diminished emotional reactions.

To try similar methods with humans who suffered phobias and other maladaptive fears, Wolpe needed to create responses other than eating that might be incompatible with anxiety. He chose three: deep muscle relaxation, interpersonal assertion, and sexual arousal. Muscle relaxation became the standard anxiety inhibitor in most cases of systematic desensitization; assertion or sexual arousal is employed mainly when the anxiety to be inhibited relates to interpersonal or sexual problems.

The most common relaxation technique is *progressive relaxation training* (e.g., Bernstein, Borkovec, & Hazlett–Stevens, 2000), a shorter version of a method pioneered by Edmund Jacobson in 1938. It involves tensing and then releasing various groups of muscles while focusing on the sensations of relaxation that follow. (You can get an idea of what the training feels like by clenching your fist for about 5 seconds and then abruptly releasing the tension.)

The next step in desensitization is for the therapist to create a *graduated hierarchy* of situations that the client finds increasingly anxiety-provoking. The content and ordering of these items (which are later to be imagined or experienced "live") is guided by the client so that each elicits just a bit more anxiety than the one before it (see Table 7.2). Too large an increase in arousal between items will make progress difficult, while too small an increase may lengthen treatment needlessly.

After relaxation training and hierarchy construction are complete, desensitization itself begins. In *imaginal desensitization*, the client relaxes and then visualizes the easiest item on the hierarchy. If the client can imagine the scene without anxiety for 10 seconds, the therapist describes the next one. If not, the client signals the anxiety and stops visualizing the scene. After regaining complete relaxation, the client again pictures the item for a shorter duration, then for gradually longer periods until it no longer creates distress. This sequence is continued until the client can handle all items in the hierarchy. Ideally, reduction of anxiety to imagined scenes transfers to their real-life equivalents, but the client is also urged to seek out real-world counterparts of the visualized scenes in order to reinforce progress and to assess the generality of treatment effects. Completion of a hierarchy typically takes three to five sessions, though it is possible to finish a short hierarchy in a single meeting. In *in vivo* desensitization, clients use their relaxation skills, and the comforting presence of the therapist, to stay calm while actually confronting gradually more threatening versions of what they fear.

Systematic desensitization can be very effective in the treatment of conditioned maladaptive anxiety. Indeed, Gordon Paul (1969b), a pioneer in research on SD, concluded that "for the first time in the history of psychological treatments, a specific therapeutic package reliably produced measurable benefits for clients across a broad range of distressing problems in which anxiety was of fundamental importance" (p. 159). However, SD may be less successful in treating anxiety-related problems, such as panic disorder and obsessive-compulsive disorder, that are more generalized or complex than specific phobias. Indeed, behavioral therapists have found that treatments involving direct exposure of the client to feared stimuli may be the treatment of choice for many of these disorders (Barlow & Wolfe, 1981).

Desensitization appears especially effective when clients are exposed slowly and carefully to real (rather than imagined) items within their hierarchy (Chambless, 1990; McGlynn et al., 1999). However, exposing clients to real situations, such as heights, airline flights, or highway situations can be difficult or expensive, and precise calibration of the desired level of exposure can be difficult to achieve. Simulated environments, which are used successfully in training airline and military pilots, offer an alternative. In *virtual reality exposure treatments*, clients can be exposed to carefully monitored levels of a stimulus. In one study, for instance, clients who feared heights wore a head-mounted virtual reality helmet that gave them the impression of standing on bridges of gradually increasing heights, on outdoor balconies at higher and higher floors, and in a glass elevator as it slowly rose 49 stories (Rothbaum, et al., 1995). The same technology has been used successfully in the treatment of a variety of anxiety disorders (Klein, 1999; Robins, 2000; Rothbaum et al., 1999, 2000).

TABLE 7.2 A Desensitization Hierarchy

In imaginal desensitization, the client relaxes while visualizing a series of increasingly frightening scenes. In *in vivo* desensitization, the client confronts real hierarchy items under controlled conditions. Here is an imaginal hierarchy used in the treatment of a seventeen-year-old woman who feared getting lice or other bugs in her hair. The numbers in parentheses indicate the session(s) of desensitization during which each item was presented.

1. Writing the words *bug* and *lice*. (1)
2. While reading in school you notice a small bug on your book. (1)
3. While walking down the sidewalk you notice a comb in the gutter. (1)
4. You are at home watching television when an ad concerning a dandruff-removing shampoo comes on. (2)
5. You are reading a *Reader's Digest* article that goes into detail concerning the catching and curing of a case of lice. (2)
6. You look at your desktop and notice several bobby pins and clips upon it. (3)
7. You are in a department store, and the saleslady is fitting a hat on you. (3)
8. At a store you are asked to try on a wig and you comply. (3)
9. You are watching a movie and they show a scene where people are being deloused. (4, 5, and 6)
10. At school, in hygiene class, the teacher lectures on lice and bugs in people's hair. (4 and 5)
11. A girl puts her scarf on your lap. (5)
12. In a public washroom you touch the seat of a commode. (6)
13. You are in a beauty shop having your hair set. (6)
14. A girl sitting in front of you in school leans her head back on your books. (6 and 7)
15. While sitting at home with your sister, she tells you that she used someone else's comb today. (7 and 8)
16. While sitting in the local snack bar a friend tells you of her experiences when she had a case of lice. (8 and 9)
17. You are combing your hair in the washroom when someone asks to borrow your comb. (9)
18. A stranger asks to use your comb and continues to ask why not when you say no. (9)
19. While standing looking at an ad in a store window, someone comes up beside you and puts their head near yours to see too. (10)
20. A stranger in the washroom at school hands you her comb and asks you to hold it for her. (10)
21. Your sister is fixing your hair when she drops the curlers on the floor, picks them up, and uses them in your hair. (11)
22. A stranger notices a tangle in your hair and tries to help you by combing it out with her comb. (11)

SOURCE: Geer, J. H. (1965). The Development of a Scale to Measure Fear. *Behaviour Research and Therapy, 3,* pp. 45–53.

Exposure Techniques

Like *in vivo* desensitization, *exposure treatments* entail direct exposure to frightening stimuli, but the idea here is not to prevent anxiety. Instead, exposure to feared stimuli is arranged so that anxiety occurs and continues until—because no harm comes to the client—it eventually disappears through the process of extinction.

Using *flooding*, for example, clients might be asked to touch and remain in contact with—for hours, if necessary—items they fear are "contaminated." While some therapists favor intense, prolonged exposures to items at the top of the client's anxiety hierarchy, others start with lower items before trying the most frightening ones (Barlow & Waddell, 1985). In either case, exposure times must be long enough for anxiety to dissipate; exposure should not be terminated while the client is still anxious because the resulting anxiety reduction would reinforce avoidance behavior.

Exposure treatments are especially popular in cases of obsessive-compulsive disorder (in which clients experience *obsessions*—persistently intrusive and fearful thoughts—and engage in *compulsions*, which are repeated behavioral rituals designed to reduce or prevent anxiety stemming from their obsessions). In such cases, exposure is usually accompanied by *response prevention*, meaning that clients are not allowed to perform the rituals they normally use to reduce anxiety (Abramowitz, 1996; Lam & Steketee, 2001; see Table 7.3). The combination of exposure and response prevention is sometimes provided in a group format, where modeling and group pressure can serve to facilitate the treatment's effectiveness (McLean et al, 2001). Exposure techniques are also used extensively with agoraphobia, a severe disorder involving fear of being away from home or some other safe place, or of being in a public place—such as a theater—from which escape might be difficult. Exposure treatments are also used for the panic attacks that often precede the development of agoraphobia.

Social Skills Training

Some psychological disorders may develop partly because people lack the social skills necessary for participating in satisfying interpersonal relationships and for gaining other reinforcers. If their skill deficits are severe, these people can become demoralized, anxious, angry, or alienated. Accordingly, behavioral therapists often include *social skills training* in the treatment of disorders such as depression (Bellack, Hersen, & Himmelhoch, 1983), anxiety disorders (van Dam-Baggen & Kraaimaat, 2000), antisocial and delinquent behavior (Stumphauzer, 1986), schizophrenia (Dilk & Bond, 1996; McQuaid et al., 2000), and social withdrawal and isolation, often with children and adolescents (Spence, Donovan, Brechman-Toussaint, 2000).

Although social skills training encompasses many techniques, *assertiveness training* is one of the most popular, especially with adults whose inability to effectively express their needs and wishes leads to resentment, aggression, or depression. All too often, these people know what they would *like* to say and do in various social situations but, because of thoughts like "I have no right to make a fuss" or "He won't like me if I object," they suffer in silence. Assertion training is designed to (1) teach clients how to express themselves appropriately if they do not already have the skills to do so, and/or (2) eliminate cognitive obstacles to clear self-expression. They are also taught that *assertiveness is the appropriate expression of feeling in ways that do not infringe upon the rights of others* (Alberti & Emmons, 1974; Wolpe & Lazarus, 1966). Thus, telling your boss that you will not agree to an unreasonable request requires assertion, but so does telling your friends that you were moved by their recent expression of sympathy.

Assertion training often takes place in groups and usually includes four components: (1) defining assertion and distinguishing it from aggression and submissiveness, (2) discussing clients' rights and the rights of others in a variety of social situations, (3) identifying and eliminating cognitive obstacles to assertion, and (4) practicing assertive behavior. This last component usually begins with role-playing or rehearsal of various social interactions, with the therapist taking the client's role and demonstrating appropriate assertiveness. Next, the client tries the same behavior. This effort is reinforced and suggestions are made for further improvement. After more refined rehearsals, the client is asked to try the new thoughts and actions outside of therapy. Successes and failures are analyzed at subsequent sessions, where further skill training and practice occur.

Although initially focused on training in the "refusal skills" many clients need to ward off unreasonable requests, assertiveness training is now also aimed at promoting a broader range of social skills, including making conversation, engaging in interpersonal problem-solving, and appropriately responding to emotional provocations (e.g., Tisdell & St. Lawrence, 1988).

Modeling

A very important mechanism in human learning is imitation, also known as *modeling* or *observational learning* (Bandura, 1969). In fact, learning through modeling is usually more efficient than learning through direct reinforcement or punishment. (Imagine if everyone had to be hit by a car before knowing how to cross streets safely!) Observing the consequences of a model's behavior can also inhibit or disinhibit an observer's imitative behavior (we are unlikely to pet a dog that just bit someone, but we are more likely to cross against a red light after watching someone else do so).

Modeling has been used to treat many clinical problems, including social withdrawal among adults and children, obsessive-compulsive behaviors, unassertiveness, antisocial conduct, physical aggressiveness, and early infantile autism (Rosenthal & Steffek, 1991). In the tradition of Mary Cover Jones (1924b), it is also commonly used to treat fears. The simplest modeling approach eliminating fearful avoidance involves having a client observe live or videotaped models as they perform behaviors that the client avoids—with the models experiencing no negative consequences. In a common variant on this basic modeling treatment called participant modeling, the client first observes live models, then makes guided, gradual contact with the feared object under controlled and protected circumstances.

Modeling treatments appear to be especially effective when the model(s) are similar to the client, have high status, and are rewarded for their actions (Bandura, 1986). One way of making models more similar to clients—while also providing instruction on how to deal successfully with fear—is to present coping models who initially display fearfulness, then cope with and overcome it (Meichenbaum, 1971). The effects of mod-

TABLE 7.3 Exposure Treatment of Obsessive-Compulsive Disorder

Here is an excerpt from a treatment session in which a client's obsessions about contamination and resulting compulsive cleaning rituals are treated with exposure methods. Notice how the therapist guides and encourages the client to confront a frightening situation (a dead animal by the side of a road) and to stay in contact with it until anxiety begins to subside.

THERAPIST: (*Outside the office.*) There it is, behind the car. Let's go and touch the curb and street next to it. I won't insist that you touch it directly because it's a bit smelly, but I want you to step next to it and touch it with the sole of your shoe.

PATIENT: Yuck! It's really dead. It's gross!

T: Yeah, it is a bit gross, but it's also just a dead cat if you think about it plainly. What harm can it cause?

P: I don't know. Suppose I got germs on my hand?

T: What sort of germs?

P: Dead cat germs.

T: What kind are they?

P: I don't know. Just germs.

T: Like the bathroom germs that we've already handled?

P: Sort of. People don't go around touching dead cats.

T: They also don't go running home to shower or alcoholing the inside of their car. It's time to get over this. Now, come on over and I'll do it first. (*Patient follows.*) OK. Touch the curb and the street, here's a stone you can carry with you and a piece of paper from under its tail. Go ahead, take it.

P: (*Looking quite uncomfortable.*) Ugh!

T: We'll both hold them. Now, touch it to your front and your skirt and your face and hair. Like this. That's good. What's your anxiety level?

P: Ick! Ninety-nine. I'd say 100 but it's just short of panic. If you weren't here, it'd be 100.

T: You know from past experience that this will be much easier in a while. Just stay with it and we'll wait here. You're doing fine.

eling treatments have increasingly been linked to their ability to increase self-efficacy, the belief that one can successfully perform certain behaviors.

Aversion Therapy

Aversion therapy is a set of techniques in which painful or unpleasant stimuli are used to decrease the probability of unwanted behaviors such as drug abuse, alcoholism, overeating, smoking, and disturbing sexual practices. Following classical conditioning principles, most aversion methods pair stimuli that elicit problematic behavior with a noxious stimulus. So, for example, an alcoholic is exposed to a foul odor as he sits at a simulated bar, smelling a glass of Scotch. Ideally, continued pairings should decrease the attractiveness of the eliciting stimuli until the unwanted behavior is reduced, if not eliminated. When aversion therapy is based on operant conditioning, electric shock or some other aversive stimulus acts as a punisher; it is delivered just after the client performs the problematic behavior (e.g., immediately after taking a drink of alcohol).

There is debate over several aspects of aversion methods. First, there is concern about whether the changes produced by aversion therapies are extensive, durable, and generalizable enough to justify the unpleasantness of the treatment. Critics also note

---

TABLE 7.3   Exposure Treatment of Obsessive-Compulsive Disorder (*Continued*)

P: (*A few minutes pass in which she looks very upset.*) Would you do this if it wasn't for me?

T: Yes, if this were my car and I dropped my keys here, I'd just pick them up and go on.

P: You wouldn't have to wash them?

T: No. Dead animals aren't delightful but they're part of the world we live in. What are the odds that we'll get ill from this?

P: Very small I guess. . . . I feel a little bit better than at first. It's about 90 now.

T: Good! Just stay with it now.

The session continues for another 45 minutes or until anxiety decreases substantially. During this period conversation focuses generally on the feared situation and the patient's reactions to it. The therapist inquires about the patient's anxiety level approximately every 10 minutes.

T: How do you feel now?

P: Well, it is easier, but I sure don't feel great.

T: Can you put a number on it?

P: About 55 or 60 I'd say.

T: You worked hard today. You must be tired. Let's stop now. I want you to take this stick and pebble with you so that you continue to be contaminated. You can keep them in your pocket and touch them frequently during the day. I want you to contaminate your office at work and your apartment with them. Touch them to everything around, including everything in the kitchen, chairs, your bed, and the clothes in your dresser. Oh, also, I'd like you to drive your car past this spot on your way to and from work. Can you do that?

P: I suppose so. The trouble is going home with all this dirt.

T: Why don't you call Ken and plan to get home after he does so he can be around to help you. Remember, you can always call me if you have any trouble.

P: Yeah. That's a good idea. I'll just leave work after he does. OK. See you tomorrow.

SOURCE: Steketee and Foa, 1985.

that aversion therapy does not teach clients alternative behaviors that can replace their maladaptive ones. Third, many therapists find it aversive to use aversion therapies. Their distaste is engendered partly by skepticism about treatment effects, but also by (1) reluctance to intentionally inflict discomfort on clients, (2) worry over possible side effects such as generalized fear or aggressiveness, and (3) overuse of the procedures by therapists who might use them simply because they can bring about quick (but temporary) changes (Masters et al., 1987).

Accordingly, aversive methods tend to be used as a last resort to control dangerous behavior (such as self-abuse or severe alcoholism) that has not responded to nonaversive methods, and even then, as part of a broader treatment approach designed to promote more adaptive behavior.

Contingency Management

Contingency management is a generic term for any operant technique that modifies a behavior by controlling its consequences. *Shaping, time out, contingency contracting, response cost,* and *token economies* are all examples of contingency management. In practice, contingency management refers to presenting and/or withdrawing rein-forcers and aversive stimuli contingent upon the appearance of certain target behav-iors. Contingency management has been applied to a broader range of problems than any other behavioral technique. Autism, temper tantrums, learning difficulties, hyperac-tivity, retardation, juvenile delinquency, aggression, hallucinations, delusions, depres-sion, phobias, sexual disorders, and physical and psychosomatic complaints are just a few of the targets that have been dealt with through contingency management.

Contingency management is so widely applied because it is so flexible. It can be tailored to clients of all ages, to the unique problems of an individual, and to the behav-ior of a group or even a whole community. Because its methods are relatively easy to learn, a client's friends, relatives, teachers, and peers can be trained to employ contin-gency management in real-life settings. Contingency management can also be used by clients to modify their own behavior. This process, known as *self-control,* can be thought of as the ability to regulate personal behaviors by arranging appropriate rein-forcement contingencies. Thus an overweight person who decides to eat only at speci-fied times, only in the kitchen, and only in the presence of family is practicing a form of self-control (Rehm et al., 1981).

Complete accounts of the wide range of contingency management techniques are available in many texts (e.g., Spiegler & Guevremont, 1993). We present five examples here.

Shaping.   Also called *successive approximation,* shaping is a procedure for de-veloping new behaviors by initially reinforcing any act that remotely resembles the de-sired behavior. The criterion for reinforcement is then made gradually more stringent until only those responses matching the final standard are rewarded. Shaping is useful for instigating behaviors that appear to exceed the client's present capacities. It has been used to teach speech to children who are mute, toilet habits to those who are in-continent, and self-help and occupational skills to severely retarded persons.

Time Out.   Time out is a special example of extinction that reduces the fre-quency of unwanted behavior by temporarily removing the person from the setting where that behavior is being reinforced. The most common example is sending a child to a quiet, boring room for a short time following some act of mischief. Time out is based on the principle that ignoring a child's "bad" behavior will decrease it, especially if alternative "good" behavior is also reinforced.

Contingency Contracting.   Contracting is a form of contingency management where a formal, often written, agreement between therapist and client spells out the con-sequences of certain client behaviors. Behavioral contracting has been applied to targets such as marital distress (Wood & Jacobson, 1985), family disruptions (Alexander & Par-sons, 1973), drug abuse (Piane, 2000), obesity (Brownell & Foreyt, 1985), and other prob-lems. Therapeutic contracts have even been used to prevent clients' dangerous or suici-dal behavior; they set up rules that forbid violent behavior or that require the client to take specific precautionary actions (calling the therapist, turning over weapons to the therapist) should he or she consider acting dangerously (Bongar, 1991).

The typical contract includes five components (Stuart, 1971): (1) responsibilities of each of the parties to the contract, (2) rewards for fulfilling the contract, (3) a system for monitoring compliance with the contract, (4) bonuses for unusual accomplishments, and (5) penalties for failures.

Response Cost. Response cost is a punishment contingency that involves the loss of a reward or privilege following some undesirable behavior. Fines for traffic violations are everyday examples of response cost. Response cost methods have been used to decrease the frequency of many clinical problems, including smoking, self-abuse, overeating, academic problems, and a range of inappropriate or aggressive behaviors in adults and children. Two major advantages of these methods are that (1) behaviors decreased through response cost remain suppressed longer than when other types of punishment are employed and (2) response cost does not carry as many unwanted side effects as other, more aversive forms of punishment (Kazdin, 1972).

Token Economies. A token economy is a system for implementing the principles of contingency management to alter a variety of behaviors, usually the behavior of adults or children in some controlled institutional setting. You might think of it as a monetary system in which clients are paid in a special currency (tokens) for performing designated behaviors.

Token economies usually include four elements, the first of which is for staff (and clients) to decide which *target behaviors* are to be changed. Common targets in hospitalized mental patients are increased social interaction and improved self-care skills. Second, a token or other medium of exchange is identified as payment for performing target behaviors. Gold stars and colored stickers are often used with children; for adults, tokens may be poker chips or specially made "coins." Third, *back-up reinforcers* are established; these are the goods or services for which tokens may be exchanged. Snacks, TV or recreational privileges, "vacations" from the hospital, and more luxurious living conditions are common back-ups. Finally, there are rules of exchange governing (1) the number of tokens to be given for performing each target behavior and (2) the number of tokens necessary to purchase each back-up reinforcer.

In the first published report on a token economy, hospitalized mental patients showed a significant increase in self-care and completed work assignments (Ayllon & Azrin, 1965). This report stimulated the development of similar token economies in numerous psychiatric hospitals, institutions for retarded people, and elementary school classrooms plagued by disruptive or delinquent behavior (Burchard, 1967; Cohen, 1968; O'Leary & Becker, 1967). Special programs for Head Start participants, alcoholics, drug addicts, and autistic children were also developed according to token economy principles. Token economies have even been designed to promote community-wide conservation and environmental protection efforts (Nietzel et al., 1977).

Biofeedback

Behavioral methods used to control heart rate, blood pressure, muscle tension and other physiological responses are known as *biofeedback*. The name refers to the fact that the behaviors to be changed are biological in nature and that special equipment is used to monitor the target response and to give the client feedback about its intensity or frequency in the form of a meter reading, graph, or auditory signal. The monitor and feedback apparatus is attached to the client, who then uses some mental or physical strategy to change the internal target response in a desired direction. In most cases, the reinforcer for improvement is simply knowledge of results provided by the feedback, but praise or monetary rewards have also been used.

Biofeedback has been widely used to treat several clinical disorders, including high blood pressure, migraine headache, Reynaud's disease (a circulatory disorder), stomach problems, bruxism (nocturnal tooth-grinding), irregular heartbeat, and other problems that involve disruptions in autonomic or musculoskeletal functioning (e.g., Carmagnani & Carmagnani, 1999; Sedlacek & Taub, 1996). It appears to produce significant improvements in many of these conditions, though it is not clear how durable these improvements are and whether they are any greater than the benefits of simpler procedures such as relaxation training (Reed, Katkin, & Goldband, 1986).

Cognitive-Behavioral Therapy

All therapeutic interventions involve thought processes, but some procedures are specifically directed toward changing clients' maladaptive cognitions. These techniques, known as cognitive therapies, attempt to modify maladaptive behavior by influencing a client's cognitions (beliefs, schemas, self-statements, and problem-solving strategies). Cognitive therapists believe that certain cognitions, particularly thoughts about the self, are especially important in the development of disorder (Salovey & Singer, 1991). Because these thoughts are usually connected to emotions, they affect how we feel about ourselves and our relationships with others. Cognitions color how we think about the past and the way we explain events that have happened to us; they affect our outlook on the future and our confidence that we will be able to cope with new demands.

The behavioral and cognitive approaches have tended to merge over the last several years. This has occurred because behaviorally-oriented therapists recognized the importance of cognitions in various disorders, and cognitively oriented therapists recognized the importance of systematically translating cognitive change into behavior change. The result is called *cognitive-behavioral therapy* or *CTB*. Cognitive-behavioral therapies have surged in popularity in the past several years. For instance, a search of the American Psychological Association's *PsychINFO ONLINE* database revealed that between 1988 and 1990, there were 48 APA journal articles with the words "cognitive-behavioral therapy" in the title. Between 1998 and 2000, there were 170, and in 2001 alone, there were an additional 144. These results mirror publication trends within psychology as a whole (see Robins, Gosling, & Craik, 1999), and within the literature on empirically-validated psychotherapies, which we discuss in Chapter 9 (see Duncan, 2001).

Beck's Cognitive Therapy. One of the most influential types of cognitive therapy is Aaron Beck's approach to the treatment of depression, an approach based on the assumption that depression and other emotions are determined by the way people think about their experiences (Beck et al., 1979; Beck & Weishaar, 1995). His version of cognitive therapy has also been applied to anxiety disorders, personality disorders, and substance use disorders (Beck et al., 1990; Linehan, 1993).

Beck says that depressive symptoms result from logical errors and distortions that clients make about the events in their lives. For example, they draw conclusions about themselves on the basis of insufficient or irrelevant information, as when a woman believes she is worthless because she was not invited to a party. They also exaggerate the importance of trivial events, as when a man decides that his vintage record collection is ruined because one record has a scratch on it. And they minimize the significance of positive events, as when a student believes that a good test score was the result of luck, not intelligence or hard work.

Cognitive therapists work to identify and correct their client's distorted beliefs using five related strategies: (1) recognizing the connections between cognitions, affect, and behavior; (2) monitoring occurrences of cognitive distortions; (3) examining the evidence for and against these distortions; (4) substituting more realistic interpretations for dysfunctional cognitions; and (5) giving "homework assignments" to practice new thinking strategies and more effective problem-coping.

Rational Emotive Behavior Therapy. Another influential cognitive therapy, one that helped pioneer cognitive-behavior, is Albert Ellis's *rational-emotive behavior therapy*, or REBT (Ellis, 1995; 2001). Ellis (1973) stated the core principles of REBT as follows:

> When a highly charged emotional Consequence (C) follows a significant Activating Event (A), A may seem to but actually does not cause C. Instead, emotional Consequences are largely created by B—the individual's Belief System. When, therefore, an undesirable Consequence occurs, such as severe anxiety, this can usually be quickly traced to the person's irrational Beliefs, and when these Beliefs are effectively Disputed (at point D), by challenging them rationally, the disturbed Consequences disappear and eventually cease to reoccur. (p. 167)

To summarize the ABCs of REBT: Psychological problems result not from external stress but from the irrational ideas people hold, which lead them to insist that their wishes must be met in order for them to be happy.

The therapist's task in REBT is to attack these irrational, unrealistic, self-defeating beliefs and to instruct clients in more rational or logical thinking patterns that will not upset them (Ellis, 1962; Ellis & Grieger, 1977; Ellis & Dryden, 1987). The REBT therapist is active, challenging, demonstrative, and often abrasive. Ellis advocates the use of strong, direct communication in order to persuade clients to give up the irrational ideas with which they indoctrinate themselves into misery. Here is a brief excerpt from an initial REBT session between a therapist (T) and a young woman (C) who presented several problems, among them the abuse of alcohol.

> C: (after being asked what is wrong) . . . my tendency is to say everything. I want to change everything; I'm depressed about everything; et cetera.

T: Give me a couple of things, for example.

C: What I'm depressed about? I, uh, don't know that I have any purpose in life. I don't know what I—what I am. And I don't know in what direction I'm going.

T: Yeah, but that's—so you're saying, "I'm ignorant!" (client nods) Well, what's so awful about being ignorant? It's too bad you're ignorant. It would be nicer if you weren't—if you had a purpose and knew where you were going. But just let's suppose the worst: For the rest of your life you didn't have a purpose, and you stayed this way. Let's suppose that. Now why would you be so bad?

C: Because everyone should have a purpose!

T: Where did you get the should?

C: 'Cause it's what I believe in. (silence for a while)

T: I know. But think about it for a minute. You're obviously a bright woman; now, where did that should come from?

C: I, I don't know! I'm not thinking clearly at the moment. I'm too nervous! I'm sorry.

T: Well, but you can think clearly. Are you now saying, "Oh, it's hopeless! I can't think clearly. What a shit I am for not thinking clearly!" You see: You're blaming yourself for that.

C: (visibly upset; can't seem to say anything; then nods)

T: Now you're perfectly able to think.

C: Not at the moment!

T: Yes you are! Want to bet?

C: (begins to sob)

T: What are you crying about now?

C: Because I feel so stupid! And I'm afraid!

T: Yeah, but "stupid" means "I'm putting myself down for acting stupidly."

C: All right! I didn't expect to be put on so fast. I expected a moment to catch my breath and see who you were; and to establish some different kind of rapport.

T: Yeah. And that would be nice and easier; but we would really waste our time.

C: Yes, I guess we would.

T: But you're really upset because you're not giving the right answers—and isn't that awful!

C: Yes. And I don't think that anybody likes to be made a fool, a fool of!

T: You can't be made a fool of!

C: (chokes a little)

T: You see, that's the point: That's impossible. Now why can't you be made a fool of?

C: (angry outburst) Why don't you stop asking me?

T: (interrupting) No! You'll never get better unless you think. And you're saying, "Can't we do something magical to get me better?" And the answer is "No!"

The REBT therapist's frontal assault on the client's irrational beliefs is not restricted to cognitive interventions. Role-playing, sensory-awareness exercises, desensitization, assertion training, and specific homework assignments are also employed in an attempt to provide behavioral complements to cognitive change.

Dialectical Behavior Therapy.   Pioneered by Marsha Linehan (Linehan, 1993; Linehan & Kehrer, 1993), *dialectical behavior therapy*, or *DBT*, is a form of cognitive-behavioral therapy often used to help clients who display the impulsive behavior, mood swings, fragile self-image, and stormy interpersonal relationships associated with borderline personality disorder (Nietzel et al., 1998; Sheel, 2000). It has also been applied to eating disorders such as bulimia nervosa (Safer, Telch, & Agras, 2001).

Initially, DBT helps these clients develop skill at containing their erratic behaviors, but after these "containment" goals have been reached, the therapist helps the client confront any traumatic experiences—such as physical or sexual abuse in childhood—that might have contributed to their current emotional difficulties. This phase of treatment concentrates on eliminating self-blame for these traumas, reducing posttraumatic stress symptoms, and resolving questions of who is to blame for the trauma. By consistently helping borderline clients see that almost all events can be thought about from varying perspectives, the dialectical therapist tries to encourage them to see the world in a more integrated or balanced way.

Relapse Prevention.   Alan Marlatt and Judith Gordon's *relapse prevention* treatment is a cognitive-behavioral intervention designed to help clients who are trying to overcome alcoholism or other substance use disorders (Marlatt & Gordon, 1985). Marlatt and Gordon believe that relapse is most likely when clients engage in thoughts (such as "I owe myself a drink.") that lead to relapse. Once a relapse episode occurs, guilt and shame tend to generate a cascade of negative self-evaluations ("I've let my family down."; "I'm a complete failure.") which increases the probability of continued drinking, an outcome known as the *abstinence violation effect* (Marlatt & Gordon, 1985).

Relapse prevention techniques teach the client to monitor risky cognitions and to replace them with different thinking strategies. For example, instead of thinking about how good it would feel to drink, clients are taught to focus on how miserable it felt to be in jail after a drunken driving arrest. They are also taught to view a relapse episode not as an excuse to resume substance use, but as a temporary setback whose recurrence can be prevented by working on better cognitive and behavioral self-control strategies.

HUMANISTIC THERAPIES

The therapies we have described so far treat human behavior as mainly the product of either intrapsychic conflicts or learning. However, as discussed in Chapter 2, a third force in clinical psychology deemphasizes these factors and focuses instead on *conscious experience* as the basis for human behavior. This *humanistic* approach views humans as creative, growthful beings who, if all goes well, consciously guide their own behavior toward realization of their fullest potential as unique individuals. When behavior disorders arise, they are usually seen as stemming from disturbances in awareness or restrictions on existence that can be eliminated through various therapeutic experiences (Fischer, 1989; Greenberg, Elliott, & Lietaer, 1994). Treatment approaches aimed at addressing and correcting these problems are known as *humanistic* (or *phenomenological/experiential*) *therapies*.

Common Features in Humanistic Therapies

Several themes unify the goals and techniques associated with humanistic treatments.

First, humanistic therapists assume that their clients' lives can be understood only when viewed from the point of view of those clients. This theme can be traced to philosophers such as Søren Kierkegaard and Jean-Paul Sartre, who emphasized that the meaning of life is not intrinsic, but is constructed by the perceiver. The idea of individually construed reality was also emphasized by a group of German psychologists—including Koffka, Köhler, and Werthheimer—known as the Gestalt school.

Second, many humanistic therapists view human beings not as instinct-driven creatures but as naturally good people who are able to make choices about their lives and determine their own destinies. Those humanistic therapists committed to European existential philosophies are less likely to argue that all clients naturally strive toward positive goals (Fischer, 1989), but all humanistic therapies do aim to promote each client's growth as a unique person. This goal is referred to as *self-actualization*. The assumption is that once clients are allowed to reach their full potential, they will find their own solutions to personal problems.

Third, humanistic therapists view the therapeutic relationship as the primary vehicle by which therapy achieves its benefits. It must be a relationship that guarantees honest, emotionally open, interpersonal experiences for both client and therapist. Focusing on the immediate, moment-to-moment experiences in this relationship is what helps clients perceive themselves more positively.

A fourth characteristic of humanistic therapies is that clients are regarded as equals. Therapists treat them as responsible individuals who are experts on their own experiences and who must ultimately be the ones to make decisions about their lives.

Finally, many humanistic therapists emphasize the importance of experiencing and exploring emotions that are confusing or painful. They use several techniques to promote emotional awareness and experience and, as research documenting the effectiveness of these techniques has accumulated (Greenberg, Elliott, & Lietaer, 1994), many therapists beyond the humanistic school have employed them. One example is called the *empty chair technique*. It is designed to increase awareness of unresolved conflicts and emotions by asking the client to imagine that a parent, child, spouse, or other person associated with the conflict or emotion is sitting in an empty chair nearby. The client is then instructed to talk to the imagined person and to express—perhaps for the first time—true feelings about him or her and about events or conflicts in which that person played a part. It is hoped that, in the process, clients will learn to take responsibility for and master these feelings.

Two prominent examples of humanisitc therapies are Carl Rogers' (1951) client-centered therapy and Fritz Perls's Gestalt therapy (Perls, 1969). More recent are the postmodern or constructivist approaches.

Client-Centered Therapy

By far, the most influential of the humanistic treatments is the *client-centered therapy* of Carl Rogers. First trained in psychodynamic therapy methods in the late 1920s, Rogers eventually became uncomfortable with the idea of therapists as authority figures who searched relentlessly for unconscious material. Rogers felt there had to be a better way to do clinical work, and an alternative began to take shape when he discovered a treatment approach advocated by Otto Rank, whose revision of Freud's ideas was mentioned earlier. To Rank, the client ". . . is a moving cause, containing constructive forces within, which constitute a will to health. The therapist guides the individual to self-understanding, self-acceptance. It is the therapist *as a human being* who is the remedy, not his technical skill. . . . The spontaneity and uniqueness of therapy lived in the present carry the patient toward health" (Meador & Rogers, 1973, p. 121; italics added).

As Rogers began to incorporate these ideas about nonauthoritarianism and the value of a good human relationship into his therapy sessions, he came to believe that "it is the client who knows what hurts, what directions to go, what problems are crucial, what experiences have been deeply buried" (Rogers, 1961, pp. 11–12). He also began to see therapy as an "if . . . then" proposition: *If* the correct circumstances are created by the therapist, *then* the client—driven by an innate potential for growth—will spontaneously improve.

Rogers's approach to treatment reflected his self-actualization theory, which, as described in Chapter 2, assumes that people are thwarted in their growth by judgments imposed on them by others. When these *conditions of worth* force people to distort their real feelings, symptoms of disorder appear. Thus, if a person really wanted to be an artist but had to ignore those feelings because of family pressure to become an accountant, depression might result. Growth would stop as the person's behavior (e.g., professing satisfaction with accounting) became increasingly discrepant, or incongruent, with real feelings.

Client-centered therapy is aimed at providing an interpersonal relationship that the client can use to further personal growth, but this growth-enhancing relationship can only appear, said Rogers, if the therapist experiences and expresses three interrelated attitudes: unconditional positive regard, empathy, and congruence.

Unconditional Positive Regard. The therapeutic attitude Rogers called *unconditional positive regard* conveys three messages: that the therapist (1) cares about the client, (2) accepts the client, and (3) trusts the client's ability to change.

The ideal form of unconditional positive regard is *nonpossessive caring*, in which genuine positive feelings are expressed in a way that makes clients feel valued, but still free to be themselves, not obligated to try to please the therapist. The therapist's *willingness to listen* is an important manifestation of unconditional positive regard. Patient, warm, and interested in what the client has to say, Rogerian therapists do not in-

Carl Rogers (1902–1987) by John T. Wood (Courtesy of Carl Rogers).

terrupt the client or change the subject or give other signs that they would rather be doing something else.

The "unconditional" aspect of unconditional positive regard is manifested in the therapist's willingness to accept clients as they are without judging them. Rogers believed that the experience of being prized as a human being, regardless of one's feelings or behaviors, can be a growth-enhancing experience for clients whose development has been hampered by conditions of worth and other evaluative pressures. Fortunately, expressing unconditional positive regard does not require *approving* of all the things a client says or does, merely *accepting* them as part of a person whom the therapist cares about. This ideal is illustrated in the following interaction:

> CLIENT: That was the semester my brother died and everything seemed to be going down the tubes. I knew how important it was to my parents that I get into medical school, but I also knew that my grades would be lousy that year unless I did something. To make a long story short, I bought a term paper and cheated on almost every exam that semester.
>
> THERAPIST: It was a really rough time for you.

Notice that the therapist focuses on the client's feelings in the situation, not on the ethics of the behavior. In other words, to express unconditional positive regard, the therapist must separate a client's worth *as a person* from the worth of the client's *behavior*.

The "positive" component of unconditional positive regard is reflected in the therapist's trust in the client's potential for growth and problem solving. Rogers believed that if clients perceive that their therapist lacks this trust, they will not develop the confidence they need to make changes. So, like other humanistic/experiential therapists, Rogerians try not to give advice, take responsibility for clients, or make decisions for them. Such restraint is sometimes difficult, especially when therapists feel that they know "what's best" for a client. However, the client must be allowed to make bad decisions or experience problems, even if they could have been averted by following the therapist's advice. That advice might prevent one problem, but would create others: The therapist would become a superior, the client would become more dependent, and, most important, both client and therapist would have less faith in the client's ability to deal independently with problems.

Empathy. To understand a client's behavior and help the client understand it as well, the therapist must try to see the world as the client sees it. In Rogerian terms, this involves striving for accurate empathy or empathic understanding. To illustrate, let's consider an excerpt from the beginning of a therapy session:

> CLIENT: I don't feel very normal, but I want to feel that way. . . . I thought I'd have something to talk about—then it all goes around in circles. I was trying to think what I was going to say. I tell you, I just can't make a decision; I don't know what I want. I've tried to reason this thing out logically—tried to figure out which things are important to me. I thought that there are maybe two things a man might do; he might get married and raise a family. But if he was just a bachelor, just making a living—that isn't very good. I find myself and my thoughts getting back to the days when I was a kid and I cry very easily. The dam would break through. I've been in the Army four and a half years. I had no problems then, no hopes, no wishes. My only thought was to get out when peace would come. My problems, now that I'm out, are as ever. I tell you, they go back to a long time before I was in the Army. . . . I love children. When I was in the Philippines—I tell you, when I was young I swore I'd never forget my unhappy childhood—so when I saw these children in the Philippines, I treated them very nicely. I used to give them ice cream cones and movies. It was just a period—I'd reverted back—and that awakened some emotions in me I thought I had long buried. (A pause. He seems very near tears.) (Rogers, 1951, pp. 32-33)

Many therapists would react to this client using what Rogers called an *external frame of reference*. They would observe the client from the outside and apply their values to what the client says (see the left side of Table 7.4). An empathic therapist, how-

---

TABLE 7.4 Some Therapist Thoughts That Reflect Internal Versus External Frames of Reference

External	Internal
I wonder if I should get him started talking.	You're wanting to struggle toward normality, aren't you?
Is this inability to get under way a type of dependence?	It's really hard for you to get started.
Why this indecisiveness? What could be its cause?	Decision making just seems impossible for you.
What is meant by this focus on marriage and family?	You want marriage, but it doesn't seem to you to be much of a possibility.
The crying, the "dam" sound as though there must be a great deal of regression.	You feel yourself brimming over with childish feelings.
He's a veteran. Could he have been a psychiatric case? I feel sorry for anybody who spent four and one-half years in the service.	To you the Army represented stagnation.
What is this interest in children? 　Identification? 　Vague homosexuality?	Being very nice to children somehow has meaning for you; but it was—and is—a disturbing experience for you.

SOURCE: Rogers, C. R. (1951), *Client-Centered Therapy,* pp. 33–34. Boston, MA: Houghton Mifflin.

---

ever, would try to adopt an internal frame of reference in an effort to understand what it must be like to be this client (see the right side of Table 7.4).

To communicate an empathic attitude to their clients, Rogerian therapists employ the active listening methods described in Chapter 4. Of particular value is *reflection,* which serves the dual purposes of (1) communicating the therapist's desire for emotional understanding and (2) making clients more aware of their own feelings. Reflection is one of the most misunderstood aspects of client-centered therapy because the therapist appears to be stating the obvious or merely repeating what the client has said. But reflection is more than repetition or paraphrasing. As suggested in Chapter 4, it involves distilling and "playing back" the client's feelings. For example, suppose a client says "This has been such a bad day. I've had to keep myself from crying three or four times. I'm not even sure what's wrong!" The therapist's response could be externally oriented (e.g., "Well what exactly happened?"), but a more empathic comment might be: "You really do feel bad. The tears just well up inside. And it sounds like it is scary to not even know why you feel this way."

At first glance, the clinician may seem to be a parrot, but look more closely. The client never *said* she felt bad; the therapist inferred it by taking the client's point of view. Similarly, the client never said her sadness frightened her—it was the clinician's ability to put himself in the client's shoes that led to this speculation. If the therapist's inferences are wrong, the client can correct them, but right or wrong, the clinician has let the client know that he wants to understand her.

Congruence. Rogers also believed that the more genuine the therapist is in relating to clients, the more helpful the therapist will be. The therapist's feelings and actions, he said, should be *congruent*, or consistent, with one another. "This means that I need to be aware of my own feelings . . . [and willing] to express, in my words and my behavior, the various feelings and attitudes which exist in me" (Rogers, 1961, p. 33). According to Rogers, when the therapist is congruent, a real human relationship occurs in therapy.

To get an idea of how congruence promotes trust, think of a time when a close friend might have told you something that you did not want to hear, perhaps that you looked silly or were wrong about something. Once you know that a friend will say what he or she really feels even if it does not make you happy, it makes it easier to trust whatever else that friend might say. However, if you know that your friend can be incongruent, telling you what you want to hear instead of what he or she genuinely feels, your faith in that person's reactions ("You really look great.") is likely to be undermined.

Here is one way that congruence can be displayed in a therapist–client interaction:

> CLIENT: I just feel so hopeless. Tell me what I'm doing wrong in my life.
>
> THERAPIST: I guess when you are feeling this bad it would be nice if someone could come along and tell you what is going wrong and how you can put everything right again. I wish I could do all that, but I can't. I don't think anyone else can either.

Notice the therapist's reflection of the client's feeling plus the direct expression of (1) a genuine wish to understand and solve the client's problems, and (2) an admission that she is not capable of such a feat.

The Nature of Change in Client-Centered Therapy. Rogers argued that as clients experience empathy, unconditional positive regard and congruence in a therapeutic relationship, they become more self-aware and self-accepting, more comfortable and less defensive in interpersonal relationships, less rigid in their thinking, more reliant on self-evaluation than on evaluations by others, and better able to function in a wide variety of roles (Rogers, 1951).

Carl Rogers was among the first to recognize the need for scientific research to substantiate the alleged value of any treatment technique, including his own. Rogers was also the first to record therapy sessions, and he conducted some of the first empirical research on the relationship between treatment outcome and therapist characteristics such as empathy and warmth (Rogers, 1942).

Gestalt Therapy

After Rogers' client-centered approach, the Gestalt therapy approach developed by Frederick (Fritz) and Laura Perls is probably the best-known humanistic treatment. Like client-centered methods, Gestalt therapy aims at enhancing clients' awareness in order to free them to grow in their own consciously guided ways. More specifically, the Gestalt therapist seeks to reestablish clients' stalled growth processes by helping them (1) become aware of feelings that they have disowned but which are a genuine part of them, and (2) recognize feelings and values that they think are a genuine part of themselves, but which in fact are borrowed from other people.

The client is encouraged to assimilate or "re-own" the genuine aspects of self that have been rejected and to reject the "phony" features that do not belong. Ideally, when clients assimilate and integrate all aspects of their personality (both the desirable and the undesirable), they start taking responsibility for themselves as they really are instead of being attached to and defensive of a partially phony, internally conflicted self-image. For example, a person who feels superior to others but who has forced this feeling out of awareness in favor of a more socially acceptable air of humility will become aware of and express both sides of the conflict ("I'm great" versus "I shouldn't brag"). Once both poles of this conflict confront each other, the client may find a resolution ("It's OK to express my feelings of competence, but I need to take the feelings of others into account as well."). As long as one side of the conflict is out of awareness, such resolution is impossible. According to Perls, when conflict resolutions occur with full awareness of both poles, the person begins to grow again.

As the following sections show, the methods of Gestalt therapy are much more active and dramatic than those of client-centered treatment.

Focus on the Here and Now. For one thing, Gestalt therapists believe that therapeutic progress is made by keeping clients in contact with their feelings as they occur in the here and now. Perls expressed this belief in a conceptual equation where "Now = experience = awareness = reality" (Perls, 1970). Any attempt by the client to recount the past or anticipate the future obstructs therapy goals. It is an escape from reality. So instead of reflecting (as a Rogerian might) the client's nostalgia for the past or thoughts about the future, a gestalt therapist will point out the avoidance and insist that it be terminated.

Role-Playing. Through role-playing or part-taking, clients explore inner conflicts and experience the symptoms, interpersonal games, and psychological defenses they have developed to keep those conflicts—and various other aspects of their genuine selves—out of awareness. By asking clients to "become" their resistance to change, for example, Gestalt therapists help them toward an experiential awareness of what the resistance is doing for and to them.

Frustrating the Client. Because it is not always this easy for clients to become aware of hidden feelings, Gestalt therapists use many other methods for self-exploration. To help clients give up their maladaptive interpersonal roles and games, for example, Perls deliberately set out to frustrate their efforts to relate to him as they normally would to others. During individual or group therapy, he put his clients on what he called the "hot seat," where all attention was focused on them, and where their symptoms, games, and resistances were pointed out and explored.

Suppose that a client begins a session by saying "I've really been looking forward to having this session. I hope you can help me." Instead of reflecting this feeling or asking why the client feels this way, a Gestalt therapist would focus on the manipulative aspect of the statement, which seems to contain the message, "I expect you to help me without my having to do much." The therapist might say, "How do you think I could help you?" The client (somewhat taken aback) might respond, "Well, I was hoping you could help me understand why I'm so unhappy." From here, the therapist would continue to frustrate the client's attempt to get the therapist to take responsibility for solving the client's problems and, in the process, would help the client recognize how he avoids responsibility for improving. He might also help the client recognize the unrealistic wish that the therapist would have a magic cure.

Use of Nonverbal Cues. Gestalt therapists pay special attention to what clients say and what they do, because the nonverbal channel often contradicts the client's words. For example:

CLIENT: I wish I wasn't so nervous with people.

THERAPIST: Who are you nervous with?

CLIENT: With everyone.

THERAPIST: With me, here, now?

CLIENT: Yes, very.

THERAPIST: That's funny, because you don't look nervous to me.

CLIENT: (suddenly clasping his hands) Well I am!

THERAPIST: What are you doing with your hands?

CLIENT: Nothing, I just clasped them together. It's just a gesture.

THERAPIST: Do the gesture again. (client reclasps his hands) And again, clasp them again, harder. (client clasps hands harder) How does that feel?

CLIENT: It feels tight, kind of constricted.

THERAPIST: Can you become that tightness? Can you get in touch with what that tightness might say to you?

CLIENT: OK, ah, I'm tight. I'm holding everything together. I'm keeping the lid on you so that you don't let too much out.

The therapist wondered *what* the clasped hands meant. Instead of asking *why* the client clasped them, she pointed out what the client did. She then asked him to concentrate on the associated feelings by repeating and exaggerating the gesture. Once the client expressed these feelings, the client was asked to elaborate on them. The result was that the client expressed a defensive feeling about being in therapy that he had originally, and inaccurately, described as nervousness.

The Use of Dreams.   In Gestalt therapy, a client's dreams are seen as messages from the client to him- or herself. Gestalt therapists help clients become aware of what the message says by asking them to first recount their dream, then to "read" it by playing the part of certain features and characters. In the process, the client may become aware of and assimilate disowned parts of the self.

Other Methods.   Gestalt therapists use several other methods to help clients increase awareness and promote "re-owning" of alienated aspects of personality.

One of these is encouraging direct and immediate messages that force clients to take responsibility for their feelings. In group therapy, for example, the client who points to another client and says "She really makes me uncomfortable" would be asked to repeat the message directly to the person involved: "You make me uncomfortable." Similarly, "I" language is substituted for "it" language. "It makes me furious to hear that" contains the message that "it" is responsible for the client's anger. The therapist would ask the client to restate the message as "I am angry at you." Clients are also asked to convert indirect *questions* into direct *statements*. The message behind the question "Do you think I'll ever feel any better than I do now?" may be "I am terrified that I'll always be depressed and maybe kill myself." If so, it is important for the client to be aware of and to express the fear.

Gestalt therapists also turn role-playing into extended "conversations" between various parts of the client, including between the client's superego (what Perls called "topdog") and the part that is suppressed by "shoulds" and "oughts" (the "underdog"). Using the *empty chair technique* described earlier, dialogues also occur between the client and persons from the past with whom the client has unfinished business; the client "talks" to these people while imagining them seated in a nearby chair. This activity is designed to promote here-and-now awareness of strong emotions in a safe environment and, in the process, allows the person to master these feelings rather than be intimidated by them. Here is an example:

> CLIENT: My sister and I used to fight an awful lot when we were kids, but we seemed closer somehow then than we are now.
>
> THERAPIST: Can you put her in that chair and say this to your sister now?
>
> CLIENT: OK. I feel so far away from you now, Rita. I want to have that feeling of being in a family again.

Clients may also be asked to clarify and release feelings toward significant people in their lives via the *unmailed letter technique*. Here, they write—but do not send—a letter in which they express important, but previously unspoken feelings.

Role-played *reversals* also are used to enhance awareness of genuine feelings. So the client who conveys an image of cool self-sufficiency and denies feelings of tenderness toward others might be asked to play a warm, loving person. In the process, this client may get in touch with some feelings that have been suppressed for many years.

Other Humanistic Therapies

Rogers' and Perls' methods of treatment represent two prominent examples of humanisitic therapies, but there are others which blend psychodynamic, Rogerian, or Gestalt methods with principles from behavioral or existential psychology (Greenberg, Elliott, & Lietaer, 1994; Kahn, 1985; Maslow, 1962, 1968; May, 1969; May, Angel, & Ellenberger, 1958).

For example, the *logotherapy* of Viktor Frankl (1963, 1965, 1967) is based on existential philosophy and is oriented toward helping clients (1) take responsibility for their feelings and actions, and (2) find meaning and purpose in their lives. Frankl believed that people can feel a lack of meaning and purpose without displaying neurotic or psychotic behaviors. He saw his approach as applicable to anyone, whether they were officially suffering mental disorder or not.

Postmodern Approaches.   *Postmodernism* is a term applied to philosophies that reject the idea of objective, absolute, or perceiver-independent truth. Postmodern approaches within psychology are called *constructivist, constructionist, intersubjectivist*, or *narrative* approaches, as are the therapies derived from them. A central theme of postmodern therapies is that people live, psychologically speaking, not in an objective reality but in a reality of their subjective making. The way they organize and understand their experiences in narratives is what matters, not what *really* happened to them. Postmodern therapies "assume that reality is, to a large extent, 'constructed' or 'invented' by individuals and groups as a function of particular personal beliefs and historical, cultural, and social contexts" (Fishman, 1999; p. xxi).

This assumption has important implications for psychotherapy. First, it makes the search for any objective "cause" of a client's problem futile. If no independent and objective reality can be established, the therapist can never be in a position of authority, knowing more about the client's problem—its origins, significance, treatment—than the client knows. Accordingly, the therapist does not lead or direct or teach. Instead, the therapist brings his or her own subjective reality to the session, combining that with the client's subjectivity. From this, the two mutually construct a view of the problem and its remedy. The model of therapist-as-expert is replaced by a model of therapist-as-collaborator. Standard DSM diagnostic classification is also rejected in these approaches, as are other aspects of psychotherapy that cast client distress as pathology. The emphasis in therapy is on helping clients "reauthor their life narratives or experiment with new constructions of the self and relationship that afford more hopeful possibilities for the future" (Neimeyer & Raskin, 2000, p. xi).

This nonpathologizing and collaborative approach to psychotherapy has gained many adherents, but it has been criticized for lacking guidelines for how therapists should practice. One criticism centers on how therapists understand a client's distress. If clients do not have a "problem," "deficit," "conflict," "illness," or "pathology," and if therapists do not have some conception of that problem that they believe is reasonably accurate (rather than merely their own invention), then what guides the therapist's behavior? Critics argue that narrative therapists probably rely on assumptions of objective reality and assumptions of psychopathology more than they are willing to admit (Erwin, 1999). Still, the constuctivist approach has attracted attention because it focuses intensely on the therapeutic relationship as a two-person social construction.

PSYCHOTHERAPY INTEGRATION AND ECLECTICISM

Our description of psychotherapy methods so far has focused on differences among the major approaches. Historically, differences among the major schools have received more attention than have the similarities among them. This is not surprising given that newer approaches often define themselves by their rejection of assumptions held dear by older approaches (e.g., behavioral approaches rejected unconscious and unobservable mental events in favor of observable behavior, humanistic approaches rejected historical deterministic assumptions in favor of here-and-now self-determination, postmodern approaches rejected objectivist assumptions about reality in favor of subjective points of view). Clinical training often compounds the perceived differences among approaches. Trained in programs favoring one theoretical orientation (i.e., psychodynamic, cognitive-behavioral, humanistic), therapists and researchers have used methods they learned in graduate school and championed their approaches over the others. The result is that clinicians from different schools appear to use extremely different methods in sessions with clients.

There are of course healthy aspects to such "turf wars." As long as a discipline is guided by basic scientific practices, competing points of view stimulate research, and research advances theory and practice. Fortunately, this has happened in clinical psychology. As we will discuss more fully in Chapter 9, years of research show convincingly that no single approach cornered the market on therapeutic effectiveness. Each of the approaches we have discussed so far is effective with certain clients in certain situations. It is this fact, more than any other, that has fueled the move toward the integration of psychotherapeutic approaches.

The move toward integration is based on the belief that no single approach is comprehensive enough to address all the problems people face. Each theory has its strengths, and each theory leads to techniques that are effective in some but not all situations. The situation is analogous to the story of the three blind men describing what an elephant is like—one felt the elephant's thigh, one the tail, and one the trunk, and each produced a partially correct description of the elephant, but the descriptions sounded vastly different.

Psychotherapy integration can take different forms. One is *eclecticism*, in which therapists adopt techniques from several approaches. Counseling and clinical psychologists identify themselves as eclectic more than any other orientation (Norcross, Karg, & Prochaska, 1997); it is now the dominant orientation in the field, with estimates of clinicians identifying themselves so ranging from near one third to two thirds (Slife & Reber, 2001). Eclecticism can mean that a therapist simply selects techniques he or she likes, cafeteria-style, but this is a rather unsystematic way to go about it. *Technical eclecticism* is when clinicians select techniques based on empirical research—those techniques that show the strongest evidence of treating a specific disorder (or helping persons with certain characteristics) are selected, regardless of the orientation from which the technique came.

Integration can also mean *combining approaches*. In this view, specific techniques are combined in treating a specific disorder. Much of cognitive-behavioral therapy is the result of combining approaches to treat specific disorders. For example, a therapist treating a client with obsessive-compulsive disorder might combine exposure and response prevention (behavioral techniques) with rational restructuring (a cognitive technique).

Another approach to integration involves looking for the *common factors* in psychotherapy. If it is true that effective therapists are more similar in practice then their disputes about theory would suggest, it would be wise to discover what effective therapists have in common and what sets them apart from less effective therapists. The focus on the therapeutic relationships is a good example of the common factors approach, as the quality of the relationship affects therapy regardless of theoretical lines. Another approach along the common factors line involves attempts to define and measure therapist competence (see Milne, Claydon, Blackburn, James, & Sheikh, 2001; Svartberg, 1999).

Efforts to identify therapist competence have been surprisingly difficult. Weissmark and Giacomo (1998) suggest that most professionals believe they know good practice when they see it, but it is difficult to operationalize because so much of therapy involves spontaneous improvisation. (We should note also that many clinicians favor *reducing* improvisations by having therapists follow manuals to conduct specific treatments. The idea here is to reduce the error associated with therapist improvisation and confine treatment to those methods with empirically demonstrated effectiveness. This will not reduce all improvisation, but it does increase the structure imposed on the therapy, which some favor.) Using an observational coding method (see Chapter 4), Weissmark and Giacomo attempted to catalog the behaviors used by effective therapists. Others (e.g., Milne et al., 2001) have suggested alternate ways of measuring competence. It is not yet clear which measures of therapist competence are best, nor is it clear how to teach behaviors associated with theory-neutral competence, but research along these lines continues.

A final approach to integration is called *theoretical integration*. Also called assimiliative integration, this approach involves blending the various theories and expressing phenomena described in one theory in the language of another theory. For instance, in classical psychoanalytic theory, the therapeutic relationship was expressed in terms of inappropriate, historically-based reactions on the part of the client or the therapist (i.e., transference and countertransference). But if we strip away the favored language of each theory, we find similarities. For instance, behaviorists might explain transference-like response biases by invoking stimulus generalization or learned habits; cognitive therapists might explain them based on schemas or faulty reasoning. Just as clinicians increasingly cross the lines in practice, researchers increasingly cross theoretical lines in their investigation. An example of research that promotes theoretical integration is an investigation conducted by Paul Kwon and Katherine Lemon (Kwon & Lemon,

2000). They investigated whether defense mechanisms (a psychodynamic concept) interacted with attributional style (a cognitive concept) in depressive symptoms. They found that persons with low defense maturity were likely to show depressive symptoms when they also had a negative attributional style. However, the presence of a positive attributional style reduced the relation of low defense maturity on depressive symptoms.

Though some clinicians remain skeptical about integration and eclecticism (see Slife & Reber, 2000), others welcome the trend. Some welcome it because they claim that working across theoretical lines is what they have been doing all along—eclectically using techniques or referring to specialists with other orientations despite having one favored orientation (McWilliams, 1999). They also welcome the trend because it reflects practice's responsiveness to empirical research, which is necessary if psychotherapy is to continue to be a viable part of the health-care system.

CHAPTER SUMMARY

Clinicians offer psychotherapy using methods based on psychodynamic, behavioral, and humanistic approaches to clinical psychology.

In Freudian psychoanalysis, clients are helped to explore the unconscious wishes, fantasies, impulses, and conflicts that are presumed to lie at the root of their psychological problems. The goals of psychoanalytic treatment include insight into these underlying causes and then understanding, or working through, the implications of the insight. To get at unconscious material, much of which is based in infancy and childhood, Freud developed a number of treatment techniques, including free association and analysis of the meaning of dreams, of everyday behaviors, of resistance to treatment, and of transference appearing in the therapeutic relationship. Interpretations of the meaning of this material help move clients toward insight and understanding.

Other psychodynamically oriented therapists have developed variations on orthodox Freudian psychoanalysis. Among the most prominent of these methods are Alexander's psychoanalytically oriented psychotherapy, ego analysis, Adler's individual psychology, object relations therapy, and Sullivan's interpersonal therapy. These therapies tend to be briefer than classical psychoanalysis and to focus more on current problems rather than childhood conflicts, more on strengthening ego functions than on analyzing id impulses, more on actively repairing damage from inadequate early caregiver relationships than on gaining insight into them, and more on changing maladaptive interpersonal relationships than on delving into their unconscious origins.

Behavioral and cognitive-behavioral therapies are based on the principles of learning and on research on cognitive psychology. Their treatment methods are aimed at directly modifying overt maladaptive behaviors, as well as the maladaptive thinking patterns that accompany those behaviors. Behavioral methods include various kinds of systematic desensitization, exposure techniques such as flooding, social skills training (including assertiveness training), several types of modeling, aversion therapy, contingency management (including shaping, time out, contingency contracting, response cost, and token economies), and biofeedback. Cognitive-behavioral methods include Beck's cognitive therapy for depression and Ellis's Rational Emotive Behavior Therapy.

Humanistic therapies are based on the assumption that people are inherently growthful and that their progress toward unique self-actualization will resume when problems that have impaired it are removed by the experience of a supportive therapeutic relationship. These problems are presumed to arise largely from socialization processes that prompt people to distort or suppress genuine feelings and wishes in order to please others, so therapy is aimed at creating a client-therapist relationship in which clients can become more aware of how they really think and feel. Therapists using Carl Rogers' client-centered therapy create this relationship by using reflection and other active listening methods to convey empathy, unconditional positive regard, and congruence as they work with clients. The same goals of self-awareness and growth are sought in a more active and direct way through Perls' Gestalt therapy, whose methods include focusing on the present, having clients role-play suppressed or disowned aspects of the self, frustrating their efforts at resistance, attending to their nonverbal behavior, and having them engage in dialogues with imaginary versions of significant people in their lives.

Chapter 8

Alternative Modes
of Clinical Intervention

In this chapter, we examine socially oriented modes of clinical intervention. These modes—group therapy, marital and family therapy, psychosocial rehabilitation and prevention, community psychology—emphasize the importance of interpersonal networks in the creation and maintenance of problems and as the focus of treatment.

THE GROWTH OF SOCIALLY ORIENTED INTERVENTION MODES

The dominant therapy model of the early 20th century, psychodynamic psychotherapy, was originally designed for treating individual clients. Though some clinicians applied psychoanalytic thought to group psychotherapy (Bion, 1959), most psychodynamic psychotherapists apply analytic techniques to one-on-one therapy. Behavioral and humanistic approaches gained recognition during the mid-20th century, but they too were also originally designed for individuals. However, since the middle of the last century, modes of therapy that focus on relationships or relationship systems have proliferated.

Group therapy was one of the first of the socially-oriented therapies. Ironically, some of group therapy's popularity was due to the rise of behavioral and humanisitic approaches as alternatives to psychodynamic psychotherapy during the middle of the last century. Though originally designed for individuals, behavioral and humanistically oriented clinicians stressed techniques that were readily adaptable to multiclient interventions. For instance, behaviorists emphasized observable behaviors, social reinforcement, modeling, and other forms of overt learning that could be enhanced by a group context. Humanistically-oriented therapists stressed attention to conscious experience and here-and-now communication. These techniques became central to most forms of group therapy and to other multi-person intervention.

Also around the middle of the last century, marital and family therapy grew as child psychologists realized they could treat behavior problems more effectively if the parents were involved. Also contributing to the rise of family therapy were research projects in the United States that examined how family influences affected schizophrenia (Street, 2000). Clinicians developed new theories about how family interactions contributed to distress, and these led to new treatment approaches for families and couples.

Many of the same factors that influenced the advancement of family therapies contributed to the development of rehabilitation and prevention interventions. For instance, clinicians interested in helping persons who were recovering from schizophrenia recognized that patterns of family interaction affected relapse of the disorder. Accordingly, they designed interventions to help family members interact in ways that lessen the chances of relapse. Many rehabilitation efforts also included helping the client within the larger community. Preventive interventions often took the emphasis on community intervention a step further. For instance, drug use prevention efforts were designed to maximize the number of persons who avoided drugs and to "immunize" them against the influence of those who did use.

These alternate modes of interventions reflect trends in psychology that view people's behavior as a reflection of the relationship systems they inhabit. Each of the approaches we review in this chapter assumes that psychological problems exist within social contexts; each emphasizes interventions built around a given social context (see Table 8.1).

GROUP THERAPY

Group therapy was first practiced at the turn of the twentieth century in Boston by Joseph Pratt, and later stimulated by the shortage of professional personnel around the time of World War II. It grew in popularity especially in the 1960s and 1970s and has since progressed to the point that it is now regarded as a valuable intervention in its own right (Klein, 1983).

Every major approach to clinical psychology offers group treatment. There are analytic groups, client-centered and gestalt groups, and behavioral groups. Groups are also popular with many nonprofessional self-help organizations (Gottlieb & Peters, 1991). Weight-control groups, assertiveness groups, consciousness-raising groups, and Alcoholics Anonymous are common examples. Accordingly, it is difficult to provide a complete and general account of group therapy, per se. What we can say, however, is that most group therapists emphasize the importance of interpersonal relationships and assume that personal maladjustment involves difficulties in those relationships. Further, as in the case of individual psychotherapy, most group therapies share a set of

TABLE 8.1 Socially Oriented Clinical Interventions

Intervention Mode	Emphasis
Group Therapy	Understand and alleviate disturbances in interpersonal relationships as revealed in a group setting
Couples Therapy	Help couples in intimate relationships to improve problem-solving and communication skills
Family Therapy	Change harmful family interaction patterns so that the family system functions better
Psychosocial Rehabilitation	Improve clients' abilities to cope with mental disorders, live in the community, and limit resulting impairment
Prevention	Head off the appearance of mental disorders by counteracting risk factors and strengthening protective factors
Community Psychology	Create beneficial changes at a community or societal level to prevent disorders or raise general levels of mental health
Self-Help	Encourage people to perform therapeutic functions for themselves, either in groups organized around a specific concern or individually through a course of study.

common features, some of which resemble those found in one-to-one treatment, but most of which are unique to groups.

Therapeutic Factors in Group Therapy

Group therapy is more than the simultaneous treatment of several individuals. Groups provide therapeutic opportunities that cannot be found in individual therapy, and group therapists must learn how to use those opportunities. We summarize these below; a fuller discussion is contained in standard references on group therapy (e.g., Corey, 1999; Bednar & Kaul, 1994; Yalom, 1995).

Sharing New Information. New information is imparted from two sources in groups: The group leader may offer advice, and advice also comes from other members of the group who share their experiences. The multiple perspectives of the group constitute a richer store of information than would usually be the case with a single therapist. The impact of all this information is magnified by its *consensuality:* While it might be tempting to discount feedback from a therapist, it is more difficult to dismiss as biased or inaccurate the similar opinions of eight or ten group members. In numbers there is strength, especially when the numbers all agree.

Instilling Hope. As with individual psychotherapy, confidence in the therapist and an expectancy that treatment can be helpful are important features of the group mode. The hopes of new group members can be buoyed not only by optimistic therapist comments, but also by special features of groups that increase the positive expectancies of their members. One of these features is the opportunity for group members to observe improvement in others. So even if some clients are impatient about their own slow pace of improvement, seeing positive changes in others may lead to the recognition that progress will eventually come; this may sustain faith in the group.

Universality.   By showing that everyone struggles with problems in living, therapy groups help their members learn that they are not alone in their fears, low moods, or other difficulties. This discovery is important because many people are secretive about their problems, which restricts their ability to find out that they are not unique. As group members share their problems they derive comfort from knowing "there are others like me." Learning about the universality of one's problems also soothes anxiety about "going crazy" or "losing control."

Altruism.   Groups give clients a chance to discover that they can help other people. Just as group therapy produces new insights into interpersonal weaknesses, it confirms the presence of interpersonal strengths. In addition to being clients, group therapy members serve as therapists for one another. Clinicians refer to the positive emotions that follow altruistic behavior as "feelings of self-worth," an outcome that is promoted by effective group therapy.

Interpersonal Learning.   When a group first forms, the interpersonal contacts between members are usually hesitant and guarded, but as group members come to know one another, their contacts become more spontaneous and direct. A properly conducted therapy group is an ideal setting to learn new interpersonal skills. It presents repeated opportunities to practice fundamental social skills with various types of people and with immediate feedback on performance. Groups also contain numerous models for imitative learning, one of the most efficient ways to learn new behaviors.

Recapitulation of the Primary Family.   Some group therapists regard the therapy group as a "reincarnation" of clients' primary families. This *family reenactment* is thought to be a curative factor because it allows clients to deal with those early family experiences that still impair their current functioning. Recapitulation of the family is group therapy's counterpart to the transference relationship in individual psychodynamic therapy.

Group Cohesiveness.   Cohesiveness is the "attractiveness of a group for its members" (Frank, 1957). Members of cohesive groups accept one another; they are willing to listen to and be influenced by the group. They participate in the group readily, feel secure in it, and are relatively immune to outside disruption of the group's progress. Cohesive groups also permit the expression of hostility, provided such conflicts do not violate the norms of the group. Attendance is reliable in cohesive groups, and premature termination of treatment is not usually a problem (Yalom, 1995).

Cohesiveness is often regarded as the most important factor underlying the beneficial effects of group therapy, partly because it enhances the development of other curative factors (Yalom, 1995). The acceptance that members receive from the group may counteract their own feelings of worthlessness. The public esteem of the group serves as a reference point that increases members' own self-esteem because groups tend to evaluate individual members more favorably than the individuals evaluate themselves. Group members, in turn, will try to change in order to confirm the group's impression. This effect is something like a group-fulfilling prophecy, where members are motivated not to let down the group. Behaviors that a client once thought were impossible may be accomplished because of the group's supportive demand that they at least be attempted.

The Practice of Group Therapy

Therapy groups usually consist of 6 to 12 members. Group leaders tend to disagree on whether groups should be *homogeneous*, consisting of members who are similar in age, sex, and type of problem, or *heterogeneous*, in which there is a mix of client types. Heterogeneous groups are easier to form. They also have the advantage of exposing members to a wider range of people and perspectives. The major advantage of homogeneous groups is that they facilitate a direct focus on the common problem that motivated each member to enter treatment. Homogeneity and heterogeneity can refer to a diagnosis or any number of personal characteristics (e.g., problem severity, ego strength, coping style, introversion-extraversion, or any number of personality variables). As a result, groups will invariably be homogeneous on some dimensions (e.g., diagnosis and problem severity) and heterogeneous on others (e.g., problem duration and coping style).

Some groups, like old soldiers, never die; they just add new members as old ones depart. Other groups meet for only a specified number of sessions. These groups may be open to new members, but more often they continue only with the initial participants because the loss of one individual and replacement with another invariably affects the dynamics of the group.

Group meetings are typically longer—usually lasting about 2 hours—than sessions of individual psychotherapy, mainly because it takes more time for, say, eight clients to talk things over. It also tends to take more time for a group to reach a meaningful level of dialogue. Especially lengthy sessions are a defining characteristic of *marathon groups*, whose meetings may last from 6 to 48 hours or more. The rationale for marathon groups is that as people get tired, they also become less defensive. As social facades erode, people are assumed to be more willing to express their true feelings. (There is little, if any, empirical evidence to support these ideas; in fact, one might just as reasonably suggest that fatigue reduces motivation and makes one more hostile toward other members of the group.)

An Example of Group Therapy

Here is a brief description of the fifth session of therapy for a group of five women and three men, all in their late 20s and 30s and all unmarried or separated. The cognitive-behavioral orientation of the group's therapist is evident in that the members are asked to concentrate on helping each other improve their coping skills and interpersonal relationships (Rose & LeCroy, 1991).

As the group settled into places on the floor or on chairs, the therapist welcomed them and asked each member to review what he or she had done throughout the week to complete the assignment of the previous week. One at a time, members described their social achievements, their success in coping with anxiety, and the frequency with which they used the relaxation exercise. Several also related unusually stressful situations they had experienced during the week.

After each had summarized her or his experiences, amid a great deal of praise and support from group members for achievements, Delores volunteered to describe in some detail her situation in which her ever-present feelings of helplessness were intensified. Her supervisor at her office, she stated, was always giving her instructions on the least little thing. "It was as if she thought I was stupid and, frankly, I'm beginning to believe it." The other members inquired as to the nature of her job, which was quite complicated. They noted that she did receive good feedback from her peers, who often consulted with her with various problems. She also noted that in a previous job no one gave her more than the briefest instructions, and she did fine. Charles wondered whether she couldn't conclude that there was a problem between her and her supervisor and not with her as a person. There was just no evidence that she was dumb in any way; in fact, she appeared to be uniquely qualified to do the job. The others agreed.

Delores said she guessed they were right, but she didn't know what to do about it, and it was making her miserable. She had thought about quitting, but it was in other ways a good job; and besides, she added, "good jobs were hard to get these days."

After careful questioning by the other clients in order to have a clear picture of what was going on, they then provided her with a number of strategies she could employ to deal with the situation and suggested what she could specifically say to herself and to her supervisor. She evaluated and selected several from among these for practice in the group.

MARITAL AND FAMILY THERAPY

In *marital therapy* and *family therapy*, the focus is on disturbed relationships rather than on individuals who happen to be in a relationship. In marital therapy, also called *couples therapy* to include relationships other than marriages, the focus is on a dyad. Family therapy focuses on relationships among one or more parents (or guardians) and their children. Because both marital and family therapy emphasize communication patterns within close relationships, therapists who work with couples often work with families and visa versa.

Prior to the 1950s, few therapists worked with couples or families (Fruzzetti & Jacobson, 1991). However, as other forms of social and multiclient intervention grew, so did family therapy. Since the 1970s, the number of practicing marriage and family therapists has increased 50-fold (American Association of Marriage and Family Therapy, 2001). Journals devoted to family psychology first appeared in the United States and Japan during the 1980s, and the Division of Family Psychology was founded within the American Psychological Association in 1985 (Koslow, 2001). Courses in family psychology are now offered by many psychology, counseling, and social work graduate programs.

Therapists who practice marital and family therapy come from all of the core mental health professions. Some are trained in programs that focus almost exclusively on marital and family interventions, while others are trained in programs that include models designed for individuals as well. Some therapists devote their practice exclusively to couple or family therapy while others include it among other therapy modalities.

Couples Therapy

Couples seek therapy for a variety of reasons. A wife who was initially attracted to her husband because of his dashing charm and playboy image might now find that these qualities threaten the emotional security she wants from their relationship. A husband might come to feel that what he once admired as spunkiness in his wife now challenges his need to dominate the marriage. Intimate relationships are frequently beset by problems in the areas of sexual satisfaction, personal autonomy, dominance-submission, responsibility for child rearing, communication, intimacy, money management, fidelity, and the expression of disagreement and hostility.

Couples therapy can be the main intervention when relationship difficulties are the primary treatment target, or it can be combined with other methods designed to address other problems. For example, when depression, alcoholism, or severe anxiety disorders affect the quality, and even the existence, of a client's marriage or intimate relationship, some mental health experts recommend couples therapy—or at least the involvement of the client's partner—in the treatment of these disorders (Jacobson, Holtzworth-Monroe, & Schmaling, 1989). In many instances, the therapist sees both members of the couple at the same time, called *conjoint therapy*. Some couples even obtain therapy to help them end a marriage or long-term relationship with a minimum of conflict. Such *separation counseling* is often desirable when questions about child-custody must be resolved. Under these conditions, the therapist might see members separately during some, or several, of the sessions.

The goals and techniques of marital therapy depend partly on which conflicts are the most pressing for a given couple and partly on the theoretical orientation of the therapist. For example, a behaviorally oriented marital therapist would be likely to help with a couple's communication problems by teaching the partners to replace hostile, unconstructive criticism with comments that clearly express feelings and directly convey requests for the behaviors that each wants from the other. To bring about quick changes in a troubled relationship, *behavioral exchange* contracts may be established. Using such agreements, whenever one partner does something on the other's "wish list" (e.g., listening without interrupting), the other partner will reciprocate by doing something that is desired by the first partner (e.g., paying a compliment).

Cognitive-behavioral marital therapists work to help couples change the way they think about their relationship and modify the attributions they make about each other (Baucom et al., 1989; Bradbury & Fincham, 1990). When couples are preoccupied with deciding who is to blame for their relationship problems, and especially when each member begins to attribute dishonorable motives to everything the other one says or does, it becomes almost impossible for the couple to even work on, let alone solve, their problems. Accordingly, the cognitive-behavioral therapist may teach each member of the couple to recognize, for example, that the other member's anger may reflect anxiety about the future of the relationship, not necessarily an effort to end it.

Marital therapists who adopt a more humanistic approach may focus on restoring the emotional bond and sense of intimacy the couple once enjoyed. Thus, the goal of emotionally focused couples therapy is to help partners become more comfortable expressing and accepting each others' emotional needs (Greenberg & Johnson, 1988). To reach this goal, the therapist may use techniques that allow each partner to get in touch with and resolve, or at least disarm, the lingering resentments or other emotional problems that always seem to be surfacing in their relationship.

Psychodynamically oriented couples therapy is also designed to help partners understand and resolve areas of conflict, but here it is assumed that the problems may be unconscious. Accordingly, the partners work to understand that the actions of each that cause unhappiness for the other may (unconsciously) arise out of unresolved conflicts experienced in their families of origin or may stem from unmet emotional needs that impair their ability to handle intimacy. The partners may also come to realize that the pairing of these individual characteristics may tend to bring out the worst in each other. Following such insights, the partners are helped to work through the emotional meaning of their problems, and to work on conscious efforts to solve them.

Regardless of theoretical orientation, however, most marital therapists tend to emphasize problem solving. The touchstone of problem solving is teaching the couple how to communicate and negotiate more effectively with each other. Among the multiple tasks involved in building better communication are teaching the couple to accept mutual responsibility for working on problems, maintaining focus on current relationship problems rather than old grudges, fostering expression of preferences rather than demands for obedience, and negotiating compromises to problems the couple decide cannot be solved.

The following brief excerpt from a couples therapy session illustrates an attempt by the therapist (T) to help a wife (W) learn new ways of communicating some of her negative feelings to her husband:

> T: I do think that what Pete is saying is an important point. There are things that are going to be different about you and each of you is going to think the things you do maybe make more sense than the other person's, and that's probably going to be pretty much of a reality. You're not going to be able to change all those. You may not be able to change very many of them. And everybody is different. They have their own predilections to do things a certain way and again what's coming through from you is sort of like damning those and saying those are wrong; they're silly, they don't make sense, I don't understand them or whatever. You may not understand them but they are a reality of each of you. That's something you have to learn how to deal with in some way. Otherwise, you . . . the reason I'm stressing this is I think it plays a large part in your criticalness.

W: Well, I do find it difficult to cater to, I guess that's the word, cater to some idiosyncrasies that I find or think are totally foolish. I am intolerant. I am, and I find it very difficult. I find it almost impossible to do it agreeably and without coming on as "Oh, you're ridiculous."

T: I guess what would be helpful would be if you could come on honestly enough to say "I don't like them" or "It doesn't sit well with me" without having to add the additional value judgment of whether they're foolish or ridiculous or whatever. That's the part that hurts. It's when you damn him because of these things—that's gonna hurt. I'm sure from Pete's point of view they make sense for his total economy of functioning. There's some sense to why he does things the way he does, just as there is for why you do things the way you do. It's not that they're foolish. They make sense in terms of where you are, what you're struggling with, and what's the best way you can deal with right now. I'm not trying to say that means you have to like them, but when you come across and say "It's ridiculous or foolish"—that's the part that makes it hurt.

W: Well, tell me again how to say it, because I find it hard to say anything except "That's really stupid—that's silly." I know you said it a minute ago but I lost it.

T: Well, anytime you can say it in terms of how it affects you and say with it, like "It's hard—I find it hard to take," that doesn't say "I find you're an ass for wanting to do that such and such a way." It's just that, I find it hard to take—I get upset in this circumstance" or whatever. Stay with what your feelings are rather than trying to evaluate Pete. (Ables & Brandsma, 1977, pp. 92–94)

Family Therapy

Just as marital therapy is aimed at changing a couple's relationship, family therapy is a mode of treatment aimed at changing patterns of *family* interaction so as to correct family disturbances (Gurman, Kniskern, & Pinsof, 1986). And like couples therapy, family therapy arose from observations that problems seen in individual psychotherapy clients have social contexts and social consequences. It was observed, for example, that clients who showed great improvement during individual therapy while hospitalized often relapsed when they returned to their families. This observation, along with other clinical insights and research, led to several early theories of psychopathology that emphasized the family environment and parent–child interactions as causes of maladaptive behavior (Bateson et al., 1956; Lidz & Lidz, 1949; Sullivan, 1953).

The basic concepts underlying family therapy differ from those of individual psychotherapy. In particular, family therapy is grounded in systems theory (von Bertalanffy, 1968), which emphasizes three principles. The first is *circular causality*, meaning that events are interrelated and mutually dependent rather than fixed in a simple cause–effect sequence. Thus, no one member of a family is the cause of another's problems; the behavior of each member depends to some degree on each of the others. The second principle is that of *ecology*, which says that systems can only be understood as integrated patterns, not as collections of component parts. In a family system, a change in the behavior of one member will radiate to affect all the others. The third principle of systems theory is *subjectivity*, which means that there are no objective views of events, only subjective perceptions filtered by the experiences of perceivers within a system. In other words, family members each have their own perception of family events.

Family therapy often begins with a focus on one family member who is having problems. Typically, this *identified client* is a male child (often of adolescent age) whom the parents label as having an unmanageable behavior problem, or a teenage girl who displays an eating disorder. Soon, however, the therapist will try to reframe the identified problems in terms of disturbed family processes or faulty family communication, to encourage all family members to examine their own contributions to the problem, and to consider positive changes that each member can make. As in marital therapy, a common goal of family therapy is improved communications, because disturbed families often rely on coercion as their major means of communication (Patterson, 1982). The message from both parents and children is, "Do what I want or you'll be sorry."

As with individual, group, and couples therapy, there is no one agreed-upon technique for conducting family therapy. Rather, therapists can select from a wide variety of techniques. For example, those operating from a *behavioral* point of view try to teach family members alternative, noncoercive ways of communicating their needs. They teach parents to be firm and consistent in their child-discipline practices, encourage each family member to communicate clearly with one another, educate family members in behavior-exchange principles, discourage blaming of the identified client for all family problems, and help all members of the family to consider whether or not their expectations of other members are reasonable.

Another influential approach is called *strategic*, or *structural* family therapy (Minuchin, 1974; Satir, 1967). Here, the therapist seeks to reframe the main problems of the identified client as a disturbed family process rather than as an individual problem. The goal is to minimize the blame being directed at a person who has become a convenient family scapegoat. For example, the therapist might suggest that an adolescent son's aggressive and defiant behavior may be a sign of teenage insecurity or a plea for more attention from his father. The structural family therapist also helps families communicate more clearly and directly. In many distressed families, emotional messages are so disguised or distorted that family members frequently talk *at* rather than *to* each other. Often they assume they can "read each others' minds," as when a daughter accuses her mother of "never believing anything I say" or when a father accuses his son of "never caring about anyone but yourself."

Therapists practicing *intergenerational* family therapy (also known as *"Bowenian"* family therapy to recognize its founder, Murray Bowen) limit the amount of direct interaction among family members during sessions. The theory here is that such limitations reduce the overall level of family anxiety and temporarily increase each persons's emotional distance from their conflicts, allowing members to more easily learn new, adaptive behaviors (Kerr & Bowen, 1988). Therapists using this approach might work with clients individually, see parents or children separately, or hold sessions with any combination of family members.

Narrative or *constructionist* approaches to family therapy focus on the way members understand the meanings of their relationships and interactions. Such approaches, coming largely from the postmodern phenomenological tradition, rely on examining the stories members tell themselves about their roles, their relationships, and each other. The therapist does not focus on verifying each person's story, but takes each construction as a valid measure of that person's understanding of themselves and their relationship. The focus of intervention is on making the narratives explicit, helping persons take responsibility for their construction, fostering a sense of self-efficacy (as constructors of stories rather than as victims), and, when possible, re-authoring family narratives.

Diagnosis in Marital and Family Therapy

One challenge for marital and family therapists is how best to understand relationship difficulties. With individual clients, psychologists have developed a classification system, the DSM (or the ICD), to better understand individuals' problems. This system is based on evidence that, though each person is unique, psychological difficulties tend to cluster into certain identifiable patterns. When disorders can be reliably classified according to certain observable patterns, more effective interventions can be developed. But with couple and family therapy, the client is not so much an individual as a *relationship* or *system of relationships*. How should we understand and diagnose relational problems? Are there are identifiable patterns for dysfunctional relationships, patterns that might eventually point the way to effective intervention techniques?

The diagnosis of relational difficulties is in its early stages. Fincham and Beach (1999) suggest that marital conflict is much better understood than it was two decades ago, but the field still lacks a unifying framework from which to develop interventions. However, the work of developing diagnostic categories for interpersonal conflicts has begun. For instance, the *Handbook of Relational Diagnosis and Dysfunctional Family Patterns* (Koslow, 1996) includes at least 30 diagnostic categories of dysfunctional relationship patterns, and Brown (2001) has suggested a framework for identifying and treating patterns of infidelity. Needless to say, much research still needs to be done to establish the reliability, validity, and utility of relational diagnoses.

The Social Contexts of Marital and Family Therapy

Some of the most important challenges for couple and family therapists come from the changing *social contexts* in which families live. Families are invariably a part of a larger social context, and their functioning is partly dependant on that context. Even something as basic as how we define a family can be an issue in family therapy. A minority of children now live in traditional families with married, heterosexual parents and one or more biological children. Modern families can also be defined as multigenerational, multicultural units, foster families, blended families, gay or lesbian couples with children, or several people living together with no legal ties but with strong mutual commitments (Koslow, 2001). To be effective, therapists must understand the special problems each type of family faces.

Therapists must also be free of biases against certain family structures. When therapists are conscious of such biases, they should refer clients elsewhere. But being human, therapists are not always conscious of their biases. It is possible, for instance, for a husband to have one set of expectations about gender roles, a wife another set of expectations, and a therapist a third set. Because of the higher probability of subtle bias and the impact of bias on therapy, therapists should strive to be conscious of how their own views of gender roles and family life might affect their therapeutic interventions.

The larger social contexts in which families operate can dramatically affect the problems families encounter and how therapists intervene. In the United States, the reality of terrorism has dramatically affected many thousands of families, posing new problems for family therapists. What family problems grow from these horrific events, and what models of family intervention best help couples and families deal with fear or loss? To answer these questions, researchers and clinicians sometimes look to psychotherapeutic practices in other cultures. In Israel, for instance, family psychologists are often among the teams that respond to community disasters. They also treat families affected by the stresses of unconventional war and terrorism. The situations producing stresses can be unique, such as when soldiers or civilians fighting unconventional war do not go away but still live at home among their families (Halpern, 2001). In several countries around the world, families must navigate dramatic social changes brought on by armed conflict or political upheaval. The plight of refugees needing to survive and relocate is an ongoing problem.

Events less dramatic than war or terrorism can still produce dramatic problems for families. In Japan, for instance, family therapy interventions have grown markedly since the 1980s largely because of the problem of school phobia among children (Kameguchi & Murphy-Shigematsu, 2001). In North America, more and more families in the United States have members who came from other cultures, and family therapists are increasingly called upon to deal with issues related to cultural diversity. Of course, this phenomenon is not unique to North America; it occurs in many countries around the world.

In short, family psychologists must adapt to the unique social and geopolitical realities encountered by those they treat. Fortunately, most forms of family therapy have been adapting to take into account cultural factors that might interfere with the treatment of families. For example, José Szapocznik and his colleagues in Miami, Florida, commonly encountered problems in providing family-based drug abuse treatment to adolescents from Hispanic, largely Cuban, backgrounds (Szapocznik et al., 1986). To get these families into treatment, and to keep them coming back, Szapocznik evaluated a set of "family engagement" procedures designed to counter four forms of resistance (Szapocznik et al., 1990): (1) refusal by the adolescent to enter treatment, (2) mothers' ambivalence about entering their families into treatment, (3) fathers' disengagement from their families, and (4) family members' concerns about disclosing secrets to strangers.

In his evaluation study, Szapocznik randomly assigned families to receive either a standard invitation to begin treatment or an experimental program which used structural family techniques to overcome the family's initial resistance to therapy. Results indicated that the experimental engagement technique was highly successful; 93% of families receiving the culturally sensitive engagement methods began treatment compared to 42% of the standard-invitation families. Further, families receiving the structured engagement method were three times more likely to complete treatment than were families in the control condition.

To deal with the effects of changing social contexts, some therapists augment their training by taking specialized courses offered by professional organizations or universities. Others try to keep abreast of research on how various cultural groups experience and understand different disorders (see Lopez & Guarniccia, 2000, for a discussion of how certain anxiety-related disorders are construed in different cultures). Other clinicians are more comfortable referring couples or families to therapists from the clients' culture of origin, or to therapists who have expertise in particular types of family interventions.

PSYCHOSOCIAL REHABILITATION AND PREVENTION

Despite the dominant status of individual, group, couples, and family psychotherapy, not all psychologists believe that these are the best modes of intervention for psychological problems. To produce truly meaningful improvements in people's lives, these critics say, psychologists must employ intervention strategies based on an *ecological perspective* on behavior disorder (Rappaport, 1977). Taking an ecological perspective means developing interventions designed to maximize the "fit" between individuals and specific environments that are likely to promote their adjustment. It means understanding the causes of disorders more broadly, and sometimes attempting to modify causes before they have an opportunity to influence individuals or groups. Examples of these interventions—which include efforts at psychosocial rehabilitation and prevention of mental disorders—are described in the next two sections.

Psychosocial Rehabilitation

The effectiveness of antipsychotic medications has allowed an increasing number of severely mentally ill people to be discharged from public mental institutions into local communities in recent decades. This trend was encouraged by the community psychology movement of the 1960s (described later), which presented evidence that severely mentally ill people could receive more beneficial (and less expensive) care as outpatients at neighborhood mental health centers (Kiesler & Sibulkin, 1987). Accordingly, the number of mental patients confined in public mental hospitals in the United States declined from approximately 550,000 in 1955 to less than 70,000 in 1999 (*Congressional Record*, 1999). With so many patients discharged, the number of available psychiatric hospital beds was reduced by roughly 90% (Torey, 1999). Deinstitutionalization has occurred in many other countries as well. In Finland, for example, the number of psychiatric beds decreased by about two-thirds (Salokangas, Honkonen, Stengard, 1998).

This deinstitutionalization process should have been a great success for the field of mental health, but for many former mental patients, release did not improve the quality of their lives, at least not on a permanent basis (Moscarelli & Capri, 1992). Sadly, thousands of them have simply "fallen through the cracks" and are not receiving any kind of regular treatment. Many have drifted into unemployment and homelessness, often becoming the unwanted responsibility of police and the criminal justice system.

Obviously, these severely mentally ill people are unlikely to enter individual or group psychotherapy on their own and, even if pushed into it by family members, may not benefit much. An alterative intervention called *psychosocial rehabilitation* teaches patients displaying schizophrenia, major mood disorders, or other severe mental disorders how to cope better with the effects of these problems, and especially how to prevent or lessen the crises that often threaten their ability to function in society. In other words, rather than trying to cure serious mental disorders, psychosocial rehabilitation helps patients normalize their lives, compensate for their impairments, and achieve the highest possible quality of life in the community (Hunter, 1995).

A goal of psychosocial rehabilitation is *empowerment* (Rappaport, 1981; 1987), the development of a belief among formerly dependent and powerless people that they can master and control their lives. Empowerment requires both an adequate understanding of the environment and skills for living effectively in it. It also includes the abilities to maintain stable housing and engage in regular, meaningful employment. Thus, psychosocial rehabilitation programs are designed to teach formerly hospitalized mental patients the basic competencies they need to live successfully and independently in the community (Stroul, 1993). These programs typically include four components.

The first is the effort to help patients understand their disorder so that they can cope with it more effectively. For example, Assertive Community Treatment (ACT)—a multicomponent program developed in Madison, Wisconsin in the late 1960s—uses mental health teams to teach patients how to recognize the early warning signs of psychological deterioration in time to avoid high-risk situations and obtain social support to avert a crisis. When patients and their families are able to detect specific symptoms, such as insomnia or auditory hallucinations, that precede psychotic "breaks" and lead to hospitalization or arrest, they can call on treatment staff for help in managing the situation (Herz & Melville, 1980).

Psychosocial rehabilitation programs also help patients learn community living skills such as making change, using public transportation, obtaining medical care, buying groceries, cooking meals, and most important, interacting with other people. Patients are helped to understand how their symptoms may affect others. They will be told, for example, that it is frightening to the average person on the street to see someone who is disheveled or is talking back to hallucinated voices. When patients understand onlookers' reactions, they can more easily learn to ignore them. Note that the goal here is not to eliminate the symptoms of mental disorder but to cope better with its consequences.

A third component of most psychosocial rehabilitation programs is case management, in which a staff person helps the client obtain services related to employment, housing, nutrition, transportation, recreation, medical care, and finances.

Finally, psychosocial rehabilitation promotes treatment efforts by maintaining a coalition among mental health professionals, family members, and patients. Often, treatment occurs in self-help groups. Organizations such as GROW and Recovery, Inc. have demonstrated that severely mentally ill people are capable of providing mutual support and effective crisis intervention services (Galanter, 1988; Rappaport et al., 1985).

Preventive Interventions

Using principles borrowed from the field of public health, Gerald Caplan (1964) described three levels at which mental health problems can be prevented.

Tertiary prevention seeks to lessen the severity of disorder and to reduce its short-term and long-term consequences. Psychosocial rehabilitation falls in this category because it seeks to minimize the severity and reduce the adverse consequences of being mentally ill. *Secondary prevention* involves interventions for people who are at risk for developing a disorder. Effective secondary prevention requires knowledge of how risk factors culminate in specific disorders. It also usually requires assessment methods that reliably and validly detect the initial signs of a disorder so that attempts can be made to intervene at the earliest possible point. *Primary prevention* involves eliminating disorders by either modifying environments or strengthening individuals so that they are not susceptible to disorder in the first place. Primary prevention programs seek to counteract risk factors and reinforce protective factors (Coie et al., 1993).

Primary prevention can focus narrowly on the risks and protective factors associated with specific problems (e.g., teen suicide or drug use), the goal being to reduce the incidence of those particular problems. Alternately, prevention can be aimed broadly toward increasing the public's general mental health or reducing social inequalities that affect disadvantaged groups, the goal being to reduce the incidence of several types of mental illness. Though broader competency-based programs have shown promising results, the more narrowly-focused programs have often been favored by policy makers (Reppucci, Woolard, & Fried, 1999).

The focus in the field now known as *prevention science* has been strongly influenced by the research reviews and recommendations contained in the reports of two study groups sponsored by the National Institute of Mental Health and the National Academy of Sciences' Institute of Medicine (Mrazek & Haggerty, 1994; NIMH, 1994). Those reports were the results of efforts begun in 1982 to fund and stimulate prevention research. That is when the U.S. National Institute of Mental Health began funding a series of Prevention Intervention Research Centers (PIRCs). The hope was to bring together scientists from fields such as psychology, anthropology, sociology, epidemiology, and psychiatry to collaborate on research on the early causes of specific disorders. The centers focus on experiments with at-risk, but not yet disordered, groups such as children living in high-stress environments or adults facing the threat of unemployment (Sandler et al., 1991; Turner, Kessler, & House, 1991).

PIRC research is geared toward first discovering the incidence of disorders, then investigating the causal mechanisms responsible for them. Prevention programs aimed at modifying risk factors for the disorders are then developed and assessed. The programs that prove effective are then transferred to new settings where their impact is again evaluated. This sequence of events has already proven its worth in a number of areas, including, for example, reducing the incidence of aggressive behavior in schoolchildren and reducing depressive disorders in adolescents (Clarke et al., 1995; Kellam et al., 1994). Assuming adequate funding will be allocated for implementing them, these blueprints for prevention science (NIMH, 1995) are sure to chart the course of preventive interventions for many years to come (Reiss & Price, 1996).

Prevention-centered research can benefit the entire field of mental health because its longitudinal nature leads to a clearer picture of the way mental disorders emerge and develop. Unfortunately, prevention programs are often very expensive, so unless federal and state legislators are convinced that the effects of these programs justify their cost, the funds to implement them may not be forthcoming. In the long run, preventing disorders in large populations costs less than treating people one at a time, but the long-term perspective is not an easy one for most politicians (and many psychologists) to take (Heller, 1996).

Still, many psychologists continue to pursue prevention programs consistent with the PIRC research model. The focus will increasingly be on intervention experiments—carried out by teams of researchers from clinical psychology, psychiatry, social work, and other fields—aimed at rigorously evaluating interventions aimed at reducing the biological, developmental, and psychological risk factors that are known to lead to specific disorders.

Primary prevention programs utilize five basic methods to try to accomplish their goals.

Encouraging Secure Attachments and Reducing Family Violence. One method is to help parents and their children form the kind of warm, nurturant, and secure early attachments that tend to be associated with mental health as the children grow. (Insecure or disrupted attachments are one of the earliest and most pernicious risk factors for many mental disorders; Nietzel et al., 1998.) Why don't healthy attachments form naturally? For one thing, some parents do not understand the importance of such attachments or may believe that if they are too responsive their baby will be "spoiled." In other cases, substance abuse or depression might leave parents unable to care properly for a child. Severe poverty can also make it difficult for parents to properly nurture children. Various types of preventive interventions can be devised to deal with these and other sources of attachment problems and, if applied early enough, can reduce the harm they might otherwise have done.

Related primary prevention programs are aimed at the reduction of family violence. The fact that at least 1 million children a year are victims of physical or sexual abuse or severe neglect—and that 3 to 4 million U.S. households may be the site of other forms of family violence every year—is tragic enough on its own, but there is also evidence that children reared in violent homes are more likely to become aggressive, abusive, or criminal adults themselves (Ollendick, 1996). Prevention programs attempt to improve parenting skills, reduce the use of corporal punishment and change parental attitudes (McInnis-Dittrich, 1996).

Teaching Cognitive and Social Skills. A second approach to primary prevention of mental disorder involves teaching children and adolescents the cognitive and interpersonal skills crucial to later development and adjustment. For example, children lacking in such skills tend to display, as early as kindergarten, a pattern of behavior that elevates their risk for later delinquency (Farrington, 1991). A core element of this pattern is impulsivity, which is manifested in refusing to wait one's turn, being disrespectful and defiant toward teachers, and constantly interrupting others. In other words, these children have trouble regulating their behavior so as to abide by rules and accommodate other people. However, there is evidence that if these children can be taught to control their impulses (Kendall & Braswell, 1985), to use effective problem-solving strategies (Spivack & Shure, 1974), and to respond nonaggressively to provocation and teasing by peers (Dodge, McClaskey, & Feldman, 1985), they can avoid developing the academic and social problems common in the backgrounds of conduct-disordered youngsters (Ollendick, 1996).

Changing Environments. A third approach to primary prevention entails making environments more supportive of adaptive behavior. Prime targets for such "re-engineering" are settings—such as homes, schools, neighborhoods, and the criminal justice system—that powerfully shape human development. For example, programs such as Head Start that expand preschool opportunities and increase the commitment of parents and children to academic success have been shown to decrease antisocial behavior in the long run, even though this was not their original goal (Schweinhart, Barnes, & Weikhart, 1993; Zigler, Taussig, & Black, 1992). Programs that help children and adolescents adjust to the transition from elementary to middle school or from middle school to high school have also been found to prevent school dropout and antisocial behavior in school (Olweus, 1995; Seidman et al., 1994).

Enhancing Stress-Coping Skills. A fourth approach to primary prevention takes the form of reducing environmental stressors and/or helping people cope more effectively with the stressors they must endure. In either case, harmful mental and physical stress reactions are likely to decrease, along with the incidence of the disorders associated with them.

For example, increasing the availability of affordable housing can reduce the frequency of household moves, a major stressor for poor families that has been linked to psychological maladjustment. Further, strengthening or creating social support for the elderly, for immigrants, and for other people facing social isolation can help protect against future problems (Felner, Farber, & Primavera, 1983). Problems might also be prevented by helping the millions of people who face ethnic prejudice every day develop new strategies for coping with unfair employment and housing practices, verbal abuse, and social rejection. Thus, some minority children who anticipate discrimination at school tend to devalue and withdraw from academic activities, but interventions designed to prevent this counterproductive coping strategy could improve these youngsters' academic performance, bolster their self-esteem, and keep them on the path to success (Basic Behavioral Science Task Force of the National Advisory Mental Health Council, 1996).

Promoting Empowerment. Finally, there are primary prevention programs designed to empower the powerless, to help those for whom old age, poverty, homelessness, ethnic minority status, physical disability, or other factors have left them without the ability or confidence to take control of their lives. Many psychologists believe that the disproportionately high levels of mental disorder seen in these groups is largely caused by the psychological and physical problems that often accompany their chronic sense of *dis*empowerment. Accordingly, prevention programs or social changes that help people gain a sense of control can be expected to decrease their risk for developing mental disorders. There is already some evidence that empowering minority parents to influence school policies or empowering neighborhoods to control crime can have long-term mental health benefits (Comer, 1987).

COMMUNITY PSYCHOLOGY

Interventions aimed at psychosocial rehabilitation and prevention have been stimulated largely by work in the field of community psychology. Let's consider the history, principles, and current status of this field.

What Is Community Psychology?

Community psychology seeks to apply psychological principles to (1) understanding individual and social problems, (2) preventing behavioral dysfunction, and (3) creating lasting social change. All of these efforts are based on the ecological perspective described earlier, which says that human behavior develops out of interactions between people and all aspects of their environment—physical, social, political, and economic. Accordingly, community psychologists argue that alleviating individual and social problems requires that we make changes in *both environmental settings and individual competencies*. Along with their emphasis on environmental factors in disorder, community psychologists also focus on the plight of the urban and rural poor and other groups whose problems have (1) tended to be underserved by traditional systems for psychotherapy service delivery and (2) appear more social than psychological and thus require social rather than individual change.

The History of Community Psychology

In the 1950s and 1960s, an array of influences came together to accelerate the development of community psychology. Some of these influences appeared within psychology itself, while others were associated with the extensive social and political changes taking place throughout North America during this period.

Prominent factors within psychology included (1) disenchantment with a clinical psychology that was then dominated by psychodynamic approaches to psychopathology (Rappaport, 1977); (2) skepticism about the reliability and validity of psychological diagnosis of disorders (Rosenhan, 1973) and about the benefits of traditional psychotherapy (Eysenck, 1952, 1966; see Chapter 9); (3) prophecies of shortages of mental health professionals to deliver individual treatment (Albee, 1959); and (4) dissatisfaction with the training models and role expectations for clinical psychologists (Korman, 1974; Peterson, 1968; see Chapters 1 and 14).

At the same time, the United States was in turmoil over the civil rights movement, black separatist ideology, urban crises, the war on poverty, and protests against the Vietnam War. These upheavals helped stimulate the growth of community psychology because they prompted many psychologists to broaden their conceptions of what the helping professions should do in the interest of social change. The roots of community psychology are also found in the 1961 report of the Joint Commission on Mental Health and Illness, which recommended the construction of multiservice comprehensive care centers to serve the mental health needs of local communities. This report led to passage in 1962 of the Community Mental Health Centers Act, which provided funds for the construction of a network of comprehensive mental health centers that could cover service areas of not less than 75,000 nor more than 200,000 people. In 1965, legislation was passed that provided grants to pay the personnel to be employed in these "comp care" centers.

The official "birth" of community psychology came in the spring of the same year when about 30 psychologists, many employed in community mental health centers, met in Swampscott, Massachusetts. The Swampscott conference participants stressed three principles for the new field. First, community psychology was not to be limited to combating mental illness; it should work for "community well-being" and "furthering normal development" (Bennett, 1965). Second, community psychology should promote community growth through planned social action and the scientific method. Finally, community psychology must be broader than the *community mental health* movement's efforts to deliver traditional mental health services in community settings.

Today, community psychology is in its fourth decade. It boasts its own division within the American Psychological Association and there are several journals—including *The American Journal of Community Psychology, The Community Mental Health Journal*, and *The Journal of Community Psychology*—devoted to reporting the research and accomplishments of its members. The training of community psychologists has also become an important activity of graduate psychology programs. In 1962 there was one program offering an MA or PhD in community psychology and community mental health. By the late 1980s, about 100 U.S. graduate programs in the United States were offering training in community psychology (Elias, Dalton, & Godin, 1987).

Principles and Methods of Community Psychology

We have already seen that community psychology takes an ecological perspective on mental disorder and that it emphasizes the importance of primary, as well as secondary and tertiary prevention programs. Let's now consider some of the other principles and methods associated with community psychology that help differentiate it from clinical psychology.

Social-System Change. In accordance with their ecological approach, community psychologists are often more interested in promoting social-system-level changes, than person-oriented changes. Social-system changes are intended to make the social institutions in our lives more growth-enhancing. Changes in social systems can occur at a low level, as when one schoolteacher begins using a reward system to increase class participation. Social changes also can occur at a higher level, as when a group of parents, dissatisfied with the quality of public education, begins its own alternative school. This is not to say that community psychologists avoid person-oriented interventions, but their preference is for social-system changes because these changes present the greatest opportunity to bring about important improvements for large numbers of people.

Clinical psychologists usually offer direct services to clients who, because they have some psychological complaint, are willing to pay for them. In contrast, community psychologists emphasize indirect services that have no particular target client, but which are expected to achieve benefits because the social-system changes they produce radiate to intended target groups. Thus, consultation with educational, social, political, and other community agencies and groups is a common activity for the community psychologist (O'Neill & Trickett, 1982).

Promoting a "Psychological Sense of Community." Community psychologists are also concerned with strengthening the ability of a community to plan and implement its own changes. To make this more likely, they work at promoting a "psychological sense of community" (Sarason, 1974). Community psychologists try to foster this sense of community by developing people's strengths rather than focusing on their weaknesses. They encourage collective action by people with common needs or interests and they seek to help these coalitions maintain their commitment to mutual problem solving. This goal involves the development of collective power mobilized for the purpose of specific reforms, a strategy described earlier as empowerment (Rappaport, 1981).

Paraprofessionals. Another example of expanding roles for community psychologists is seen in their preparation of nonprofessionals for behavior-change functions that had previously been reserved for professionals. These *paraprofessionals* then act as child care workers, mental health workers, peer counselors, abortion counselors, and in many other roles. Many of these helpers are known as *indigenous paraprofessionals* because they are drawn from the very groups that will receive their services. Indeed, their cultural rootedness in the to-be-served group is one of their fundamental assets. Community psychologists also train clients' relatives (Guerney, 1969), peers (Harris & Sherman, 1973), teachers (Meyers, 1975), and friends (Sulzer, 1965) to initiate behavior-change programs or to maintain programs that were introduced during a professional intervention.

Because paraprofessionals are generally paid less than clinical psychologists, they are an attractive option for those concerned about health-care costs. Bachelor's-level paraprofessionals trained in administering specific interventions and supervised by a doctoral-level psychologist could provide services at lower costs than could several clinical psychologists. Models for such interventions have been suggested in settings such as forensic hospitals (Jones, Menditto, Geeson, Larson, & Sadewhite, 2001) and rehabilitation centers (Holland, 1998).

Use of Activism. Social activism refers to the use of power to accomplish social reform. This power may be economic, it may be political, or it may be the coercive power of civil disobedience. Power can be manipulated through publicity, and it is for this reason that community psychologists cultivate media contacts to spread their influence. Finally, power resides in positions of leadership. Accordingly, some community psychologists seek employment where they have access to the formation of social policy—on urban-planning teams, as consultants to city councils, as advisors to legislators, as directors of citizen's advocate groups, or heads of social-service agencies.

Social action has been considered both an essential contribution and an unnecessary evil in community psychology. Advocates of activist tactics claim that professionals' willingness to provoke, agitate, and confront accounts for a large measure of their effectiveness in promoting change. Opponents of professional social action argue that such activity is incompatible with the objective empiricism that is the scientist's defining characteristic.

Use of Research as a Form of Intervention. George Fairweather, a psychologist at Michigan State University, coined the phrase "experimental social innovation" to describe research which, after demonstrating the value of a new community psychology program, can be used to support that program's implementation. Research as intervention is also exemplified by what is called *dissemination research*. This is experimentation designed to evaluate alternative methods of implementing programs that initial studies have shown to be successful. In the course of finding the most effective means of persuading other communities to adopt a given program, that program is, by necessity, adopted.

The best example of dissemination research is Fairweather's experimental project on the effectiveness of various approaches to persuading mental hospitals to adopt an outpatient "lodge program" designed as a form of supported housing and employment for chronic mental patients (Fairweather, Sanders, & Tornatzky, 1974). The research investigated which techniques were most effective in activating the lodge program once a decision had been made to adopt it and explored the procedures used in spreading the lodge approach to other mental health programs (Fairweather, 1980).

Some Final Comments on Community Psychology

Despite its innovativeness and obvious good intentions, community psychology has evoked a number of concerns. One fear is that community programs, particularly those aimed at prevention, may threaten people's privacy, individual freedom, and other rights to live their lives the way they please (Halleck, 1969). This fear is probably exaggerated, mainly because Americans are notably resistant to controls and coercion. Our mistrust of undue regulation from any source, whether political, military, or medical, has been effective protection against excessively intrusive control. At present, this quality appears sufficiently strong to prevent abuses by even the most zealous community psychologist.

Other critics fear that community psychology's emphasis on prevention will distract professionals from offering the intensive treatment severely disturbed clients require (Lamb & Zusman, 1981). This outcome, too, appears unlikely, since professional mental health fields suffered from an insufficiency of professional personnel long before community psychology came along.

There is uncertainty about exactly who in a community decides the goals of community interventions. Is it the psychologist, the recipients of the program, the majority of the community, or only influential leaders? Community psychologists assure us that the aims of their interventions are directed by the people they serve (Zax & Specter, 1974), but the notion of community participation is a complex ideal made all the more difficult by the frequent value conflicts between community residents and professional psychologists. Community psychologists must be cautious about overplaying their empirical hands. Few people disagree with community psychology interventions when they are supported by empirical research. But to the extent that community interventions outpace their empirical support, they become political advocacy at risk of being discredited when the political pendulum swings against them.

SELF-HELP INTERVENTIONS

If the popularity of an intervention is reflected in the number of books published about it, psychotherapy cannot hold a candle to self-help. A recent search of the amazon.com database yielded 10,959 matches for the term "psychotherapy" and twice that (22,225) for "self-help." The growing popularity of self-help groups of all forms has led some to suggest that they may soon rival all other forms of treatment (Barlow, Burlingame, Nebeker, & Anderson, 2000). For many persons, self-help is the prime source of psychological advice and treatment (Norcross, Santrock, Campbell & Smith, 2000). John Norcross (2000) has referred to the self-help movement as a "massive, systemic, and yet largely silent revolution" (p. 370).

The self-help movement has its roots in programs such as Alcoholics Anonymous (AA), one of the earliest such interventions. Persons involved in the community psychology movement were instrumental in advancing the numbers and scope of self-help groups. Self-help interventions are similar to psychotherapy in that they provide a structured way of understanding and dealing with a problem (e.g., by a 12-step approach). Members assist one another by exchanging information, providing social support, and discussing mutual problems (Backer & Richardson, 1989; Jacobs & Goodman, 1989). Group cohesiveness and other factors that operate in group therapy contexts can also occur in self-help interventions.

Most group self-help interventions fall into one of five subtypes (Powell, 1987). *Habit disturbance groups* such as Alcoholics Anonymous and Gamblers Anonymous focus on a specific behavior-change goal. *General-purpose groups* address a wide range of difficulties such as dealing with the death of a child (Compassionate Friends) or helping psychiatric patients cope with crises (GROW; Recovery, Inc.). *Lifestyle organizations* support individuals—such as single parents (Parents Without Partners) or the elderly (Gray Panthers)—who feel their interests are underserved by society. *Significant-other organizations* provide advocacy, education, support, and partnership for relatives of disturbed persons; examples include Gam-Anon (relatives of compulsive gamblers) and Al-Anon (relatives of alcoholics). Finally, *physical handicap organizations* such as Mended Hearts and the Cerebral Palsy Association provide support to heart surgery or cerebral palsy patients.

With the development of electronic media, self-help groups are no longer restricted by geographical boundaries. Many on-line support and self-help groups now exist, most of them offering bulletin boards to which members post comments and replies (such interchanges are called "asynchronous communication"). Some are monitored by a professional, others by paraprofessionals or members, and others are not monitored.

Many self-help groups are not strictly "self-help" but are run by or supervised by professionals. In face-to-face groups, the professional might orient new members and act as a consultant to the group. In on-line groups, the professional might supervise the web-site design, suggest links to sources of information, and maintain the supportive milieu by encouraging communication, providing information, or trying to limit access by disruptive members.

The self-help interventions are not restricted to face-to-face, telephone, and virtual (internet) groups. *Bibliotherapy*, reading books to treat psychological problems, is a large component of the self-help movement. A walk through your local bookstore is all that's needed to get a sense of the prevalence of self-help books. Some books, such as Burns's (1999) *Feeling Good Handbook*, are based on established psychological theory and research (Burns's book is based on cognitive therapy principles). Others are not.

Many psychologists are concerned that some self-help books and groups ignore or distort scientific findings and that books, in particular, may replace science in favor of the rule "anything that sounds good and sells." Publishers are typically more concerned with a book's potential sales than with its empirical foundations. There is real danger of miseducating and harming the public, and even if no immediate harm is done, the proliferation of self-help methods without solid claims of efficacy can only increase the public's perception that psychology is a discipline where anything goes and one person's theory is as good as the next one's. Fortunately, some psychologists have made efforts to help the public wade through the immense jungle of self-help. John Norcross and colleagues published the *Authoritative Guide to Self-Help Resources in Mental Health* (Norcross et al., 2000). The work reports the results of surveys of professionals on the value of individual self-help resources (books, groups, internet sites, etc.) for various disorders, ranking each one. Because the self-help movement was designed to free persons from reliance on professionals, it is doubtful whether professionals will ever have oversight on the myriad of self-help treatments offered to the public, but efforts such as this help.

Professionals' attitudes about self-help are mixed. Some professionals are deeply committed and involved in assisting self-help (many books are written by psychologists), while others are skeptical (Shepherd, Shoenberg, Slavich, Wituk, Warren, & Meissen, 1999). Many psychologists refer clients to self-help interventions but do not follow up to assess the results. As you might expect, clinicians who believe professionally led groups are significantly better than self-help groups are less likely to refer (Salzer, Rappaport, & Segre, 2001).

CHAPTER SUMMARY

Psychotherapy can involve modes of intervention that focus on and attempt to use the social contexts in which people's problems are embedded. Interventions can be conducted with groups, couples, and families, using methods that combine those employed in individual psychotherapy with specialized techniques unique to these special formats. Group therapy seeks to change the way individuals interact in a wide range of interpersonal relationships, while couples therapy addresses these issues within the context of an intimate dyad. Marital and family therapy focus on understanding and changing the forces within a family that affect the functioning of each of its members. These approaches often rely on systems-theory approaches, and diagnosis and treatment are aimed at changing a system rather than changing individuals.

Psychosocial rehabilitation is a mode of intervention that aims to help people displaying mental disorders to cope with the occupational, economic, family, and environmental effects of those disorders. Intervention programs emphasizing prevention attempt to modify social, economic, and environmental factors that lead to disorders in vulnerable populations or to strengthen qualities that protect individuals from developing disorders.

Community psychology is a field that applies psychological principles to understanding individual and social problems, preventing behavior disorders, and creating beneficial social changes. One of the offshoots of community psychology—self-help groups—has grown into a broad industry. Professionals' involvement in, and attitudes toward, the self-help movement is mixed.

Chapter 9

Research on Clinical Intervention

In Chapters 6, 7, and 8, we described the wide array of interventions that clinical psychologists employ in their efforts to help troubled clients. How well do these methods work? In this chapter, we first review the research methods that are used to evaluate clinical interventions in general and psychotherapy in particular. Next, we discuss what those methods have revealed about the effects of the various forms of psychotherapy that clinicians offer to individuals, groups, couples, and families. We then consider the results of clinical and community psychologists' efforts to promote psychosocial rehabilitation and to prevent mental disorders. Finally, we summarize the ways in which the results of evaluative research have combined with economic forces to shape today's clinical intervention methods.

The results of research on the effects of psychotherapy and other clinical interventions are of interest to three audiences, each with somewhat differing perspectives on mental health and the criteria used to assess it (Newman & Tejeda, 1996; Strupp & Hadley, 1977). First are clients, who have an obvious stake in the success of interventions designed to help them. Clients tend to ask two questions: "Did the intervention help me?" and (if they paid for treatment) "Was it worth the expense?" The second audience is made up of psychotherapists and others who implement clinical intervention programs. They want to know whether or not their efforts are worthwhile and whether and how the effects of their efforts can be improved. The third audience evaluating clinical interventions is society, by which we mean all "third parties" who are interested in the ability of those interventions to produce desirable changes in clients. Third parties can include the client's spouse or companion, parents, friends, or teachers, as well as police, judges, and the insurance companies or health maintenance organizations responsible for covering mental health care costs. The combined concerns of this third audience are that clinical intervention should not only benefit clients, but—by reducing crime, family stress and violence, human suffering, and health-care-related expenses—should also benefit society at large.

METHODS FOR EVALUATING PSYCHOTHERAPY

Because it is the most prominent form of clinical intervention, researchers have tended to focus most of their attention on evaluating the effects of various forms of psychotherapy. For a long time the main question posed by clinical researchers was "Is psychotherapy effective?", but they gradually discovered that this question was too broad. Starting in the 1970s, therapy outcome research began to be influenced by Gordon Paul's (1969a) more specific reformulation: "What treatment, by whom, is most effective for this individual with that specific problem, under which set of circumstances, and how does it come about?" (p. 44).

Alan Kazdin (1982b) translated Paul's "ultimate question" into a list of outcome research goals including (1) determining the efficacy of a specific treatment; (2) comparing the relative effectiveness of different treatments; and (3) assessing the specific components of treatment that are responsible for particular changes. Today, psychotherapy research also seeks to assess the durability of the benefits of particular treatments, identify any negative side effects associated with a treatment, determine how acceptable a treatment is to various kinds of clients, map the cost-effectiveness of various treatments, and discover whether a treatment's effects are clinically significant and socially meaningful (Howard et al., 1996; Kazdin & Wilson, 1978).

Designing Outcome Experiments on Psychotherapy

To reach all these goals, psychotherapy researchers must design and conduct their treatment outcome evaluations in such a way that the results can be interpreted unambiguously. For example, it is one thing for clients, therapists, relatives, and even test scores to suggest that a client has improved following a program of psychotherapy, but it is quite another to demonstrate scientifically that it was psychotherapy itself that caused the improvements. Of all the research designs that can evaluate the presence of a cause–effect relationship between therapy and improvement, the most powerful is the controlled experiment (Jacobson & Christensen, 1996).

An experiment is an attempt to discover the causes of specific events by making systematic changes in certain factors and then observing changes that occur in other factors. The factors that experimenters manipulate are called *independent variables*, while the factors in which resulting changes are observed are called *dependent variables*. In psychotherapy-outcome research, the independent variable is usually whether (or what type of) therapy is given, and the dependent variable is the amount and kinds of change seen in clients.

Most psychotherapy-outcome experiments employ either within-subject or between-subject research designs, both of which allow the experimenter to examine the effects of varying treatment conditions (the independent variable) on clients' thinking and behavior (the dependent variables). Generally speaking, within-subject designs alter a treatment variable and observe the effects of that manipulation on the same client(s) at different points in time. In between-subject research, different groups of clients are exposed to differing treatments, whose effects are then compared across the groups.

Within-Subject Research

The within-subject experiment requires that the dependent variables (client behaviors) be measured on several repeated occasions. The first of these observations usually takes place during a pretreatment, or baseline, period that provides a measure of the client's problematic behavior against which to compare subsequent changes. Once baseline measures have established a stable picture of the client's typical behavior, the intervention phase of the experiment begins. Here, the experimenter manipulates the independent variable by introducing some form of treatment and watches the dependent variable for any changes from its baseline level. Several types of within-subject experiments are used in clinical treatment research (Hayes, 1983; Kazdin, 1982a), but the two most popular versions are the reversal design and the multiple-baseline design.

In the reversal, or ABAB, design, a no-treatment baseline period (A) is alternated with a treatment period (B). The length of the A and B phases is determined by many factors, but usually each phase continues until the client's behavior becomes relatively stable. What can be learned from repeatedly presenting, then withdrawing, treatment? The logic underlying this design suggests that if behavior changes reliably and substantially only during each treatment period, and returns toward the baseline each time treatment is discontinued, the experimenter gains confidence that the treatment is responsible for the changes (see Figure 9.1).

Especially in situations where there are clinical or ethical concerns about interrupting treatment, experimenters may prefer the multiple-baseline design, which allows them to evaluate the effect of an intervention without repeatedly discontinuing it. Instead, the researcher observes several dependent measures at once, but applies a treatment to only one of them. If the treatment has a specific effect, the only aspect of the client's behavior that should change is the one that was treated. The treatment is then applied to additional targets, one at a time, and the effect on each is observed. Confidence in the causal effects of the treatment increases if each dependent measure changes when, and only when, treatment is applied to it. However, if behaviors change whether or not they were specifically targeted, the experimenter can assume that improvement may have been caused by some combination of treatment and some more general factors, such as the client's positive expectations about treatment.

To illustrate, suppose an experimenter wants to evaluate the effects of a contingent social-reinforcement program on the behavior of hospitalized mental patients. The dependent variables in this hypothetical experiment are three behaviors needing improvement: personal grooming, attending occupational therapy, and socializing with other patients. Each of these targets is first observed during a pretreatment baseline

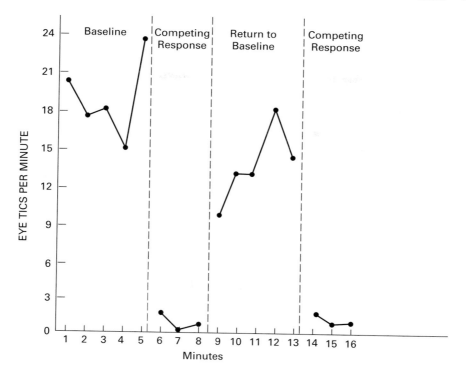

FIGURE 9.1   Evaluating treatment with a reversal design. The client in this study was a nine-year-old girl with a severe eye tic. The frequency of tics observed during the first baseline period declined dramatically when the intervention was introduced (it consisted of teaching the girl to blink softly every five seconds as a competing response to the tic). Notice that the tics increased when treatment was withdrawn during the second baseline period, but nearly disappeared when the competing response treatment was resumed during the second treatment period. (From N. H. Azrin & A. L. Peterson, 1989, Reduction of an eye tic by controlled blinking. *Behavior Therapy, 20,* 467–473.)

period, after which social reinforcement from hospital staff is first provided whenever the patients display improved grooming, then when they attend therapy sessions, and finally when they socialize. If the results of this treatment program are as shown in Figure 9.2, it becomes highly unlikely that factors other than treatment accounted for the outcome.[1]

---

[1]Tests of the statistical significance of treatment effects are not used in single-subject research, mainly because the researchers are interested in demonstrating that a client's behavior was reliably affected by manipulations of the independent variable. If such results are not obvious in a graph of the client's behavior, the change, though perhaps statistically significant, would be seen as irrelevant. When within-subjects designs employ groups of clients, however, researchers sometimes do employ statistical techniques to measure the magnitude and significance of changes appearing over time (Kraemer & Thiemann, 1989; Kratochwill, Mott, & Dodson, 1984).

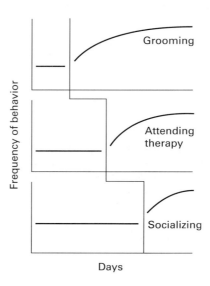

FIGURE 9.2 Hypothetical data from a multiple-baseline design. Notice that each targeted dependent variable improves when, *and only when*, social praise was made contingent on it. Such a pattern of results bolsters confidence that the treatment had a causal effect on behavior. (From A. E. Kazdin & S. A. Kopel, "On resolving ambiguities of the multiple baseline design: problems and recommendations," *Behavior Therapy*, 1975, 6, 601–608. © 1975 by Academic Press, New York. Reprinted by permission.)

Within-subject research can be conducted with a small number of clients, sometimes as few as one at a time. Indeed, "single-subject" or "$N = 1$," research is a popular treatment evaluation strategy because, first, it permits the intensive study of clinical phenomena—such as multiple personality—that are too rare to allow large-group designs (Barlow & Hersen, 1984; Kazdin, 1993, 1994; Morgan & Morgan, 2001). Second, the $N = 1$ approach encourages the integration of clinical research and clinical practice; it gives individual clinicians a way to empirically evaluate the treatment they deliver to individual clients (Hayes, 1983). Third, the fine-grained study of a particular client over time makes it possible for clinicians to address therapy "process" questions—such as which events in therapy were followed by what changes—as well as the more obvious outcome questions (e.g., whether their treatment caused changes in their clients). Indeed, the intensive study of how interactions, events, or sequences within a psychotherapy session are related to important changes in a client has become a major focus of psychotherapy research (e.g., Greenberg, 1986; Greenberg, Elliott, & Lietaer, 1994). A goal of this kind of "process research" is to discover *how* psychotherapy produces change in a client so that therapists can learn how to bring about more therapeutic "good moments" (Mahrer & Nadler, 1986) in which clients show change or improvement.

Between-Subject Research

The simplest example of a between-subjects experiment on therapy outcome is one in which the researcher manipulates an independent variable by giving treatment to one group of clients—the *experimental* group—and compares any observed changes to those seen in members of a *control* group, which received no treatment. Measures of the clients' problematic behavior (the dependent variable) are made for both groups prior to the experiment (the *pretest*), shortly after the treatment period ends (the *posttest*), and perhaps also at longer posttreatment intervals (the *follow-up*).

It is important that clients be *randomly assigned* to experimental or control groups because, given a large enough number of clients, this procedure makes it likely that the treatment and control groups will be approximately equivalent in age, severity of disorder, socioeconomic status, and other important variables that might affect treatment outcome. If clients are not randomly assigned to conditions, any between-group differences in client behavior seen at the end of the experiment might be attributed to differences that existed between groups before the experiment ever began. If, for example, the most disturbed clients were put in the no-treatment group, the cards are stacked in favor of the treatment being evaluated. Thus, treated clients might improve much more than untreated clients, but because they were less disturbed to begin with, the treated clients might have improved even without treatment. When experimental designs are flawed, or *confounded*, in this way, we do not know whether to attribute improvement to treatment or to other uncontrolled factors. Once the pretest equivalence of the experimental and control groups is established, differences between the groups at posttest or follow-up can more confidently be attributed to the treatment that only the experimental group received. The significance of observed differences between treatment and control groups is tested via standard statistical analyses that help the researcher determine how likely it was that these differences might have occurred by chance.

Comparisons between treatment and no-treatment groups is just a first step in therapy-outcome research. After all, even large and statistically significant differences between a treatment and a no-treatment group can tell us little more than giving treatment appears to be more effective than doing nothing. The simple treatment/no-treatment design cannot shed much light on the more complex questions that psychotherapy-outcome researchers want to address. Was treated clients' improvement caused by specific therapeutic techniques, characteristics of the therapist, or the capacity of therapy to generate expectancy for improvement? Is the treatment tested better than various alternative treatments available?

One way of answering questions like these is to design *factorial experiments*, so named because they allow the researcher to examine the impact of various factors that might be responsible for the changes seen in treated clients. In a typical factorial outcome study, one group of clients might receive a complete treatment package, while another gets only that part of treatment thought to be most important to its effectiveness. A third group might be exposed to procedures that are impressive enough to generate expectations for improvement but involve no formal treatment methods (a *placebo-control* condition). A *no-treatment* group might also be included to assess the impact of the mere passage of time. By comparing the changes seen in all four groups, the experimenter can begin to determine whether the effects of the complete treatment package is better than no treatment, placebo effects, and a less extensive version of treatment. If a fifth group of clients is given a completely different form of treatment, the experimenter could also compare the first approach with that alternative.

Between-subject research designs have been popular among psychotherapy researchers because they allow manipulation of several independent variables simultaneously rather than sequentially, as required by within-subject designs. Between-subject designs are expensive, however; it usually takes many clients and a large research staff to compose and treat the groups necessary for the statistical analyses used. In addition, between-subject designs are not as suitable for evaluating the effects of a sequence of interventions; that type of question is better addressed by within-subject designs.

PRACTICAL PROBLEMS IN PSYCHOTHERAPY RESEARCH

Whether they employ within-subject or between-subject methods, psychotherapy researchers' overriding goal is to design experiments whose results are as high as possible on both internal and external validity so that they can serve as useful guides to clinicians in choosing treatments and charting progress in individual cases (Goldfried & Wolfe, 1996; Howard et al., 1996; Newman & Tejeda, 1996; Cook & Campbell, 1991; Shadish, 2002).

Threats to Internal and External Validity

An experiment is said to have high *internal validity* if its design allows the researcher to confidently assert that observed changes in dependent variable(s) were caused by manipulated independent variable(s), not by some unknown, unintended, or uncontrolled confounding factor(s). The experimenter wants to be able to say, for example, that clients' reduced depression was caused by the cognitive therapy they received, not by the confidence they had in the treatment or by a TV show they happened to see.

Experiments are high on *external validity* if their results are applicable, or generalizable, to clients, problems, and situations other than those included in the experiment. External validity does not always follow from internal validity. For example, a study evaluating systematic desensitization for claustrophobia might feature random assignment to groups and include all the control conditions necessary to conclude that desensitization was responsible for clients' improvement. However, suppose this internally valid design employed expert desensitization therapists who treated only European-American female college students with mild cases of claustrophobia. These restrictions on therapist and client variables might reduce the study's external validity because its results may not apply to therapists in general, to clients from varying age or ethnic groups, or to clients who display more disabling phobias.

Most researchers agree that the best way to assess the outcome of psychotherapy is to conduct research on the treatments actually offered by clinicians to clinically disordered clients in real treatment settings. The ideal experimental outcome study, then, would select a large random sample of clients seeking help for depression or some other specific problem, assign them randomly to varying treatments or to specialized control conditions, have practicing therapists give them real or placebo treatments, then measure therapeutic change through data collected by unbiased persons who are unaware of which clients were in which treatment or control groups.

Unfortunately, numerous practical obstacles make these ideal arrangements virtually unachievable. For one thing, both clinical and ethical considerations sometimes prevent randomly assigning real clients to various treatment and control conditions. Few clients seeking treatment would be happy about being placed in a placebo or no-treatment group simply for the sake of promoting good science. Therapists, too, are reluctant to allow clients to be assigned to conditions that have little chance of bringing about beneficial changes. Other more basic impediments to research on psychotherapy include the fact that few clinical settings can offer researchers a sufficient number of clients who meet all the demographic, health, and disorder criteria that are ideal for inclusion in a controlled experiment. Add to these obstacles the practical problems of enlisting experienced therapists to participate in a study, convincing agency administrators to invest resources in the research, preventing subjects from prematurely dropping out of treatment, and collecting meaningful long-term outcome measures from clients, and you can understand why some psychotherapy researchers shy away from attempting to conduct real-life evaluations of treatment outcome.

Dealing with Threats to Validity

Several approaches are available to solve these psychotherapy-outcome research problems. The first is for researchers to use all their creativity and tenacity to conduct the best clinical research they can, while recognizing that certain questions about psychotherapy cannot be answered with certainty outside a laboratory, while others cannot be answered with certainty inside the laboratory.

Single-Subject and Case Study Research. Another approach, as mentioned earlier, is the use of within-subject designs to conduct fine-grained research on the "good moments" that occur in real-world therapy settings. A variant on this approach is the *case-study* model, in which therapists develop a specific treatment formulation for each client, then assess therapy's effects for that client using techniques appropriate to single-subject design research (Howard et al., 1996; Kazdin, 1993; Persons, 1991).

Clinical Trials. Investigators can also conduct cooperative outcome studies in which they combine therapy results for similar types of clients being treated by many different therapists at several clinical centers. This type of study, known as a *clinical trial*, allows experimental procedures such as random assignment to be used to investigate psychotherapy as it is practiced in real clinical settings. A prime example of this strategy is the NIMH Collaborative Study on the treatment of depression (Elkin, Gibbons, Shea, Sotsky, Watkins, & Pilkonis, 1995; Zlotnick, Elkin, & Shea, 1998). Similar multisite studies are currently evaluating the treatment of other mental disorders.

Laboratory Analogues. Yet another approach is to bring psychotherapy research questions into the laboratory. Approximating clinical conditions in a controlled experimental setting is called *analogue research*. Its advantages include the ability to (1) control the client, therapist, and environmental variables that tend to fluctuate in unknown ways in clinical settings, (2) recruit (even advertise for) a sufficient number of clients who display a particular problem and who meet other demographic criteria, (3) train therapists to conduct treatment(s) in specified ways, and (4) keep the number and length of treatment sessions constant for all clients.

The similarity between clinical and analogue settings can be assessed along four dimensions (Bernstein & Paul, 1971). The first of these involves *client characteristics* and recruitment. The degree to which an analogue experiment's results can be generalized to a clinical population depends on the extent to which the subjects are similar to clients who seek treatment.

The second dimension is the nature of the *target problem*. Certain target problems selected for analogue study, such as the fear of small animals or insects, may bear so little resemblance to the problems that most clients bring to clinics that they distort our understanding of the potency of therapeutic techniques.

A third dimension of interest relates to *therapist characteristics*. In many analogue studies, the therapists are graduate students in clinical psychology who have far less experience in general, or with the particular treatment being evaluated, than the average practicing clinician. (As we will see later, however, this factor may not necessarily hamper the ability of inexperienced therapists to help their clients.)

Finally, clinical and analogue studies can be compared in terms of the *treatment techniques* they employ. As noted, analogue treatments can be standardized for all clients. This often means that therapists are given manuals that specify how a treatment should be conducted during the analogue study (e.g., Moncher & Prinz, 1991). In most clinics, however, therapists use methods that are tailored to the unique needs of each client. If manualized treatment techniques are simplified, altered, shortened, or otherwise changed in ways that do not fairly represent their use in clinical practice, the results of these analogue methods may say little about the therapies they were designed to evaluate.

Client Surveys. A recent and somewhat controversial approach to evaluating psychotherapy has been to conduct surveys of how real clients fared after receiving psychotherapy as it is practiced in their communities. The survey approach obviously places far more emphasis on external rather than internal validity because, unlike within- or between-subject experiments, it exerts no experimental control over anything (Jacobson & Christensen, 1996). Later, we describe a survey in which readers of *Consumer Reports* magazine answered a series of questions about the treatment and treatment results they experienced when they sought help for mental health problems (Seligman, 1995).

Necessary Compromises in Therapy Research

Notice the dilemma inherent in any approach to designing valid psychotherapy research: In order to exert the experimental control necessary to maximize internal validity, researchers may be forced to study clients, therapists, problems, treatments, and treatment settings that may not allow for high external validity. At the same time, if the researcher tries to maximize external validity by conducting research on real clients with real problems in community treatment settings, the resulting lack of experimental control may be lethal to internal validity. Given this dilemma, we must recognize that the results of well-controlled experiments can be used to draw only limited conclusions about therapies being conducted in clinical practice (Weisz, Weiss, & Donenberg, 1992). At the same time, we must be wary of evaluative data coming from less well-controlled research in clinical settings. Indeed, any conclusions drawn from the results of any outcome study must be tempered by awareness of the compromises in research design and methods that were made in an effort to strike a reasonable balance between internal and external validity.

In short, answering Paul's ultimate outcome question ("What treatment, by whom, is most effective for this individual, with that specific problem, under which set of circumstances, and how does it come about?") will require many researchers to conduct many different kinds of studies over many years. Let's now consider what they have discovered so far about the outcome of individual psychotherapy.

EFFECTIVENESS OF INDIVIDUAL PSYCHOTHERAPY

Although therapists have studied the outcome of psychotherapy for a long time, the modern era of outcome research began in 1952 when Hans Eysenck, a British psychologist, reviewed several experiments and concluded that the recovery rate is about the same for patients who receive therapy as for those who do not. Eysenck argued that the rate of "spontaneous remission" (improvement without any special treatment) was 72% over 2 years compared to improvement rates of 44% for psychoanalysis and 64% for eclectic therapy (Eysenck, 1952). In later reviews, Eysenck (1966) evaluated more studies and, while persisting in his pessimism about the effectiveness of traditional therapy, claimed that behavior therapy produced superior outcomes.

Box Score Reviews

Eysenck's conclusions sparked heated debate among clinicians. Many critics attacked his thoroughness, fairness, and his methods of statistical analysis. Others conducted their own reviews of the outcome literature and reached more optimistic conclusions about the effectiveness of psychotherapy. For example, Allen Bergin (1971) asserted that "psychotherapy on the average has modestly positive effects" (p. 228), a belief he later amended to "clearly positive results" (Bergin & Lambert, 1978). Another review found that more than 80% of psychotherapy outcome studies produced positive results (Meltzoff & Kornreich, 1970). Indeed, most reviews have concluded that most forms of psychotherapy produce better outcomes than no treatment and that various types of therapy are equally effective with most clients (e.g., Lambert, Shapiro, & Bergin, 1986; Luborsky, Singer, & Luborsky, 1975; Shadish et al., 2000; Smith, Glass, & Miller, 1980; Stiles, Shapiro, & Elliott, 1986). But there were also reviews that supported Eysenck's claim that (1) traditional psychotherapy is no better than no treatment, and (2) for several kinds of problems, behavior therapy is especially effective (Borkovec &

Costello, 1993; DeRubeis & Crits-Cristoph, 1998; Lambert & Bergin, 1994; Weisz et al., 1995).

Among the many reasons for the discrepant, sometimes contradictory results of therapy outcome reviews is the fact that different researchers have used differing standards in (1) selecting the outcome studies they survey, (2) evaluating the quality of these studies, (3) interpreting the magnitude of therapy effects, and (4) combining the results of many studies to reach their conclusions.

The traditional approach to summarizing outcome research has been the narrative, or *box score,* review. In a box score review, the researcher makes categorical judgments about whether each outcome study yielded positive or negative results and then tallies the number of positive and negative outcomes. Reviewers who use this method have been criticized (including by each other) for being subjective and unsystematic in the way they integrate research studies. Another problem with narrative reviews is that the sheer number of outcome studies makes it difficult for reviewers to weigh properly the merits and results of each study. Disagreements over these results made it clear that an alternative to box score analyses was needed, an alternative that would allow researchers to quantify and statistically summarize the effects of each outcome study, separately and in the aggregate.

Meta-Analytic Studies

One such alternative is *meta-analysis*, a quantitative technique that standardizes the outcomes of a large number of studies so they can be compared or combined (Rosenthal, 1983). The first application of meta-analysis to psychotherapy research came in 1977 and led Mary Smith and Gene Glass to conclude that, on the average, psychotherapy was very effective (Smith and Glass, 1977). Later, they published a much larger meta-analysis which encompassed 475 psychotherapy-outcome studies (Smith, Glass & Miller, 1980). In this monumental meta-analysis, therapy effectiveness was evaluated by computing effect sizes for all the treatments used in all the studies. An effect size was defined as the treatment group mean on a dependent measure minus the control group mean on the same measure divided by the standard deviation of the control group. Thus, an effect size indicates the average difference in outcome between treated and untreated groups in each study. There can be as many effect sizes for a treatment as there are measures on which that treatment is evaluated—including clients' self-reports of how they feel, therapists' opinions about how much a client has changed, pre- and posttreatment psychological test scores, and observers' ratings of how well clients are doing—although there are statistical reasons why it is best to derive one average effect size for each treatment (Hedges & Olkin, 1982). Looking at effect sizes measured immediately after therapy ends, or in some cases, months after treatment, indicates how much better off the average treated client was compared with the average person in a no-treatment control group.

Several other research teams have performed meta-analyses using different statistical methods or differently selected sets of studies (e.g., Andrews & Harvey, 1981; Brown, 1987; Grissom 1996; Lambert & Bergin, 1994; Landman & Dawes, 1982; Lipsey & Wilson, 1993; Shapiro & Shapiro, 1982; Wampold, et al., 1997). In general, these analyses have confirmed the conclusion that psychotherapy is an effective intervention for a wide variety of psychological disorders. In addition, these second and third-generation meta-analyses have led to the following conclusions about the effects of psychotherapy:

1. Many meta-analyses found no consistent differences in effectiveness among the various forms of psychotherapy. Indeed, this conclusion has been reached by so many analyses that psychotherapy researchers jokingly call it the "Dodo bird verdict" (Luborsky et al., 1975), in reference to Lewis Carroll's tale of *Alice in Wonderland*. In the story, Alice and several other characters run a race, but they run in different directions. When they ask the Dodo bird to name the winner, he answers diplomatically: "Everybody has won and all must have prizes." In the race among various psychotherapies, too, all appear to have crossed the outcome finish line together. As we shall see below, the Dodo bird verdict has been brought into question by researchers using different methods.

2. Therapist training and experience do not appear to affect the success of treatment as much as most clinicians assume (Berman & Norton, 1985; Dawes, 1992; Durlak, 1979; Hattie, Sharpley, & Rogers, 1984; Henry, et al., 1993; Stein & Lambert, 1984). Experienced professionals sometimes produce outcomes that are superior to those of novice or nonprofessional therapists (Stein & Lambert, 1995), but the fact that most studies fail to find large advantages associated with professional training or experience is remarkable.

3. The problems of a small percentage of clients do become worse after psychotherapy—about 10% of effect sizes in major meta-analytic studies of psychotherapy have been negative (Shapiro & Shapiro, 1982; Smith et al., 1980)—but the causes and course of deterioration or negative change are not well understood.

4. It appears that, for about half of treated clients, the benefits of psychotherapy begin to appear after the first 6 to 8 sessions, and that 75% of those who show improvement typically do so by the 26th session (Howard et al., 1996). Continued benefits occur as treatment continues, but the rate of progress tends to slow, probably because the client's most difficult problems tend to be addressed in later sessions. The relatively quick response to psychotherapy by most clients has led to the increased use of "brief therapies" that aim to produce benefits in 25 sessions or less (Koss & Shiang, 1994).

5. The effects of psychotherapy tend to be maintained over periods of 6 to 18 months (Andrews & Harvey, 1981; Nicholson & Berman, 1983; Robinson, Berman, & Neimeyer, 1990). These data serve to counter fears that gains attributed to psychotherapy might be short lived; there is even some evidence that clients show continuing improvement during follow-up periods (Gallagher-Thompson, Hanley-Peterson, & Thompson, 1990).

Criticisms of Meta-Analysis. Despite its popularity, meta-analysis has been criticized on the grounds that it (1) is subject to the same biases and arbitrariness encountered in narrative reviews; that is, certain studies are omitted and others are combined into categories that may not be reliably defined; (2) involves an "apples-and-oranges" approach to evaluation (combining varying treatments for varying problems on varying clients) that obscures important distinctions in treatments and outcomes; (3) pays insufficient attention to the research quality of individual studies of psychotherapy; and (4) is based on several statistical assumptions that, if violated, can invalidate the results obtained (e.g., Eysenck, 1978; Wilson, 1985; Wilson & Rachman, 1983).

Each of these criticisms has been answered by proponents of meta-analysis who argue that (1) meta-analysis makes explicit the rules for selecting and combining studies (in narrative reviews, these rules are often not explicitly defined); (2) if one is interested in evaluating psychotherapy as a general intervention, combining different treatments is not an error (just as it is not an error to combine apples and oranges if one is evaluating fruit); (3) as noted earlier, it is the better-designed studies, not the weaker ones, that are producing the largest therapy effect sizes; and (4) corrections are available for remedying most of the statistical problems that can threaten a meta-analysis.

Client Satisfaction Surveys

The conclusions about psychotherapy reached by most box score analyses and meta-analyses are reflected in the *Consumer Reports* study mentioned earlier (Seligman, 1995). In that survey, about 4,100 of the 7,000 respondents had seen a mental health professional in the past 3 years. As a group, these clients were well-educated and predominantly middle-class; about half were women, and their average age was 46. Although these characteristics are not representative of the U.S. population as a whole, they are a reasonably good approximation of the type of client who normally seeks out professional treatment for psychological problems. The respondents were asked to rate (1) the degree to which formal treatment had helped with the problem that led them to therapy, (2) how satisfied they were with the treatment they received, and (3) how they judged their "overall emotional state" after treatment.

Responses indicated that about 90% of these clients felt better after treatment, that there was no difference in the improvement of clients who had psychotherapy alone versus psychotherapy plus medication, that no particular approach to psychotherapy was rated more highly than others, and that while all types of professionals appeared to help their clients, greater improvements were associated with treatments by psychologists, psychiatrists, and social workers compared to family physicians or marriage counselors.

Empirically Supported Treatments (ESTs)

Despite repeated findings that there appear to be no significant differences in the outcome of various types of treatment, empirically oriented clinicians (and others) found it difficult to believe that all forms of psychotherapy were equally effective for all clients and all psychological problems. Accordingly, in 1993, the American Psychological Association's Division of Clinical Psychology (Division 12) convened a special task force to determine which psychological interventions were empirically validated. The *Task Force on Promotion and Dissemination of Psychological Procedures* first established a set of criteria for evaluating the effectiveness of clinical interventions. They then began reviewing the massive psychotherapy literature to determine which interventions meet these criteria. In 1995, the Task Force published a preliminary list of 25 treatments identified as efficacious (Task Force, 1995). The list was updated in 1996 and again in 1998. The 1998 list included 71 treatments (Chambless, et al., 1998). By 2001, the Task Force, along with other work groups whose methods were compatible with the Task Force, had classified 108 treatments for adults and 37 for children as either *well-established/efficacious* (category-I) or *probably/possibly efficacious* (category-II). They also included a third category, *promising*, for treatments that had shown preliminary success (Chambless & Ollendick, 2001).

Controversy has accompanied questions about psychotherapy's effectiveness even before Eysenck's review, yet few publications in clinical psychology have generated as much controversy as have the attempt to identify *empirically supported treatments (or ESTs)*.[2] Many psychologists praised the work as the most comprehensive and systematic attempt yet to identify which of the more than 400 psychological treatments available actually work. Others criticized the effort, claiming that the Task Force's criteria were arbitrary, overly restrictive, or congenial toward some types of therapy but not others (Beutler et al., 1996; Silverman, 1996).

Criteria and Outcomes for EST Research.

The Task Force had some difficult decisions to make when selecting the studies to review for evidence of therapy effectiveness. For example, what kinds of study designs should they include? Should they choose only randomized, between-subjects designs? What about single-subject designs, naturalistic designs, case-study designs, and descriptive or qualitative designs? Should they use only studies in which clients' disorders were categorized according to the standard diagnostic system (DSM-IV)?

In the end, the Task Force decided to favor studies with strong *internal validity*—studies whose designs allowed for strong inferences about therapy effects based on unambiguously causal relationships between treatments and outcomes. To make stronger claims about the effects of specific treatments, the Task Force favored studies that sought to reduce therapist variability. In practice, this meant choosing studies in which therapists treated each client in substantially the same manner, typically by following relatively detailed treatment manuals (Chambless & Ollendick, 2001).

Variability in clients' problems was also a concern. For instance, in a study on the effectiveness of a cognitive-behavioral treatment for panic disorder, it will be easier to evaluate the specific effects of that intervention if all clients were suffering only from panic disorder, and were not also troubled by, say, substance abuse or depression. Because the task force's goal was to identify which interventions were effective for clients

---

[2]The 1995 report labeled as *empirically validated* those interventions that met the Task Force's criteria. However, many clinicians, even some favorable to the Task Force's efforts, believed that the word "validated" was too strong and contained unwanted connotations. The Task Force eventually replaced it with the term *empirically supported*. The two terms—empirically validated and empirically supported—are sometimes used interchangeably in the literature.

experiencing specific problems, studies in which clients had clear DSM-IV diagnoses but no comorbid conditions were favored.

Given its overriding concerns for internal validity and treatment specificity, the Task Force relied especially on studies using randomized clinical trials (experiments in which clients were randomly assigned to conditions) though they also used single-client designs when there were enough such studies available to establish generalizable patterns.

Using these criteria, the Task Force identified empirically supported treatments. Table 9.1 is a partial listing of empirically supported treatments, focusing only on ESTs for anxiety disorders and depression. This partial list conveys prominent features of empirically supported treatments. Perhaps the most noticeable feature of the table is the preponderance of behavioral and cognitive-behavioral treatments listed as ESTs. Another important feature is that some disorders appear particularly responsive to just one or a few specific treatments while other disorders show no such *specificity*. For instance, several investigators have found that obsessive-compulsive disorder appears most effectively treated with exposure plus response prevention (ERP). Many of the anxiety disorders show similar treatment specificity. However, far less specificity occurs when it comes to depression; there are no apparent differences in effectiveness among cognitive-behavior therapy, cognitive therapy, interpersonal therapy, and brief dynamic therapies for depression (Elkin et al.,1989; Thompson et al., 1987). One study even found that cognitive-behavioral therapy for depression was as effective when it contained only one of its components (assignment of activities to build mastery and positive mood) as when it contained its full package of components (Jacobson et al., 1996). In short, EST research has found that treatment specificity exists for some disorders but not others.

Criticisms of EST Research. EST research has been criticized on several grounds. One concerns whether the treatments shown to be effective in controlled settings generalize to clinical settings. When a treatment produces outcomes for a given condition that are clearly superior to no treatment (or are equivalent to that achieved by an established treatment) under well-controlled conditions, it is said to have shown *efficacy*. But efficacy is not the same as *effectiveness* (Seligman, 1995), which refers to how a treatment works in clinic settings, not in controlled clinical trials. It is also unclear whether the effects from such studies are *clinically significant*, as well as statistically significant (Sechrest, McKnight, & McKnight, 1996). The authors of one recent meta-analysis of controlled studies of the efficacy of ESTs in treating depression, panic, and generalized anxiety disorder concluded that the screening procedures and limited range of outcomes reported in many of these studies raised questions about whether their positive results would generalize to real-world clinical situations (Westen & Morrison, 2001).

Much of the criticism of the EST research has focused on the criteria used to select studies. For instance, though the Task Force occasionally used research that classified client samples according to cut-off scores on diagnostic questionnaires (Chambless & Ollendick, 2001), many of these studies relied on *DSM diagnoses* to describe the client population. As we discussed in Chapter 3, some critics believe that DSM diagnostic classification may not be the best way to classify clients for psychotherapy research.

Other critics have disputed the assumption inherent in most EST research that treatment of psychological disorders follows a *medical model* (Wampold, Ahn, & Coleman 2001; Strupp, 2001). In the medical model, treatment success is assumed to result from matching a treatment (e.g., amoxicillin) with an illness (e.g., ear infection). In the strict version of medical model, the doctor's characteristics (e.g., bedside manner) and the patient's characteristics (e.g., optimism) are less important than choosing the correct treatment and applying it in the proper dosage to a disease; as long as the right treatment is given, the patient is expected to improve. In psychotherapy, the specific intervention techniques are analogous to the "active ingredients" in medications, and the psychological disorders are analogous to the illness.

Critics of EST research point to evidence such as a recent meta-analysis of 27 studies that investigated the effects of therapy's "active ingredients." In these studies, the effects of complete psychotherapy packages were compared with those same packages which had been altered by subtracting one theoretically important component or by adding an extra component (Ahn & Wampold, 2001). This analysis found no differences in the effect sizes of the various comparison packages, suggesting that the supposedly essential aspects of some treatments are not necessarily essential. In fact, in most psychotherapy research, specific treatment techniques typically account for only a small proportion of psychotherapy's outcome variance while client, therapist, and other factors each account for larger proportions of variance (Lambert, 1992; Messer, 2001).

The *use of treatment manuals* in some of the psychotherapy research reviewed by the Task Force drew especially sharp criticism. Critics have complained that therapists rarely use such manuals in actual clinical practice (Garfield, 1996; Seligman, 1995). Indeed, one survey found that 23% of psychologists in practice said that they had never even heard of treatment manuals (Addis & Krasnow, 2000). Others claim that manuals can act as "straightjackets" or "cookbooks," restricting therapists' ability to individualize treatment and leading to poorer outcomes for clients (Garfield, 1996; Goldfried & Wolfe, 1998; Silverman, 1996).

It is important to note that the use of treatment manuals in research studies does not eliminate variability among therapists. In one such study, one particular therapist did better than others in cognitive-behavioral interventions even though all were using the same manual (Shapiro, Firth-Cozens, & Stiles, 1998). Another study reports that among clinicians who participated in more than one experiment using manuals, two individuals showed consistently superior results while one showed consistently inferior results (Luborsky et al., 1997). Still another study found that outcomes varied according to therapists' competence, not according to the manual they used (Shaw et al., 1999). Reviewing the evidence, Wampold (2001) argued that strict *adherence* to manuals is unrelated to outcome. Instead, he argues, the therapists' *allegiance* to whatever therapy is given affects outcomes—therapists who strongly believe in what they are doing tend to produce better outcomes.

In short, critics contend that by controlling much of what influences psychotherapy outcomes—nonspecific client, therapist, and relationship factors—EST research ignores these major influences on therapy effectiveness.

TABLE 9.1   Empirically Supported Treatments for Anxiety Disorders and Mood Disorders (Adults)

Condition	Treatment	I[b]	II[c]	III[d]
Anxiety Disorders				
Agoraphobia/panic disorder with agoraphobia	CBT	3	1	
	Couples communication training as adjunct to exposure			2
	Exposure	4	1	
	Partner-assisted CBT		2	
Blood injury phobia	Applied tension		1	
	Exposure			1
Generalized anxiety disorder	Applied relaxation	1	3	
	CBT	4	1	
Geriatric anxiety	Relaxation		1	
	CBT			2
Obsessive-compulsive disorder	ERP	4	1	
	Cognitive therapy		2	1
	RET + exposure			1
	Family-assisted ERP + relaxation		1	
	Relapse prevention		1	
Panic disorder	Applied relaxation	1	3	
	CBT	4	1	
	Emotion-focused therapy			1
	Exposure	1	2	
Post-traumatic stress disorder	EMDR			2
	Exposure	1	2	
	Stress inoculation	1	2	
	Stress inoculation in combination with CT + exposure	1	2	
	Structured psychodynamic treatment			1
Public speaking anxiety	Systematic desensitization		1	
Social anxiety/phobia	CBT	2	3	
	Exposure	1	4	
	Systematic desensitization		1	
Specific phobia	Exposure	3	1	
	Systematic desensitization		1	
Stress	Stress inoculation	1		

The column headers under "Empirical Support Category[a]" are I[b], II[c], III[d].

TABLE 9.1   Empirically Supported Treatments for Anxiety Disorders and Mood Disorders (Adults) *(Continued)*

Condition	Treatment	Empirical Support Category[a]		
		I[b]	II[c]	III[d]
Mood Disorders				
Bipolar disorder	Psychoeducation		1	
	CBT for medication adherence		1	
	Family therapy			1
Geriatric depression	Behavior therapy	2	2	
	Brief psychodynamic therapy	2	2	
	CBT	2	3	
	Interpersonal therapy		1	
	Problem-solving therapy		2	
	Psychoeducation	1		
	Reminiscence therapy (mild-moderate)	1		
Major depression	Behavior therapy	2	1	
	BMT (for marital discord)	1	1	
	Brief dynamic therapy		1	1
	CBT	4	1	
	Interpersonal therapy	3	2	
	Self-control therapy		2	
	Social problem solving		2	

[a] In addition to the Division 12 Task Force, various work groups have contributed to the list of ESTs: Spirito (1999); *Journal of Clinical Child Psychology* (1998); Kendall & Chambless (1998); Roth & Fonagy (1996); Nathan and Gorman (1998); Wilson & Gil (1996); and Gatz et al. (1998). In this table, the number in the columns indicates the number of work groups identifying that treatment as having a particular level of support. Some caution is advised in interpreting the numbers because work groups did not use identical criteria. Most, but not all, work groups made distinctions similar to those used by the Task Force between the various levels of support (described below).

[b] Category I = *well-established/efficacious and specific* based on at least two rigorous randomized controlled trials in which treatment showed superiority to placebo control conditions or another bona fide treatment, or based on a large series of rigorous single-case experiments.

[c] Category II = *efficacious/probably efficacious/possibly efficacious* based on at least one rigorous randomized controlled trial in which treatment showed superiority to placebo control conditions or another bona fide treatment, or based on a small series of rigorous single-case experiments.

[d] Category III = *promising* based on studies with a lower level of evidence than Category I or II.

SOURCE: Adapted from Chambless & Ollendick (2001)

Empirically Supported Treatments in Perspective. You might have noted a contrast between the findings of meta-analyses and the finding of studies investigating ESTs. Meta-analyses generally reached the conclusion that no form of therapy is clearly superior to the others. Indeed the "Dodo bird verdict" was perhaps the most robust finding in psychotherapy research during the 20th century. Studies investigating ESTs, on the other hand, have found the majority of efficacious treatments to be of the cognitive-behavioral variety. Critics of EST research have claimed that this result stems from the use of narrow criteria that stacked the deck in favor of cognitive-behavioral treatments, which are more easily "manualized" than other treatment approaches. These critics also contend that EST criteria excluded research that shows the significant contributions to therapy outcome made by therapist, client, and relationship factors.

The Task Force has been responsive to such criticisms, modifying their criteria and asking critics to join with them to study the issues involved. Beutler et al. (1996), for instance, studied the question of whether the task force's conclusions would be different if criteria for research were to be expanded. They concluded that, if the criteria had been expanded:

1. There would be stronger evidence for nonspecific therapy effects, particularly for long-term treatments, which tended to produce superior results.
2. Therapist factors would be given relatively more weight.
3. Cognitive therapy would still predominate as an effective treatment approach.
4. Psychoanalytic therapies would continue to make a poor showing.
5. The question of whether expert or advanced training is needed beyond that necessary for conducting competent manualized treatment would go unresolved. (Beutler, 1998)

Much of the criticism of the effort to establish ESTs concerns what EST researchers have *not* done rather than what they have done. What the Task Force—and other work groups following similar procedures—*have* done is to provide a partial answer to the question of what constitutes evidence-based psychotherapy. What they have not done is provide a final answer. Chambless and Ollendick (2001) conclude their discussion of ESTs this way:

> Almost all ESTs rely on therapists' having good nonspecific therapy skills. For example, in the NIMH Treatment of Depression Collaborative Research Program, two ESTs (interpersonal therapy and cognitive therapy) for depression, in which therapists followed elaborate treatment manuals, treatment effects varied according to therapists' competence (Shaw et al., 1999). Client characteristics such as ability to form an alliance with the therapist (Krupnick et al., 1996) and initial functioning (e.g., Elkin et al., 1995) also proved to be important in predicting treatment outcome. Research on the interaction of client characteristics (e.g., personality) with treatment approaches is in its early stages (e.g., Beutler et al., 1991). Such research is difficult to conduct because of the large sample size required for sufficient power. Yet such research has great potential for addressing practitioners' questions about which among several ESTs might be best for a particular client. Thus

the practice of evidence-based psychotherapy is a complex one, and ESTs are only one piece of the puzzle. (p. 712)

Research on Common or Nonspecific Factors

Because therapy outcomes are only partly explained by treatment techniques and client diagnoses, researchers have also focused attention on the therapist, the client, and other features of the therapeutic situation, particularly the therapeutic alliance. They look for characteristics, behavioral patterns, and process variables that correlate with positive therapeutic outcomes. Collectively, these variables are sometimes called *common factors* or *nonspecific treatment variables*. These variables are independent of the specific treatment techniques used, though they can interact with treatment variables, as we will see below.

Therapist Variables. What therapist characteristics or behaviors—apart from the therapist's adherence to a specific treatment method—predict positive therapy outcomes? It has proven surprisingly difficult to answer this question because the characteristics proposed by theorists and qualitative researchers seldom predict therapy outcomes in clinical research. Though some therapists consistently have better outcomes than others, the reasons for this are elusive.

One factor that may be important, however, is the therapist's empathy. Keijsers, Schaap, & Hoogduin (2000) reviewed the empirical literature in cognitive-behavioral therapy and concluded that treatment outcomes are best for therapists who express high levels of empathy and unconditional positive regard. These "Rogerian" qualities—empathy, warmth, positive regard—are consistently among the qualitites that therapists look for in a therapist when seeking treatment for themselves (Neukrug & Williams, 1993).

As mentioned earlier, a therapist's commitment or allegience to the kind of psychotherapy offered is also related to outcomes. Belief in, and commitment to, a particular type of therapy may affect how a therapist explains the treatment to a client, which in turn affects the clients' comprehension, commitment, sense of hope, and the therapeutic relationships (Addis & Carpenter, 2000; Keijsers et al., 2000).

What about a therapist's level of experience? As noted earlier, meta-analytic studies found little or no relationship between experience and therapeutic outcome. However, recent well-designed studies have found that therapists with more experience do tend to have better outcomes. For instance, Huppert et al. (2001) found that therapists' experience was positively related to some outcome measures in a multi-site study of cognitive-behavioral psychotherapy for depression. Of particular interest is that it was general clinical experience, not experience with cognitive-behavioral therapy specifically, that predicted more positive outcomes. The findings in this area are neither clear nor robust, but it appears that in randomized clinical trials using experienced therapists who vary in their years of experience, therapist experience does have a small but significant effect on outcomes (Beutler et al., 1994; Crits-Christoph & Mintz, 1991).

Though randomized clinical trials have not produced a very detailed picture of the competent therapist, other research designs have. One study, for example, used a peer-nomination method to identify 10 clinicians considered by their colleagues as exceptionally skillful (Jennings & Skovholt, 1999). After interviewing these "master therapists," the authors concluded that highly-skilled therapists possess characteristics that fall into three domains: cognitive (e.g., they are voracious learners who value complexity and learn from their failures), emotional (e.g., they are mentally healthy and sensitive to how deviations in their health affect treatment), and relational (e.g., they believe that therapy is strongly affected by relationship factors and are skilled in relationship building). This type of *qualitative research* offers a promising way to identify important therapist variables, but it should be interpreted cautiously until and unless those variables are associated with superior treatment outcomes in controlled experiments.

Whatever factors make it up, therapist competency appears to be relatively stable. As mentioned earlier, certain therapists consistently have above-average outcomes, while others consistently have below-average outcomes. One study (Svartberg, 1999) found that therapists who began a psychotherapy intervention with higher competency ratings retained that status. Another (Siqueland et al., 2000) found that therapists with higher competency ratings prior to training in cognitive-behavioral therapy benefitted more from the training.

Therapist factors and treatment factors interact. Specifically, the range of outcomes produced by different therapists is smaller when the therapists use highly structured (manualized) treatment protocols, and it is greater when they use less structured treatments (Crits-Christoph et al., 1991; Huppert et al., 2001). This phenomenon probably occurs because in less-structured treatment, the more-skilled therapists use treatment flexibility to capitalize on their relationship-building skills, while less-skilled therapists find that any deficits they have in these areas are magnified by any ambiguity in the treatment protocol.

The finding that certain therapists have consistently better outcomes than others, even when offering relatively structured treatments, has caught the attention of managed care providers. If research indicates that therapist skill predicts outcome better than type of treatment does, would it not make sense for managed care companies to evaluate therapists and refer clients to therapists based on some measure of those therapists' skills? This may be exactly what is happening (Messer, 2000), and this trend will put considerable pressure on clinicians to demonstrate their effectiveness. Requesting that clinicians (or practice groups) gather data to demonstrate their effectiveness is part of the movement to improve therapist *accountability* (also called *quality management* or *quality assurance*), which we will discuss in Chapter 14.

Client Variables. It has been suggested that the client is the single most important common factor in psychotherapy outcome (Bohart, 2000), but the client factor has been largely neglected in psychotherapy research (Duncan & Miller, 2000). Not everyone agrees with these assessments—one observer (Carere-Comes, 2001) warns against replacing the old hero in psychotherapy (the therapist) with a new one (the client). Nevertheless, evidence suggests that a few client characteristics do exert consistent, though modest, influences on therapy outcomes.

One of these is the client's *openness* or *level of resistance* (Orlinsky et al., 1994). Clients who are open and offer higher levels of disclosure from the beginning of therapy tend to have better outcomes (Kahn, Achter, & Shambaugh, 2001). A client's *level of distress* can also affect therapy, but the relationship between distress and outcome may not be straightforward. Some early studies found that clients with greater distress showed more improvement (e.g., Stone et al., 1961). However, more recent studies tend to find that it is clients with higher levels of distress who tend to have worse outcomes (Garfield, 1994). One possible explanation for these divergent results is that the relationship between distress and outcome may not be linear, but curvilinear (Miller & Gross, 1973). That is, the best outcomes may come to clients who are at intermediate levels of distress, while those clients with little distress and clients with extreme distress benefit less.

Like therapist variables, client variables may interact with other factors to affect outcomes. For example, one study found that clients who are impulsive and externalizing in their coping style benefit more from behavioral and cognitive-behavioral interventions than they do from insight-oriented therapies. However, for clients less externalizing in their coping style, the relationship is reversed (Beutler & Harwood, 2000). Similarly, nondirective and paradoxical therapy techniques are more effective than directive ones for clients entering therapy with high levels of resistance, but directive treatments are more effective for clients with low levels of resistence (Beutler & Harwood, 2000).

Relationship Variables. In Chapter 6, we discussed various views of the therapeutic relationship, and its measurement. Here we summarize the results of research investigating its influence on therapy outcome.

A large research literature on the therapeutic alliance now exists, including two meta-analyses conducted nearly a decade apart (Hovarth & Symonds, 1991; Martin et al., 2000). Results of these analyses reveal that the alliance is consistently one of the better predictors of therapeutic outcome. Theorists of many different persuasions support this conclusion, which has been demonstrated in many randomized clinical trials (Kopta et al., 1999). Indeed, some see overwhelming evidence for the assertion that the therapeutic relationship is the most important single factor in client change (e.g., McGuines, 2000; Sexton & Whiston, 1994). Though, again, not everyone agrees, it does appear that the therapeutic alliance has effects on therapy outcome over and above the effects of specific therapy techniques, and that it acts as both a context for treatment and an ingredient in treatment success. Still, questions about the therapeutic relationship remain: Is the relationship more important in treating certain disorders or when using certain therapies? Can the quality of the relationship be predicted before therapy starts? How can therapists be trained to improve their relationships with clients? Questions such as these are currently under investigation.

EFFECTIVENESS OF ALTERNATIVE MODES OF INTERVENTION

Less research exists on the outcome of groups, couples, and family therapies, but available results suggest that, in general, these formats for psychotherapy can have benefits that are at least equal to those of individual treatment.

Effectiveness of Group Therapy

Empirical evidence confirms that group therapy can be an effective form of treatment, especially when group members clearly understand how the group is run and what will be expected of them (Bednar & Kaul, 1994). Certain group therapy interventions appear on lists of empirically supported treatments (e.g., supportive group therapy for schizophrenia; Chambless & Ollendick, 2001), and recent meta-analyses support the efficacy of group therapy for depression (McDermut, Miller, & Brown, 2001). Better outcomes are achieved when the group is cohesive, provides accurate feedback to members, and encourages interpersonal learning and supportive interactions.

Despite these generally supportive findings, research on group therapy's effectiveness lags well behind research on the effects of individual therapy. Though some research finds that group treatment can be as beneficial as one-to-one psychotherapy (e.g., Orlinsky, Grawe, & Parks, 1994) the number of studies is small; more research is needed in order to compare group therapy with individual therapy and determine if it has specific advantages (McDermut et al., 2001). Proponents of group therapy (e.g., Scheidlinger, 2000) contend that evidence of its effectiveness will lead to its increased use because of the cost savings for clients and insurance companies.

Effectiveness of Couples Therapy

Compared with no-treatment control groups, almost all forms of marital therapy can produce significant improvements in couples' happiness and adjustment (Alexander, Holtzworth-Monroe, & Jameson, 1994). However, the magnitude or clinical significance of these improvements is frequently disappointing. More than half of treated relationships remain distressed, and even among couples who show improvement, the changes are often not large enough to allow them to view their relationship as successful or happy (Christensen & Heavy, 1999). Further, the few available long-term follow-ups on the effects of successful marital therapy indicate that 30 to 40% of couples treated with behavioral marital techniques, at least, relapse into marital discord or divorce (Jacobson, Schmaling, & Holtzworth-Munroe, 1987; Snyder, Wills, & Grady-Fletcher, 1991). One review of research in this area (Christensen & Heavey, 1999) concluded that couples therapy usually produces positive effects lasting through a 6-month follow-up, but that most couples relapse to distressed states 1 to 4 years posttreatment.

Studies comparing the effects of different theoretical approaches to marital therapy have found no major advantages for any of them in terms of immediate benefits (Snyder & Wills, 1989; Snyder, Wills, & Grady-Fletcher, 1991; Wills, Faitler, & Snyder, 1987). In one of the most comprehensive of these comparative outcome studies, Doug Snyder and his colleagues assessed the fate of 79 unhappily married couples who had been randomly assigned to behavioral marital therapy, insight-oriented marital therapy, or a wait-list control group. All treatments were conducted by well-trained and closely-supervised clinicians. After 25 sessions of therapy, both behavioral and insight couples reported significant improvements in marital satisfaction and individual adjustment compared to their pretreatment status and to couples on the waiting list. At a follow-up assessment 6 months later, these improvements tended to be well-maintained. In short, both therapies proved to be about equally effective (Snyder & Wills, 1989). Four years later, however, about half the remaining couples in both conditions reported substantial marital difficulties since termination of treatment. We say "remaining" because by that time 38% of the couples who had behavioral treatment had divorced; only 3% of the couples in the insight-oriented treatment had done so (Snyder, Wills, & Grady-Fletcher, 1991).

Though these results call into question the long-term benefits of behavioral marital therapy, critics of the study note that the form of behavioral therapy used in Snyder's research excluded many contemporary behavioral techniques, including some procedures that were offered in the insight-oriented treatment (Jacobson, 1991). Still, these results suggest to many that achieving long-term gains in a couple's happiness is difficult because it requires understanding and resolving persistent emotional conflicts, not just negotiating solutions to specific problems.

Programs aimed at enriching marital relationships or preventing marital problems in new marriages generally show positive initial effects relative to no-treatment controls (Giblin, 1986; Halweg & Markman, 1988), but, as with most forms of marital therapy, it has not been shown that these programs can produce lasting changes in long-term relationships (Christensen & Heavey, 1999; Bradbury & Fincham, 1990).

Couples therapy is sometimes used as a treatment for the couple, and sometimes used as an adjunct to treatment for one partner's individual disorders. For instance, it has been used in the treatment of depression, anxiety disorders, substance abuse, sexual disorders, and others. The involvement of a partner has obvious treatment advantages, and some of these couples interventions have shown efficacy (Chambless & Ollendick, 2001). Couples therapy has also been used in cases of domestic violence with some success (Brannen & Rubin, 1996). These are promising directions for couples therapy, yet researchers must still address the biggest problem in this area—that the initial benefits of couples therapy typically degrade over time.

Effectiveness of Family Therapy

Families who complete a course of therapy together usually show significant improvements in communication patterns and in the behavior of the family member whose problems prompted therapy in the first place (e.g., Szapocznik et al., 1986). This outcome is typically reported in empirical research on family therapy for several kinds of identified-client and family problems (Hazelrigg, Cooper, & Boudin, 1987; Shadish et al., 1993). Family therapies aimed at improving parental discipline techniques and at decreasing family members' criticism of, and emotional overinvolvement with, mentally ill relatives have proven particularly effective (e.g., Hooley, 1985; Serketich & Dumas, 1996).

Certain types of family therapy appear more successful than others. Behavioral and structural family therapies have received the strongest empirical support. Though research in this area too often focuses on nonclinical samples (Hawley et al., 2000), the superiority of these approaches in well-controlled studies is still evident. As noted in Chapter 8, each of these approaches emphasizes pragmatic changes in the way families interact and go about solving problems. Psychodynamic or humanistic family therapies that do not stress direct modification of specific symptoms and problems tend to show smaller effects.

Effectiveness of Psychosocial Rehabilitation

Recall from Chapter 8 that, unlike individual, group, couples, or family therapy, psychosocial rehabilitation programs are designed to help people with mental disorders cope with—and minimize the impact of—their problems. Do these programs reach their goals?

Several research studies have shown that psychosocial rehabilitation programs can help severely mentally ill patients learn new skills such as administering their own medication, monitoring their symptoms, engaging in appropriate social conversations, and caring for their own health and safety (Benton & Schroeder, 1990; Brekke & Long, 2000; Dilk & Bond, 1996). Such programs also show improvements in subjective variables such as client self-esteem. In a review and meta-analysis of the psychosocial rehabilitation literature, Burton (1999) concludes that psychosocial rehabilitation has strongly demonstrated its effectiveness. His research suggests that it reduces costs of treatment by more than 50%, mostly by reducing subsequent hospitalizations.

Comprehensive psychosocial rehabilitation programs have also been shown to reduce relapse rates and other crises such as arrests or imprisonment (Bond et al., 1990; Olfson, 1990). In some cases, these outcomes are achieved even though the overall rate of symptom expression has not declined significantly. In one well-conducted evaluation of Assertive Community Treatment (ACT), severely mentally ill patients were randomly assigned to either ACT or a drop-in center where they could socialize with other patients, obtain food, and engage in recreational activities (Bond et al., 1990). Outcome assessments after one year suggested that there were large differences in how often clients actually participated in their assigned services; 76% of ACT patients were active in treatment, compared to only 7% of drop-in center patients. Further, ACT patients were admitted to the state mental hospital significantly less often during the treatment year than were the drop-in center clients, they had significantly fewer contacts with the legal system, and maintained more stable housing arrangements in the community.

No particular brand of psychosocial rehabilitation has demonstrated superiority. In one study, for example, there was no difference at 2-year follow-up between supportive counseling and cognitive-behavioral therapy, though both were clearly superior to routine care (Tarrier et al., 2000). In fact, it appears to be nonspecific variables involved in longer and more intense rehabilitations, not the specific treatments used, that are associated with positive outcomes (Brekke & Long, 2000). If rehabilitation programs are not continued for at least 2 years, clients are more likely to deteriorate, be rehospitalized, and experience a reduced overall quality of life (Wallace, 1993). These results are not particularly surprising. Given that disorders such as schizophrenia impair almost all aspects of functioning, it is to be expected that, to be effective, treatment should be comprehensive and continuous.

Effectiveness of Preventive Interventions

In Chapter 8, we described a number of community psychology programs aimed at preventing mental disorders. Recall that these primary prevention programs are designed to modify social, economic, and environmental risk factors that lead to disorders or to strengthen positive qualities that can protect vulnerable individuals from developing disorders.

Some prevention programs aim at one causal variable, while others address a multitude of influences. Some are small-scale innovations funded on a shoestring; others, like Head Start, are multibillion dollar national efforts. Most important, some of these programs have been flops, while others have produced impressive successes (Burchard & Burchard, 1987; Edelstein & Michelson, 1986; Mrazek & Haggerty, 1994; Price et al., 1988). Evaluative research on prevention programs have taught community psychologists and other mental health professionals several important lessons about what makes these programs work (Coie et al., 1993; Reppucci et al., 1999).

They have learned, first, that certain risk factors—such as poverty, child abuse and family violence, infant–caregiver attachment problems, stressful life events, academic failure, and low self-esteem—can have such widespread effects on human development that they should be the main targets of prevention programs.

Second, because most mental disorders are caused by a host of social, economic, and psychological risk factors (Petraitis, Flay, & Miller, 1995), prevention programs must address these multiple risks if they are to be effective. Consistent with psychology's historical focus on the individual, earlier prevention programs focused on the individual, identifying risks and building strengths (e.g., by teaching social skills). But an approach on the individual alone is often inadequate. For example, preventing school failures among low-income children might require study-skill tutoring programs, but these programs will not help children whose parents cannot bring them to the sessions because they lack reliable transportation. An effective prevention program for these families would have to provide transportation as well as tutoring, and it would need to address social and economic influences as well.

Third, researchers have learned that the longer mental-disorder risk factors operate, the more serious their consequences (Rutter, 1997). For example, severe parental conflict early in a child's life may impair the parents' ability to supervise the child and thus make it harder for the child to achieve success in the early school years. As school performance declines, the child may suffer rejection by more successful peers, thus leading the child to affiliate with other children who are doing poorly in school. By early adolescence, these groups of unsuccessful, disaffected youngsters tend to increasingly reject prosocial expectations, which puts them at risk for antisocial behavior and substance abuse. Recognizing this "domino effect," prevention-oriented psychologists now seek to defuse risk factors as early as possible (Zigler, Taussig, & Black, 1992).

They also realize that, partly because of the "domino effect," certain risk factors are particularly dangerous during particular developmental stages. For example, the appearance of criminal activity associated with antisocial behavior disorders is most closely linked to inadequate parental monitoring and discipline in the preschool years, to disengagement, misbehavior, and poor academic performance in the primary school years, and to peer influences in adolescence. To effectively prevent these disorders, psychologists must design their programs to address the right risk factor at the right time in clients' lives (Yoshikawa, 1994).

Fourth, prevention programs must also take into account the cultural norms and traditions of the people they aim to help. In California, for instance, European

Americans now make up less than half of the state's population. By the year 2050, it is estimated that African-Americans, Hispanic-Americans, Asian-Americans, and Native Americans will be nearly 50% of the U.S. population. These demographic changes pose a fundamental challenge to preventionists because programs that work well in one cultural setting may not work well in another (Reppucci et al., 1999).

Community psychologists and other mental health professionals are using what they have learned to develop preventive interventions that are based on empirically supported theories. Recent efforts have focused especially on domestic violence, youth violence, child maltreatment, drug and alcohol use, smoking, and HIV/Aids prevention. In most cases, targeted groups have better outcomes than controls. In some instance, however, the gains from interventions do not last as long as we would like. For instance, when victims of domestic violence made use of post-shelter advocacy services, improvements that had been evident just after the intervention diminished after 6 months and sometimes disappeared in longer follow-ups (Reppucci et al., 1999).

Obstacles to Progress in Prevention. Progress toward the primary prevention of mental disorders is hampered by several problems. For one thing, many of the people for whom prevention programs are intended do not acknowledge that they are at risk for anything and may view preventive services as unnecessary or intrusive. In other words, those most in need are sometimes the least interested in what prevention scientists have to offer. Community psychologists debate the wisdom of trying to convince these people of their high-risk status because doing so can have unintended consequences that raise serious ethical questions. For example, educating people about their mental health risks might create enough anxiety about the appearance of mental disorder that the warning becomes a self-fulfilling prophecy.

The reluctance of some high-risk people to take part in prevention programs also creates a problem in evaluating these programs. If the people who end up participating in a program are at lower risk for disorder than the population for which the programs were intended, researchers may overestimate what their prevention program can accomplish in the community as a whole (Stein, Bauman, & Ireys, 1991).

Prevention programs are often initiated before there is sufficient research to support them. This happens because policy makers feel the need to address problems quickly and not wait for research, which can be very slow to emerge. As a result, some prevention programs are initiated without careful forethought about evaluation.

Finally, even when a new prevention program demonstrates success with high-risk groups, its results may not be replicable. Demonstration projects—with their full funding and large and enthusiastic staffs—are often hard to duplicate in less well-funded agencies where overworked, underpaid, and unappreciated staffers do not have the time or commitment to follow through on the project (Bauman, Stein, & Ireys, 1991).

Effectiveness of Self-Help Groups

The effects of self-help groups (SHGs) are seldom evaluated empirically. Most SHG members are simply convinced that their groups are valuable and thus see formal outcome research on them as unnecessary or even undesirable. Evaluation is further complicated by the fact that the goals of SHGs are often hard to describe precisely. The few outcome evaluations that are available have produced mixed results (Barlow et al., 2000; Moos et al., 2001; Nietzel, Guthrie, & Susman, 1991), but it generally appears that active members value their involvement in the group and experience moderate improvements in some areas of their lives. It would be helpful if SHGs were more receptive to empirical research so that clinicians could learn more about their beneficial effects and how they occur.

CLINICAL INTERVENTIONS TODAY

Social and economic realities strongly affect the research agendas and practices of clinical psychologists. Psychotherapy has been affected by the long-term trend to regard all health care as a business. From this perspective, psychotherapy research is not concerned with effectiveness so much as with *cost-effectiveness*. This change in emphasis can be see in the shifting language of psychotherapy research—the field has moved from talking about whether psychotherapy works to talking about efficacy, effectiveness, specificity, accountability, quality assurance, and continuous quality management. In this final section, we consider some of the outcomes and trends that have resulted from applying a marketplace perspective to psychotherapy and psychotherapy research.

The Influence of Managed Care

As discussed in Chapter 1, passage of the Health Maintenance Organization Act of 1973 set in motion a chain of events that transformed clinical practice. What used to be a two-party fee-for-service transaction between clients and therapists became a three-party transaction between clients, therapists, and HMOs or managed care companies. In the United States today, the kind of treatment clients receive—and the duration of that treatment—is influenced not only by therapists' judgments and preferences but also by the preferences and policies of the insurance companies and health maintenance organizations that pay those therapists' bills.

Because these managed care "third-party payers" are businesses motivated by profits, they naturally want to cover only treatments that are cost-effective and necessary. Ideally, the focus on effective treatments should maximize benefits for clients, but for many years the managed care companies' preoccupation with short-term profitability made the reality otherwise (Reed et al., 2001). Between 1988 and 1998, health care costs rose, but spending on mental health benefits were cut approximately in half (McCarthy, 1998). Under direction of managed care companies, mental health services were restricted. Reed et al. (2001) suggest that managed care companies are now realizing that severely restricting mental health benefits saves money in the short run but results in increased costs in the long run. For instance, during the years when mental health services were most drastically cut, mental health disability claims more than doubled (Owens, 1997). Particularly costly in terms of average number of days of work missed were claims for depression, heart disease, and other mental health disorders.

Fortunately, there are signs that the drastic reductions in covered services and the "shortest treatment is always best" philosophy are changing. For years, many managed care companies have attempted to contain their costs by doing *utilization reviews*. In such a review, a case manager looks at the nature of the client's problems, the therapist's treatment plan, and the therapy progress notes. The case manager—who is not likely to be a mental health professional—then determines whether the managed care plan will pay for the treatment and, if so, for how many sessions of which specific types of therapy. A case manager may decide, for example, that a depressed client can receive no more than eight sessions of psychotherapy, even though the therapist says the client's problems require more extensive treatment.

Utilization reviews have created two problems. The first is simply that these reviews are not always cost-effective. It takes personnel and infrastructure to have someone from an insurance company oversee each treatment, and those resources are often better used elsewhere. The second problem is that utilization reviews do not always result in the most effective treatments. As discussed earlier in this chapter, optimal treatment decisions are rarely a simple matter of matching a treatment and a disorder. It can be difficult for a person not well-versed in clinical psychology research to understand the results of psychotherapy research. Many clinicians argue that they are in the best position to decide on appropriate treatments, not nonclinician case managers.

As problems with case-by-case utilization reviews have become more apparent, managed care companies have considered alternate ways to reduce costs (see Reed et al., 2001, for a more extended discussion). For example, in a *risk shifting* approach, the managed care companies pay fixed monthly or yearly fees to a clinical practice and let the clinicians manage the money. For instance, if a large clinical practice contracted to provide services to 15,000 members in an insurance plan, the managed care company might pay $1 per member per month, or $15,000 per month to the practice, regardless of how many clients actually required services. Under such an arrangement, the managed care company has a fixed cost, making their financial planning easier and cheaper, and now it is the clinical practice that must worry about how to distribute the money they receive. This particular form of risk shifting is called *capitation*. State funding agencies sometimes use this approach when funding other programs, such as drug treatment. Various treatment providers might compete for the state contract, and the provider to whom the contract is awarded then has to manage the budget and provide services.

Another alternative under consideration is to require clinicians to collect and report data on the outcome of their treatment. In other words, clinicians must *demonstrate* to the insurance company the effectiveness of their work, as individuals or as a group practice. Insurance companies would then simply compare data sets and pay providers who are effective. If providers consistently fail to obtain expected outcomes with a client, managed care companies could stop paying the provider or require remedial action such as further training or a probationary period.

A related approach being considered also relies on detailed case information collected by clinicians. In this approach, third party providers would perform periodic audits of clinicians' records. These audits would require empirical data on clients for normative comparisons (e.g., how does this client's response to therapy compare with the response of the average client experiencing the same disorder or having the same characteristics?). Such audits are routinely done within the medical profession and by agencies that accredit universities, but they are a relatively new idea in the realm of psychotherapy.

These are only some of the innovative approaches taken by managed care companies in the current psychotherapy marketplace. The U.S. has no national health care system, so psychotherapy is being conducted in an environment which has been described as ". . . a scramble of market driven realignments with new roles, novel expectations, accountabilities, and unexpected winners and losers (Hacker, 1997)" (O'Neil, 2000, p. 265).

Time-Limited Therapies

Managed care reviewers' affinity for treatments that are as brief as possible tends to discourage long-term, insight-oriented therapies, and certainly much of this is justified, based on the empirical research. However, as described in Chapter 7, the idea of relatively brief treatment and the development of alternatives to psychoanalysis appeared long before the advent of managed care. These trends began in the 1930s with Franz Alexander's psychoanalytically oriented psychotherapy and gained prominence in the 1960s as clinicians found that behavioral, cognitive-behavioral, and humanisitc methods could produce benefits in months rather than years (Garfield & Bergin, 1994). By the 1980s, according to some surveys, the average psychotherapy client was being seen for only 8 to 10 sessions (Olfson & Pincus, 1994; Taube et al., 1988), but it was not lost on managed care organizations that, when clients paid a fixed health care fee instead of being charged for each session, treatment lasted an average of nearly 17 sessions (Manning, Wells, & Benjamin, 1986).

Clinicians and managed care personnel who advocate brief treatments point to evidence from meta-analyses and other sources suggesting that most improvements take place early in the therapy process, and they conclude from this evidence that treatment need not be lengthy to be effective (Austed & Berman, 1991; Bloom, 1992; Kopta et al., 1991; Steenbarger, 1994). Other clinicians challenge the validity of this conclusion (e.g., Miller, 1996a) and argue further that even if brief treatments can be effective, they may not be right for every client. Choices about the duration of treatment, they say, should reside mainly with clinicians; they are concerned that cost-driven pressure for shorter treatments will discourage comprehensive pretreatment clinical assessments and deprive some clients of the amount of treatment they need to experience long-term benefits. They point to studies showing, for example, that not all symptoms of depression improve at the same rate and that clients who received 16 therapy sessions show more permanent improvement than those whose treatment lasted only 8 sessions (Barkham et al., 1996a, 1996b). We have also reviewed evidence that longer treatments tend to produce better outcomes for clients recovering from schizophrenia.

Psychotherapy and Drug Treatments

Managed care organizations' emphasis on brief, efficient treatment has also fostered a trend toward the use of drugs, or drugs plus psychotherapy, as a way of quickly reducing the symptoms of mental disorder, especially in cases of anxiety and depression. Of course, the use of drugs in the treatment of these and many other psychological problems began almost as soon as the drugs appeared in the 1950s, well before managed care came along. But whereas only 27% of psychiatric outpatients were given drugs in 1975, that figure grew to 55% by 1988, and today, psychiatrists prescribe antidepressants, anxiolytics (anti-anxiety), and other psychotropic medication for up to 90% of their patients (Glenmullen, 2000; Olfson, Pincus, & Sabshin, 1994). These drugs are also routinely prescribed by most general practice physicians for patients complaining of anxiety, depression, eating disorders, sleep disorders, and a wide variety of other problems. In the United States alone, hundreds of millions of drug prescriptions are written every year for the treatment of mental disorders.

Combining drugs and psychotherapy can in fact be quite helpful and, in some cases, may be better than either approach alone (e.g. Hollon, 1993), but most studies have found that, for anxiety disorders and depression, at least, combined treatments do not greatly improve on what either treatment can achieve on its own (Antonuccio, Danton, & DeNelsky, 1995; Conte et al., 1986; Wexler & Cicchetti, 1992). Other studies have found that, for these disorders, psychotherapy can result in benefits that are greater and more enduring than drug treatments (e.g., Hollon & Beck, 1994; Weissman & Markowitz, 1994). Nevertheless, many clients who might once have received psychotherapy alone are now getting drugs, or drugs and psychotherapy, even though they might have done just as well without them (Barlow, 1996).

The Emergence of Practice Guidelines

Numerous sets of practice guidelines are now being published in the United States by health care corporations, by professional organizations such as the American Psychiatric Association (APA, 1995) and the American Association of Applied and Preventive Psychology (Hayes et al., 1995), and by federal government bodies such as the National Institutes of Health and the Agency for Health Care Policy and Research (Depression Guideline Panel, 1993). Guidelines are also appearing in the United Kingdom, Australia, New Zealand, and many other countries (e.g., Barlow, 1996; Roth & Fonagy, 1995; Quality Assurance Project, 1985). These guidelines are designed to steer mental health care providers toward treating specific problems—such as anxiety disorders, depression, schizophrenia, bipolar disorder, eating disorders, and substance-use disorders—with methods that maximize effectiveness while minimizing cost (VandenBos, 1993).

Practice guidelines have proven controversial because (1) they are perceived as restricting clinicians' freedom; (2) the empirical basis, and thus the validity, of some recommendations has been questioned; (3) recommendations from differing sources may be inconsistent; and (4) they tend to "medicalize" the treatment of many disorders that can be effectively treated without drugs. Indeed, the American Psychological Association has published a set of suggestions for evaluating recommendations contained in various practice guidelines (APA Board of Professional Affairs Task Force, 1995).

In an attempt to remedy the problems created by the proliferation of numerous uncoordinated practice guidelines, the Association for the Advancement of Behavior Therapy and the American Association for Applied and Preventive Psychology jointly sponsored a National Planning Summit on Scientifically Based Behavioral Health

Practice Guidelines (Hayes, 1996). The idea behind this meeting—which took place in November of 1996 and was attended by representatives of managed care organizations, government agencies, and organizations of psychiatrists, psychologists, counselors, nurses, and social workers—was to begin working toward a set of empirically based treatment guidelines that can be confidently used by all mental health practitioners, regardless of which third-party payer is involved in a client's treatment. Accomplishing this goal is a tall order, to say the least, so it is unlikely that universally agreed-upon practice guidelines will be adopted in the near future. At this point, significant problems still accompany the use of practice guidelines (Strickler, Abrahamson, Bologna, Hollon, Robinson, & Reed, 1999).

In summary, both hopeful and discouraging signs are evident in the recent trends in clinical practice. The hopeful signs suggest clinical research on effectiveness and market research on cost-effectiveness may be converging toward the realization that while some disorders are treatable with specific short-term interventions, others are best treated with longer nonspecific interventions or with combinations of therapeutic and preventive interventions. In other words, long-term effectiveness may ultimately prove to be the most cost-effective. The discouraging signs come from the continued dominance of large-scale business models in psychotherapy, which, in some formulations, run the risk of pitting client welfare against therapist or corporate profit. Clinicians will need to develop business skills that they never envisioned necessary while in graduate school, and market forces may make it more difficult for individual clinical practice, long a mainstay of clinical psychology, to survive.

CHAPTER SUMMARY

Evaluative research on clinical interventions has focused mainly on the effects of various forms of psychotherapy. The goals of this research are to answer questions about the efficacy of specific treatments, the relative effectiveness of different treatments, the components of treatment responsible for improvement, the durability of treatment benefits, the negative side effects associated with treatment, client acceptance of treatment, the cost-effectiveness of various treatments, and their clinical and social significance.

The main method for establishing a causal relationship between therapy and improvement is the controlled experiment, in which the researcher makes systematic changes in certain factors (called independent variables) and then observes changes occurring in other factors (called dependent variables). In psychotherapy-outcome research, the independent variable is usually the type of therapy given, and the dependent variable is the change seen in clients. Within-subject experiments (including reversal, or ABAB, designs) manipulate a treatment variable and observe its effects on the same client(s) at different points in time. Between-subject experiments randomly assign clients to different groups, each of which is exposed to differing treatments whose effects are compared.

Psychotherapy-outcome experiments should be designed to be as high as possible on both internal and external validity. If an experiment is high on internal validity, the researcher can be confident that observed changes in clients were actually caused by treatment, not by uncontrolled confounding factor(s). An experiment is high on external validity if its results are generalizable to clients, problems, and situations other than those included in the experiment. Unfortunately, in order to exert the experimental control necessary to maximize internal validity, researchers are usually forced to use clients, therapists, problems, treatments, and settings that may not be representative enough to allow for high external validity. External validity can be increased by studying real clients with real problems in real treatment settings, but the loss of experimental control in such studies may impair internal validity.

In spite of Hans Eysenck's initial claim that traditional psychotherapy is no more beneficial than receiving no treatment, most subsequent reviews, meta-analyses (studies that quantitatively summarize the results of many outcome experiments), and client surveys suggest that most forms of psychotherapy do produce better outcomes than no treatment. It also appears that therapists' training and experience has a less-than-expected impact on the success of treatment. The benefits of therapy often begin to appear early, in six to eight sessions, and the effects of psychotherapy are relatively durable, though often less so for couples therapy.

Perhaps the most surprising result from decades of box score reviews, meta-analyses, and surveys was that the various types of therapy are about equally effective. Despite this finding, many clinicians (and others familiar with psychotherapy), doubted whether all forms of treatment were equally beneficial for all types of clients. The movement to identify empirically supported treatments sought to address this doubt and resulted in publications of efficacious and possibly efficacious treatments, the majority of which were behavioral or cognitive-behavioral. Critics disputed the criteria used to determine ESTs, and they pointed to common or nonspecific factors that often account for more of the variance of treatment outcome.

A much smaller body of research exists for group, couples, and family therapy, though some interventions are among the empirically supported treatments. Psychosocial rehabilitation programs can help mental patients function at maximum capacity and avoid rehospitalization, especially if the patients participate in these programs for an extended period. The effects of a wide variety of programs designed to prevent mental disorders are mixed; the best of them tend to intervene early in people's lives in order to alter many of the risk factors known to be associated with specific disorders.

Today's clinical interventions are shaped not only by research on psychotherapy, psychosocial rehabilitation, and prevention programs, but also by the economic realities of health care. The policies of managed care companies, which derive from concerns about cost-effectiveness, influence how psychotherapy is practiced and how it is researched. The health care environment in which psychotherapy is practiced has been very fluid and will likely continue to change for the foreseeable future.

Chapter 10

Clinical Child Psychology

The history of clinical child psychology reveals something of a paradox. On the one hand, clinical psychology has its roots in the assessment and treatment of childhood disorders, but for much of the 20th century, behavior disorders in childhood were largely overlooked in favor of adult disorders (Rubenstein, 1948). Indeed, the study of childhood disorder was, for a long time, simply ". . . a downward extension and extrapolation from the study of psychopathology in adults" (Garber, 1984, p. 30).

This longstanding adult-oriented perspective on childhood disorders reflects the history of the very concept of childhood itself. Only recently have children been considered and treated as something other than miniature adults. This "adultomorphic" view was reinforced by psychoanalytic and behavioral approaches to therapy, both of which tended to downplay the unique nature of childhood problems (Gelfand & Peterson, 1985). Because Freud's theory focused so much on early childhood development, it may seem paradoxical to accuse psychoanalysis of adultomorphism, but Freud did not see children as good candidates for psychoanalytic treatment, and ". . . many analysts' formulations of patients' problems seem remarkably little affected by their patients' ages" (Gelfand & Peterson, 1985, p. 41). In similar fashion, the radical behavior therapy that was so influential in the 1960s and 1970s ignored the unique nature of childhood disorders. Its guiding principle was "an organism is an organism," be it a rat, a child, or an adult. Because all organisms are subject to the same laws of learning, developmental level became an irrelevant issue in treatment planning (Baer, 1973).

During the last three decades, this adult-oriented approach to children's behavior disorders has given way to a more child-centered approach. This new approach highlights several aspects of childhood that make it inappropriate to try using adult models of psychopathology to understand children's disorders. Clinical child psychologists are also discovering that traditional adult-oriented methods of classification, assessment, and intervention may have limited relevance for childhood disorders. The changing approach to child clients appeared in DSM-III, which was the first version of DSM to make specific recommendations concerning developmental considerations in the diagnostic criteria for childhood disorders. Today, DSM-IV contains more than two dozen Axis I disorders specific to children. In addition, since 1970 several major new journals have appeared—such as the *Journal of Abnormal Child Psychology*, the *Journal of Clinical Child and Adolescent Psychology*, and *Development and Psychopathology*—devoted entirely to research on childhood behavior disorders. At the start of the millennium, two new divisions of the APA were created devoted entirely to children's behavioral, learning, and medical problems—Division 53 (Clinical Child and Adolescent Psychology) and Division 54 (Pediatric Psychology). Finally, a new field of study known as developmental psychopathology has evolved to study childhood disorders from a developmental perspective. Scientists working in this field focus on how various adaptive and maladaptive patterns of behavior are manifested during various stages of development (Rutter & Sroufe, 2001). Developmental psychopathologists also study how children develop competencies as well as disorders (Masten, 2001), and they try to learn about protective factors that prevent some children at risk for disorders from actually developing them (Mash & Dozois, 1996). Developmental psychopathologists also are interested in how the study of normal child development can enhance our understanding of disordered development.

After so many years of neglect, why is so much attention being devoted to understanding and treating childhood psychopathology? First, psychopathology is relatively common in childhood; 8 to 22% of children are diagnosed with a behavioral, emotional, or learning disorder (Mash & Dozois, 1996; U.S. Surgeon General, 1999). Second, many childhood disorders (e.g., conduct disorders, learning disabilities, autism) have lifelong consequences for the affected individual, the family, and society at large. Third, most adult disorders have their roots in childhood disorders, many of which go undiagnosed and untreated. One study found that fewer than 15% of children with a diagnosable psychiatric disorder had received any outpatient mental health services in the preceding year (Goodman et al., 1997). Fourth, by studying the risk factors, causes, and courses of childhood disorders, we may be better able to develop effective early intervention programs that prevent childhood problems from escalating into adult psychopathology. Finally, media attention devoted to some high-profile, child-related problems—school violence, the potential misuse of Ritalin, the increase in reported child abuse cases—has caused society to reevaluate the mental health status of children, and has led to the development of a number of national task forces, a Surgeon General's Report on children's mental health (U.S. Public Health Service, 2000), and White House conferences devoted to understanding and ameliorating childhood mental health problems.

In this chapter, we discuss several characteristics and concerns that differentiate clinical child psychology from the general field of clinical psychology. We first provide an overview of clinical child psychology, and then focus on the classification, assessment, and treatment of childhood disorders.

CHARACTERISTICS UNIQUE TO CLINICAL CHILD PSYCHOLOGY

In dealing with their young clients, clinical child psychologists must pay special attention to a number of factors that differentiate childhood disorders from those seen in adult disorders. These include the nature of the referral process, developmental considerations, infant temperament factors and the quality of infants' early attachments, the reciprocal nature of parent–child interactions, and the unique impact of childhood stressors. A guiding principle of clinical child psychology is that children exist in a number of contexts (e.g., the family, school, the peer group), and in order to understand a given child's problems, it is necessary to understand the problems within the situational contexts in which the child resides.

Referral Processes

When adults feel distressed they can seek professional help, but children must depend on parents, teachers, or other significant people in their lives to determine whether they need the help of a mental health professional. A child may suffer considerable distress, but if the parents are unaware of, or are indifferent to, the problem, the child will not receive needed attention. Conversely, as noted in our discussion of family therapy in Chapter 8, children may be referred to a mental health professional for reasons that have more to do with parental or family problems than with the child's emotional or behavioral characteristics (Christensen, Margolin, & Sullaway, 1992). Among the parental factors that influence whether children will be referred for psychological help is the parents' level of tolerance for certain behaviors. For example, parents who perceive noncompliance as temporary and manageable are less likely to seek help for their child than are parents who see the same behavior as permanent and unmanageable (Shepherd, Oppenheim, & Mitchell, 1971; see also, Johnston & Freeman, 1997).

Maternal depression is another factor that may influence the referral of children for clinical intervention. Research consistently shows that the more depressed mothers feel, the more likely they are to see their children as behaviorally disordered (Griest, Wells, & Forehand, 1979; Webster-Stratton, 1988). There are several possible explanations of these correlational findings (Richters, 1992). Maternal depression may indeed lead mothers to view their children as disordered; depressed individuals see many aspects of their world in a negative light. Or, it might be that unmanageable child behavior contributes to the mothers' feelings of helplessness and depression. It may even be that a third factor, such as the father's indifference or abusive behavior, could account for both the mother's depression and the child's behavioral problems. Whatever the case, results such as these suggest that mothers' emotional states may influence how they perceive their children's behavior, their own capacity to cope with it, and thus the likelihood of referring children for professional help. (Fathers' emotional states appear less influential; Webster-Stratton, 1988.) The message for child clinicians is that the child's referral must be understood in terms of family contextual factors that may be contributing to the child's problem and/or the parents' perception of the problem. As we will see, this has implications for the assessment data collected, the manner in which the child's problems are conceptualized, and the treatment that is undertaken.

Developmental Considerations

The particularly rapid physical, psychological, and social developments that occur in childhood have profound implications for clinical child psychology. For one thing, clinicians must evaluate the appropriateness or inappropriateness of a child's behavior relative to developmental norms in the child's culture. Thus, intense fears or bedwetting might be considered normal in young children, but symptoms of disorder in older children (Campbell, 1989). In fact, most symptoms of childhood disorders tend to be seen as appropriate, or at least typical, behavior at an earlier stage of development. With the exception of symptoms associated with autism, mental retardation, and other severe disorders, the appropriateness of children's behavior must be evaluated in light of their developmental stage (Mash & Dozois, 1996).

Theoretical explanations of children's problems also must take developmental factors into account. For example, learned helplessness—the belief that one cannot control future events—is a powerful model for explaining depression in adults. Adults susceptible to such beliefs tend to attribute their failures to permanent internal characteristics ("I failed the test because I am stupid"), whereas a psychologically healthier response would be to make temporary, external attributions ("The test was unfair" or "I did not study enough this time"). A major premise of this model is that failures produce a sense of helplessness among some adults when they perceive there is nothing they can do to alter outcomes. However, a developmental study of causal attributions found that younger children (kindergarten, first-, third-graders) were less susceptible to helpless attributions following failure than were older children (fifth-graders; Rholes et al., 1980). One reason for the difference may be that younger children do not see ability as a stable attribute, so failures do not imply stable limitations on their likelihood of future successes. Younger children's attributional style may protect them against the onset of perceived helplessness. With increasing age, children may become more realistic—and perhaps more pessimistic—about their capabilities (Ruble & Rholes, 1981).

If clinicians are to avoid making errors in identifying or explaining children's disorders, it is important that they familiarize themselves with the developmental literature on what is normative at different stages of development, as well as on theories that underlie the development of normal and dysfunctional behavior (Rutter & Sroufe, 2001). Thus, a clinician working with children needs to have a strong background in normal developmental psychology in addition to training in abnormal child psychology.

Infant Temperament

Child clinicians need a good understanding of the role of individual differences, including differences in *infant temperament* in creating risk for or protection against subsequent behavior problems. Several landmark studies have discovered reliable temperamental differences that appear at birth and have both short-term and long-term implications (Thomas, Chess, & Birch, 1968; Thomas & Chess, 1977; Chess & Thomas, 1986).

"Easy" children adapt well to new situations, are not easily upset, show regularity in biological functions such as feeding and sleeping, and pose few problems for their parents. Parents whose first child displays this "easy" temperament often wonder why other parents complain so much about child-rearing problems. The reason is that some of them have a "difficult" child, who is easily upset, is irregular in biological functioning, shows intense and often negative reactions to environmental changes, and in general drains the parents' energy and patience. Indeed, the parents of a "difficult" first child may wonder at times whether they ever want to have another child. The "slow-to-warm-up" child falls somewhere between the "easy" and "difficult" types, and tends to be shy and anxious.

One of the most important implications of infant temperament for clinical child psychology is that "difficult" infants tend to be at greatly increased risk for developing conduct problems, stormy relationships with peers, and academic difficulties when they enter first grade (Thomas et al., 1968). Further, temperament at age 3 has also been found to predict behavioral problems 12 years later (Caspi et al., 1995) and personality traits 15 years later (Caspi & Silva, 1995). These data suggest that some childhood behavioral problems are partly a function of the child's innate biological characteristics. These findings have created a renewed interest in the diathesis-stress model of psychopathology, which, as described in Chapter 2, emphasizes the interaction between biological predisposition and environmental stressors in producing behavior problems.

Jerome Kagan's (1989) research on overly inhibited children provides an excellent example of how early temperament can act as a diathesis in the development of subsequent clinical difficulties. Kagan found that 10 to 15% of very young children are constitutionally shy and inhibited in unfamiliar situations. Compared to noninhibited children, they tend to be more behaviorally cautious, motorically tense, and physiologically aroused. When asked to fall backwards onto a mattress, for example, overly inhibited children are more likely to fall into a sitting position rather than relax and let gravity take over completely. Similarly, overly inhibited children have higher heart rates and increased cardiac acceleration in response to mild stressors. Being overly inhibited appears to be a stable characteristic that places these children at increased risk for developing various anxiety disorders, much as children with difficult, underinhibited temperaments tend to be at higher risk for conduct disorders (Nietzel et al., 1998). In short, children at opposite ends of the temperament spectrum seem to carry a diathesis for different kinds of disorders. Whether the children actually display these disorders, of course, depends on the influence of various risk (e.g., school failure, parental depression) and protective (e.g., close relation with an adult, high IQ, good problem-solving skills) factors.

Thus, almost all childhood disorders are seen now as an interaction between the child's characteristics (e.g., predispositions) and the environmental contexts in which they find themselves. An excellent example of this interaction effect is a study by Lynam et al. (2000), which found that childhood impulsivity was a risk factor for juvenile offending but that this risk was greatly enhanced if the child lived in a poor neighborhood. Interestingly, nonimpulsive children who lived in poor neighborhoods were at no increased risk for offending.

Early Attachment

Another developmental consideration for understanding children's behavior disorders is the nature and quality of the *attachment* that develops between infants and their caregivers. According to the object relations theories described in Chapter 7, the nature and quality of the infant-caregiver attachment—especially in the first year of life—play a crucial role in shaping the child's later personality and behavior (Jones, 1996). Attachment theory has led many clinical child psychologists to look for links between the nature of infants' early attachments and the appearance of psychopathology in childhood, adolescence, and adulthood (Cicchetti, Toth, & Lynch, 1995).

According to attachment theory, infants have an innate need to form a strong emotional bond with at least one caregiver, and they arrive with a built-in repertoire of behaviors—such as smiling and cooing—designed to maintain proximity to the caregiver. Separation from the caregiver produces crying and other distress reactions designed to get the caregiver's attention and services (Beck, 1991; Bowlby, 1969). From an evolutionary perspective, these behaviors are adaptive because they increase the likelihood that the caregiver will meet the infant's needs, thereby increasing its chances for survival.

John Bowlby, a British psychiatrist and psychoanalyst, developed an influential version of attachment theory while assessing the mental health needs of very young children who were orphaned and left homeless by World War II (Bowlby, 1969; Zeanah, 1996). Inspired by earlier research on insitutionalized infants, (Spitz, 1946), Bowlby suggested that the depression, weight loss, and other psychological and physical problems shown by some of these infants stemmed from the fact that, although orphanages were meeting their charges' physical needs, there were not enough caregivers available to allow the infants to form a firm attachment to at least one caregiver. This idea is consistent with the results of experiments by Harry Harlow (e.g., Harlow & Zimmerman, 1959) in which monkeys deprived of attachment experiences from infancy displayed a variety of emotional problems.

Mary Ainsworth, an American psychologist, is credited with developing an experimental procedure, called the Strange Situation, for measuring the nature and quality of 1- to 2-year-old children's attachments to their caregivers (Ainsworth & Wittig, 1969). The Strange Situation exposes children to several stressors and observes their reactions to each. First, the mother and child enter a playroom and the clinician observes the child's ability to separate from the mother and explore. Then, a stranger enters the room and starts talking with the mother. Shortly thereafter, the mother leaves the room for approximately 3 minutes, then returns. In another episode, the baby is left alone in the room for up to 3 minutes.

The child's responses to separations from the mother and to subsequent reunions with her are the primary targets of measurement. Using the Strange Situation, Ainsworth found that most babies (about 70%) displayed what she called *secure attachment,* while the rest showed insecure forms of attachment. Subsequent work has identified three types of insecure attachments: *avoidant, resistant/ambivalent*, and *disorganized/disoriented* (Beck, 1991). Securely attached babies, even if distressed by their mother's departure, are easily comforted by her return. Insecurely attached infants either avoid the mother when she returns (the avoidant type) or approach her but are not comforted by her (the resistant/ambivalent type). The disorganized/disoriented group display the greatest apparent insecurity, and their responses are often contradictory (e.g., approaching the mother but looking away). According to attachment theory, these different patterns of responding are assumed to be determined by the babies' experiences with their caregivers. Securely attached infants have been found to have warm, loving mothers who are sensitive to their needs, whereas insecurely attached infants tend to have distant, rejecting, or inconsistent mothers (Cicchetti et al., 1995).

Attachment theorists argue that people's view of themselves, as well as the quality of all subsequent relationships, are colored by the kind of attachment they had with their caregiver in infancy. For example, infants whose attachment was impaired by the behavior of distant, insensitive mothers may come to view themselves as unworthy of love, and, in adulthood, they may never find close relationships capable of meeting their emotional needs. Work in this area has also suggested that infants who experienced different types of insecure attachments may be at risk for different types of disorders (Cicchetti et al., 1995). Thus, aggressive behavior in children has been found to be associated with the disorganized/disoriented pattern of attachment (Lyons-Ruth, 1996), whereas depressive disorders tend to be associated with insecure-avoidant attachment (Cicchetti et al., 1995). Researchers also have found evidence of early attachment types in the behavior of adolescents and adults (Main, 1996) and have related these patterns to the appearance of a variety of disorders (del Carmen & Huffman, 1996). It is interesting to note, however, that a recent cross-cultural analysis reveals that what is considered a healthy attachment style in our Western culture, with its emphasis on independence and individuation, may not be considered the child rearing ideal in Eastern cultures, such as Japan, with their emphasis on dependence and collectivism (Rothbaum, Weisz, Pott, Miyake, & Morelli, 2000).

Given the apparent relation between insecure attachment and later behavior problems, recent work has attempted to develop therapeutic interventions to counteract the negative effects of insecure attachments. These interventions focus on increasing the mother's sensitivity toward her infant by training the mothers first to recognize their infants' attachment signals and then to respond to them quickly and appropriately (van Ijzendoorn, Juffer, & Duyvesteyn, 1995). A meta-analysis of the initial intervention studies suggests that the interventions are successful in decreasing parental insensitivity, but much less successful in decreasing the insecure attachment of the child (van Ijzendoorn et al., 1995). The findings of this meta-analysis raise an important cautionary note about intervention directed toward altering the infant-caregiver attachment. Although caregivers obviously play a crucial role in the attachment process, it is important not to give them all the credit or blame for the kind of attachment that develops with their babies. It is also the case that infants differ in their ability to form attachments with a caregiver, and differences in temperament may make it easier or harder for caregivers to form attachments to them. Indeed, the quality of attachment probably results from the mutual influence of caregiver and infant characteristics (Greenberg, Speltz, & DeKlyen, 1993; Sroufe, 1985).

Parent–Child Interaction Patterns

Research on infant temperament and the related emphasis on the diathesis-stress model has influenced clinical child psychologists to pay closer attention to what the *child* brings to the parent-child relationship (Thomas & Chess, 1977). These studies showed, for example, that initial assessments of parent–child interactions across the three infant-temperament categories showed few differences. During subsequent assessments, however, the parents of "difficult" infants issued more controlling statements and engaged in more punitive interactions with their children. These results suggest that, to some extent, at least, it is the child's difficult behavior that creates—or triggers—parents' inappropriate reactions.

This temperament-related interpretation of parent–child interactions contrasts with the traditional view that child psychopathology is mainly the result, not the cause, of faulty parenting. For example, researchers have found that the punitive behavior often shown by the parents of children with ADHD has more to do with the children's behavior than the parents' disciplinary style. In one study, when children with ADHD were given medication that improved their behavior, their parents immediately behaved more positively toward them (Barkley & Cunningham, 1979). Similar effects have been seen in the behavior of the teachers and peers of such children (Cunningham, Siegel, & Offord, 1985; Whalen, Henker, & Dotemoto, 1980).

A final example of the powerful effects of children's behavior on their parents comes from a study that investigated the relation between adult alcohol consumption and child behavioral problems (Pelham et al., 1997). Parental alcohol problems can certainly contribute to behavior disorders in their children, but this study addressed the reciprocal question: Can child behavior disorders contribute to adult alcohol consumption? To find out, 60 parents of normal children were asked to interact with either a normal child or a boy trained to act like a child with ADHD. The parents were told that the purpose of the study was to examine the effects of adult alcohol consumption on child behavior. After this initial, baseline interaction, the parents were allowed to drink as much of their preferred alcoholic beverage as they wanted before going back for a second interaction. The second interaction never took place, however, because the researchers were interested only in how much alcohol the parents consumed and how distressed they reported feeling during the first interaction. The results indicated that parents who interacted with the "hyperactive" child were significantly more distressed than those who spent time with the normal child, and they consumed significantly more alcohol than did parents in the "normal" condition. Thus, having a distressing interaction with a difficult-to-manage child was associated with significantly greater distress and alcohol consumption.

In summary, clinical child psychologists now realize that it is overly simplistic to attribute all children's behavioral problems to faulty parenting. It is equally unlikely, however, that all child psychopathology can be understood exclusively in terms of the child's characteristics. The parent–child relationship, like all dyadic interactions, is reciprocal in nature; the child's temperament and behavior affect the parents, and parental tolerance and responses alter the child's behavior. The term *goodness-of-fit* has been used to capture the idea that whether a child develops a behavioral problem is partially a function of the degree to which the child's temperament and the parental response style are concordant (Thomas & Chess, 1977). The greater the mismatch (e.g., rigid parents with a "difficult" infant), the greater the likelihood that the child will be at risk for subsequent problems.

Many of the advances in understanding and treating childhood behavior disorders that have occurred in the last three decades have been made by theorists who take this reciprocal or bidirectional view of parent–child interactions. An example of just such a perspective, and how it has advanced our understanding of children's behavior problems, can be seen in Patterson's (1976, 1982) "coercion-escalation hypothesis" of aggressive behavior, which focuses on the reciprocal nature of interactions between aggressive children and their parents. As would be expected from our earlier discussion, Patterson's detailed observations in the homes of normal and aggressive children showed that in both kinds of homes, parents' behavior alters the probability of certain child responses, just as the children's behavior alters the likelihood of certain parental responses (Patterson et al., 1969). However, Patterson also saw important differences in the family interactions of normal versus aggressive children. For example, aggressive children were twice as likely as nonaggressive children to persist in their aversive behavior following parental punishment (Patterson, 1976).

Rather than seeing this pattern as reflecting parents' ineffective punishment tactics or children's insensitivity to the consequences of their behavior, Patterson looked at how parents and children "teach" each other to adopt and rely on coercive, aversive control tactics that can lead to childhood aggressiveness. Here is a simple example: Suppose that Mrs. Jones has just picked up her 3-year-old son, Billy, from day-care and they are now at the grocery store, buying food for dinner. As they pass a freezer case, Billy asks for an ice cream bar but Mrs. Jones says, "No, you'll spoil your dinner." Billy responds by throwing a temper tantrum, which creates a problem for Mrs. Jones because she needs to finish her shopping and, besides, it is embarrassing to have her child acting out-of-control in public. Mrs. Jones solves the problem by giving Billy an ice cream bar, but with the admonition that this is the last time he will get one this close to dinner. Billy's tantrum stops immediately, and the shopping proceeds.

What do Billy and his mother learn from this interaction? First, Billy learns that if he throws a temper tantrum when his mom says "No," he can get his way (tantrum-throwing is positively reinforced). At the same time, Mrs. Jones is reinforced for acceding to Billy's demands—especially when he throws a tantrum in public—because doing so terminates his aversive and humiliating behavior. The principles of operant conditioning outlined in Chapter 7 suggest that both Billy and his mother will behave in similar ways when confronted with similar situations in the future. Billy will throw tantrums, and Mrs. Jones, despite her best intentions to the contrary, will give in to them. Indeed, not giving in will probably cause Billy to escalate the intensity of his tantrum—perhaps including physical aggression or damage to property—until Mrs. Jones feels she has no choice but to give him what he wants. This family dyad has fallen into what Patterson (1982) called the "reinforcement trap"—each obtains a short-term benefit at the expense of undesirable long-term consequences. As Billy becomes harder to manage, his parents may resort to more aversive methods to control him.

As discussed later, Patterson's work on understanding children's aggressive behavior from the perspective of reciprocal interactions between parents and children has led to the development of a systematic and widely employed behavioral intervention program for dealing with such problems (Patterson & Forgatch, 1987). The program focuses on changing the parents' interactions with their children to decrease the occurrence of coercive exchanges.

Childhood Stressors

Adopting a diathesis-stress model of psychopathology requires clinical child psychologists to look not only at diatheses (such as temperament, attachment problems, cognitive deficits, and genetic influences), but also at a variety of environmental stressors that are likely to make expression of disorder more likely. Among these stressors are maladaptive parenting (including physical or sexual abuse), parental disability, psychopathology or discord, multiple hospitalizations, loss of a parent through divorce or death, the birth of a sibling, exposure to poverty, and the trauma of war (Freud & Burlingham, 1943; Garmezy, 1983; Lyons, 1971). Here we focus on three common childhood stressors—starting school, parental marital conflict, and abuse.

Starting School. Because it is mandatory in North America and many other cultures, going to school constitutes the single greatest source of stress for many children. Indeed, the age of 6—when most children enter first grade—is the peak referral point for childhood disorders, including learning disabilities, attention deficit hyperactivity disorder, conduct and oppositional disorders, and peer relationship difficulties. Most of these problems stem from, arise in, or are exacerbated by the school environment.

What is it about school that makes it such a potent stressor? For most children, the school environment offers a major change in the expectations placed on them and the rules to be followed. Consider what is required of children entering first grade. They must sit quietly for what seems to them to be long periods of time while focusing their attention on mastering complex new skills (e.g., reading, math) that make heavy demands on the children's cognitive resources. Further, they need a certain amount of social skill in order to be accepted by and succeed with their peers. Finally, children must constantly comply with their teacher's requests. Children who fail at one or more of these tasks are very likely to be labeled as displaying one of the primary behavior disorders of childhood, which tend to involve learning difficulties, noncompliance, peer conflicts or rejection, and attentional problems and disruptive behavior.

Because most child referrals involve some form of school-related difficulties, clinicians routinely collect assessment data directly from the school setting (usually in the form of teacher ratings or observations) or from school-related measures such as achievement tests. Accordingly, clinical child psychologists must be knowledgeable about what is considered normal and abnormal in school functioning—including how learning disabilities are assessed and diagnosed—as well as about legal issues affecting school referrals and placements. Clinical treatment of children often takes place in the school and may involve training teachers in classroom management procedures (Walker, Colvin, & Ramsey, 1995) or helping them develop social-skills training programs for their students (Goldstein & McGinnis, 1997). In addition, clinical child psychologists may find themselves seeking compromises between the wishes of the school (e.g., to place a disruptive child in a special class) and the concerns of parents (e.g., to avoid stigmatizing their child with a "special class" label). Working in school settings also helps clinical child psychologists understand how those settings can either increase or decrease the likelihood of behavioral and learning problems (Rutter et al., 1979) and how important school-based programs can be in efforts at primary prevention of behavior disorders (see Chapter 8).

Parental Conflict and Divorce. Exposure to parental conflict and divorce creates several sources of stress, all of which can have significant effects on children's physical, psychological, and behavioral functioning. For one thing, the child's standard of living often falls as parents shoulder the financial burden of maintaining two households. Children also may be caught up in the turmoil of a custody battle between their parents, and even if not, may have to shuttle between, and adapt to, differing home environments and parenting practices. Further, parenting skills often deteriorate, partly because each parent may now have to work alone, and partly because they may be experiencing depression, anger, and other psychological problems that impair their effectiveness as sources of discipline, guidance, and support. Finally, should one or both parents remarry, children must deal with a stepparent and, perhaps, stepsiblings (Hetherington & Arasteh, 1988). Even then, the children of divorce are not out of the woods, because remarried parents are at increased risk for subsequent separations and divorce (Hetherington, Stanley-Hagan, & Anderson, 1989).

When children are exposed to so many stressors at once, the likelihood of mental health problems increases dramatically (Rutter, 1981). Boys, especially, tend to show marked increases in aggressive and noncompliant behavior, as well as disruptions in school work and peer relations during the two years following their parents' divorce. For girls, the findings are not as dramatic or clear-cut. The post-divorce problems that girls display tend to be less severe and to disappear in a year or so. This sex difference may be attributed to the tendency for boys to act out their problems and for girls to internalize them, thus making them less obvious. However, there is some evidence that divorce-related stress may result in delayed problems for girls, especially regarding heterosexual relations, early pregnancy, and decreased educational achievement (Hetherington et al., 1998).

Individual differences in children can influence the effects that divorce has on them. For example, temperamentally "difficult" children show more adverse effects of divorce than do "easy" children (Hetherington et al., 1998). Age is also a factor. Preschool children often respond to divorce with behavioral regression and separation anxiety, whereas the most striking response of older children is intense anger at one or both parents (Wallerstein, Corbin, & Lewis, 1988).

Exactly how does divorce produce negative consequences in children? Is it the fact that the child now lives mainly with one parent (the mother, typically) and sees the other one much less frequently, if at all? The consensus among clinical child psychologists is that separation per se does not produce the adverse behavioral consequences associated with divorce (Emery, 1982). Instead, the active component appears to be the amount and intensity of marital conflict taking place prior to, during, and after the divorce. Relatively amicable divorces produce much less psychological and behavioral disturbance in children than stormy ones.[1] Thus, when parents in distressed relationships ask clinical psychologists whether they should stay together for the benefit of the children, a common response is, "not if there is a high degree of conflict between you."

Clinical child psychologists are paying increasing attention to helping parents and children cope with the stressors associated with the dissolution of marriage or other long-term relationships (Grych & Fincham, 1992). For example, one program designed to help children cope with separation and divorce emphasizes three goals: (1) social support, whereby children are taught to share their feelings with other children facing similar situations; (2) self-statement modifications, in which the children are trained to identify problem areas which they can and cannot control; and (3) training in appropriate ways of expressing anger (Pedro-Carroll & Cowen, 1985). Intervention programs have also been created for divorcing parents (Bloom, Hodges, & Caldwell, 1982). In these programs, parents are taught how to cope with their own feelings and how to help their children adjust to the disruptions in their lives (Grych & Fincham, 1992).

Child Abuse. The scope and seriousness of child abuse only came to public attention in the United States in the late 1960s and early 1970s, as signaled by the publication of a book called *The Battered Child Syndrome* (Helfer & Kempe, 1968). In 1974, the U.S. Congress passed the Federal Child Abuse Prevention and Treatment Act, and, since then, reports of abuse have increased dramatically. Between 1986 and 1993 the rates of reported abuse doubled (Mash & Wolfe, 2002), and it is now estimated that child abuse results in 570,000 serious injuries a year (Sedlak & Broadhurst, 1996). The increase in abuse reports may reflect some increase in the incidence of abusive behavior, but it also reflects major changes in public and professional sensitivity to and awareness of the problem of abuse. Thus, in 1976, only 10% of the U.S. population thought abuse was a serious problem; 90% of the population thought so 10 years later (Wicks-Nelson & Israel, 1991). All U.S. states have made it a legal requirement that any teacher, physician, psychologist, or other health professional who suspects abuse must report the case to the appropriate social agencies.

The battered child syndrome originally centered on severe physical abuse (Helfer & Kempe, 1968). It was diagnosed from evidence of inexplicable or repeated injuries detected in X-rays and physical examinations. However, the definition of child abuse has now broadened to include neglect, psychological abuse, sexual abuse, and exploitation. Neglect refers to failure to sufficiently meet children's physical and/or emotional needs. Psychological abuse has proven more difficult to define; it consists of verbal and emotional assaults against the child, including rejection, degradation, and terrorizing (Hart & Brassard, 1987). Today, physically battered children make up only a minority of reported abuse cases. Not surprisingly, the primary perpetrators of neglect and physical and sexual abuse are parents, although siblings and other relatives, babysitters and day-care workers also may be responsible.

---

[1]Obviously, a major confound in these studies is that conflict-filled divorces are more likely in families in which there had been higher rates of discord and aggression all along. Thus, children in these families may have been predisposed to aggressive and noncompliant behavior (Block et al., 1986).

It is a common misconception among the public and professionals alike that if you were abused as a child, you are doomed to perpetuate the cycle by becoming an abusing parent. However, there is evidence that only about a third of abused children become abusive parents (Kaufman & Zigler, 1987). Although this tragic figure greatly exceeds the rate for nonabused children, it still means that the majority of abused children do not become abusive parents. Another misconception is that the vast majority of abusive parents suffer from mental disorders. In fact, most of these people do not meet diagnostic criteria for any psychiatric disorder (Mash & Wolfe, 2002). So what does cause parents to abuse their children? Three general factors have been identified (Wicks-Nelson & Israel, 1991): (1) social and cultural influences, including poverty, stress, and a tolerance for violence and harsh disciplinary procedures; (2) parents' personal characteristics, including a history of abuse, low frustration tolerance, and aggressiveness; and (3) difficulties in the parent–child interaction, including inappropriate parental expectations or explanations for the child's behavior, ineffective disciplinary practices, and a temperamentally "difficult" child.

Research suggests that abused children are at increased risk for behavioral and emotional problems, though not for any specific disorder (Browne & Finkelhor, 1986). Abused children are prone to later school failure, aggressiveness, depression, peer problems, and impaired sexual and marital relationships. In addition, these children tend to develop insecure attachments, to view interpersonal relationships as coercive, threatening, and unpredictable, and to interpret the behavior of others in a hostile and suspicious manner (Mash & Dozois, 1996). Finally, as many as 20% of abuse victims show serious psychopathology in adulthood, including depression, substance use, sexual dysfunctions, eating disorders, and personality disorders (Finkelhor & Browne, 1988). In addition, anywhere from 25 to 50% of children and adolescents who have been abused meet criteria for PTSD (Mash & Wolfe, 2002).

Historically, the primary intervention for abused children has been to place them in foster care. The goal, obviously, is to remove children from dangerous environments and provide them with a stable and therapeutic setting. However, foster care has been criticized for several reasons. First, it is expensive. Second, although it was designed to be short-term in nature, it is not uncommon for abused children to spend many years living in a series of foster homes. Foster care placement is also designed to provide a respite for abusing parents during which time they could learn more appropriate parenting skills, but the necessary training often does not occur and when periods of separation are extended, it becomes difficult to reintegrate the child into the family home.

Today, treatment and prevention of child abuse focuses on working with both the victims and their parents (Wolfe, 1987). Intervention with parents usually concentrates on helping them to improve their disciplinary practices so as to reduce out-of-control incidents, on educating them about realistic expectations for their child's behavior, on training them in anger control and stress management, and on providing social support for those who feel isolated. Treatment also may focus on alleviating parents' marital discord, depression, or other problems that heighten the likelihood of child abuse. Interventions with abused children may involve an environmental enrichment program for those who exhibit developmental delays due to neglect or abuse. Alternatively, the intervention may be directed at specific behavioral or emotional problems arising from the abusive environment. For example, social skills training may be offered to socially withdrawn children, whereas impulse (or anger) control training or supportive therapy may be used with children experiencing emotional problems. Finally, some form of individual or group therapy may be provided for the victims of abuse. The goal of this therapy is to provide a safe environment in which children can express their feelings and gain a better understanding of what happened to them—including the fact that they are not responsible for their parents' abusiveness (Wenar, 1994). The therapy sessions also give children a chance to form a supportive relationship with an adult. There is evidence that having such a relationship with one adult can serve as a buffer against the effects of adverse environmental events, including maladaptive parenting.

CLINICAL ASSESSMENT OF CHILDREN

For both children and adults, the assessment process is designed to serve a number of purposes, including arriving at a diagnosis, making treatment recommendations, and offering information about long-term prognosis. However, as we noted at the beginning of this chapter, clinical child psychologists must take special note of the child referral processes, developmental considerations, mandatory school attendance policies, and social/familial factors that make childhood disorders different from adult disorders.

Recognition of these special issues also influences how clinicians collect assessment data regarding childhood disorders. For one thing, because parents and teachers refer children for mental health services, paramount attention is given to information supplied by these adults during interviews and on behavior rating scales. In contrast, less attention is given to the reports offered by the child clients themselves about their problems. The validity of child self reports tends to be limited by the children's often unreliable memories and concrete cognitive styles (Edelbrock et al., 1985). Second, children's behavior is context dependent, so that child assessment must be comprehensive, gathering information from multiple sources reflecting the child's major life domains, including school, family, and peer group (Kamphaus & Frick, 1996). Because the majority of child referrals pertain in some fashion to school-based problems, the clinical assessment of children routinely includes an evaluation of school performance, including intelligence and achievement testing as well as actual school behavior. Third, children's emotional and behavioral states depend heavily on the nature of their family life. Accordingly, assessment of children often includes exploration of the child's behavior within the family (e.g., observations of mother–child interactions), as well as assessment of parental functioning (e.g., maternal depression, marital discord). Thus, a standard assessment battery for children includes behavior rating scales from multiple informants, clinical interviews, intelligence and achievement testing, structured observations, and an evaluation of family functioning.

We noted in Chapter 3 that market forces (e.g., restrictions imposed by third-party payers) have fostered a trend toward briefer, more problem-focused assessment in clinical practice. Child assessment is not immune to these forces. For example, as noted in this chapter, observations of the child in the home or school, which were once quite routine, are now almost never undertaken. However, because children's problems can occur in several different domains (e.g., home, school, peer group), clinical assessment still must be comprehensive. Fortunately, as described later, reliable and valid data can be obtained from parents and teachers through the use of inexpensive behavior rating scales. Further, legal mandates require intellectual and achievement testing if a question of a learning disability arises. As a result, it may well be that child assessments will never be as brief and focused as those done with adults.

Behavior Rating Scales

Behavior rating scales have become a standard part of almost all child assessment batteries. The rating scales generally consist of a list of child behavior problems (e.g., fidgets, easily distracted, shy and withdrawn), and the parent or teacher rates each behavior according to how much it represents a problem for the child (e.g., not at all, a little bit, somewhat, or a great deal). Behavior rating scales differ in their coverage, with some focusing on specific disorders (e.g., the *Child Depression Inventory*; Kovacs, 1992) whereas others cover most areas of child behavior problems (e.g., the *Child Behavior Checklist*; Achenbach, 1991).

Many aspects of behavior rating scales make them a valuable addition to childhood assessment batteries. They are inexpensive and easy to administer. The forms can be completed and returned in advance of a clinic appointment so the information can be evaluated before the formal assessment begins, or parents can complete the forms while they are in the clinic's waiting room. Some scales, such as the Child Behavior Checklist (CBCL) (Achenbach, 1991), can be computer-scored, thereby increasing their accuracy and utility. Standard rating scales cover most of the most common childhood behavioral problems, so they give clinicians a broad overview of the child's problem areas, including conduct and anxiety problems as well as social relations and school functioning. In addition, extensive normative data are available on many rating scales, thus allowing the child's behavior to be evaluated in comparison to a large group of children of similar age and sex. Rating scales can be collected from significant adults in the child's life (e.g., parents, teachers), allowing for an examination of the child's behavior in different contexts and from different perspectives. Finally, because they are easy to administer, rating scales can be used on repeated occasions, such as when monitoring the effectiveness of an ongoing treatment program. They also allow for the collection of standardized follow-up data, even after families have moved away.

The most frequently used behavior rating scales show high test–retest reliability and good validity (Kamphaus & Frick, 1996). For example, scores on the Conners (1989) ten-item *Teacher Rating Scale* can differentiate attention-deficit hyperactivity disorder (ADHD) children from children with other behavior problems, and can distinguish children with ADHD on medication from those on placebo. This rating scale can even detect behavioral changes associated with differing dosages of medication. Similarly, the parent version of the Child Behavior Checklist does an excellent job of differentiating children with various types of behavior problems (Kamphaus & Frick, 1996). Together, parent and teacher ratings offer reliable, valid, economical, and useful information on children's functioning.

However, like all assessment instruments, rating scales do have their limitations. The data are subject to the information-processing biases discussed earlier, as well as errors stemming from rater characteristics. Parents' mood, tolerance or intolerance of their children's behavior, and their desire to make their children look "good" or "bad" all can influence ratings (Webster-Stratton, 1988). The value of behavior ratings also is limited by the fact that they convey global impressions of children's behavior but offer little information about important situational determinants of that behavior (Cairns & Green, 1979). Information about global traits may be helpful in diagnosing a child's problems, but it does not say what environmental factors trigger or reinforce problematic behavior. As we shall see later, knowing about these factors can be crucial in establishing an effective treatment program. Rating scales also can be criticized for focusing primarily on a child's problems, with little attention to areas of competence and resilience. Finally, it is not always clear how to interpret rating scale responses from multiple informants when the informants (e.g., parents and teachers) disagree about the nature or extent of the problem (Achenbach, McConaughy, & Howell, 1987). What should the clinician conclude if the mother says the child is noncompliant but the father disagrees, or the teacher says the child is hyperactive but the parents disagree? This is why child assessments should be comprehensive, gathering data from multiple informants and using a number of different assessment procedures.

Clinical Interviews

As in adult cases, clinical interviews are central to the assessment of childhood disorders. The clinician will usually interview the parents, and depending on the child's age and cognitive maturity, the child as well. When interviewing the parents, the clinician has the following goals in mind:

1. Establish rapport. Developing a close working relationship with the parents will make it easier for them to reveal personal information about themselves, the referred child, and the family. This relationship also will be valuable if the clinician ends up helping the parents with their own psychological and parenting problems.

2. Obtain specific details about the child's problem. What is it? When and where and how often does it occur? How do the parents and siblings respond? Interviews allow the clinician to follow up on rating scale responses by obtaining specific examples of problematic behaviors and situations.

3. Chart the course of the problem. When did it start? Is there a specific event or developmental stage that appeared to trigger the onset of the problem? Is it continuous or does it come and go?

4. Gather a developmental history of the child, including information on major developmental milestones, transition periods (e.g., starting school), and factors that may have disrupted normal development (e.g., hospitalizations, parental divorce).

5. Explore family factors that may exacerbate the child's problem. These factors might include marital discord, sibling rivalry, and parental mental disorder. When

both parents are interviewed, the clinician will evaluate the degree to which they agree about the nature and origins of their child's problems, and will estimate the parents' abilities to participate in programs for dealing with those problems.

As described in Chapter 4, the validity of any interview can be threatened by various kinds of bias or error, and this is certainly true when parents describe their children's problems. Parents' memories are fallible, they have limited normative data on which to base judgments about the appropriateness of their children's behavior, they may have emotional problems that may distort their responses, and they may be motivated to present their children in either a positive or negative light (especially during interviews relating to child custody battles or school placement decisions). Still, information from parental interviews is crucial in piecing together the diagnostic puzzle.

Interviews with referred children themselves can offer valuable information about them and the environments in which their problems occur (La Greca, 1990; Mash & Terdal, 1988). The goals of child interviews often differ from those described for the parent interview and include the following:

1. Establish rapport. Children often do not know why they are being interviewed and may misunderstand what their parents told them about the clinical evaluation. Some parents tell the child nothing about the clinic visit, or present only vague information (e.g., "We're going to take you to the doctor's office."). It is important to correct any misconceptions the child may have.

2. Evaluate the child's understanding of the problem that led to referral. Does the child feel there is a problem and, if so, what does he or she think is the cause?

3. Evaluate the child's explanations of problematic behavior. This goal is important in assessing the child's habitual way of thinking about the world. For example, does the child see others as hostile and threatening? Does the child believe that he or she is powerless to forestall failure at school (Diener & Dweck, 1978)?

4. Obtain a description of the fear, sadness, anxiety, anger, or low self-esteem associated with problems such as childhood depression and anxiety disorders (Ialongo et al., 1994).

5. Observe the child during the interview. By doing so, clinicians can confirm or revise impressions gained from interviewing the child's parents. These observations also can provide information about the child's cognitive maturity, activity level, and degree of compliance (Edelbrock et al., 1985). It is important to remember, however, that informal observational assessments have limited validity. For example, one study found that 80% of children diagnosed with hyperactivity displayed no signs of overactivity in the physician's office (Sleator & Ullmann, 1981).

As valuable as child interviews can be, clinicians do not usually rely on them very much in determining the severity of behavioral problems, in making a diagnosis, or in choosing a treatment approach because—especially when children are under the age of 10—these interviews tend to have low reliability (Edelbrock et al., 1985). The reliability of child interviews increases with age of the child; adolescents are as reliable as, and sometimes more reliable than, their parents in reporting their behavioral problems. A new set of interview methods known as *narrative elaboration* has been shown to improve the accuracy of young children's self-reports (Saywitz & Snyder, 1996), but it will take further research to determine if these methods—which include visual recall cues as well as training in, practice with, and reminders to use memory retrieval skills—can aid memory without influencing its content.

Intelligence and Achievement Tests

Poor school performance accounts for a large number of child referrals for mental health services, with first grade being the peak period for such referrals. Further, behavior problems and academic difficulties are intertwined in complex ways, with the former contributing to the latter and the latter contributing to the former (Hinshaw, 1992). Finally, in order for children with behavior or academic difficulties to receive the school support services (e.g., tutoring, special placement) to which they are legally entitled, they must receive standardized and individualized intelligence and achievement testing. For these reasons, such testing is a routine aspect of child assessment batteries. There are other reasons why IQ and achievement tests are commonly employed by clinical child psychologists:

1. Compared to all other tests or interview procedures, IQ and achievement tests have the best normative data available, allowing for precise statements about the child's functioning relative to other children of the same age.

2. Excellent reliability and validity data exist for both types of tests. IQ scores are the single best predictor of children's current and future academic and occupational functioning.

3. Because the majority of child referrals involve academic and/or behavioral difficulties in the classroom, it is necessary to determine what contribution learning problems, low intelligence, or inappropriate parent or teacher expectations may make to these problems. For example, a child who is struggling academically may become disruptive to avoid the frustration and failure associated with the schoolwork.

4. These tests assess specific strengths and weaknesses in the child's academic and cognitive functioning (e.g., memory or visual-spatial deficits) and this information can be used to make recommendations concerning treatment, special school placements, remediation, and even vocational planning.

5. Testing gives the clinician a standardized situation in which to observe the child's activity level, ability to follow instructions, speed of response, distractibility and attention span, friendliness, flexibility in thinking, anxiety, and response to feedback about success and failure (Sattler, 2001).

Against these advantages, the clinician must balance the following limitations of intelligence and achievement testing (Sattler, 2001):

1. The test environment is somewhat artificial and may yield an inaccurate picture of the child's performance in the classroom. Test anxiety may impair the performance of some children, whereas for others—such as children with ADHD—the structured nature of testing may raise performance above what normally appears in the classroom.

2. IQ and achievement tests may be biased against minority children or children for whom English is a second language. Further, too much credence can be given to a single IQ score, so that lowered expectations about a child's ability become self-fulfilling prophesies that lead to declining performance (Rosenthal & Rubin, 1978). Factors other than intelligence (e.g., proper nutrition, teacher expectancies) also can influence success in the classroom.

3. Classification systems, which often require definitive yes/no decisions, can be quite arbitrary and not consistent with what is known about the measurement error associated with psychological tests. Special support services in the schools often have rigid selection criteria, so that a specific IQ score (e.g., 69) may entitle a child to receive special support services whereas a statistically comparable score (e.g., 72) may not.

It is probably clear why so much controversy surrounds the use of IQ tests with children. Legitimate arguments can be made both in defense of, and against the use of, such tests. Further, the decisions made from the results of these tests are often not inconsequential—such information helps determine whether and what type of school support, services, and placements a child may receive. Despite this controversy, most child clinicians recognize the important role of intellectual and achievement testing in identifying a child's strengths and weaknesses, especially as they relate to academic functioning and school behavior. Further, as long as the law requires such testing for determination of special education services, intelligence and achievement testing will remain an important part of the assessment of children.

Projective Tests

Projective testing with children represents the domain in which the discrepancy is greatest between what research findings support and what clinicians actually do (Kamphaus & Frick, 1996). Many clinicians' assessment batteries still include the Rorschach inkblot test, as well as projective tests specifically designed for children—including story-telling procedures such as the *Children's Apperception Test* (Bellak, 1954) and the *Mutual Story-Telling Technique* (Gardiner, 1971), and drawing techniques such as the Draw-a-Person (Koppitz, 1968) and House-Tree-Person techniques (Buck, 1948)—in spite of research showing that projectives fail to offer much valid or useful assessment information about children (Martin, 1988).

Test–retest and interrater reliabilities for these tests are often unacceptably low (Lilienfeld, Wood, & Garb, 2000), especially among child samples (Gittelman-Klein,

1986), and there is little evidence that the tests measure what they purport to measure (Gittelman-Klein, 1986; Lilienfeld et al., 2000). Finally, there is no evidence for the incremental validity of projective tests. In other words, even if they did allow valid inferences about children (e.g., that signs of aggression on the CAT predicted aggressive behavior), it is usually the case that this same information is already available through interviews, observations, or other simpler, more valid means. One investigator put it this way: projective tests with children "sometimes . . . tell us poorly something we already know" (Gittelman, 1980, p. 434).

Given their dismal track record, why do projective tests remain popular in the assessment of children? The answer is partly that drawing pictures or telling stories offer excellent ways for children to express themselves. Many clinical child psychologists would agree that "[drawings] must be looked upon as a universal language of childhood whereby children of all races and cultures express their ideas of the world about them" (Goodenough, 1931, p. 505). The courts also recognize the importance of children's nonverbal expressions; judges routinely allow child witnesses to use anatomically correct dolls to help describe incidents of sexual abuse (Haugaard & Reppucci, 1988). Similarly, clinicians who work with children know that often the best way to break the ice and build rapport is to ask the child to draw a picture or tell a story. The problem is not in using play materials to break the ice with children, but instead lies in attempting to use the play behavior diagnostically. There is no good evidence that clinical interpretations of these pictures or stories offer especially accurate insights into children's personalities and underlying drives, or especially accurate predictions about children's behavior outside the testing situation.

Behavioral Observations

More so than for adult disorders, behavioral observations are an integral part of the assessment of childhood disorders. Because children's problems usually occur in the home or school, observations in these settings give clinicians the opportunity to validate, or get new perspectives on, reports made by parents and teachers through rating scales and interviews. Thus, observations allow a more naturalistic assessment of the child's behavior, providing real-world information that interviews and tests cannot offer. Observational assessments are also vital to the behavioral techniques that have become the treatment of choice for many childhood disorders. These techniques require systematic observation of behaviors that are the targets of treatment, as well as of the environmental stimuli that either elicit or reinforce those behaviors. Unlike rating scales, which offer global impressions, observations allow fine-grained analyses of these important stimulus–behavior–consequence relations (Mash & Wolfe, 2002).

Gerald Patterson and his colleagues were pioneers in the development of home observation systems. They first recorded the rate of noxious child behaviors (e.g., noncompliance, teasing, whining), then compared rates of inappropriate (and appropriate) behaviors across deviant and nonreferred children to quantify the characteristics of disturbed family interactions. They also tried to isolate those parent or sibling behaviors that elicited noxious responses from referred children. For example, one important finding was that "sibling teases" can be a powerful stimulus for deviant responses, something that Patterson and his colleagues probably would not have learned from interviews or rating scales. Observational data allowed Patterson and his colleagues to develop his coercion-escalation model, discussed earlier, of how children's aggressive behavior begins and is maintained. Later, we describe an intervention program Patterson developed based on this model for altering dysfunctional family interactions.

School observation systems focus primarily on classroom behavior (Kamphaus & Frick, 1996), although playground behavior also may be monitored (Walker, Colvin, & Ramsey, 1995). Classroom observations often concentrate on behaviors associated with ADHD, including off-task behavior, out-of-seat, disruptiveness, and noncompliance.

Despite the benefits offered by observational assessment in the home or school, many clinicians hesitate to use these methods. For one thing, observation is expensive and time-consuming. Obtaining reliable and representative observational data requires a professional or paraprofessional observer to travel to the child's home or school and remain there for extended periods often over several days. If interrater reliability data are to be obtained, a second observer is needed. Home observations usually require that observers visit during the evening, when the entire family is present (and when hourly pay rates for observers may be higher). Many clinicians also worry that placing observers in the child's home can change the environment enough to alter the family's interactions and thus undermine the validity of observational data. For example, Patterson's (1982) system requires that all family members be in sight, and that they not watch television or talk on the telephone. In such circumstances, if everyone tries to be on their best behavior, the clinician may not learn much about typical family life, or the child's problems.

To overcome some of these problems, clinicians often arrange for observations to be made in the clinic setting (Mash & Barkley, 1986). Clinic observations can be recorded on videotape by cameras, making it unnecessary for trained observers to be present when the family comes in; tapes of families can be evaluated later, at an observational analysis session. Further, clinic observations can be made under standardized conditions in which each child or family can be exposed to identical situations. For example, some clinics feature a simulated classroom that can be used to assess child behaviors related to ADHD (Milich et al., 1982). Alternatively, Rex Forehand and his colleagues have employed a clinic observation system for assessing children's rates of noncompliance with parental commands (Forehand & McMahon, 1981). The parent is given a series of tasks that she/he must get the child to complete, and the clinician observes how the parent issues the command, whether the child complies, and how the parent responds to the compliance or noncompliance. Not only are such observations valuable in assessing the problems in the parent-child interaction, but the videotape can be used therapeutically to demonstrate the problems to the parent.

Family and Peer Interaction Measures

Children live in a number of important social worlds, including home, school, and peer group, and clinicians often attempt to assess the impact of these multiple social environments.

Assessment of Children's Peer Relations.   In the last three decades, interest among clinical child psychologists in the assessment of children's peer relations has increased (Landau & Milich, 1990). This is not surprising; just thinking back to childhood can help us recall how our emotional development was affected by how well, or how poorly, we got along with our peers (Hartup & Stevens, 1997).

Clinicians are also interested in children's peer relations because many social skills (e.g., sharing, taking turns, cooperating) are learned best through peer interactions, and because disturbed peer relations are one of the strongest predictors of later behavioral and psychological problems (Parker & Asher, 1987).

Although mothers, teachers, or children themselves can provide some information about peer relations, a child's peer group offers the most reliable and valid data. In an assessment procedure known as peer sociometics, children evaluate their classmates or playmates by answering two simple questions: "Whom do you like?" and "Whom don't you like?" The answers to these questions allow any child in a group to be assigned two scores: a popularity index, which is the total number of classmates indicating they like the child; and a rejection index, which is the total number who dislike the child. Neglected children (low popularity, low rejection) differ in important ways from rejected (low popularity, high rejection) and popular (high popularity, low rejection) children. Neglected children make few social overtures, whereas both rejected and popular children initiate many social interactions. The overtures of popular children are successful, but those of the rejected children are rebuffed.

Although peer sociometric data are quite reliable and valid, collecting these data can be difficult, and there are concerns that—especially at school—the use of sociometry risks stigmatizing rejected children (Hayvren & Hymel, 1984). Accordingly some clinicians prefer to assess a child's social interactions via teacher ratings (Greenwood et al., 1979) or by asking the child for self-reports on social anxiety, loneliness, and social goals (Asher & Wheeler, 1985; La Greca et al., 1988; Renshaw & Asher, 1983).

Assessment of Family Interactions.   Just as a thorough child assessment involves examining the child in the context of the school and peer group, it is also necessary to assess the child within the context of the family. Some of this is accomplished with the parent-child and home observations described earlier. However, assessment of the family context usually goes beyond observations and may include the following areas (Kamphaus & Frick, 1996):

1. *Family history data.* Given the evidence documenting the powerful effects of both genetics and the environment, family history data can offer valuable leads for which disorder(s) the child may be at risk. Thus, for example, mothers with anxiety disorders are more likely to reinforce separation problems in their children, as well as pass on anxiety producing genes.

2. *Parental psychopathology.* A clinical assessment of the child often includes some measure of parental psychopathology, such as the MMPI or a depression scale. Such information can be valuable in identifying the strengths and weaknesses of the parents in managing the child's behavior, and also can reveal factors that may bias the parents' perception of the child (Webster-Stratton, 1988).

3. *Marital relationship.* As noted earlier, divorce and, especially, marital conflict can be a major contributor to a child's behavior problems. In addition, marital discord may interfere with the parents' ability to agree on treatment goals and how to implement them.

4. *Child-rearing methods.* Child noncompliance is one of the most common referral complaints, especially for preschool age children. Thus, clinicians often will try to assess parents' expectations about their child's behavior, how the parents attempt to manage this behavior, what has worked and what has not, agreement or inconsistencies between the two parents, and the parents' willingness to learn new, more effective procedures.

5. *Stress and perceived support.* Stress in the family, be it due to marital discord, parental psychopathology, or unemployment and financial problems, contributes to childhood behavior problems. Further, stressors can limit the resources the parents have available to cope with the child's problems. Thus, child assessment routinely includes an evaluation of the stressors experienced by the parents as well as their means of coping, such as social support systems (see Wahler, 1980).

CLASSIFICATION OF CHILDHOOD DISORDERS

One purpose of the assessment of childhood problems is to diagnose mental disorders. Classification of childhood disorders has followed a different path than adult disorders, although they both have the same objectives (see Chapter 1). There has been a greater emphasis on *empirically derived* classification systems for children, whereas adult disorders have been classified mainly into *clinically derived* diagnostic categories. Empirically derived systems rely on statistical analyses of large amounts of data to determine the symptoms that make up a diagnostic category. In contrast, clinically derived systems rely on the judgments of experts, who use their clinical and research experience to determine the diagnostic criteria.

There are at least two reasons for the emphasis on the empirical approach among childhood researchers. First, as already noted, early versions of the clinically derived DSM systems virtually ignored the unique aspects of childhood disorders. The empirical approach to classifying childhood disorders arises also from the referral process described earlier. Because children do not refer themselves for help, standard assessment procedures rely on information from parents, teachers, and other significant people in the child's life. The most common procedure for gathering this information is to have knowledgeable adults complete behavior rating scales on the referred child. Child psychiatry clinics routinely collect such data on large numbers of children. The advent of high-speed computers made it possible to quickly analyze these data to determine which symptoms tend to cluster together in children.

Here, we consider both empirical and clinical approaches to the classification of childhood disorders, as well as the similarities and differences in the disorder category systems derived from each.

Clinically Derived Systems

As described in Chapter 3, clinically derived classification systems, such as the DSM, are developed by panels of experts who identify appropriate diagnostic categories, as well as the specific symptoms most typical of each. These experts rely on their clinical experience with a variety of disorders, as well as their reading of the research literature, to arrive at an agreed-upon classification system. However, even when experts observe similar patients and read the same empirical reports, they may not always agree on the diagnostic criteria for a given disorder. In short, reaching a consensus on these decisions often involves compromise, just as legislators must amend proposed legislation to produce a bill that will receive support sufficient for passage.

Clinicians and researchers interested in childhood disorders have had differing responses to the way these disorders have been classified in the various editions of the DSM. Many felt satisfied that, beginning with DSM-III, childhood problems were finally recognized as unique and worthy of clinical attention. Others questioned whether the revisions were a step forward or backward in terms of classifying childhood disorders (Rutter & Shaffer, 1980). Let's consider the improvements and shortcomings of DSM-III, DSM-III-R, and DSM-IV classifications of childhood disorders.

One improvement has been greater breadth of coverage; DSM-IV contains more than four times as many childhood categories as DSM-II (Bemporad & Schwab, 1986). These categories reflect five domains of functioning: intellectual problems (e.g., mental retardation), behavioral problems (e.g., conduct disorders), emotional problems (e.g., anxiety disorders), physical problems (e.g., enuresis), and developmental problems (e.g., autism). However, some clinicians have criticized this increased breadth of coverage. They argue that disorders such as mental retardation and learning disabilities, which are included in recent versions of the DSM, are educational problems rather than psychiatric disorders and therefore should not be included in a psychiatric classification system (Rutter & Shaffer, 1980). Some psychologists fear that broadening coverage of childhood disorders represents an attempt by psychiatrists to assume control of problems outside their expertise (Garmezy, 1978).

As noted in Chapter 3, operational criteria for defining mental disorders began appearing in DSM-III, an improvement that benefited the diagnosis of childhood as well as adult problems. For example, whereas DSM-II contained only one sentence listing the possible symptoms of hyperactivity, DSM-IV includes explicit diagnostic criteria about the number and types of specific symptoms that must appear before this diagnosis can be made, along with information about onset and duration of the disorder, and exclusionary criteria.

Still, even DSM-IV falls short of using fully operational criteria. It does not specify how to measure criterion behaviors, and terms such as "often" and "easily" are used without guidance about the severity of the problems they represent. What does it mean to say a child "is often easily distracted by extraneous stimuli?" A major goal of the newest DSM was to introduce a developmental framework to the classification of the childhood disorders. Unfortunately, the only consistent developmental data offered are age of onset and course of disorders. The diagnostic criteria are not adjusted to reflect developmental differences for any disorder. For example, DSM-IV offers the clinician no guidelines for diagnosing the presence of attention problems in children of differing ages. In addition, for several disorders (e.g., depression, generalized anxiety), no specific childhood criteria are offered. Instead, the clinician is instructed to use the adult criteria, somehow adjusting them to reflect how the symptoms may manifest themselves in childhood. Similarly, the DSM-IV offers the same diagnostic criteria for boys and girls, even though evidence exists that for some disorders (e.g., aggression), the problems may be manifested differently for the two sexes. Finally, the recent DSM versions offer too little coverage of disorders seen in infancy and early childhood (Mash & Dozois, 1996).

The developers of DSM-IV have relied far more than their predecessors on empirical investigations to identify the symptoms of specific disorders (Widiger et al., 1991), and this is especially the case for childhood disorders (Mash & Dozois, 1996). Still, to the clinical child psychologist, perhaps the most frustrating aspect of the DSM approach to diagnosis is that the criteria for given disorders (and the names of the disorders as well) change, often substantially, with each edition of the manual. For example, in DSM-III, a diagnosis of attention deficit disorder (ADD) required that a child display inattention, impulsivity, and hyperactivity. In DSM-III-R, the symptoms from these three subcategories were collapsed into one list, and a child could receive an ADHD diagnosis merely by displaying a certain number of them, regardless of which subcategories they represented. DSM-IV contains only two symptom subcategories (inattention and impulsivity/hyperactivity), and a child can receive one of three ADHD diagnoses—Inattentive Type, Hyperactive/Impulsive Type, or Combined Type—depending on whether they meet the criteria for one or both of the subcategories.

Empirically Derived Systems

In contrast to the clinical approach, the empirical approach to classification makes no initial assumptions about which symptoms are interrelated, or what diagnostic categories may exist, although a priori decisions are involved in determining which behavioral symptoms to enter into the statistical analyses. In other words, the data are allowed to speak for themselves about the extent to which symptoms appear in the same child. The primary statistical technique for determining the interrelationship among behavioral symptoms is *factor analysis*. This procedure involves examining the correlations among all symptoms and determining which behaviors tend to correlate or occur together. Those symptoms that show the highest correlations among themselves form factors or dimensions. This is the *dimensional approach* to psychopathology, which assumes that all children display all of the behaviors being studied, but to varying degrees. Children who score high on particular disorder factors are considered to suffer to a greater degree from the problems associated with those factors. This approach contrasts with clinically derived *categorical systems*, which assume that children either do or do not have a given disorder. One way to contrast these two approaches is to consider intelligence and mental retardation. Intelligence represents the dimensional approach—all children have a measurable intelligence, but IQ scores can range from very low to very high. Mental retardation represents a categorical approach—you either have the disorder or you do not (see Chapter 3).

The empirical approach to the diagnosis of childhood psychopathology is embodied in the work of Thomas Achenbach (1978; Achenbach & Edelbrock, 1979, 1981), who developed rating scales for assessing more than 100 of the most common problems of childhood. He asked thousands of parents and teachers to complete these rating scales in relation to both referred and nonreferred boys and girls ranging in age from 4 to 18. Although the results differed somewhat depending on the child's age and sex, several factors emerged that reflect a variety of childhood behavioral problems. Figure 10.1 offers examples of the factors that typically arise from such analyses, along with the behavioral characteristics associated with each.

Historically, the majority of childhood behavior disorders have been subsumed under two broad factors (Achenbach & Edelbrock, 1978; Quay, 1986). One of these

---

Conduct Disorder
  Fighting, hitting
  Disobedient, defiant
  Temper tantrums
  Destructiveness
  Impertinent, imprudent
  Uncooperative, resistant
Attention Problems
  Poor concentration, short attention span
  Daydreaming
  Clumsy, poor coordination
  Preoccupied, stares into space
  Fails to finish, lacks perseverance
  Impulsive
Motor Overactivity
  Restless, overactive
  Excitable, impulsive
  Squirmy, jittery
  Overtalkative
  Hums and makes other odd noises
Social Ineptness
  Poor peer relations
  Likes to be alone
  Is teased, picked on
  Prefers younger children
  Shy, timid, lacks self-confidence
  Stays with adults, ignored by peers
Somatic Complaints
  Headaches
  Vomiting, nausea

Stomach aches
Muscle aches and pains
Elimination problems
Socialized Aggression
  Has "bad" companions
  Truant from home
  Truant from school
  Steals in company with others
  Loyal to delinquent friends
  Belongs to a gang
Anxious-Depressed Withdrawal
  Anxious, fearful, tense
  Shy, timid, bashful
  Withdrawn, seclusive
  Depressed, sad, disturbed
  Hypersensitive, easily hurt
  Feels inferior, worthless
Schizoid Unresponsive
  Won't talk
  Withdrawn
  Sad
  Stares blankly
  Confused
Psychotic Disorder
  Visual hallucinations
  Auditory hallucinations
  Bizarre, odd, peculiar
  Strange ideas and behavior
  Incoherent speech
  Repetitive speech

This table lists nine factors typically obtained from factor analyses of behavior rating scales. The behavioral items that frequently load on each factor are listed under the factor name.
SOURCE: Quay (1986).

FIGURE 10.1 Factors typically derived from factor analysis of rating scales, and characteristics frequently associated with each.

factors describes *externalizing* or undercontrolled problems; the other, *internalizing* or overcontrolled problems. The externalizing factor refers to acting-out behavior—such as hyperactivity, aggression, and delinquency—that is aversive to others in the child's environment. The internalizing factor refers to problems in which the child experiences depression, anxiety, somatic problems, and other significant discomfort that may not be evident, let alone disturbing, to others. These two broad factors offer a reliable and valid way of differentiating childhood behavioral problems. Generally, children who display externalizing problems tend to be male, have academic problems, and to have worse prognoses than those with internalizing disorders. Given the aversive nature of the externalizing disorders, as well as their more negative prognosis, it is not surprising that, until recently, more attention has been devoted to these problems than to the internalizing disorders.

Although the dimensions of externalizing and internalizing disorders have served as a useful heuristic for summarizing the types of problems children experience, it is now generally agreed that a more complete understanding of children's behavior problems requires a more fine grained analysis of the empirical data. Thus, whereas in the 1960s and 1970s clinicians and researchers were content to talk about the externalizing disorders, it is now widely accepted that there are important distinctions within this broad category, and that a child's functioning and level of impairment may differ dramatically depending on whether he/she has attention deficit hyperactivity disorder, conduct disorder, or both. Similarly, distinctions are being made among the internalizing disorders, especially in differentiating anxiety from depression as well as among various types of anxiety disorders.

The computer-driven empirical approach avoids the biases in judgment that may be associated with the clinical approach. As noted in Chapter 3, clinicians sometimes misperceive associations between symptoms; they sometimes even perceive correlations that do not exist. For example, clinician's biases have often led to a perceived association between bedwetting and firesetting even though there is, in fact, no association (Achenbach, 1985). The problem is compounded when clinicians are asked to make judgments about associations among numerous symptoms and disorders.

A second strength of empirical classification systems is their quantitative approach to decision making. Large-scale normative investigations have resulted in objective, operational rules for defining inclusion and exclusion criteria for specific syndromes. In one study, for example, rating scale data from 1,300 parents of nonreferred children (aged 4 to 16) allowed researchers to calculate means and standard deviations for disorder factor scores (Achenbach & Edelbrock, 1981). This normative information then was used to compare referred children's scores on specific factors to developmental norms of peers of the same age and sex (see Figure 10.2).

A final strength of the empirical approach is that it allows evaluation of childhood disorders from the perspectives of both parents and teachers. Factor analyses of these separate ratings can show, for example, that certain behavioral problems are more significant in some situations than others, meaning that teachers may be less aware of delinquency problems than mothers, but the converse may be true for problems in peer relationships.

A major problem with the empirical approach to classifying childhood disorders relates to the data used in the factor analyses. Most of the conclusions about the

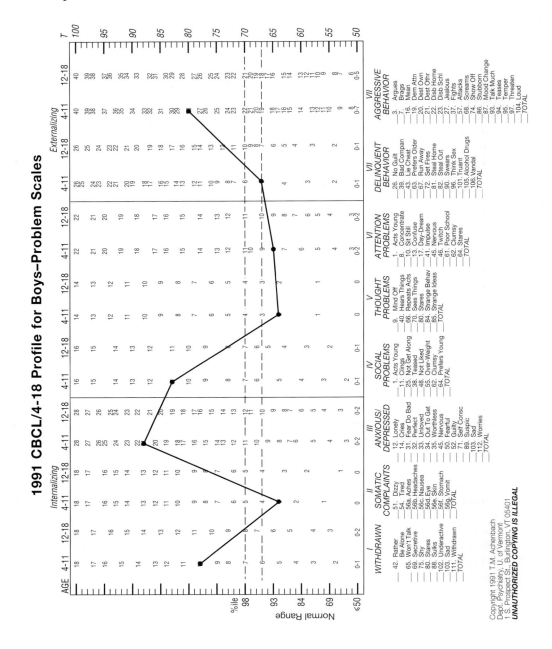

1991 CBCL/4-18 Profile for Boys–Problem Scales

dimensions underlying childhood disorders have been based on symptom ratings by parents and teachers. These ratings may be biased by personal factors, such as parental depression, that have little to do with the child's behavior. The factors derived from rating scale items also depend on how parents and teachers interpret those items. For example, DSM-IV includes "often doesn't seem to listen" as an example of inattention. However, mothers tend to interpret "doesn't seem to listen" to mean active noncompliance and thus tend to associate it with oppositional or conduct disorders (Milich, Widiger, & Landau, 1987). Further, the empirical approach is not good at identifying rare disorders. For example, empirical analyses of behavior checklist data almost never generate factors describing autism (see Nietzel et al., 1998), yet this disorder does exist.

SPECIFIC CHILDHOOD DISORDERS

In this section, we offer descriptions of four types of childhood disorders that clinical child psychologists often encounter in their assessment and treatment activities: attention deficit hyperactivity disorder (ADHD; an externalizing disorder), childhood depression (an internalizing disorder), learning disabilities (a developmental disorder), and childhood autism (a pervasive developmental disorder).

Attention Deficit Hyperactivity Disorder

Attention deficit hyperactivity disorder is considered the most common childhood behavior disorder, affecting approximately 5% of school-age children. Although this figure represents, on average, only one child per classroom, it is enough to seriously disrupt the learning environment, as any teacher will confirm. ADHD primarily affects boys (the boy-to-girl ratio ranges from 4:1 to 10:1) and, although it appears prior to first grade, the problems it creates are intensified by the demands of the school environment.

As already noted, the core features of ADHD are inattention, impulsivity, and overactivity. The attention problems consist primarily of children having difficulty sustaining their focus; they fail to finish school assignments, and they do not stay on task in the classroom (Barkley, 1998). In addition, they are distracted by highly appealing and salient extraneous stimuli (Lorch et al., 2000). Impulsivity refers to the fact that these children act before they think. Although it is agreed that children with ADHD are impulsive, operationally defining this construct is difficult (Milich & Kramer, 1984). Be-

FIGURE 10.2 An example of a profile from the 1991 Child Behavior Checklist (CBCL). Here is the profile of a 6-year-old boy's scores on the mother's rating version of the Child Behavior Checklist (CBCL). The CBCL contains scales for two age groups: 4 to 11 and 12 to 18. Scores falling above the dotted line occur in less than 2% of nonreferred children in the age range and are considered especially problematic. This type of profile resembles, and offers many of the same diagnostic features as, those generated by the MMPI (see Chapter 5). In this case, the profile is typical of a young child displaying aggression, peer difficulties, and depression. (Adapted from Achenbach, 1991).

haviors typical of this problem include difficulty waiting to take turns, interrupting, and being impatient. Children with ADHD exhibit overactivity in both gross motor movements (e.g., running around the room, standing on chairs), and fine motor movements, (e.g., fidgeting and squirming, restlessness, and playing with objects).

In addition to these core features, children with ADHD are likely to display a myriad of other behavioral and learning problems, including aggressive and delinquent behavior, oppositional and noncompliant reactions to adult requests, and problems in social interactions. Even relatively brief interactions with unfamiliar peers often leads to social rejection (Diener & Milich, 1997), and the reputation that these children develop among their peers is so negative that merely telling a normal child that he or she is about to meet a boy with ADHD will adversely affect the subsequent interaction, even if the boy does not actually display ADHD behaviors (Harris et al., 1990).

As ADHD children develop, the primary features of the disorder lessen and, in adulthood, some show few effects of their childhood disorder. Nevertheless, two-thirds of the children still have the disorder in their 20s (Barkley, 1998). Among these young adults, a number are at significant risk for residual academic, social, and emotional problems. For example, they may work at jobs that are below what their socioeconomic background would predict, and may report having fewer friends and being less happy than their age mates (Weiss & Hechtman, 1993). Still others experience more serious legal or psychiatric complications, including depression and substance use disorders. Anywhere from one-third to one-half of adults who had displayed ADHD in childhood will be arrested at least once for a serious offense, compared to 10% of a non-ADHD control group (Satterfield, Hoppe, & Schell, 1982). Having a stable family background, a high IQ, and low levels of aggression in childhood seem to protect children with ADHD against this last outcome.

Numerous investigations have been undertaken to determine what treatments may work for children with ADHD, and the findings are quite consistent—stimulant medication and behavior modification techniques are both effective in improving the behavior across all major areas of functioning, including in the classroom, with the peer group, at home, and even on the ballfield (Pelham, Wheeler, & Chronis, 1998). In fact, there is a growing literature suggesting that the combination of medication and behavior modification together may be the most effective treatment for these children (Pelham & Murphy, 1986). The strengths of one treatment seems to offset the weaknesses of the other. For example, medication is relatively fast acting but it does not teach the child new skills. Behavioral approaches are slower to take effect but they focus on teaching new skills.

Childhood Depression

Increased attention to internalizing disorders has made it clear that childhood depression is similar to adult depression in terms of its emotional, cognitive, behavioral, and physical manifestations, but that the specific symptom picture may differ depending on the child's developmental stage (Kaslow & Rehm, 1985). Indeed, there is considerable debate over the fact that DSM-IV lists the same criteria for diagnosing depression in both children and adults. For example, there are several important ways in which childhood depression seems to differ from adult or even adolescent depression. The sex ratio in childhood (1:1) is different from the 2:1 (female:male) ratio consistently found in adolescence and adulthood. Further, the suicide rate is much lower in childhood, bereavement appears to be less common and less severe, and children may not show the same degree of vegetative symptoms (e.g., sleep or eating problems) that are a common aspect of adult depression. In addition, depression in childhood is more likely to be associated with and even result from other disorders (e.g., conduct disorders) than occurs in adulthood (Rutter & Sroufe, 2001). Finally, as the DSM-IV acknowledges, the specific symptom presentation may differ for children so that, for example, instead of irritability you may see temper tantrums.

Research on the assessment of childhood depression has focused on the reliability and validity of children's self-reports (Saylor et al., 1984), as well as on the validation of behavioral observation measures (Kazdin et al., 1985). Unfortunately, as noted earlier, young children's self reports can be unreliable, and some research suggests that parents may be better informants of their child's depressive state than is the child him/herself (Kazdin et al., 1985). Researchers are also looking at whether causal theories of adult depression, such as learned helplessness, apply to childhood depression (Kaslow, Rehm, & Siegel, 1984; Seligman et al., 1984).

Given that our attention to and understanding of childhood depression has lagged far behind what is known about the externalizing disorders, it is not surprising that the same is true in terms of treatment. In fact, very few controlled studies have systematically examined the psychological (or even medication) treatment of childhood depression, and to date no treatment has met the APA criteria for a well established, empirically validated treatment (Kaslow & Thompson, 1998). This contrasts to the hundreds of intervention studies that have been undertaken for the externalizing disorders.

Learning Disabilities

Learning disabilities refer to the problems some children have in mastering one or more basic academic tasks (such as reading or math), despite having average or above intelligence and sufficient motivation and environmental stimulation. Learning disabilities appear in all cultures, although the rates may differ from one to another. It is estimated that learning disabilities affect from 5 to 10% of school-age children, with many more boys than girls being identified. These developmental disorders have been around for as long as children have been going to school, but it was not until the 1970s that they were officially recognized. Prior to that time, children with learning disabilities were considered either unmotivated or oppositional and often were held back repeatedly in school until they either dropped out or were expelled.

Clinicians agree that there are several types of learning disabilities, although there is less agreement on how to subdivide the different types. One approach is to categorize children by the subject matter in which they have a problem (e.g., reading disability, math disability). Another is to refer to the mental processing problems involved (e.g., language disorder, visual-spatial disorder). One group of children with language disorders shows a Verbal IQ lower than their Performance IQ, a good sight vocabulary, but problematic phonetic skills. Thus, they can read familiar words readily, but have great difficulty with new ones. In contrast, another group of children with visual-spatial problems tends to have a Performance IQ lower than their Verbal IQ and to display good phonetic skills but have a problematic sight vocabulary.

The Individuals with Disabilities Education Act (IDEA; 1997) guarantees that all children with handicapping conditions, including those with learning disabilities, receive a free public education designed to meet their unique needs in the least restrictive environment possible. Because the law's definition of learning disabilities is vague, the individual states have developed operational definitions that usually incorporate three basic features. First, there must be a significant discrepancy between a child's potential and actual performance (e.g., obtaining a reading achievement score that is significantly below the level predicted by the child's IQ). Second, the child's deficit must be due to "basic psychological processes." These deficits must be inferred from the child's performance on tests, but unfortunately, no tests exist that can offer reliable and valid assessments of such processing deficits (Wong, 1986). Accordingly, attention has shifted to a third definitional feature, namely exclusionary criteria. This involves inferring a deficit in basic psychological processes when subpar academic performance cannot be explained by emotional disturbance, educational disadvantage, poor motivation, or other causes. Because it is impossible to rule out many of these alternative causes, many states, fearing litigation, define learning disabilities exclusively in terms of a significant, and quantifiable, discrepancy between a child's measured aptitude and achievement (Wong, 1986).

Not surprisingly, given the important role that schools play in children's development, children who have learning disabilities exhibit a number of associated features. Some of these (e.g., ADHD) may contribute to their learning problems. Others (e.g., low self-esteem, peer difficulties) may be a consequence of continual exposure to failure in one of life's most important domains.

A number of educational and psychological interventions have been developed for children with learning disabilities, and several of these have shown considerable promise in alleviating the academic difficulties experienced by these children. In general, the earlier the intervention, and the more intensive the intervention, the greater the success. For children with specific reading disabilities, the most effective interventions are those that place great emphasis on training in phonics, along with many opportunities to practice these skills with meaningful texts (Lyon & Cutting, 1998). However, to date the long-term follow-up of children with reading problems does not paint a pretty picture. In one representative study, 75% of the children at age 5 with speech and language problems still showed deficits in these areas 7 years later (Beitchman et al., 1994).

Childhood Autism

The pervasive developmental disorder known as autism is one of the most unusual and baffling disorders seen in childhood. It is unusual because of the symptom picture it presents, and baffling because no adequate theory has been proposed to account for these symptoms. Children with autism have severe problems in social functioning and language development, and display a variety of bizarre and inappropriate behaviors.

The movie *Rain Man* presents an accurate, although not necessarily representative, portrayal of an adult with autism.

The social difficulties experienced by these children consist of complete indifference to others. They do not seek interactions with others and even as infants they avoid making eye contact, resist physical contact, and show little or no emotion. They do not play with other children, do not imitate the behavior of others, and do not engage in pretend play.

Approximately half of these children do not develop normal, useful language and those who do, speak in an unusual manner, occasionally using language for noncommunicative purposes. For example, they may engage in echolalia, in which they repeat whatever they hear. Unlike children with hearing impairments, they will not sign or point to get their message across. They also have great difficulty talking about situations or events that are not present, and are very poor at understanding the perspective of other individuals. Finally, their speech sounds different from that of other children, often being flat and lacking inflection, so that it has been described as sounding similar to computer-generated language.

The bizarre behavior exhibited by children with autism often involves abnormally under- or overreactivity to environmental events. Thus, the child may be oblivious to the comings and goings of other individuals but may be hypersensitive to the rustling of paper. In addition, they often are overly sensitive to any changes in their environment and may scream in protest if one of their favorite objects is touched or moved. They also engage in unusual, repetitive behaviors that appear to serve a self-stimulatory purpose. Thus, they may repeatedly flap their hands or engage in self-injurious behavior, such as hitting or biting themselves. In addition, these children may gaze at spinning objects (e.g., fans) for long periods of time, or constantly twirl an ashtray or a piece of string.

Autism is presumed to be present at birth, although it may not become evident until around the age of 2, when the child still has not begun using language. Fortunately, it is a relatively rare disorder, only occurring in approximately 4 children per every 10,000. The majority of children with autism are mentally retarded, with only approximately 20% with an IQ score above 70. Obviously, these children are difficult to test, and, for some, their IQ scores may be underrepresentations of their actual abilities. However, for most of these children, their IQ scores and adaptive functioning levels (e.g., self-care skills) are consistent with a diagnosis of mental retardation. The child's IQ score and use of language are the two best predictors of long-term outcome, and many of these children need to be institutionalized as adults.

Historically, many different psychological (e.g., play therapy), language (e.g., sign language), and medication interventions have been tried with children with autism, with very limited success, leading to the conclusion that nothing can help these children. However, work by Lovaas (1987) offered the first glimmer of hope for this most handicapping of conditions. Lovaas developed a very intensive behavioral intervention for children with autism, starting in the preschool years. The intervention requires approximately 40 hours per week of one-on-one instruction, and lasts for 2 to 3 years. The intervention, "discrete trial training," involves parsing the behaviors to be learned (e.g., eye contact) into very small steps and then using applied behavior modification techniques (e.g., cueing, shaping, immediate reinforcement) to train the discrete behaviors. The results of this intensive intervention have been remarkably encouraging. Not only did Lovaas see dramatic improvements in the treated children's behavior compared to children who received standard interventions, but the improvements were maintained for a 6-year follow-up period, to age 13. Even more noteworthy, at follow-up 9 of the 19 children in the treated group were indistinguishable from their normal classmates on measures of intelligence and adaptive behavior. If other investigators can replicate Lovaas's findings, this will prove to be one of the most remarkable findings in the child treatment literature.

A CLINICAL CASE

So far, our discussion of the assessment and classification of childhood disorders has remained mainly at an abstract, conceptual level. However, the assessments and disorders we have described involve not abstract entities, but real children whose problems do not always fit neatly into diagnostic categories, and for whom clinical assessment data are not always clear or unambiguous. To highlight these realities, and to illustrate how various sources of assessment data are combined in making decisions about diagnostic classification and treatment, we offer the case of "Billy," a boy who was seen by one of the authors. As is common in clinical case presentations, our description will be organized in terms of referral questions, history of the problem, behavioral observations, assessment results, diagnostic conclusions, and treatment recommendations.

Referral Questions

When first seen, Billy was 11 years and 8 months old and in the 5th grade at school. He was referred by the school social worker because he was displaying a number of behavioral problems, both at home and in class. He was sometimes quite aggressive, he did not do what others asked of him, he was manipulative, and he was cruel to animals. Billy was described as having a high activity level, being difficult to discipline, often displaying temper tantrums when he did not get his way. The teacher in his special, "behavior problem" classroom described him as impulsive, difficult to motivate, likely to fail to complete assignments, and having poor attentional skills. He was also said to constantly move his head and make unusual noises. Billy had little self-confidence, had difficulty making friends, and even had talked about killing himself.

In a complex clinical case like Billy's, a number of diagnoses must be considered, including both externalizing (i.e., ADHD, conduct disorder, oppositional defiant disorder) and internalizing (i.e., depression) disorders. In addition, the clinical child psychologist must consider whether a learning disorder may be involved in the clinical picture and whether the constant head movements and unusual noises might be an early indication of Tourette's syndrome, a neurological disorder. To evaluate all these possibilities, clinical assessment must address a number of questions: (1) what is the nature and extent of Billy's aggressive behavior?; (2) how serious is his suicidal ideation?; (3) what is the nature of his home life and what skills do his parents have for handling him?; and (4) how are his attentional problems, his poor motivation and his academic difficulties related—what is causing what?

History of the Problem

Billy's parents said that he had no real problems until he entered school at age 5, but teachers have had great difficulty disciplining him ever since. School records include repeated references to problems of inattention and impulsivity, and the parents noted that his "motor was running all of the time." For a time, he had been treated with Ritalin (a medication for ADHD described later), but this only made him worse. In the 5th grade, when he was placed in the behavior problem class, his suicidal talk began. Billy's medical history and exam were considered unremarkable, except that he was somewhat slow in developing. He did not walk until the age of sixteen months. He was noted to be markedly obese, being three standard deviations above the mean weight for his age. He also needed glasses to do school work, but he often refused to wear them.

Behavioral Observations

Billy frequently whined, complained, and displayed other strikingly immature behavior during the testing phase of clinical assessment. He was noncompliant and oppositional, constantly testing the patience of the examiner. However, as testing progressed and limits were firmly enforced, his oppositional behavior diminished. Billy showed a generally short attention span and was easily distracted. He also often responded to test materials too quickly and without sufficient regard for his responses. The examiner also noted intermittent shoulder shrugs, which may have been consistent with the head movements reported by the school.

Assessment Results

An interview with the parents, who had been married for 15 years, revealed that they were in constant conflict with Billy at home, and that—consistent with Patterson's coercion-escalation hypothesis—these encounters frequently escalated into verbal fights. They said that Billy displayed a number of conduct disorder symptoms, including bullying neighbor children, setting fires, frequent lying, and stealing money from home. His mother reported that she was held back in school because of math difficulties and that her father was an alcoholic. The father reported no significant problems, although he quit school after the 10th grade. Finally, the parents said that, while they are "getting to the end of their rope" in dealing with Billy, his only sibling, a sister, displayed no significant problems.

The results of Billy's intellectual and achievement tests presented an inconsistent and somewhat confusing picture. His Full Scale IQ was 81, putting him in the borderline-low range of normal functioning. However, there was considerable inconsistency among his scores on various subtests, with scores ranging from 4 to 11 (10 is average). This variability suggested that his intellectual capabilities were probably somewhat greater than the score of 81 he received, but that poor motivation and/or learning problems may have impaired his performance. Achievement testing presented a somewhat different picture. Billy tested at his age-appropriate grade level, and above what his IQ results would predict, for both reading and spelling. However, he was 2 years below grade level in arithmetic. Thus, while he clearly did not have a learning disability in reading and spelling, he may have had one in arithmetic. It is hard to be sure about this, however. His arithmetic score of 71 was not significantly below his IQ score, but the IQ itself may have been spuriously low because of his motivational problems. As noted earlier, such considerations often complicate the diagnosis of learning disabilities.

Observations made at school revealed that Billy did indeed have difficulty settling down to tasks and that he constantly fiddled with objects. He also complained a great deal and could be quite "mouthy." He was observed to be "off-task" 41% of the time during seatwork and 61% of the time during classroom instruction time. However, in a small group setting he was off-task only 4% of the time, highlighting the importance of contextual factors in children's behavior.

Conclusions and Recommendations

On the basis of all the assessment information available, the clinician concluded that Billy clearly demonstrated a significant conduct disorder, as well as attention-deficit hyperactivity disorder. The possibility of a learning disability in math was considered but not diagnosed, pending further testing. Additional neurological testing was also required before any conclusion could be drawn about whether Billy was showing signs of Tourette's disorder. He was not judged to be clinically depressed, although it was obvious that he did have self-esteem problems resulting from academic and behavioral difficulties.

Because of the severe nature of Billy's conduct disorder, his large size (which made him difficult to manage), and the fact that his parents acknowledged that they were no longer confident about being able to handle him, the clinician recommended that Billy be placed in a residential treatment center.

Follow-up Evaluation

The clinician evaluated Billy again 2 years after the initial assessment program. Unfortunately, his problems had continued. He was still at the residential treatment center, and he was not doing well there. In addition, his movement disorder symptoms had worsened, and he was receiving medication for Tourette's. Billy was also exhibiting signs of anxiety, insecurity, and low self-esteem, so that concern about depression was raised again and became a focus of further attention.

TREATMENT OF CHILDHOOD DISORDERS

The treatment of childhood disorders differs in important ways from clinical interventions for adults. As is the case with assessment, child therapy poses a special challenge for clinicians because children do not self-evaluate or self-report effectively, and because they do not refer themselves for help, their contact with a therapist requires parental motivation and cooperation. The significance of these and related issues will be apparent in the following brief review of the major forms of therapy for childhood disorders.

Psychodynamic Therapy

Children are usually not considered appropriate candidates for traditional psychoanalytic therapies (Johnson, Rasbury, & Siegel, 1986), partly because they are seldom motivated to participate in such an intensive therapy experience. Further, they are unlikely to understand the need for introspection and the active role they must play in orthodox psychoanalysis. Their immature language and incomplete cognitive development, too, may hamper verbal reasoning and abstract problem solving, thus limiting their ability to profit from a therapist's interpretations. In addition, psychoanalysis assumes the presence of established psychological defenses and a relatively stable personality structure. Depending on their age and developmental status, children may not exhibit such consistencies. Finally, many childhood problems appear to result from environmental forces (e.g., school, parents) rather than from intrapsychic conflicts.

Given that research evidence and clinical practice suggest that standard psychoanalytic therapies are not well suited to children (Achenbach, 1982; Johnson et al., 1986), psychodynamically oriented therapists tend to adopt variations on usual analytical procedures—such as using play rather than free association as the main communication medium between client and therapist. They also may pursue less ambitious treatment goals, such as helping a child successfully pass through a crucial stage of development rather than focusing on prior fixations (Gelfand & Peterson, 1985).

Various forms of psychodynamically oriented play therapy focus on helping children become aware of and resolve inner conflicts without relying heavily on the verbal skills required in adult treatment. Play therapy is designed to allow children to express their inner concerns not by talking about them directly, but through the way they play with, and the voices they give to, puppets, dolls, and modeling clay. All the while, the therapist creates an accepting and empathic atmosphere in which children can feel secure to explore their feelings (Axline, 1976). Traditional psychoanalysts tend to interpret the child's verbal and nonverbal behavior during play as revealing unconscious motivation and conflicts, whereas object-relations therapists (see Chapter 7) are more likely to see it as indicative of the quality of a child's attachment to caregivers. Therapists who adopt a client-centered therapy approach are also likely to use play as a method for helping children explore their feelings and their problems.

Although these various "traditional" therapies differ somewhat in their underlying theories and their therapeutic approaches, Weisz (2001) identifies several common factors among them. These include: talking or playing with the child; listening reflectively and empathically; building a warm relationship with the child; and being supportive and encouraging.

Behavioral Therapy

Various forms of behavioral therapy, especially operant procedures, have been the most frequently employed interventions for childhood problems during the last three decades. Approximately 50% of child therapists identify with this approach (Mash,

1989), which is characterized by several notable features reminiscent of adult versions of behavioral treatment. These include (1) an emphasis on the principles of learning as the basis of behavior disorder and treatment; (2) a focus on observable situational determinants of behavior (e.g., rewards and punishments, instead of inferred intrapsychic problems); (3) treating problems by altering observable stimuli that control behavior today, not by exploring hypothesized underlying problems from the past; and (4) using empirically validated treatments and collecting objective, observable outcome data on treatment results.

Behavioral interventions often involve teaching parents or teachers to administer effective behavior management procedures (Dangel & Polster, 1984; Walker et al., 1995). The rationale for this aspect of behavioral treatment is that parents and teachers are often in a better position than therapists to control the environmental antecedents and consequences that maintain problem behaviors in children at home and at school, and these adults spend many more hours with the child during the week than the one hour session typically associated with therapy (see Figure 10.3).

There are several reasons why behavioral interventions have become the treatment of choice for many childhood disorders. First, the community mental health movement of the 1960s emphasized preventive interventions, including training non-professionals as change agents. Behaviorally oriented parent and teacher training programs fit well with these goals. Second, there was dissatisfaction with traditional psychodynamic treatment methods, especially for children with externalizing disorders or severe psychopathology (e.g., autism). Operant conditioning procedures, in particular, gave parents and teachers concrete solutions for previously intractable child behavioral problems. Third, in the late-1970s the federal government began to stress accountability in the treatment of school children with handicapping conditions. IDEA requires Individual Education Plans (IEPs) for all special education children. For every identified child, schools must develop an IEP that contains a list of treatment goals for the child, a plan for reaching those goals, and a report on the outcome. Behavioral interventions, with their clearly defined targets, specific treatment strategies, and systematic data collection components, lend themselves well to such an accounting.

There is evidence that behavioral therapies are effective for a wide range of childhood disorders, especially for externalizing disorders involving aggression (Brestan & Eyberg, 1998), stealing (McMahon & Wells, 1998), and ADHD (Pelham, Wheeler, & Chronis, 1998). Behavioral procedures also have proven effective for a number of internalizing problems, including bedwetting (Mellon & McGrath, 2000), fears (Barrios & O'Dell, 1998), and school avoidance (Last, Hansen, & Franco, 1998). Finally, operant approaches have shown to effectively maximize the skills and potential of children with severe mental disorders, including mental retardation and autism (Lovaas, 1987). Behavioral interventions are also cost-effective; most can be completed in less than 20 sessions. In addition, by training parents and teachers as change agents in the natural environment, clinicians increase the likelihood that positive changes will be maintained after therapy is terminated, and that positive effects may generalize to other, nonreferred children (siblings, classmates). Finally, the theory behind the behavioral approach is easy to understand, the treatments can be implemented in a relatively

Because many childhood behavioral disorders reflect problems in the home, behavioral parent training procedures focus on systematically teaching parents how to manage their children better. A variety of approaches have been proposed, although those developed by Patterson (1975) and Forehand and McMahon (1981) are the most widely implemented. Whatever the specific orientation, all behavioral parent training procedures include the following five steps.

1. *Pinpoint the target behavior.* Parents must define the problem behavior explicitly so that it can be measured. Often, parents present vague or global complaints about their child's behavior ("He won't mind," "He's got a bad attitude") that make it difficult for the clinician to design the intervention. Parents are encouraged to identify inappropriate behaviors to be decreased as well as appropriate behaviors to be increased.

2. *Chart the target behavior.* Parents are then asked to keep records of the target behaviors. There are two purposes to this data collection. First, these data offer a baseline against which subsequent interventions can be assessed. Second, merely by observing their child's behavior more systematically, parents begin to note the stimuli and consequences that elicit or reinforce the undesirable behavior

("Whenever his sister teases him he hits her and she starts crying").

3. *Develop an intervention.* Behavioral parent training employs an operant perspective, which assumes that behaviors are elicited by the stimuli that precede them and maintained by the consequences that follow. Separating where two children sit at the dinner table is an example of altering antecedents to decrease the rate of fighting during dinner. Giving the children extra TV time for each 5 minutes of dinner that passes without fighting is an example of altering the consequences to modify the same behavior.

4. *Assess the intervention.* Throughout the intervention, the parents keep records of the target behaviors. These data indicate whether the intervention is effective or whether changes need to be made. For example, if a shaping procedure is employed, the data indicate when the parents should increase the behavior criterion required to earn reinforcement.

5. *Fade out the program.* The ultimate goal of all behavioral interventions is that naturally occurring antecedents and consequences will elicit and maintain the desired behaviors. Therefore, if an intervention is successful, the therapist will help the parents fade out the program so that the treatment gains can be maintained after the treatment has ended.

FIGURE 10.3   Behavioral parent training.

straightforward manner, and the results can be quantified in a way that allows parents and teachers to chart improvements as they occur.

Despite its popularity and proven effectiveness, the behavioral approach does have some limitations. For one thing, it does not help all children. For example, Patterson (1982) found that he was unsuccessful with at least one-third of the aggressive children he treated. These children tended to live in families in which there was serious parental psychopathology (e.g., maternal depression) or powerful environmental stressors (e.g., poverty, divorce). Indeed, behaviorally oriented therapists have recognized that simple parent training may not be sufficient for insular families (those with few social resources), and that a multimodal approach, addressing parental as well as child problems, may be necessary (Griest et al., 1982). A second limitation of the behavioral approach is that although producing generalized treatment effects is a desirable goal, achieving that goal is often difficult. Often, initial successes are not maintained, or behavioral changes seen in one setting (e.g., school) do not carry over to other settings (e.g., home). Finally, there are some childhood problems—depression and certain anxiety disorders, for example—that may not lend themselves to operant conditioning or other traditional behavioral interventions. Behavioral clinicians are now turning to cognitive-behavioral interventions to help them deal with such disorders.

Cognitive-Behavioral Interventions

Adult versions of the cognitive-behavioral treatment approach have focused on anxiety disorders and depression, where they have a long history of significant success (see Chapter 9). The use of cognitive-behavioral methods with children, however, has appeared only relatively recently. At first, these methods were used almost exclusively in cases of externalizing disorders, especially impulsivity, hyperactivity, and conduct disorders (Abikoff & Gittelman, 1985; Kazdin et al., 1987; Lochman, 1992; Meichenbaum & Goodman, 1971). Today they are as likely to be applied to children's anxiety and depressive disorders as to ADHD and conduct disorders (Kendall & Panichelli-Mindel, 1995).

The cognitive-behavioral approach to externalizing disorders involves training children to improve their problem-solving skills (Kazdin et al., 1987), to engage in careful planning before making verbal responses in social situations (Meichenbaum & Goodman, 1971), and to learn to control their anger (Lochman, 1992). In other words, children with behavior disorders are taught to bring their inappropriate behavior under cognitive (rational) control. Several techniques are employed in these interventions, including:

1. Problem-solving training (Kazdin et al., 1987). Here, the child is taught to assess the problem (e.g., Billy teased me); generate as many solutions as possible (ignore him, hit him, discuss the problem with him, tell the teacher); and evaluate the consequences of these alternative solutions (if I hit him, I may get in trouble; if I tell the teacher he may stop teasing me but I will lose face with the other children, etc.). Once all of the solutions have been evaluated, the child chooses the best one for him/her and then practices this solution in role-playing scenarios.

2. Impulse-control training. This approach involves training impulsive children (e.g., those with ADHD) to slow down and evaluate response alternatives before responding—to "stop, look, and listen" (Douglas, 1972).

3. Perspective-taking. Children are trained to evaluate the effects of their misbehavior (e.g., stealing, lying) on others, and to be sensitive to the thoughts and feelings of others. This approach is frequently employed with delinquent and aggressive children (Chandler, 1973; Kazdin et al., 1987).

4. Attribution retraining. Based on Dodge's (Crick & Dodge, 1994) theory of hostile attributional biases among aggressive children, attribution retraining instructs such children that there may be several explanations why an event occurred (e.g., the milk was spilled by accident rather than intentionally). Such training is

designed to help aggressive children realize, as nonaggressive children already recognize, that most actions are not performed with hostile intentions.

Initially, cognitive-behavioral approaches were heralded as a clinical breakthrough for treating the externalizing disorders. Training children to think carefully before they act was assumed to produce the kind of generalizable treatment effects that had been missing from more traditional operant interventions. Further, whereas operant approaches require a parent, teacher, or other adult to elicit and reinforce the desired behavior, cognitive interventions are designed to help children carry out a change strategy within themselves, whether or not an adult is present. Unfortunately, this does not always happen. A review of cognitive-behavioral interventions with ADHD children led to the conclusion that, "The expectation that the development of internalized self-regulation skills would facilitate generalization and maintenance has not been realized" (Abikoff, 1985, p. 508). Although other reviews are less pessimistic (Dush, Hirt, & Shroeder, 1989; Kazdin et al., 1987), the general conclusion has been that these interventions may be less effective with seriously disturbed children (Baer & Nietzel, 1991).

One promising line of work has been reported by Alan Kazdin and his colleagues, who employed cognitive-behavioral therapy to treat severely conduct-disordered children (Kazdin et al., 1987, 1989). In two studies, intensive problem-solving training (compared to social-relationship therapy) significantly improved the children's behavior, as indicated by parent and teacher ratings. Even more noteworthy, these improvements were maintained at a 1-year follow-up.

The cognitive-behavioral approach to internalizing disorders tends to focus on the following skills:

1. Recognizing anxiety-arousing feelings and the thoughts that may trigger these feelings. Once the feelings and thoughts are identified, problem-solving procedures are employed to counter them (Kendall, 1994).
2. Identifying biased, dysfunctional, and misguided cognitions and learning to make more appropriate and adaptive cognitions (Mash & Dozois, 1996). Dysfunctional cognitions may include helpless attributions, self-blame for uncontrollable events, and overly harsh self-judgments (Kaslow, Rehm, & Siegel, 1984).

Cognitive-behavioral interventions for internalizing disorders are still quite new, and not enough studies are available to draw firm conclusions about their effectiveness (Kaslow & Thompson, 1998; Kendall & Panichelli-Mindel, 1995).

Psychopharmacological Interventions

Although they are very popular in the treatment of adult mental disorders, until recently medications were not employed widely in the treatment of childhood disorders. For example, when antidepressants are prescribed for children, it is often in relation to problems other than depression (bedwetting, school avoidance, ADHD). Drug treatments are used less frequently with children than adults mainly because still-developing children may be especially vulnerable to the adverse side effects associated with various drugs. Further, research evaluating the effectiveness and safety of psychoactive medications has not received widespread financial support, either from the pharmaceutical firms or the federal government. However, stimulated by a recent White House conference on the use of medication for children's behavior and learning problems, federal funds are now more readily available to study the efficacy and safety of these drugs for children. Such medications are beginning to be used by physicians to treat children's behavior and emotional problems, even in the absence of empirical validation (Mash & Wolfe, 2002).

Stimulant Medication Treatment of ADHD Children. The main exception to physicians' tendency not to medicate children for behavior disorders is seen in the use of methylphenidate (Ritalin) and other stimulant medications in the treatment of attention-deficit hyperactivity disorder. As many as 5% of school-age children in the United States are currently taking these medications for behavioral or learning problems (Safer & Krager, 1994; Jensen et al., 1999), and hundreds of careful studies have shown that stimulant medication dramatically improves the behavior of ADHD children (Swanson, McBurnett, Christian, & Wigal, 1995). The children remain seated longer, finish more academic work, give correct answers more often, and show improved social interactions with peers, parents, and teachers. ADHD boys even pay attention better while playing baseball while on medication than placebo (Pelham et al., 1990).

Nevertheless, controversy continues to surround the use of stimulants for children. It seems that, at least once a year, Ritalin makes the cover of a major news magazine or newspaper. The DEA reports that production of Ritalin has increased more than sevenfold in the last decade, and prescriptions for this drug have increased 60%. Further, the illegal use of this prescribed medication has increased dramatically among 12- to 14-year-olds, from an annual prevalence of 0.1% in 1992 to an annual prevalence of 2.8% in 1997 (NIDA Research Report, 2001). In addition, several lawsuits have claimed that stimulant medication is responsible for a variety of negative outcomes, including suicides and homicides. Most professionals dismiss these claims as overly sensational, but many questions about stimulant medication have not yet been resolved.

For example, even though medication may produce behavioral improvements, it may also give children the message that their improvements are not attributable to their own efforts, but to the medication. Critics worry that children who get such a message may exert less effort at self-control when they are not being medicated, thus creating a form of dependency on the drug. This may not always be the case, however. One study examined the impact of medication on ADHD boys' self-evaluations, self-esteem, and mood, as well as the explanations they offered for improved performance (Pelham et al., 1992). On medication days, compared to placebo days, these boys were significantly more likely to report positive behavioral changes, including increased compliance and fewer rule violations. They also reported feeling happier and liking themselves better on medication days. However, when asked to account for their good performance on medication days, the boys were likely to say that they tried hard, rather than the pill helped them. These results indicate that children with ADHD recognize the effects of medication, but are also willing to take personal credit for improved behavior.

Is Psychotherapy Effective in Treating Childhood Disorders?

As we note in Chapter 9, clinical psychologists have always been interested in evaluating scientifically the effectiveness of psychotherapy, and this desire has intensified of late due to pressures from managed care systems. As a result, meta-analytic reviews of the adult therapy literature have been undertaken (Smith et al., 1980), and task forces have been formed to identify empirically validated treatments (Chambless, 1995). Clinical child psychologists are also interested in determining the effectiveness of their interventions, and similar reviews have been undertaken (Weisz, Donnenberg, Han, & Weiss, 1995) and task forces formed (Lonigan, Elbert, & Johnson 1998). Interestingly, meta-analytic reviews of child therapy produce effect sizes comparable to those found in the adult reviews, with effect sizes ranging from .7 to .8 (Casey & Berman, 1985; Weisz et al., 1995). Even more encouraging, those studies that followed up their samples found that these positive effects persisted for at least 6 months (Weisz, 2001). Further, the effects appeared to be comparable for both internalizing and externalizing disorders (Mash & Wolfe, 2002).

Despite these positive effects, several caveats need to be offered concerning these meta-analytic reviews. First, the overwhelming majority (>75%) of the studies reviewed have involved behaviorally oriented or cognitive-behavioral approaches. This reflects the fact that such therapists are more interested in empiricially testing their interventions, and the behavioral approach lends itself more readily to scientific scrutiny. A review of 14 studies evaluating traditional (e.g., talking) therapies for children obtained an effect size of 0.0 (Weisz, 2001), suggesting that these therapies offer no documented benefits to their clients. This finding held even for studies that averaged 60 or more individual therapy sessions with the child (Weiss, Catron, Harris, & Phung, 1999), or when the services offered to the families in the treatment group were more extensive (and more costly) than those services offered to the comparison families (Bickman, 1996). Nevertheless, child clinicians continue to employ these traditional therapies at depressingly high rates (Weisz, 2001).

A second potential limitation of these meta-analytic reviews is that the vast majority of the reviewed studies concerned externalizing disorders rather than internalizing disorders. This conclusion is most evident in the reports of the task forces on empirically validated child treatments (Lonigan et al., 1998), in which a number of interventions were found to be "well established" for both ADHD (Pelham et al., 1998) and conduct disorder (Brestan & Eyberg, 1998), but no treatments met this criterion for childhood depression (Kaslow & Thompson, 1998) or for anxiety disorders other than simple phobias (Ollendick & King, 1998). This reinforces a point we made earlier that research on the childhood internalizing disorders lags far behind what is known about the externalizing disorders.

A third potential concern raised about the meta-analytic reviews of child therapy studies is that the interventions employed in these studies may not reflect accurately what happens in real clinical practice (Weisz et al., 1992). As we note in Chapter 9, the concerns raised include the unrepresentativeness of the study samples (e.g., less co-morbidity, less severe symptomatology) and the strict adherence to manualized treatment, which occurs much less frequently in clinical practice. In fact, Weisz (2001) argues that the major problem in child therapy is not the absence of effective interventions but that everyday practitioners do not routinely employ those validated treatments that do exist. Weisz attributes this problem to a lack of knowledge on the part of clinicians as to what the literature supports, as well as the difficulty in making validated treatments more accessible to these clinicians.

An Integrative Approach to Treating Childhood Disorders

Even this brief review shows that a variety of approaches have been employed in the treatment of childhood disorders. Although these interventions are often beneficial in the short-run (Weisz et al., 1995), long-term improvement in most serious childhood problems—especially attention-deficit hyperactivity disorder, conduct disorder, and delinquency—is not nearly as likely (Pelham & Murphy, 1986; Zigler, Taussig, & Black, 1992).

Why have psychological interventions so consistently failed to demonstrate long-term gains? First, interventions for serious childhood disorders tend to be reactive rather than proactive. Regardless of whether the problem is delinquency, school failure, or child abuse, there has been a tendency for clinicians to wait until the problem is well established before taking action. As described in Chapter 8, a more effective approach would be to identify at-risk children and then try to intervene before their problems have become entrenched and resistant to treatment.

The second problem with current approaches to childhood treatment is that they are often not comprehensive enough. Serious childhood disorders such as delinquency are caused by a multitude of economic, social, and psychological factors. For interventions to be effective, they must address as many of these factors as possible (Zigler et al., 1992). Too many treatments today address only one or two causal factors. In delinquency, for example, a large number of causal factors has been identified, including temperament, inhibitory control problems, faulty or abusive parenting, school failure, poverty, parental discord, and peer difficulties (Zigler et al., 1992). A comprehensive treatment package for this disorder should include interventions that focus on most, if not all, of these factors. It might consist of medication to decrease the child's inhibitory problems, academic tutoring to lessen the risk of school failure, training in problem solving to improve peer interactions, anger-control training to decrease inappropriate responses to frustration, marital therapy for parents to decrease discord in the home, parent training to improve disciplinary procedures, and early childhood education to decrease the adverse effects of poverty. An example of such a comprehensive intervention is the ongoing study examining the effectiveness of the FAST Track Program (Conduct Problems Prevention Research Group, 2000).

A third factor limiting the long-term effectiveness of psychological treatments for serious childhood disorders is their relatively brief duration. For example, the typical parent-training program lasts from eight to twenty weeks. However, as Alan Kazdin

(1997) persuasively argues, chronic disorders need continual treatment. Using an analogy from medicine, he notes that a physician treating diabetes would not discontinue insulin treatment after the diabetes comes under control. Similarly, psychological interventions with children should not end when the problem shows initial improvement.

In short, serious childhood disorders require early, comprehensive, and long-term interventions. Unfortunately, the expense of such interventions makes it difficult to find funding for early prevention strategies, even though the initial expenditures would save money in the long run. For example, insurance companies generally do not pay for treating children who are at risk for problems, and although governments will spend $40,000 a year to incarcerate a juvenile offender (Zigler et al., 1992), they tend to refuse to spend a fraction of that amount on programs to prevent delinquent behavior. This short-sighted perspective may be changing, however. The U.S. government has awarded a major grant for a pilot project designed to evaluate the long-term effectiveness of comprehensive treatments for at-risk conduct-disordered children (Conduct Problems Prevention Research Group, 2000). These treatments include many of the procedures described above (the intervention even pays for telephones to be installed in children's homes to help decrease their mothers' social isolation). If this pilot project proves effective in decreasing the risk of delinquency among these children, the government may decide to provide broader support for such programs.

THE FUTURE OF CLINICAL CHILD PSYCHOLOGY

Predicting the future is a hazardous business. However, the history of clinical child psychology clearly shows that its advances have lagged several decades behind developments in adult clinical psychology. Therefore, the future of clinical child psychology is likely to shadow recent developments in the adult area. Specifically, we predict that research into the neurobiological functioning of children and its influence on behavior and learning problems will receive a great deal of attention in the next decade. We further believe that pediatric psychology and cognitive-behavioral interventions—especially for internalizing disorders—will burgeon in the near future. In addition, school violence and the use/misuse of psychoactive medications with children are receiving national attention, including recent White House conferences. This heightened attention at the level of the federal government will translate into increased federal funding to stimulate research in these areas. Finally, the identification of risk factors for substance use, and the development of prevention or treatment programs to combat this problem, are now receiving millions of dollars of federal funding and a great deal of scientific and public attention.

In terms of neurobiological functioning, high-technology advances (neuroimaging of brain functioning) are allowing major breakthroughs in the understanding of the role of brain functioning in the development of many childhood disorders, including learning disabilities (Shaywitz & Shaywitz, 1999), ADHD (Zametkin, Ernst, & Silver, 1998), and autism (Rumsey & Ernst, 2000). In pediatric psychology, programs are being developed to help children cope with diabetes and other chronic illnesses (Drotar, 1999). Further, now that it is recognized that children infected with the AIDS virus suffer profound social and psychological problems, clinicians will be working on interventions designed to help children cope with the prolonged hospitalization, social stigma, and physical disabilities associated with this disease (Task Force on Pediatric AIDS, 1989). In the area of cognitive-behavioral therapy, more attention will be directed toward the identification and subsequent treatment of children with internalizing disorders, especially anxiety and depression (Kendall, 2000).

The recent dramatic increase in the rate of school shootings, despite the fact that adolescent violence has actually decreased of late, has led society to demand safer schools (Brener, Simon, Krug, & Lowry, 1999). As part of this agenda, efforts have been undertaken to identify children at-risk for such violence, as well as to develop interventions that can decrease the factors that may lead to such violence. For example, the last decade has seen a dramatic increase in research on bullying and victimization (Perry, Hodges, & Egan, 2001), a major contributing factor to school shootings.

The last decade also has seen a sharp increase in the use of medications to improve the functioning of children with mental health problems. Unfortunately, the use of such medication has far outstripped the research supporting this use. Thus, for example, the use of the SSRIs in treating children with depression has increased dramatically, although there is little empirical evidence to support this use (Mash & Wolfe, 2002), and these drugs have not received FDA approval for use with children. It is anticipated that the next decade will see a large increase in studies examining the safety and efficacy of psychoactive medications for a wide variety of childhood problems.

Just as the use of prescribed medications for children increased, during the 1990s illegal substance use by children and adolescents dramatically increased, too, although this increase may be leveling off. In response, researchers set out to identify risk factors (e.g., personality, peer, and home factors) for substance use/abuse, as well as prevention/intervention programs to counteract this problem (Bryant, Windle, & West, 1997). Unfortunately, we have a much better understanding of what the risk factors are than of how to prevent or treat substance abuse. For example, Project DARE, the most widespread prevention program in the U.S., consistently has been shown to be ineffective in altering children's later use of drugs (Lynam et al., 1999). Work on identifying effective prevention and intervention programs for substance use among children and adolescents certainly will continue for the next decade at least.

Finally, in response to the bombing of the federal building in Oklahoma City and the September 11, 2001 terrorist attacks, it is quite conceivable that the future may see an increase in anxiety disorders among children, including separation anxiety disorder and, especially, posttraumatic stress disorder. The latter has received very little attention in the child literature in the past, but this will most likely change in the future.

CHAPTER SUMMARY

Clinical psychologists' longstanding focus on assessing and treating adults has changed over the last three decades to the point that clinical child psychologists have become a prominent subgroup in the field. Clinical psychologists have developed methods of classification, assessment, and intervention that are specialized for use with young clients.

In dealing with these clients, clinical child psychologists pay special attention to referral issues, developmental considerations, infant temperament factors, the quality of infants' early attachments, the nature of parent–child interactions, and the impact of childhood stressors.

Taking all these special considerations into account leads clinical child psychologists to ask assessment questions about child clients that they would usually not ask about adults, and to use assessment methods (e.g., behavior rating scales, third-party interviews, intelligence and achievement tests, and family and peer interaction measures) that are less frequently used with adult clients.

Unlike the clinically derived disorder classification systems used with adults (which rely on the judgments of experts to determine diagnostic criteria), classification of childhood disorders has tended to emphasize empirically derived systems which rely on statistical analyses of large amounts of data to determine the symptoms of given diagnostic categories. Empirically derived systems have identified two main kinds of childhood disorders: externalizing problems such as hyperactivity, aggression, and delinquency and internalizing problems such as depression, anxiety, and somatic problems. Other significant childhood problems include developmental disorders such as learning disabilities, and pervasive developmental disorders such as childhood autism.

Treatment of child clients poses special challenges because children may not give accurate self-reports and because their presence in therapy requires parental motivation and cooperation. Specialized forms of psychodynamic, behavioral, and cognitive-behavioral treatment have been developed for use with children, and although some (such as operant and cognitive-behavioral approaches) have proven successful with a wide range of problems, the benefits may be of rather short duration and may not generalize beyond the settings in which treatment took place. Although, in general, drugs tend to be used only rarely in treating childhood disorders, methylphenidate (Ritalin) and other stimulant medications are widely prescribed and widely effective in dealing with attention deficit hyperactivity disorder. Rather than dealing with childhood disorders after they appear, clinical child psychologists would prefer early, comprehensive, and long-term interventions designed to prevent these disorders before they emerge.

Chapter 11

Health Psychology

In this chapter and the next, we discuss two specialized areas of clinical psychology—health psychology and neuropsychology—that illustrate how important it is for psychologists to study relationships between psychological and biological factors. We have selected these areas because they have been some of clinical psychology's best "growth stocks" in the past 25 years. New research discoveries and expanding professional roles for clinicians have increasingly attracted psychologists to these areas.

WHAT IS HEALTH PSYCHOLOGY?

Health psychology is a specialty that emerged in the 1970s and is devoted to studying "psychological influences on how people stay healthy, why they become ill, and how they respond when they do get ill" (Taylor, 1995, p. 3). This subfield has enjoyed such rapid growth over the last 25 years that it now has its own division in the APA (Division 38) and its own journal, *Health Psychology*. Health psychology research is also often published in the *Journal of Behavioral Medicine* and *Psychological Medicine*. Related professional organizations include the Society of Behavioral Medicine and the American Psychosomatic Society. Many clinical psychology training programs now include a "track" that specializes in the training of health psychologists, and some programs have developed health psychology as their major focus.

Health psychology is closely related to the larger field of *behavioral medicine*, which involves the integration of knowledge from the social/behavioral sciences (e.g., psychology, sociology, and anthropology), the biological sciences, and medicine into an interdisciplinary science focused on understanding and treating all types of medical disorders in the broadest possible ways. Health psychology and behavioral medicine follow a *biopsychosocial* model which holds that physical illness is the result of biological, psychological, and social disruptions. They study how psychological conditions and behavioral processes are linked to illness and health.

Sir William Osler, a physician, is generally considered the father of modern behavioral medicine because he insisted that psychological and emotional factors must be considered in order to understand and treat various diseases. In 1910, Osler gave a lecture in which he suggested that many symptoms of heart disease "are brought on by anger, worry, or sudden shock." These ideas are remarkably similar to contemporary proposals about how key psychological factors may be linked to heart disease.

Osler's views were made more relevant by significant changes in the nature of illness in Western cultures during the 20th century. As recently as 100 years ago, most Americans died of acute infectious diseases such as pneumonia, typhoid fever, and tuberculosis. However, advances in education, sanitation, and vaccination have all but eliminated these diseases, leaving chronic illnesses—heart disease and cancer, for example—as the major threats to life (Blumenthal, 1994). Further, the major risk factors for developing chronic illnesses are behaviors such as smoking, unhealthy eating, sedentary lifestyles, and alcohol abuse.

These changes in the major threats to health, along with changing ideas about illness, spurred research on how psychological, behavioral, and medical conditions are related. It became clear, for example, that psychological factors contribute to the onset or severity of heart disease, ulcers, asthma, stomach disorders, cancer, arthritis, headaches, and hypertension. Indeed, until recently, these illnesses were called *psychosomatic* or *psychophysiological*, disorders in recognition of the mixture of psychological and biological determinants operating in them. But categorizing just a few illnesses as psychosomatic implies that psychological factors are not relevant in other conditions. Today's health psychologists consider psychological factors to be potential influences on almost all diseases.

The more we learn about any human disorder, the more difficult it becomes to draw a line that clearly divides those that are "physical" from those that are "mental." For example, schizophrenia and major depression, two of our most serious mental disorders, almost always entail a mixture of physical and psychological causes and symptoms. Further, depression often adversely affects the course of diseases such as diabetes; and many cases of diabetes ultimately lead to clinical depression.

Physicians and other health professionals are also becoming increasingly interested in contributions of health psychologists. Indeed, up to 60% of all physician office visits are related to emotional distress (Pallak et al., 1995). Because physicians are seldom prepared to deal with these aspects of disease, prevention and treatment increasingly fall to persons in the health psychology field. In short, health psychology has grown because evidence strongly shows that it no longer makes sense to treat patients ". . . from either the head up or the neck down" (Dornelas, 2001, p. 1261).

Several books provide more detailed discussions of the history and status of health psychology and behavioral medicine (e.g., Baum, Revenson, & Singer, 2001;

Ogden, 1996; Taylor, 1999). In this chapter, we discuss four areas of research and practice that occupy many health psychologists (Blumenthal, Matthews, & Weiss, 1994):

1. Understanding how environmental stressors, psychological processes, social forces, and physiological factors interact to influence illness and health,
2. Identifying risk factors for sickness as well as protective factors for health,
3. Developing and evaluating techniques for promoting healthy behaviors and preventing unhealthy ones, and
4. Developing and evaluating psychological interventions that contribute to the effective treatment of illness.

STRESS, COPING, AND HEALTH

Stress is the negative emotional and physiological process that occurs as people try to adjust to or deal with environmental circumstances that disrupt, or threaten to disrupt, their daily functioning (Taylor, 1999). The environmental circumstances (such as job demands, exams, personal tragedies, or even annoying daily hassles) that cause people to make adjustments are called *stressors*. The physical, psychological, and behavioral responses (such as increased heart rate, anger, and impulsiveness) that people display in the face of stressors are called *stress reactions*. It is important to remember that stress is not the result of events per se, but the result of responses to events.

Barbara Dohrenwend (1978) suggested a four-stage model of how stressors and stress reactions contribute to physical illness and/or psychological disorder. In the first stage, stressful life events occur, followed in the second stage by a set of physical and psychological stress reactions. In the third stage, these stress reactions are mediated by environmental and psychological factors that either amplify or reduce their intensity. Factors likely to reduce stress reactions include things like adequate financial resources, free time to deal with stressors, a full repertoire of effective coping skills, the help and support of friends and family, a strong sense of control over stressors, a tendency to be optimistic, and a view of stressors as challenges. Stress-amplifying factors include things like poverty, lack of social support, inadequate coping skills, pessimism, a sense of helplessness, and seeing stressors as terrifying threats. In stage four, the interaction of particular stressors, particular people, and particular circumstances results in physical and/or psychological problems that may be mild and temporary (some anxiety, a headache, or a few sleepless nights) or severe and persistent (e.g., an anxiety or mood disorder, or physical illness). Exactly how stressors and stress reactions might contribute to physical illness is not clearly understood, but part of the story is told by their impact on the nervous system and the immune system.

Stress and the Nervous System

Physiological reactions to stress include a pattern of responses in the central and autonomic nervous system that Hans Selye (1956) called the *general adaptation syndrome* or GAS. The GAS begins with an *alarm reaction* which is often called the fight-or-flight response because it helps us combat or escape stressors. The alarm reaction releases into the bloodstream a number of "stress hormones," including adrenal corticosteroids, catecholamines (e.g., adrenaline), and endogenous opiates (the body's natural pain-killers), all of which increase heart rate, blood pressure, and respiration, pupillary dilation, muscle tension, release of glucose reserves, and concentration of attention on the stressor.

If the stressor persists, or if new ones occur in quick succession, alarm is followed by the *stage of resistance*, during which less dramatic, but more continuous biochemical efforts to cope with stress can have harmful consequences. For example, prolonged release of stress hormones can create chronic high blood pressure, damage muscle tissue, and inhibit the body's ability to heal.

If stressors continue long enough, the *stage of exhaustion* appears as various organ systems begin to malfunction or break down. Here, people experience physical symptoms ranging from fatigue, weight loss, and indigestion to colds, heart disease, and other more serious problems.

Stress and Immune System

Another important effect of prolonged stress is suppression of the immune system, the body's defense against disease-causing agents (Herbert & Cohen, 1993; Maier & Watkins, 1998). For example, chronic stressors (e.g., taking care of a seriously ill relative) have been shown to lower immune system functioning, and even brief stressors like final-exam periods have been associated with a decline in the activity of immune system cells that fight viruses and tumors (Kiecolt-Glaser & Glaser, 1992). In one particularly interesting study of the relationship between stress and illness, researchers injected volunteer subjects with cold viruses or a placebo and then measured the amount of stress experienced by the volunteers over a given time period (Cohen, Tyrell, & Smith, 1991). The results showed that the appearance of colds and infections was correlated with the amount of stress the subjects encountered. Many researchers now suspect that *immunosuppression* is the basis for the association between stressors and increased risk for illnesses, such as some forms of cancer (e.g., Cohen & Rabin, 1998).

Measuring Stressors

To study the relationship between stress and illness, it is necessary to measure stress accurately, and health psychologists have tried to do so in several ways. One example is a questionnaire called the *Schedule of Recent Experiences* (SRE) (Amundson, Hart, & Holmes, 1986), which contains a list of 42 events involving health, family, personal, occupational, and financial matters. Respondents check the events that have happened to them during the past 6, 12, 24, and 36 months, and then give each event a weight based on the amount of adjustment needed to deal with it (1 = very little adjustment; 100 = maximal adjustment). These weights are summed to give a *Life Change Unit Score*.

Criticism of the SRE led other researchers to develop stress assessment instruments that differ in how they weight the occurrence of an event, the time periods surveyed, and the content of the events themselves (Zimmerman, 1983). For example, the

Life Experiences Survey (Sarason, Johnson, & Siegel, 1978) allows respondents to rate the positive or negative impact of each listed event, and to add stressful events that are not listed. These more individualized ratings are designed to make the LES and similar instruments more sensitive to the stressors experienced by people of diverse ethnic and cultural backgrounds.

Health psychologists have theorized that the cumulative effects of many minor daily annoyances can produce as much or more stress as one major event, so they have also developed "chronic strain" inventories, such as the *Hassles Scale* (Kanner et al., 1981). On this scale, respondents indicate how severely they have been hassled in the past month by events such as "misplacing or losing things," "unexpected company," "auto maintenance," "too many meetings," and "filling out forms." Another approach to measuring stress involves examining the effects of specific life crises such as crime victimization (e.g., Burnam et al., 1988) on later adjustment.

The results of research with even the best stress assessment scales shows that while there is undoubtedly a relationship between stress and illness, the strength of that relationship is relatively weak. In other words, even though people who are exposed to significant stressors are more likely overall to become ill than those exposed to fewer stressors, most people who experience stressors do not become ill. This realization has led health psychologists to search for variables that might explain how people are protected from the assumed health-harming effects of stress. Among several *vulnerability or resistance factors* (Kessler, Price, & Wortman, 1985), three variables—coping strategies, positive psychological states, and social support—have sparked the most interest.

Coping Strategies

Coping refers to people's cognitive, emotional, and behavioral efforts at modifying, tolerating, or eliminating stressors that threaten them (Folkman & Lazarus, 1980). People vary in how they cope with stress. Some try to eliminate or otherwise deal with stressors directly; others attempt to change the way they think about stressors to make them less upsetting; still others concentrate on managing the emotional reactions that stressors cause (Lazarus, 1993).

Research groups at the University of California (Berkeley) and at the State University of New York at Stony Brook have developed instruments to measure how people cope with stress. At Berkeley, Richard Lazarus and Susan Folkman developed a *Ways of Coping* checklist consisting of 68 items that describe how 100 middle-aged adults said they coped with stressful events in their lives (Folkman & Lazarus, 1980). These items fall into two broad categories: *problem-focused* and *emotion-focused coping* (see Table 11.1). The 100 respondents reported on a total of 1,332 stressful episodes, and in 98% of them, said they used both coping methods. Their choice was not random, however. The typical respondent emphasized problem-focused methods for coping with some stressors and emotion-focused methods for others. Problem-focused coping was favored for stressors related to work, while emotion-focused coping was used more often when the stressors involved health. Men tended to use problem-focused coping more often than women in certain situations, but men and women did not differ in

TABLE 11.1   Ways of Coping

Problem-focused and emotion-focused coping are two major ways in which people deal with stressors.

Coping Skills	Example
Problem-focused coping	
Confronting	"I stood my ground and fought for what I wanted."
Seeking social support	"I talked to someone to find out more about the situation."
Planful problem solving	"I made a plan of action and I followed it."
Emotion-focused coping	
Self-controlling	"I tried to keep my feelings to myself."
Distancing	"I didn't let it get to me; I tried not to think about it too much."
Positive reappraisal	"I changed my mind about myself."
Accepting responsibility	"I realized I brought the problem on myself."
Escape/avoidance (wishful thinking)	"I wished that the situation would go away or somehow be over with."

SOURCE: Adapted from Folkman, S., Lazarus, R. S., Gruen, R. J., & DeLongis, A. (1986). Appraisal, coping, health status, and psychological symptoms. *Journal of Personality and Social Psychology*, 50, 571–579.

their use of emotion-focused coping. Other researchers using different instruments have reached similar conclusions (Stone & Neale, 1984).

The distinction between problem-focused and emotion-focused coping has been particularly useful, guiding research for the last two decades (Tennen, et al., 2000). Surprisingly, however, results from thousands of coping checklist studies have produced few other findings of significant value (Coyne & Racioppo, 2000; Lazarus, 1998;). Most effects are small or inconsistent, and it is still unclear what processes operate during successful long-term coping or what effects coping has on stress (Somerfield & McCrae, 2000). Because of the lack of theoretically useful findings, it has been difficult to develop a broad range of clinical interventions based on coping strategies.

Still, coping research is continuing. *The American Psychologist* published two multi-article collections on coping and its close cousin, *positive psychology* (discussed below), in the year 2000 and another in 2001. In addition to the types of research discussed above, researchers are examining how personality variables or cognitive factors such as implicit memory, selective attention, and out-of-awareness decision making impact coping. (These cognitive factors can also be called defense mechanisms; see Cramer, 2000; Vaillant, 2001.) It appears that a comprehensive theory of coping is yet to be developed, but interest in this area has accelerated, and interventions intended to enhance coping often work, even if we can't yet fully explain why.

Positive Psychology.   Research on the impact of successful coping strategies is only one aspect of a cross-disciplinary field called positive psychology. Researchers working in this increasingly popular field examine how positive subjective states, individual traits, and situations influence health and well-being. Positive psychology developed partly as a reaction against the traditional focus on pathology and negative emotions that has prevailed in much of health psychology and psychology in general (Seligman & Csikszentmihalyi, 2000). Psychologists interested in positive psychology examine a variety of personality and cognitive characteristics, including optimism (Peterson, 2000), resilience, (Fredrickson, 2001), faith and hope (see Myers, 2000), and adaptive defense mechanisms (Valliant, 2000), all of which can be part of adaptive coping.

Researchers who study positive psychology, and the mechanisms associated with it, have found that although adaptive coping can promote health, the benefits of positive attitudes do have their limits. For example, it may not be a good idea simply to act happy when you're not. Efforts to inhibit or suppress negative emotions may have some short-term benefits, but may, in the long run, be harmful to health (Salovey et al., 2000). In fact, it appears beneficial to acknowledge and, to some degree, express feelings about negative experiences. One study on this point found that rheumatoid arthritis sufferers who talked about stressful events more tended to have better outcomes than those who talked about it less (Kelley, Lumley, & Leisen, 1997). And James Pennebaker (1995) has shown that persons who write about stressful experiences over successive days have better health outcomes than those who do not. Findings such as these are consistent with evidence that disclosure of negative emotions in therapy is related to positive physical health, and why inhibition is generally not (Miller & Cohen, 2001).

Other researchers in this area have investigated the role in physical and mental health of optimistic beliefs, including slightly over-optimistic distortions of reality ("positive illusions"). A recent review of literature in social psychology and related areas reveals, for example, that positively biased perceptions of reality are more common in people who are not depressed (Taylor et al., 2000). Healthy or mature defense mechanisms such as sublimation, altruism, suppression, and humor also appear to safeguard health and lessen the effects of some diseases (Vaillant, 2000).

Several questions about coping and positive psychology remain unanswered. One of these concerns the optimum balance of positive and negative expectations—is it better to be optimistic or realistic? Optimism can often lead to self-deception and less-careful cognitive processing, but without a certain amount of optimism, people may be more vulnerable to stressors (see Schneider, 2001). Another question relates to how positive and negative experiences aggregate over time to affect health. Finally, we have yet to delineate clearly which features of maladaptive coping are deeply ingrained and therefore difficult to change through therapy (i.e., personality characteristics), and which are less deeply ingrained and are therefore teachable.

Social Support

Social support has been defined in many ways (Schradle & Dougher, 1985), but its essential element appears to be the experience of being cared for, loved, esteemed, and part of a network of communication and mutual obligation (Baumeister & Leary, 1995).

Social support, then, involves more than the presence of others. It provides relationships in which emotional support, feedback, guidance, assistance, and values are exchanged.

Several studies have shown that the relationship between stress and illness is weaker among individuals who perceive high levels of social support in their lives (e.g., Broman, 1993; Wickrama, Conger & Lorenz, 1995). Several possible reasons are given for why this might be so (Cohen & Wills, 1985; Uchino, Cacioppo, & Kiecolt-Glaser, 1996). The most popular explanation is that social support acts as a *buffer* against stress. The buffer model claims that social support enables people who face intense stressors to neutralize their harmful effects. By serving as an additional resource in a person's attempts at managing stressful problems, social support offers more opportunities for self-disclosure and bolsters their efforts at constructive coping (Myers, 2000; Thoits, 1986), and may lessen the chances of self-defeating strategies such as excessive drinking. In short, people's perception of social support can strengthen their belief that others care for and value them; it may also enhance their self-esteem and increase feelings of confidence about handling stress in the future. Another view, sometimes termed the *direct-effect* model, holds that social support is helpful regardless of whether stressful events are experienced because there is a general benefit to being embedded in supportive relationships that manifests itself in better health (Baumeister & Leary, 1995). A third explanation for the apparent benefits of social support is that high levels of support, good health, and low levels of stress all reflect the influence of some underlying characteristic such as *social competence*, which has positive effects on many areas of functioning.

Of course, some combination of all three models may be operating. What does seem clear is that lack of social support, particularly lack of emotional support, puts people at higher risk for both physical and psychological disorders (Cohen & Wills, 1985; Kessler et al., 1985) and even death (House, Robbins, & Metzner, 1982).

Despite its general advantages, social support is not always associated with protection against illness. Social ties can create conflicts if others' helping efforts leave the recipient feeling guilty, overly indebted, or dependent. If a recipient is not able to reciprocate helping efforts, she or he may feel disadvantaged in future interactions with the donor. In other instances, potential helpers may behave in misguided ways (giving too much advice or becoming upset when their advice is not followed) that lead the recipient to feel invaded, incompetent, or rejected (Broman, 1993; Malarkey et al., 1994; Wortman & Lehman, 1985).

RISK FACTORS FOR ILLNESS

Anything that increases a person's chances of developing an illness is called a risk factor for that illness. Some risk factors stem from biological and environmental conditions such as genetic defects or exposure to toxic chemicals (Stokols, 1992). Others come in the form of health–risky patterns of behavior. For example, smoking, overeating, lack of exercise, and consumption of a high-fat, low-fiber diet have all been identified as risk factors for two of North America's leading killers: cardiovascular disease and cancer

(VandenBos, DeLeon, & Belar, 1991). Conversely, certain behaviors or lifestyles tend to promote health. For example, people who eat breakfast regularly, rarely snack between meals, exercise regularly, do not smoke, get 7 to 8 hours of sleep per night, and do not use alcohol excessively live an average of 11 years longer than people who practice none of these behaviors (Breslow, 1979).

Psychological risk factors, too, can influence illness and health in a number of ways. To take but one example, aggressive people are likely to seek out competitive situations which, because they often entail conflict, frequently produce physiological arousal. This arousal may ultimately increase the risk of illness. At the same time, aggressive people may be less likely to receive stress-reducing social support from others. Because they are often competitive and in a hurry, aggressive people may be less likely to take time to get medical check-ups that might detect diseases in their early stages. So a personality trait such as aggressiveness may make three contributions to an illness—especially in people who are genetically predisposed toward it—by increasing physiological arousal, by suppressing social support, and by interfering with healthy behavior.

Behavioral and psychological risk factors appear to combine with other risks to create a strong overall relationship between socioeconomic status (SES) and health. (SES, which reflects a person's social standing relative to others in a society, is measured in terms of income, education, and occupation.) The lower one's SES, the greater one's chances of suffering chronic illness and unexpectedly early death (e.g., Adler et al., 1994). This relationship makes sense when viewed in light of the fact that low SES is linked to poorer nutrition, greater exposure to environmental hazards, less adequate medical care, and other sources of stress-related illness.

The prevalence of health-risky behaviors also tends to be inversely related to SES. Smoking, for example, is more common among less educated people, and people who work in lower status occupations are less likely to engage in physical exercise. Each of these habits have direct negative effects on health, but they can also act in concert with each other, and with other variables, to magnify health problems. Thus, lack of exercise is associated with obesity, which itself is more common among low SES groups (Ernst & Harlan, 1991). Obesity, in turn, significantly increases risks for serious illnesses such as hypertension, diabetes, and coronary heart disease (e.g., Foster & Kendall, 1994). Similarly, people who drink alcohol excessively or abuse illegal drugs are also much more likely to smoke (Sobell, Toneatto, & Sobell, 1994), thereby constituting a double dose of behavioral risk. The negative physical consequences of unhealthy behaviors may also lead to increased levels of stress, depression, discouragement, and consequent impairment in coping skills (Baum & Posluszny, 1999; Vaillant, 1994).

The multifaceted influence of behavioral, psychological, and social risk factors is seen in several serious illnesses, including heart disease, cancer, and AIDS.

Risk Factors for Cardiovascular Disease

About half of the deaths each year in North America result from cardiovascular diseases, which include coronary heart disease (CHD), high blood pressure, and stroke. That works out to more than 2,600 people per day, an average of one death every 33 seconds. In 2001, cardiovascular disease cost the United States an estimated $299 billion dollars in health care costs and lost productivity (Centers for Disease Control, 2001a).

The numerous risk factors for CHD have been classified as either causal, conditional, or predisposing (Grundy, 1999). *Causal risk factors* include cigarette smoking, elevated serum cholesterol, and hypertension. *Conditional risk factors*, such as serum triglycerides and coagulation factors, are those that have not as yet been identified as an independent cause of CHD but are often seen as contributing to its appearance. *Predisposing risk factors* affect CHD by influencing causal and conditional factors. The list of predisposing factors is long, and most of them are of direct relevance to health psychologists. They include family history, ethnicity, depression, anxiety, obesity, sedentary lifestyle, social isolation, hostility, and work-related stress (Schneiderman, et al., 2001). Let's consider the role of stressors and other psychological factors in CHD.

The Role of Stressors.   Some of the first strong evidence for the role of stressors in cardiovascular disease came from research on monkeys' responses to various types of stress (Manuck, Kaplan, & Clarkson, 1983; Manuck et al., 1988). Researchers wanted to know whether increases in cardiovascular and endocrine reactivity caused by stressors can, if repeated many times over several years, produce the kinds of changes in the heart or peripheral arteries seen in cardiovascular diseases. The answer appears to be yes; animals showing the greatest increase in heart rate in response to stressors also had significantly more plaque—a build-up of cholesterol and other fatty substances—in their coronary arteries than did animals whose reaction was less extreme.

As noted earlier, people, too, react to threatening stimuli and other stressors with increases in heart rate—as well as with pronounced changes in blood pressure, and secretion of epinephrine, norepinephrine, and other stress hormones (Anderson, 1989; Krantz & Manuck, 1984). In the short run, these changes have little significance for cardiovascular functioning, which returns to normal soon after a stressor ends. However, if repeated stressors continually stimulate cardiac activity, the small arteries at the body's periphery may undergo permanent constrictions that result in increased blood pressure (Obrist, 1981).

Demographic variables such as ethnicity, gender, and age are related to a tendency to overreact physiologically to stressors (Adler & Matthews, 1994). This relationship may explain why certain people are at greater risk for heart disease than others. For instance, CHD is about half as common among Chinese- or Japanese-Americans as among European- or African-Americans, while high blood pressure is about twice as common among African-Americans as European-Americans. Males, African-Americans of both genders, and older people all suffer higher-than-average rates of heart disease *and* have larger-than-average blood pressure responses to certain stressors. Why these differences occur is not yet clear, although physical factors—such as diet—and cultural factors such as living in stressful environments are almost certainly important contributors. Thus, the heightened risk of cardiovascular disease among African-Americans may be related to the fact that many of them are, because of lower socioeconomic status, exposed to higher-stress environments. Because they face more social adversity and obstacles than other groups, African-Americans may also be more likely to feel anger and express hostility. The increased risk of CHD for men in general may stem from their tendency to behave aggressively or competitively in social situations, while the risk for older people may lie in a gradual erosion of social support that increases the impact of stressors.

Psychological Factors in CHD.

Psychological Factors in CHD.   As noted earlier, the impact of stressors can be mediated by psychological factors, including whether we think about stressors as threats or challenges, and whether we believe we can control them. People who feel helpless in the face of what they see as threats are likely to experience more intense physiological reactivity and emotional upset. On the other hand, those who view stressors as challenges, and feel confident about coping with them, may experience less reactivity and distress (Lazarus & Folkman, 1984).

The psychological risk factors for CHD that have attracted the most attention in the past twenty years are associated with the *Type-A behavior pattern* that a pair of cardiologists noticed was typical of many patients with heart disease (Friedman & Rosenman, 1974). Type-A people are described as displaying (1) explosive, accelerated speech; (2) a heightened pace of living; (3) impatience with slowness; (4) attempts to perform more than one activity at a time; (5) preoccupation with self; (6) dissatisfaction with life; (7) evaluation of accomplishments in terms of numbers; (8) competitiveness; and (9) free-floating hostility (Matthews, 1982). In contrast to Type-A persons, Type-B persons are more relaxed and feel less time pressure. They appear less competitive, controlling, and hostile. *The Structured Interview* (Rosenman, 1978) is one of the most common ways of measuring Type-A behavior (Matthews, 1988).

Early research suggested that Type-A behavior and thinking is an important risk factor for the development of CHD. For example, in the Western Collaborative Group Study (WCGS), 3,500 men between the ages of thirty-nine and fifty-nine were classified as Type A or Type B. Of 257 men who suffered heart attacks during the eight-and-a-half-year study, 178 (69%) of them were Type A's. In other words, Type A's were more than twice as likely to have had heart attacks as Type B's (Rosenman et al., 1975). The impact of Type A on CHD risk remained even after the researchers statistically controlled for several other risk factors, including family history of heart disease, high cholesterol, high blood pressure, and cigarette smoking.

The effects of Type-A on heart disease appears across genders and cultures. For example, one study compared the personality characteristics of 290 Japanese men and women who had suffered nonfatal heart attacks to those of 489 healthy control participants (Yoshimasu et al., 2001). The Type-A behavior pattern was significantly associated with risk, especially among Japanese women.

It appears that when encountering a stressor, people who are classified as Type-A experience faster heart rates and higher blood pressure than those classified as Type B (Harbin, 1989; Lyness, 1993). These differences in reactivity are strongest in response to stressors that generate interpersonal conflict, mobilize competitiveness, or involve criticism. These are precisely the kinds of situations that are most likely to trigger anger and hostility. Likewise, chronically hostile people experience high levels of cardiovascular reactivity and sodium consumption, most notably in response to interpersonal stressors (Miller et al., 1998; Suls & Wang, 1993).

So it may be that Type-A behavior or chronic negative emotions are linked to CHD because people with these characteristics consistently overreact physiologically to situations that threaten them or make them angry. In addition, their competitiveness and hostility create ever more opportunities for conflict, to which they then overreact. In the long-run, this physiological overarousal could put a strain on arteries and increase the chances for other cardiovascular defects. The link between these psychological characteristics and CHD might also be forged in another way. Frequent angry outbursts or other negative emotions may be accompanied by rapid swings in the levels of stress hormones, the corticosteroids and catecholamines. A constant barrage of hormonal changes could, in turn, bring about various chemical changes that weaken arteries. In addition, many of these people are "too busy" to go to a doctor, eat a balanced diet, get enough sleep, or engage in regular exercise; they may also consume excessive caffeine and smoke tobacco. The interaction of these unhealthy behaviors with emotionally driven wear and tear may prove to be the most complete explanation of the psychological risks for CHD because it is more specific than the global association between Type-A behavior and CHD.

In fact, we now know that the relationship between Type-A behavior and CHD is indeed much more complex than was originally believed. For one thing, being a Type-A person does not mean that you are highly likely to suffer a heart attack or other form of CHD. Notice that even though Type As in the WCGS were twice as likely to develop CHD as Type Bs, the vast majority of Type As never developed CHD. Second, careful reanalysis of other research (Eaker et al., 1989), some more recent follow-up data on the WCGS sample (Ragland & Brand, 1988), and data from prospective studies conducted with Asian-American men (Cohen & Reed, 1985) suggest that not all aspects of Type-A behavior are risk factors for CHD (Matthews, 1988; Miller et al., 1991). It appears that the most health-risky aspect of the Type-A pattern is *hostility*, a feature that not all Type As display (Williams & Barefoot, 1988; Williams, 2001). Because Type-A behavior includes both "toxic" and "nontoxic" elements, recent research has focused less on the global pattern and more on those elements of personality or behavior that are more specifically associated with risk (e.g., Birks & Roger, 2000).

Depression also plays a role in CHD. Depression among patients who have had a myocardial infarction (commonly known as a "heart attack") is as high as 20%, with an additional 27% showing some symptoms of depression (Burg & Abrams, 2001). After suffering an attack, those who are depressed tend to have poorer long-term outcomes, even after controlling for other factors (e.g., cardiac history). In fact, depression is a serious problem for many chronic illnesses. Depression is also associated with lifestyle choices that are more likely to produce additional disease, so treatment of depression as part of an integrated treatment plan is critical.

Risk Factors for HIV/AIDS

It has been estimated that as many as 1 million people in the United States are infected with HIV, the virus that causes acquired immune deficiency syndrome (AIDS). As of 2000, over 770,000 cases of AIDS had been reported in the United States (Centers for Disease Control, 2001b). Homosexual males and intravenous drug users are at highest risk, but the incidence of HIV infection is growing especially fast among low-income African-Americans and Hispanic-American adolescents. The problem is much worse in other parts of the world. Globally, over 36 million persons, 47% of them women, are estimated to be living with HIV/AIDS, and 95% of the cases are in the developing countries (Centers for Disease Control, 2001c).

Health psychologists have helped focus attention on the fact that most cases of AIDS can be prevented by avoiding several risky behavior patterns: (1) sexual activity without the use of condoms or other protective devices, (2) sexual contact with multiple partners and/or partners with an unknown sexual history, (3) heavy use of alcohol or other drugs prior to sexual activity (because drugs impair judgment about the necessity of using condoms), and (4) for intravenous drug users, sharing injection needles. Stress is also a risk factor for AIDS (as it is for many other diseases) because people are more likely to engage in impulsive behaviors such as drug use or unprotected sex when they are under higher levels of stress (e.g., Testa & Collins, 1997).

ILLNESS PREVENTION AND TREATMENT PROGRAMS

Health psychologists have collaborated with physicians, health educators, and other professionals to develop programs for preventing and treating a variety of illnesses. The prevention programs are designed to reduce behavioral and psychological risk factors in specified populations, typically by helping people make healthy changes in diet, exercise, and smoking and drinking habits (Dornelas, 2001; Matarazzo & Carmody, 1983). Health psychology treatment programs usually focus on helping medical patients, individually or in small groups, minimize or cope with the symptoms of their illnesses. The success of these methods and the promise of new advances account in part for the rapid increase in the number of health psychologists employed in hospitals and other health care settings.

In this section, we highlight health psychology interventions related to cardiovascular diseases, pain, cancer, and HIV/AIDS. More extensive discussions of these activities can be found in health psychology textbooks (e.g., Baum et al., 2001; Taylor, 1999).

Cardiovascular Diseases

As noted earlier, many people who do not currently have CHD or hypertension are at risk for these diseases because of the way they tend to behave and think. These people can benefit from preventive interventions designed to reduce their risk.

For example, several treatment programs have been developed to reduce Type-A behavior (Nunes, Frank, & Kornfeld, 1987; Thoreson & Powell, 1992). Among the many techniques available, relaxation training, self-monitoring, and training in coping skills appear to have the largest effects on Type-A behavior. Interventions aimed at changing Type-A behavior can also have beneficial effects on some of the biological factors presumed to be at the root of CHD; reduced cholesterol, lowered systolic blood pressure, and slowed heart rate have all been associated with reductions in Type-A behavior.

Many studies have evaluated the effects of programs for changing Type-A behavior. For example, in the Recurrent Coronary Prevention Project, over 800 patients who had already suffered a heart attack received periodic counseling over a 3-year period (Friedman et al., 1986). For some, the counseling focused on the importance of changing diet, exercise, and smoking habits, and adherence to prescribed medications. Others received this counseling along with advice on how to reduce Type-A behavior. At the end of the 3-year program, only 7.2% of the patients who regularly attended the counseling-plus-Type A modification sessions had suffered another heart attack. The heart attack rate was 13.2% for those who had received counseling alone. It is not yet clear, however, if similar programs with healthy Type-A people would have similar effects.

In another approach to preventing CHD, health psychologists have developed programs aimed at eliminating smoking and other harmful habits and at promoting regular exercise, good diet, and other healthy habits (e.g., Jeffery, 1988). Some of these programs focus on a specific risk factor, such as obesity; others address several risk factors at once. The settings for implementing these programs also vary. Workplace interventions have become popular because corporations believe they reduce the cost of health care and because occupational health promotion programs permit the control and investigation of several motivational and environmental variables (Glasgow & Terborg, 1988). Mass media, correspondence, and agricultural extension programs have also been attempted.

Prominent examples of multiple-component prevention programs are the Multiple Risk Factor Intervention Trial (MRFIT, 1982), which attempted to lower blood pressure, smoking, and blood cholesterol in thousands of high-risk individuals; the North Karelia, Finland project (designed in the context of the international Know Your Body Program; Williams, Arnold, & Wynder, 1977); and the Minnesota Heart Health Program, a 5-year educational intervention targeting multiple heart disease risk factors (Blackburn et al., 1984). A special feature of the latter two programs is that their interventions were aimed at children and adolescents. Schools were the primary setting for these interventions, which concentrated on improving knowledge about health, changing peer norms about habits like cigarette smoking, and educating families about risk factors (Perry et al., 1988).

Pain

Pain may be the single most common physical symptom experienced by medical patients (Turk & Rudy, 1990), so pain management is an important objective in psychological interventions with many disorders. Health psychologists have concentrated their pain research and treatment on a few areas: chronic pain conditions, headache, and rheumatoid arthritis. For headache and chronic pain, biofeedback and relaxation training methods have a long record of success, and cognitive-behavioral techniques have also proved effective (e.g., Azar, 1996; Blanchard, 1992). Arthritis pain has generally been treated effectively via stress management and cognitive-behavioral therapy techniques (Young, 1992). These treatments also have some positive effects on the overall physical impairment associated with arthritis.

Cancer

Cancer prevention programs typically focus on stopping unhealthy behaviors (e.g., smoking or overeating) and beginning healthy ones (e.g., exercise). Once a person is diagnosed with cancer, treatment programs focus on factors that can affect the progression of the disease or factors affecting subjective appraisals of the quality of life.

Health psychologists have developed a number of interventions designed to address several aspects of cancer (Andersen, 1992; Baum, Reveson, & Singer, 2001). Their goal is to promote a higher quality of life for cancer patients by helping them (1) understand and confront the disease more actively, (2) cope more effectively with stressors associated with cancer, and (3) develop emotionally supportive relationships in which they can disclose their fears about the disease (Andersen, 1992). Behavioral techniques, such as relaxation training, hypnosis, stress management, and cognitive restructuring have proven especially useful.

For example, many drugs used to treat cancer cause severe nausea and vomiting. After several treatments, some patients become nauseated even before they receive the drugs, an effect known as *anticipatory nausea*. This reaction, in turn, makes some of these patients reluctant to continue treatment. (Anticipatory nausea is probably a conditioned response elicited by cues associated with the sights and smells of the hospital environment where the unconditioned stimulus—chemotherapy—is delivered.) Standard antiemetic drugs have not proven very successful in reducing or preventing anticipatory nausea and vomiting, so attention has turned to the use of behaviorally oriented psychological treatments such as relaxation training with guided imagery, systematic desensitization, and biofeedback (Redd et al., 1987).

In one study, patients receiving chemotherapy were randomly assigned to receive either psychological treatment or no treatment (Burish et al., 1987). Before their first session of chemotherapy, patients in the treatment group were trained to use muscle relaxation and calming imagery to cope with the stress of the cancer-treatment procedures. No-treatment patients were told about the advantages of staying relaxed during chemotherapy and were urged to do so, but they were given no training in relaxation or coping skills. Patients receiving the relaxation training reported significantly less nausea, vomiting, and anxiety than did no-treatment control patients. These improvements were still apparent as long as three days after chemotherapy sessions.

A number of other psychological interventions, including educational programs and various kinds of supportive individual and group therapy, have been shown to improve the mental and physical well-being of some, but not all, cancer patients (Fawzy et al., 1995; Goodwin et al., 2001; Helgeson, Cohen, & Fritz, 1998).

HIV/AIDS

As many as one-third of HIV-positive people continue unprotected sexual practices after learning that they are HIV infected (Kalichman et al., 2001). Therefore, the main focus for health psychologists working on the problem of AIDS is to reduce the unprotected sexual contact and needle sharing that are known risk factors for HIV infection (e.g., Bowen & Trotter, 1995; Kalichman, Cherry, & Browne-Sperling, 1999; Taylor, 1999).

In one program, for example, 233 men and 99 women infected with HIV/AIDS were randomly assigned to either a five-session group intervention focused on practicing safe sex behavior or a five-session health-maintenance support group (a standard-of-care comparison). The safe-sex practices intervention included emphasis on information, motivation, and behavioral skills. At 6-month follow-up, participants who had completed safe-sex practices intervention engaged in significantly less unprotected intercourse and greater condom use (Kalichman et al., 2001). In another program, gay men participated in twelve group sessions of role-playing, behavioral rehearsal, and problem-solving techniques designed to promote condom use and other safe sex practices. Compared to a control group of gay men who did not receive training, program participants significantly increased their use of condoms, their resistance to sexual coercion, and their knowledge of AIDS risks (Kelly et al., 1989).

In a study of an HIV/AIDS program aimed at African-American teenagers at risk for HIV infection, participants were randomly assigned to either a single class on the basic facts about HIV transmission and prevention, or to an eight-session program combining the same basic information with behavioral skill training, role-playing, and group support for sexual abstinence, safe sex practices, and resisting pressure to engage in unsafe sex (St. Lawrence et al., 1995). Teenagers in the behavioral skills group decreased their rate of unprotected intercourse significantly more than those in the single-class group, and this difference was still evident a year later. Further, among those who had been sexually abstinent when the study began, 88.5% of the teens in the behavioral training program remained so during the follow-up, while only 69% of the one-session information group were still abstinent. Success has also been reported following similar programs aimed at adult African-American women in inner-cities (e.g., Kalichman, Rompa, & Coley, 1996).

With the help of health psychologists, many large U.S. cities have established AIDS education programs, clean needle exchanges, condom distributions, and publicity campaigns encouraging safe sex (Kelly & Murphy, 1992). There are also AIDS prevention programs in many other countries, including those of sub-Saharan Africa, Asia, and parts of the Caribbean where women's AIDS risks are increasing dramatically. A major goal of AIDS prevention programs in these countries is to empower women to (1) learn about HIV transmission, (2) take greater control of their sexual lives, (3) obtain protective devices such as female condoms or vaginal microbicides, and (4) become less economically dependent on men and therefore less subject to coerced or commercialized sex.

Other psychological interventions attempt to help patients cope with HIV/AIDS itself. For example, in a study conducted at the University of Miami, 47 gay men who were unaware of their HIV status agreed to be tested for HIV (Anntoni et al., 1991; LaPerriere et al., 1990). Five weeks before being notified of their HIV status, the men were randomly assigned to either a 10-week cognitive-behavioral stress management (CBSM) program, a 10-week group aerobic exercise program, or a no-treatment control group. The main goals of treatment were to buffer the anxiety and depression associated with being notified of HIV infection and to lessen the immunological impairments that often occur with the stress of being notified that one has HIV. Men receiving CBSM training received assertiveness role-playing, training in muscle relaxation, cognitive restructuring to help reduce feelings of stress and helplessness, and basic information about HIV risks and transmission. Men in the CBSM group whose tests showed they had HIV displayed less depression and less significant impairments in immune system functioning than did HIV-positive subjects in the no-treatment group.

Another study compared the effectiveness of different individual psychotherapies for treating depression among HIV-positive patients (Markowitz et al., 1998). In this study, cognitive-behavioral therapists focused on helping clients restructure their appraisals and replace irrational thoughts with more rational ones. Interpersonal therapists focused on mood and helped clients relate moods to environmental events and social roles. Supportive psychotherapy involved client-centered therapy with an added educational component about depression. A fourth condition, supportive psychotherapy plus imipramine was also included. Reductions in depression appeared in each therapy, but reductions were significantly better for interpersonal therapy and supportive psychotherapy plus medication.

Cognitive factors appear to play a significant role in the progression of HIV/AIDS. In one study, for example, men were placed in two groups based on their self-reported acceptance of their illness. Those scoring high in realistic acceptance responded affirmatively to items such as, "I tried to accept what might happen" and "I go over in my mind what I will do about this problem" and negatively to items such as "I refuse to believe that this problem has happened." Men who scored higher on this realistic acceptance factor died an average of nine months *earlier* than those scoring low (Reed et al., 1994). Other studies have also found that negative expectancies are related to less-favorable health outcomes, even when controlling for health habits. Shelley Taylor and her colleagues have suggested that factors such as optimism and beliefs about one's control over an illness affect the actual course of the disease (Taylor, et al., 2000). Apparently, even overly optimistic or unrealistically positive beliefs can have this effect. (Of course cognitive factors such as realistic or optimistic expectancies are invariably infused with affect, so the distinction between cognition and emotion is probably fuzzy, in much the same way as the distinction between mental and physical health is.)

Evidence so far suggests that stress management and positive affect are associated with better outcomes for persons diagnosed with HIV, but negative affect is associated with less favorable outcomes. For instance, Vassend, Eskild, and Halvorsen (1997) studied 104 HIV-positive patients in Norway and concluded that negative affect was associated with progression of the disease. Several studies have found stress reducing intervention techniques useful in helping persons diagnosed with HIV (Baum & Posluszny, 1999).

A Health Psychology Intervention Case

Robert E. Feinstein and Marilyn Sommer Feinstein (2001) describe a case example that illustrates many of the conditions encountered by health psychologists. Perhaps the most prominent feature of their work with "Karen" was the co-occurrence of several conditions that are of both medical and psychological concern. Karen, A 42-year-old female, was married with two children (one a step-child). When she came to the clinic for help with smoking cessation, she was 30 pounds overweight, drank excessively, had high cholesterol, and symptoms of depression. In some areas of her life she functioned reasonably well, however.

Rather than relying on a traditional theoretical orientation for assessment and intervention (i.e., psychodynamic, humanistic, or cognitive-behavioral), Feinstein and

Feinstein adopted a Transtheoretical model (Prochaska et al., 1994). This model is designed to assess a client's readiness and ability to inhibit certain behaviors (e.g., smoking) or perform others (e.g., exercise), and interventions are shaped accordingly.

The Transtheoretical model is one of several models within health psychology that address cognitive factors involved in people's decision to change health-related behaviors (see Rothman, 2000). The model takes into account a person's readiness to change. Prochaska and colleagues have suggested that successful change involves five steps; the first three involve cognitive readiness (Prochaska, DiClemente, & Norcross, 1992):

1. *Precontemplation.* The person does not perceive a health-related behavior as a problem and has not formed an intention to change.
2. *Contemplation.* The person is aware that a health-related behavior should be changed and is thinking about it.
3. *Preparation.* The person has formed a strong intention to change.
4. *Action.* The person is engaging in behavior change. (Relapse and backsliding are common at this stage.)
5. *Maintenance.* After behavior changes have begun, the person must continue performing and/or avoiding specified behaviors.

Karen's treatment planning began with a patient history, then, empirical evidence about the health risk for items in that history were collected. Data on success rates for the various methods available to deal with the patient's various problems were also reviewed. These data provided an estimate of how easy or difficult change generally is. Karen and her therapists discussed her personal priorities for treatment and her hopes and expectations about its success. For instance, they considered Karen's motivation and expectations about change in light of the health threats she faced and her probability of achieving change. Through a process known as *informed shared decision making*, Karen and her therapists jointly developed an intervention plan.

Karen and her therapists decided to begin a program of once-a-week treatment sessions focused on her depression and lack of exercise. These targets were chosen because, given her history and current situation, efforts at dealing with them appeared to have the greatest chance of success.

Karen's case illustrates an important aspect of health psychology treatment, namely that therapists often must consider conducting interventions outside of the normally-defined roles of clinical psychologists. Helping clients to increase exercise is one of these areas (Pollock, 2001). Such nontraditional interventions are indicated because of research evidence that exercise can be as effective as other, more traditional clinical interventions. For instance, Babyak and colleagues (2000) found that exercise was at least as effective as antidepressant medication in reducing the symptoms of depression, and more effective in preventing remission.

Maintaining Behavior Change

Psychological interventions aimed at disease prevention or symptom reduction often result in immediate improvements, but unfortunately, these changes may not be maintained long enough to promote a healthier life (Blanchard, 1994). Maintaining behavior change remains one of the most vexing problems in health psychology. For example, smoking cessation programs are usually followed by significant rates of abstinence, but more than 50% of smokers resume their habit within a year (Jason et al., 1995; Shiffman et al., 1996). A similar picture exists for the treatment of obesity. Although behavior modification appears to be the most effective psychological intervention for obesity, maintenance of weight loss and learning new eating habits are major difficulties for most people. For example, most psychologically oriented weight-reduction interventions can achieve reductions of about 1 pound per week, but it is much more difficult to maintain these reductions beyond 1 or 2 years (Brownell & Wadden, 1992). Similar difficulties are found even when patients try to alter their lifestyles after a heart attack. It would seem reasonable to assume that such a traumatic event might jolt people into permanent lifestyle changes, but as many as 50% of cardiac rehabilitation participants drop out of their programs within 1 year (Burke et al., 1997).

Most theories of change in health psychology assume that the factors responsible for initiating behavior change are also the factors that will maintain those changes, but this might not always be the case (Rothman, 2000). For example, there is an interesting contrast between long-term success in smoking cessation programs and dieting programs, both of which involve inhibition of behaviors. Dieters are typically motivated by expectations of becoming thin. They are highly optimistic at the beginning of treatment and quite ready to make changes. In contrast, smokers are usually motivated by a desire to avoid health threats. Even those entering smoking cessation programs are often initially hesitant in their resolve. But after 6 months of success, relapse rates are significantly higher for weight-control clients than for smoking cessation participants. Rothman (2000) suggests that these differences in outcome should alert health psychologists to the importance for long-term success of (1) clients' motivation to attain a positive goal versus avoid a negative one, and (2) the dangers of overly optimistic client expectations. Factors such as these will undoubtedly be important to understand as health psychologists seek their goal of improving the long-term effects of risk reduction programs.

IMPROVING COMPLIANCE WITH MEDICAL TREATMENT REGIMENS

The effectiveness of treatment of an illness depends first on its being the correct treatment, and second on the patient's continued cooperation with the treatment. The extent to which patients adhere to medical advice and treatment regimens is called *compliance* or *adherence* (Rodin & Salovey, 1989). Noncompliance in taking prescribed medication may occur in up to half of all patients, at least part of the time (Haynes, 1982), and this figure may be as high as 80% among adolescents (Rickert & Jay, 1995). They may not take prescribed medications at all, may take it less frequently or more frequently than instructed, or they may ignore rules about the need to take medicine with food or not to consume alcohol while on medication. Noncompliance tends to be even more common in relation to treatments that are complicated or involve substantial lifestyle changes. Health psychologists have been involved in efforts to understand the causes of noncompliance and in developing interventions to improve compliance.

Causes of Noncompliance

The chief cause of noncompliance appears to be miscommunication between physicians and patients. Patients frequently do not understand what physicians tell them about their illnesses or their treatments. As a result, they are confused about what they should do or they forget what they have been told. One study showed that, 5 minutes after seeing their physician, general-practice patients had forgotten 50% of what the doctor had told them (Ley et al., 1973). The emotional aspects of patient–physician communication also are correlated with compliance. A common pattern of troubled communication involves patient antagonism toward the physician, accompanied by physician withdrawal from the patient. Compliance may also be reduced by the sheer complexity, inconvenience, or discomfort associated with some kinds of treatment. Finally, noncompliance with treatment may appear because patients do not have a good system for reminding themselves about what to do, and when to do it.

A social-psychological theory called the *Health Belief Model* (HBM) (Rosenstock, 1974) has been applied to understanding the reasons for patient noncompliance (Becker & Maiman, 1975). According to the HBM, patients' compliance with treatment depends on factors such as (1) how susceptible to a given illness they perceive themselves to be and how severe the consequences of the illness are thought to be; (2) how effective and feasible versus how costly and difficult the prescribed treatment is perceived to be; (3) the influence of internal cues (physical symptoms) plus external cues (e.g., advice from friends) in triggering health behaviors; and (4) demographic and personality variables that modify the influences of the previous three factors.

Interventions to Improve Compliance

Attempts to improve compliance with treatment can be classified into three general approaches: (1) educating patients about the importance of compliance so that they will take a more active role in maintaining their own health, (2) modifying treatment plans to make compliance easier, and (3) using behavioral and cognitive-behavioral techniques to increase patients' ability to comply (Masur, 1981).

Education. One direct and effective intervention for improving compliance with short-term treatments is to give patients clear, explicit, written instructions that supplement oral instructions about how treatment is to proceed. Educating physicians about the causes and management of noncompliance may also be beneficial. In one study (Inui, Yourtee, & Williamson, 1976), physicians who had been educated about the HBM and ways to improve compliance had more compliant patients at a 6-month reassessment. Education can also counteract inaccurate or naive theories of illness that some clients may have.

Modification of Treatment Plans. A second strategy for increasing compliance is to reorganize treatment to make it easier for patients to comply with it. Examples include timing daily doses of medication to coincide with daily habits (e.g., taking pills right after brushing teeth), giving the treatment in one or two injections rather than in several doses per day, packaging medicine in dosage strips or with pill calendars, and scheduling more frequent follow-up visits to supervise compliance. These procedures have shown promise (e.g., Boczkowski, Zeichner, & DeSanto, 1985), but many of them entail additional manufacturing costs and extra time from service providers, two characteristics that tend to limit their usefulness.

Behavior Modification. Health psychologists have used a number of behavioral techniques, including the use of postcard reminders, telephone calls, wristwatch alarms and other environmental cues to prompt patients to take pills or perform other aspects of treatment plans (Rickert & Jay, 1995). They have also set up written *contingency contracts* between patient and physician that specify what behaviors the patient must perform in order to earn rewards (e.g., more conveniently timed office appointments). Such contracts encourage a more collaborative relationship between patient and physician and have been successful in improving compliance (Swain & Steckel, 1981). Token economies (see Chapter 7) have also been employed to encourage compliance. In one study, three children with kidney failure were given points for maintaining recommended weight, potassium, and nitrogen levels (Magrab & Papadopoulou, 1977). The points could be exchanged for rewards in the hospital. In comparison to baseline levels, these children were able to achieve substantial weight gains, and two of them showed improvements in the other indices.

Behavior modification procedures have also been used to reduce noncompliance motivated by the discomfort associated with essential medical procedures or treatments. The best-known illustration of these methods was described earlier in relation to behavioral treatments for the control of anticipatory nausea in cancer patients undergoing chemotherapy. Other examples include teaching children to use breathing exercises and distraction techniques to help them overcome fear of routine vaccination shots (Blount et al., 1992), employing hypnosis to reduce pain in burn patients who are undergoing debridement procedures (Patterson et al., 1992), and using relaxation, systematic desensitization, and participant modeling to help fearful patients get the dental work they need, but have been avoiding (e.g., Kleinknecht & Bernstein, 1978).

CHAPTER SUMMARY

Health psychology is a specialty devoted to studying psychological influences on health, illness, and coping with health problems. It is closely related to the larger field of behavioral medicine, which involves the integration of knowledge from many disciplines in understanding and treating medical disorders. Both fields adopt a biopsychosocial model, seeing physical illness as the result of biological, psychological, and social disruptions. Health psychologists seek to (1) understand how these factors interact to influence illness and health, (2) identify risk factors for sickness and protective factors for health, (3) promote healthy behaviors and prevent unhealthy ones, and (4) create interventions that contribute to medical treatment of illness.

Stress is the negative emotional and physiological process that occurs as people try to deal with environmental circumstances, called stressors, that disrupt or threaten daily functioning. Stress reactions can be physical, psychological, and behavioral. Physical stress reactions include the general adaptation syndrome, which begins with an alarm reaction and, if stressors persist, continues into the stages of resistance and exhaustion. Prolonged stress can result in immunosuppression, impairment of the body's disease-fighting immune system. Stressors can be measured by the Life Experiences Survey and other paper and pencil tests.

People's stress-coping efforts can be problem-focused (aimed at modifying or eliminating stressors), emotion-focused (aimed at blunting the emotional impact of stressors), or both. The impact of stressors tends to be lessened in people with better social support systems. Lack of social support increases risk for physical disorders.

Anything that increases the chances of developing an illness is called a risk factor for that illness. Behaviors associated with risk for coronary heart disease (CHD) and cancer include smoking, overeating, lack of exercise, and consumption of a high-fat diet. Stressors, Type-A personality, and especially the negative emotions associated with both, also appear to be a risk factor for CHD. Risk factors for AIDS include unprotected sexual activity and, for intravenous drug users, sharing injection needles.

Illness prevention programs in health psychology seek to reduce risk factors for cardiovascular disease, chronic pain, cancer, AIDS, and other diseases by working with individuals, groups, and whole communities to alter health-risky behaviors. Health psychologists often treat individuals with multiple health problems, and decisions must be made about which conditions have priority. Though many types of interventions are initially successful, long-term behavior change is difficult in some areas, particularly those involving smoking, substance abuse, and overeating.

Health psychologists' efforts to improve patients' compliance with prescribed medical treatments include education about the importance of compliance, modifying treatment plans to make compliance easier, and using behavioral techniques to increase patients' ability to comply.

Chapter 12

Clinical Neuropsychology

Neuropsychology is the field of study that endeavors to define the relationship between brain processes, human behavior and psychological functioning. Neuropsychologists are interested in a wide range of human abilities, including cognitive functioning (e.g., language, memory, attention, mathematical, and visual-spatial skills), motor functioning (e.g., gross and fine motor skills), emotional functioning (e.g., the ability to comprehend and express emotion, anxiety, depression, euphoria), social functioning (e.g. activities of daily living, social judgment, interpreting social information) personality traits (e.g., extraversion, neuroticism), and psychological disorders (e.g., post-traumatic stress disorder, clinical depression, and schizophrenia).

Historically, the main source of data in neuropsychology has been the study of behavior after brain damage. By observing the effects of specific kinds of brain damage on behavior, neuropsychologists were able to make inferences about the organization of the brain. More recently, the development of methods that allow neuropsychologists to study the organization of the brain in people without brain damage has made it possible to confirm and expand our understanding of brain–behavior relationships. The power of the neuropsychological approach is revealed by the insights it has provided about brain functioning and about psychological disorders such as learning disabilities, anxiety, depression, and schizophrenia.

Knowledge that has been garnered from neuropsychological research is often applied by *clinical neuropsychologists*, who work with children and adults who have had trauma or injury to the brain, or who are experiencing problems in some area of functioning that may be related to a brain impairment. Often, the clinical neuropsychologist is called upon to assess how damage to the brain expresses itself in behavioral, cognitive, emotional and social difficulties. (The difficulties or *deficits* on test performance are quantified by comparing a patient's performance relative to the level shown by a normative, or average, group of people, or relative to the level shown by a patient on an earlier occasion.) Clinical neuropsychologists typically seek to answer one or more of the following questions (Jones & Butters, 1983)

1. Does the client show difficulties or deficits in test performance that suggest organic brain damage?
2. If there is an impairment, how severe is it and what is the prognosis or likely course?
3. Can the impairment be localized to a specific area of the brain?
4. What is the probable cause of the impairment?
5. What are the consequences of the impairment for the client's daily, occupational, and interpersonal functioning?
6. What recommendations are there for rehabilitation of the impairment?

In answering these questions, clinical neuropsychologists must integrate data and knowledge from several sources. First, they must be proficient in the general assessment skills we described in Chapters 3 through 5. Neuropsychological assessment should not be isolated from an assessment of the entire person, including social and family background, personality dynamics and emotional reactions to possible brain dysfunction. Second, the clinical neuropsychologist must be well versed in the neurosciences, including neuroanatomy (the study of the structures of the nervous system and the functions of these structures), neuropharmacology (the study of drugs that affect the functioning of the nervous system), and neurophysiology (the study of the physiology of the nervous system, including the chemistry of nerve tissue and the relationship between the nervous system and endocrine functions). Third, clinical neuropsychologists must be knowledgeable about a wide range of human abilities—including cognition, language, and perception—and developmental psychology (including behavioral genetics and life-span psychology). Fourth, the need to distinguish brain impairments from nonorganic psychopathology and the ability to design effective rehabilitative programs require an in-depth understanding of clinical psychology. Finally, clinical neuropsychologists must be thoroughly trained in the specialized methods of neuropsychological assessment.

HISTORICAL DEVELOPMENT OF NEUROPSYCHOLOGY

Neuropsychology has only recently been defined as a field of study; the term appears to have been first used in the late 1940's. Of great importance to the development of neuropsychology were several lines of research in the 1800s that focused on possible relationships between selected behaviors and specific areas of the brain. At its extreme, anatomists Franz Gall and his associate, Johann Spurzheim, popularized this study of *localization of function* as phrenology. As noted in Chapter 1, phrenologists claimed that individual differences in personality and intelligence could be assessed by measuring the bumps and indentations on the surface of the skull. These features supposedly corresponded to the part of the brain responsible for the characteristic in question. Phrenology was very popular with the public but was disdained by most scientists.

Discoveries made by Pierre Flourens earned greater scientific respectability. Flourens surgically destroyed parts of animals' brains and then observed the behavioral consequences of the loss. He concluded that although there was some localization of cortical function, the hemispheres of the cortex functioned more like an interrelated unit. This view was later supported by the work of Karl Lashley, who emphasized the capacity of one area of the cortex to take over for the functions of a destroyed area, a capacity he described as *equipotentiality*.

Although the excesses of phrenology discredited early ideas about localization of brain functions, careful work in behavioral neurology eventually provided convincing support for cortical localization of many cognitive functions. Paul Broca, a French physician, is often credited with the discovery that expressive speech is controlled by an area in the left frontal area. Broca had the opportunity to confirm, by autopsy, that a patient with a profound speech problem but otherwise normal intelligence had damage to the left frontal lobe. By 1863, Broca had collected a series of eight cases and had argued his case in such a way that localization of function was indisputable.

Another early clinical insight into localization of function was made by two Italian ophthalmologists: Antonio Quaglino, a professor at the University of Pavia, and Giambattista Borelli, a practicing ophthalmologist in Turin. In 1867, they published a paper describing the case of a man who lost the ability to recognize familiar faces after a cerebral hemorrhage that mainly damaged the right hemisphere of the brain. The loss of the capacity for facial recognition is known today as *prosopagnosia*, and recent neuroimaging research has made great strides in describing the neural circuits involved (e.g., Katanoda, Yoshikawa, & Sugishita, 2000; Halgren et al., 2000).

Development of Neuropsychological Assessment Techniques

By the turn of the 20th century, Alfred Binet had begun assessing children with brain damage in Paris. Although these tests are usually considered the beginning of modern intelligence testing (see Chapter 5), they also foreshadowed neuropsychological assessment. Many of the disorders commonly assessed today with neuropsychological techniques had been identified by Binet's time. *Aphasia* (disordered language abilities), *apraxia* (impaired abilities to carry out purposeful movements), amnesia (disorders of memory), and *seizure disorder* had all been classified, studied, and, in some cases, treated by the 1920s. In Russia, a Psychoneurological Institute was formed in 1907 to study the behavioral consequences of brain damage, and throughout the first decade of the 1900s, several investigators in the United States had begun to use psychological tests to study the effects of brain damage on behavior.

A crucial development in the history of neuropsychology was the work of Ward Halstead, who established a neuropsychology laboratory in 1935 at the University of

Chicago. Halstead began his work by observing persons with brain damage in natural settings. These observations led him to identify several characteristics of behavior, which he then tried to assess more thoroughly through existing psychological tests or new ones he developed himself. After testing a large number of patients who had been referred to him, Halstead compared the results of the referral cases to a group of control cases and selected 10 measures for his assessment battery based on the ability to discriminate patients from controls (Reitan & Davison, 1974). Halstead's first graduate student, Ralph M. Reitan, started his own neuropsychology laboratory in 1951 at the Indiana University Medical Center. Reitan revised Halstead's test battery by eliminating two tests and adding several new ones, including the Wechsler intelligence scale and the MMPI. This revised battery became known as the *Halstead-Reitan Battery*, and is still one of the most widely used neuropsychological batteries in existence.

Basic research in neuropsychology and advances in assessment methods grew dramatically following World War II. Jones and Butters (1983) list five groups of scientists who made especially noteworthy contributions to the field in this period.

1. The Montreal Neurological Institute-McGill University Group, especially Brenda Milner and Doreen Kimura, who studied the effects of many types of specific, or focal, brain lesions on behavior. The Montreal investigators developed several neuropsychological assessment techniques, and their research (e.g., Branch, Milner, & Rasmussen, 1964; Kimura, 1967) led to widespread acceptance of the view that each hemisphere of the brain has special importance for specific types of behavior.

2. Hans-Lukas Teuber who, along with several colleagues at the New York University College of Medicine and the Massachusetts Institute of Technology, studied the behavioral effects of combat injuries to the brains (particularly the frontal lobes) of World War II veterans.

3. The Boston Veterans Administration and Boston University School of Medicine group, including Edith Kaplan, Nelson Butters, and Harold Goodglass, who carefully classified various forms of aphasia and amnesia and who emphasized the need to study the process that contributes to objective performance deficits. Noting that patients may do poorly on the same neuropsychological tests for different reasons, the Boston group advocated assessments that measure not only the extent of deficits but also the qualitative problems that lead to the deficits. This approach has come to be known as the process approach.

4. Arthur L. Benton, at the University of Iowa, who, in 1945, developed the Benton Visual Retention Test, a test of visual memory still in use today. Benton also made numerous discoveries about the different behavioral effects of lesions in the right versus the left hemisphere and developed a number of other neuropsychological tests with admirable psychometric properties (see e.g., Benton, Hamsher, Varney & Spreen, 1983).

5. Alexander Luria, a Russian scientist whose unique approach to neuropsychology became enormously influential in the West following the translation of his book, *Higher Functioning in Man*, in 1966 and the systematic description of his

assessment methods by the Danish psychologist Anna-Lise Christensen in 1975. Luria's theory of functional systems in the brain is founded on important principles of brain functioning which we will examine in more detail later.

Split-Brain Research

Another important part of the history of neuropsychology is the development of neuropsychological techniques that allowed for more precise localization of functions in the brain. In this respect, the work of Roger Sperry and his colleagues at the California Institute of Technology (Sperry, 1961, 1982) deserves special mention. These investigators studied the behavioral effects of cutting the *corpus callosum*, the band of fibers that connects the brain's two hemispheres and allows them to communicate with each other. This particular surgical procedure is occasionally used to prevent the spread of epileptic seizures from one side of the brain to the other in cases where the pharmacological treatment is ineffective. When the corpus callosum is severed, there is no direct pathway between the hemispheres. Although vast sections of brain tissue devoted to complex information processing were presumably rendered incommunicado by this surgery, previous research in the 1940s had failed to note any significant differences between normal people and so-called split-brain patients. It was not until Roger Sperry (who won the Nobel Prize in 1981 for his work) and his associates used more sophisticated experimental procedures to test patients with split-brains that it became possible to identify a disconnection syndrome (e.g., Sperry, 1968).

Normative Studies

Split-brain research stimulated an enormous number of studies investigating the brain organization of people without brain damage. These studies often used a *tachistoscope*, which is a stimulus presentation device that takes advantage of the fact that when the eyes are focused on a central point, stimuli in the left visual field are perceived first by the right hemisphere, whereas stimuli in the right visual field are perceived first by the left hemisphere. To get the information *directly* to both hemispheres, a person would have to move the eyes so as to place the information that was formerly in one visual field in the other. To forestall this possibility, the tachistoscope is designed to have split-second accuracy in the timing of the lights that illuminate the stimuli. Because it takes about 200 milliseconds to move the eyes, the stimuli are lit up for that amount of time or less. Researchers can thus be fairly certain that the only way each hemisphere can obtain information from the opposite hemisphere's visual field is to receive a "second-hand copy" via the fibers of the corpus callosum.

Using tachistoscopic methods, experimenters were able to direct visual stimuli to one hemisphere or the other and measure a person's accuracy of performance or reaction time in response. Similarly, dichotic listening techniques, which direct auditory input simultaneously to both ears, rely on the tendency to ignore or suppress information in the ear opposite the hemisphere that is less adept at the task. Both approaches were based on the fact that pathways for sensory input are predominantly crossed in the nervous system.

By measuring the relative accuracy of responses for the two visual fields (for tachistoscopic presentation) or for the two ears (dichotic presentation), researchers have been able to document and confirm unique hemispheric superiorities for a wide variety of cognitive and perceptual tasks (Kimura, 1961, 1966, 1967; Pirozollo & Rayner, 1977).

BASIC PRINCIPLES OF NEUROPSYCHOLOGY

A thorough understanding of brain functioning is obviously beyond the scope of this chapter; it is even beyond the scope of any single book devoted to the topic. However, certain principles of brain–behavior relationships are so fundamental to neuropsychology that it is essential to review them before describing any neuropsychological assessment procedures.

Localization of Function

As we have already mentioned, the idea that certain parts of the brain control specific behaviors became the prevailing view of scientists in the 19th century. Localization theories portray the brain in a compartmentalized fashion with different parts responsible for different skills or senses. Localization of function continues to be an important idea among modern neuropsychologists, while they also recognize that the different areas of the brain are intricately interrelated and may even take over some of the functions formerly directed by an injured area.

Theorists who emphasize the interrelatedness of brain areas and who stress the holistic quality of brain functioning are sometimes known as *globalists*. John Hughlings Jackson, Karl Lashley, and Kurt Goldstein are three of the more influential globalists, but it was Alexander Luria, who, more than any other scientist, proposed a theory of brain organization that emphasized its integration rather than its specificity.

Luria's theory was that the brain is organized into three functional systems: (1) a system for regulating a person's overall tone or waking state, which involves the brain stem; (2) a system located in the posterior (back) portion of the cortex for obtaining, processing, and storing information received from the outside world; and (3) a system for planning, regulating, and verifying mental operations that is located mainly in the anterior (front) portion of the cortex. It is important to recognize that Luria, like all other globalists, still believed the brain had some specialized division of labor.

Today, when neuropsychologists map the brain according to specific functions, they do so in a way that reflects both localization and global perspectives (Walsh, 1987). For example, the concept of *modularity* implies that different regions of the brain function are specialized units that process particular types of information or perform specific kinds of tasks. Different modules interact with each other to produce a seamless sequence of behaviors. Modules are organized in a fashion that reflects both the structure and function of the brain. Thus, the brain can be conceptualized as having several levels of organization, ranging from the global to the local. For example, the various areas identified in Figure 12.1 are associated with functions that can be distin-

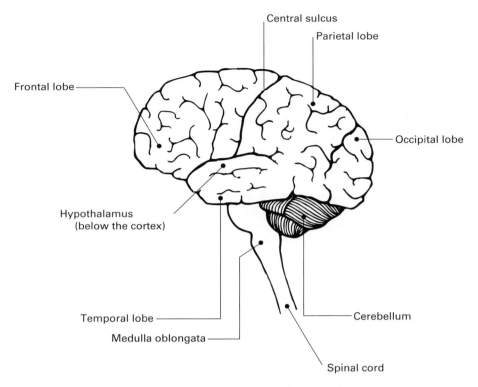

Central sulcus

Parietal lobe

Frontal lobe

Occipital lobe

Hypothalamus
(below the cortex)

Temporal lobe

Medulla oblongata

Cerebellum

Spinal cord

FIGURE 12.1 A lateral view of the human cerebral cortex and other brain structures.

guished by whether they primarily process incoming information (sensory) or program outgoing behavior (motor). They can also be distinguished by modality (for example, whether they primarily process visual or auditory information). In general, brain regions behind the central sulcus are more involved in the reception of sensory information involving touch, pressure, temperature, and body position, whereas brain regions in front of the central sulcus are more involved in programming motor output.

The lobes of the cerebral cortex are also associated with particular functions. For example, the *occipital lobes* are involved in processing visual information. Signals from the eyes' retinas are carried by the optic nerves to the thalamus and then to several regions in the occipital lobes. Because of the way the nervous system is organized, visual information is represented *topographically* in the brain; in other words, neighboring parts of the brain respond to neighboring areas of the visual field. A similar arrangement for other types of specific sensory and motor information has given rise to the rather comical maps of the *homunculus* (literally, "little man") which display the relative size of cortical areas representing sensory information or motor output to and from various regions on the opposite side of the body; see Figure 12.2.

A Sensory homunculus **B** Motor homunculus

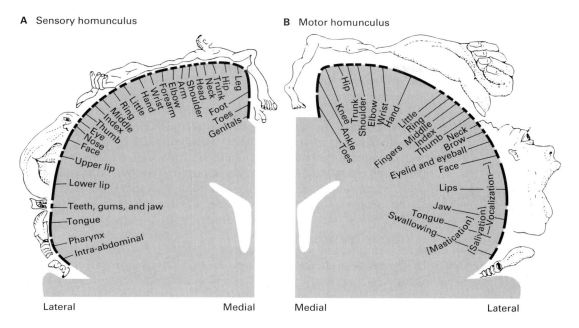

Lateral   Medial   Medial   Lateral

FIGURE 12.2 Sensory and motor areas of the human brain. These maps show where on the human cortex sensory information is received (left) and where motor functions are controlled (right). Note that areas of the body that are more sensitive to sensory information (such as the tip of the tongue or the fingers) are represented by more cortical area than areas that are less sensitive (such as the back of the head or the upper leg). Source: Kandel, Schwartz, and Jessell (1991). Reprinted with the permission of Macmillan Publishing Company from *The Cerebral Cortex of Man* by Wilder Penfield and Theodore Rasmussen. © 1950 Macmillan Publishing Company. Copyright renewed © 1978 Theodore Rasmussen.

After visual information is processed in the occipital lobes, it is relayed to association areas in the *parietal lobes*. They are called "association" areas because they combine and integrate sensory information from a variety of sources. Because the parietal lobes are the meeting ground for visual, auditory, and sensory input, they are uniquely involved in creating a unified perception of an object. For example, when we pick up a rose, the pathways that convey its smell are separate from those that convey its visual image, and these are separate from the ones that convey the painful prick of its thorns. Yet we experience the rose as a single, unified object. Patients with damage to the parietal lobes often have difficulty recognizing objects, even highly familiar ones, in this unified way.

The parietal lobes are also involved in creating a spatial map of our environment and the objects in it, an organization that doesn't depend on the orientation or position of our bodies. Because of this specialty, the parietal lobes play a unique role in attention and awareness of spatial location. Patients with damage to the parietal lobe on only one side of the brain often display an intriguing deficit called *hemi-neglect*, in which they ignore the side of the body and the side of space opposite the damaged hemisphere. For example, a person who has had damage to the right parietal region might not eat the food on the left side of his or her plate, forget to comb hair on the left side of his or her head, and neglect to button the shirt-sleeve on the left arm. They might ignore words on the left side of the page and fail to notice when a doctor or family member approaches from the left. Hemi-neglect can be so extreme that patients sometimes believe that parts of their bodies belong to other people. In an anecdote reported by Oliver Sacks in *A Leg to Stand On* (1990), a patient woke up in the middle of the night and tried to throw his leg out of bed, thinking that a stranger had gotten into bed with him. This syndrome is most common after damage to regions of the right parietal lobe (probably because of the unique specialization of the right hemisphere for processing spatial information), but it can occur after damage to the left parietal lobe as well.

Clinical neuropsychologists typically assess the presence of parietal lobe deficits by using tests such as the *Benton Test of Facial Recognition*, tests of object recognition in which the patient is shown an object and asked to name it or point to it, and tests of visual-spatial skills. Asking the patient to draw a clock or a flower often assesses hemi-neglect. Problems are revealed when patients put all the numbers on the clock, or all the petals on the flower, on only one side. Other tests of neglect include letter cancellation tasks, where individuals are asked to cross out all of the letters or symbols on a page, or line bisection tasks where they are asked to bisect a line in the middle.

Once information is integrated in the parietal lobes, the *temporal lobes* come into play by categorizing, classifying, and storing the information in long-term memory. Although the temporal lobes are also involved in processing auditory information, the most dramatic effect of temporal lobe damage is the disruption of memory. Researchers at McGill University discovered that patients who underwent brain surgery that removed a structure called the *hippocampus* from both temporal lobes had complete amnesia for all new information (Scoville & Milner, 1957). These persons cannot remember how to find their way around in unfamiliar places, nor can they remember the name of someone they met minutes earlier. Every event, no matter how often repeated, is perceived as if it is happening for the first time. Interestingly, their memory loss is most evident on a conscious level. Thus, while these patients may not be aware of having seen a particular object in the past, they sometimes show *unconscious recognition*, as evidenced by changes in heart rate or skin conduction in response to familiar stimuli (Gazzaniga, Fendrich, & Wessinger, 1994; Jacoby & Kelley, 1987; Milner & Rugg, 1992).

The temporal lobes are also important in attaching appropriate emotional or motivational significance to particular stimuli. People with temporal lobe epilepsy, for example, often display a collection of emotional traits, which some researchers have termed the "temporal lobe personality" (Bear & Fedio, 1977). One of these traits is a tendency to see mundane events as imbued with personal emotional significance, a tendency that can lead to paranoid thinking. Patients with temporal lobe epilepsy have also been described as "hypergraphic," which refers to their tendency to do a lot of writing, or to be "sticky" (a tendency to have difficulty disengaging from a conversation).

Clinical neuropsychologists typically assess problems associated with temporal lobe pathology by using a variety of memory tests, such as *Benton's Visual Retention Test*, the *Wechsler Memory Scale*, or the *California Verbal Learning Test*. They also compare patients' memory for verbal material, which would indicate left temporal lobe disorder, with their memory for visual-spatial material, which would indicate right temporal lobe disorder.

The brain's *frontal lobes* are seen as primarily involved in executive functions, a term that includes many abilities such as planning, initiating behavior, purposive action, self-regulation, judgment, assimilating new information and adapting to novel situations (e.g., Kolb & Whishaw, 1990; Banich, 1997; Levin, Eisenberg & Benton, 1991). As befits a position of such responsibility, the frontal lobes receive input from most other parts of the brain. This input is necessary because making appropriate decisions about responses and actions requires taking into account as much current information as possible from the environment (including the position and current state of the body). This new information must also be compared to previous information, and its motivational and affective significance must be assessed. Only then can appropriate motor responses be sequenced in time and space.

Damage to the frontal lobes often profoundly affects social and emotional functioning. The classic case of Phineas Gage, a railroad worker who sustained a frontal lobe injury in 1848 when a steel rod blew through his skull during an explosion, is widely cited as an example of the effects of frontal lobe damage. His friends and family noted that Phineas was a "different" person. He had been socially appropriate, but after the accident, he was loud and profane. He was irresponsible and did not follow through with plans. In fact, patients with frontal lobe damage may have problems with any stage of a goal-directed behavior. For example when cooking a meal, they may have difficulties planning the meal, breaking down the overall task into its necessary components, timing each component, or making adjustments, as when someone is overcooking. Eslinger and Damasio (1985) have reported a case of a patient whose performance on an entire battery of neuropsychological tests was unimpaired; yet he was unable to hold down a job, plan or conduct chores around the house, or even decide what to do next. Despite wholly intact perceptual abilities and intellectual skills, he was unable to integrate all the information available to him and apply it to daily activities in an adaptive fashion. In other cases, frontal lobe damage can result in a tendency to *perseverate* (an inability to inhibit behavior even when it is inappropriate), to be emotionally labile, and have a low tolerance for frustration.

Typically, clinical neuropsychologists test for frontal lobe function by examining sequences of motor behavior, the ability to generate behavioral strategies, and the tendency to perseverate. Two tests commonly used to assess frontal lobe damage are the *Wisconsin Card Sorting Test* and the *Categories Test* from the *Halstead-Reitan Battery*. Both tests use feedback from the examiner to cue patients how to proceed, by informing them on each trial whether they were right or wrong. This feedback is designed to signal them to change their strategy for matching or categorizing information.

Patients with frontal lobe lesions will often perseverate in the same strategy regardless of whether it is successful.

Lateralization of Function

The cortex of the brain is divided into hemispheres, and each hemisphere is associated with different kinds of functions. Historically, this concept has been referred to as cerebral dominance, with the left hemisphere being viewed as the dominant and the right as the nondominant or minor hemisphere. Current conceptualizations of cerebral dominance view each hemisphere as dominant for specific types of functions or processes.

Specialization of the Left Hemisphere. In most right-handers, the left hemisphere is specialized to handle speech and other aspects of linguistic processing, such as the ability to understand and produce language. Thus, in right-handers, the right hemisphere has no direct access to speech mechanisms. Brain organization in left-handed people is more variable. Evidence that the left hemisphere is specialized for speech comes from a variety of sources. In addition to studies documenting language deficits in patients with left hemisphere damage (Rasmussen & Milner, 1975), data from a number of neurosurgical procedures have provided comprehensive evidence for the left hemisphere's special language abilities. For example, before beginning brain surgery, neurosurgeons typically locate, and then try to avoid, regions of the brain that are crucial for language. They do this by electrically stimulating particular areas, and, if this renders the patient unable to speak when instructed to, they conclude that the area is important for language. Such explorations have shown that stimulation of the left, but usually not the right, hemisphere leads to disruptions in speech production and language processing. Furthermore, the disruptions are consistent with the general area of function subserved by particular regions of the brain reviewed earlier. Thus, stimulation of the left temporal lobe disrupts verbal memory functions, whereas stimulation of the left frontal lobe disrupts speech production (because it involves complex motor sequences).

Another technique often used to investigate language lateralization involves injecting sodium amytal into the internal carotid artery (Wada & Rasmussen, 1960). This procedure temporarily puts one hemisphere "to sleep," during which time the neuropsychologist or neurologist can test the patient. Milner (1974) and others have found that when the left hemisphere is put to sleep, nearly all right-handers lose their ability to speak. Split-brain research has also provided powerful evidence for left hemisphere dominance in language functions. For example, a patient with a severed corpus callosum might be asked to sit in front of a screen that makes it impossible to see objects that are placed in their hands. To identify the object, these patients must depend entirely on tactile information carried by the sensory nerves from the hand to the brain. Like most nerve pathways, these sensory nerves cross over the midline before they reach information processing areas in the cortex. As a result, information from the left hand is initially sent to the right side of the brain, and information from the right hand is sent to the left side of the brain. In a normal brain, the corpus callosum transfers this information to the opposite hemisphere in a split-second, but because the corpus callosum is severed in these patients, the only way their opposite hemisphere can obtain information about a touched object is if they look at it. What happens when the screen blocks the patient's view? Roger Sperry and his associates (e.g., Sperry, 1974) found that these patients have no difficulty naming objects being held in the right hand (which is connected to their left hemisphere), but when asked to name objects they were holding in the left hand (which is connected to the right hemisphere), the patients were reduced to silence. When they were asked to use their left hand to pick out a picture of the object, however, they could do so correctly every time. The obvious conclusion is that the right hemisphere is mute—it has no access to speech mechanisms that are housed within the left hemisphere.

Specialization of the Right Hemisphere. Although the right hemisphere appears to lack speech functions, it plays a very important role in human communication. As Sperry and his colleagues showed, given a nonverbal means of communication, the right hemisphere is able to perform on a level equal to that of the left. Indeed, one of the greatest contributions of split-brain research has been to demonstrate the right hemisphere's high-level information-processing capability. We now know that the right hemisphere is crucial for analyzing a vast array of spatial and nonverbal information, including the highly complex signals involved in social communication. The right hemisphere is superior to the left in its understanding of the relationships between objects in space and time. It seems to specialize in perceiving the gestalt, or whole picture presented by the world. Thus, when we look at a wooded landscape the left hemisphere would be more likely to focus on individual trees, but miss the perception of a forest. The right hemisphere will likely see the forest but ignore the trees. These tendencies are revealed in the drawings produced by patients with brain damage. For example, patients with right-hemisphere damage are reasonably good at drawing the parts of an object, but they are likely to place the *parts* incorrectly relative to each other. Patients with left-hemisphere damage are reasonably good at drawing an object's overall shape, but they tend to leave out the details.

Processing nonverbal information involves understanding the highly complex signals that are involved in social and emotional communication. Only part of the important information in a conversation is carried by the actual content of the utterances; a great deal of information is conveyed by *how* words are said rather than by *what* is said. The right hemisphere is especially good at perceiving and decoding gestures, tone of voice, facial expressions, body language, and other nonverbal information, and then integrating them into a coherent message.

Even the domain of language, long thought to be under the sole purview of the left hemisphere, depends, in part, on the right hemisphere. The right hemisphere plays an important role in understanding linguistic devices like metaphors. For example, persons with right-brain injury might interpret statements like, "I cried my eyes out" as if they were literally true. Similarly, right-brain injury can affect the appreciation of humor and the ability to "get a joke" (Gardner, Brownell, Wapner, & Michelow, 1983).

The difficulties patients with right-brain damage have in judging situations appropriately, in relating to others, and in accurately perceiving social cues is compounded by another problem—they are often unaware of their deficits. The inability to comprehend the magnitude and severity of one's difficulties is called *anosognosia*. For example, several days after sustaining a right-brain injury, a pilot with left hemiparesis (paralysis on one side of the body) and serious cognitive difficulties assumed that he would soon be able to go back to work. Anosognosia poses a serious obstacle to rehabilitation programs because few remedial strategies will be effective if the person does not perceive that he or she has a problem.

THE PROFESSION OF CLINICAL NEUROPSYCHOLOGY

Our understanding of brain–behavior relationships has been enriched and expanded remarkably by research, and these findings have been increasingly applied in clinical settings. The field of clinical neuropsychology has grown tremendously in the past several decades. Clinical neuropsychologists likely see a wide variety of clients. Many adult clients are referred by the staff of rehabilitation, psychiatric, or geriatric facilities. Child and adolescent clients may be referred by teachers, school psychologists or social workers, or family physicians. Many clients are referred to clinical neuropsychologists by physicians or other medical staff because of suspected brain damage caused by a brain injury, stroke, or dementing illness.

In the last two decades, clinical neuropsychology has rapidly developed, and educational and training guidelines have been articulated. Several events marked the development of clinical neuropsychology. In the late 1960s, the *International Neuropsychological Society* (INS) was founded by scientists interested in brain-behavior relationships, and in the 1970s clinical neuropsychology emerged as a distinctive professional specialty. The *Division of Clinical Neuropsychology* (Division 40) was formed within the American Psychological Association (APA) in 1980, and in 1983 clinical neuropsychology was recognized as a specialty by the American Board of Professional Psychology (ABPP). (Division 40 is now one of the largest divisions of the APA!) Another important event was the APA's designation of clinical neuropsychology as a specialty (similar to clinical, counseling, or health psychology) in 1996.

The increasing demand for clinical neuropsychologists has prompted many clinical psychologists to list neuropsychology as one of their specialties. This rush to neuropsychology has led to serious questions about the education necessary to ensure competency in the field. Part of the task of Division 40 has been to define the training and educational experiences necessary to become a competent clinical neuropsychologist, and to institute a procedure by which to obtain the credentials to demonstrate such competence. As a result, an *American Board of Clinical Neuropsychology* has been established as a component of the *American Board of Professional Psychology* (see Chapter 14). Individuals who have undergone the proper training and have had sufficient experience in the practice of clinical neuropsychology can apply to take the examination for diplomate status in clinical neuropsychology.

The education of a competent clinical neuropsychologist is a lengthy process requiring courses in several disciplines, a large body of basic knowledge, research sophistication, supervised experience, and clinical acumen. The following statement defining a clinical neuropsychologist was adopted by the Executive Committee of Division 40 at the APA meeting on August 12, 1988:

> A Clinical Neuropsychologist is a professional psychologist who applies principles of assessment and intervention based upon the scientific study of human behavior as it relates to normal and abnormal functioning of the central nervous system. The Clinical Neuropsychologist is a doctoral-level psychology provider of diagnostic and intervention services who has demonstrated competence in the application of such principles for human welfare following:
>
> 1. Successful completion of systematic didactic and experiential training in neuropsychology and neuroscience at a regionally accredited university;
> 2. Two or more years of appropriate supervised training applying neuropsychological services in a clinical setting;
> 3. Licensing and certification to provide psychological services to the public by the laws of the state or province in which he or she practices;
> 4. Review by one's peers as a test of these competencies.

Attainment of the ABCN/ABPP Diploma in Clinical Neuropsychology is the clearest evidence of competence as a clinical neuropsychologist because it assures that all of these criteria have been met.

In September 1997, a group of specialists and educators met in Houston to "advance an aspirational, integrated model of specialty training in clinical Neuropsychology." The convention resulted in the "Houston Conference" guidelines for training of clinical neuropsychologists. The guidelines specify core knowledge bases and skills. Core knowledge bases include: 1) general psychology (including statistics and methodology, learning, cognition and perception, social psychology, biological bases of behavior, life span development, history, cultural and individual differences), 2) general clinical (including psychopathology, psychometric theory, interviewing, assessment, intervention, and ethics, 3) foundations for the study of brain–behavior relationships (including neuroanatomy, neurological and related disorders and their etiology, pathology, course and treatment, non-neurological conditions affecting central nervous system functioning, neuroimaging and other neurodiagnostics, neurochemistry of behavior, and neuropsychology of behavior), and 4) foundations for the practice of clinical neuropsychology (specialized assessment, intervention, research design and analysis, ethics and practical implications of neuropsychological conditions). Core skills include: 1) assessment, 2) treatment and intervention, 3) consultation, 4) research, and 5) teaching and supervision. Individuals acquire these skills and competencies in graduate school, internship and postdoctoral residency.

Clinical neuropsychologists may also specialize in particular areas which require additional training. For example, *pediatric clinical neuropsychologists*—who work mainly with children—need further training because many disorders have particular manifestations in children, and the problems that arise are unique. This training will help them recognize, for instance, that family dynamics can play an important role in managing children with seizure disorders. Pediatric clinical neuropsychologists must also have experience in evaluating the educational programs and resources available to the client. The Houston Conference guidelines suggest that specialization within clinical neuropsychology will become more common in the future, and appropriate guidelines and competencies will be delineated.

NEUROPSYCHOLOGICAL ASSESSMENT TECHNIQUES

Whatever their special interests, clinical neuropsychologists employ a number of techniques to assess their patients' cognitive, emotional, or behavioral functioning, and to link any difficulties in this functioning to what is known about the human brain. In addition to specific tests, a clinical neuropsychologist will conduct a thorough interview and examination of medical records, including records of previous assessments. Information about *premorbid* (before the onset of the disorder) functioning, demographic, familial, linguistic, and educational history allows the clinician to place the current levels of functioning within a context. Several authors (e.g., Fletcher-Janzen, Strickland & Reynolds, 2000) have recently underscored the importance of cultural competence in neuropsychology. The basic principles underlying this cultural competence include: 1) using appropriate assessment norms when available, 2) being aware of potential test biases (for example, some tests of intellectual functioning draw on knowledge that may be unfamiliar to minority clients), 3) understanding the influence of age, education, gender, socioeconomic status and acculturation on standardized test performance, and 4) adapting the testing environment, when possible, to be sensitive to varying cultural norms. Other authors have also suggested that examining the social and institutional factors involved in particular patients' adjustment to brain injury and dysfunction may allow clinicians to do a better job of helping these patients recover (e.g, Mukherjee, Heller, & Alper, 2001).

Neuropsychologists have historically relied on a deficits approach to understanding brain–behavior relationships. As mentioned earlier, a deficit is a deficiency in a patient's performance in comparison to the level shown by a normative or average group of persons or, more importantly, from a level shown by the patient at an earlier time. The determination of an individual's performance before any suspected brain damage is called a *premorbid* assessment of functioning. Often, information, such as the individual's age, educational level, occupation, and geographic region can be used to estimate what the person's premorbid functioning was likely to have been. Repeated testing of the same person can yield information about how rapidly a difficulty is progressing, or how general or specific the difficulty is. These data are useful for diagnosing brain disorders and making a prognosis.

Clinical neuropsychologists typically follow one of two approaches to assessing individuals suspected of having sustained brain damage. The first approach is to administer a predetermined, standardized set of tests combined into a *battery*. Test batteries contain uniform assessment techniques for all patients. The second approach is the *individualized method*, in which a few tests are routinely given to every patient, but the remaining tests are tailored to the specific diagnostic questions, as well as to what is discovered from the initial core of tests.

Both approaches have advantages. Batteries are comprehensive, their standardization is useful for research, and they can be given by paraprofessionals, because there is no need for expert judgments about what tests to use. (It is worth noting that one federal court accepted evidence from a Halstead-Reitan Neuropsychological Battery but barred evidence from two flexible batteries; Reed, 1996.) Individualized approaches allow in-depth assessment of particular problems, permit the use of new tests as they are developed, and focus more thoroughly on specific difficulties.

Each approach has disadvantages as well. Batteries can be inefficient because they assess functions that are not impaired in many patients; also, because of their fixed nature, batteries may become obsolete; it is difficult to revise them to incorporate new and potentially better tests. Individualized approaches require their users to have more training and sophistication, and because of the different combinations of tests they employ, research comparing different patients is more difficult.

Batteries

The most widely used battery developed for neuropsychological assessment in the United States is the Halstead-Reitan Battery (HRB). It is suitable for persons aged 15 and older, but two other versions can be used for children aged 9 to 14, and children between 5 and 8 years of age.

The Halstead-Reitan Battery. Currently, most examiners who use the HRB also administer a Wechsler Intelligence Scale, tests of memory, and other tests of specific functions such as the Minnesota Multiphasic Personality Inventory (MMPI-2), a personality test (e.g., Reitan and Wolfson, 1993). (Weschler tests and the MMPI-2 are discussed in more detail in Chapter 5.) The core tests include the following:

1. *The Categories Test* requires a patient to form correct categorizations of the visual stimuli presented in 208 slides. Initially the task is simple but becomes more difficult as it goes along. This test measures mental efficiency, the ability to derive a rule from experience, and the ability to form abstract concepts.

2. *The Tactual Performance Test* presents a board with spaces into which ten blocks of various shapes can be fitted, somewhat like a big jigsaw puzzle. The patient is asked to fit the blocks into the spaces as quickly as possible, while blindfolded. The patient performs this task three times; first with the preferred hand, next with the nonpreferred hand, and finally with both hands. Following the final trial, the blindfold is removed, the board is removed from view, and the patient is asked to draw the board and its blocks in their proper places from memory. This test measures abilities such as motor speed, tactile and kinesthetic perception, and incidental memory.

3. *The Seashore Rhythm Test* presents 30 pairs of rhythmic beats. The patient's task is to say whether the rhythms are the same or different. The test measures nonverbal auditory perception, attention, and concentration.

4. *The Speech-Sounds Perception Test* requires that the patient match spoken non-sense words to words on written lists. Language processing, verbal auditory perception, attention, and concentration are measured by this task.

5. *The Finger Oscillation or Finger Tapping Test* is a simple test of motor speed in which the patient taps a small lever with the index finger as fast as possible for 10 seconds. Several trials with each hand are used, allowing comparison of lateralized motor speed.

6. *The Trail-Making Test* is a kind of "connect-the-dots" task involving a set of circles that are numbered or lettered. The circles must be connected in a consecutive sequence, thus requiring speed, visual scanning, and the ability to use, and switch between, different sets.

7. *The Dynamometer or Strength of Grip Test* gives a right- versus left-side comparison of physical strength. The patient simply squeezes a dynamometer twice with each hand.

8. *The Sensory-Perceptual Exam* assesses whether the patient can perceive tactile, auditory, and visual stimulation when presented on one side of the body at a time (unilaterally) and on both sides simultaneously (bilaterally). Each of the three senses is assessed separately and with standard variations in the location of the stimulation used.

9. *Tactile Perception Tests* employ various methods to assess the patient's ability to identify objects when they are placed in the right and left hand, to perceive touch in different fingers of both hands, and to decipher numbers when they are traced on the fingertips while the patient's eyes are closed.

10. *The Aphasia Screening Test* measures several aspects of language usage and recognition, as well as abilities to reproduce geometric forms and pantomime simple actions.

Reitan recommended four procedures for evaluating performance on the Halstead-Reitan Battery. Practitioners generally follow these procedures today, although there are variations in the extent each of them is emphasized. First, *level of performance* is assessed by comparing the patient's performance to that of normative groups; an impairment index is calculated based on the number of tests for which the patient's performance falls into a clinically deficient range. Second, *patterns of performance* are analyzed. Pattern analysis examines variations in performance on different components of a test; the most common example is the comparison of scores on verbal versus performance scores on a Wechsler Intelligence Scale. Third, emphasis is placed on *comparing right-side to left-side performance* and drawing inferences about hemispheric functioning when large differences appear. Fourth, the neuropsychologist looks for *pathognomonic signs*, which are specific deficits that are so strongly indicative of organic problems that their presence almost always indicates a disorder.

The Luria-Nebraska Neuropsychological Battery.   In an attempt to administer and evaluate the neuropsychological approach pioneered by Luria in a standardized and reliable manner, Charles Golden and his colleagues at the University of

Nebraska (Golden, 1981; Golden, Purisch, & Hammeke, 1985) compiled a neuropsychological test battery based on Luria's methods but with explicit rules for presenting the test items and quantitatively scoring the results. The latest version of this battery, known as the *Luria-Nebraska Neuropsychological Battery*, consists of items organized into 12 content scales, which test motor functions, rhythm and pitch, tactile and kinesthetic functions, visual functions, receptive language, expressive language, reading, arithmetic, writing, memory, intermediate memory, and intelligence. In addition, a pathognomonic scale is composed of items that are rarely missed by normal subjects but rarely passed by individuals with brain damage. A left-hemisphere scale and a right-hemisphere scale also measure motor and sensory functions of the right and left sides of the body, respectively. Scales for localization and lateralization have also been described, but have not been as thoroughly validated as the initial scales (e.g., McKay & Golden, 1979).

A patient's performance on each test item is scored 0 (normal performance), 1 (borderline performance), or 2 (defective performance). The summed items from each scale are then converted to T-scores, allowing creation of a profile much like those derived from the MMPI (see Chapter 5). In addition to profile analysis, the Luria-Nebraska can be interpreted qualitatively by analyzing patterns of item failures or the presence of pathognomonic signs. T-scores can also be adjusted for age and education, making the score cutoffs used to assess impairment specific to such characteristics.

Evaluation of Batteries

Both the Halstead-Reitan and the Luria-Nebraska batteries have shown impressive validity in discriminating patients with brain damage from controls (Golden, Hammeke, & Purisch, 1978; Reitan, 1955; Vega & Parsons, 1967). The Halstead-Reitan has also demonstrated good validity in detecting the lateralization and localization (Reitan, 1964) of brain damage, but it does a relatively poor job of discrimination between brain damage and serious psychological disorders such as schizophrenia (Jones & Butters, 1983). Although strong claims have been made for the Luria-Nebraska's ability to discriminate patients with brain injury from patients with schizophrenia, this battery has been severely criticized for flawed test construction, improper data analysis, inadequate standardization, and a distortion of Luria's original methods, which simply may not be translatable into items on a battery (see Lezak, 1995, for a review of these criticisms).

Individualized Approaches

One of the most thorough and best-described individualized approaches is that of Muriel D. Lezak, a psychologist at the Oregon Health Sciences University and the Portland, Oregon, Veterans Administration Hospital. Lezak's strategy, as described in her book, *Neuropsychological Assessment* (1995), is to give all patients several standard tests that assess major functions in the auditory and visual receptive modalities as well as in the spoken, written, graphic, and constructional response modalities. Following this initial battery, which usually takes 2 to 3 hours, Lezak proceeds with "hypothesis testing," during which she shifts the focus of the assessment from one set of functions to another as the data indicate what may be the most impaired abilities.

> The addition of specialized tests depends on continuing formulation and reformulation of hypotheses as new data answer some questions and raise others. Hypotheses involving differentiation of learning from retrieval, for instance, will dictate the use of techniques for assessing learning when retrieval is impaired. . . . every other function can be examined across modalities and in systematically varied formats. In each case, the examiner can best determine what particular combinations of modality, content, and format are needed to test the pertinent hypothesis. (Lezak, 1995, p. 721–722)

The Boston group, including Edith Kaplan, Harold Goodglass, and Nelson Butters developed the other well-known individualized approach to neuropsychological assessment. Their assessment begins with a core set of eleven tests that measure areas such as intelligence, memory, attention, construction, and sensory-perceptual abilities. The additional tests that are administered depend on the nature of the referral plus the results of initial testing. Attention to the strategies and processes involved in patients' failures and successes in test performance partially determines the selection of additional tests. Even more importantly, the emphasis on process and strategy contributes to a more than usually detailed analysis of patients' test performance deficits, with the recognition that superficially similar deficits can reflect quite distinct underlying processes (Jones & Butters, 1983; Kaplan, 1990).

It is difficult to assess the validity of individualized approaches because they are tailored to each patient's needs and hence are not given in exactly the same form to sufficient numbers of patients to permit large-scale comparisons. Furthermore, individualized approaches depend much more than batteries do on the skill of the examiner using them. It thus becomes difficult to separate the validity of the tests from the clinical acumen of the examiner. Despite these limitations, individualized approaches offer a promising strategy when they are based on theoretical models that specify the impairments that one is likely to encounter with various types of brain damage (Satz & Fletcher, 1981). In other words, individualized approaches usually reflect a theoretical justification for the use of particular tests while the typical neuropsychological battery does not; its construction depends only on the ability of its items to empirically differentiate patients with brain damage from those without damage. This difference is another example of the distinction between empirical versus rational approaches to test construction that we outlined in Chapter 5.

Neurodiagnostic Procedures

The neuropsychological assessments we have described have often been compared to and validated against methods used by neurologists. Those *neurodiagnostic procedures* are designed to directly observe damage to central nervous system tissue or to monitor some biophysical function of the brain that suggests impairment. In other words, whereas the neuropsychologist examines how patterns of behavior are related to possible brain lesions, the neurologist either observes lesions themselves or looks for chemical or physical evidence that a lesion is present.

Despite their growing sophistication in recent years, these neurological methods are not infallible. In the first place, some of them are valid indicators of certain disorders but not of others. For example, the EEG is an excellent test for patients with seizure disorders, but it is not sensitive to Alzheimer's disease or brain infections. Second, some neurological tests may show abnormalities in patients who actually have no brain damage. The EEG is susceptible to this "false-positive" mistake, particularly in children. A third difficulty with some of the neurodiagnostic techniques listed below is that they are risky for the patient. This is especially true of exploratory surgery, arteriograms, and repeated X-rays.

Neurological Clinical Examination. In this procedure, the physician screens the patient's sensory abilities, eye movements, cognitive and perceptual abilities, language, motor and postural irregularities, and symptom history. The examination is a preliminary investigation of brain disturbance.

Lumbar Puncture. This involves extracting spinal fluid from the spinal cord by inserting a needle. Examination of the fluid's chemistry as well as its pressure upon extraction can help diagnose brain infections, hemorrhages, and some tumors. It is often not performed when any of several conditions are present (e.g., brain abscess), and it has some complications, the most common of which is headaches.

Electroencephalogram (EEG). The EEG monitors the electrical activity of the cerebral cortex. It is especially useful in the diagnosis of seizure disorders and some vascular diseases affecting large blood vessels in the brain. It is safe, but it yields a relatively high rate of false-positives.

Other Electrical Tests. Electromyogram (EMG), evoked potentials, and nerve conduction velocities all measure electrical activity of some sort—in muscles (EMG), in the brain when elicited by an external stimulus (evoked potentials), or in peripheral nerves (nerve conduction velocities). These tests are useful in the diagnosis of muscle disease, nerve disease caused by conditions such as diabetes, and certain sensory deficits.

X-rays. There are many variations of x-ray pictures of brain structure. The technology of X-rays was revolutionized in the 1970s by the introduction of computerized tomography (CT scans), which provides computer-enhanced three-dimensional pictures of successive "slices" of the living brain. CT scans are very valuable in the diagnosis of tumors, traumatic damage, degenerative diseases like Alzheimer's, and cerebrovascular disease.

Positron Emission Tomography (PET). PET scans show changes not just in the structure of the brain, but also in its metabolic function. It does this by tracking the rate at which a radioactive chemical injected into the brain is consumed by brain cells. Since diseased tissue uses the chemical at a different rate than normal tissue, PET scans can reveal specific areas of abnormal brain physiology. PET is a relatively invasive procedure.

Single Photon Emission Computed Tomography (SPECT). The SPECT procedure is similar to the PET scan, but because it uses a radioactive chemical that lasts longer than those used in PET, it permits imaging of cortical and subcortical brain sections from several different angles.

Arteriography. Arteriograms involve injection of a dye into arteries, and then a series of x-rays reveals the condition of the arteries as a dye passes through them. This test is used primarily to diagnose cerebrovascular disease, especially strokes and hemorrhages. Arteriograms can be very uncomfortable and sometimes dangerous.

Magnetic Resonance Imaging (MRI) and Functional MRI (fMRI). MRI works by tracking the activity of atoms in the body as they are "excited" by magnets in a chamber or coil placed around the patient's head. MRI allows imaging of brain structure whereas functional MRI (fMRI) is similar to PET and SPECT in that it measures the activity of the brain. fMRI provides a measure of blood flow. Increases in blood flow are presumed to reflect increases in the activity or work that is being done by a particular region of the brain. MRI and fMRI are advantageous in that they do not require exposure to X-rays or radioactive substances. A great deal of recent research has relied on fMRI techniques during cognitive processing, and as a result our models of the neural circuitry associated with various kinds of information processing are becoming more precise.

Biopsies and Exploratory Surgery. These procedures involve direct examination of suspect brain tissue. Although they are risky, they can give a definitive diagnosis of some neurological conditions.

NEUROPSYCHOLOGICAL APPROACHES TO PSYCHOPATHOLOGY

Research in neuropsychology has contributed to our understanding of a number of psychological disorders, including depression and schizophrenia. Neuropsychological research has also expanded our knowledge of several childhood problems, especially learning disabilities.

Depression

Neuropsychologists have been interested in depression ever since Gainotti (1972) documented in a systematic fashion that localized brain damage can produce emotional effects. For example, individuals with right brain damage often show a rather cheerful, inappropriate, unconcerned reaction to their impairment and hospitalization. This "euphoric" or "indifference" reaction is often accompanied by anosognosia, or unawareness of deficit. In contrast, individuals with left brain damage often show a "catastrophic" reaction, which is characterized by tearfulness, despair, and other symptoms of depression. Subsequent studies confirmed that one-third to two-thirds of patients become depressed after experiencing damage to the left side of the brain (Starkstein & Robinson, 1988). These studies have also shown that the probability of depression rises with increasing proximity of the lesion to the front part of the brain. The closer the lesion is to the frontal pole of the left hemisphere, the more severe the depression.

It appears that these emotional responses are not simply a reaction to the experience of being impaired and that the degree of depression does not correlate with the severity per se of the disability (e.g., Folstein, Maiberger & McHugh, 1977). These asymmetry findings have been corroborated by electroencehpalographic (EEG) and hemodynamic (PET, fMRI) research measuring brain activity in the left versus the right hemisphere. The left hemisphere in people who are clinically depressed is typically less active than the right; similarly, when people who are not clinically depressed are feeling sad, the left hemisphere is less active than the right hemisphere. These differences in brain activity are most evident over the frontal regions of the brain, confirming their importance for these emotional effects. Some research has indicated that this asymmetry in favor of the right hemisphere in depression is superimposed upon bilateral decreases in activity in regions of prefrontal cortex. Heller and Nitschke (1997) and others (e.g., Mayberg, 1997) have suggested that these patterns of brain activity can account for a variety of deficits in executive, memory, and attentional functions that have been documented in depression.

Tachistoscopic studies have also shown that, when visual stimuli are projected to both hemispheres, the left hemisphere typically rates pictures as more positive than the right hemisphere—even though each hemisphere has seen the exact same pictures (Heller, 1990). These results suggest that in the normal brain, frontal regions of the left hemisphere play some role in maintaining a positive perspective on things. It appears that negative mood states result when a lesion or other condition causes these left-side areas to be underactive relative to those in the right hemisphere.

In contrast to increases in right frontal activity, other studies have found that depression is associated with decreases in right posterior activity (Heller & Nitschke, 1997). People who are depressed show some of the same cognitive deficits displayed by patients with damage to parietal-temporal regions of the brain. They have difficulty with visual-spatial information processing and show a number of attentional problems that are similar to patients with right brain damage. These effects may be caused by the interrelationship of the frontal and posterior regions of the brain. Because frontal regions often inhibit activation in posterior regions, relatively greater activation in the right frontal region compared to the left may be producing too much inhibition of the right posterior regions.

These neuropsychological findings have implications not only for our understanding of depression, but also for its diagnosis and treatment after brain damage. For example, it is important to consider the possibility that in addition to having problems with impaired language comprehension or expression, a patient with brain injury may also be depressed. This is why neuropsychologists typically ask individuals and family members whether the individual is sleeping and eating normally, or recovering as expected. If not, an underlying depression may be present, and may require treatment with antidepressant medication. People who are depressed (with no apparent brain damage) can also display deficits on neuropsychological assessment measures. With proper treatment of the depression, these deficits are typically reduced. For this reason, an assessment of depression is an important part of any neuropsychological evaluation.

Schizophrenia

Neuropsychologists have been deeply involved in studying brain functioning in people with schizophrenia. Early studies, most of which used tachistoscopic methods, suggested the possibility that schizophrenia is characterized by an overactivation of the brain's left hemisphere (Gur, 1978). Current studies continue to implicate the left hemisphere, but the picture is now more complicated.

Both structural (Harrison, 1999) and functional (Berman & Weinberger, 1986) abnormalities have been demonstrated in the prefrontal cortex of schizophrenics. Studies measuring regional cerebral blood flow and glucose metabolism suggest that the left prefrontal region of persons with schizophrenia is abnormal because it is not activated during performance on tests like the Wisconsin Card Sort Test. In contrast, subcortical regions of the same hemisphere show a hyperactivation compared to controls (Rubin et al., 1991). Many researchers believe that the results of neuropsychological and brain imaging studies suggest that dysfunction of the prefrontal regions, particularly of the left hemisphere, is a fundamental characteristic of brain function in schizophrenia (Andreasen et al., 1986; Buschbaum et al., 1992; Rubin et al., 1991; Carter, et al., 1998).

These results are compatible with several observations regarding the symptoms of schizophrenia. First, many individuals with schizophrenia display what are termed negative symptoms, which include flat affect, lack of initiative, lack of energy, absence of social engagement, and loss of spontaneity. These same symptoms are encountered in certain patients with prefrontal lesions. Second, the disruption in linear reasoning, logical thought, working memory, and language (positive symptoms) typically seen in schizophrenia is consistent with some kind of damage to the specialized regions of the left hemisphere.

In addition, some research suggests that schizophrenia may be accompanied by deficits in right-hemisphere processing as well, since the right hemisphere has been associated with affective and social functions and is also disrupted in schizophrenia. Another area of vigorous research has raised the possibility that disconnections between frontal and temporal, and perhaps other, brain regions, may also be related to the pathology of schizophrenia (Meyer-Lindenberg et al., 2001). However, an integrative neuropsychological account of schizophrenia is still lacking.

Learning Disabilities

Given neuropsychologists' interest in cognitive abilities, it is not surprising that learning disabilities would be a popular area of research, assessment and intervention. Several neuropsychological studies have found, for example, that dyslexia (disruptions in the ability to read) is usually related to dysfunction of the left hemisphere. Tachistoscopic studies and other behavioral measures have found that children with reading problems tend to show a reduction in the advantage normally seen in the left hemisphere relative to the right (Obrzut, 1988). Indeed, these children tend to rely more on right than left hemisphere processes in learning to read. Dyslexia is correlated with other difficulties in language skills; for example, children with reading difficulties often are slow to acquire spoken language.

Several studies have reported the results of brain autopsies in people who were known to have had dyslexia. These studies have found that the structure of the left hemispheres is different from that of people without dyslexia, and researchers have also found evidence for misplaced brain cells, called *ectopias*, in the left hemisphere. These misplaced cells are likely to "get lost" during the development of the brain, when cells normally migrate to their proper places in the cortex. Such misplacements could cause developmental delays and deficits in the functioning of the left hemisphere. It should be noted, however, that while there are some biological correlates of learning disabilities, clinical neuropsychologists will also consider and evaluate behavioral, environmental, and social explanations for the difficulties.

Pediatric clinical neuropsychologists can often help delineate the specific difficulties in left hemisphere functioning and help design remedial strategies. In fact, children with difficulties in school ranging from attentional difficulties manifested in attention deficit disorder, to memory and language problems, to social and emotional problems—including depression and anxiety—will often be referred to a pediatric clinical neuropsychologist. The clinician will typically conduct a thorough examination and then consult with teachers and parents on how best to help the child.

Nonverbal Learning Disabilities

A different type of learning disability involves deficits in visual-spatial and visual-motor skills, as well as in other abilities that depend on the right hemisphere. This syndrome of *nonverbal learning disability* was first described in the mid-1970s (Myklebust, 1975), but neuropsychological research has only recently been helping to delineate this disorder and communicate its significance to teachers and mental health professionals. Children with nonverbal learning disabilities may have long escaped the notice of professionals because they are often talkative and show high levels of verbal intelligence. Consequently, they sound as though they should be more skillful in the nonverbal realm than they actually are. Children with nonverbal learning disabilities often have difficulty keeping up with other children on nonverbal tasks. They are slow to learn skills like tying shoes, dressing, eating, and organizing their time and their environment. Because their difficulties are less obvious, they are likely to be labeled as having an emotional or behavioral problem, not a learning disability. Unfortunately, when these children have been viewed as bad, uncooperative, or "a problem" long enough, they may end up behaving accordingly. Early diagnosis and treatment of children with nonverbal learning disabilities should help prevent some of these subsequent psychological and behavioral problems.

Nonverbal learning disabilities may result from right-hemisphere deficits early in childhood which can dramatically interfere with normal development (Rourke, 1989). These difficulties inhibit a child from exploring the environment, learning the consequences of actions, and gaining essential experience in coordinated visual-motor skills. They also interfere with the process of attachment between an infant and its caretakers, which depends on nonverbal cognitive processes. Because mother–infant interaction predicts the quality of attachment during the toddler phase, and because quality of attachment predicts social adjustment in early and middle childhood, problems in right-brain functioning can not only create early motoric and cognitive difficulties, but can also lead to abnormalities in social relationships that place the children at risk for emotional difficulties later in life. Other difficulties in social development are probably related to their inability to meet the intense demands for nonverbal information processing in social situations. Overwhelmed by the task of integrating information about other children's facial information, tone of voice, physical activity, and verbal content, they fail to follow even simple exchanges. Over time, their lack of experience and interaction with other children can cause them to feel isolated, lonely, and depressed. It has even been suggested that nonverbal learning disability may be a risk factor for the development of schizophrenia.

In assessing nonverbal learning disabilities, pediatric clinical neuropsychologists look first for a discrepancy between Verbal and Performance IQ on the Wechsler Intelligence Scale for Children. Often, Verbal IQ will be average or well above average, with Performance IQ significantly lower. If the pattern persists on other tests comparing verbal and visual-spatial/visual-motor skills, a nonverbal learning disability is likely to be diagnosed. Often, although not always, the pattern of poor performance on right hemisphere tasks is accompanied by signs on the Halstead-Reitan Battery suggesting impaired right-hemisphere performance.

As in the case of verbal learning disabilities, pediatric clinical neuropsychologists work to devise remedial programs for children with nonverbal learning disabilities. They encourage parents and teachers to take advantage of the child's verbal skills in ways that can help compensate for a lack of understanding in nonverbal domains. They also recommend that these children get individual attention from a learning disabilities specialist or tutor; otherwise, like children with verbal learning disabilities, their academic achievement is likely to fall behind as the demands of school increase. The children's impaired social skills can often be addressed by group therapy, social skills workshops, individual therapy, or facilitation of structured peer interactions or participation in after-school programs.

FUTURE DIRECTIONS IN NEUROPSYCHOLOGY

One of the most obvious trends in neuropsychological research and practice is the increasing reliance on hemodynamic (blood flow) measures of brain functioning such as fMRI and other indices of regional cerebral activation and organization. Continued development and refinement of these techniques are likely, and they will become more accessible to researchers and clinicians. In combination with other measures of psychophysiological, neuropsychological, cognitive, attentional, and emotional functioning, hemodynamic brain activity measures will provide a new database for the field. Joseph Matarazzo (1992) predicted that these measures will eventually be used to assess individual differences in brain structure and cognitive ability, "thus heralding the first clear break from test items and tests in the Binet tradition in a century" (p. 1012). Ten years later, basic research is still the focus of investigation using these measures, and their clinical utility is still in its infancy.

Matarazzo also argued that the future will bring refinement in the specificity of tests of ability as psychologists learn more about cognitive organization. At the same time, the links between specific kinds of abilities and the parts of the brain involved in those abilities will become clearer. Consequently, it will become easier to design tasks to measure even more precisely the functioning of particular brain regions, and to link these to individual differences in ability levels. Increasing the sensitivity of the measures we have available, along with an improved ability to link these measures to specific brain regions, bodes well for our understanding of brain–behavior relationships in a variety of conditions. For example, demographic trends suggest that the incidence of Alzheimer's and other dementing illnesses will increase. Mapping the relationship between memory functions and the activity of specific brain regions promises to advance both basic knowledge about the problem as well as efforts to improve clinical assessment and intervention.

In addition to pursuing their assessment and diagnostic activities, neuropsychologists are also becoming more involved in designing effective interventions to help individual patients. Many of these neuropsychologists work in rehabilitation settings where their efforts to design and implement appropriate services for patients and patients' families take into account the cognitive, social and emotional consequences of brain damage, as well as the long-term needs of people living with such damage. In short, neuropsychologists' contributions to providing patients with integrated and comprehensive diagnostic, assessment and intervention plans will continue to be very important.

CHAPTER SUMMARY

The field of neuropsychology seeks to define the relationship between brain processes and human behavior and psychological functioning including cognitive and motor abilities, emotional characteristics, personality traits, and mental disorders. Clinical neuropsychologists apply the results of neuropsychological research in their work with children and adults who have had trauma or injury to the brain, or who are experiencing other problems related to a brain impairment.

Neuropsychology was not defined as a scientific field until the late 1940s, and clinical neuropsychology did not emerge as a distinctive professional specialty until the 1970s.

One of most important organizational principles underlying brain behavior relationships is localization of function, which refers to the fact that different parts of the brain are responsible for different skills or senses. Lateralization of function is another vital feature of the brain's organization that has important implications for behavior. In most right-handers, the left hemisphere is specialized to handle speech and other linguistic processing, including the ability to understand and produce spoken language. The right hemisphere is crucial for analyzing spatial and other nonverbal information, including complex signals involved in social communication.

Clinical neuropsychologists use a variety of tools and one of two main approaches to assess patients' cognitive, emotional, or behavioral deficits, and to relate these deficits to specific impairments in brain functioning. In the fixed-battery approach, a standardized set of tests is given to all patients, while in the individualized approach, a flexible battery of tests is selected depending on the characteristics of each patient. The most widely used fixed battery is the Halstead-Reitan Neuropsychological Test Battery. It consists of ten specific tests, and is combined with the MMPI and an IQ test. The Luria-Nebraska Neuropsychological Battery can be given in less time and the scores can be organized into an MMPI-like profile. Two prominent individualized approaches have been developed by Murial D. Lezak, and by Edith Kaplan, Harold Goodglass, and Nelson Butters. The results of neuropsychological assessments are often compared to and validated against neurological assessments, including EEG, various brain imaging techniques, and even exploratory surgery.

Today neuropsychology research is helping clinicians better understand a variety of psychological disorders, including depression, schizophrenia, and verbal and non-verbal learning disabilities.

APA's Division of Clinical Neuropsychology has defined the training and educational experiences necessary to become a clinical neuropsychologist and established criteria for demonstrating competence in this specialty.

Chapter 13

Forensic Psychology

In the 4th edition of this book, published in 1994, we predicted that forensic psychology—a specialty that applies psychological principles and knowledge to legal issues and proceedings—would be a "growth stock" for clinical psychologists. Our prediction was accurate. It is now clear that the demand for psychologists to contribute in various ways to the legal system has grown to the point that forensic psychology has become a major professional activity and a focal point of scholarship among clinical psychologists. Numerous signs indicate this growth surge. For example, the American Psychology-Law Society (Division 41 of the American Psychological Association) now lists almost 2,000 members and publishes its own journal, *Law and Human Behavior*, a newsletter, *American Psychology-Law Newsletter*, and a book series, *Perspectives in Law and Psychology*. In 1995, APA itself inaugurated publication of *Psychology, Public Policy, and Law*, another journal devoted to psychology and the law. There are several other journals devoted to legal issues, including *Behavioral Sciences and the Law*, *Law and Psychology Review*, *Journal of Forensic Neuropsychology*, *Journal of Forensic Psychology Practice*, and *Psychiatry, Psychology, and the Law*.

Perhaps the most significant indication of the expansion of field was the American Psychological Association's approval, in 2001, of forensic psychology as a specialty area of applied psychology, joining clinical, counseling, school, and other practice areas. *The American Board of Forensic Psychology* (ABFP) was established in 1978 for the purpose of contributing to the development and maintenance of forensic psychology as a specialized field of study, research, and practice. It certifies psychologists specializing in forensic psychology, issuing the Diplomate in Forensic Psychology to practitioners who meet its rigorous examination and experience standards.

THE SCOPE OF FORENSIC PSYCHOLOGY

Clinical psychologists play a variety of roles in the legal system, including in the areas of (1) law enforcement psychology, (2) the psychology of litigation, (3) correctional psychology, and (4) forensic psychology, the area we will focus on in this chapter.

Law enforcement psychology involves conducting research on the activities of law enforcement agencies and providing direct clinical services in support of these agencies (Super, 1999). A clinician working in this area might test candidates for police work to screen out those who are not psychologically fit (i.e., Gaines & Falkenberg, 1998), offer crisis intervention to police officers involved in violent encounters, consult with detectives about what kind of individual might have committed a certain type of crime, or help question witnesses in ways that enhance their recollections of crimes (i.e., Cassel, 2000; National Institute of Justice, 1999).

The *psychology of litigation* is concerned with the effects of various legal procedures used in civil or criminal trials. Clinicians working in this area may offer advice to attorneys about jury selection, study the factors that influence jury deliberations and verdicts such as eyewitness testimony (Loftus, 1993), and analyze the effects of specific portions of trials, such as opening statements, examination of witnesses, or closing arguments (Marcus, Lyons, & Guyton, 2000).

Correctional psychology is concerned primarily with the delivery of psychological services to individuals serving jail sentences after having been convicted of a crime (Milan, Chin, & Nguyen, 1999). Most clinicians working as correctional psychologists are employed in prisons, penitentiaries, or juvenile facilities, but they may also operate out of a probation office or be part of a special community-based correctional program.

Forensic psychology (and forensic psychiatry) involves the application of mental health knowledge and expertise to the assessment and treatment of individuals who, in some way, are involved in the legal process or legal system (Hess, 1999). The term "forensic" comes from the Latin word "forensis," meaning "of the forum," where the law courts of ancient Rome were held.

Clinical psychologists working in the forensic area may be involved in addressing a wide range of legal issues, including whether 1) an individual is sufficiently mentally ill and potentially dangerous to justify involuntary hospitalization; 2) a person charged with a crime is mentally competent to stand trial, 3) a perpetrator of an illegal act was sane at the time of the offense, 4) a person suffered psychological harm as the result of an injury or trauma, and if so, how serious it is. Forensic psychologists might also be involved in questions relating to child custody, guardianship, and execution of wills. Clinical psychologists answer these and many other questions that arise in particular cases by applying the results of empirical research and the skills and techniques of their profession and offering their opinions during testimony at civil and criminal trials or other legal proceedings.

In this chapter, we illustrate the practice of forensic psychology by describing several areas:

1. Competence to stand trial and take criminal responsibility;
2. Predicting dangerousness of defendants;
3. Psychological damages in civil trials;
4. Competencies in civil (i.e., non-criminal) areas;
5. Psychological autopsies and criminal profiling;
6. Child custody and parental fitness.

Our discussion will describe the basic psycho-legal questions experts must address in each area, examine the techniques clinicians typically use to evaluate these questions, and summarize the empirical evidence and legal status associated with psychologists' activities in these areas. Remember, though, that our review of these five areas is merely an introduction to what is going on at the interface of psychology and law. New research issues are constantly being addressed, and professional psychological services are continually expanding in the legal arena. You can review these advancements in the journals mentioned above as well as in textbooks on law and psychology (e.g., Cassel & Bernstein, 2001; Hess & Weiner, 1999; Monahan & Walker, 2002; Wrightsman, 2001; Wrightsman et al., 2002).

CRIMINAL COMPETENCE AND RESPONSIBILITY

No area of law illustrates the controversies surrounding expert testimony as dramatically as the question of whether a defendant was insane while committing a crime. Proving insanity can result in a defendant's being acquitted, in which case the finding is not guilty by reason of insanity (NGRI). If found NGRI, the defendant will be hospitalized until he or she is no longer suffering from a mental disorder and no longer believed to be dangerous. Alternately, the defendant can be found to be guilty but mentally ill (GBMI). If found GBMI, the defendant will be sentenced as any other convicted defendant, but be ordered to receive such mental health treatment as the correctional institution deems appropriate.

Courts allow defendants' mental condition to be considered at trial because our society believes that it is immoral to punish people who, as a result of a mental disorder, either do not know that their actions are wrong or cannot control their conduct.

Criminal Competence

In the United States, it is not even permissible to continue criminal proceedings against a defendant who is unable to understand the nature and purpose of those proceedings. Thus, forensic psychologists also assist in determining a defendant's competence to stand trial. The legal standard for *competence to stand trial* has not changed since the U.S. Supreme Court enunciated it in 1960: "The test will be whether [the defendant] has sufficient present ability to consult with his lawyer with a reasonable degree of rational understanding, and whether he has a rational as well as a factual understanding of the proceedings against him" (*Dusky v. Unites States*, 362 U.S. 402).

Competence focuses on the defendant's "present ability" to proceed to adjudication, and is to be distinguished from retrospective inquiries regarding criminal responsibility (such as the insanity defense) which focus on the defendant's mental state at the time of the offense. A defendant is considered competent unless and until the defendant convinces the judge otherwise. Defendants must be competent not only at the time of the trial, but also at the time of sentencing, and, if they received a death sentence, at the time of execution. Clinical psychologists and other mental health experts are also asked to evaluate other kinds of competence in criminal defendants, including competence to confess to a crime, competence to waive the right to an attorney, competence to choose not to invoke the insanity defense, and competence to be sentenced and punished (perhaps with the death penalty).

The law requires defendants to be competent for several reasons (Melton et al., 1987). First, legal proceedings are more likely to arrive at accurate results with the participation of competent defendants. Second, as noted earlier, punishment of convicted defendants is morally acceptable only if they understand why they are being punished. Finally, the perceived fairness of our adversary system of justice requires participation by defendants who have the capacity to defend themselves against charges brought by the state. Here is one example of a case in which the question of competence to stand trial was raised (Wrightsman et al., 2002, p. 297):

> Jamie Sullivan was a twenty-four-year-old clerk charged with arson, burglary, and murder in connection with a fire he set at a small grocery store in Kentucky. Evidence in the case showed that, after closing time, Sullivan returned to the store where he worked and forced the night manager, Ricky Ford to open the safe and hand over $800. Sullivan then locked Ford in a small office, doused the store with gasoline, and set it on fire. Ford was killed in the blaze. Police arrested Sullivan within hours at his grandmother's apartment on the basis of a lead from a motorist who saw Sullivan running from the scene.
>
> If convicted on all charges, Jamie Sullivan could have faced the death penalty, but he was mentally retarded. He had dropped out of school in the eighth grade, and a psychologist's evaluation at that time reported his IQ to be 68. He could read and write only his name and a few simple phrases. He had a history of drug abuse and had spent several months in a juvenile correctional camp at the age of fifteen after vandalizing five homes in his neighborhood. When he tried to enlist in the Army, he was turned down because of his limited intelligence and drug habit. Jamie's attorney believed that Sullivan's mental problems might render him incompetent to stand trial and therefore asked a psychologist to conduct an evaluation. The psychologist asked Jamie a series of questions about his upcoming trial, to which he gave the following answers:
>
> QUESTION: What are you charged with?
>
> ANSWER: Burning down that store and stealing from Ricky.
>
> Q: Anything else?
>
> A: They say I killed Ricky too.
>
> Q: What could happen to you if a jury found you guilty?
>
> A: Electric chair, but God will watch over me.

Q: What does the judge do at a trial?

A: He tells everybody what to do.

Q: If somebody told a lie about you in court, what would you do?

A: Get mad at him.

Q: Anything else?

A: Tell my lawyer the truth.

Q: What does your lawyer do if you have a trial?

A: Show the jury I'm innocent.

Q: How could he do that best?

A: Ask questions and have me tell them I wouldn't hurt Ricky. I liked Ricky.

Q: What does the prosecutor do in your trial?

A: Try to get me found guilty.

Q: Who decides if you are guilty or not?

A: That jury.

After interviewing and testing Sullivan, the psychologist found that his current IQ was 65, which fell in the mentally retarded range, that he did not suffer any hallucinations or delusions, but that he expressed strong religious beliefs that "God watches over his children and won't let nothing happen to them." At a hearing to determine whether Jamie was competent to stand trial, the psychologist testified that the defendant was mentally retarded and consequently his understanding of the proceedings was not as accurate or thorough as it might otherwise be. However, the psychologist also testified that Sullivan did understand the charges against him as well as the general purpose and nature of his trial. The judge ruled that Jamie Sullivan was competent to stand trial. A jury convicted him on all the charges and sentenced him to life in prison.

It is estimated that, like Jamie Sullivan, between 24,000 and 60,000 competency evaluations per year are performed on criminal defendants in the United States (Poythress et al., 2001). The question of a defendant's competence can be raised by the prosecutor, the defense attorney, or the presiding judge at any point in the criminal process. Though typically it is defense attorneys who raise the competence question, the judge can also do so.

Assessing Competence

If a question of competence is raised, the judge will order a psychological evaluation. Most assessments take place at local community mental health centers, but if the defendant is suffering from severe depression or a severe disorder such as schizophrenia, the evaluation may be performed at an inpatient facility, such as a state mental hospital. In most states, psychiatrists, psychologists, and social workers are authorized to perform competency evaluations, and they often use special structured interviews to do so (see Table 13.1).

Though the burden of proving incompetence is only by a "preponderance of the evidence" (which is sometimes quantifiable as at least a 51 percent chance), 70 to 90% of defendants referred for such evaluations are found competent. The more rigorous

---

TABLE 13.1   Assessing Competence to Stand Trial

An assessment for a defendant's competence to participate in criminal proceedings usually begins with a mental status examination, a brief focused interview designed to evaluate the defendant's memory, mood, orientation, thinking, and ability to concentrate. The assessor usually then administers one or more specialized instruments, such as the Competency Screening Test (CST), the Competency Assessment Instrument (CAI), or the MacArthur Competence Assessment Tool–Criminal Adjudication (MacCAT-CA) (Heilbrun & Collins, 1995; Monahan, 1996).

The instruments are designed to determine the defendant's ability to:

1. Understand the charges filed;
2. Understand the nature and range of possible criminal penalties if convicted;
3. Understand the adversarial nature of the legal process (prosecution versus defense);
4. Disclose to a defense attorney pertinent facts surrounding the alleged offense;
5. Relate to and communicate with the defense attorney;
6. Assist the defense attorney in planning a defense;
7. Realistically challenge the testimony of prosecution witnesses;
8. Behave appropriately in the courtroom;
9. Give relevant testimony in court; and
10. Engage in self-beneficial, as opposed to self-defeating, behaviors throughout the process. (Heilbrun & Collins, 1995)

---

the evaluation, the more likely it is that the defendant will be found to be competent (Heilbrun & Collins, 1995), but most states have a very low threshold for competence.

What sort of person is usually judged to be incompetent? One study showed that of more than 500 defendants who were found incompetent, many were "marginal" men—undereducated, deficient in job skills, and with long histories of contact with both the legal and mental health systems (Steadman, 1979). Substance abuse problems were common, and minorities were overrepresented relative to their presence in the general population. Other studies have found relatively high percentages of psychosis and lower intelligence among incompetent defendants (Nicholson, Briggs, & Robertson, 1988; Roesch & Golding, 1980; Ustad et al., 1996). One other consistent finding is that incompetent defendants are charged with more serious crimes than defendants in general. Overall then, the typical incompetent defendant is likely to have a history of psychosis for which treatment has been received, to currently exhibit symptoms of serious mental disorder, and to be single, unemployed, and poorly educated (Nicholson & Kugler, 1991).

If a competency evaluation finds a defendant competent, the legal process resumes and the defendant faces trial. If the defendant is found incompetent, the picture becomes more complicated. For crimes that are not serious, the charges might be dropped, sometimes in exchange for requiring the defendant to receive treatment, usually psychotropic medication. If the charges are serious, the defendant usually will be returned to an institution for treatment designed to restore competence, which, if successful, will result in the defendant ultimately standing trial. In most states, this mandatory treatment can last up to 6 months (4 months if they are being tried under federal law), after which, if the person is still judged incompetent, the prosecutor may seek a civil commitment by showing that the defendant is a danger to self or others. In the case of a minor, nonviolent offense, the person might be released. Most incompetent defendants are restored to competency through psychotropic medications, at which time they are returned to jail to await trial.

Can a mentally ill defendant be forced to take medication solely to be made competent to stand trial? At least one federal court and several state courts have said yes. Consider the case of Russell Weston, Jr., who, on July 24, 1998, stormed the U.S. Capitol building with a .38 caliber handgun. He was looking for the "Ruby Red Satellite System" that he claimed was spreading a deadly disease. During the attack, Weston shot and killed two police officers. Because of a history of schizophrenia and his manifestation of paranoid delusions at the time he was captured, he was sent to the federal prison medical facility in Butner, North Carolina and evaluated for competency. In interviews with psychiatrists, who diagnosed him as suffering from paranoid schizophrenia, Weston expressed the delusion that the purpose of his trial would be to expose the threat of "cannibalism." When asked if he understood the nature of the death penalty that may be sought against him, he was nonchalant, saying that he could "wake up" whenever he wanted to. Indeed, he said he could "bring back" the victims at will. These statements, and others, indicated that he clearly did not understand the nature of the proceedings nor could he assist his attorneys in his defense.

The judge ordered that Weston receive psychotropic medications so that he could be tried. His attorneys objected to his being medicated because the prosecution might seek the death penalty. Legal wrangling over this issue were not resolved until December 2001, when the U.S. Supreme Court refused to hear the appeal of the court's medication order (Tucker, 2001). It remains to be seen if Weston will ever be restored to competence. The time limit on hospitalization for incompetent defendants does not apply to Weston since he has fought efforts to restore his competency.

The Insanity Defense

A crime is an intentional act (or failure to act) that is a violation of criminal law and committed without a defense or excuse. But even acts that are prohibited by law generally will not rise to the level of criminal conduct unless the accused person possesses *mens rea*, the mental element of culpability. Mens rea literally means "guilty mind," or intent to do wrong.

Criminal defendants are presumed to have *mens rea* and to be legally responsible for the crimes with which they are charged. Therefore, if defendants plead not guilty by reason of insanity (NGRI), they must present evidence that they lacked the state of mind necessary to be held responsible for a crime. Because insanity is a legal term, not a psychological concept, it is defined by legal standards that have evolved over time, and vary from state to state.

These standards began to be formalized in 1843, when an Englishman named Daniel McNaughton tried to assassinate the British prime minister, Robert Peel.

McNaughton suffered paranoid delusions that Peel was conspiring against him, so he waited outside the prime minister's house at Number 10 Downing Street, where he shot and killed Peel's secretary, whom he mistook for the prime minister. McNaughton was charged with murder, but pleaded not guilty by reason of insanity, claiming that he did not know the difference between right and wrong. Nine medical experts testified that McNaughton was insane and, after hearing instructions from the judge, the jury did not even leave the courtroom before deciding that McNaughton was not guilty by reason of insanity. This verdict infuriated the British public, and Queen Victoria was particularly upset because she herself had been the target of several assassination attempts. She demanded that Britain toughen its definition of insanity.

After extended debate in the House of Lords and among the nation's highest judges, a definition of insanity known as the *McNaughton rule* was enacted: ". . . to establish a defense on the grounds of insanity it must be clearly proved that, at the time of committing the act, the accused was laboring under such a defect of reason, from disease of the mind, as not to know the nature and quality of the act he was doing or, if he did know it, that he did not know what he was doing (was) wrong" (quoted in Post, 1963, p. 113).

In the United States today, the criteria for insanity varies slightly from state to state; the federal system has its own rule as well. But generally all insanity laws require defendants to prove that, at the time of their crimes, they were suffering from a serious mental disease or defect and 1) lacked substantial capacity to appreciate the criminality or wrongfulness of their conduct or 2) were unable to conform their behavior to the requirements of law. The defendant has the burden of proving insanity.

Misperceptions of the Insanity Defense. At the time that John Hinckley used the insanity defense during his trial for the attempted assassination of President Ronald Reagan, press secretary James Brady, and three other people in 1982, the federal law under which Hinckley was tried did not require his lawyers prove that he was insane. Instead, it required the prosecution to prove that he was sane, a difficult task since Hinckley had a clear history of disordered behavior (Bonnie, Jeffries, & Low, 2000). And after Hinckley was found not guilty by reason of insanity, public pressure led to a revision of the federal law to require defendants to prove insanity, as is the case now in most state laws.

The uproar over the Hinckley verdict illustrates widespread dissatisfaction with the insanity plea, a dissatisfaction based mostly on misperceptions about the frequency of its use and about its outcomes. Many people believe that criminals routinely claim insanity to evade punishment. The fact is, that insanity pleas occur in only 1 out of every 200 criminal cases and are successful in only 2 of every 1,000 cases. (Applebaum; 1994; Silver, Cirincione, & Steadman, 1994). For each successful insanity plea, dozens are unsuccessful, including that of Jack Ruby, killer of Kennedy assassin Lee Harvey Oswald; Sirhan Sirhan, assassin of Robert Kennedy; and serial killers John Wayne Gacey, Jeffrey Dahmer, David Berkowitz (the "Son of Sam"), and Kenneth Bianchi (the "Hillside Strangler").

The typical defendant who is found not guilty by reason of insanity is similar to the typical defendant who is found incompetent to stand trial. This is not surprising, since most successful insanity pleas involve defendants who at one point were deemed incompetent to be tried. NGRI acquittees are generally seriously mentally ill, unemployed white males in their 20s and 30s, who have a history of hospitalization for mental illness and/or arrest. Few have high school educations. Most are suffering from a psychotic disorder such as schizophrenia and have been charged with nonviolent crimes.

Do NGRI Acquittees Get Away With Murder? A common misperception is that NGRI acquittees walk away from the courtroom, literally "getting away with murder." In fact, according to one study, only 1% of insanity acquittees are released without any restrictions and a mere 4% are placed on conditional release; however, 95% were hospitalized (Steadman, 1993). In most states, the defendant's mental status is reviewed periodically. Defendants judged no longer mentally ill and dangerous (a two-prong test) cannot be confined further, a mandate from the U.S. Supreme Court in *Foucha v. Louisiana*[1] (1992). NGRI acquittees generally spend twice as long—or longer—locked up in state mental hospitals than they would have spent in prison had they been convicted (Steadman, 1993). Investigation into the incarceration of NGRI acquittees in Virginia found that 25% of those confined had committed misdemeanors—offenses that would carry a maximum of 1-year in jail. Yet, the average time they spent in mental hospitals was 7 years. Two men diagnosed with paranoid schizophrenia were locked up for 17 and 16 years, respectively—both for stealing goods having a value of less than $200 (Rein, 2001). It is no surprise then, that John Hinckley has been hospitalized in St. Elizabeth's hospital in Washington, D.C., since 1982 and that, in spite of his annual efforts to be released, he is unlikely to get out as long as anyone is alive who can remember the day President Reagan was shot (Miller, 2000). McNaughton,, whose case gave us the insanity defense, died after 20 years in an insane asylum.

The Role of Expert Witnesses in the Insanity Defense. In federal courts and most states, expert witnesses are not allowed to give an opinion as to whether or not the defendant was "sane" or "insane" at the time of committing the offense. That is a legal question which only the judge or jury can answer. The expert witness can only testify as to the symptoms, behaviors, and diagnosis of the defendant. Even before this restriction was codified in state and federal rules of criminal procedure, the American Psychiatric Association took the position that "[No] expert witness testifying with respect to the mental state or condition of a defendant in a criminal case may state an opinion or inference as to whether the defendant did or did not have the mental state or condition constituting an element of the crime charged or a defense thereto. Such ultimate issues are for the trier of fact alone" (APA, 1994).

Indigent defendants have the right to experts to assist in their insanity defense, but not to the expert of their choice, according to the 1985 U.S. Supreme Court decision in *Ake v. Oklahoma*.[2] Absent a showing of some special circumstances or unusual disease or defect, indigents are evaluated by state or federal government-employed

---

[1] 112 S. Ct. 1780(1992).
[2] 105 S. Ct. 977 (1985).

mental health professionals, most of whom are highly qualified and competent witnesses. Of course, a person who can afford more than one expert, or the most expensive expert, might mount a more impressive insanity defense than a less affluent defendant, but this economic reality applies to any kind of defense.

Reforming the Insanity Defense

Two major changes have been made over the past 15 years that make it more difficult for mentally ill defendants to obtain the benefit of the insanity defense: Some states have abolished the insanity plea altogether, while others have added the "guilty but mentally ill" (GBMI) verdict mentioned earlier.

The Guilty But Mentally Ill Verdict. For many decades, juries deliberating cases involving the insanity defense could only reach verdicts of guilty, not guilty, or not guilty by reason of insanity. Since 1976, however, twenty states have passed laws allowing juries to find defendants guilty but mentally ill (GBMI). This verdict option is available only for defendants who plead NGRI. A defendant found GBMI is usually sentenced to the same period of confinement as any other defendant convicted of the same crime. The order of sentence provides that the mentally ill defendant be treated in the correctional facility. However, such treatment is rarely adequate, if provided at all, because GBMI convicts have no guarantee of medical care beyond the minimal level required by law for other convicts (Slobogin, 1985; Steadman, 1993). In one Michigan study, 75% of GBMI offenders went directly to prison without any treatment (Sales & Hafemeister, 1984). The intent of GBMI laws is to offer a compromise verdict that will decrease the number of defendants found NGRI. But research of verdicts indicates that when states allow both GMBI and NGRI, jurors usually require stronger proof of insanity before returning the NGRI verdict (Roberts, Sargent, & Chan, 1993) and render GBMI verdicts when they believe defendants may not have been sane enough to be held legally responsible for their actions, but culpable enough to warrant punishment (Sales & Shuman, 1996).

Abolishing the Insanity Defense. A few U.S. states, including Idaho and Montana, have abolished the insanity defense altogether. This did not—and could not—eliminate consideration of defendants' mental state, however because a crime requires *mens rea*, a concept we discussed at the beginning of this section. Some states have a special form of *mens rea* defense, in which a defendant can introduce evidence designed to show not insanity, but merely that he or she had "diminished capacity" to know right from wrong or to control behavior. This defense does not seek to abolish the defendant of responsibility, but asks for conviction of a lesser charge (i.e., manslaughter instead of murder) because of the defendant's incapacity to form meaningful premeditation. Former San Francisco County Supervisor Dan White, who in 1978 shot and wounded the mayor and killed another elected official, was found to have had a "diminished" capacity for murder based on the now famous "Twinkie defense." White claimed that his reasoning was clouded by eating too much junk food. The jury found him guilty of manslaughter instead of murder. Shortly after was released from serving his 6-year sentence, White took his own life. In 1982, California abolished the diminished capacity defense.

Assessing Sanity

It is relatively straightforward to assess a defendant's competence, requiring a determination of the defendant's present mental status. But assessing a defendant's mental condition during a criminal act that took place weeks, months, or even years earlier is a much tougher challenge for mental health professionals. To accomplish this, a variety of methods are used, including a review of the defendant's family, educational, employment, and medical history; ascertaining if the defendant has a history of prior criminality or mental disorder and treatment; listening to the defendant's version of the crime; and administering a variety of psychological assessment instruments.

Assessments typically used include a structured interview, in which a defendant is asked a predetermined sequence of questions, intelligence tests (usually either the Weschler Adult Intelligence Scale or the Stanford-Binet Intelligence Scale), and several personality assessments such as the Minnesota Multiphasic Personality Inventory (MMPI-2), the Psychopathy Checklist-Revised (PCL-R), and projective personality tests like the Rorschach Inkblot Test and the Thematic Apperception Test (TAT). Defendants whose history, observed behavior, or IQ test results suggest the possibility of brain dysfunctions may be given neurological tests like the Halstead-Reitan or Luria-Nebraska Batteries. These instruments measure abilities in areas such as information processing, attention, concentration, language, and perception of visual, auditory, and tactile stimulation. If there is a history of head trauma, brain injury, or recent change in personality or behavior, brain imaging procedures (such as an MRI and CT scan) may help determine if brain function or structure are compromised by disease or injury. (Each of the above tests are discussed in more detail in Chapter 5, except the Halstead-Reitan, Luria-Nebraska Batteries, MRI, and CT scan, which are discussed in Chapter 12).

Although it is estimated that 20 to 25% of defendants attempt to fake or "malinger" their mental illness, assessment instruments and astute clinicians are very successful in detecting malingering (Schretlen et al., 1992). One famous malingerer was the "Hillside Strangler," who was believed to have murdered more than a dozen young women in California and Washington in the 1970s. Although four experts had diagnosed him with having multiple personality disorder (now known as dissociative identity disorder), a savvy prosecution expert detected that Bianchi was faking the presence of "alter" personalities. His cover blown, Bianchi abandoned his insanity plea and pled guilty to murder in exchange for the prosecutor's not seeking the death penalty (Cassel & Bernstein, 2001).

PREDICTING DANGEROUSNESS

Russell Weston, Jr. had been had been suffering from paranoid schizophrenia long before his attack on the U.S. Capitol building. Two years earlier, Weston had been involuntarily committed to a Montana mental hospital because of his paranoid delusions and odd behavior, which included claims that President Clinton was his close friend and that he was being spied by devices planted in television satellite dishes and cable boxes. Weston was released before the court-ordered stay of his confinement ended, because hospital officials deemed him to be no risk for violent behavior if he took his medications. That was a big "if," to be sure. But could psychologists have known in 1996 that Weston would kill people in 1998?

As we discussed in Chapter 3, mental health professionals are called upon by the courts to predict a person's potential for future dangerous behavior in several contexts. Should someone charged with murder be free on bond pending trial? Or pending appeal of a conviction? Should a NGRI acquittee be committed to the penal division of a state mental hospital for a lengthy period of time, or has the mental breakdown that accounted for the crime passed so that the person can be supervised in the community? (Remember that NGRI defendants cannot be confined in a hospital just because they have a mental diagnosis—they must be dangerous to society.) And then, as in the case of John Hinckley, is a NGRI acquittee who was committed well enough after years of confinement to be released? Is someone guilty of a capital offense so dangerous to society that they should receive the ultimate penalty—that of death? In a civil context, psychologists will be asked to determine whether someone is such a danger to self that he or she should be put in a mental hospital to protect his or her health and welfare.

PSYCHOLOGICAL DAMAGES IN CIVIL TRIALS

In December 2001, David Diaz, a security guard at a Marilyn Manson concert, filed a lawsuit in which he claimed that, during a concert, Manson grabbed Diaz's head and held it against his hips as he "gyrated" in front of the crowd, ignoring Diaz's protests to stop. Diaz sought $75,000 damages for emotional distress and other injuries. If the case goes to trial, Diaz will likely have a psychological expert testify about nature and extent of his emotional suffering (Associated Press, 2001).

Diaz's suit is a *tort action* for which he is seeking money to compensate him for his emotional suffering. A *tort* is a wrongful act that causes harm to an individual. Tort law provides a mechanism for *individuals* to seek redress for the harm they have suffered from the wrongful acts of another party. It thus differs from *criminal law* which—acting on behalf of society as a whole—prosecutes defendants for wrongful behavior and seeks to punish them in an attempt to maintain society's overall sense of justice.

Definition of a Tort

Many kinds of behavior can constitute a tort. Slander and libel are torts, so are cases of medical malpractice, the manufacture of defective products resulting in a personal injury, and intentional or negligent behavior producing harm to another person.

A person can suffer various kinds of damage from a tort, including destruction of personal property, physical injuries, and emotional distress (sometimes called "pain and suffering"). A plaintiff may sue for psychological damages that arise either out of a defendant's "negligent" wrongful behavior or "intentional" wrongful conduct. In both kinds of cases, clinical psychologists are often called upon to give expert testimony on the nature and extent of the plaintiff's psychological suffering. Intentional misconduct is described variously as "willful," "wanton," "reckless," "malicious," or "outrageous." Most successful claims for emotional damages arise out of intentional conduct that most people would find offensive. If what Diaz says is true, Manson's conduct would likely fall in that category. Damages for negligent behavior are limited to "compensatory" damages, meaning those that compensate the plaintiff for their suffering and things like lost wages and medical expenses. Recovery for intentional torts allows "punitive" damages, an order to pay money that is designed to punish and deter egregious behavior.

Assessing Psychological Damage in Tort Cases

When clinical psychologists conduct assessments with civil plaintiffs, they typically perform an evaluation that, like most clinical assessments, includes a social history, a clinical interview, psychological testing, interviews with others, and a review of available records (see Chapter 3). Based on these data, the clinician will reach a decision about what, if any, psychological problems, the person might be suffering. This aspect of the forensic evaluation is not much different from what a clinician might do with any client, whether or not the client is involved in a lawsuit.

The far more difficult additional question the clinician must answer is whether the psychological problems were caused by the tort, were aggravated by the tort, or existed prior to the tort. While there is no established procedure for answering this question, most clinicians try to locate all clinical records and other sources of data that might help establish the point in time at which any diagnosed disorder began to appear. When plaintiffs allege that they were targeted for harassment or some other intentional tort because the defendants knew they had a psychological problem that made them especially vulnerable, the clinician must take this prior condition into account in reaching conclusions about the effects of the tort.

Workers' Compensation Cases

When a worker is injured on the job, the law provides for the worker to be compensated, but it does so via a streamlined system that avoids the necessity of proving a tort. This system, known as *workers' compensation law*, is in place in all 50 states and in the federal government. In workers' compensation systems, employers contribute to a fund that insures their workers who are injured at work, and they also waive their right to blame the worker or some other individual for the injury. For their part, workers give up their right to pursue a tort against their employers; the award they receive will be determined by the type and duration of the injury and the amount of their salary at the time of the injury. Workers can seek compensation for (1) physical and psychological injuries sustained at work, (2) the cost of the treatment they receive for their injuries, (3) lost wages, and (4) the loss of future earning capacity.

Because psychological injuries or mental disorders arising from employment can be compensated, clinical psychologists are often asked to evaluate injured workers and render an opinion about the existence, cause, and implications of any mental disorders that might appear in a given case. Claims for mental disability usually arise in one of three ways.

First, a physical injury or job-related threatening event can cause a mental disorder and psychological disability. A common pattern in these *physical–mental* cases is for a worker to sustain a serious physical injury—a broken back or severe burns, for example—that results in chronic pain. As the pain continues, the worker experiences an overlay of psychological problems, usually depression and anxiety (see Chapter 11). These problems worsen until they become full-fledged mental disorders, resulting in further impairments in overall functioning.

The second work-related pathway to mental disability is for an individual to suffer a traumatic incident at work or to undergo a long period of continuous stress that leads to psychological difficulties. The night clerk at a convenience store who is the victim of an armed robbery and subsequently develops post-traumatic stress disorder exemplifies such *mental–mental* cases, as does the clerical worker who, after years of overwork and job pressure, experiences an anxiety disorder, perhaps post-traumatic stress disorder. (In a third kind of case, known as mental–physical, work-related stress is blamed for the onset of a physical disorder such as high blood pressure. Many states have placed special restrictions on these types of claims, and psychologists are seldom asked to evaluate them.)

In recent years, the number of psychological claims arising in workers' compensation litigation has increased dramatically. In the 1980s, stress-related mental disorders became the fastest growing occupational disease category in the United States (Hersh & Alexander, 1990), with claims more than doubling from 1985 to 1990. It is not clear what accounts for this surge in psychological claims, but three explanations have been proposed. It might be caused, first, by the growing proportion of women in the workforce. Women are more often diagnosed with anxiety and depressive disorders than men are (Sparr, 1995). A second possibility is that shifts in the job market from manufacturing and industrial jobs to service-oriented jobs have produced corresponding increases in interpersonal and other psychological stressors and decreases in physical injuries. Job violence, or the threats of violence at work, are having a significant impact on stress-related job claims. After the terrorist attacks on the Pentagon and World Trade Centers on September 11, 2001, followed by Anthrax scares at post offices and other government buildings, job-related stress soared—including the appearance of post-traumatic stress disorder—and claims for related damages are expected to skyrocket, especially in New York City and Washington, D.C.

CIVIL COMPETENCIES

The concept of mental competence extends to many decisions that individuals must make throughout their lives. In our earlier discussion of competence to stand trial, we focused on the tasks required of defendants during the course of a criminal trial. However, the question of mental competence is raised in several noncriminal situations as well. We refer to these other situations as involving *civil competencies*.

Questions of civil competency focus on whether an individual has the capacity to understand information relevant to making a particular decision and then making an informed choice about what to do. For example, civil competency questions are commonly asked about whether a person is capable of managing personal financial affairs, making decisions about accepting or refusing medical or psychiatric treatment, or executing a will that directs how property should be distributed to heirs or other beneficiaries.

The legal standards used to define competence have evolved over many years, but scholars who have studied this issue agree that four abilities are essential to competent decision-making (Appelbaum & Grisso, 1995). A competent individual is expected to be able to (1) understand basic information relevant to making a decision, (2) apply that information to a specific situation in order to anticipate the consequences of various choices that might be made, (3) use logical, rational thinking to evaluate the pros and cons of various strategies and decisions, and (4) communicate a personal decision or choice about the matter under consideration.

The specific abilities associated with each of these general criteria vary, depending on the decision the person must make. Deciding whether to have risky surgery demands different kinds of information and thinking processes than does deciding whether to leave one's estate to one's children versus a charitable organization.

Clinical psychologists interested in psycho-legal issues have focused considerable research attention on the competence of individuals with severe mental disorders to make decisions and give informed consent about their own psychiatric treatment. Can persons with serious mental disorders make competent treatment decisions? Do their decision-making abilities differ from persons who do not suffer mental disorders? These questions have been the focus of the MacArthur Treatment Competence Study, which has led to the development of a series of structured interview measures to assess the four basic abilities discussed earlier in relation to competence in criminal cases. Standardized interviews were conducted with three groups of patients—those with schizophrenia, major depression, and heart disease—and with groups of healthy persons from communities who were demographically matched to the patient groups (Grisso & Applebaum, 1995). Only a minority of the persons in all of the groups showed significant impairments in competent decision making about various treatment options, and patients were capable of significantly better understanding when treatment information was presented to them in small bits, one element at a time. However, the patients with schizophrenia and major depression tended to have a poorer understanding of treatment information and used less adequate reasoning in thinking about the consequence of the treatment than did the heart patients or community sample.

Since the Supreme Court decision in *Cruzan v. Director, Missouri Department of Health*[3] (1990), which recognized that states may allow patients to formalize their desire not to receive life-sustaining medical treatment should they become incapacitated or terminally ill, mental health professionals may be called upon to determine the competence of a person to make what are known as advance medical directives. The

---

[3]497 U.S. 261 (1990).

ethical and practical issues involved in determining patients' competence to make prospective end-of-life decisions are enormous; but the trend is to recognize that patients have a high degree of autonomy in accepting or rejecting a variety of treatments and health-care provisions (Cantor, 1998; Rich, 1998). The state of Oregon, which has the only physician-assisted suicide law in the country (allowing physicians to provide their terminally ill patients with enough barbiturates to end their lives), requires psychological evaluations to rule out depression as a contributing factor in patients' decisions to end their lives.

Questions relating to civil competencies illustrate that mental health laws and policies are not just theoretical concepts or abstract principles; these laws and policies can have significant positive or negative effects on the treatment that individual patients receive, and how well that treatment works. Accordingly, many mental health professionals and attorneys point out that legal rulings in this area have far-reaching social consequences. This perspective, known as *therapeutic jurisprudence*, concentrates on the law's impact on emotional life and psychological well-being. It is a perspective that regards the law (rules of law, legal procedures, and roles of legal actors) itself as a social force that often produces therapeutic or anti-therapeutic consequences. It does not suggest that therapeutic concerns are more important than other consequences or factors, but it does suggest that the law's role as a potential therapeutic agent should be recognized and systematically studied and that mental health laws and decisions should be evaluated to determine their impact on individuals and society (Stolle, Wexler, & Winnick, 2000). Principles of therapeutic jurisprudence are being applied to criminal areas as well, influencing the establishment of drug and mental health courts and public policy relating to trying juveniles as adults and civilly committing dangerous sexual offenders.

PSYCHOLOGICAL AUTOPSIES AND CRIMINAL PROFILING

As already mentioned, most forensic assessments, like most other clinical assessments, include interviewing, observing, and testing clients in order to arrive at an understanding of them. In a few unusual circumstances, however, clinicians may be called upon to give opinions about a deceased person's state of mind prior to death. In such cases, obviously, the clinician must conduct the evaluation without that person's participation. These postmortem psychological evaluations are known as psychological autopsies or equivocal death analyses (Ogloff & Otto, 1993).

Psychological Autopsies

The first *psychological autopsies* are believed to have been done in the 1950s, when a group of social scientists in Los Angeles began assisting the County Coroner's Office in determining whether suicide, murder, or accident was the most likely cause of death in certain equivocal cases. Since then, psychological autopsies have become commonplace, especially when it is important to determine whether someone died by accident or suicide (this question is often raised by insurance companies in cases in which death benefits could be denied if a policy holder died by suicide). Psychological autopsies are also used (1) in workers' compensation cases when an employee's family claims that stressful working conditions or work-related trauma contributed to their relative's suicide or accidental death, (2) to decide whether a deceased individual had the mental capacity necessary to competently execute or modify a will, and (3) to support the argument made by criminal defendants that the person they allegedly killed died by suicide, not homicide.

There is no standard format for conducting psychological autopsies, but most clinicians rely heavily on documents and other life records that a person leaves behind, as well as on interviews with those who knew the decedent (Ebert, 1987). Some clinicians concentrate on evidence from the time just before the person's death. What was the person's mood? How was the person doing at work? Were there any pronounced changes in the person's behavior? Those who take a psychodynamic approach to clinical psychology look for evidence about family dynamics and personality traits appearing early in the person's life. As a child, how did the person interact with parents or other caregivers? What was the individual's approach to school? To competition with peers?

How valid are psychological autopsies—that is, do they accurately portray a person's state of mind at the time of death? There are certainly reasons to doubt their validity. For one thing, most of the assessment information comes "secondhand," because the person about whom inferences are to be made is not available for interviewing or testing. Further, as noted in Chapter 4, information obtained through third-party interviews may be distorted by memory lapses or by efforts to describe a person in an especially good, or bad, light. Unfortunately, no empirical research is available concerning the validity of psychological autopsies, mainly because the decedent's "true" state of mind prior to death is unknown, and thus cannot be compared to conclusions later drawn by clinicians. This problem may be partially solved if, in future studies, researchers were to see how well-reputed experts do when given psychological autopsy information about cases in which the cause of death appears ambiguous but is actually known. Studying the accuracy of these experts' conclusions, and the reasons behind them, may go a long way toward establishing the validity of psychological autopsies.

In the absence of such research, judges have had mixed reactions to psychological autopsy evidence. In cases involving workers' compensation claims and questions of whether insurance benefits should be paid, the courts have usually admitted psychological autopsy testimony. They have been much more reluctant to do so in criminal cases and in cases involving the question of whether a person had the mental capacity to draft a will (Ogloff & Otto, 1993), because these cases may involve testimony about the ultimate issue to be decided in a case, a concept we discuss in the last section of this chapter.

Criminal Profiling

In some ways, psychological autopsies resemble a technique known as *criminal profiling*. In both cases, clinicians draw inferences about an individual's motives and state of mind on the basis of life records or other data a person has left behind. In psychological autopsies, however, the identity of the person being assessed is known, and the question is what they did, and why. In criminal profiling, the person's behavior is known, and the question is "who did it."

Clinicians' involvement in criminal profiling is based on the assumption that criminals commit their crimes in distinctive ways, leaving clues to their psychological makeup—much as DNA or fingerprints point to their physical identity or ballistics tests reveal the kind of firearm they used. Indeed, evidence is accumulating that certain psychological characteristics are linked to certain patterns of criminal behavior and that these links can be detected by a psychological analysis of crime scenes. Accordingly, police are now using criminal profiling to focus their search for suspects in certain kinds of crimes to people who possess the behavioral and psychological characteristics that tend to be associated with such crimes. Profiles have also been developed to help investigators identify persons who are likely to be hijackers, drug couriers, and illegal aliens (Monahan & Walker, 1990).

One of the first examples of successful criminal profiling came in 1957, with the arrest of George Matesky, the so-called "Mad Bomber" of New York City. After trying for over a decade to identify the person responsible for more than 30 bombings in the New York area, the police consulted Dr. James Brussel, a local psychiatrist. Brussel examined pictures of the bomb scenes and analyzed letters sent to police by the bomber. Based on these data, Brussel advised the police to look for a heavyset, middle-aged, Eastern European, Catholic man who was single and lived with a sibling or an aunt. Brussel also concluded that the man loved his mother and valued neatness. He even predicted that, when the man was found, he would be wearing a buttoned double-breasted suit. When the police finally arrested Matesky, this profile turned out to be uncannily accurate, right down to the suit (Brussel, 1968).

Today, the major source of research and development on criminal profiling is the FBI's Profiling and Behavioral Assessment Unit. This unit is composed of about a dozen profilers who have training in behavioral science and who work with a very small number of psychologists and other mental health professionals who are involved in profiling activities. The unit analyzes about 1,000 cases a year (Homant & Kennedy, 1998), and has amassed large amounts of data on the backgrounds, family characteristics, current behaviors, and psychological traits of various types of criminal offenders (Douglas & Olshaker, 1995). The unit has concentrated on the study of violent offenders, especially those who commit bizarre or repeated crimes, including rapists, arsonists, sexual homicides, and mass and serial murderers. A key element of the unit's research is the interviewing of various types of known offenders in order to discover how each type selects and approaches their victims, how they react to their crimes, what demographic or family characteristics they share, and what personality features predominate among them. For example, as part of its study of mass and serial killers, the FBI has conducted detailed interviews with many notorious killers, including Charles Manson, Richard Speck, and David Berkowitz (Ressler & Shachtman, 1992).

One review of criminal profiling (Homant & Kennedy, 1998) concluded that different kinds of crime scenes can in fact be classified with reasonable reliability and that various kinds of crimes do correlate with certain offender characteristics. At the same time, research on profiling suggests several reasons for caution about its value. For one thing, in contrast to the "mad bomber" case, inaccurate profiles are quite common.

Second, many of the evaluation studies have been conducted by FBI profilers themselves, and have focused on a rather small number of cases. Finally, the concepts and approaches actually used by profilers have often not been objectively and systematically defined. In fact, a survey of 152 police psychologists found that 70% of them had serious questions about the validity of crime scene profiling (Bartol, 1996), and for good reason. Recall that, after a bomb exploded at the 1996 Olympics, Atlanta police almost immediately—and incorrectly, as it turned out—focused their suspicions on Richard Jewell, an Olympic Park security guard. Jewell was singled out because he fit an FBI profile for this kind of bombing; he is a white, single, middle-age male who craves the limelight, sometimes as a police "wannabe." In this case, the profile was wrong.

CHILD CUSTODY AND PARENTAL FITNESS

One of the fastest growing areas for clinical psychologists in forensic psychology is the assessment of families in crisis.

Parental Fitness

Sometimes clinicians are asked to conduct evaluations of *parental fitness*. In these cases, the evaluator must determine if a parent's custody rights over their children should be terminated—and the children removed from their home—because the individual is unfit to be a parent. The legal definition of parental unfitness varies from state to state (Azar & Benjet, 1994), but in general, the law makes it rather difficult to take children away from their biological parents. To prove parental unfitness in Kentucky, for example, it must be shown that the parent (1) inflicted, or allowed someone else to inflict, physical injury, emotional harm, or sexual abuse on the child, (2) is morally delinquent, (3) abandoned the child, (4) is mentally ill, or (5) fails to provide essential care for the child for some reason other than poverty (*Davis v. Collinsworth*,[4] 1989). In most other states, too, it must be shown that one or more of these conditions is substantially threatening a child's welfare, and the evidence proving this threat must usually be "clear and convincing" (Azar & Benjet, 1994), which is quantified as a 75% chance. This high standard, along with the unrealistic caseloads of child protective service social worker, results in numerous children being killed or severely abused by their parents.

Child Custody Disputes

More commonly, clinical psychologists' involvement in the legal aspects of family crises comes when parents are separating or divorcing. Here, the clinician is usually asked to conduct a *child custody evaluation* and to offer recommendations to help a court settle disputes over which parent can best meet their children's needs and which, therefore, should retain custody of them. The growth in these assessment

---

[4]Ky. 771 S.W. 2d 329 (1980).

activities is attributable, first, to the fact that, with half of all marriages in the United States now ending in divorce, child custody issues arise in millions of families. One-third of U.S. children living today will spend some time living in a stepfamily and over half will spend time in a single-parent household (Arnold, 1998). Second, the preference for maternal custody that marked most of the 20th century gave way in the 1980s to gender-neutral laws that put parents on equal footing, in principle at least. Courts now routinely want to know about the parenting abilities of each parent before making a decision about custody (Liss & McKinley-Pace, 1999).

Most states permit two kinds of custodial arrangements—joint or sole custody. The law prefers joint custody, in large part because of mental health experts' educating the courts that children's needs are best met when both parents are involved in their lives. But there are two categories of joint custody—legal and physical. Although parents may be likely to have joint legal custody, meaning they jointly make decisions about their children's welfare (such as those related to education and health care), generally one parent has sole physical custody, with the other parent having visitation rights. Compared to sole legal custody, joint legal custody distributes the frequency of child contact more evenly between the two parents, leads to more interaction between the divorced parents (and generates more demands for cooperation concerning their children), and results in more variation in caregiving arrangements (Clingempeel & Repuccci, 1982).

Clinicians conduct custody evaluations under any of three sets of circumstances. In some cases, a judge appoints a clinician to conduct a custody evaluation that will be available to all the parties. In others, each party retains a different expert to conduct independent evaluations, and in still others, the two sides agree to share the cost of hiring one expert to conduct a single evaluation (Weissman, 1991). Most informed observers, including attorneys, prefer either the first or third option because they minimize the hostilities and adversarial pressures that usually arise when separate experts are hired by each side (Keilin & Bloom, 1986).

Although the methods used in custody evaluations vary a great deal depending on the specific issues in each case, the American Psychological Association and the Association of Family and Conciliation Courts have published guidelines for conducting custody evaluations. Most evaluations include clinical and social histories, standardized testing of the parents and the children, observation of parent-child interactions, interviews with individuals who have had opportunities to observe family members, and a review of documents that might be relevant to the case, including medical records of children and parents.

A national survey of mental health professionals who conduct child custody evaluations found that these experts devoted an average of thirty hours to each custody evaluation (Ackerman & Ackerman, 1997). A substantial amount of this time is spent interviewing and observing the parties in various combinations. More than two-thirds of the respondents indicated that they conducted individual interviews with each parent and each child, observed each parent interacting (separately) with each child, and conducted formal psychological testing of the parents and the children. The MMPI was the test most often used with parents; intelligence tests and projective personality tests were the most common instruments used with the children (see Chapter 5). An increasing number of clinicians report using one or two instruments specifically designed for child custody evaluations: the Bricklin Perceptual Scales and the Ackerman-Schoendorf Scales for Parent Evaluation of Custody (ASPECT), with the ASPECT having better empirical support (Nicholson, 1999).

These experts also reported how often they recommended different kinds of custodial arrangements. The most common recommendation was limited joint custody, in which parents share the decision making, but one parent maintains primary physical custody. Single-parent custody without visitation was the least recommended alternative.

Do children adapt and function better when raised in joint custody or sole custody arrangements? One might expect it could go either way, because while joint custody allows the child to maintain close ties to both parents, sole custody simplifies custodial arrangements and minimizes children's confusion over where their home is. Indeed, most studies report either no major differences between children in the two types of custody or only somewhat better adjustment by joint-custody children (Bender, 1994; Crosbie-Burnett, 1991). For example, in a study of 78 stepfamilies with adolescent children, Margaret Crosbie-Burnett (1991) found that joint custody was associated with greater family cohesion, improved adjustment by these adolescents, and better relationships with their stepparents. However, the gender of the child moderated the impact of the custodial arrangement on adjustment. Consistent with the results of earlier research (Emery, 1982; Hetherington & Arasteh, 1988), Crosbie-Burnett (1991) found that continuing hostility and conflicts between the parents—regardless of the type of custody in force—was associated with poorer adjustment on the part of the children. It appears that the quality of the relationship between divorced parents is more important to the adjustment of their children than whether the children are raised in sole-custody or joint-custody arrangements (Hughes, 1996; Rodriguez & Arnold, 1998).

Many mental health professionals believe evaluations regarding child custody and parental fitness are among the most ethically challenging and clinically difficult of all forensic cases. For one thing, the emotional stakes are extremely high, and both parents are often willing to spare no expense or tactic in the battle over who will win custody. Associated with this conflict is the fact that the children are usually forced to live, for months if not years, in an emotional limbo where they do not know with whom they will eventually live, where they will be going to school, or how often they will see each parent. Second, to conduct a thorough family assessment, the clinician must evaluate the children, both parents, and, when possible, other people who have observed the family's interaction. Often, not all parties agree to such evaluations or do so only under coercion, a fact that often creates a lengthy and unfriendly assessment process. Third, to render an expert opinion, the clinician must possess a great deal of knowledge—not only about the particular children and parents being evaluated—but also about infant–parent attachment, child development, family systems, the effects of divorce on children, adult and childhood mental disorders, and several different kinds of testing.

Complicating the situation, too, are changes in traditional definitions of a "family." Increasing tolerance of variability in lifestyles has forced clinical psychologists and legal scholars to confront questions about whether parents' sexual orientation or ethnicity should have any bearing on custody and adoption decisions. For instance, the highest court in New Jersey has given gay men and lesbians the right to adopt children. This is not the case, however, in some other states (e.g., Virginia).

Finally, child custody evaluations are usually highly adversarial processes, in which one side will challenge the procedures or opinions of any expert with whom it disagrees. Clinicians who conduct custody evaluations must therefore brace themselves for all sorts of attacks on their clinical methods, scholarly competence, personal character, and professional ethics.

Custody Mediation

Because divorce is such a potent stressor for children and because protracted custody battles tend to leave a trail of emotionally battered family members in their wake, clinicians are devoting increasing attention to helping parents and children cope with these transitions or to finding alternatives to custody battles (Grych & Fincham, 1992; Kelly, 1991).

Custody mediation services are now being used more often in lieu of adversarial court procedures. The job of the mediator, who often is a layperson rather than a mental health professional or a lawyer, is to try to help the parties resolve their differences through an agreement by providing a safe environment for communication and by helping them explore options (Stahl, 1994). Psychologists can facilitate mediation by helping the parties emotionally accept the divorce, resolve disputes, and establish a good coparenting relationship (Melton et al., 1997).

Early promoters of mediation asserted that mediation would reduce competition between parents, improve children's adjustment, reduce constant relitigation of custody matters, and increase compliance with custody agreements. Has mediation lived up to that promise?

To assess the impact of mediated versus adversarial child custody procedures, Robert Emery and his colleagues at the University of Virginia randomly assigned divorcing couples to settle their custody disputes either through mediation or litigation. They found that while mediation greatly reduced the number of hearings and total amount of time required to reach a resolution, parents who mediated did not differ in terms of psychological adjustment from those who litigated. There was a consistent gender difference in satisfaction with the two methods, however. Fathers who went through mediation were much more likely to report feeling satisfied with the process than did fathers who litigated; mothers who went through mediation, on the other hand, were less likely to express satisfaction with its effects, and some measures showed better adjustment for mothers who litigated their dispute (Emery, Matthews, & Wyer, 1991; Emery, Matthews, & Kitzmann, 1994). To date, there is little evidence showing that mediation, relative to litigation, has improved post-divorce adjustment of either parents or their children (Melton et al., 1997). Further, mediation may even be counterproductive or harmful when domestic violence or substance abuse has led to one partner having more power in the relationship (Liss & McKinley-Pace, 1999).

MENTAL HEALTH EXPERTS IN THE LEGAL SYSTEM

Testifying as an expert witness is one of the most visible of clinical psychologists' forensic activities. Clinical psychologists (and psychiatrists) have testified in some of the most notorious criminal proceedings in recent U.S. history, including those of the Menendez brothers, O.J. Simpson, Jeffrey Dahmer, John Hinckley, Theodore Kaczynski, and Timothy McVeigh. By legal definition, an expert witness is someone with scientific, technical, or other specialized knowledge who may testify in the form of an opinion or otherwise if certain requirements are met:

1. An expert testifies at the discretion of the judge—there is no right for a party to present expert testimony—if he or she believes that the testimony will assist the judge or the jury in understanding evidence or determining a fact in issue.
2. The witness must be qualified by knowledge, skill, experience, training, or education to testify about a scientific, technical, or other specialized matter.
3. The expert's testimony must be based on reliable principles or methods (i.e., reliably and accepted research methods) that are established by acceptance within the expert's field (i.e., acceptance by academics and researchers).
4. The principles and methods must be applicable to the facts or data in the case.

These standards are codified in Federal Rule of Evidence 702, Testimony by Experts, which reflects significant litigation in the 1990s concerning the reliability of scientific expert testimony (*Daubert v. Merrell Dow Pharmaceuticals*,[5] 1993; *General Electric v. Joiner*,[6] 1997; and *Kumho v. Carmichael*,[7] 1999). Although the Federal Rule applies only to trials in federal court, the majority of states are applying its standards. Other states have differing requirements for admissibility, but require, at the least, that the testimony be based on established and accepted scientific evidence (*Frye v. United States*,[8] 1923; Shuman & Sales, 1999).

Testimony of experts is limited by law to descriptions of parties' symptoms, behavior, and demeanor; explanation of the evaluation and assessment instruments used, and opinions about the party's mental status, including a diagnosis of mental disorder. Experts are *not* allowed to give an opinion as to whether or not a defendant is competent to stand trial or was sane at the time of an offense, whether a party was competent to make a will, which of two parents would make a better custodian of children, or any other opinion that goes to the ultimate issue before the court. Offering "ultimate opinion testimony" would be drawing a legal conclusion that usurps prerogative of the judge and jury to apply the law to the facts and opinions given by the expert (Cassel & Bernstein, 2001).

---

[5]509 U.S. 579 (1993).
[6]522 U.S. 136 (1997).
[7]526 U.S. 137 (1999).
[8]293 F. 1013 (D.C. Cir. 1923).

Psychological and psychiatric expert testimony has, along with all other types of scientific expert evidence, grown rapidly in recent years. It is estimated that psychologists and psychiatrists testify in approximately 8 percent of all trials held in federal civil courts, and mental health witnesses participate in as many as a million cases each year (O'Connor, Sales, & Shuman, 1996).

Expert testimony is frequent because there are many topics for psychologists to testify about (see Table 13.2). As scientists learn more about human behavior, attorneys are likely to find their research results helpful in court cases. The press usually focuses on testimony concerning criminal competence and responsibility, but testimony about these topics is actually relatively rare compared to those involving experimental, developmental, industrial/organizational, and social psychology.

Psychological expert testimony has often been criticized as lacking in reliability, validity, propriety, and usefulness. Former federal appellate judge David T. Bazelon, a supporter of legal rights for the mentally ill, (1974) once complained that, "In no case is it more difficult to elicit productive and reliable testimony than in cases that call on the knowledge and practice of psychiatry." This view was echoed by Warren Burger (Burger, 1975), a former Chief Justice of the Supreme Court who chided experts for the "uncertainties of psychiatric diagnosis." Sharply worded critiques of psychologists' expert testimony can be found in several other sources (Bonnie & Slobogin, 1980; Ennis & Litwack, 1974; Morse, 1978), and one well-known guidebook is devoted entirely to the subject of how to cross-examine the expert testimony of psychologists (Ziskin & Faust, 1988).

Tightening the evidentiary standards, as Federal Rule 702 and case decisions have done, forces psychological experts to address some of the concerns lawyers, judges, and appellate courts have had in the past (Smith, 1989), such as the unreliable nature of some of their opinions that were not based on valid research. But judges and juries still have to contend with the problems attributable to attorneys who are not knowledgeable enough about psychology as a science to properly examine and cross-examine the experts, and with experts who are not good witnesses. These deficits deprive the fact finder of the benefits of a well-presented and effectively challenged opinion, for jurors cannot be influenced by testimony they do not understand. Studies recommend that experts take the role of teachers and try to present complex concepts in simple terms, using charts, videos, photographs, and models to help jurors visualize and comprehend the material (Sleek, 1998).

Another problem with psychological expert testimony is that juries are confused and frustrated by the "battle of the experts" that is joined when opposing sides have numerous contradictory experts. When the parties (e.g., defense and prosecution, divorcing parents, siblings fighting over a will) present contradictory mental health testimony, jurors tend to throw out the expert opinions and base their decision on nonexpert testimony. In a Maryland case in which a wealthy real estate developer pleaded NGRI to a charge of hiring a hit man to murder her husband, jurors deadlocked and were unable to reach a verdict. So many mental experts were called that the jurors reported paying no attention to any of them. They reasoned that if the experts could not agree on the defendant's mental condition, they were not going to try to figure out which expert to believe. Other data support this anecdotal evidence (Brekke et al.,

TABLE 13.2 Topics for Expert Psychological Testimony

Expert witnesses from psychology testify about topics in criminal trials, civil litigation, and domestic disputes. In fact, expert testimony is given on these topics much more often than on claims of insanity. Here are fourteen of the more common subjects of expert psychological testimony.

Topic of Testimony	Main Question Addressed in Testimony
1. Insanity	What is the relationship between the defendant's mental condition at the time of the alleged offense and the defendant's responsibility for the crime?
2. Criminal competency	Does the defendant have an adequate understanding of the legal proceeding in which he or she is involved?
3. Sentencing	What are the prospects for the defendant's rehabilitation? What deterrent effects do certain sentences have?
4. Eyewitness identification	What factors affect the accuracy of eyewitness identification?
5. Civil commitment	Does a mentally ill person present a danger, or threat of danger, such that hospitalization is necessary?
6. Psychological damages in civil cases	What psychological consequences has an individual suffered as a result of wrongful conduct? To what extent are the psychological problems attributable to a preexisting condition?
7. Negligence and product liability	How do environmental factors and human perceptual abilities affect an individual's use of a product?
8. Trademark litigation	Is a certain product name or trademark confusingly similar to that of a competitor?
9. Discrimination	What psychological evidence is there that equal treatment is being denied or that certain procedures and decisions discriminate against women and minorities in the schools or in the workplace?
10. Guardianship and conservatorship	Does an individual possess the necessary mental ability to make decisions concerning his or her health and general welfare?
11. Child custody	What psychological factors will affect the best interests of the child whose custody is in dispute?
12. Adoption and termination of parental rights	What psychological factors affect the best interests of a child whose parents disabilities may render them unfit to raise and care for the child?
13. Professional malpractice	Did a mental health professional's conduct fail to meet the standard of care owed to the client?
14. Mitigating psychosocial factors in litigation	What are the effects of pornography, violence, spouse abuse, and the like on the behavior of litigants who claim that their conduct was affected by one of these influences?

1991). Even uncontradicted mental health testimony does not always influence juries or judges, who often perceive psychology and psychiatry to be "soft sciences" that are too dependent on subjective interpretations (Rohde, 1999). In spite of these findings, the U.S. Supreme Court's opinion in *Barefoot v. Estelle*[9] (1983)—that jurors are capable of separating reliable from unreliable mental health evidence and opinion—is controlling, though the new federal rule discussed above gives judges the role of "gatekeepers" to determine what testimony is sufficiently reliable and probative for the jury to hear.

Several suggestions have been made that would, if implemented, reduce the overly adversarial nature of scientific and technical experts within all disciplines, not just psychology. These include (1) limiting the number of experts each side may introduce to testify about a given topic, (2) requiring that the experts be chosen from an approved panel of individuals reputed to be objective and highly competent, and (3) allowing testimony only from experts who have been appointed by a judge—not those hired by opposing attorneys. A number of scientific and professional organizations have come forward with proposals to aid the courts in finding skilled experts, an initiative supported by U.S. Supreme Court Justice Stephen Bryer (2000). The National Conference of Lawyers and Scientists, a joint committee of the American Association for the Advancement of Science and the Science and Technology Section of the American Bar Association, has developed a pilot project to test the feasibility of increased use of court-appointed experts in cases that present technical issues. The project will recruit a slate of candidates from science and professional organizations to serve as court-appointed experts in cases in which the judge decides that adversarial experts are unlikely to yield the information that is necessary for a well-reasoned resolution of the disputed issues. The project also is developing educational materials that will be helpful to scientists who are unfamiliar with the legal system (Bryer, 2000).

In the words of Justice Bryer, "In this age of science, we must build legal foundations that are sound in science as well as in law" (Bryer, 2000). Mental health experts can do their part by learning more about the legal system and enhancing their own professional skills so as to insure that their expertise can be fully utilized for the betterment of the law.

CHAPTER SUMMARY

Clinical psychologists are becoming increasingly involved in forensic psychology, a specialty that applies mental health knowledge and expertise to questions about individuals involved in legal proceedings. The nature of forensic assessment depends on the questions being asked, but, like most clinical assessments, it often includes a social history, a clinical interview, psychological testing, a review of life records, and perhaps interviews with a variety of third parties.

Evaluating competence to stand trial requires assessment of whether defendants can understand the nature of their trial, participate in their defense, or consult with

---

[9]463 U.S. 880 (1983).

their attorney. Most defendants referred for such evaluations are ultimately found competent.

At their trials, defendants who plead not guilty by reason of insanity (NGRI) must present evidence that they lacked the state of mind necessary to be held responsible for a crime. Psychologists and other mental health experts evaluate these defendants to determine if they meet the legal definition of insanity. This definition has changed over time, and can vary from one state or country to another, but the essence of the laws are that a defendant be unable to understand the nature of criminal act, or to know that the act was wrong as a result of a mental disease or defect. A variety of reforms—including abolition of the insanity defense, further changes in the definition of insanity, and the advent of the guilty but mentally ill verdict—have been enacted in order address public and political criticisms of the insanity defense.

Mental health professionals are called upon to assess the dangerousness of criminal defendants, a task that requires them to look into the future and predict which persons will reoffend.

In tort lawsuits, where plaintiffs seek compensatory and punitive damages for wrongful acts they claim caused them psychological harm, psychologists often testify about the nature, extent, and impact of that harm.

Psychologists also conduct assessments designed to determine questions about civil competency, such as whether a person is mentally capable of making decisions about financial affairs, medical or psychiatric treatment, or disposition of assets in a will.

Some clinicians involved in conducting psychological autopsies seek to determine the case of a suspicious death, usually at the behest of courts and insurance companies and often to rule out suicide. Psychologists with expertise in law enforcement may also be involved in criminal profiling, a practice that seeks to determine the perpetrator of especially heinous or serial crimes.

A growing area of forensic activity for clinical psychologists is assessing families in crisis. They offer opinions about the fitness of parents to retain custody over their children, and whether joint custody, sole custody, or some other arrangement would be best for the children when parents divorce. Many clinicians are also involved in efforts to mediate, rather than litigate, custody battles.

While expert testimony by psychologists is common, critics doubt the reliability, validity, propriety, and usefulness of such testimony. A variety of reforms, including enactment of procedural rules that govern the type of limits of expert testimony and creating registries of experts that will serve the court itself, not individual parties, may enhance the reputation of psychological expert testimony.

Chapter 14

Professional Issues in Clinical Psychology

If Lightner Witmer returned from the dead to review the field he founded, he would not recognize many modern clinicians as his colleagues. A few might match his original psychoeducational, child-oriented model. But many others would bewilder Witmer, because they practice something very different from the clinical psychology of the early twentieth century.

After reading the previous 13 chapters, you should be able to sympathize with Witmer's confusion. Clinical psychology is an expanding profession that is becoming more and more difficult to summarize in a single volume. As we saw in Chapter 1, clinicians now fill a long list of professional roles. However, no list does full justice to the complexity of clinical psychology, because it does not indicate either the multiple functions required by each job or the new specialties yet to emerge in the years to come. Noting an almost geometric growth in the number of clinicians, a proliferation of alternative roles, and increasing specialization, commentators struggle for an apt description of clinical psychology's current status. A favorite summary is that clinical psychology is in a transitional state.

This claim understates the changes in clinical psychology on at least two counts. First, it suggests that transition is a novel era in an otherwise tranquil history. This, of course, is not correct. Clinical psychology has been in constant transition. Witmer would not have had to wait until the 21st century to be surprised by changes in clinical psychology; he would have seen them by the 1920s.

The words "transitional state" also underestimate the pace of change in clinical psychology. The rate of transition has been accelerating like an object falling through space. Each decade since World War II has seen more extensive changes in the field than any preceding period.

Consider just three examples. First, in 1947 there were 787 members in American Psychological Association's Division 12, the Division of Clinical Psychology. In 1964, there were 2,883 members (Shakow, 1968), and in 2001 the membership of Division 12 stood at more than 7,000, over eight times its original size (The Society of Clinical Psychology, 2001). Second, in the first 50 years of clinical psychology, only one conference was offered on professional training. Since that time five national training conferences have taken place. In addition, several other conferences addressing specific issues in the training of clinical psychologists have been held; we discuss some of these conferences later in this chapter. Finally, early proposals for training in clinical psychology discouraged clinicians from entering private practice; only a handful of psychologists did so. Independent practice later became the leading type of employment for clinical psychologists, with more than one-third of clinicians employed full-time or part-time in some type of independent practice. Recently, however, the growth of independent practice has slowed, again signaling change within clinical psychology

These changes—along with the community mental health movement, health care reform, the appearance of behavioral medicine and other new psychological specialties, and society's increasing demand for mental health services—suggest that it is more accurate to portray clinical psychology not so much in transition, as in an entirely new era. It has been an era in which clinicians struggled for autonomy, got it, and became determined to retain it.

The professionalization and current status of clinical psychology are our primary topics in this final chapter. It is a story that has many subplots because the professionalization of clinical psychology involves several overlapping developments that have reshaped clinical psychology's identity. We focus on five issues crucial to clinical psychology's struggle for professional recognition:

1. *Professional training.* What training does one need to become a clinical psychologist, and what are the options for obtaining it?

2. *Professional regulation.* What are the mechanisms for insuring that a clinical psychologist possesses minimum skills and meets minimum requirements to function professionally?

3. *Professional ethics.* What principles guide clinicians in determining the ethical standards for their profession? How is unethical behavior handled?

4. *Professional independence.* What is the relationship between clinical psychology and other mental health professions?

5. *Perils of professionalization.* Has the professionalization of clinical psychology been an asset or a detriment? Has the public benefitted? Has the quality of clinical psychology improved?

PROFESSIONAL TRAINING

The first four decades of the twentieth century saw little progress in the creation of advanced training for clinical psychologists. For clinicians of that period, experience was not only the best teacher, it was practically the only one. Psychologists were involved increasingly in clinical work during this time, but their training for these activities was unsystematic.

During the late 1940s, social needs brought about by World War II and the financial support provided by the Veterans Administration and the U.S. Public Health Service combined to offer clinical psychology a unique opportunity to establish its identity, expand its functions, and elevate its status. It was then that training became a central concern.

The psychologist most influential in the development of clinical training programs was David Shakow, for many years the chief psychologist at Worcester State Hospital in Massachusetts and later an important figure at the National Institute of Mental Health. As early as 1942, Shakow saw the need for a 4-year doctoral-level training program in clinical psychology that included an internship during the 3rd year (Shakow, 1942). Shakow attracted the attention of Carl Rogers, who was then president of the APA. Rogers asked Shakow to chair a Committee on Training in Clinical Psychology, with the task of formulating a recommended clinical training program. The committee prepared a report entitled "Recommended Graduate Training in Clinical Psychology," which APA accepted in September 1947 and published that same year in APA's official journal, the *American Psychologist*. The Shakow report set the pattern for clinical training and remains, with surprisingly few exceptions, a standard against which modern clinical programs can be evaluated.

Three important recommendations of the Shakow report on clinical training were:

1. A clinical psychologist should be trained first and foremost as a psychologist.
2. Clinical training should be as rigorous as that for nonclinical areas of psychology.
3. Preparation of the clinical psychologist should be broad and directed toward assessment, research, and therapy.

The Shakow report also advocated several other principles for graduate clinical programs:

4. The core of clinical training programs should involve six areas: general psychology, psychodynamics of behavior, diagnostic methods, research methods, related disciplines, and therapy.
5. The program should offer basic courses in principles as opposed to a large number of courses on special techniques.
6. Training should integrate theory with practice. This emphasis on integrated training was a hallmark of Shakow's plan; mechanisms for integrating theory with practice are suggested in every one of his many articles on training.

7. Throughout the entire program, beginning in the first year, students should have contact with clinical material.

8. Opportunities should also be provided for contact with "normal" persons who never establish clinical contacts.

9. The training atmosphere should encourage maturity and the continued growth of desirable personality characteristics.

10. The program should promote a sense of responsibility for clients.

11. Representatives of related disciplines should teach clinical trainees, and joint study with students in these related disciplines should be arranged.

12. The program must emphasize the research implications of clinical phenomena.

13. Trainees "must acquire the ability to see beyond the responsibilities they owe the individual patient, to those they owe society" (Shakow, 1978, p. 151).

The Shakow report suggested a year-by-year curriculum to achieve these goals. This schedule was not offered as a blueprint for training but as an illustration of an adequate clinical program. In this model, first-year clinical students would become acquainted with the foundations of general psychology. They would also be trained in observational techniques. The second year would be devoted primarily to the experimental, diagnostic, and therapeutic content of clinical psychology. In addition to didactic material, students would acquire direct, practical experience through practicum courses and clinical placements. The third year would be the internship, a year of intensive and extensive experience with clinical phenomena at a hospital, clinic, or medical center. Shakow regarded the internship as an essential component that fostered students' sense of professional identity and immersed them in practical clinical experience. Several objectives were to be met during the fourth year. The dissertation would be completed; the student would take a seminar on professional problems and ethics as well as seminars involving related disciplines; and the student would undergo a period of self-evaluation. Self-evaluation usually meant being in individual psychotherapy, which would help the student uncover biases, attitudes, and personality problems that might interfere with later clinical work.

Many of today's clinical training programs are much like Shakow's prototype (see Table 14.1). However, it usually takes about 6.5, rather than 4, years to complete the entire training sequence (Gaddy et al., 1995), and the internship is now usually taken in the 4th or 5th year.[1] The major reasons for the extra years are that most programs require a master's thesis (usually in the second year), some universities still retain requirements such as a foreign language, and many clinical programs have added required

---

[1]The process of matching internship applicants with internship sites has always been cumbersome and stressful. For over 25 years, students have rank ordered preferences and waited anxiously to be called by internship sites making offers. Everyone was called on the same day. However, in 1998 to 1999, the process of matching internship applicants with internship sites changed dramatically. In that year, the Association of Psychology Postdoctoral and Internship Centers (APPIC) went to a computer matching system. Internship selection can still be stressful, but initial reports of the computer matching suggest that it is now more efficient (Keilin, 2000).

TABLE 14.1   Sample Schedule for Ph.D. Program in Clinical Psychology

Although there are many variations in the curricula of APA-accredited clinical training programs, the schedule shown here approximates what students encounter in most of them.

Fall Semester	Spring Semester
	First Year
Psychological Statistics I	Psychological Statistics II
Introduction to Interviewing	Clinical Assessment II
Clinical Assessment I	Selected Proseminar (Social Psychology, Developmental Psychology, Psychology of Learning, Physiological Psychology)
Practicum in Assessment	
History and Systems of Psychology	Theories and Research in Personality
	Second Year
Psychopathology	Psychotherapy Practicum
Selected Proseminar (choose one from list above)	Clinical Seminar (Group Therapy, Behavior Modification, Child and Family Therapy, Health Psychology, Community Psychology)
Systems of Psychotherapy	
MA research	MA research
	Third Year
Psychotherapy Practicum	Advanced nonclinical seminar
Clinical Seminar (choose one from list above)	Clinical or nonclinical research seminar
Clinical Research Seminar (Research in Personality, Psychopathology Research, Research in Psychotherapy)	Psychotherapy Practicum
Advanced nonclinical Seminar	

A written qualifying examination is to be taken during the third year of graduate work, but no later than the beginning of the fourth year. Only those students who have completed their MA thesis are permitted to register for the qualifying examination.

	Fourth Year
	Internship
	Fifth Year
Clinical or nonclinical research seminar	Same as Fall Semester
Advanced nonclinical seminar	
Research on dissertation	

courses on professional ethics as well as such specialty areas as human diversity, substance abuse, sexual problems, and organic disorders.

The greatest impact of the Shakow report was that it prescribed that special mix of scientific and professional preparation that has typified most clinical training programs ever since. This recipe for training—described as the scientist–professional model—was officially endorsed at clinical psychology's first major training conference held in Boulder, Colorado, in 1949 (Raimy, 1950).

The Boulder Conference

The Boulder Conference on Training in Clinical Psychology was convened with the financial support of the Veterans Administration and the U.S. Public Health Service, which requested APA to (1) name those universities that offered satisfactory training programs and (2) develop acceptable programs in universities that did not have them.

The Boulder conferees accepted the recommendations of Shakow's committee for a scientist–professional model of training. Clinical psychologists were expected to be proficient in research and professional practice and to have earned a PhD in psychology from a university-based graduate program. A supervised, year-long internship would also be required. Shakow's plan thus became known as the Boulder model.

The Boulder conferees further agreed that some mechanism was necessary for monitoring, evaluating, and officially accrediting clinical training programs and internship facilities. As a result, APA formed an Education and Training Board whose Committee on Accreditation was charged with these tasks. Currently, clinical training sites are visited by an APA accreditation team about every 5 years; the longest permissible interval between site visits is 7 years. The team consists of three psychologists (selected by the visited program from a list of available choices) who evaluate how well the program is meeting its own training goals and APA's training standards. The most recent version of APA's criteria for accreditation was published in 1996 (APA Office of Program Consultation and Accreditation, 1996). These new standards, developed by APA over several years, apply to areas of "professional psychology," which include clinical, counseling, and school psychology (Sheridan, Matarazzo, & Nelson, 1995). Programs that emerge in new areas of professional psychology would also be subject to these accreditation guidelines.

The results of accreditation site visits are published each year in the *American Psychologist.* In 2000, there were approximately 300 accredited doctoral programs. Roughly 70% of them were in clinical psychology, with the remainder in counseling psychology, school psychology, and professional schools. ("Accredited doctoral programs," 2000).[2] In addition, many doctoral training programs function without APA

---

[2]To acquaint prospective clinical students with the array of training possibilities, APA publishes annual editions of a book called *Graduate Study in Psychology and Associated Fields*, which lists all graduate programs in psychology, along with a brief description of requirements and training features. In addition, almost all clinical programs offer information—through brochures and/or internet websites—about their orientation, faculty interests, admission and course requirements, and financial support opportunities (see Appendix).

approval, either because the program has not requested a site visit or because approval has not been granted after an accreditation visit.

The Conferences at Stanford, Miami, and Chicago

The Boulder model remains the pivot point for discussions of clinical psychology training today. However, ever since its birth in 1949, some clinicians have expressed discontent with it. This discontent has grown in recent years, and major alternatives to the Boulder model now exist. The alternatives took shape during several post-Boulder training conferences, which we briefly describe below.

Approaches to clinical training were debated during two conferences held during the 1950s, and though neither altered the Boulder Model significantly, they did focus attention on changes in the profession. Named for its location at Stanford university, the 1955 *Stanford Conference* (Strother, 1956) stressed the need to prepare clinicians for the new professional roles that community mental health would offer. During the 1958 the *Miami Conference* (Roe et al., 1959), conferees again concluded that the PhD program should be retained as the primary training vehicle, and empirical research should be emphasized, but they encouraged departments to develop programs that suited their own resources and needs.

The 1965 *Chicago Conference* on the Professional Preparation of Clinical Psychologists was the first conference to seriously consider alternative models of clinical training. A theme of this conference was that, while the scientist–professional model should be continued, the value of a purely professional model of training should also be appreciated.

Interest in a professional model that stressed training in the delivery of clinical services stemmed from two sources. First, the need for psychological service providers was burgeoning, due in large part to the community mental health movement. Second, only a small minority of psychologists, probably about 10%, publish research in psychology. Critics of the Boulder model argued that too much time was being spent training students for activities that, as professionals, they were unlikely to actually perform. At the same time, research-oriented departments of psychology were accepting increasing numbers of practice-oriented graduate students. The fit was often a bad one, which left both students and faculty dissatisfied.

Participants at the Chicago conference debated the wisdom of replacing the scientist–professional with a professional program (Zimet & Throne, 1965). Conferees continued to emphasize a broad training in diagnostics, therapy, and prevention, but they changed the emphasis of the scientific training of clinicians. Rather than broad scientific training, they favored science training sufficient only to make clinicians sophisticated evaluators of new clinical methods. They also dropped the doctoral dissertation or foreign language requirements.

In the end, the conferees refused to endorse a purely professional model, preferring instead a flexible scientist–professional plan that would not short-change training in clinical activities. Training programs were urged to add faculty who were practicing clinicians and also to broaden their criteria for acceptable research activities.

Diversity in training was encouraged by calling for pilot programs that would experiment with innovative ways of implementing the professional model. Special interest focused on the first PsyD degree (Doctor of Psychology, which we describe later) program, then under development at the University of Illinois at Urbana-Champaign. The appropriate levels (doctoral and subdoctoral) and locations (department of psychology, medical center, independent professional school) of clinical training were also debated at Chicago.

The Chicago conference was important because, while professional training models and subdoctoral programs were not officially endorsed, they had gained considerable support among clinical psychology's leadership. Many of the ideas considered for the first time at Chicago were adopted by the participants at psychology's next training conference.

The Vail Conference

The National Conference on Levels and Patterns of Professional Training in Psychology was held in 1973 in Vail, Colorado. Supported by a grant from the National Institute of Mental Health (NIMH), the *Vail Conference* brought together representatives from a wide range of psychological specialties and training orientations, and included graduate students and psychologists from various ethnic minority groups. In only 5 days the conference passed 150 resolutions, which introduced sweeping changes in the training of psychologists. These recommendations addressed professional training models, levels of training, and desirable characteristics of training programs (Korman, 1976).

Professional Training Models. The conference officially recognized professional training as an acceptable model for programs that defined their mission as the preparation of students for the delivery of clinical services. These "unambiguously professional" programs were to be given status equal to their more traditional scientist–professional counterparts. Professional programs could be housed in a number of settings, including academic psychology departments, medical schools, or specially established professional schools. When emphasis was on the delivery and evaluation of professional services, the PsyD would be the appropriate degree. When emphasis was on the development of new knowledge in psychology, the PhD would be preferred.

Levels of Training. The conferees believed that priority should be given to programs that provided multiple levels of training or demonstrated coordination with degree programs at varying levels. They advocated the idea of a career lattice, a structure that would allow upward professional mobility through continued, integrated training.

One of the most controversial of the Vail recommendations was that persons trained at the master's level should be considered professional psychologists. This sentiment reversed the opinion of previous conferences, which envisioned psychology as strictly a doctoral-level profession. The Vail participants, however, felt that many services performed by doctoral psychologists could be performed just as well by personnel trained at the master's or submaster's level. The conference called for professional master's programs and full membership in APA for people trained at the master's level. Soon, universities in several states developed MA training programs in clinical psychology. Today, master's-level clinical, counseling, and school psychology programs accept more applicants than doctoral-level programs do, and two to three times as many students graduate with master's degrees as graduate with PhDs (Morgan & Korschgen, 2001; Pate, 2001).

The MA proposal was short-lived because the tide later turned against the MA as a recognized degree for the professional psychologist. In 1977 the APA voted that the title of *psychologist* should be reserved for those who have completed a doctoral training program, a policy that remains in effect today, although it is coming under intense attack as the number of MA psychology graduates continues to grow.

The status of the MA clinician was also jeopardized by Vail advocates who, while willing to endorse MA-trained persons as professionals, were unwilling to recommend that they be eligible for licensing as psychologists (a process described later). Another obstacle for the master's-level clinician has been a political one. Quite simply, the status of psychology as a profession vis-a-vis psychiatry is threatened by lumping MA holders along with PhD psychologists. Most observers agree that the professional autonomy of psychology is best preserved by defining it exclusively as a doctoral-level enterprise. Financial considerations have also militated against granting full standing to MA recipients. Psychologists' eligibility for reimbursement as health care providers is strengthened by portraying clinical psychology as a doctoral-level profession (we return to this topic later).

The Salt Lake City Conference

The 6th national conference on graduate education in psychology was held in July, 1987 at the University of Utah in Salt Lake City. The conference was convened for several reasons, chief among which was the need to evaluate several changes that had taken place in the training of professional psychologists since the Vail conference. There was also a desire to reduce growing tensions between scientists and practitioners over numerous training and organizational issues. Three of the most important of the conference's 67 resolutions are listed below (see also Bickman, 1987, and a special issue of the *American Psychologist*, December 1987):

1. Students in graduate programs seeking accreditation must be trained in a core of psychological knowledge that should include research design and methods; statistics; ethics; assessment; history and systems of psychology; biological, social, and cognitive-affective bases of behavior; and individual differences.

2. By 1995, in order to be accredited by the APA, doctoral training programs must be academic units within a regionally accredited institution of higher education or must be formally affiliated with a regionally accredited university. This resolution was aimed at gaining tighter control of over "free-standing" professional

schools of psychology not associated with a university. We discuss those schools in more detail later.

3. Education in psychology occurs along a continuum that includes precollege, undergraduate, graduate, and postdoctoral levels. Training at the lower levels should be broad, with greater depth and specialization introduced at the advanced levels.

Clinical Psychology Training Today

What does training in clinical psychology look like after six national training conferences, several smaller conferences, countless hours of discussion, debate, and argument among clinicians, educators, and students, and, most recently, a lengthy process of revising APA's accreditation guidelines? There is no easy answer to that question, but we can provide a general summary.

First, the scientist–professional model has proven to be a tough competitor that is still "the champ" in terms of the number of programs professing it as their training philosophy (see Belar, 2000; O'Sullivan & Quevillon, 1992; Peterson, 2000). The original Boulder model now comes in an increasing number of different packages, however. Most programs have increased the time devoted to professional training in psychotherapy, usually at the expense of courses in psychodiagnostics or general psychology. Some follow a particular theoretical approach—cognitive-behavioral or psychoanalytic, for example—which offers students a relatively narrow perspective on clinical psychology. Other programs emphasize a specialty such as health psychology, clinical-child psychology, or community psychology.

Second, many programs that favor the scientist–professional model are still struggling to find the best way to train clinical psychologists so that their practical skills are well integrated with a solid foundation of scientific knowledge. This struggle stems from at least two sources: (1) the increasing tendency for accreditation standards to create additional course requirements that may not promote integration of science and practice and (2) the difficulty that clinical faculty members have in providing a scientist-professional role model for students.

In 1990, concern over these issues led to the calling of a National Conference on Scientist–Practitioner Education and Training for the Professional Practice of Psychology. Taking place in Gainesville, Florida, this conference reaffirmed the Boulder model as the best foundation for training clinicians and stressed the need for such training to involve more than just equal attention to practice and science (Belar & Perry, 1992). The basic principle for scientist-practitioner training, said the conferees, is that students must be trained to "embody a research orientation in their practice and a practice relevance in their research" (p. 72). This principle should be realized in all aspects of the curriculum, including coursework, research training, and practicum experiences, they said, and must be modeled as much as possible by clinical faculty.

The ideals put forth at the Gainesville conference were reflected in the establishment, in 1994, of the Academy of Psychological Clinical Science. This academy, affiliated with the American Psychological Society[3] and made up of graduate training programs committed to clinical science, was created in response to concerns that recent developments in health care reform and licensure and accreditation requirements are threatening to erode the role of science and empirical research in the education of clinical psychologists. Representatives of programs in the academy were particularly concerned that professional training—divorced from its research base—is beginning to dominate accreditation decisions. The goals of the academy, which included 26 member programs by 1996, are to strengthen the role of science-based education by (1) encouraging the training of students for careers in clinical research, (2) improving the integration of clinical science research with other scientific areas, (3) developing new opportunities for training, funding, and careers in clinical science, (4) providing for the dissemination of clinical science knowledge to policy-makers, consumers, and other professionals, and (5) fostering the application of clinical science to human problems in responsible, empirically justifiable ways (APS, 1996). For example, one special issue endorsed by many Academy programs is a commitment to training students in interventions that are empirically supported (see Chapter 9).

As mentioned earlier, other training programs with different philosophies about how to train clinicians have also been created in the past few decades. These programs envision clinicians mainly as health care or human-service professionals and therefore tend to deemphasize the integration of science and practice. Two training models of this type—the PsyD program and the professional school of psychology—are discussed next.

The Doctor of Psychology (PsyD) Degree

One of the earliest and most influential professional training programs was the Doctor of Psychology (PsyD) program begun by the Department of Psychology at the University of Illinois (Urbana-Champaign) in 1968, and discontinued there in 1980. Unlike Boulder model programs, PsyD programs provide training that concentrates on professional skills and clinical services. The emphasis is on the skills necessary for the delivery of a range of assessment, intervention, and consultation services. A master's thesis is not required, nor is a research-oriented dissertation, although most PsyD programs do require a written, doctoral-level report of professional quality.

The number of APA-accredited PsyD programs continues to grow. Clinical psychology programs produce approximately 600 to 700 PsyDs per year (Norcross et al., 1998). One recent survey of graduate school departments found that 33% of doctoral-level psychology students were enrolled in PsyD programs. When only *new* enrollments were considered, the figure was 39% (Pate, 2001). Nonetheless, many clinicians have leveled criticisms at PsyD training. One observer summarized the initial objections

---

[3]The American Psychological Society is the second largest—after APA—national organization of psychologists. Its membership is made of a broad spectrum of psychologists, some of whom also belong to APA, but APS has a higher proportion of research-oriented psychologists employed in academia, while APA has a higher proportion of practitioners. The presence of two national organizations of psychologists, APA and APS, reflects the different perspectives (and underlying tensions) between research and application in psychology generally, and in clinical psychology in particular.

as follows: (1) the PsyD program is likely to acquire second-class status in the eyes of faculty, students, and the public; (2) the fact that support for the alternate doctorate comes from the unlikely quarter of academic psychology is suspected as being a device for shunting aside the bothersome problem of professional training in clinical psychology; (3) the profession of clinical psychology is in a state of flux, with new roles and practices emerging, making this a particularly inappropriate time to create a new profession with activities that are only dimly foreseeable at present and whose present clinical skills may soon be obsolete; (4) two parallel programs, producing two different degrees, will tend to separate clinical practice from the rest of psychology even further, thus cutting the profession off from its scientific roots; (5) expert practitioners, necessary in a professional degree program, are likely to find it as difficult to be appointed and later promoted at the university as is the case now of competent clinical professors who do not publish research findings; and (6) future graduates of such programs are likely to be stigmatized because of their different degree and different training (Goldenberg, 1973, p. 85).

Were these concerns justified? One study at the University of Illinois found that PsyD and PhD students there performed equivalently on qualifying exams and course grades, and showed similar attrition rates (Peterson & Baron, 1975). Other research showed that clinical internship supervisors did not differentiate the quality of work by PhD versus PsyD interns (Shemberg & Leventhal, 1981; Snepp & Peterson, 1988). However, there are certainly some important differences between PsyD and PhD programs. For instance, compared to the average PhD program, the average PsyD program accepts a higher percentage of applicants, a larger absolute number of applicants (two to three times as many as the average PhD program), and applicants with lower GRE scores. PsyD students are also much less likely to be involved in research activities than PhD students are (Norcross et al., 1998).[4] There are also general differences among faculty in these programs as well. The percentage of psychodynamically-oriented faculty is higher among PsyD programs (36%) than among PhD programs, while the percentage of cognitive behaviorally-oriented faculty are higher among PhD programs (48%) (Norcross et al., 1998). Finally, there are differences that reflect the emphases of the two degrees: Compared to PsyD students, PhD-program graduates are more likely to be employed in academic settings, to pursue post-doctoral degrees, and to be engaged in research as a regular part of their work week (Cherry, Messenger, & Jacoby, 2000; Kohout & Wicherski, 1999).

These differences do not seem to justify the gloomy early predictions about PsyD programs, but they do still raise some concerns. Although proponents continue to call for expanded PsyD training opportunities (Shapiro & Wiggins, 1994), others have serious questions about the quality of training in some PsyD programs (Peterson, 1985; Strickland, 1985). Two areas of concern are 1) that too many PsyD programs employ part-time faculty to train large numbers of students in settings that do not encourage comprehensive education, and 2) too few PsyD graduates are involved in research of any kind.

---

[4]PsyD students tend to finish their clinical programs about 1.5 years sooner than PhD students do (Gaddy et al., 1995).

Professional Schools of Psychology

As noted earlier, professional schools of psychology are free-standing clinical training units, some with no ties to university departments of psychology. This independent arrangement is thought to free clinical psychology training from the academic constraints of the university, to allow rewards for professional as well as scholarly achievements, and to provide students with faculty role models who are actively practicing clinicians.

Though some professional schools of psychology (at Rutgers or Yeshiva, for example) are housed within a university, most of the more than fifty professional schools in the United States—such as the Minnesota or Chicago Schools of Professional Psychology—are free-standing organizations. The first of these free-standing schools was the California School of Professional Psychology, founded in 1969 under the auspices of the California Psychological Association. With campuses at Los Angeles, Berkeley, San Diego, and Fresno, it is generally regarded as the leading free-standing professional school of psychology in the United States. Some free-standing schools award the PhD, while others grant the PsyD (Peterson, 1985); the Fresno, Los Angeles, and San Diego campuses of the California School offer both.

For the academic year 1999 to 2000, more students were enrolled in clinical programs in professional schools than in traditional academic clinical programs (Pate, 2001). The average entering class of a professional school is about five times larger than the typical first-year class in a university psychology department.

The appearance and growth of the professional schools was stimulated by several influences. First, well-intentioned, competent psychologists have had honest disagreements among themselves about the best way to educate clinical students (Bourg et al., 1989). Second, the curricula of professional schools reflect the desire—expressed by most clinical graduate students—to be trained as providers of psychological services rather than as academicians and researchers. Third, professional schools provide a training atmosphere that many students find more comfortable than what they expect to find in academic programs. The professional schools' emphasis on clinical practice and the availability of faculty who are practitioner role models create a culture in tune with the applied interests of most of today's clinical students. Fourth, economic factors and changing employment opportunities encouraged more psychologists to start independent and group practices, work in health-care facilities, and take other clinical service positions for which professional school training appears especially relevant. Finally, professional schools provided the further-training venue sought by large numbers of people who hold master's degrees in psychology but who have not been admitted to traditional PhD training programs in clinical psychology. In short, professional schools challenged the nature of clinical training. They forced clinicians to consider seriously the type of knowledge upon which their services should be based and the standards against which they should evaluate their practices.

Do different training models produce clearly different "kinds of" professionals? In certain ways, they do. For instance, Cherry et al. (2000) compared three models: 1) the *scientist-practitioner model*, which follows the Boulder model and provides for approximately equal emphasis on research and application to practice (common in traditional programs and in some professional schools); 2) the *practitioner-scholar model*, which follows the Vail model and stresses human service delivery and places proportionately less emphasis on scientific training (common in professional schools); and 3) the *clinical scientist* model, which grows out of the Academy of Psychological Science approach and places proportionately more emphasis on scientific research (more common in university settings). As expected, graduates of the practitioner-scholar model spent the least time in clinical research, while graduates of clinical scientist programs spent the most time. These findings raise concerns in those who fear that professional school programs do not sufficiently value clinical research.

On the other hand, advocates of the professional school approach have complained that researchers often do not sufficiently value clinical practice, and there is some support for this assertion. A recent survey found that 44% of PhD-level clinical psychologists employed in traditional academic settings reported *no* involvement in clinical practice (Himelein & Putnam, 2001). And compared with students who took academic jobs after completing clinical Ph.D. programs, their classmates who became full-time practitioners were generally less satisfied with their graduate education (Thelen & Rodriguez, 1987). These findings concern practitioners who fear that research-oriented programs offer too little appreciation of, or training in, the realities of clinical practice.

It is important to note that when practitioners or researchers fail to follow the Boulder model, it is not always because they reject it—indeed, most think the scientist-practitioner model is a good idea (Peterson, 2000). Rather, professionals often fail to follow the Boulder model—which stressed the integration of science and practice—because the incentives in their work environments do not to support it. For instance, academic settings seldom offer support or incentives for clinical faculty who wish to work with clients in a part-time private practice (Himelein & Putnam, 2001), and few independent practice clinicians have the resources to conduct the kind of research that is published in professional journals. These differing reward structures can reinforce attitudes and behaviors that further split the field into practitioners versus researchers. But as Belar (2000) points out, this a problem with implementation, not a problem with the model. It sometimes seems that the Boulder model is a good idea that has yet to be fully implemented (see Stricker, 2000).

Concluding Comments on Clinical Psychology Training

Clinical psychology training has been in a state of transition for over 50 years, yet we know relatively little about the comparative outcomes of various training models. Most of the research comparing different training models focuses on the time students or professionals spend in various activities, where they are employed, how much they publish, or how they view the training they had. There is little information about whether different training models ultimately lead to different outcomes, such as success in treating clients. This is unfortunate, but as suggested by meta-analytic and other studies of psychotherapy outcome (see Chapter 9), we would not be surprised if specific training models account for relatively small proportions of the variance in some arenas of clinical performance. Does this mean that there are no important differences across models, or that it is impossible to evaluate them? We think the answer to both questions is no.

Our view is that clinical training programs can be evaluated in light of whether they produce produce clinicians who are competent at performing the professional functions that their work demands. This kind of technical competence is not enough, however. Despite the attraction exerted by programs that focus on producing practitioners, we believe that the single most important goal in training competent clinical psychologists is to teach them to choose and evaluate whatever services they offer in light of research that employs the empirical methods of science. We think that training programs should emphasize the teaching of those clinical services that have been empirically confirmed as effective; they should not offer training in services or roles that, while perhaps being professionally appealing or financially lucrative, have failed to gain research support. We also believe that if clinical training moves too far from its foundation in psychological science and concentrates only on teaching therapy techniques, assessment methods, and other professional skills, the clinical psychologist of the 21st century will become a narrowly specialized practitioner for whom research is of only passing interest. As a result, clinical psychology will become a poorer science, and ultimately, a weaker profession. If you are interested in further discussions of the pros and cons of professional and Boulder model training, you might enjoy the American Psychologist's (February, 2000) special issue on the Boulder Conference. There are several other excellent sources available (e.g., Belar & Perry, 1991; Bickman & Ellis, 1990, Fox, 1994; Matarazzo, 1987; Peterson, 1985, 1995; Shapiro & Wiggins, 1994; Stricker, 1992; Stricker & Trierweiler, 1995).

PROFESSIONAL REGULATION

One major responsibility of any health care or human-service profession is to establish standards of competence that members of the profession must meet before they are authorized to practice. The primary purpose of such *professional regulation* is to protect the public from unauthorized or incompetent practice of psychology by impostors, untrained persons, or psychologists who are unable to function at a minimum level of competence. Although some critics doubt the value of regulation in meeting this goal (e.g., Gross, 1978; Hogan, 1983), psychology has developed an active system of professional regulation.

Certification and Licensure

The most important type of regulation lies in state laws that establish requirements for the practice of psychology and/or restrict the use of the term *psychologist* to persons with certain qualifications. This legislative regulation comes in two kinds of statutes: certification and licensure. The legal basis of these laws rests in the right of the state to pass legislation that protects its citizens. Caveat emptor ("let the buyer beware") is an inadequate protection when buyers are not sufficiently informed about the services to know what to beware of.

Certification laws restrict use of the title psychologist or *certified psychologist* to people who have met requirements specified in the law. Certification protects only the title of psychologist; it does not regulate the practice of psychology. Licensure is a more restrictive type of statute. Licensure laws define the practice of psychology by specifying the services that a psychologist is authorized to offer to the public. The requirements for licensure are usually more comprehensive than for certification. To distinguish between certification and licensure, remember the following rule of thumb: Certification laws dictate who can be called a psychologist, while licensing laws dictate both the title and what psychologists do.

Licensing laws are administered by *state boards of psychology*, which are charged by legislatures to regulate the practice of psychology in the states. State boards of psychology have two major functions: (1) determining the standards for admission to the profession and administering procedures for the selection and examination of candidates, and (2) regulating professional practice and conducting disciplinary proceedings involving alleged violators of professional standards.

Thus, in the United States and Canada, having a PhD in clinical psychology does not automatically allow a person to "hang out a shingle" and start to practice psychology. The steps involved in becoming licensed differ somewhat from place to place, but there is enough uniformity in the procedures of most U.S. states to offer a rough sketch of how the aspiring clinical psychologist would approach this task (see Table 14.2). Today, all 50 states, the District of Columbia, and all Canadian provinces have certification or licensure laws. Many states combine their certification and licensure laws into one statute.

As various states passed licensing statutes, there evolved an obvious need for an organization to coordinate the activities of the state boards of psychology and to bring about uniformity in standards and procedures. To answer these needs, the American Association of State Psychology Boards (AASPB) was formed in 1961. In 1991, this organization was renamed the *Association of State and Provincial Psychology Boards* (ASPPB). ASPPB has also developed a Code of Conduct for psychologists that consists of rules of professional behavior intended to protect the public from unscrupulous, incompetent, and unethical psychologists. The ASPPB has also developed a standardized, objective test for use by state boards in examining candidates for licensure. First released in 1964 and revised frequently since then, this *Examination for Professional Practice in Psychology* is sometimes called the *multistate* or *national exam* because all jurisdictions can use it as a part of their examination procedure. A person must meet the requirements for licensure to take the exam, which, beginning in 2001, is available continuously at various computer vendor sites (ASPPB, 2001).

In most states, psychologists are required to keep their license or certificate up to date by paying a periodic renewal fee and by documenting involvement in *continuing professional education* (CPE). Continuing professional education is usually provided in special postdoctoral institutes, seminars, or workshops conducted by experts on particular topics. The ASPPB also helped develop a system of *reciprocity*, meaning that someone licensed in one state can usually transfer licensure to another jurisdiction.

Many other countries also have also established regulatory control over psychological practice. For instance, every European state that has a well-developed

---

TABLE 14.2   So You Want to Be a Licensed Psychologist?

Imagine you have just completed a doctoral program in clinical psychology and are now interested in becoming a licensed clinical psychologist. What steps would you have to take? The following hurdles will be encountered in most states. First, you must ask that the state board of psychology review your credentials to determine your eligibility for examination. Their decision is based on several criteria:

1. *Administrative Requirements.* You must have reached a certain age, be a U.S. citizen, and have been a resident in the state for some minimum period. Not too much can be done about these requirements; you either meet them or you do not. One bit of advice: Don't commit any felonies, engage in treason, or libel your governor. These activities are judged to be indicative of poor moral character and may leave you plenty of time to fantasize about licensure while in prison.

2. *Education.* Most states require a doctoral degree in psychology from an accredited university (accreditation in this case refers not to APA approval but to accreditation of the university by a recognized accrediting agency). Official graduate and undergraduate transcripts are required.

3. *Experience.* This usually amounts to one, or more commonly two, years of supervised professional experience in a setting approved by the board. Some of the experience must be postdoctoral; letters of reference will be required from your supervisor(s). If, after scrutinizing your credentials, the board finds you are eligible for examination, you will be invited to take an exam. Here is what to expect:

Examination Fee. There is a charge for the examination; it is usually between $200 and $300.

The Examination. Many states use a national exam that contains about 200 objective items covering general psychology methodology, applications of psychology, and professional conduct and ethics. Because many candidates want to practice a specialty like clinical, school, or industrial psychology, boards also prepare essay examinations in these areas. You may also be required to take an oral examination given by the board in which any material relevant to psychology may be covered.

Reexamination. If you fail any part of the exam, you will be given another chance to take that portion. Most boards feel that twice is enough, however; so if you fail the second time, it might be wise to reconsider the advantages of the family business.

---

profession of psychology now has some form of regulation (Lunt, 1999). If you are interested in reading more about professional regulation, consult the *Handbook of Licensing and Certification Requirements for Psychologists in the United States and Canada*, which is revised each January and available from the ASPPB.

Over the years, licensure of psychologists has been criticized on several grounds. A major objection is that licensure does not assure competence of practitioners because the examination procedures do not adequately assess professional abilities. Some critics further contend that licensure may be detrimental to the public interest because it functions to curtail competition and increase the cost of psychologists' services. Legal challenges to licensure of psychologists involving alleged due process violations and antitrust considerations have been attempted by disgruntled parties, but these attacks have had limited success. Today, licensure laws are applauded by a majority of clinicians and are upheld by courts if there is a plausible reason to believe they protect the public.

In 1975, the first edition of the *National Register of Health Service Providers in Psychology* was published. The register is a listing of psychologists who possess the training and experience adequate to qualify them as health service providers. The register is used primarily to (1) identify psychologists who specialize in delivering health services and (2) help various organizations identify those psychologists whose mental health services are eligible for reimbursement. Thousands of psychologists are listed in the register, and hundreds of organizations, including many of the largest insurance companies, subscribe to it.

ABPP Certification

Another type of professional regulation is certification by the American Board of Professional Psychology (ABPP). ABPP was founded in 1947 as a national organization that certifies the professional competence of psychologists. Its certification is signified by the award of a diploma in one of several specialty areas including clinical, counseling, industrial/organizational, school, family, forensic, health, and neuropsychology. In 1992, the ABPP reorganized itself so that each of these specialty areas has its own board (all organized under the ABPP umbrella) that develops and administers its own exams and awards its diplomas.

Though it carries no special legal authority, an ABPP diploma is considered more prestigious than licensure. While licensure signifies a *minimal* level of competence, diplomate status is an endorsement of professional expertise, an indication that the person so designated possesses a masterful knowledge of some specialty field. Accordingly, requirements for the ABPP diploma are more rigorous than for licensure. Three years of experience is a prerequisite to even take the ABPP examination, which is conducted by a group of diplomates who observe the candidate dealing directly with clinical situations (e.g., giving a test or interacting with a therapy client).

Other Forms of Legal Regulation

An interesting by-product of psychology's increasing professionalization is greater legal scrutiny of the profession. Historically, courts have been disinclined to pass judgment on what constitutes acceptable psychological treatment, but this reluctance has recently given way to a willingness to evaluate the legality of mental health care. Courts are no longer willing to permit what they see as violations of clients' rights, despite the hazards inherent when nonexperts try to evaluate treatment methods. A comprehensive review of the legal status of psychological treatments would be beyond our purposes here, but we will highlight four legal principles that have been used to challenge some forms of intervention. The first two, known as *right to treatment* and *informed consent*, are usually concerned with institutionalized persons such as mental patients or prison inmates. The third, known as *privileged communication* is particularly relevant to outpatient psychotherapy clients. The fourth form of legal control over professional interventions is through *malpractice litigation*.

Right to Treatment. The concept of a right to treatment for patients committed to psychiatric hospitals found legal support in the landmark *Rouse v. Cameron*[5] decision. In this case, the patient, Charlie Rouse, had been confined in a hospital for four years after being found not guilty by reason of insanity (see Chapter 13) on a weapons charge. Rouse was not receiving any treatment, and his period of confinement was longer than the 1-year maximum prison sentence he would have received if convicted. He petitioned the court to release him from the institution, and the appellate court agreed, further ruling that hospitals must make at least a reasonable effort to treat committed patients.

The court considered the *standards* for treatment in the case of *Youngberg v. Romeo*,[6] which involved a profoundly retarded, 33-year-old man named Nicholas Romeo who had been committed to the Pennhurst State Hospital in Pennsylvania after his father died and his mother could no longer care for him. Nicholas frequently engaged in self-mutilation and was injured several times during his first few years in the hospital, both by his own actions and by other patients. As a protective step, he was restrained in bed for long periods. Upset with how her son was being "treated" at Pennhurst, Nicholas' mother filed suit, alleging that Pennsylvania had violated his 14th Amendment due process rights by not providing him a safe environment and by failing to train him adequately. The case ultimately reached the U.S. Supreme Court which held that the Constitution guarantees involuntarily committed patients the following rights: (1) adequate food, shelter, and clothing, (2) adequate medical care, (3) a safe environment, (4) freedom from restraint, unless restraint is necessary to protect the patient or others, and (5) such training as may be required to ensure the above rights. The Court also concluded that the form of training provided should remain largely a matter of professional judgment.

Although Youngberg laid a constitutional "floor" below which no state can fall in treating committed patients, individual states are free to set higher standards of care for the mentally ill, and several states have done so. For example, in the celebrated 1971 case of *Wyatt v. Stickney*,[7] a federal court in Alabama ruled that involuntarily committed patients have the right to individualized treatment which they can help plan, to clothing of their choice, and to a certain number of mental health professionals per patient in order to assure that treatment will be provided.

In 1975, the U.S. Supreme Court considered the case of *O'Connor v. Donaldson*.[8] Kenneth Donaldson was a 49-year-old man who had been diagnosed with paranoid schizophrenia and confined to the Florida State Hospital at Chattahoochee for 15 years. His father had him committed because he was supposedly delusional and dangerous, but the evidence for his dangerousness at the time of commitment was questionable. Indeed, hospital staff notes and testimony later revealed that Donaldson was never dangerous to himself or anyone else. Donaldson repeatedly asked to be released from the hospital on the grounds that he was not receiving treatment, that he was not a threat,

---

[5]2373 F. 2d 451 (D.C. Cir. 1966).
[6]457 U.S. 301 (1982).
[7]344 F. Supp. 373 (1972)
[8]422 U. S. 563 (1975)

and that he could live effectively outside the hospital. After his requests were denied, Donaldson filed a lawsuit against Dr. J. B. O'Connor, the superintendent of the hospital for most of the time Donaldson was confined. A jury agreed with Donaldson that he had been improperly confined and awarded him $38,500 in damages. The wisdom of this decision was supported by the fact that, immediately upon his release, Donaldson obtained a job in hotel administration.

The state of Florida appealed the jury's verdict to the U.S. Supreme Court. *O'Connor* was a landmark case because it was the first time the Supreme Court heard arguments about the constitutional rights of a civilly committed mental patient, and it required the Court to evaluate a state's justifications for involuntarily committing the mentally ill to a hospital. Writing for the Court, Justice Potter Stewart ruled that a "state cannot constitutionally confine . . . a nondangerous individual who is capable of surviving safely in freedom by himself or with the help of willing and responsible family and friends." The effect of this decision, and others since then (*Foucha v. Louisiana*[9]), is to limit the state's powers such that it can not force the hospitalization of persons who, even though mentally ill, are not dangerous and can live outside the hospital on their own or with the support of others.

The Right to Refuse Treatment and Informed Consent.

The claim that institutionalized persons have a right to treatment is complicated by the suggestion that they also may have a right to refuse at least some treatments. Fundamental questions are raised when a mental patient does not want to take medication that a physician has prescribed. Should society "help" such patients by ordering treatment against their will? Does the need for treatment outweigh an individual's right to privacy and autonomy? Does it make sense to commit patients to a hospital and then allow them to refuse treatments that could help them regain their freedom?

People's control over their treatment usually takes the form of giving or withholding informed consent. Full informed consent involves several elements, including full specification of the nature of treatment; a description of its purpose, risks, and likely outcomes; notification that consent may be terminated at any time without prejudice to the individual; and, as discussed in Chapter 13, demonstration of a mental capacity to consent. Written informed consent is usually required for treatments of an experimental, intrusive, or aversive nature. The rules of informed consent assume that patients are competent to make decisions about their treatment. However, for many decades, informed consent procedures were not applied to mental patients because it was presumed that they were incompetent to make such important decisions.

However, concerns about the side effects of psychoactive drugs, about patients' rights to privacy, and about patients' control over what goes into their bodies led federal district courts in Massachusetts (*Rogers v. Okin*[10]) and New Jersey (*Rennie v. Klein*[11]) to hold that mentally ill patients do have the right to refuse medications, even if those medications are likely to be beneficial. However, the courts held that this right

---

[9]112 S.Ct. 1780 (1992)
[10]478 F. Supp. 1342, 1369 (Mass. 1979).
[11]462. F. supp. 1131 (D.N.J. 1978).

to refuse was not absolute. A patient's desire not to be medicated can be overridden in three general situations: (1) if the patient is behaving dangerously toward self or others, (2) if the patient is so ill as to be unable to make a competent decision about treatment, and (3) if there is an emergency that, in a physician's judgment, makes forced medication necessary. In the 1990 case of *Washington v. Harper,*[12] for example, the U.S. Supreme Court held that a mentally ill prisoner cannot be medicated against his will unless it is determined by the application of professional standards that the medication was necessary for safety reasons.

The U.S. Supreme Court has also refused to hold that mentally ill patients have a Constitutional right to refuse treatment. Instead, it has used a doctrine of deferring to the professional judgment of physicians who are treating the patient. Thus, in the Youngberg v. Romeo case mentioned earlier, the Court held that honoring the rights of patients cannot be used to restrict unnecessarily the professional judgment of treating physicians. Some states still allow patients a right to refuse treatment, but there are so many ways to override a patient's refusal, that the right to refuse is actually more of a right to object to treatment and to have the treating physician review the medical necessity of the treatment (Brooks, 1986). In reality, few patients refuse medication over a long period of time (Appelbaum, 1994), and those who persistently do so typically have their refusal ultimately overridden (Appelbaum & Hoge, 1986; Godard et al., 1986).

Informed consent is a concern in other areas of clinical work as well. For instance, ethical principles require that clients be told, in language that they understand, of potential risks of treatment. Certain of the outcomes of psychotherapy could be considered risks: clients could fail to improve, married clients entering marital therapy could decide to divorce. There are even risks that clients could recover—or erroneously believe they have recovered—memories of past sexual abuse during treatment (a topic which is discussed later in this chapter; Cannell, Hudson, & Pope, 2001). Bernstein and Hartsell (2000) suggest that the best way for clinicians to deal with (and document) informed consent is by having new clients complete a detailed intake and consent form.

Privileged Communication. Numerous states have laws establishing a psychotherapist–client privilege (see Glosoff, Herlihy, & Spence, 2000). *Privilege* is a legal right granted to clients in order to protect them from having therapists publicly disclose confidences without the clients' permission. Privilege is similar but not identical to confidentiality. The main difference is that *confidentiality* is an ethical obligation imposed on members of a profession, not a legal requirement. Therapist–client privilege statutes are on the books mainly because of the widespread belief that successful psychotherapy depends in part on assuring clients that the information they reveal to a therapist in confidence will remain private.

Prior to 1996, federal judges had been free to decide on a case-by-case basis whether to protect communications between therapists and clients or to force therapists to reveal their contents. In that year, however, a U.S. Supreme Court decision in the case of *Jaffee v. Redmond*[13] assured protection of confidential communications

---

[12]494. U.S. 210 (1990).
[13]133 L. 2d 758 (1996).

between a therapist and client in federal cases. The case involved the death of Ricky Allen, a young man who was killed by Mary Lu Redmond, a police officer in Illinois. Redmond had been called to an apartment to break up a fight. When she arrived and saw Allen about to stab another man, she shot Allen. His family claimed that Allen was unarmed and sued officer Redmond and her police department for violating his civil rights. When the family discovered that Redmond had undergone therapy with a social worker after the shooting, they petitioned to have the therapy notes made available. Both Redmond and her social worker refused to turn over the notes. After trial jurors were told by the judge that they could assume these notes contained material unfavorable to officer Redmond, they returned a verdict for the plaintiff in the amount of $545,000. In its review of the case, the U.S. Supreme Court held that therapists could not be forced to testify about confidential communications. Writing for the Court, Justice John Paul Stevens stated, "effective psychotherapy . . . depends upon an atmosphere of confidence and trust in which the patient is willing to make a frank and complete disclosure of facts, emotions, memories, and fears."

As desirable as it may be, a client's right to privileged or confidential communications—like the right to refuse treatment—is not absolute. A therapist may be forced to breach confidentiality (1) if a therapist believes that a client needs to be involuntarily committed to a hospital, (2) if a client raises the issue of his or her mental condition in a trial and the therapist testifies on the client's behalf, (3) if a client has undergone a court-ordered evaluation of his or her psychological condition, (4) if the therapist learns that a client is abusing other people, or (5) if a client tells a therapist of an intent to harm another person.

This last exception to maintaining confidentiality poses a particularly difficult situation for clinicians. On the one hand, therapists cannot be expected to treat a client's impulses toward violence without discussing them. On the other hand, if therapists know they might be compelled to disclose such information despite their clients' wish to keep it confidential, they have a reason to avoid the topic of violence in therapy, even if it is important. One specific dilemma brings this issue into particularly sharp focus: Should a therapist who has heard a client threaten to harm another person be required to break confidentiality in order to protect the intended victim? This was the question raised in the now-famous case of *Tarasoff vs. Regents of the University of California*.[14] The answer, in several states at least, is yes.

In the Tarasoff case, a couple sued the University of California, psychotherapists employed by the university, and the campus police to recover damages for the murder of their daughter (a UC student) by a client of one of the psychotherapists. A lower court sustained the defendants' answers to the suit, but the Supreme Court of California reversed that decision and found for the plaintiffs.

Here are the facts of the case. The client, Prosenjit Poddar, told his psychotherapist, Dr. Lawrence Moore, that he intended to kill a young woman, Tatiana Tarasoff. The therapist informed his superior, Dr. Harvey Powelson, of this threat. The campus police were called and were also asked, in writing, to confine the client. They did so briefly, but then released him after concluding that he was rational and believing his

---

[14]529 P. 2d 553 (Col. 1974) Vac. Reheard in bank and affirmed 131 Cal. Prtr. 14, 551 P. 2d 334 (1976).

promise that he would stay away from the Tarasoff's home. He didn't do so. After terminating his relationship with his therapist, Poddar killed Tatiana. He was later convicted of murder. No one had warned the woman or her parents of the threat. In fact, Powelson had asked the police to return Moore's letter and further ordered that all copies of the letter and Moore's therapy notes be destroyed.

In reaching its decision, the court weighed the importance of confidential therapy relationships against society's interest in protecting itself from dangerous persons. The balance was struck in favor of society's protection. The therapist's situation was like that of a physician who would be held liable for failing to warn persons about a contagious disease: "The protective privilege ends where the public peril begins."

The analogy between potentially dangerous clients and potentially contagious patients is particularly apt for psychotherapists who see clients with HIV. With such clients, what are the limits of confidentiality? Do clients present a risk to others? Do Tarasoff principles apply? The case law on these questions is mixed; a review of relevant cases revealed that courts favored maintaining confidentiality in roughly half of them and favored at least limited disclosure in the other half (Webber, 1999). Obviously, therapists dealing with such clients must consider the foreseeability of harm, the identifiability of potential victims, ethical guidelines, and state or federal laws when evaluating possible courses of action (Chenneville, 2000).

The *Tarasoff* decision that therapists have a duty to protect specific victims from clients that the therapist believes or should believe to be dangerous has been implemented in some other U.S. states, but it is not legally binding in all states—a fact that even many psychologists misunderstand. About a third of the states have now passed laws that specify the conditions under which a therapist is liable for failing to take precautions to protect third parties from the dangerous acts of the therapist's clients. Some other states have extended "Tarasoff liability" to persons other than those specifically threatened. But state laws can change with new rulings (see Davis, Davis, & Davis, 1999; Felthous & Kachingian, 2001; Wettstein, 1999). One thing is clear: Therapists are responsible for knowing what their state requires regarding protection of third parties.

More than 20 years have passed since the Tarasoff case was decided. What impact has it had? It appears that the decision has made therapists more aware of the potential complications involving client dangerousness and how they should respond to it. At the same time, considerable evidence suggests that Tarasoff has not had the adverse impact that many clinicians predicted. For one thing, therapists have not stopped seeing potentially dangerous clients (Givelber, Bowers, & Blitch, 1984). When therapists have had to break confidentiality because of a client's dangerousness, it has not inevitably led to negative effects on the client, particularly when the therapist has first discussed with the client the need to take precautionary steps. Finally, even before Tarasoff, many therapists had been breaking confidentiality to warn potential victims in emergency situations, so the decision did not necessarily require clinicians to change their existing practices.

Regulation Through Malpractice Lawsuits. Civil lawsuits brought by clients who allege they have been harmed by the malpractice of professionals constitute another form of regulating clinical psychologists. If a jury agrees with the client's claim, it may order the clinician to pay the client monetary damages to compensate for the harm. To prove a claim of professional malpractice, four elements must be established:

1. A special professional relationship had to exist between the client/plaintiff and the therapist. Establishing this element usually requires proving that the plaintiff was receiving formal services from the clinician in exchange for a fee.

2. It must be shown that the clinician was negligent in treating the client. Negligence does not simply mean that a bad outcome occurred; nor does it require that the therapist intended any harm to occur. Negligence involves a violation of the standard of care, defined as the treatment that a reasonable practitioner facing circumstances similar to those of the plaintiff's case would be expected to give.

3. Even if the professional was negligent, it must be shown that the client suffered harm.

4. The therapist's negligence must then be shown to be the cause of the harm suffered by the client.

Until about 30 years ago, malpractice claims against clinical psychologists were almost nonexistent. Plaintiffs were reluctant to sue a therapist if it meant they might have to talk about their psychological problems in court. Further, there were few agreed-upon standards of care for treating mental disorders so it was difficult to show that a therapist had violated accepted practice. The tide began to turn, however, during the turbulent 1960s. Lawsuits against mental health professionals are still not nearly as frequent as those against medical specialists in obstetrics, gynecology, and surgery, but the number of malpractice charges against clinical psychologists has increased, and so has the cost of malpractice insurance. Estimates are that only 1 to 2% of clinicians will be sued for malpractice (Baerger, 2001), though one study (Montgomery, Cupit, & Wimberley, 1999) found the chances of being to be somewhat higher.[15] Even among filed claims, however, few go to trial, and the large majority of these are won by clinicians (Baerger, 2001).

Malpractice actions against clinicians often arise over claims that they (1) failed to provide appropriate care to hospitalized inpatients, (2) failed to prevent a client from committing suicide, (3) failed to carry out Tarasoff duty-to-protect obligations, (4) failed to make a proper referral of a client when the therapist terminated treatment, or (5) misrepresented their professional qualifications (Baerger, 2001; Smith, 1996). Among psychotherapists conducting outpatient treatment, the most common basis for malpractice claims involves charges that they engaged in sexual intimacies with a current or recently terminated client. Since the ethical codes of all mental health professions strictly forbid such behavior, and since there is empirical evidence that sexual contact between therapist and client is usually harmful to the client (Feldman-Summers

---

[15]The estimate in this study may be higher because in suits that name large practices or hospitals, each person on the staff might be named, even though they did not directly treat the person or persons filing the suit (Montgomery et al., 2000).

& Jones, 1984; Pope & Tabachnick, 1994), plaintiffs who prove such contact can win large malpractice awards. According to several surveys, about 5 to 8% of mental health professionals have engaged in intercourse or other sexual intimacies with a client (Haspel et al., 1997). The rate of sexual contact with clients is about four to five times greater for male therapists than for female therapists (Report of the APA Ethics Committee, 2001). Further, therapists who have engaged in sex with clients once are likely to do so again (Pope & Vasquez, 1991).

A few large malpractice verdicts have also been returned in cases in which therapists are accused of influencing clients to falsely recall allegedly *repressed memories* of physical or sexual abuse in childhood. Such "de-repression" techniques have been advocated by popular books on incest and by therapists who believe that unless severe childhood traumas are recalled and defused, they will continue to cause mental problems. In addition to being asked to dredge up repressed memories of trauma, suspected victims are sometimes encouraged by their therapists to join special support groups—such as Survivors of Incest Anonymous—that urge their members to aggressively search for buried memories of abuse.

Many researchers and clinicians are skeptical about the accuracy of memories of trauma that resurface years after the alleged incidents—and only after aggressive memory-recovery therapy (Loftus & Polage, 1999; Wakefield & Underwager, 1992; Walcott, 2000). Skeptics point out that most people who suffer severe trauma do not lose their memory of it; in fact, many of them suffer intrusive recollections of it for years afterward (Pope et al., 1998). Skepticism is also fueled by the fact that some alleged victims claim to recall traumas that happened when they were less than 1 year old, a feat contradicted by almost all research on memory and "infantile amnesia."

Loftus and Polage (1999) note that there are two aspects of the repressed memory controversy: 1) whether real memories can be repressed and later recovered, and 2) whether false memories can occur as a result of suggestion or other factors. Regarding the first, cognitive psychologists have not found evidence for a mechanism that causes repression (McNally et al., 2000b; McNally, Clancy, & Schacter, 2001; Pope et al., 1998). That does not mean that repression does not occur—reports of people who are known to have been abused sometimes include no memory for the abuse—only that it is unclear whether repression is the best explanation for people's failure to recall or report past events.

Regarding the second aspect, considerable evidence suggests that memory can be changed by post-event suggestion or by repeated rehearsal of inaccurately recalled past events. It is also clear that some people have difficulty distinguishing real and false memories (Garry & Polaschek, 2000; Johnson & Raye, 1998). People who score high on tests of introversion, fantasy-proneness, and dissociation—the latter of which includes a tendency toward lapses of memory, and attention—are more likely than others to develop false memories and may also be more likely to report the recovery of repressed memories (McNally et al. 2000; Porter et al. 2000). The fact that no one is immune from memory errors, and that some people are more prone than others to develop false memories, makes forensic evaluation much more difficult.

In one highly publicized trial of supposedly-recovered memories, Gary Ramona— once a highly paid executive in the California wine industry—sued family counselor Marche Isabella and psychiatrist Richard Rose for planting false memories of trauma in his daughter, Holly, when she was their 19-year-old patient. Ramona claimed that the therapists told Holly that her bulimia and depression were caused by having been repeatedly raped by him when she was a child. They also told her that the memory of this molestation was so traumatic that she had repressed it for years. According to Ramona, Dr. Rose then gave Holly sodium amytal (a so-called truth serum) to confirm her "recovered memory." Finally, Isabella was said to have told Holly's mother that up to 80% of all bulimics had been sexually abused (a statement for which there is no scientific support).

At the trial, the therapists claimed that Holly suffered flashbacks of what seemed to be real sexual abuse. She also became increasingly depressed and bulimic after reporting these frightening images. Holly's mother, Stephanie, who divorced her husband after Holly's allegations came to light, testified that she suspected her husband had abused Holly and listed several pieces of supposedly corroborating evidence. Gary Ramona emotionally denied ever sexually abusing his daughter.

The mental health experts who testified on Romana's behalf criticized the therapists for engaging in dangerous techniques. Elizabeth Loftus (1993), a leading critic of aggressive memory therapy, testified that therapists often either suggest the idea of trauma to their clients, or are too uncritical in accepting the validity of trauma reports that occur spontaneously. Another defense witness, Martin Orne, a renowned authority on hypnosis, condemned the use of sodium amytal interviews as "inherently untrustworthy and unreliable" and concluded that Holly's memory had been so distorted by her therapists that she no longer knew what the truth was.

The jury decided that Holly's therapists had planted false memories in her and, in May of 1994, awarded damages to Gary Ramona in the amount of $500,000. Since then, according to the False Memory Syndrome Foundation, a group devoted to uncovering abuses associated with memory recovery therapy, the number of "false memory" cases against therapists has grown.

The increase in "false memory" litigation adds to the already difficult challenges therapists face when trying to help adult clients who have suffered a traumatic childhood. It is obvious that recovered memory therapy has led to some very bad outcomes and very real damage to clients and their families. It is also obvious that the trauma of child abuse does occur and that it can leave deep, painful, and long-lasting emotional scars. Accordingly, therapists must be sympathetic listeners and helpful counselors when clients remember only too well real horrors from childhood; these clients need support in talking about and coping with what they remember. At the same time, therapists must be cautious and avoid suggesting that clients' problems come from traumas that might never have happened.

PROFESSIONAL ETHICS

A code of professional ethics is a set of principles that encourages or forbids certain professional conduct. Ethics are normative statements that justify certain goals and behaviors. All professions have ethical principles about the proper way for professionals to behave toward the public and toward each other. As psychology moved into its professional era, it needed to articulate its own ethical principles.

Ethical Standards of The American Psychological Association

Psychology's first code of ethics was published in 1953 (APA, 1953). A unique feature of this code was the way it was developed. True to their empirical foundations, psychologists submitted to an APA committee a large number of "critical incidents" involving some ethical dilemma that had occurred in a professional context. By analyzing this real-life material, the committee distilled a comprehensive ethical code, which was summarized in a set of general principles 6 years later (APA, 1959). After this version was used for 3 years, it was amended and formally adopted (APA, 1963). The ethical principles underwent several revisions through the 1960s, 1970s, and 1980s, and they are regularly reviewed and revised by the APA's Ethics Committee Task Force (ECTF). As of the time of this writing, the 1992 *Ethical Principles of Psychologists and Code of Conduct* were in still force, but a new edition of the Ethical Principles was expected to be ready for publication in 2002 (Report of the Ethics Committee, 2000, 2001). The Ethical Principles document consists of a Preamble, General Principles, and a large number of specific Ethical Standards. The Preamble and General Principles of the 1992 document, presented in Table 14.3, are not enforceable rules; they are statements of the aspirations of psychologists to attain their highest ideals, and they provide guidance to psychologists who are evaluating what would be ethically desirable behavior in certain situations.

It is the Ethical Standards that establish enforceable rules of conduct for psychologists. They apply to members of APA and may be used by other organizations, such as state boards of psychology and courts, to judge and sanction the behavior of a psychologist, whether an APA member or not. These standards are organized under the following headings:

> *General Standards.* Rules prohibiting discrimination, sexual and other types of harassment, and misuse of work products are included here, as are rules about maintaining competence, recognizing the limits of one's competence, proper record keeping, fees, and financial relationships.
>
> *Evaluation, Assessment, or Intervention.* Rules pertaining to the use and interpretation of tests are listed here.
>
> *Advertising and Other Public Statements.* Standards that control the way psychologists publicize their services and their professional credentials are presented under this category.
>
> *Therapy.* Rules about the structuring, conduct, and termination of therapy are identified here. Specific standards prohibit psychologists from having sexual intimacies with current clients and from accepting persons as clients if they have had previous sexual intimacies with them. Furthermore, psychologists should not have sexual intimacies with former therapy clients for at least two years after the termination of therapy, and even then only if the psychologist can demonstrate that no exploitation of the client has occurred.
>
> *Privacy and Confidentiality.* These rules cover psychologists' obligations to protect their clients' rights to confidentiality and privacy.

Teaching, Training, Supervision, Research and Publication. This section contains several ethical standards that control psychologists' conduct as they teach and supervise students and perform psychological research.

Forensic Activities. When performing forensic evaluations or other services, psychologists must comply with special rules about such services.

Resolving Ethical Issues. This last section contains standards about how psychologists are to resolve ethical questions or complaints.

APA's Casebook on Ethical Standards

In 1967, the APA published its first *Casebook on Ethical Standards of Psychologists,* which contained a restatement of the 1963 ethical principles as well as descriptions of factual cases drawn from discussions of the APA's Committee on Scientific and Professional Ethics and Conduct between 1959 and 1962. The Casebook, now in a revised edition (APA, 1987a) is intended as a guide to applying APA's ethical principles and standards in situations that psychologists face in their everyday professional activities. It is the source most psychologists study in order to educate themselves about the profession's ethical standards. Periodically, summaries of actual ethical cases and their resolutions are published in the *American Psychologist,* and several books on psychology ethics are now available (Bernstein & Hartsell, 2000; Bersoff, 1999; Koocher & Keith-Spiegel, 1998; Small & Barnhill, 1998; Canter et al., 1994).

Most psychologists take great pains to deal with complex and ethically ambiguous situations in accordance with the highest standards of professional conduct. But because many situations often involve moral and cultural questions and do not match exactly the cases presented in guidelines or case books, there is often no clear course of action, no right answer. How do psychologists manage such ethical problems? They begin with awareness of acceptable and unacceptable practices within their area. Proper informed consent procedures, release of information forms, and case documentation are also important risk management procedures (Montgomery et al., 1999). Beyond that, professionals consult books, such as those mentioned above, or professional journals, which periodically publish articles about ethics (for instance, Baerger, 2001, suggested risk management practices with suicidal patients; Hansen & Goldberg, 1999, suggest a seven-category matrix for decision making in ethical problems). Finally, consultation with colleagues and professional organizations is often highly advisable. Though these efforts do not provide immunity for psychologists from malpractice suits or other legal actions, they do reflect a conscientious effort to do the right thing, and documentation of such efforts is likely to be looked upon favorably by professional organizations and courts.[16]

---

[16]The APA's Ethics Office can provide information to psychologists to help them in ethical dilemmas. Other organizations, such as the American Counselor's Association and the National Association of Social Workers also have established codes of ethics and can help their members with ethical questions. Because there are often no clear "right answers," guidance from professional organizations is often advisory—it does not tell the professional what to do. APA's commitment to providing education about ethics is reflected in the Ethics Office's recent announcement of a $1000 prize, plus a free trip to APA's national convention, to be awarded to the graduate student who writes the best paper on psychology and ethics (Behnke, 2001).

TABLE 14.3 Preamble and General Principles in the APA Ethical Principles of Psychologists and Code of Conduct

---

Preamble

Psychologists work to develop a valid and reliable body of scienctific knowledge based on research. They may apply that knowledge to human behavior in a variety of contexts. In doing so, they perform many roles, such as researcher, educator, diagnostician, therapist, supervisor, consultant, administrator, social interventionist, and expert witness. Their goal is to broaden knowledge of behavior and, where appropriate, to apply it pragmatically to improve the condition of both the individual and society. Psychologists respect the central importance of freedom of inquiry and expression in research, teaching, and publication. They also strive to help the public in developing informed judgments and choices concerning human behavior. This Ethics Code provides a common set of values upon which psychologists build their professional and scientific work.

This Code is intended to provide both the general principles and the decision rules to cover most situations encountered by psychologists. It has as its primary goal the welfare and protection of the individuals and groups with whom psychologists work. It is the individual responsibility of each psychologist to aspire to the highest possible standards of conduct. Psychologists respect and protect human and civil rights, and do not knowingly participate in or condone discriminatory practices.

The development of a dynamic set of ethical standards for a psychologist's work-related conduct requires a personal commitment to a life-long effort to act ethically; to encourage ethical behavior by students, supervisees, employees, and colleagues, as appropriate; and to consult with others, as needed, concerning ethical problems. Each psychologist supplements, but does not violate, the Ethics Code's values and rules on the basis of guidance drawn from personal values, culture, and experience.

General Principles

Principle A: Competence

Psychologists strive to maintain high standards of competence in their work. They recognize the boundaries of their particular competencies and the limitations of their expertise. They provide only those services and use only those techniques for which they are qualified by education, training, or experience. Psychologists are cognizant of the fact that the competencies required in serving, teaching, and/or studying groups of people vary with the distinctive characteristics of those groups. In those areas in which recognized professional standards do not yet exist, psychologists exercise careful judgment and take appropriate precautions to protect the welfare of those with whom they work. They maintain knowledge of relevant scienctific and professional information related to the services they render, and they recognize the need for ongoing education. Psychologists make appropriate use of scientific, professional, technical, and administrative resources.

Principle B: Integrity

Psychologists seek to promote integrity in the science, teaching, and practice of psychology. In these activities psychologists are honest, fair, and respectful of others. In describing or reporting their qualifications, services, products, fees, research, or teaching, they do not make statements that are false, misleading, or deceptive. Psychologists strive to be aware of their own belief systems, values, needs, and limitations and the effect of these on their work. To the extent feasible, they attempt to clarify for relevant parties the roles they are performing and to function appropriately in accordance with those roles. Psychologists avoid improper and potentially harmful dual relationships.

(continued)

TABLE 14.3   Preamble and General Principles in the APA Ethical Principles of Psychologists and Code of Conduct (*Continued*)

Principle C: Professional and Scientific Responsibility

Psychologists uphold professional standards of conduct, clarify their professional roles and obligations, accept appropriate responsibility for their behavior, and adapt their methods to the needs of different populations. Psychologists consult with, refer to, or cooperate with other professionals and institutions to the extent needed to serve the best interests of their patients, clients, or other recipients of their services. Psychologists' moral standards and conduct are personal matters to the same degree as is true for any other person, except as psychologists' conduct may compromise their professional responsibilities or reduce the public's trust in psychology and psychologists. Psychologists are concerned about the ethical compliance of their colleagues' scientific and professional conduct. When appropriate, they consult with colleagues in order to prevent or avoid unethical conduct.

Principle D: Respect for People's Rights and Dignity

Psychologists accord appropriate respect to the fundamental rights, dignity, and worth of all people. They respect the rights of individuals to privacy, confidentiality, self-determination, and autonomy, mindful that legal and other obligations may lead to inconsistency and conflict with the exercise of these rights. Psychologists are aware of cultural, individual, and role differences, including those due to age, gender, race, ethnicity, national origin, religion, sexual orientation, disability, language, and socioeconomic status. Psychologists try to eliminate the effect on their work of biases based on those factors, and they do not knowingly participate in or condone unfair discriminatory practices.

Principle E: Concern for Others' Welfare

Psychologists seek to contribute to the welfare of those with whom they interact professionally. In their professional actions, psychologists weigh the welfare and rights of their patients or clients, students, supervisees, human research participants, and other affected persons, and the welfare of animal subjects of research. When conflicts occur among psychologists' obligations or concerns, they attempt to resolve these conflicts and to perform their roles in a responsible fashion that avoids or minimizes harm. Psychologists are sensitive to real and ascribed differences in power between themselves and others, and they do not exploit or mislead other people during or after professional relationships.

Principle F: Social Responsibility

Psychologists are aware of their professional and scientific responsibilities to the community and the society in which they work and live. They apply and make public their knowledge of psychology in order to contribute to human welfare. Psychologists are concerned about and work to mitigate the causes of human suffering. When undertaking research, they strive to advance human welfare and the science of psychology. Psychologists try to avoid misuse of their work. Psychologists comply with the law and encourage the development of law and social policy that serve the interests of their patients and clients and the public. They are encouraged to contribute a portion of their professional time for little or no personal advantage.

Dealing with Ethical Violations

On those rare occasions when, as fallible human beings, psychologists behave in a questionable manner, they are subject to censure by local, state, and national organizations whose task it is to deal with violations of ethical practice. The largest number of ethical violations involve (1) sexual intimacy between a therapist and a client, (2) violations of state or federal laws (e.g., fraudulent billing practices), and (3) breaches of confidentiality. In addition to clear-cut violations, a large number of questionable behaviors often occur that raise possible ethical problems.

Once a complaint of unethical behavior is brought against an APA member and the appropriate committee has decided that the conduct in question was in fact unethical, the question of punishment must be decided. The most severe APA sanction is to dismiss the offender from the association and to inform the membership of this action. This penalty is embarrassing for most transgressors, humiliating for a few, but seldom devastating for any. Unethical conduct can also cause psychologists to have their professional license taken away by the board of psychology in the state where they practice. Other actions can include censure, censure with probation, or a decision that no cause for action is warranted.

Other Ethical Standards

Because of increasing public concern, new governmental research regulations, and outrage about the alleged mistreatment of animals in some laboratories, APA has found it necessary to supplement its ethical standards with a detailed set of guidelines covering psychologists' research with animals, called the *Guidelines for Ethical Conduct in the Care and Use of Animals* (APA, 1992).

Clinical psychologists are also responsible for knowing about other standards that govern their research and delivery of psychological services. As mentioned in Chapter 9, there are numerous guidelines. Examples of more general guidelines include: *Ethical Principles in the Conduct of Research with Human Participants* (APA, 1982), *Standards for Educational and Psychological Testing* (APA, 1985), and the *Publication Manual of the American Psychological Association* (APA, 2001). Specialty guidelines in particular have proliferated. Examples include: *Guidelines for the Evaluation of Dementia and Age-Related Cognitive Decline* (APA, 1998a); *Guidelines for Psychological Evaluations in Child Protection Matters* (APA, 1998b); *Guidelines for Psychotherapy with Lesbian, Gay, & Bisexual Clients* (APA, 2000a). The American Psychological Association has recently published a *Criteria for Evaluating Treatment Guidelines* (APA, 2000c), which should be of help to clinical psychologists in sorting through the numerous guidelines (see Chamberlin, 2000).

PROFESSIONAL INDEPENDENCE

Clinical psychologists must consult and collaborate with other professionals in many aspects of clinical practice. They often work closely with educators, attorneys, ministers, social workers, nurses, physicians, and other psychologists. For the most part, psychology's interprofessional relationships are healthy, profitable, and characterized by good will. The most obvious sign of this harmony is the frequency of referrals made across groups. A teacher with a child whose classroom misbehavior is related to a serious emotional problem is likely to suggest that the family consult a psychologist. Similarly, when psychologists encounter clients who are in legal trouble, they urge such clients to hire an attorney.

Unfortunately, psychologists have had considerable friction with physicians, particularly psychiatrists. In fact, clinical psychology's most persistent interprofessional problem has been its wary, often stormy, relationships with the medical profession. Saul Garfield (1965) observed that as early as 1917, psychiatrists were critical of psychologists, particularly "those who have termed themselves 'clinical psychologists'" and work in "so-called 'psychological clinics'" and provide "so-called expert testimony." It is no wonder, then, that clinical psychology and psychiatry have waged several battles. The first involved the independent practice of psychotherapy by psychologists. Later, the two fields argued over whether psychologists should have privileges to practice independently in hospitals (*CAPP v. Rank*[17]). More recently, the squabble has concentrated on psychologists' eligibility for reimbursement under an increasing array of public, private, and prepaid mental health plans. Although these controversies are related, we will look at two of them—the independent practice of psychotherapy and reimbursement issues—in separate sections that clarify the development of each.

Independent Practice of Psychotherapy

As long as psychologists confined themselves to research, consultation, and testing, physicians did not interfere. Psychologists, by the same token, found no problem with the fact that physicians were the authority on physical disorders or organic treatments such as medication, electroconvulsive therapy, and surgery. Disagreement, when it came, centered on psychotherapy, which both professions (along with several others) offered to the public.

When psychologists began to engage in the independent practice of psychotherapy, psychiatrists objected and insisted that a psychotherapist must be either a physician or under the supervision of a physician. The psychiatrists' rationale was that physicians are the experts on the functioning of the whole person and that with many types of abnormal behaviors it is essential that the therapist differentiate mental and physical aspects of the disorder and treat both aspects thoroughly. For their part, psychologists contended that the vast majority of mental disorders involve psychological and social processes rather than physical ones, and that they are better trained about these processes than physicians are. In addition, when physical causes and/or medical treatments are indicated, psychologists are aware of their ethical obligations to refer such clients to physicians. Finally, psychologists pointed out that many of the most influential therapists over the years have been nonphysicians (e.g., Anna Freud, Carl Rogers, Erich Fromm, Erik Erickson).

It is ironic that psychologists themselves were once opposed to practicing psychotherapy independently (Humphreys, 1996). In 1949, the APA discouraged the

---

[17]CAPP v. Rank, 51 Cal. 3d, 793 P.Sd (1990).

practice of psychotherapy by psychologists who were not working in collaboration with psychiatrists (Goldenberg, 1973). Psychologists reconsidered their position on the independent practice of psychotherapy (APA, 1958), but psychiatrists did not. In fact, the American Medical Association (AMA, 1954) adopted an official policy that psychotherapy was a medical procedure to be performed only by medically trained personnel. The strategy of the AMA in this battle was to oppose certification and licensure of psychologists. This strategy was unsuccessful, a fact for which most clinical psychologists are grateful. By the end of the 1950s, psychology had ended psychiatry's dominance over psychotherapy, and psychologists now provide more office-based mental health care than do psychiatrists (McGuire, 1989). At the same time, there are indications that psychiatrists themselves are spending less time then ever doing psychotherapy. A survey of psychiatrists between 1985 and 1995 showed that office-based visits with psychiatrists were shorter in 1995 than they had been in 1985, and that they less often included formal psychotherapy (Olfson, Marcus, & Pincus, 1999).

Relations between psychologists and psychiatrists improved throughout the 1970s and early 1980s. Psychiatrists came to accept psychologists as professionals and were less inclined to treat them with the condescension of earlier days. In turn, psychologists shed some of their defensive armor and were less prone to feel that they constantly must guard against psychiatrists. Both fields were strengthened by the growing number of well-qualified persons who entered the two professions.

By the 1990s, however, relations between psychologists and psychiatrists had again become strained. This time the tensions are primarily economic, although they also involve questions about whether psychologists should continue to be excluded from offering professional services—such as the prescription of psychoactive medications—that had historically been the sole right of physicians. These issues are made more urgent by changes occurring in the way health care is funded in the United States.

The Economics of Mental Health Care

Having won the battles over licensure and recognition of psychology as an independent profession in the 1970s and 1980s, clinicians turned to struggles involving the economic aspects of mental health care. The initial focus of these struggles was whether psychologists should be eligible for reimbursement for their services by insurance companies. Physicians opposed psychologists' inclusion, claiming that it would be too costly to third-party payers and consumers. Physicians also argued that if psychologists were to be included, their services should be reimbursed only when they were treating clients referred and supervised by physicians. As a result, many major health insurance companies (such as Blue Cross/Blue Shield), run by and for physicians, excluded psychologists from third-party payments except when billing under a physician's supervision.

As members of a profession that aspired to full autonomy, psychologists found this arrangement intolerable. As a result, in the late-1960s and early-1970s psychologists began lobbying state legislatures to pass *freedom-of-choice* laws, which mandate that services rendered by qualified mental health professionals licensed to practice in a given state shall be reimbursed by insurance plans covering such services regardless of whether the provider is a physician. Physicians fought hard against such legislation, using the term *medical psychotherapy* to refer to the only services they believed should be reimbursable. This term was condemned by psychology as a political maneuver intended to guarantee that physicians would be the only professionals identified as appropriate providers of psychotherapy.

Psychologists argued that there is nothing "medical" about psychotherapy. They also presented data to counter claims that including them as providers or even including coverage of mental disorders treated by any provider would be too costly for third-party payers. For example, one study showed that *a single session of psychotherapy* reduced subsequent use of medical resources by 60% among the recipients, and that there was about a 75% reduction in medical utilizations by patients receiving two to eight sessions of psychotherapy (Cummings, 1977; see also Olbrisch, 1977). Psychologists contended that, far from being economically disadvantageous, reimbursing for psychotherapy can be cost effective because it saves money that would otherwise be spent for more expensive medical services. This reduction, known as *medical offset* has been replicated in larger studies (e.g., Holder & Blose, 1987) and has become a rallying point for clinical psychologists who claim that psychotherapy is a highly effective and efficient addition to the health care system (Fraser, 1996; Groth-Marnat & Edkins, 1996).

Over the years psychologists have succeeded in having freedom-of-choice laws enacted in most U.S. states. By 1983, 40 states covering 90% of the U.S. population had passed legislation that provided free choice of licensed psychologists as reimbursable providers of mental health services (Lambert, 1985). Additional legislation at the federal level promoted recognition of psychologists as independent clinicians. The Rehabilitation Act of 1973 (PL 93-112) provided parity for psychologists with physicians in both assessment and treatment services. Services provided by clinical psychologists are reimbursable under both the Federal Employee Health Benefits Act (PL 93-363) and the Federal Work Injuries Compensation Program (PL 94-212). Licensed psychologists are also recognized as *independent providers* by CHAMPUS (The Civilian Health and Medical Program of the Uniformed Services), a federal program covering several million beneficiaries in all 50 states and the District of Columbia.

For three decades, psychologists have fought for legislative changes that would make it possible for them to be directly reimbursed for their services under Medicaid (a shared federal/state program for the medically needy) and Medicare (a federal program for elderly and disabled clients). Physicians have strenuously lobbied against such amendments, repeating the refrain that including psychologists would be too costly and that psychologists are not qualified to diagnose and treat many mental disorders without the supervision of a physician.

However, the tide has now turned. With respect to Medicare, the federal program that provides health care funds for more than 30 million aged and 3 million disabled recipients, an amendment allowing psychologists to be included and reimbursed as direct Medicare providers was signed into law. Psychologists have been less successful in obtaining coverage for their services under Medicaid (DeLeon et al., 1992). This program, established by Congress in the 1960s to help the states supply health care to the poor and needy, grew dramatically in the last decade; federal expenditures for Medicaid increased from $14 billion to $41 billion. The individual states are free to determine their own criteria for recipient eligibility and to control which services will be covered at what cost. As a result, states that have been concerned about excessive use of mental health services have limited the kinds of treatment they will reimburse (see below).

Unfortunately, some insurance companies will ignore state or federal freedom-of-choice laws, unless forced to abide by them. For example, it took nearly four years of litigation to force Blue Cross/Blue Shield of Virginia to comply with that state's freedom-of-choice law (Resnick, 1985). A related area of litigation lies in suits challenging the practice of denying hospital staff privileges to nonphysicians. California, North Carolina, Washington, D.C., Georgia, and several other states have passed laws allowing hospital privileges for psychologists, but physician-based attacks on California's law required psychologists to go to court to protect the original law.

The Effects of Changing Health Care Systems.   As noted in Chapter 1, the delivery, financing, and organization of health care—including mental health care—changed at an unprecedented rate in the 1990s. Several forces have given rise to these changes. First, the costs of health care have skyrocketed and now account for approximately 13% of the U.S. gross domestic product (Cowen, et al., 2001). The United States spends a higher percentage of its GDP on health care than any other country, but it lags behind many other developed nations in the quality of that care as measured by a variety of indices. For instance, it is an irony of the United States health system that it has many of the most advanced medical facilities and specialists in the world and yet one of the highest rates of infant mortality among the developed nations (Berk, 2002). One likely reason is that the focus of health care in the United States has been mainly on acute care, surgical procedures, and hospitalization—a focus that favors expensive medical procedures and medical specialization (Reed et al., 2001). Accordingly, prevention, early intervention, and less acute medical and psychological conditions have received less attention.

Changes that have occurred in the U.S. health care system over the last decade have been largely driven by efforts to contain high costs. With these changes have come numerous challenges to the practice of clinical psychology. In particular, psychologists have been forced to recognize that (1) the nature, quality, and availability of health care is often determined by health care economics, and (2) changes in health care financing can nullify all the victories psychologists won in freedom-of-choice legislation battles. If clinical psychology is to remain an active player in the health care market, clinicians have to be prepared to adjust to the financing changes already in place, and those likely to come in the near future (Humphreys, 1996; Keisler, 2000; Reed et al., 2001).

There is continuing debate over how to reform the organization and financing of the U.S. health care system so as to provide basic health care for all citizens while controlling health care costs. The outcome of this debate will have a tremendous impact on mental health services. The two questions of greatest interest to clinical psychologists are what mental health services will be covered in the basic package of guaranteed care and whether psychologists delivering these services will be reimbursed as independent professionals. Whatever system ultimately appears, containing costs and easing people's access to care will be primary goals. Accordingly, clinical psychologists will need to become increasingly able to integrate their mental health services into ever evolving new general health care approaches. Perhaps the most dramatic changes to clinical practice have come about because of health care reform known as managed care.

Managed Care Systems.   *Managed care* developed under the assumption that fee-for-service health care (as dominated medical and psychological care in previous decades) provides incentives for escalating costs, whereas prepaid comprehensive plans that provide financial oversight of services could control or reduce costs (Reed et al., 2001). A managed care system develops methods of allocating health services to a group of people in order to provide the most appropriate care while still containing the overall cost of these services.

Managed care can be organized in several different ways, including, for example, as employee assistance programs (EAPs), health maintenance organizations (HMOs), preferred provider organizations (PPOs), integrated delivery systems (IDSs), and independent practice associations (IPAs). In general, these organizations provide specific packages of health care services to subscribers for a fixed, pre-paid price.

Mental health care in the United States has been increasingly offered in the context of one of these managed behavioral health care plans. By one estimate, approximately 75% of persons with health care insurance are covered under some type of managed mental health program (see Kiesler, 2000). How have mental health services been affected by managed care?

One of the first and most noticeable effects was the *reduction in spending for mental health services*. By one estimate, reimbursement for mental health services decreased during the 1990s by 670%, a far larger reduction than any other area of health care (Reed et al., 2001). Managed care companies found that they could save money by denying payment for the expensive, long-term psychotherapy that a fee-for-service system encouraged. They could also save money by denying services for any therapeutic procedures that did not have clearly documented benefits (most of the time, benefits were assessed over short time periods; see our discussion of this topic in Chapter 9).

During the 1990s, the states began experimenting with new ways of delivering mental health services to Medicaid recipients. One popular approach is known as the *carve-out*, in which a state creates a separate organization that is responsible for "carving out," delivering, and integrating all the mental health services to which Medicaid recipients are entitled. Carve-outs typically involved managed care companies contracting for services with providers. They are called carve-outs because such contracts are not an integrated part of the (primarily medical) health care plans. Carve-outs became the norm in mental health delivery during the 1990s, accounting for 88% of mental health services under managed care (Kiesler, 2000).

Carve-out services typically involve the managed care company paying a fixed amount per client to a mental health service provider, a system referred to as *capitation*. As discussed in Chapter 9, capitation is a popular way of shifting financial risks away from managed care companies and toward providers. Here is how a simple capitation system might work: The Acme Insurance Company agrees to pay a mental health corporation $3.00 per month for every subscriber to its Positive Mental Health Plan. This arrangement limits the insurance company's financial risk by putting a "cap" on its costs. If the Positive Mental Health Plan enrolls 60,000 members, Acme pays it $180,000 every month from the premiums Acme collects from its customers. Obviously, the fewer treatment sessions Positive Plan clients receive from therapists working for the Plan, the more profit it will make. The more clients that must be treated, or the longer their treatments last, the smaller the profit to Positive. These considerations will affect the kinds and duration of treatment received by positive plan subscribers.

Managed care has also exerted increasing control over the types and length of treatments through a system known as *utilization review*. In this system, a case manager working for a managed care company may make decisions about the appropriateness of treatment. The case manager, who more than likely is not a mental health professional, determines whether the managed care company will pay for particular treatments and, if so, for how many sessions. Generally, managed care reviewers discourage comprehensive clinical assessments and insight-oriented, longer term therapies in favor of medications and short-term therapies. Thus, a case manager may decide, for example, that a depressed client can receive no more than eight sessions of psychotherapy, even if the therapist believes that the client's problems require more extensive treatment. As discussed in Chapter 9, other forms of utilization review are now being considered, such as requiring therapists to provide data on their effectiveness.

As you might imagine, the advent of managed care has caused great concern among mental health professionals. Some of their most serious criticisms are that managed care systems (1) are more interested in cutting costs and raising profits than in assuring excellent heath care, (2) result in many clients receiving too little treatment, (3) threaten the confidentiality of therapy by requiring that too much information about clients be included in the utilization review, (4) allow untrained personnel to conduct the utilization reviews, (5) collect inadequate data on the outcomes of their treatments, and (6) exclude from the system clients who have pre-existing disorders.

So while most clinicians welcome incentives that encourage their use of the most effective and efficient treatments available (Patricelli & Lee, 1996), they oppose incentives that put profits before quality of treatment and that are determined by case managers who know very little about the nature and treatment of mental disorders. Indeed, the major concern about managed care is that it usually focuses on management of costs, not quality health care. If cost containment is promoted over treatment quality, if inappropriate limits are set on the duration of psychotherapy, and if case managers intrude too often into the confidentiality of therapy, managed mental-health care systems will ultimately fail to bring about the cost-effective treatment they promise.

As mentioned in Chapter 9, there are signs that these concerns are beginning to change the way managed care operates. Evidence is mounting that there can be substantial long-term costs associated with not treating or under-treating psychological disorders—particularly chronic disorders or those that are most likely to be accompanied by depression or addiction. As managed care companies digest this information, they may be more willing to forsake short-term gains for long-term profitability. Charles Kiesler (2000) suggests another important change that is in the wings: the move from mental health carve-outs to mental health *carve-ins*. He suggests that managed care companies are moving from an era of cost containment to an era characterized by assessment of value. That era, he contends, would focus on *evidence-based medicine* and favor empirically-based psychological services. Rather than reduce the dollars allocated to mental health, it would reduce the inefficiencies in mental health delivery. Given the speed of changes in health care in the United States, it is very difficult to predict what clinical services will be like in 5 or 10 years, but like Kiesler, other observers, (e.g., Cummins, quoted in Simon, 2001) also see greater integration of medical and psychological practice in the future.

The Costs of Protecting Professional Independence

It is almost inevitable that the legal struggles and political combat over issues of professional independence will have negative effects on psychology in general, and clinical psychology in particular. For one thing, litigation is very expensive for the APA, the state psychological associations, or the other organizations of psychologists that bear most of the costs. Further, money spent on litigation cannot be spent for other activities (e.g., sponsorship of research or prevention programs) that might be of greater interest to academic or nonclinical psychologists, who are justifiably concerned that clinicians will bankrupt psychological associations by expending their resources in court cases. Clinicians need to take seriously the questions that nonclinical psychologists raise about the best use of organized psychology's limited resources.

Another risk of litigation is that, as previously described in relation to psychology's high-profile marketing strategy, psychologists may be tempted to exaggerate their accomplishments and claims for success, particularly in psychotherapy. The profession will not be well served by promising more than it can deliver, especially when consumers must bear whatever additional costs expanding health care coverage might bring. Finally, there are disadvantages in maintaining an adversarial stance toward psychiatry. As one observer put it, "today's adversaries are tomorrow's allies" (Resnick, 1985, p. 983). Psychology and psychiatry have mutual interests in several areas and these interests will be jeopardized by continued interprofessional sparring. For example, some forms of managed care might seek to omit mental health services, an exclusion that both psychology and psychiatry would surely oppose. Members of both professions may find that the most serious threats to their status as mental health care providers come not from each other, but from outside forces and that countering these threats requires a cooperative and unified response.

PERILS OF PROFESSIONALISM

Have the first 50 years of clinical psychology's professional era made it a better profession, or have they simply made it more of a guild that employs meaningless membership criteria? Has clinical psychology become a better profession by endorsing standards of training, competence, and service, or is it merely a more closed profession? We consider such questions in these final pages.

The ultimate justification for the professionalization of any discipline is that the public will benefit from the standards that govern the profession. Of course these restrictions also benefit members of the profession because they control the profession's population and thus reduce competition. There is little objection to this latter function when it is a by-product of protecting the public from unqualified practitioners. The problem arises when the priorities of a profession are reversed, so that the promotion of its members' interests takes precedence over its obligations to the public.

As early as 1951, Fillmore Sanford, then executive secretary of the APA, warned about the perils of professionalization. In an effort to call psychology's attention to its obligations as a profession, Sanford proposed sixteen principles that should be considered "the criteria of a good profession" (Sanford, 1951, p. 667; see Table 14.4). He hoped that these criteria would guide the development of psychology as a socially useful and responsive profession.

Sanford's statement remains timely. Although it was written as an idealistic vision of what psychology should strive for, it can be used today as a yardstick for measuring

---

TABLE 14.4   Fillmore Sanford's Criteria for a Good Profession

1. A good profession is motivated by a sense of social responsibility.

2. A good profession is sufficiently perceptive of its place in society to guide its practices and policies so they conform to the best and changing interests of that society.

3. A good profession is continually on guard lest it represent itself as able to render services that are beyond its demonstrable competence.

4. A good profession continually seeks to find its unique pattern of competence and concentrates its efforts on the rendering of the unique service based on its pattern of competencies.

5. A good profession devotes relatively little of its energy to "guild" functions, to the building of its own in-group strength, and relatively much of its energy to the serving of its social function.

6. A good profession engages in rational and non-invidious relations with other professions having related competencies and common purposes.

7. A good profession devotes a proportion of its energies to the discovery of new knowledge.

8. A good profession develops channels of communication between the discoverers of knowledge and the appliers of knowledge.

9. A good profession does not relegate its discovers of knowledge to positions of second-rate status.

10. A good profession is free of nonfunctional entrance requirements.

11. A good profession provides preparatory training which is validly related to the ultimate function of the members of the profession.

12. A good profession is one in which the material benefits accruing to its members are proportional to social contributions.

13. A good profession is one whose members are socially and financially accessible to the public.

14. A good profession has a code of ethics designed primarily to protect the client and only secondarily to protect the members of the profession.

15. A good profession facilitates the continuing education and training of all its members.

16. A good profession is continually concerned with the validity of its techniques and procedures.

what psychology has become. The first two criteria deal with the need for psychologists to adjust to social needs and changes. At several points we have emphasized that clinical psychology has responded to the social, political, and economic events surrounding it. The growth of the profession itself was a reaction to social upheaval and virtually unprecedented human needs. In a similar fashion, the evolution of such disparate psychological activities as assessment, psychotherapy, community psychology, and behavior modification was rooted in the fact that psychology has always been well tuned to the current *zeitgeist*.

Several criteria (3, 4, 13, and 14) are concerned with professional ethics. Psychologists are justifiably proud of their code of ethics because it remains the only set of professional standards developed through explicitly empirical procedures. This pride has not fostered complacency, however, because, as mentioned earlier, the code continues to be revised and supplemented with other statements about ethics in specific areas.

Three criteria (10, 11, and 15) relate to professional training. Clinical psychology is committed to training programs that are appropriate for the roles clinicians are asked to fill. The Boulder model of training is still valued, but in the context of experimentation with other systems of training intended to prepare psychologists who will deliver clinical services.

The sixth of Sanford's criteria concerns interprofessional relationships. This issue, especially the relationship between clinical psychologists and psychiatrists, continues to be the focus of much attention. An adequate response to our sometimes troubled relations with psychiatry requires a balancing act. Clinicians must search for new opportunities to collaborate and cooperate with all professions, but at the same time, psychology must also be a free profession, unwilling to enter into a Faustian pact where the goodwill of the medical profession is purchased with acquiescence to its domination of psychology.

The largest number of Sanford's criteria discuss the priorities of the profession, the essential contributions it should make to the public. Like many psychologists before and after him, Sanford affirmed research and advancement of new knowledge as psychology's primary activity. The creation of basic knowledge is the one function that separates the professional from the technician, who applies methods based on existing knowledge. This conclusion seems especially important for a relatively new profession like clinical psychology, where "the fewer its techniques of demonstrable utility, the more of its resources it should devote to research" (Sanford, 1951, p. 669).

THE FUTURE OF CLINICAL PSYCHOLOGY

When authors reach the end of their books, they often assume the role of prophets who cast an eye toward the future and predict the development of their fields. We, too, cannot resist this temptation. Our outlook for the future of clinical psychology emphasizes the following expectations:

1. The number of clinicians will begin to level off. Clinical psychology has had a growth spurt over the past few decades. Whether one considers the number of training programs established, the number of students graduated, or the number of psychologists licensed to practice, the field has expanded enormously. Some analysts suggest that the number of clinical psychologists (approximately 33 per 100,000, based on licensing board data) now exceeds national needs, and they recommend reducing the entering class size of clinical doctoral students as a way to avoid an oversupply (Robiner & Crew, 2000). Psychology is just one of many areas of health care currently threatened by oversupply, a condition brought about largely by managed care's influence on market conditions (O'Neil, 2000). Supply and demand are difficult to predict, but one thing is clear: the psychological workforce has grown at a much faster rate than the population for many years now, and that trend cannot go on forever.

Although we believe the rate of increase in the production of clinical psychologists will slacken over the next decade, we think that the overall number of clinicians available will be a less important issue than two others—for what roles will clinicians be trained and how good will that training be? We agree with Pion, Kohout, & Wicherski (2000) that it is important to identify specific areas of oversupply and undersupply.

Several of those areas will continue as "growth stocks" for clinicians. As described in Chapters 11 and 12, health psychology, behavioral medicine, and clinical neuropsychology are likely to remain important specialty areas because of the contributions psychologists can make to treatment and the promotion of physical health. Although these activities pose exciting opportunities for psychologists, we must be realistic in our claims of success so as not to promise more than our knowledge allows us to deliver, and realistic in the number of clinicians who can enter these areas of practice before saturation occurs. Forensic psychology, described in Chapter 13, will also continue to be a growing specialty area as psychologists will continue to be consulted on a range of topics relevant to the legal system (Cassel & Bernstein, 2001; Sales & Shuman, 1996; Wrightsman, Nietzel, & Fortune, 1998). Although the demand for psychologists is gratifying and potentially lucrative, psychologists must be careful not to testify on matters that exceed their competence and not to exaggerate the scientific support for the conclusions they report.

Clinical child psychology is yet another area in which clinical psychologists' services will be in increasing demand. Assessment and treatment of childhood disorders have advanced remarkably in the past decade, as has basic research on child development and the etiology of child psychopathology. Recently, these efforts increasingly include programs for the prevention of drug and alcohol abuse among children and adolescents. Finally, new opportunities for employment appear to be developing for psychologists in government, administration, and research (Kohout & Wicherski, 1999; Pion, Kohout, & Wicherski, 2000).

2. Clinical psychology will take on a more notable consumer orientation. This trend is apparent in the growing emphasis on professional accountability and in the expectation that psychologists must develop their own standards as health service providers. As a result of these developments, clinicians will need to better evaluate both the effectiveness of their interventions and the financial costs of producing certain outcomes. This trend is supported by the increasing appearance of publications instructing practitioners in evaluating their own outcomes (e.g., Cone, 2000). Increasingly, psychologists will be expected to prove that their services lead to substantial improvements in clients' health and functioning. The psychologist as researcher will always have a place in the future.

3. The growing emphasis on service evaluation will be accompanied by abandonment of a "brand name" approach to psychotherapy and a shift toward offering treatments that have been empirically validated as effective. As research indicates the effectiveness of behavior-change techniques, regardless of their theoretical origins, clinicians may find little advantage in identifying themselves as behaviorists, gestaltists, or analysts. Training will also begin to deemphasize adherence to particular orientations and stress integration and eclecticism.

4. Controversy will continue over the question of how clinical psychologists should be trained. Currently, there is enthusiasm for preparing clinicians to work with specialty problems and/or groups such as the chronically mentally ill, children and youth, rural populations, substance abusers, and older patients. NIMH has directed training grant funds toward these "underserved groups," and they will probably remain a focus of training for some clinical programs in the future.

As for more general training trends, we anticipate a continuing gap between Boulder model programs that stress training in research methods and psychology's scientific traditions and more professionally oriented programs that concentrate on developing practitioner skills. This gap may ultimately be accompanied by the development of alternative or competing systems of accreditation—one for clinical scientist programs and one for professional practitioner programs. Programs of all types should expect to face rising expectations that their students are trained in interventions that enjoy the highest levels of empirically validated effectiveness (Crits-Christoph et al., 1995).

5. Psychologists will continue to push for the freedom of their profession. Not only will organized psychology intensify its political efforts for inclusion in all types of health care plans, but individual psychologists will strive to keep abreast of the most modern clinical techniques so that they can continue to offer top-quality services.

The most controversial of these political efforts will continue to be the one aimed at enabling psychologists to prescribe psychoactive medication for their clients. The idea that, like psychiatrists, psychologists should have *prescription privileges* emerged in the mid-1980s and was based on two main arguments: (1) it is in clients' interests that psychologists be able to offer a full range of treatment alternatives; and (2) it worked out well when optometrists, podiatrists, physician assistants, dentists, nurses, and other non-physician groups acquired prescription privileges (Cullen & Newman, 1997).

Psychologists' involvement in prescribing medications is not new. For some time now, a few psychologists employed by the federal government have been authorized to prescribe drugs—under the supervision of a physician—aboard Navy ships and in the Indian Health Service. The Department of Defense has also explored the possibility that psychologists might be prepared to prescribe psychotropic medications more widely. Perhaps more importantly, a recent survey of 596 practicing psychologists found that *virtually all* reported that they were "involved in making recommendations for medication evaluations, consulting with physicians about which medications to use with specific patients, and discussing medication-related issues with patients." (Vanderbos & Williams, 2000; p. 615).

In 1996, the American Psychological Association's Council of Representatives officially endorsed the pursuit of prescriptive authority for psychologists. The Council also recommended a draft of model legislation to be introduced in states seeking authorization of psychologist prescribers and a model postdoctoral curriculum (covering neurosciences, pharmacology, physiology, physical and laboratory assessments, and clinical pharmacotherapeutics) to be used in training prescribers (Cullen & Newman, 1997). Today, psychologists show a consistently high level of support for prescription privileges (Pimental et al., 1997; Sammons, Gorny, Zinner, & Allen, 2000).

Still, opponents of prescription privileges for psychologists (DeNelsky, 1996; Hayes & Heiby, 1996) question the long-term impact of prescription authority, either for clinical psychology or for the clients it serves. They are concerned that this authority would detract from the nonmedical identity and services that psychology has traditionally offered to the public (Albee, 2000). Some psychologist educators, too, remain skeptical about prescription privileges, largely because they fear it would unduly lengthen their training programs, displace other important subject matter in the traditional clinical psychology curriculum, and cost too much (Evans & Murphy, 1997). Finally, as you might imagine, the idea of prescription privileges for clinical psychologists has met with fierce opposition from organized psychiatry and physicians in general (Bell, Digman, & McKenna, 1995).

Although the debate is far from resolved, it does appear that the pro-prescription contingent is strong and has steadily gained support. Psychologists' attitudes toward prescription privileges have become more favorable, and the more they learn about the prescription privilege, the more they tend to endorse it. A growing number of state psychological associations are working to secure prescription privilege legislation, and in 2002, New Mexico became the first state to pass such legislation.

Of course, none of these forecasts tells us what clinical psychology should strive for and what it should avoid. For that kind of wisdom we continue to rely on the ideas of a clinical psychologist who gave the question a career's worth of attention:

> Clinical psychology, after a long period spent as part of an academic discipline, is in the early stages of becoming a profession. It is going through the natural disturbances and difficulties which attend a growth process of this kind. However, if it selects its students carefully, for personality as well as intellect; if it trains thoroughly, in spirit as well as letter; if it trains broadly, recognizing that "specialists" . . . are not clinical psychologists; if it remains flexible about its training and encourages experimentation; if it does not become overwhelmed by immediate needs at the cost of important, remoter goals; if it maintains its contact with its scientific background, remaining aware of the importance of theory as well as practice; if it remains modest in the face of the complexity of its problems, rather than becoming pretentious—in other words, if it finds good people and gives them good training—these disturbances and difficulties need not be of serious concern. Its future, both for itself as a profession and for society in the contribution it can make, is then assured. Fortunately, there are many reasons for believing that these are the prevailing aspirations in clinical psychology. (Shakow, 1948, p. 246)

These comments were written by David Shakow in 1948. We believe that the aspirations Shakow expressed can be realized by clinical psychology only if, in the future, it firmly establishes itself, in Stanley Schneider's (1991) eloquent phrase, as "a profession based on science that is informed by practice." We hope this book plays a role in moving some of you to join in the creation of that future.

CHAPTER SUMMARY

Five professional issues are of prime importance as clinical psychology continues to develop its scientific and professional identity in the 21st century. These issues involve training, regulation, ethics, independence, and the perils associated with the professionalization of clinical psychology.

Beginning in the late-1940s, clinical training programs have typically followed some version of the Boulder model, a scientist–practitioner curriculum which emphasizes psychology's scientific foundation more than the development of clinical service skills. Several training conferences since that time have reaffirmed the Boulder model, but training models that emphasize professional skills are also available now. These include Doctor of Psychology (PsyD) programs and practice-oriented PhD programs offered in psychology departments, medical schools, and, especially, in free-standing schools of professional psychology.

Professional regulation of clinical psychologists comes in several forms, including (1) laws that establish criteria for who may use the title of "psychologist" (certification laws) and perform psychological services (licensing laws), (2) laws and court rulings that give institutionalized clients the right to receive treatment and the right to give informed consent for it, (3) laws establishing client–therapist discussions as privileged communication, and (4) lawsuits alleging clinical malpractice.

Psychology's code of ethics is unique because it was developed on the basis of psychologists' experiences with real ethical dilemmas. The current version, called "Ethical Principles of Psychologists and Code of Conduct," includes a Preamble, General Principles, and a large number of Ethical Standards covering a wide range of specific topics, from advertising services and testing to rules about confidentiality and sexual contact with clients.

Clinical psychology's struggle to gain, and retain, its status as a profession that is authorized to offer independent services has been long, difficult, and continuing. It first involved the right of clinicians to offer psychotherapy. Later, the issue was whether clinical psychologists could practice independently in hospitals, and whether psychologists should be eligible for reimbursement under various public, private, and pre-paid mental health insurance plans. While these rights are now reasonably well established in most states, some of them may be made irrelevant by the continuing growth of managed care systems whose provisions are making it increasingly difficult for clinical psychologists to function outside of HMOs, group medical practices, or other health-related organizations.

Today, clinical psychology confronts the formidable challenge of shaping its training programs and service functions to meet client needs in the era of managed care while still maintaining the highest standards of professionalism, which includes letting itself be guided by the empirical research tradition that launched the field a hundred years ago.

Appendix

Getting into Graduate School in Clinical Psychology

John P. Fiore, M.Ed.
Associate Head for Undergraduate Affairs
Department of Psychology
University of Illinois at Urbana-Champaign

Richard Milich, Ph.D.
Professor and Associate Chair
Department of Psychology
University of Kentucky

Students ask a number of questions when they are thinking of applying to graduate school in clinical psychology. The purpose of this Appendix is to answer some of those questions, and to pose other questions that potential applicants need to consider. We will begin by addressing several questions that you need to ask yourself when considering whether to apply to graduate school in clinical psychology: (1) In what type of program am I interested? (2) Am I ready to make the commitment required for a doctoral program in clinical psychology at this time in my life? (3) Are my credentials strong enough for admission to graduate school? (4) Given my credentials, to what type of program can I realistically aspire? Let's consider some things you should take into account as you answer these and related questions.

WHAT TYPES OF GRADUATE PROGRAMS WILL HELP ME MEET MY CAREER GOALS?

In thinking about life after college, the first questions you need to ask yourself are, "What type of career do you want?" and "What types of graduate programs are available to meet your career goals?" If your primary interest is in research or if you want to receive significant research training, the PhD program in clinical is probably your best option. If your interest is primarily in clinical work, there are a variety of options available. Many students seem to think that if they want to do clinical work, they must enter a PhD program in clinical psychology. In fact, approximately three times as many students get master's degrees in psychology as get the doctoral degree (Morgan & Korschgen, 2001). Many of the students who are considering clinical PhD programs probably could get their educational and employment needs met in an MA program or in other types of programs that offer training leading to careers in the mental health professions. At the doctoral level, PsyD programs may provide training with a stronger emphasis on clinical skills than on research (issues related to these programs are discussed further below). Programs in counseling psychology, school psychology, and social work all offer extensive training and experience in clinical work, and graduates of these programs enter many of the same positions as do clinical psychologists. As noted in Chapters 1, 9, and 14, recent trends in our health care system have led to increased enrollment in health maintenance organizations (HMOs), many of which are saving costs by hiring increasing numbers of master's-level professionals rather than individuals who have received their doctorates in clinical psychology. Indeed, there are those who believe that master's-level professionals from psychology and related fields will enjoy increased opportunities for direct service roles, while doctoral-level clinical psychologists will tend to take on more administrative, supervisory, grant writing, consulting, and program evaluation roles.

Thus, the MA in clinical psychology may be a more marketable degree than it has been in the past. Further, what is seen as the biggest drawback to the MA degree—the need for continual supervision from a licensed PhD psychologist—may be changing. The state of Kentucky, for example, has recently passed legislation that allows MA level psychologists to be licensed to work independently after they had met certain training (e.g., 60 graduate credit hours in psychology) and professional experience (e.g., 5 years of full-time supervised practice) requirements. Thus, before investing all of your efforts in applying to doctoral programs in clinical psychology, you may want to explore the clinical job opportunities available to professionals trained at the master's level, as well as those available to doctoral and subdoctoral professionals trained in related fields. This is especially the case if you are committed to a full-time clinical career, with little interest in spending a considerable amount of your graduate education on research related activities.

AM I READY TO MAKE THE COMMITMENT REQUIRED IN DOCTORAL PROGRAMS AT THIS TIME IN MY LIFE?

After exploring the career options available with MA and PhD degrees, and after careful consideration of what you want to achieve, you have decided that a doctoral program in clinical psychology offers you the most career flexibility and the best chance to obtain your research and clinical goals. The next question you have to ask yourself is whether you are prepared to make the type of commitment required for such a program.

A doctoral program in clinical psychology requires that you make major emotional, financial, and time commitments. On average, five to seven years are needed to complete such a program, during which time you will be living on subsistence wages, at best. In addition, new licensing requirements almost guarantee that you will need to take a one- to two-year postdoctoral position after you graduate in order to obtain the necessary clinical supervision for licensure. Thus, it may take anywhere from seven to nine years after starting graduate school before you are ready to venture into the job market. Further, it is quite likely that you will incur some debt during your graduate school and postdoctoral years, and depending on the financial support you receive in graduate school, it is possible that the debt could run quite high. For example, the *APA Monitor* (May, 2000) reported that some graduates of PsyD programs, where tuition is often relatively high and financial support is not guaranteed, have run up debts upon graduation approaching $100,000. High debt is particularly likely for students in professional schools and nontraditional doctoral programs (see Chapter 14). In addition, the starting salaries for clinical psychologists are not so great as to make paying off this debt easy. In fact, the job market for PhDs is in something of a transition period, due to the emergence of managed care, and it is not clear how this will play out in the next 5 to 10 years.

In addition to the financial costs associated with doctoral programs in clinical psychology, you will be expected to make major time and effort commitments. You will be asked to work harder than you have in previous academic endeavors. For example, typical requirements may involve a full course load of academic work as well as a 20-hour-per-week job either as a teaching or research assistant or at a placement in a clinical agency. In addition, you will be expected to find time to make continual progress on your independent research toward completion of your thesis and dissertation. Thus, it is not unusual for graduate students in clinical programs to work 60 hours or more per week, 12 months per year. Unlike college, summer is not a time for rest and relaxation for doctoral students.

It is not only the time and effort that make doctoral programs so demanding. The academic expectations and requirements are aimed at a higher level than those with which most students are familiar. Compared to college, much more independent thinking and work are expected of graduate students. First, the method of instruction shifts dramatically compared to that encountered in undergraduate courses. Most graduate classes are taught in a small seminar format, which involves discussion and student-directed presentations rather than faculty lectures. Second, journal articles, rather than textbooks, are the primary reading material, and the amount of reading material assigned is typically at least twice that of the typical college course. Finally, the professors' expectations are higher because the students are on average much stronger academically than those found in the typical college class. Admission to PhD programs in clinical psychology is so competitive that the faculty can offer admission to the brightest and most conscientious students, thereby setting very high standards for the graduate classes.

The purpose of this admittedly sobering introduction is not to discourage you from applying to doctoral programs in clinical psychology. Rather, these issues are raised to help you prepare better for the initial decision making process through which all potentials applicants should go before they spend the hundreds of dollars and numerous hours needed to apply successfully to graduate programs in clinical psychology. How can you determine whether you are ready for graduate study in clinical study? The answer may depend on how you feel about the prospect of graduate study, in light of the issues we raised above. It is appropriate to be somewhat apprehensive; indeed, a certain amount of anxiety can serve as an effective motivator for increased effort. However, if you are ambivalent about committing 5 to 7 years of your life to graduate school, where the stress level is high and you will be living on minimal income while incurring some debt, consider taking some time off before pursuing further education. Most graduate programs are so demanding and stressful that ambivalence on your part is likely to interfere with your ability to complete your PhD successfully. You may want to consider applying to a master's level program in psychology, which may require only a two- to three-year commitment before you are eligible to enter the work force.

Students often wonder whether a delayed application will hurt their chances for admission. Contrary to what you might have heard, your application to graduate school in clinical psychology will not be jeopardized if you decide to take some time off after completing your undergraduate studies. Graduate admissions committees are seeking the best candidates for their programs, and what you do during your "time off"—along with accompanying changes in your attitude, commitment, maturity, and motivation—may actually enhance your application, thus making admission more, not less, likely. In fact, some clinical programs prefer applicants who have had work experience after completing the undergraduate degree. It is also possible that a period of time off may also help you decide that graduate study in clinical psychology is not for you. Whatever the case—whether you need to be away from school for a while before making a final decision about applying, or you need to work for a year or more in order to accumulate sufficient funds to pay for your education—rest assured that your delayed application will be taken seriously.

If you do decide to take time off before applying to graduate school, there are several things that you can do to enhance your application. First, try to obtain a position in the field, either as a research assistant or as a mental health worker in a clinical setting. Both of these options will help document your commitment to the field, as well as give you valuable experience and further insight in helping to decide your future. If you cannot obtain paid research or clinical positions, try to obtain a volunteer position in these areas. Second, if you are located near a university, consider taking one or more graduate courses. Once again, this will help document your commitment to the field and may help you decide whether graduate school is for you. Although your inclination may be to take clinically related courses, graduate admissions committees will probably be more impressed if you take (and do well in) graduate courses in nonclinical areas, such as statistics, research design, or psychology proseminars (e.g., learning or personality theory). In addition, you may receive credit for these latter courses when you enter a graduate program, whereas clinical programs often require that you repeat any clinically related courses you may have taken previously.

ARE MY CREDENTIALS STRONG ENOUGH FOR GRADUATE SCHOOL IN CLINICAL PSYCHOLOGY?

In order to evaluate your credentials objectively, and to be aware of your strengths and weaknesses, it is important to understand the criteria employed by graduate admissions committees in clinical psychology. Surveys of directors of clinical training programs suggest that the four main criteria employed in the selection of new graduate students are: (1) Graduate Record Exam (GRE) scores; (2) grade point average (GPA); (3) letters of recommendation; and (4) research experience, especially independent research such as an honors thesis. Each graduate program may weigh these criteria differently, of course, and programs will examine other factors (e.g., personal statements, interviews) as well, but all of these criteria tend to be used, to some extent at least, by all doctoral clinical programs. Notice that clinical experience was not included on the list. Indeed, such experience can be valuable in helping students decide whether the mental health profession is the field for them, and in which clinical areas (e.g., child, substance use) they are especially interested, but clinical experience appears not to be deemed especially important in the graduate selection process, especially for PhD programs in clinical psychology. Other types of programs (e.g., MA clinical or counseling psychology), which put more emphasis on clinical training, may value undergraduate clinical experience to a greater degree.

GRE Scores

Students often do not like to hear this, but performance on the GRE is an important predictor of success in graduate school, and thus one of the most important selection criteria used by graduate admissions committees. One study found, for example, that GRE scores were more useful than college GPA in predicting performance in a graduate program in clinical psychology (Dollinger, 1989). A recent meta-analysis (Kuncel, Hezlett, & Ones, 2001) found that, across all disciplines, both GRE scores and undergraduate GPA were significant and powerful predictors of performance in graduate school, as measured by a variety of outcome measures (e.g., graduate GPA, publication citation counts, faculty ratings). Interestingly, the meta-analysis revealed that the GRE Subject Test was the single best predictor of performance in graduate school, suggesting that graduate admission committees may well give more weight to this test in future admission decisions than probably has occurred in the past.

Besides the GRE's predictive validity, there are other reasons why these scores are valued by admissions committees. The GRE represents the only data for which direct comparisons can be made across all applicants. All students take exactly the same test, so performance is not influenced by differences in collegiate standards, as are letters of recommendation and college grades. A score of 600 on the verbal subtest for a student at the University of Washington means the same as a 600 for someone at the University of Florida. Thus, the GRE is widely viewed as providing a valid indicator of a student's potential for successful performance in graduate school. In addition, the GRE and undergraduate GPA together can serve as relatively objective screening instruments that help admission committees reduce the several hundred applicants to a more manageable number. With this dramatically smaller pool of applicants, the admissions committee can then give much closer scrutiny to the other, more qualitative and time consuming selection criteria, such as the personal statement, letters of recommendation, and personal interview (Morgan & Korschgen, 2001).

Students often ask what scores are necessary on the GREs to get past the initial screenings undertaken by admission committees. This is a difficult question to answer, for several reasons. First, programs vary considerably in the range of GRE scores they expect from their incoming students. Second, graduate programs often do not have strict cutoffs for the GRE scores but instead they employ guidelines as to what they are looking for. For example, the minimally acceptable GRE scores reported by schools in the graduate guide books tend to be considerably below the median scores of the entering graduate classes (Morgan & Korschgen, 2001). In other words, if your GRE scores are just at or a little above the minimally acceptable scores reported by a school (e.g., an average of 500 per subtest), you probably will not be admitted to that program. Surveys of the GRE scores of students admitted to PhD clinical programs suggest that you would want to average at least 550 to 600 on each of the GRE subtests in order to be a viable candidate for such programs. (Norcross et al., 1996). Finally, scores on the GRE and other standardized quantitative tests tend not to be given as much weight when evaluating applications from members of ethnic minority groups, international students, students with disabilities, and other "nontraditional" or disadvantaged students whose potential might not be captured fully by such tests.

Grade Point Average

If the GRE is seen as a reliable and valid predictor of your overall ability, your GPA is seen as an excellent indicator of the effort you have exerted in college and your willingness to work up to or even beyond your predicted potential. Thus, an outstanding undergraduate GPA may offset to some degree a less than desired GRE score. Conversely, outstanding GRE scores combined with a mediocre GPA could raise serious concerns about an applicant. This is why the GRE and GPA make such excellent screening instruments—together they offer valid and objective measures of both academic potential and willingness to work hard.

There are several things admission committees will look for when examining an applicant's GPA. First, they will focus primarily on your psychology GPA, although they will want to make sure you are a serious student and that you did not just "blow off" your other courses because these may have been outside your major. However, the committees tend to be forgiving if you started off in another area of study (e.g., as a pre-med student) and did poorly in these courses. Second, the admissions committees will look to see that you maintain or improve your GPA as you progress through college, rather than have it fall. Thus, they are more forgiving of poorer grades early in your college career rather than later. Admission committees also may pay close attention to "less popular" required courses such as statistics and experimental methods. Even though you are applying to a clinical program, there is a heavy emphasis on research in graduate school, and the admissions committees want to ensure that you do as well in your research related courses as you do in the more popular clinical courses, such as abnormal psychology.

Once again, it is impossible to offer absolute guidelines as to what PhD clinical programs are looking for when they examine an applicant's undergraduate GPA. Surveys of entering classes in PhD clinical programs suggest that a psychology GPA of 3.5 or 3.6 (on a 4-point scale) is necessary, at a minimum, to be a strong candidate for admission (Norcross et al., 1996). Thus, if you have obtained a somewhat marginal GPA, seriously consider repeating those courses in which you did poorly to improve your GPA. For example, if you earned a B− in undergraduate statistics, you would be well advised to retake the course to improve your grade. Otherwise, admission committees will be concerned about your ability to handle more difficult graduate statistics courses, where a B− is the minimally acceptable grade.

Letters of Recommendation

When reading letters of recommendation, admissions committee members tend to look for comments relating to the applicant's overall potential for graduate school, willingness to work hard, level of interpersonal skills, and likelihood of success in clinical work. Letter writers are not likely to learn these things about you through classroom contacts alone. Even if you received one of the top grades in the course, if that is the professor's only contact with you, there is not much he/she can write about you. Thus, it is crucial that you develop means of interacting with faculty outside the classroom. The best way to do this is to get involved as a paid or volunteer member of one or more faculty member's research groups. In addition, make a point of stopping by professors' offices outside of class to talk with them about class content that has intrigued you. Most professors welcome students stopping by to talk, especially if it does not concern complaining about a grade received or explaining why an assignment was missed. A good way to think about letters of recommendation is that, ideally, the professor should be able to write about your motivation, your conscientiousness, your ability to think intelligently about the subject material, your ability to take on independent responsibility, and your maturity, among other factors. You need to do whatever you can to give the professor enough samples of your behavior in these domains so that he/she can write a positive and knowledgeable letter about you.

Research Experience

There are many reasons why you should gain research experience prior to applying to doctoral programs in clinical psychology. First, the PhD in clinical psychology is both a research degree and a clinical degree, and you may well spend as much if not more of your graduate training on research as on clinical work. Therefore, admissions committees want to ensure that applicants understand what is involved in research, and that they enjoy participating in such activities. In a similar fashion, working on several research projects will give you an excellent understanding of what graduate school will be like. Thus, for example, if you find that research is really not for you, then you may want to reconsider whether to apply to programs offering a PhD in clinical psychology, since much of your graduate training will focus on research activities. Second, as just noted, working with faculty on their research is an excellent way to obtain letters of recommendation that define more precisely your potential for graduate school. Third, working on research projects can help you decide which research areas you would (and would not) like to pursue in graduate school. This information, in turn, will help you apply to those psychology departments whose faculty are working in the areas of your greatest interest. Finally, research experience serves as an excellent basis for discussion with faculty during any faculty interviews that you might have. In fact, recent years have seen a trend where an increasing number of interviewees for PhD programs have undertaken independent honors theses or capstone research experiences. Thus, applicants who do not have such experiences are at a distinct disadvantage during the interview process, because they do not have the depth of knowledge of a specific research project that is associated with having undertaken an honors thesis study.

GIVEN MY CREDENTIALS, TO WHAT TYPE OF PROGRAM CAN I REALISTICALLY ASPIRE?

One of the most difficult things you need to do when applying to graduate school is to be realistic about evaluating your credentials. Unfortunately, the credentials of many applicants are not strong enough to gain entry to PhD programs in clinical psychology. PhD clinical programs routinely receive anywhere from 100 to 400 applicants, and these programs generally accept anywhere from five to ten students. Thus, these programs are extremely competitive, and shortcomings in any of the selection criteria described above can undermine your chances of receiving an offer of acceptance. Unless you have pursued other options as well, you may be setting yourself up for failure and disappointment. Fortunately, several such options are available. For example, master's (MA) programs in clinical psychology usually have lower criteria for admission, in terms of expected GRE scores and GPA, than PhD programs. You might want to consider these programs either to earn a terminal master's degree or as the first step toward a PhD program. Counseling, school, or other psychology programs that offer clinical training also tend to be less competitive than PhD programs in clinical psychology. As noted earlier, students in these programs often receive as much applied training and experience as students in clinical psychology programs, and master's-level job openings, and even potential licensure, appear to be on the rise. Finally, nonclinical PhD programs in psychology (e.g., developmental, social) tend to attract fewer applicants, and have lower admission criteria, than do clinical programs. If you are committed to the field of psychology, and want to remain in a research environment, you may find a nonclinical PhD program in psychology more rewarding than a mental-health-related doctoral or master's level program in another field.

In short, PhD programs in clinical psychology are not for everyone; they are highly competitive, they place great demands on their students, they take five to seven years to complete, and they emphasize research training as much as if not more than clinical experience.

Having offered some guidelines to help you assess your credentials and aspirations, and to determine whether you should apply to doctoral programs in clinical psychology, we now consider some more general issues that you will need to address before beginning the application process.

GENERAL ISSUES

I Have Decided to Apply to Graduate School in Clinical Psychology. What Should I Do First?

In choosing graduate programs, you will want to make sure they provide the training and professional environment that will meet your needs. Therefore, you should clarify your personal goals, objectives, and plans. Are you most interested in research, balanced training in clinical practice and research, or primarily in clinical practice? Are you interested in doctoral-level or master's-level programs? Do you have an interest in a specific client population? These are but a few of the questions you should be asking yourself before the application process begins. You will not have definitive answers for all possible questions, but you will have some, and these will probably indicate what is most important to you in choosing a graduate program. In addition, the stronger your credentials, the more freedom you will have to use these factors in deciding to which programs to apply. Thus, students with a 3.5 GPA in psychology and an average of 550 on each GRE subtest will probably need to be concerned with getting into any PhD program they can, whereas students with a 4.0 GPA and 700 per GRE subtest probably have the luxury of identifying programs that are ideally suited for their needs in terms of relevant factors (e.g., faculty research interests, financial support offered, geographical location).

Should I Apply to a Master's Degree Program and Complete It Before I Apply to a Doctoral Program?

As noted earlier, there are various routes you can take to earn the doctorate in clinical psychology. A number of graduate programs provide master's degree training only. Many graduates from these programs terminate their formal education at the master's-degree level; others go on to doctoral programs. Most PhD clinical programs are designed to prepare doctoral-level clinicians only. They may award the master's degree after a minimum number of credits and a master's thesis have been completed, but it is important to recognize that these departments accept applications for the doctoral degree only.

How Does Earning a Master's Degree Affect My Chances for Admission to a Doctoral Program Later On?

Generally, the possession of a master's degree has little impact on a student's application. Graduate schools are interested in the best candidates they can find. If your credentials are excellent, your chances for being admitted to a doctoral program are good. Some students who feel they need to improve their credentials may find master's-degree work helpful in achieving that goal, but doctoral admission committees consider all academic work when making their decision. A mediocre undergraduate academic record is not disregarded because it has been supplemented with a master's degree and good graduate school grades, but these graduate credentials can improve a student's chances for being seriously considered.

If I Choose to Terminate my Training After Earning a Master's Degree, Will My Opportunities for Doing Clinical Work be Limited?

Historically, the doctorate is considered the standard of the profession. You also need to consider that all U.S. states employ some form of licensing or certification for psychologists (see Chapter 14). Though requirements vary from state to state, an earned doctorate is a prerequisite in most of them. So while the growth of managed care systems has stimulated the job market at the master's-degree level for those seeking a career in direct service, be certain that such jobs match your career expectations before deciding to prepare for clinical work by earning a master's degree. This is especially true if your ultimate goal is to have an independent clinical practice. Having said this, the recent change in the licensure law in Kentucky and other states suggests that the future for independent practice for MA level clinicians may be more promising. Given the impact of managed care systems and the changes in the licensure laws, it is impossible to predict exactly how the job market for MA (and even PhD) clinical psychologists will look in 5 to 10 years.

Are All Doctoral Programs in Clinical Psychology Research-Oriented?

All university-based PhD programs in clinical psychology provide training in research as well as in clinical functions, but there are differences in emphasis from one institution to another. It is worth your effort to learn of each program's emphasis when you are gathering other information about the program. Programs that are strictly research-oriented make this fact clear in their descriptive information and may even refrain from using "clinical psychology" as a program title (experimental psychopathology is a common substitute). Similarly, subtle differences in a program's description (e.g., scientist practitioner vs. clinical scientist; see Chapter 14) may reveal a great deal about the program's training emphasis.

Some graduate programs offer a doctor of psychology (PsyD) degree in addition to, or instead of, a traditional PhD. As noted in Chapter 14, this degree puts the emphasis on clinical training while reducing the emphasis on research. These programs still require their students to acquire knowledge of research tools, but do not require students to do basic research. In other words, students still develop their knowledge of statistics and research methods but may not be required to do an empirically based thesis or dissertation.

A relatively recent development in the field is the rise in professional schools offering the PsyD degree. What is unique about these programs is that they often are not affiliated with a specific psychology department or even with a university. On the surface, these programs often are attractive to student for two reasons. They generally have considerably lower selection criteria than PhD clinical programs. Thus, in a survey of clinical psychology directors Mayne, Norcross, and Sayette (1994) found that 23% of students applying to PsyD programs were accepted compared to 6% for research-oriented PhD programs. Another reason for the popularity of PsyD programs is that they put a greater emphasis on clinical training while downplaying the research requirements. However, several cautionary notes are necessary. First, because these programs are stand-alone institutions, they usually have to support themselves financially from student tuition. Thus, similar to medical schools and law schools, the tuition can be quite high with little financial assistance available. In contrast, most clinical PhD programs offer their students some financial support, including tuition remission and RA or TA positions. Mayne et al. (1994) found that students were six times less likely to receive financial support as were students in PhD clinical programs. Thus, students in professional schools often amass considerable debt during their graduate years. PsyD students also tend to have much higher debt when they graduate, probably because, compared to PhD programs, PsyD programs rarely offer graduate assistantships or other forms of financial assistance. The median debt reported by 1997 clinical PsyD graduates was $53,000; for clinical PhD graduates, it was $22,000 (Kohout & Wicherski, 1999). However, unlike medical or law students, the job market is not so promising and the starting salaries are much more modest, making it more difficult for PsyD graduates to pay off their debt (*APA Monitor*, May, 2000). Second, PsyD programs often need to accept large entering classes (e.g,. as many as 100 students) in order to make the program succeed financially. Thus, students may not get the same individual attention that they would in a PhD program, where the entering class may be five to ten students.

How Do I Identify "Good" Graduate Programs?

It is difficult to label graduate programs as "good" or "bad." The real question to be answered is whether a particular university, department, and program fit your needs. Part of the answer will lie in the "research" versus "clinical" emphasis of each program and you can gather information about that by corresponding with current graduate students and faculty located there. You should also consider the size of the department and the program, whether there are faculty undertaking research in areas of interest to you, the student/faculty ratio, opportunities for a variety of practicum experiences, the size and location of the campus and the community, the type and extent of department resources, and the theoretical orientation(s) or approaches that may exist in or dominate the program.

Finally, be cautious about generalizing about the quality of a clinical program on the basis of the reputation of the department in which it resides. There are some psychology departments that are considered to be the "best" by many psychologists, but if your interest is in clinical psychology, do not assume that the clinical program is also one of the best. It very well may be, but be sure to identify what is the best for you and to judge each program against your own personal criteria. In addition, as noted above, the weaker your credentials, the more you need to search for programs that are less competitive, which may mean having to forego applying to programs that may appear to be an ideal fit for you.

What Does American Psychological Association (APA) Accreditation of a Clinical Psychology Graduate Program Mean?

APA accreditation means the program has met a minimum standard of quality (see Chapter 14). The APA publication *Graduate Study in Psychology* explains that APA accreditation should be interpreted to mean:

1. The program is recognized and publicly labeled as a doctoral program in clinical, counseling, or school psychology (or combination thereof). It is located in and supported by an institution of higher education, which itself is accredited by one of six regional accrediting bodies also recognized by COPA.

2. The program voluntarily applied for accreditation and, in so doing, engaged in extensive self-study of its program objectives, educational and training practices, its resource support base, and its faculty, students, and graduates. The program also par-

ticipated in a peer review of its operations by a site-visit team of distinguished professional colleagues.

3. The program was thoroughly evaluated by the APA Committee on Accreditation (comprised of professional and public members) and judged to be in sufficient compliance with the APA Criteria for Accreditation to warrant accreditation status. Those criteria against which a program is evaluated include institutional support; sensitivity to cultural and individual differences; training models and curricula; faculty; students; facilities; and practicum and internship training.

Accreditation, in summary, applies to educational institutions and programs, not to individuals. It does not guarantee jobs or licensure for individuals, though being a graduate of an accredited program greatly facilitates such achievement. It does speak to the manner and quality by which an educational institution or program conducts its business. It speaks to a sense of public trust, as well as professional quality (APA 1996, p. ix).

Thus, graduating with a Ph.D. from any accredited program is seen as a laudatory accomplishment, regardless of the school's apparent reputation. Further, many APA-approved internships will only accept applicants from APA approved graduate programs. Thus, if you are thinking about a PhD in clinical psychology, there are many reasons to limit your search only to APA-approved programs.

A list of APA-accredited programs in clinical psychology is published each year in the December issue of the APA's main journal, the *American Psychologist*. In addition, the APA also accredits PhD programs in other areas, including counseling and school psychology, as well as a number of PsyD programs. In contrast, MA programs are not accredited by APA, making it more difficult to identify high quality master's programs.

APPLICATION PROCEDURES

It is now time to review the steps you will need to take in order to file admission applications for graduate programs in clinical psychology. In addition, there are a number of other valuable resources available that can help in all stages of the application process. Three helpful books are *Majoring in Psych? Career Options for Psychology Undergraduates* (Morgan & Korschgen, 2001), *Getting in: A Step-by-step Plan for Gaining Admission to Graduate School in Psychology* (APA, 1997), and *Insider's Guide to Graduate Programs in Clinical and Counseling Psychology* (Mayne, Norcross, & Sayette, 2000). Another valuable resource for gaining information about graduate schools and the application process is the APA website (www.apa.org).

Applying to graduate school is a major undertaking, not something to be done on the spur of the moment. Here is a list of the different tasks you must complete to successfully accomplish this undertaking:

Study for and take the GRE General and Subject tests, at least once each.

Search the websites for appropriate programs to which to apply, and identify at least 10 to 15 appropriate programs.

Obtain information on these programs, and fill out the application and financial aid forms for each program.

Arrange for your transcripts from all of your undergraduate institutions to be sent to each graduate program.

Arrange for your GRE scores to be sent to each program.

Identify three professors who are willing to write letters of recommendation for you, and get them the necessary forms and information about your undergraduate career at least one month prior to the first application deadline.

Write a personal statement and revise it as often as necessary, based on feedback you have received from one or more faculty members.

Applying to graduate school can be considered the work equivalent of taking a demanding undergraduate course. Like taking a course, the application process will last approximately the length of a semester, starting around Labor Day and ending the middle of December. Similarly, like a course, the more effort you put into the process, and the more conscientious you are in your efforts, the more successful you will be. However, unlike any single undergraduate course, the attention you devote to applying to graduate school has profound implications for your future career options. This is not something you want to approach casually! The book, *Getting In* (APA, 1997), has a very helpful timeline that you can follow to make sure you are accomplishing all of the necessary tasks in a timely fashion.

How Do I Get Initial Information About Graduate Schools?

There are several sources of information and you should use all of them. Some of the best of these are the psychology faculty you know, especially those who are clinical psychologists. In preparing for courses, doing research, and keeping current for clinical practice, these faculty members carefully review new ideas and research, attend professional meetings, and participate in continuing education workshops. This exposure to the field helps faculty members learn about various departments, programs, schools, training and research staff, the nature and theoretical orientations of different programs, recent changes in the direction of certain departments, and other pertinent information. Though it is not reasonable to expect the faculty to know about all or even most doctoral programs, they will be able to provide you with good information about many of them. In addition, the faculty may have personal contacts at schools that may help your application. A personal recommendation from a faculty member can be a valuable help in highlighting your credentials and increasing the attention your application receives.

Professional journals and related publications are information sources that many applicants overlook. An excellent way to find programs that meet your needs is to use these sources to identify faculty who are studying topics that interest you. A thorough search of the literature—using CD-ROM services such as Psychlit, and various on-line search services—will very likely highlight faculty with whom you might like to study, and indicate where they can be reached. For specific address information, consult the American

Psychological Association and the American Psychological Society membership directories (most psychology departments have recent editions), or visit these organizations' Worldwide Web Homepages. A very valuable website is http://www.psychwww.com/resource/deptlist.htm, which connects you to most psychology departments in North America. The Internet and World Wide Web offer an enormous amount of information about many universities, psychology departments, and clinical programs. With a few clicks of a mouse, you can quickly gather information about graduate programs, faculty rosters and research programs, department facilities, and the e-mail addresses and phone numbers you might need in order to request additional information and application materials. In many cases, you can even download the application forms you will need. In fact, many universities are moving toward having students submit their applications for graduate school via the web, and within the next decade it is likely that this may be the only acceptable way to apply to graduate programs.

There are also numerous books that list graduate schools and programs. We have already mentioned the best of these for psychology: the American Psychological Association's *Graduate Study in Psychology*. This book, which is updated bi-annually, contains over 500 pages of information, including application addresses, types of programs and degrees offered by each institution, number of faculty, financial aid information, tuition costs, degree and admission requirements, average grades and entrance test scores for students admitted the previous year, comments about the program, and other valuable information. If your departmental or school library does not have a copy, or if you want your own copy, you can order the book directly from the APA website (www.apa.org).

How Many Potential Programs in Clinical Psychology Should Be on My Initial Application List?

Your initial list should include as many programs as possible. The APA's *Graduate Study in Psychology* lists almost every clinical psychology program in the United States and Canada. As you use the various sources of information mentioned above and decide about location preferences, degree preferences, and the like, you will begin to systematically eliminate programs from your initial list. Once you have eliminated as many programs as possible by using the information you have compiled, you should contact each remaining program to request more detailed descriptions. This will allow you to continue to reduce the list on the basis of new information.

When Should I Contact Graduate Programs for Information?

You should request information in August or September, approximately a year before your desired admission date (e.g., September for the following fall admission). Requesting material earlier than this sometimes gets you old information or merely places you on a waiting list until material is available. If you make a request too late, the material may not arrive in time for you to make effective use of it. Remember, you may have questions which arise from your reading of the material and you may wish to correspond with some departments before a final decision is made about whether to apply to them. This all takes some time—give yourself plenty!

What Application Information Should I Ask for and What Format Should I Use?

At minimum, you should ask for information about the clinical psychology program, and request appropriate department and graduate school application forms, a graduate school program and course catalog, financial aid information, financial aid application forms, and a list of faculty and their research interests.

Your request for information need not be elaborate. A post card, form letter, or e-mail message addressed to the department's graduate admission committee can be used, but be sure it includes a request for all the information you will need. Many departments now enable you to gather all of the necessary information directly off of their website.

When Should I Apply?

Department application deadlines vary, but most fall between January 1 and February 15. A few come as early as December while others (mostly for master's degree programs) run as late as August. Some departments (primarily MA level programs) that have later deadlines often select students as applications arrive for processing. If you apply to schools that use this "rolling admissions" plan, it is to your advantage to submit your application early in the process.

Submitting very early applications (September or October) is usually of no particular value since departments are not "tooled-up" for the admission process until later in the fall. Also, required testing (to be discussed later) may not be available to you this early in the school year.

To How Many Programs Should I Apply?

It is difficult to identify a specific number of applications that is appropriate for all students. We are reminded of two cases: One student applied to 6 schools and was admitted to all of them, while another applied to 27 and was admitted to 1. Since competition for admission to PhD programs is keen, the general rule is to apply to as many programs as you can reasonably afford. The larger the number of applications, the better your chances of being accepted. It is our experience that even students with relatively strong credentials will want to apply to 10 to 15 programs, to ensure at least one offer of acceptance and to increase their chances of receiving financial aid offers as well.

Once you have decided on a final list of schools, ask yourself what you will do if you are not accepted by any of them. Perhaps at this point you may want to add one or two "safety valve" programs to fall back on. However, do not apply to programs that are really not acceptable to you. Such applications waste admission committee time, your time, and perhaps most importantly, your money.

How Much Does It Cost to Apply?

Applying to graduate school is an expensive process, in terms of the time and effort involved as well as the money spent. Total GRE and other testing costs usually run somewhere close to $250. Departmental application fees usually vary from $20 to $50.

Transcript costs (usually $2 to $5 each), additional test report fees (e.g., $13 for GRE scores to be sent to each school), postage, and photocopies can add up very quickly. Someone applying to ten graduate programs can expect an average cost of $75 to $100 per application. This is why it is important to choose the programs you apply to with care, and to realistically appraise your chances of receiving an offer. A good strategy is that after you have selected your initial list of schools show the list to a faculty member for feedback. Ideally, you will want a mix of a few long-shots, several relatively sure-bet programs, and a number of reasonable-risk programs.

What Kinds of Courses and Experiences Will Help My Application?

Your undergraduate department will have designed a graduate preparatory major to meet your course needs. This will probably include a core program of introductory psychology, statistics, and experimental psychology (including a laboratory). These are the minimum requirements for most graduate programs, regardless of specialization area.

In addition to standard course work, independent research such as an honors thesis and/or experience as a faculty research assistant is very helpful, in general, and essential for PhD programs. As noted earlier, such research activity not only provides you with desirable experience, but also allows faculty supervisors to observe your potential for scholarly endeavors and to include their evaluations and impressions in letters of recommendation.

As also noted earlier, having clinical experience may not be a very important criterion for admission—psychology departments do not expect you to be a trained clinician when you arrive—but it is helpful to provide some evidence of experience in "helping relationships." Clinically relevant volunteer work, for example, will assist you in establishing that your career decision is based partly on firsthand knowledge of the field.

Participation in extra-curricular activities, including psychology clubs and honor societies is not usually considered in the admission process except as it might indicate your involvement in psychology, your interpersonal skills, your willingness to work hard, and the like. Thus, simply being a member of Psi Chi, for example, will not strengthen your application much. However, it could help a lot if your participation as a member showed your creative leadership in developing effective and impressive programs and led to strong letters of support from faculty advisors and campus or community leaders. These activities, and glowing letters about them, will not substitute for the grades, GRE scores, and research experience required for admission, but they may make a difference when admissions committees are trying to decide between candidates who are equally strong on quantitative criteria.

What Testing Is Involved in Applying to Graduate School?

Most graduate schools use standardized tests to assist them in evaluating applicants. As already noted, the most common example is the Graduate Record Examination (GRE), including both the General Test and the Psychology Subject Test. Detailed information about the GRE (e.g., description, fees, registration) can be found at www.gre.org. The General Test is described on the website as follows:

> "The General Test measures verbal, quantitative, and analytical skills that have been acquired over a long period of time and that are not related to any specific field of study. The test consists of three scored sections:
>
>   Verbal (V): 30-minute section (30 questions)
>   Quantitative (Q): 45-minute section (28 questions)
>   Analytical (A): 60-minute section (35 questions)
>
> The verbal measure tests your ability to analyze and evaluate written material and synthesize information obtained from it, analyze relationships among component parts of sentences, and recognize relationships between words and concepts. The quantitative measure tests your basic mathematical skills and your understanding of elementary mathematical concepts, as well as your ability to reason quantitatively and solve problems in a quantitative setting. The analytical measure tests your ability to understand structured sets of relationships, deduce new information from sets of relationships, analyze and evaluate arguments, identify central issues and hypotheses, draw sound inferences, and identify plausible causal explanations.

The Subject Test In Psychology, which is required by approximately 2/3 of doctoral programs in psychology, is described on the website as follows:

> The test has about 215 questions drawn from courses most commonly offered at the undergraduate level, in three categories:
>
> 1. Experimental or natural science oriented (about 40% of the questions), including learning, language, memory, thinking, sensation and perception, ethology, and physiological psychology.
> 2. Social or social science oriented (about 43% of the questions), including clinical and abnormal, developmental, personality, and social psychology.
> 3. General (about 17% of the questions), including the history of psychology, applied psychology, measurement, research designs, and statistics."

A computer-based version of the GRE General Test is currently employed, and more than 250 test centers around the world give the GRE General Test, by appointment, using PC-type computers. One advantage of taking the test on a computer is that you can learn the results immediately after you have finished; written score reports are then mailed to you and the schools you designate within fifteen days. In addition, you can take the computer-based version of the test almost any day of the year, although you can only take the test once per calendar month. Remember, however, that the computerized version is available only for the GRE General Test.

One feature of the computer-based GRE testing that worries some students is the fact that it is not possible to reconsider the answer given for previous questions. Indeed, once a question is answered, the computer program selects the next questions based on the accuracy of the previous answer. Thus, it is also not possible to make a first pass through the test to answer "easy" questions and then go back and spend more time on those that take more thought. This restriction has tended to raise the pretest anxiety level of some students because it forces them to change the way they have learned to take multiple-choice tests. This is an excellent reason why you should consider taking the practice computer-generated exams sold by ETS.

Other students report that they actually like the computer-generated test because it (1) takes significantly less time than the paper-based exam, (2) provides immediate results to the student and forwards these results to the graduate programs within 10 to 15 days, and (3) can be taken by appointment throughout the year at a date that is convenient for the student. Whatever you may feel about the computer-generated exam, research by ETS shows that the scores obtained through this approach are comparable to those produced by the paper-based test.

As noted earlier, the GRE subject test is not currently available in a computer-based format, so you must sign up to take it on one of the three standard testing dates. The Educational Testing Service reports that it takes approximately six weeks to score paper-based tests and have the results in the mail, so the latest you can take the subject test is on a scheduled date that is at least six weeks before your earliest application deadline. Thus, for example, if January 1 is the first deadline date for the schools to which you are applying, only the November test date will meet that deadline.

One consideration in selecting test dates is whether you wish to use the results to shape decisions about where to apply (a very good strategy, given the expense of applying to programs). If you choose test dates that are sufficiently early, you will be able to look over your scores, consult with advisors, and review resource material such as APA's *Graduate Study in Psychology* book. Applying to certain graduate programs before you know what your GRE scores are can be a waste of time and money. Having scores at the 90th percentile makes it reasonable to apply to the most competitive schools; scores at the 40th percentile require a more conservative strategy.

A second factor that should influence your choice of test dates is that you may well want the option of retaking the GRE if you are not satisfied with your scores. One test-scheduling strategy that has worked well for some students is to take the general test near the end of their junior year. They then spend the summer reviewing for the subject test in psychology and/or studying to retake the general test, which they take early in their senior year. This plan allows time for retaking both tests, if necessary, and for using test results in deciding where to apply.

Can I Study for the GRE?

You can, and should, study for the GRE! The GRE website describes the types of questions found on the general test, along with a number of strategies you can use in taking the computer-based test. A free full-length sample GRE general test, which includes instructions for evaluating your performance, is available from the GRE program at the Educational Testing Service. ETS also sells practice material, including GRE general tests and GRE subject tests actually administered in previous years. In addition, ETS now sells software that allows you to practice the computer version of the test and receive feedback on your performance. All of this material can help you become familiar with the types and forms of questions you are likely to encounter on the GRE and it can also give you practice at pacing yourself during the actual examination.

You should review for the quantitative portion of the General Test, especially if you have been away from mathematics for a while. Brushing up on basic algebra and geometry will help you during this part of the exam by reducing the time you will need to recall how to solve particular problems. Students report that the quantitative portion of the GRE is not difficult, but that it is fast-paced. Know your basic math "cold," so you can work quickly and accurately.

You can also prepare for the GRE general test via test preparation courses (presented live or on videotape) and annually-revised test preparation books. Because courses and tapes can be quite expensive, most students tend to use the test preparation books. These books usually provide a mathematics and vocabulary review, tips on test taking, and a set of sample test items. Some of the more frequently used "how to prepare" books are published by Barron's Educational Series, Arco Publishing Company, and Monarch Press. They are readily available at most bookstores.

Deciding on test preparation courses versus self-preparation is an individual decision. Some students do not have the time or inclination to design a disciplined preparation study schedule and, for them, the expense of test preparation courses is worth it because they provide needed structure. An alternative strategy is to do the self-preparation for the first time you take the test, and then if you are not satisfied with your scores, you can try the more formal test preparation courses. Whether you decide on a formal course or a do-it-yourself approach, it is important to prepare for the GRE general test in some way! The stakes are rather large—whether you receive an offer to a PhD program and/or the type of financial aid you receive depend to a large degree on how well you do on the GRE tests.

As for the subject test in psychology, remember that it covers all areas of the discipline. Names, theories, and definitions are likely to be covered on the test, as are basic concepts. No one is expected to know about every area, so if you have not been exposed to certain aspects of psychology, you will no doubt have trouble with some questions. You can prepare for the subject test in psychology by thoroughly reviewing a comprehensive introductory psychology textbook. In addition, books that present the history of psychology, and/or systems and theories in psychology, provide information that is particularly useful in preparing for the psychology subject test.

Will I Need Letters of Recommendation for Graduate School Application? If So, How Many and From Whom?

Three letters of recommendation are required by the overwhelming majority of graduate programs in clinical psychology. At least two letters should be academic references—that is, from psychology faculty familiar with your academic ability. Ideally, at least one of the letters should be from a faculty member who has supervised you in research related activities. If faculty from other disciplines can provide an additional picture of your academic achievement and potential for graduate study, feel free to ask them for letters.

A letter from someone who supervised a clinically related experience or (relevant) job generally is not given much weight by admissions committees. Similarly, letters from "important people" such as senators, governors, and ministers do not help your application. Generally, these say nothing more than "I've been asked to write . . ." and "please give this student full consideration." Such letters are likely to leave the impression that you feel incapable of "making it" on your own. Unless the writer is in a position to judge the candidate's potential as a graduate student or a clinician, such "prestige" letters should not be submitted.

What Should I Know About Asking for Letters of Recommendation?

First, ask permission before you use someone's name as a reference. Many faculty will want to talk with you about your academic and career plans and objectives before agreeing to write a letter. Some will ask you to provide additional written information about yourself and may want to discuss this information with you. Be prepared to do this!

It is appropriate for you to provide faculty with information about yourself because faculty meet many students and can easily forget what each individual did in class, what role they served on the research project, and other details. Also, it is not unusual for faculty to know little about a student other than what they have observed in the laboratory or in the classroom. Information about your activities, accomplishments, and job experiences can supplement classroom contacts in a way that enhances the tone and thrust of a recommendation letter.

Here is a list of items you should provide to faculty who are writing letters of recommendation for you (see also, Morgan & Korschgen, 2001, p. 107):

1. Your full name.
2. Major, minor, curriculum, and specialization.
3. A computation of the grade average in your major, in all college work, and in courses taken since the end of your sophomore year.
4. A transcript of your college courses and grades.
5. A list of the psychology laboratory courses you have had.
6. A description of other research experiences, including comments about the full extent of your participation (include a copy of any major research papers you wrote or contributed to).
7. A list of honor societies, clubs, and organizations to which you belong, along with comments on your participation (be sure to mention positions of responsibility you held).
8. A brief discussion of jobs you have held and volunteer work you have done. Some students carry heavy work loads while being enrolled as full-time students in order to pay for their education; this information should be included, too.
9. An outline of your personal and professional plans and goals.
10. Any other information that might be helpful to the person in writing your letter of recommendation.

Be sure to ask for letters and provide all appropriate recommendation information and other materials early, at least one month before the first application is due. Remember, faculty often write letters for many students; give them plenty of time to prepare yours. To reduce the possibility of error and to speed the process, you want to minimize the work the faculty has to do in putting the recommendation material together, thereby minimizing any errors that may occur. Therefore:

1. Include a stamped, addressed envelope for each program for which a recommendation is to be sent.

2. When forms are included, be sure to type your name and other information which is not part of the formal recommendation in the appropriate spaces. Do not hand blank forms to the letter writers. Attach the appropriate envelope to each form.

3. Include a list of all the schools—and their application deadlines—to which a recommendation letter is to be sent. Indicate which schools have provided forms to be completed and which have not provided such forms. This information can then be used by the letter writer as a checklist as the letters and forms are completed.

Will I Be Able to See My Recommendation Letters?

Letters of reference are not confidential unless you waive your right to see them. We encourage you to consider doing so because many admissions committee members feel that letter writers are more likely to provide candid evaluations when they know that the student will not see them. If you are concerned about what the letter might include, ask potential letter-writers if they can write in support of your application, not just if they will write a letter of reference. Most faculty are more than willing to indicate whether they can write a favorable letter for you.

What Should I Write About in my Personal Statement?

Most applications require that you include some form of a personal statement, usually two to three pages in length. Bottoms & Nysse (APS Observer, December, 1999) offer excellent advice on writing a personal statement, and there is a list of very helpful tips in the book, *Getting in* (APA, 1997). Generally, variations on the same personal statement can be used for all of your applications, but the essay certainly should be revised to reflect how your research and clinical interests mesh with the particular faculty and program to which you are applying. Programs differ in how much weight they give to the personal statement, and what you write in the personal statement may not help your application a great deal, but it certainly can hurt your chances. Any grammatical or typographical errors can reflect negatively on your writing skills, your conscientiousness, and your attention to details. Therefore, it is absolutely imperative that you have someone else, preferably a faculty member, read your statement for coherence and writing style, as well as to discover and correct any grammatical or typographical errors.

What should go into a personal statement? Contrary to its title, it should not be too personal. In other words, it is not a mini memoir—don't bring up childhood experiences that may have shaped your life. Nor should the statement get into any personal problems that you or family members may have had, even if these experiences did influence your decision to apply to clinical psychology programs. Instead, the personal statement is your chance to convince the admissions committee that you are a good match for their graduate program. The fact that the committee is reading your personal statement means that you have already passed their initial screen and they feel your credentials are appropriate for their program. Thus, in writing your statement you need to think about what graduate programs are looking for in their applicants, and then describe how you meet these criteria. As noted earlier, graduate programs generally are looking for students who are intellectually curious, highly motivated, hard working, and have a good familiarity with the science of psychology, especially as it relates to research experience. These are the factors that you should be addressing in some fashion in your personal statement. Bottoms and Nysse (1999) note that a personal statement should cover four key components: your previous research experience, current research interests, other relevant experience, and future career goals. Included under current research interests is some brief discussion of how your interests coincide with ongoing research undertaken by the faculty at the program to which you are applying. Many programs assign accepted students to faculty for research mentoring, so it should be crystal clear how your interests can match with those of one or more of the program's faculty.

Are Personal Interviews Required?

Interviews may be part of the admissions procedure, but if so, they are likely to come only after the admissions committee has considerably narrowed the number of applicants. Interviews are usually held on the school's campus, giving the candidate and the department a chance to size each other up. If you are invited to come for an interview, try to do so regardless of the inconvenience or expense involved. If departments have to choose between two equally qualified students, only one of whom they've interviewed in person, this individual probably has the advantage. Telephone interviews are the exception rather than the rule. However, some programs do an initial screening interview on the phone to gauge the applicant's interest in and appropriateness for the program before actually inviting the candidate for an on-site interview. With this in mind, you might want to try a bit of strategy used by one successful applicant. Near his telephone at home, he kept information about each of the programs to which he had applied (e.g., faculty names, particular emphases and strengths) along with notes about his career interests and goals. He felt that if he received a call from a school to which he had applied, having this information handy would reduce his anxiety about the conversation and help him organize his responses so that his emphasis would be appropriate for each institution. This plan also assured that he would include all the points he wanted to make during a call, and thus avoid regret over failing to mention something important. He did receive a call and his strategy worked.

Though interviews are not always part of the applicant review process, once you have received a letter of acceptance it is appropriate to visit the school and talk with department representatives and graduate students about their program. It is not appropriate to show up unannounced and expect department representatives to be available.

Make an appointment well ahead of time by calling the director of clinical training and asking to meet with clinical psychology faculty and graduate students. Be prepared to outline briefly the nature of your questions and have a number of alternative dates in mind before you call.

Often, students want to schedule interview appointments before they apply to a school or before they are admitted. Some departments, especially those offering only a master's degree, welcome early interviews. However, other departments have so many applicants that it is impossible for them to accommodate such requests. Usually, the information you gather through the methods mentioned earlier—including collecting printed material from various programs—will be sufficient to help you decide whether to apply to each of them. If the written material you received is not sufficiently informative to give you a clear picture of a particular program, contact the department for additional details. (Before doing so, be sure to carefully read what you have in hand so that you do not ask about things a department has already covered in its printed material.) Once you are admitted, however, campus visits and interviews can help you to compare programs and make your "accept" or "reject" decisions.

How Do I Prepare for an On-Site Interview?

If you are invited for an interview by a program, this means that you are in their final, relatively small (e.g., 20–30) pool of applicants. Thus, you have an excellent chance of eventually receiving an offer from this program. You will want to optimize the impact of your interview, both in terms of the information you gather and the impression you make. To do so requires preparation and practice! There are several things you should do prior to your interview.

1. Gather and read as much information about the program as you can. Read and become familiar with everything the program has sent you, as well as any additional information you can get off of the website.

2. Read and become familiar with several published articles by the faculty members with whom you are most interested in working. As you read these articles make notes on topics that interest you and questions that the research raises.

3. Prepare yourself to talk at length about your own research experience. You should be able to describe the purposes of the research, the methodology, the primary results, and the lessons you have learned from this experience. It is a good strategy to prepare in advance a brief description of your research experience, and to practice presenting this brief summary. Don't assume you can just show up at the interview and spontaneously describe your research in a coherent and knowledgeable fashion.

4. Plan in advance questions that you will want to ask the faculty. The faculty will assume that you will have such questions, and if you are not prepared the interview will end early on a negative note. Try not to ask questions that can be answered by the written materials (e.g., what courses will I take in my first year?). In addition, many of the "nuts-and-bolts" issues (e.g., financial support) are handled in group information sessions. Instead, in your faculty interview you primarily will want to ask substantive questions that better inform about what it would be like

to be a graduate student in this program. Thus, appropriate topics include the faculty member's mentoring style, the strengths and weaknesses of the program, graduate student-faculty relations, and the types of internships and jobs obtained by graduates from the program.

During the visit, you will want to spend some time talking with current graduate students in the program. Some programs offer to have their graduate students provide housing for you during the visit. It is a good strategy to take them up on this offer. It is an excellent opportunity for you to spend further timing asking the graduate students about the program. You may want to ask them many of the same questions that you ask the faculty, especially those dealing with mentoring, student-faculty relations, and strengths and weaknesses of the program. A word of caution, however—it is very likely that the graduate students will offer feedback to the faculty regarding the applicants they have met. Therefore, don't let your guard down too much and say things that contradict what you told the faculty. Further, if the students should happen to take you out on the town after the interview be very careful about the amount of alcohol you may consume. Most faculty can recount instances in which an applicant's chances for admission were ruined by things said late at night to the graduate students.

During the interview you will want to come across as poised, mature, motivated, thoughtful, and interpersonally skilled. Remember that clinical programs not only have to evaluate you in terms of your potential as a graduate student but also as someone whom the faculty feel comfortable sending out into clinical settings. Obviously, applicants will differ in the degree to which they possess the aforementioned attributes. Nevertheless, there are at least two things you can do to maximize the positive impact you make during the interview, and these are summarized by the terms "preparation" and "practice." In terms of preparation, make notes on everything of importance that you learn about a program, the articles you have read, the questions you want to ask, and anything else you can think of. The interview process can be quite stressful and our memory can fail us at inopportune times. Thus, for example, it is a good strategy to review your notes about a faculty member's research just before entering the interview. In terms of practice, a good strategy is to do one or more role-play interviews prior to going on the visit. This can be with a roommate or, better yet, with a faculty member. Make the interview as realistic as possible. Dress appropriately, shake the person's hand, introduce yourself, and in all ways interact as if the interview were the real thing. If you can arrange to videotape the interview, all the better. Look at the videotape, get feedback from the interviewer, and consider doing another role-play interview, attempting to correct the problem areas. Given the importance of the interview in the final selection process, you want to do everything you can to ensure that you present yourself in the best possible light.

Are My College Transcripts Required?

Most programs will ask for a transcript of courses and grades from each institution at which you have studied after high school. Notations of transfer credit summarized on the transcript from the last school you attended is not usually accepted—separate transcripts are required from each school. Call all the schools you have attended, find out how much they charge to send transcripts, and then send a letter to the director of student records at each school, enclosing a list of institutions to which a copy of your transcript is to be sent. Include a check to cover the cost.

FINANCIAL AID

What Kind of Financial Aid is Available for Graduate Study?

Most PhD programs in clinical psychology offer some form of financial aid to the students accepted into their program. PsyD- and MA-level programs are much less likely to do so. Financial aid comes in several forms: loans, fellowships, tuition remission, and work programs. The major source of financial aid for graduate students is the university in which they are enrolled, though aid may also be available through guaranteed loan programs (many of which are government sponsored) and national awards which are competitive and have specific criteria for application. These awards are given directly to students for use at the school of their choice.

The availability of awards and loans changes regularly, so you should check with the financial aid officer at your college or at the institutions to which you are applying for current information. Because your financial support is most likely to come through the program to which you are admitted, the aid information you will receive with your application material is very important—read it carefully!

Loan programs exist on most campuses as a way of assisting students to invest in their own futures. These loans usually carry a low interest rate, and repayment begins only after the student leaves graduate school.

Fellowships and scholarships are given on many campuses as outright grants to support and encourage students with outstanding academic and research potential. These are few in number and competition for them is fierce.

Assistantships come in two forms: research assistantships and teaching assistantships. As their names imply, both entail working at jobs that require the graduate student to assist faculty in research projects or in teaching responsibilities (e.g., as a discussion leader, laboratory instructor, or paper grader). Assistantships usually require ten to twenty hours of work each week.

Some graduate programs receive grants from the federal government to provide *traineeships* in clinical psychology. As a result, there may be training grant funds available for a limited number of students at some institutions. Like fellowships, these are usually outright gifts, but they require that you carry a full academic load. They, too, are few in number and there is keen competition for them.

Finally, many programs offer some form of tuition remission. They may offer complete remission, meaning that the student pays no tuition at all, or they offer some portion of remission (e.g., 50%). Alternatively, the program may waive the out-of-state tuition and only require that the student pay in-state tuition, even if the student is coming from out-of-state.

Not all types of aid are offered at all schools. Again, carefully read the financial aid information you receive to be sure you understand what is potentially available at each school you are considering. Further, tuition costs differ dramatically across schools. If the program does not guarantee tuition remission to its students, then you need to factor the university's tuition costs into the equation when deciding to which schools to apply.

Are There Assistantships Available From Departments Other Than the One to Which I Have Applied?

Assistantships of various types may be available on a campus. If you are accepted to a clinical psychology program that offers little or no financial aid, it is well worth your time to check on the availability of assistantships in departments outside psychology. For example, administrators of campus residence halls may hire graduate students to serve as hall counselors. Further, departments offering large undergraduate courses may not have enough graduate students in their programs to fill the teaching assistant-ships available and thus may "import" assistants from related areas. Identify your skills and experiences and seek out jobs that fit them.

Do All Financial Aid Packages Involve About the Same Amount of Money?

Financial aid will vary from campus to campus, among departments on the same cam-pus, and even among students in the same program. For example, one school may give more money than others, but also require graduate students to pay their own tuition. Others will give a smaller sum of money, but pay tuition and fees. Some residence hall assistantships provide room and board only, while others provide room, board, tuition, and fees. If financial aid is an important factor in your selection of a graduate program, be sure you know both the amount you will receive and the costs you will incur before you make a final decision to accept or reject an offer of admission.

Are Separate References Required When Applying for Financial Aid?

Sometimes, separate application deadlines and reference letters are involved in the process of seeking financial aid. Usually, any required letters of recommendation are simply copies of those used by departments in the admission process. Still, read your application material carefully to determine exactly what is required in order to apply for financial aid, and remember that deadlines for financial aid applications are some-times earlier than deadlines for applying to clinical psychology graduate programs.

OTHER IMPORTANT QUESTIONS

Are There Any Last-Minute Things I Need to Do When Applying?

Once you have sent in your applications, check with each department to which you have applied to assure that your application has been received and is complete. Each year, some applications are not considered because students were unaware that their applications were incomplete. Some departments notify students when letters of reference or GRE scores are missing, but many do not. To eliminate this potential problem, be sure to enclose with each application a stamped, self-addressed envelope or postcard for the department to use to verify that your application is complete.

When I Am Admitted to a Program, How Long Will I Have to Make a Decision About Whether to Accept?

Most admissions offers are made with a specific deadline for accepting or rejecting them. For doctoral programs, this is usually April 15 and is tied to financial aid offers. This date was adopted by the Council of Graduate Departments of Psychology to protect students from being pressured to make decisions before having full information about their alternatives. The Council's statement reads as follows:

> Acceptance of an offer of financial aid (such as graduate scholarship, fellowship, traineeship, or assistantship) for the next academic year by an actual or prospective graduate student completes an agreement which both student and graduate school expect to honor. In those instances in which the student accepts the offer before April 15 and subsequently desires to withdraw, the student may submit in writing a resignation of the appointment at any time through April 15. However, an acceptance given or left in force after April 15 commits the student not to accept another offer without first obtaining a written release from the institution to which a commitment has been made. Similarly, an offer by an institution after April 15 is conditional on presentation by the student of the written release from any previously accepted offer. It is further agreed by the institutions and organizations subscribing to the above Resolution that a copy of the Resolution should accompany every scholarship, fellowship, traineeship, and assistantship offer. (APA, 1996, p. viii)

However, this resolution was subsequently modified by the Council of Graduate Departments of Psychology to read:

> An acceptance given or left in force after April 15 commits the student not to solicit or accept another offer. Offers made after April 15 must include the proviso that the offer is void if acceptance of a previous offer from a department accepting this resolution is in force on that date. These rules are binding on all persons acting on the behalf of the offering institution. (APA, 1996, p. viii)

Most recently, the following motion was passed:

> That the currently prevailing procedures dealing with the offering and acceptance of financial aid are intended to cover graduate admissions as well as offers of financial aid. To protect candidates against the need to make premature decisions, graduate programs should allow applicants until April 15 to make final decisions. (APA, 1996, p. viii)

Still, if you have decided not to accept an offer, courtesy dictates that you inform the department of your decision as soon as possible. This will be appreciated by the department and may provide space for another student. If you do not receive an acceptance letter in April, you may receive one later because space does become available as accepted students decline offers.

Will I Be Successful in Gaining Admission?

Obviously, we can't answer this question with certainty, but we hope the information and suggestions presented here are helpful to you. A careful examination of your own credentials and the advice of those who have experience with students applying to graduate school in clinical psychology will help you apply to appropriate programs, and to maximize your chances of admission. We wish you success!

References

Abdel, K. A. M. (1994). Normative results on the Arabic Fear Survey Schedule III. *Journal of Behavior Therapy and Experimental Psychiatry, 25,* 61-67.

Abikoff, H. (1985). Efficacy of cognitive training interventions in hyperactive children: A critical review. *Clinical Psychology Review, 5,* 479-512.

Abikoff, H., & Gittelman, R. (1985). Hyperactive children maintained on stimulants: Is cognitive training a useful adjunct? *Archives of General Psychiatry, 42,* 953-961.

Ables, B. S., & Brandsma, J. M. (1977). *Therapy for couples.* San Francisco: Jossey-Bass.

Abood, L. G. (1960). A chemical approach to the problem of mental illness. In D. D. Jackson (Ed.), *The etiology of schizophrenia* (pp. 91-119). New York: Basic Books.

Abramowitz, J. S. (1996). Variants of exposure and response prevention in the treatment of obsessive-compulsive disorder: A meta-analysis. *Behavior Therapy, 27,* 583-600.

Abramson, L. Y., Seligman, M. E. P., & Teasdale, J. D. (1978). Learned helplessness in humans: Critique and reformulation. *Journal of Abnormal Psychology, 87,* 49-74.

Accredited doctoral programs in professional psychology: 2000. *American Psychologist, 55,* 1473-1488. (No authorship indicated)

Achenbach, T. M. (1978). The Child Behavior Profile: I. Boys aged 6-11. *Journal of Consulting and Clinical Psychology, 46,* 478-488.

Achenbach, T. M. (1982). *Developmental psychopathology* (2nd ed.). New York: John Wiley.

Achenbach, T. M. (1985). *Assessment and taxonomy of child and adolescent psychopathology.* Newbury Park, CA: Sage.

Achenbach, T. M. (1991). *Manual for the Child Behavior Checklist/4-18 and 1991 profile.* Burlington, VT: University of Vermont.

Achenbach, T. M. (1994). Child behavior checklist and related instruments. In M. E. Maruish (Ed.), *The use of psychological testing for treatment planning and outcome assessment.* Hillsdale, NJ: Erlbaum.

Achenbach, T. M. (1997). What is normal? What is abnormal? Developmental perspectives on behavioral and emotional problems. In S. S. Luthar, J. A. Burack, D. Cicchetti, & J. R. Weisz (Eds.), *Developmental psychopathology: Perspective on adjustment, risk, and disorder* (pp. 93-114). New York: Cambridge University Press.

Achenbach, T. M., & Edelbrock, C. S. (1978). The classification of child psychopathology: A review and analysis of empirical efforts. *Psychological Bulletin, 85,* 1275-1301.

Achenbach, T. M., & Edelbrock, C. S. (1979). The child behavior profile II: Boys aged 12-16 and girls aged 6-11. *Journal of Consulting and Clinical Psychology, 47,* 223-233.

Achenbach, T. M., & Edelbrock, C. S. (1981). Behavioral problems and competencies reported by parents of normal and disturbed children aged four to sixteen. *Monographs of the Society for Research in Child Development, 46,* Serial No. 188.

Achenbach, T. M., & Edelbrock, C. S. (1991). *Manual for the Childhood Behavior Checklist and Revised Child Behavior Profile.* Burlington, VT: University of Vermont Press.

Achenbach, T. M, McConaughy, S. H., & Howell, C. T. (1987). Child/adolescent behavioral and emotional problems: Implications of cross-informant correlations for situational specificity. *Psychological Bulletin, 101,* 213-232.

Ackerman, M. J., & Ackerman, M. (1997). Custody evaluation practices: A survey of experienced professionals (revisited). *Professional Psychology: Research and Practice, 28,* 137-145.

Ackerman, N. W. (1958). *The psychodynamics of family life.* New York: Basic Books.

Addis, M. E., & Carpenter, K. M. (2000). The treatment rationale in cognitive behavioral therapy: Psychological mechanisms and clinical guidelines. *Cognitive and Behavioral Practice, 7,* 147-156.

Addis, M. E., & Krasnow, A. D. (2000). A national survey of practicing psychologists' attitudes toward psychotherapy treatment manuals. *Journal of Consulting and Clinical Psychology, 68,* 331-339.

Adler, A. (1933). *Social interest: A challenge to mankind.* Vienna, Leipzig: Rolf Passer.

Adler, N. E., Boyce, T., Chesney, M. A., Cohen, S., Folkman, S., Kahn, R. L., & Syme, S. L. (1994). Socioeconomic status and health: The challenge of the gradient. *American Psychologist, 49,* 15-24.

Adler, N. E., & Matthews, K. (1994). Health psychology: Why do some people get sick and some stay well. *Annual Review of Psychology, 45,* 229-259.

Ahn, H., & Wampold, B. E. (2001). Where oh where are the specific ingredients? A meta-analysis of component studies in counseling and psychotherapy. *Journal of Counseling Psychology, 48,* 251-257.

Ainsworth, M. D. S., & Wittig, B. A. (1969). Attachment and the exploratory behavior of one-year-olds in a strange situation. In B. M. Foss (Ed.), *Determinants of infant behavior* (Vol. 4, pp. 113-136). London: Methuen.

Albee, G. W. (1959). *Mental health manpower trends.* New York: Basic Books.

Albee, G. W. (1996). Revolutions and counterrevolutions in prevention. *American Psychologist, 51,* 1130-1133.

Albee, G. W. (2000). The Boulder Model's fatal flaw. *American Psychologist, 55,* 247-248.

Alberti, R. E., & Emmons, M. L. (1974). *Your perfect right: A guide to assertive behavior.* San Luis Obispo, CA: Impact.

Alexander, F. M., & French, T. M. (1946). *Psychoanalytic therapy*. New York: Ronald Press.

Alexander, J. F., Holtzworth-Munroe, A., & Jameson, P. B. (1994). The process and outcome of marital and family therapy: Research review and evaluation. In A. E. Bergin & S. L. Garfield (Eds.), *Handbook of psychotherapy and behavior change* (pp. 595–630). New York: John Wiley and Sons.

Alexander, J. F., & Parsons, B. V. (1973). Short-term behavioral intervention with delinquent families: Impact on family process and recidivism. *Journal of Abnormal Psychology, 81*, 219–225.

Allen, G. J. (1971). The effectiveness of study counseling and desensitization in alleviating test anxiety in college students. *Journal of Abnormal Psychology, 77*, 282–289.

Alliger, G. M., Lillienfeld, S. O., & Mitchell, K. E. (1996). The susceptibility of overt and covert integrity tests to coaching and faking. *Psychological Science, 7*, 32–39.

Allport, G. W., Vernon, C. E., & Lindzey, G. (1970). *Study of values* (rev. manual). Boston: Houghton-Mifflin.

American Association of Marriage and Family Therapy. (2001). *Who are marriage and family therapists?* Retrieved September 7, 2001 from http://www.aamft.org/faqs/whoare.htm.

American Medical Association. (1954). Report of committee on mental health. *Journal of the American Medical Association, 156*, 72.

American Psychiatric Association. (1952). *Diagnostic and statistical manual of mental disorders*. Washington, DC: Author.

American Psychiatric Association. (1968). *Diagnostic and statistical manual of mental disorders* (2nd ed.). Washington, DC: Author.

American Psychiatric Association. (1980). *Diagnostic and statistical manual of mental disorders* (3rd ed.). Washington, DC: Author.

American Psychiatric Association. (1983). *Statement on prediction of dangerousness*. Washington, D.C.: American Psychiatric Association.

American Psychiatric Association. (1987). *Diagnostic and statistical manual of mental disorders* (3rd ed.-Revised). Washington, DC: Author.

American Psychiatric Association. (1994). *Diagnostic and statistical manual of mental disorders* (4th ed.). Washington, DC: American Psychiatric Association.

American Psychiatric Association. (1995). Practice guideline for the treatment of patients with substance abuse disorders: Alcohol, cocaine, opioids. *American Journal of Psychiatry, 152* (Suppl. 11), 5–59.

American Psychiatric Association. (2000). *Diagnostic and statistical manual of mental disorders, text revision* (4th ed.). Washington, DC: Author.

American Psychological Association. (1947). Recommended graduate training programs in clinical psychology. *American Psychologist, 2*, 539–558.

American Psychological Association. (1953). *Ethical standards of psychologists*. Washington, DC: Author.

American Psychological Association. (1958). Committee on Relations with Psychiatry, Annual Report. *American Psychologist, 13*, 761–763.

American Psychological Association. (1959). Ethical standards of psychologists. *American Psychologist, 14*, 279–282.

American Psychological Association. (1963). Ethical standards of psychologists. *American Psychologist, 18*, 56–60.

American Psychological Association. (1967). *Casebook on ethical standards of psychologists.* Washington, DC: Author.

American Psychological Association. (1981). *Specialty guidelines for the delivery of services by clinical psychologists.* Washington, DC: Author.

American Psychological Association. (1982). *Ethical principles in the conduct of research with human subjects.* Washington, DC: Author.

American Psychological Association. (1985). *Standards for educational and psychological tests.* Washington, DC: Author.

American Psychological Association. (1986). *Guidelines for computer-based tests and interpretations.* Washington, DC: Author.

American Psychological Association. (1987a). *Casebook on ethical standards of Psychologists.* (Rev. ed.). Washington, DC: Author.

American Psychological Association. (1987b). *General Guidelines for Providers of Psychological Services.* Washington, DC: Author.

American Psychological Association. (1987c). General guidelines for providers of psychological services. *American Psychologist, 42,* 712–723.

American Psychological Association. (1992a). Ethical principles of psychologists and code of conduct. *American Psychologist, 47,* 1597–1611.

American Psychological Association. (1992b). *Guidelines for ethical conduct in the care and use of animals.* Washington, DC: Author.

American Psychological Association. (1993). Guidelines for providers of psychological services to ethnic, linguistic, and culturally diverse populations. *American Psychologist, 48,* 45–48.

American Psychological Association. (1994). *Publication manual of the American Psychological Association* (4th ed.). Washington, DC: Author.

American Psychological Association. (1995a). *Report of the task force on the changing gender composition of psychology.* Washington, DC: Author.

American Psychological Association. (1995b). *1993 directory survey, with new member updates for 1994 and 1995.* Washington, DC: APA Research Office.

American Psychological Association. (1996). *Guidelines and principles for accreditation of programs in professional psychology/Accreditation operating procedures.* Washington, DC: Author.

American Psychological Association. (1997). *Getting in: A step-by-step plan for gaining admission to graduate school in psychology.* Washington, DC: American Psychological Association.

American Psychological Association. (1998a). *Guidelines for the Evaluation of Dementia and Age-Related Cognitive Decline.* American Psychological Association.

American Psychological Association. (1998b). *Guidelines for Psychological Evaluations in Child Protection Matters.* American Psychological Association.

American Psychological Association. (2000a). *Guidelines for Psychotherapy with Lesbian, Gay, & Bisexual Clients.* Washington, DC: American Psychological Association.

American Psychological Association. (2000b). Table 3: *Current major field of APA members by membership status, 2000.* Retrieved December 13, 2001 from http://research.apa.org/member.

American Psychological Association. (2000c). *Criteria for Evaluating Treatment Guidelines.* Washington, DC: American Psychological Association.

American Psychological Association. (2001). *Publication manual of the American Psychological Association* (5th ed.). Washington, DC: American Psychological Association.

American Psychological Association Board of Professional Affairs Task Force. (1995). *Template for developing guidelines: Interventions for mental disorders and psychosocial aspects of physical disorders*. Washington, DC: American Psychological Association.

American Psychological Association Division of Neuropsychology. (1989). Definition of a neuropsychologist. *The Clinical Neuropsychologist, 3,* 22.

American Psychological Association Ethics Committee. (1992). Ethical principles of psychologists and code of conduct. *American Psychologist, 47,* 1597–1611.

American Psychological Association Office of Program Consultation and Accreditation and Education Directorates. (1996). *Guidelines and principles for accreditation of programs in professional psychology.* Washington, DC: Author.

American Psychological Association Public Interest Directorate. (2001). Guidelines for Psychotherapy with Lesbian, Gay, and Bisexual Clients. Retrieved December 13, 2001 from http://www.apa.org/pi/lgbc/guideline.html.

American Psychological Society. (1996). A new alliance of doctoral training programs form. *APS Observer, 9,* pp. 22, 37, 39, 44.

American Psychologist. (2000). Accredited doctoral programs in professional psychology. *American Psychologist, 55,* 1473–1488. (No authorship indicated)

Amundson, M. E., Hart, C. A., & Holmes, T. H. (1986). *Manual for the schedule of recent experience.* Seattle: University of Washington Press.

Anastasi, A. (1988). *Psychological testing* (6th ed.). New York: Macmillan.

Anastasi, A. (1992). What counselors should know about the use and interpretation of psychological tests. *Journal of Counseling and Development, 70,* 610–615.

Anastasi, A., & Urbina, S. (1997). *Psychological testing.* (7th ed.) Upper Saddle River, NJ: Prentice Hall.

Anchin, J. C., & Kiesler, D. J. (Eds.). (1982). *Handbook of interpersonal psychotherapy.* New York: Pergamon Press.

Andersen, B. L. (1992). Psychological interventions for cancer patients to enhance the quality of life. *Journal of Consulting & Clinical Psychology, 60,* 552–568.

Anderson, N. B. (1989). Racial differences in stress-reduced cardiovascular reactivity and hypertension: Current status and substantive issues. *Psychological Bulletin, 105,* 89–105.

Andreasen, N. C. (1997). Linking mind and brain in the study of mental illnesses: A project for a scientific psychopathology. *Science, 275,* 1586–1593.

Andreasen, N. C., Arndt, S., Swayze II, V., Cizadlo, T., Flaum, M., O'Leary, D., Ehrhandt, J. C., & Yuh, W. T. C. (1994). Thalamic abnormalities in schizophrenia visualized through magnetic resonance image averaging. *Science, 266,* 294–298.

Andreasen, N., Nasrullah, H., Dunn, V., Olson, S., Grove, W., Erhardt, J, Coffman, J., & Crosett, J. (1986). Structural abnormalities in the frontal system in schizophrenia. *Archives of General Psychiatry, 43,* 136–144.

Andrews, G., & Harvey, R. (1981). Does psychotherapy benefit neurotic patients? A re-analysis of the Smith, Glass, and Miller data. *Archives of General Psychiatry, 38,* 1203–1208.

Andrews, J. D. W. (1989). Integrating visions of reality: Interpersonal diagnosis and the existential vision. *American Psychologist, 44,* 803–817.

Anson, D. A., Golding, S. L., & Gully, K. J. (1993). Child sexual abuse allegations: Reliability of criteria-based content analysis. *Law and Human Behavior, 17,* 331–341.

Antoni, M. H., Baggett, L., Ironoson, G., Laperriere, A., August, S., Klimas, N., Schneiderman, N., & Fletcher, M. A. (1991). Cognitive-behavioral stress management intervention buffers distress responses and immunologic changes following notification of HIV-1 seropositivity. *Journal of Consulting and Clinical Psychology, 59,* 906-915.

Antonuccio, D. O., Danton, W. G., & DeNelsky, G. Y. (1995). Psychotherapy vs. medication for depression: Challenging the conventional wisdom with data. *Professional Psychology: Research and Practice, 26,* 574-585.

Appelbaum, P. S. (1994). *Almost a revolution: Mental health law and the limits of change.* New York: Oxford University Press.

Appelbaum, P. S., & Grisso, T. (1995). The MacArthur Treatment Competence Study. I: Mental illness and competence to consent to treatment. *Law and Human Behavior, 19,* 105-126.

Appelbaum, P. S., & Hoge, S. K. (1986). The right to refuse treatment: What the research reveals. *Behavioral Services and the Law, 4,* 279-292.

Archer, R. P., Maruish, M., Imhof, E. A., & Piotrowski, C. (1991). Psychological test usage with adolescent clients: 1990 survey findings. *Professional Psychology: Research and Practice, 22,* 247-252.

Arkes, H. A. (1981). Impediments to accurate clinical judgment and possible ways to minimize their impact. *Journal of Consulting and Clinical Psychology, 49,* 323-330.

Arnold, C. (1998). Children and families: A snapshot. Retrieved December 12, 2001 from http://www.clasp.org/pubs/familyformation/stepfamiliesfinal.BK!.htm.

Asarnow, R. F., Nuechterlein, K. H., Fogelson, D., Subotnik, K. L., Payne, D. A., Russell, A. T., Asamen, J., Kuppinger, H., Kendler, K. S. (2001). Schizophrenia and schizophrenia-spectrum personality disorders in the first-degree relatives of children with schizophrenia: The UCLA family study. *Archives of General Psychiatry, 58,* 581-588.

Asher, S. R., & Wheeler, V. A. (1985). Children's loneliness: A comparison of rejected and neglected peer status. *Journal of Consulting and Clinical Psychology, 53,* 500-505.

Associated Press. (2001, December 5). Guard sues Marilyn Manson. Retrieved December 7, 2001 from http://news.findlaw.com/ap/e/1403/12-5-2001.

Association of State and Provincial Psychology Boards. (2001). Licensure requirements in general. Retrieved December 21, 2001 from http://www.asppb.org/reqs.htm.

Atkins, D. C., & Christensen, A. (2001). Is professional training worth the bother? A review of the impact of psychotherapy training on client outcome. *Australian Psychologist, 36,* 122-131.

Atkinson, D. R., Brown, M. T., Parham, T. A., Matthews, L. G., Landrum-Brown, J., & Kim, A. U. (1996). African American client skin tone and clinical judgments of African American and European American psychologists. *Professional Psychology: Research and Practice, 27,* 500-505.

Atkinson, J. W. (1981). Studying personality in the context of an advanced motivational psychology. *American Psychologist, 36,* 117-128.

Auld, F., Jr., & Murray, E. J. (1955). Content-analysis studies of psychotherapy. *Psychological Bulletin, 52,* 377-395.

Austed, C. S., & Berman, W. H. (1991). Managed health care and the evolution of psychotherapy. In C. S. Austed & W. H. Berman (Eds.), *Psychotherapy in managed health care: The optimal use of time and resources* (pp. 3-18). Washington, DC: American Psychological Association.

Axin, W. G. (1991). The influence of interviewer sex on responses to sensitive questions in Nepal. *Social Science Research, 20,* 303-318.

Axline, V. M. (1976). Play therapy procedures and results. In C. Schaefer (Ed.), *The therapeutic use of child's play*. New York: Jason Aronson.

Ayllon, T., & Azrin, N. H. (1965). The measurement and reinforcement of behavior of psychotics. *Journal of the Experimental Analysis of Behavior, 8*, 357-383.

Azar, B. (1996, December). Behavioral interventions are proven to reduce pain. *APA Monitor*, 22.

Azar, S. T., & Benjet, C. L. (1994). A cognitive perspective on ethnicity, race, and termination of parental rights. *Law and Human Behavior, 18*, 249-267.

Azrin, N. H., & Peterson, A. L. (1989). Reduction of an eye tic by controlled blinking. *Behavior Therapy, 20*, 467-473.

Baare, W. F. C., van Oel, C. J., Hushoff, H. E., Schnack, H. G., Durston, S., Sitskoorn, M. M., & Kahn, R. S. (2001). Volumes of brain structures in twins discordant for schizophrenia. *Archives of General Psychiatry, 58*, 33-40.

Babiker, G. (1993). Projective testing in the evaluation of the effects of sexual abuse in childhood: A review. *British Journal of Projective Psychology, 38*, 45-53.

Babyak, M., Blumenthal, J. A., Herman, S., Khatri, P., Doraiswamy, M., & Moore, M., et al. (2000). Exercise treatment for major depression: Maintenance of therapeutic benefit at 10 months. *Psychosomatic Medicine, 62*, 633-638.

Backer, T. E., & Richardson, D. (1989). Building bridges: Psychologists and families of the mentally ill. *American Psychologist, 44*, 546-550.

Baekeland, F., & Lundwall, L. (1975). Dropping out of treatment: A critical review. *Psychological Bulletin, 82*, 738-783.

Baer, D. M. (1973). The control of development process: Why not? In J. R. Nesselroade & H. W. Reese (Eds.), *Life-span developmental psychology*. New York: Academic Press.

Baer, R., & Nietzel, M. T. (1991). Cognitive and behavioral treatment of impulsivity in children: A meta-analytic review of the outcome literature. *Journal of Clinical Child Psychology, 20*, 400-412.

Baerger, D. R. (2001). Risk management with the suicidal patient: Lessons from case law. *Professional Psychology: Research and Practice, 32*, 359-366.

Bandura, A. (1969). *Principles of behavior modification*. New York: Holt, Rinehart & Winston.

Bandura, A. (1978). The self system in reciprocal determinism. *American Psychologist, 33*, 344-358.

Bandura, A. (1982). Self-efficacy mechanism in human agency. *American Psychologist, 33*, 122-147.

Bandura, A. (1986). *Social foundations of thought and action: A social cognitive therapy*. Englewood Cliffs, NJ: Prentice Hall.

Bandura, A. (2001). Social cognitive theory: An agentic approach. *Annual Review of Psychology, 52*, 1-26.

Bandura, A., Ross, D., & Ross, S. A. (1963). Imitation of film-mediated aggressive models. *Journal of Abnormal and Social Psychology, 66*, 3-11.

Banich, M. T. (1997). *Neuropsychology: The neural bases of mental function*. Boston: Houghton Mifflin.

Barkham, M., Rees, A., Stiles, W. B., Shapiro, D. A., Hardy, G. E., & Reynolds, S. (1996a). Dose-effect relations in time-limited psychotherapy for depression. *Journal of Clinical and Consulting Psychology, 64*, 927-935.

Barkham, M., Rees, A., Shapiro, D. A., Stiles, W. B., Agnew, R. M., Halstead, J., Culverwell, A., & Harrington, V. M. G. (1996b). Outcomes of time-limited psychotherapy in applied settings: Replicating the second Sheffield psychotherapy project. *Journal of Clinical and Consulting Psychology, 64,* 1079–1085.

Barkley, R. A. (1998). *Attention deficit-hyperactivity disorder.* New York: Guilford.

Barkley, R. A., & Cunningham, C. E. (1979). The effects of Ritalin on the mother-child interaction of hyperactive children. *Archives of General Psychiatry, 36,* 201–208.

Barlow, D. H. (1996). Health care policy, psychotherapy research, and the future of psychotherapy. *American Psychologist, 51,* 1050–1058.

Barlow, D. H., & Hersen, M. (1984). *Single-case experimental designs: Strategies for studying behavior* (2nd ed.). New York: Pergamon Press.

Barlow, D. H., & Waddell, M. T. (1985). Agoraphobia. In D. H. Barlow (Ed.), *Clinical handbook of psychological disorders* (pp. 1–68). New York: Guilford Press.

Barlow, D. H., & Wolfe, B. (1981). Behavioral approaches to anxiety disorders: A report on the NIMH-SUNY, Albany, research conference. *Journal of Consulting and Clinical Psychology, 49,* 448–454.

Barlow, S. H., Burlingame, G. M., Nebeker, R. S., & Anderson, E. (2000). Meta-analysis of medical self-help groups. *International Journal of Group Psychotherapy, 50,* 53–69.

Barr, C., Mednick, S., & Munk-Jorgensen, P. (1990). Exposure to influenza epidemics during gestations and adult schizophrenia: A 40-year study. *Archives of General Psychiatry, 47,* 869–874.

Barrett, G. V., & Depinet, R. L. (1991). A reconsideration of testing for competence rather than for intelligence. *American Psychologist, 46,* 1012–1024.

Barrett, M. S., & Berman, J. S. (2001). Is psychotherapy more effective when therapists disclose information about themselves? *Journal of Consulting and Clinical Psychology, 69,* 597–603.

Barrick, M. R., & Mount, M. K. (1996). Effects of impression management and self-deception on the predictive validity of personality constructs. *Journal of Applied Psychology, 81,* 261–272.

Barrios, B. A., & O'Dell, S. L. (1998). Fears and anxieties. In E. J. Mash & R. A. Barkley (Eds.), *Treatment of childhood disorders* (2nd ed., pp. 249–337). New York: Guilford.

Barron, J. W. (Ed.). (1998). *Making diagnosis meaningful: Enhancing evaluation and treatment of psychological disorders.* Washington, DC: American Psychological Association.

Barthell, C. N., & Holmes, D. S. (1968). High school yearbooks: A nonreactive measure of social isolation in graduates who later became schizophrenic. *Journal of Abnormal Psychology, 73,* 313–316.

Bartlett, C. J., & Green, C. G. (1966). Clinical prediction: Does one sometimes know too much? *Journal of Counseling Psychology, 13,* 267–270.

Bartol, C. (1996). Police psychology: Then, now, and beyond. *Criminal Justice and Behavior, 23,* 70–89.

Bartol, C. R., & Bartol, A. M. (1994). *Psychology and law: Research and application.* Pacific Grove, CA: Brooks/Cole.

Barton, A. (1974). *Three worlds of therapy: An existential-phenomenological study of the therapies of Freud, Jung, and Rogers.* Palo Alto, CA: National Press Books.

Barton, R. (1999). Psychosocial rehabilitation services in community support systems: A review of outcomes and policy recommendations. *Psychiatric Services, 50,* 525–534.

Basic Behavioral Science Task Force of the National Advisory Mental Health Council. (1996). Basic behavioral science research for mental health. *American Psychologist, 51,* 722–731.

Bateson, C., Jackson, D. D., Haley, J., & Weakland, J. H. (1956). Toward a theory of schizophrenia. *Behavioral Science, 1,* 251-264.

Baucom, D. H., Epstein, N., Sayers, S., & Sher, T. G. (1989). The role of cognitions in marital relationships: Definitional, methodological, and conceptual issues. *Journal of Consulting and Clinical Psychology, 57,* 31-38.

Baum, A. & Posluszny, D. M. (1999). Health psychology: Mapping biobehavioral contributions to health and illness. *Annual Review of Psychology, 50,* 137-163.

Baum, A., Reveson, T. A., & Singer, J. E. (Eds.). (2001). *Handbook of health psychology.* Hillsdale, NJ: Erlbaum.

Baum, C. G., Forehand, R., & Zeigob, L. E. (1979). A review of observer reactivity in adult-child interactions. *Journal of Behavioral Assessment, 1,* 167-178.

Bauman, L. J., Stein, R. E. K., & Ireys, H. T. (1991). Reinventing fidelity: The transfer of social technology among settings. *American Journal of Community Psychology, 19,* 619-640.

Baumeister, R. F., & Leary, M. R. (1995). The need to belong: Desire for interpersonal attachments as a fundamental human motivation. *Psychological Bulletin, 117,* 497-529.

Bayley, N. (1965). Comparisons of mental and motor test scores for ages 1-15 months by sex, birth order, race, geographic location, and education of parents. *Child Development, 36,* 379-411.

Bayne, R. (1995). *The Meyers-Briggs type indicator: A critical review and practical guide.* New York: Chapman & Hall.

Bazelon, D. (1974). Psychiatrists and the adversary process. *Scientific American, 230,* 18-23.

Bear, D. M., & Fedio, P. (1977). Quantitative analysis of interictal behavior in temporal lobe epilepsy. *Archives of Neurology, 34,* 454-467.

Beck, A. T. (1976). *Cognitive therapy and the emotional disorders.* New York: International Universities Press.

Beck, A. T., Freeman, A., & Associates (1990). *Cognitive therapy of personality disorders.* New York: Guilford Press.

Beck, A. T., Rush, A. J., Shaw, B. F., & Emery, G. (1979). *Cognitive therapy of depression.* New York: Guilford Press.

Beck, A. T., Ward, C. H., Mendelson, M., Mock, J., & Erbaugh, J. (1961). An inventory for measuring depression. *Archives of General Psychiatry, 4,* 561-571.

Beck, A. T., & Weishaar, M. E. (1995). Cognitive therapy. In R. J. Corsini & D. Wedding (Eds.), *Current psychotherapies* (5th ed., pp. 229-261). Itasca, Illinois: Peacock Publishers, Inc.

Becker, M. H., & Maiman, L. A. (1975). Sociobehavioral determinants of compliance with health and medical care recommendations. *Medical Care, 13,* 10-24.

Bednar, R. L., & Kaul, T. (1994). Experiential group research. In A. E. Bergin & S. L. Garfield (Eds.), *Handbook of psychotherapy and behavior change* (pp. 631-663). New York: Wiley & Sons.

Behnke, S. (2001). Ethics matters: A prize for graduate students. *Monitor on Psychology, 32,* Online version retrieved December 23, 2001 from http://www.apa.org/monitor/nov01/ethics.html.

Beitchman, J. H., Brownlie, E. B., Inglis, A., Wild, J., Mathews, R., Schachter, D., Kroll, R., Martin, S., Ferguson, B., & Lancee, W. (1994). Seven-year follow-up of speech/language-impaired and control chldren: Speech/language stability and outcome. *Journal of the American Academy of Child and Adolescent Psychiatry, 33,* 1322-1330.

Belar, C. D. (1995). Collaboration in capitated care: Challenges for psychology. *Professional Psychology: Research and Practice, 26,* 139–146.

Belar, C. D. (2000). Scientist-practitioner =/= science + practice: Boulder is bolder. *American Psychologist, 55,* 249–250.

Belar, C. D., Bieliauskas, L. A., Larsen, K. G., Mensh, I. N., Poey, K., & Roelke, H. J. (1989). The national conference on internship training in psychology. *American Psychologist, 44,* 60–65.

Belar, C. D., & Perry, N. W. (Eds.). (1991). *Proceedings: National conference on scientist-practitioner education and training for the professional practice of psychology.* Sarasota, FL: Professional Resource Press.

Belar, C. D., & Perry, N. W. (1992). National conference on scientist-practitioner education and training for the professional practice of psychology. *American Psychologist, 47,* 71–75.

Bell, P. F., Digman, R. H., & McKenna, J. P. (1995). Should psychologists obtain prescribing privileges? A survey of family physicians. *Professional Psychology: Research and Practice, 26,* 371–376.

Bellack, A. S., & Hersen, M. (Eds.). (1988). *Behavioral assessment: A practical handbook* (3rd ed.). New York: Pergamon Press.

Bellack, A. S., & Hersen, M. (Eds.). (1998). *Behavioral assessment: A practical handbook* (4th ed.). Needham Heights, MA: Allyn & Bacon.

Bellack, A. S., Hersen, M., & Himmelhoch, J. M. (1983). A comparison of social skills training, pharmacotherapy and psychotherapy for depression. *Behaviour Research and Therapy, 21,* 101–107.

Bellack, A. S., Hersen, M., & Kazdin, A. E. (Eds.). (1990). *International handbook of behavior modification and therapy* (2nd ed.). New York: Plenum Press.

Bellak, L. (1954). *The Thematic Apperception Test and the Children's Apperception Test in clinical use.* New York: Grune & Stratton.

Bellak, L. (1986). *The Thematic Apperception Test, the Children's Apperception Test, and the Senior Apperception Technique in clinical use* (4th ed.). New York: Grune & Stratton.

Bellak, L. (1992). *The TAT, CAT, and SAT in clinical use* (5th ed.). Odessa, FL: Psychological Assessment Resources.

Belter, R., & Piotrowski, C. (2001). Current status of doctoral-level training in psychological testing. *Journal of Clinical Psychology, 57,* 717–726.

Bemporad, J. R., & Schwab, M. E. (1986). The DSM-III and clinical child psychiatry. In T. Millon & G. L. Klerman (Eds.), *Contemporary directions in psychopathology: Toward the DSM-IV* (pp. 135–150). New York: Guilford Press.

Ben-Porath, Y. S., & Butcher, J. N. (1991). The historical development of personality assessment. In C. E. Walker (Ed.), *Clinical psychology: Historical and research foundations* (pp. 121–158). New York: Plenum Press.

Ben-Porath, Y. S., & Waller, N. G. (1992). "Normal" personality inventories in clinical assessment: General requirements and potential for using the NEO Personality Inventory. *Psychological Assessment, 4,* 14–19.

Bender, L. A. (1938). A visual motor Gestalt test and its clinical use. *American Orthopsychiatric Association Research Monograph,* No. 3.

Bender, W. N. (1994). Joint custody: The option of choice. *Journal of Divorce and Remarriage, 21,* 115–131.

Benjamin, L. S. (1980). *INTREX users' manual.* Madison, WI: INTREX Interpersonal Institute.

Benjamin, L. S. (1993). *Interpersonal diagnosis and treatment of personality disorders*. New York: Guilford Press.

Bennett, C. C. (1965). Community psychology: Impressions of the Boston conference on the education of psychologists for community mental health. *American Psychologist, 20,* 832–835.

Benton, A. L. (1974). *Revised visual retention test: Clinical and experimental applications* (4th ed.). New York: Psychological Corporation.

Benton, A. L., Hamsher, K., Varney, N. R., & Spreen, O. (1983). *Contributions to neuropsychological assessment: A clinical manual*. New York: Oxford University Press.

Benton, M. K., & Schroeder, H. E. (1990). Social skills training with schizophrenia: A meta-analytic evaluation. *Journal of Consulting and Clinical Psychology, 58,* 741–747.

Berg, I. A. (1955). Response bias and personality: The deviation hypothesis. *Journal of Psychology, 40,* 61–71.

Bergin, A. E. (1971). The evaluation of therapeutic outcomes. In A. E. Bergin & S. L. Garfield (Eds.), *Handbook of psychotherapy and behavior change: An empirical analysis* (pp. 217–270). New York: John Wiley.

Bergin, A. E., & Lambert, M. J. (1978). The evaluation of therapeutic outcomes. In S. L. Garfield & A. E. Bergin (Eds.), *Handbook of psychotherapy and behavior change: An empirical analysis* (2nd ed., pp. 139–190). New York: John Wiley.

Berk, L. E. (2002). *Infants, children, and adolescents* (4th ed.). Boston, MA: Allyn and Bacon.

Berman, J. S., & Norton, N. C. (1985). Does professional training make a therapist more effective? *Psychological Bulletin, 98,* 401–406.

Berman, K. F., Zec, R. F., & Weinberger, D. R. (1986) Physiologic dysfunction of dorsolateral prefrontal cortex in schizophrenia, II: Role of neuroleptic treatment, attention, and mental effort. *Archives of General Psychiatry, 43,* 126–135.

Bernstein, B. E., & Hartsell, T. L. (2000). *The portable ethicist for mental health professionals*. New York: John Wiley & Sons.

Bernstein, D. A. (1973). Behavioral fear assessment: Anxiety or artifact? In H. Adams & P. Unikel (Eds.), *Issues and trends in behavior therapy* (pp. 225–267). Springfield, IL: Charles C. Thomas.

Bernstein, D. A., Borkovec, T. D., & Hazlette-Stevens, H. (2000). *Progressive relaxation training: A manual for the helping professions* (2nd ed.). New York: Praeger.

Bernstein, D. A., Clarke-Stewart, A., Penner, L., & Roy, E. J. (2002). *Psychology* (5th ed.). Boston, MA: Houghton Mifflin.

Bernstein, D. A., & Nietzel, M. T. (1977). Demand characteristics in behavior modification: A natural history of a "nuisance." In M. Hersen, R. M. Eisler, & P. M. Miller (Eds.), *Progress in behavior modification* (Vol. 4, pp. 119–162). New York: Academic Press.

Bernstein, D. A., & Paul, G. L. (1971). Some comments on therapy analogue research with small animal "phobias." *Journal of Behavior Therapy and Experimental Psychiatry, 2,* 225–237.

Berry, D., Baer, R., & Harris, M. (1991). Detection of malingering on the MMPI: A meta-analysis. *Clinical Psychology Review, 11,* 585–598.

Bersoff, D. N. (1999). *Ethical conflicts in psychology* (2nd ed.). Washington, DC: American Psychological Association.

Bertelsen, A. (1999). Reflections on the clinical utility of the ICD-10 and DSM-IV classifications and their diagnostic criteria. *Australian & New Zealand Journal of Psychiatry, 32,* 166–173.

Bettleheim, B. (1967). *The empty fortress*. New York: Free Press.

Beutler, L. E. (1991). Have all won and must all have prizes. Revisiting Lubrosky et al.'s verdict. *Journal of Consulting and Clinical Psychology, 59,* 226-232.

Beutler, L. E. (1998). Identifying empirically supported treatments: What if we didn't? [Electronic version] *Journal of Consulting and Clinical Psychology, 66,* 113-120 [pp. 1-12 in Electronic version].

Beutler, L. E. (2000). David and Goliath: When empirical and clinical standards of practice meet. *American Psychologist, 55,* 997-1007.

Beutler, L. E., & Harwood, T. M. (2000). *Prescriptive psychotherapy: A practical guide to systematic treatment selection.* New York: Oxford University Press.

Beutler, L. E., Kim, E. J., Davison, E., Karno, M., & Fisher, D. (1996). Research contributions to improving managed health care outcomes. *Psychotherapy, 33,* 197-206.

Beutler, L. E., Machado, P. P. P., Neufeldt, S. A. (1994). Therapist variables. In A. Bergin and S. Garfield (Eds.), *Handbook of psychotherapy and behavior change* (4th ed.). New York: Wiley.

Beutler, L. E., Mohr, D. C., Grawe, K., Engle, D., & McDonald, R. (1991). Looking for differential effects: Cross cultural predictors of differential psychotherapy efficacy. *Journal of Psychotherapy Integration, 1,* 121-142.

Bickman, L. (1987). Graduate education in psychology. *American Psychologist, 42,* 1041-1047.

Bickman, L. (1996). A continuum of care: More is not always better. *American Psychologist, 51,* 689-701.

Bickman, L., & Ellis, H. (Eds.). (1990). *Preparing psychologists for the 21st century.* Hillsdale, NJ: Erlbaum.

Bieri, J., Atkins, A. L., Briar, S., Leaman, R. L., Miller, H., & Tripoldi, T. (1966). *Clinical and social judgment: The discrimination of behavioral information.* New York: John Wiley.

Bijou, S. W., Peterson, R. F., & Ault, M. H. (1968). A method to integrate descriptive and experimental field studies at the level of data and empirical concepts. *Journal of Applied Behavior Analysis, 1,* 175-191.

Bion, W. R. (1959) *Experiences in groups.* New York: Basic Books.

Birks, Y., & Roger, D. (2000). Identifying components of type-A behavior: "Toxic" and "nontoxic" achieving. *Personality and Individual Differences, 28,* 1093-1105.

Blackburn, H., Luepker, R. V., Kline, F. G., Bracht, N., Carlaw, R., Jacobs, D., Mittelmark, M., Stauffer, L., & Taylor, H. L. (1984). The Minnesota Heart Health Program: A research and demonstration project in cardiovascular disease prevention. In J. D. Matarazzo et al. (Eds.), *Behavioral health: A handbook of health enhancement and disease prevention* (pp. 1171-1178). New York: John Wiley.

Blanchard, E. B. (1992). Psychological treatment of benign headache disorders. *Journal of Consulting and Clinical Psychology, 60,* 537-551.

Blanchard, E. B. (1994). Behavioral medicine and health psychology. In A. E. Bergin & S. L. Garfield (Eds.), *Handbook of psychotherapy and behavior change* (pp. 701-733). New York: Wiley & Sons, Inc.

Blatt, S. J., & Lerner, H. (1983). Psychodynamic perspectives on personality theory. In M. Hersen, A. E. Kazdin, & A. S. Bellack (Eds.), *The clinical psychology handbook* (pp. 87-106). New York: Pergamon Press.

Blatt, S. J., Sanislow, C. A., III, Zuroff, D. C., & Pilkonis, P. A. (1996). Characteristics of effective therapists: Further analyses of data from the National Institute of Mental Health Treatment of

Depression Collaborative Research Program. *Journal of Consulting & Clinical Psychology, 64,* 1276–1284.

Blau, T. H. (1988). *Psychotherapy tradecraft: The technique and style of doing therapy.* New York: Brunner/Mazel.

Block, J. H., Block, J., & Gjerde, P. F. (1986). The personality of children prior to divorce: A prospective study. *Child Development, 57,* 827–840.

Bloom, B. L. (1992). *Planned short-term psychotherapy: A clinical handbook.* Boston: Allyn & Bacon.

Bloom, B. L., Hodges, W. F., & Caldwell, R. A. (1982). A preventive program for the newly separated: Initial evaluation. *American Journal of Community Psychology, 10,* 251–264.

Blouke, P. S. (1997). Musings of a bureaucratic psychologist. *Professional Psychology: Research and Practice, 28,* 326–328.

Blount, R. L., Bachanas, P. J., Powers, S. W., Cotter, M. C., Franklin, A., Chaplin, W., Mayfield, J., Henderson, M., & Blount, S. D. (1992). Training children to cope and parents to coach them during routine immunizations: Effects on child, parent, and staff behavior. *Behavior Therapy, 23,* 689–705.

Blumenthal, S. J. (1994). Introductory remarks. In S. J. Blumenthal, K. Matthews, & S. M. Weiss (Eds.), *New research frontiers in behavioral medicine* (pp. 9–15). Washington, DC: National Institute of Mental Health.

Blumenthal, S. J., Matthews, K., & Weiss, S. W. (Eds.). (1994). *New research frontiers in behavioral medicine.* Washington, DC: National Institute of Mental Health.

Boczkowski, J. A., Zeichner, A., & DeSanto, N. (1985). Neuroleptic compliance among chronic schizophrenic outpatients: An intervention outcome report. *Journal of Consulting and Clinical Psychology, 53,* 666–671.

Bodmer, W., & McKie, R. (1994). *The book of man: The human genome project and the quest to discover our genetic heritage.* New York: Scribner.

Bogels, S. M. (1994). A structured-training approach to teaching diagnostic interviewing. *Teaching of Psychology, 21,* 144–150.

Bohart, A. C. (2000). The client is the most important common factor: Clients' self-healing capacities and psychotherapy. *Journal of Psychotherapy Integration, 10,* 127–149.

Bohart, A. C., O'Hara, M., & Leitner, L. M. (1998). Empirically violated treatments: Disenfranchisement of humanistic and other psychotherpies. *Psychotherapy Research, 8,* 141–157.

Boice, R., & Myers, P. E. (1987). Which setting is healthier and happier, academe or private practice? *Professional Psychology: Research and Practice, 18,* 526–529.

Bond, G. R., Witheridge, T. F., Dincin, J., Wasmer, D., Webb, J., & Graff-Kaser, R. (1990). Assertive community treatment for frequent users of psychiatric hospitals in a large city: A controlled study. *American Journal of Community Psychology, 18,* 865–891.

Bongar, B. (1988). Clinicians, microcomputers, and confidentiality. *Professional Psychology: Research and Practice, 19,* 286–289.

Bongar, B. (1991). *The suicidal patient: Clinical and legal standards of care.* Washington, DC: American Psychological Association.

Bonnie, R., & Slobogin, C. (1980). The role of mental health professionals in the criminal process: The case for informed speculation. *Virginia Law Review, 66,* 427–522.

Bonnie, R. J., Jeffries, J. C., Jr., & Low, P. W. (2000). *A case study in the insanity defense: The trial of John W. Hinckley, Jr.* (2nd ed.). New York: Foundation Press.

Boone, D. E. (1993). WAIS-R scatter with psychiatric patients: II. Intersubtest scatter. *Psychological Reports, 73,* 851-860.

Boothby, H., Mann, A. H., & Barker, A. (1995). Factors determining interrater agreement with rating global change in dementia: The CIBIC-plus. *International Journal of Geriatric Psychiatry, 10,* 1037-1045.

Bootzin, R. (1996, January). Random samplings. *APS Observer, 9.*

Bordin, E. S. (1979). The generalizability of the psychoanalytic concept of the working alliance. *Psychotherapy: Theory, Research, and Practice, 16,* 252-260.

Borgata, L. (1995). Analysis of social interaction and sociometric perception. *Sociometry, 17,* 7-32.

Boring, E. G. (1950). *A history of experimental psychology* (2nd ed.). New York: Appleton-Century-Crofts.

Borkovec, T. D., & Costello, E. (1993). Efficacy of applied relaxation and cognitive-behavioral therapy in the treatment of generalized anxiety disorder. *Journal of Consulting & Clinical Psychology, 61,* 611-619.

Borkovec, T. D., & O'Brien, G. T. (1976). Methodological and target behavior issues in analogue therapy outcome research. In M. Hersen, R. M. Eisler, & P. M. Miller (Eds.), *Progress in behavior modification* (pp. 133-172). New York: Academic Press.

Borum, R. (1996). Improving the clinical practice of violence risk assessment. *American Psychologist, 51,* 945-956.

Borum, R., & Grisso, T. (1995). Psychological test use in criminal forensic evaluations. *Professional Psychology: Research and Practice, 26,* 465-473.

Boston Channel, The. (2001, October 21). Boston Strangler's body exhumed. Retrieved December 21, 2001 from http://www.thebostonchannel.com/news/1033316/detail.html.

Bouchard, T. J. (1984). Twins reared together and apart: What they tell us about human diversity. In S. W. Fox (Ed.), *Individuality and determinism*. New York: Plenum.

Boudin, H. (1972). Contingency contracting as a therapeutic tool in the deceleration of amphetamine use. *Behavior Therapy, 3,* 604-608.

Bourg, E. F., Bent, R. J., McHolland, J., & Stricker, G. (1989). Standards and evaluation in the education and training of professional psychologists: The National Council of Schools and Professional Psychology Mission Bay Conference. *American Psychologist, 44,* 66-72.

Bowen, A. M., & Trotter, R. T., II (1995). HIV risk in intravenous drug users and crack cocaine smokers: Predicting stage of change for condom use. *Journal of Consulting and Clinical Psychology, 63,* 238-248.

Bowlby, J. (1969). *Attachment and loss, Vol 1: Attachment*. New York: Basic Books.

Bowlby, J. (1988). Developmental psychiatry comes to age. *American Journal of Psychiatry, 145,* 1-10.

Boyle, G. J. (1995). Meyers-Briggs type indicator (MBTI): Some psychometric limitations. *Australian Psychologist, 30,* 71-74.

Bradbury, T. N., & Fincham, F. D. (1990). Attributions in marriage: Review and critique. *Psychological Bulletin, 107,* 3-33.

Braden, J. P. (1995). Review of the Wechsler Intelligence Scale for Children, 3rd ed. In J. C. Conoley & J. C. Impara (Eds.), *Twelfth mental measurements yearbook*. Lincoln, NE: Buros Institute.

Braginsky, B. M., Grosse, M., & Ring, K. (1966). Controlling outcomes through impression management: An experimental study of the manipulative tactics of mental patients. *Journal of Consulting Psychology, 30,* 295–300.

Braginsky, B. M., Braginsky, D. D., & Ring, K. (1969). *Methods of madness: The mental hospital as a last resort.* New York: Holt, Rinehart & Winston.

Branch, C., Milner, B., & Rasmussen, T. (1964). Intracarotid sodium amytal for the lateralization of cerebral speech dominance. *Journal of Neurosurgery, 21,* 399–405.

Brand, J. L. (1995). Does contemporary cognitive psychology favor or oppose psychoanalytic theory? *American Psychologist, 9,* 799–800.

Brannen S. J., & Rubin A. (1996). Comparing the effectiveness of gender-specific and couples groups in a court mandated spouse abuse treatment program. *Research in Social Work Practice, 6,* 405–424.

Brauer, B. A. (1993). Adequacy of a translation of the MMPI into American Sign Langauge for use with deaf individuals: Linguistic equivalency issues. *Rehabilitation Psychology, 38,* 247–260.

Bray, J. H., & Rogers, J. C. (1995). Linking psychologists and family physicians for collaborative practice. *Professional Psychology: Research and Practice, 26,* 132–138.

Breier, A., Buchanan, R. W., Elkashef, A., Munson, R. C., Kirkpatrick, B., & Gellad, F. (1993). Brian morphology and schizophrenia: A magnetic resonance imaging study of limbic, prefrontal cortex, and caudate structures. *Archives of General Psychiatry, 49,* 921–926.

Brekke, J. S., & Long, J. D. (2000). Community-based psychosocial rehabilitation and prospective chance in functional, clinical, and subjective experience variables in schizophrenia. *Schizophrenia Bulletin, 26,* 667–678.

Brekke, N. J., Enko, P. J., Clavet, G., & Seelau, E. (1991). Of juries and court-appointed experts: The impact of nonadversarial expert testimony. *Law and Human Behavior, 15,* 451–477.

Brems, C., Thevenin, D. M., & Routh, D. K. (1991). The history of clinical psychology. In C. E. Walker (Ed.), *Clinical psychology: Historical and research foundations* (pp. 3–36). New York: Plenum Press.

Brener, N. D., Simon, T. R., Krug, E. G., & Lowry, R. (1999). Recent trends in violence-related behaviors among high school students in the United States. *Journal of the American Medical Association, 282,* 440–446.

Breslow, L. (1979). A positive strategy for the nation's health. *Journal of the American Medical Association, 242,* 2093–2094.

Brestan, E. V., & Eyberg, S. M. (1998). Effective psychosocial treatments of conduct-disordered children and adolescents: 29 years, 82 studies, and 5,272 kids. *Journal of Clinical Child Psychology, 27,* 180–189.

Bridges, N. (2001). Therapist's self-disclosure: Expanding the comfort zone. *Psychotherapy: Theory, Research, Practice, Training, 38,* 21–30.

Broman, C. L. (1993). Social relationships and health-related behavior. *Journal of Behavioral Medicine, 16,* 335–350.

Brooks, A. (1986). Law and antipsychotic medications. *Behavioral Sciences and the Law, 4,* 247–264.

Brotemarkle, B. A. (1947). Fifty years of clinical psychology: Clinical psychology 1896–1946. *Journal of Consulting Psychology, 11,* 1–4.

Brown, E. M. (2001). *Patterns of infidelity and their treatment* (2nd ed). Philadelphia, PA: Brunner-Routledge.

Brown, J. (1987). A review of meta-analyses conducted on psychotherapy outcome research. *Clinical Psychology Review, 7,* 1-24.

Brown, L. S. (1990). Taking account of gender in the clinical assessment interview. *Professional Psychology: Research and Practice, 21,* 12-17.

Brown, T. T., Chorpita, B. F., & Barlow, B. F. (1998). Structural relationships among dimensions of the DSM-IV anxiety and mood disorders and dimensions of negative affect, positive affect, and autonomic arousal. *Journal of Abnormal Psychology, 107,* 179-192.

Brown, W. H., Odom, S. L., & Holcombe, A. (1996). Observational assessment of young children's social behavior with peers. *Early Childhood Research Quarterly, 11,* 19-40.

Browne, A., & Finkelhor, D. (1986). Impact of child sexual abuse: A review of the research. *Psychological Bulletin, 99,* 66-77.

Brownell, K. D. (1981). Assessment of eating disorders. In D. H. Barlow (Ed.), *Behavioral assessment of adult disorders* (pp. 329-404). New York: Guilford Press.

Brownell, K. D., & Foreyt, J. P. (1985). Obesity. In D. H. Barlow (Ed.), *Clinical handbook of psychological disorders* (pp. 299-343). New York: Guilford Press.

Brownell, K. D., & Wadden, T. A. (1992). Etiology and treatment of obesity: Understanding a serious, prevalent, and refractory disorder. *Journal of Consulting and Clinical Psychology, 60,* 505-517.

Brugha, T. S., Nienhuis, F., Bagchi, D., Smith, J., Meltzer, H. (1999). The survey form of SCAN: The feasibility of using experienced lay survey interviewers to administer a semi-structured systematic clinical assessment of psychotic and non-psychotic disorders. *Psychological Medicine, 29,* 703-711.

Brunswick, E. (1947). *Systematic and representative design of psychological experiments with results in physical and social perception.* Berkeley: University of California Press.

Brussel, J. A. (1968). *Casebook of a crime psychiatrist.* New York: Bernard Geis Associates.

Bryant, K. J., Windle, M., & West, S. G. (1997). *The science of prevention: Methodological advances from alcohol and substance abuse research.* Washington, DC: APA.

Bryer, Stephen. (2000, Summer). Science in the courtroom. *Issues in Science and Technology.* Retrieved December 8, 2001 from http://www.nap.edu/issues/16.4/breyer.htm.

Buck, J. N. (1948). The H-T-P technique: A qualitative and quantitative scoring manual. *Journal of Clinical Psychology, 4,* 319-396.

Burchard, J. D. (1967). Systematic socialization: A programmed environment for the habitation of antisocial retardates. *Psychological Record, 17,* 461-476.

Burchard, J. D., & Burchard, S. N. (Eds.). (1987). *Prevention of delinquent behavior.* Newbury Park, CA: Sage.

Burg, M. M., & Abrams, D. (2001). Depression in chronic medical illness: The case of coronary heart disease. *Journal of Clinical Psychology/In Session, 57,* 1323-1337.

Burger, W. E. (1975). Dissenting opinion in O'Connor v. Donaldson. *U.S. Law Week, 42,* 4929-4936.

Burisch, M. (1984). Approaches to personality inventory construction: A comparison of merits. *American Psychologist, 39,* 214-227.

Burish, T. G., Carey, M. P., Krozely, M. G., & Greco, F. A. (1987). Conditioned side effects induced by cancer chemotherapy: Prevention through behavioral treatment. *Journal of Consulting and Clinical Psychology, 55,* 42-48.

Burke, L. E., Dunbar-Jacob, J. M., & Hill, M. N. (1997). Compliance with cardiovascular disease prevention strategies: A review of the research. *Annals of Behavioral Medicine, 19,* 239-263.

Burnam, M. A., Stein, J. A., Golding, J. M., Siegel, J. M., Sorenson, S. B., Forsythe, A. B., & Telles, C. A. (1988). Sexual assault and mental disorders in a community population. *Journal of Consulting and Clinical Psychology, 56,* 843–850.

Burns, D. D. (1999). *The feeling good handbook.* New York: Plume.

Burns, D. D., & Spangler, D. L. (2000). Does psychotherapy homework lead to improvements in depression in cognitive-behavioral therapy or does improvement lead to increased homework compliance? *Journal of Consulting and Clinical Psychology, 68,* 46–56.

Buros, O. K. (Ed.). (1938). *The 1940 mental measurements yearbook.* Highland Park, NJ: Gryphon Press.

Burton, L. (1999). A psychoanalyst in a medical school's student health psychiatric service. *Journal of Psychotherapy: Practice and Research, 8,* 201–203.

Buschbaum, M., Haier, R., Potkin, S., Nuechterlein, K., Bracha, H., Katz, M., Lohr, J., Wu, J., Lottenberg, S., Jerabek, P., Trenary, M., Tafalla, R., Reynolds, C., & Bunney, W. (1992). Frontostriatal disorder of cerebral metabolism in never-medicated schizophrenics. *Archives of General Psychiatry, 49,* 935–942.

Butcher, J. N. (Ed.). (1987). *Computerized psychological assessment: A practitioner's guide.* New York: Basic Books.

Butcher, J. N., Dahlstrom, W. G., Graham, J. R., Tellegen, A., & Kaemmer, B. (1989). *Manual for administration and scoring of the MMPI-2.* Minneapolis: University of Minnesota Press.

Butcher, J. N., & Keller, L. S. (1984). Objective personality assessment. In G. Goldstein & M. Hersen (Eds.), *Handbook of psychological assessment* (pp. 307–331). New York: Pergamon Press.

Butcher, J. N., & Williams, C. L. (1992). *Essentials of MMPI-2 and MMPI-A interpretation.* Minneapolis: University of Minnesota Press.

Butcher, J. N., Williams, C. L., Graham, J. R., Archer, R., Tellegen, A., Ben-Porath, Y. S., & Kaemmer, B. (1992). *MMPI-A: Manual for administration, scoring, and interpretation.* Minneapolis, MN: University of Minnesota Press.

Butcher, J. N., Perry, J. N., & Atlis, M. M. (2000). Validity and utility of computer-based test interpretation. *Psychological Assessment, 12,* 6–18.

Byne, W., Buchsbaum, M. S., Kemether, E., Hazlett, E. A., Shinwari, A. Mitropoulou, V., & Siever, L. J. (2001). Magnetic resonance imaging of the thalamic mediodorsal nucleus and pulvinar in schizophrenia and schizotypal personality disorder. *Archives of General Psychiatry, 58,* 133–140.

Cacciola, J. S., Alterman, A. I., Rutheford, M. J., McKay, J. R., & May, D. J. (1999). Comparability of telephone and in-person Structured Clinical Interview for DSM-III-R (SCID) diagnoses. *Assessment, 6,* 235–242.

Cairns, R. B., & Green, J. A. (1979). How to assess personality and social patterns: Observations or ratings? In B. Cairns (Ed.), *The analysis of social interactions: Methods, issues, and illustrations* (pp. 209–226). Hillsdale, NJ: Lawrence Erlbaum Associates.

Callaghan, G. M. (1996). The clinical utility of client dream reports from a radical behavioral perspective. *The Behavior Therapist, 19,* 49–52.

Camara, W. J., Nathan, J. S., & Puente, A. E. (2000). Psychological test usage: Implications in professional psychology. *Professional Psychology: Research and Practice, 31,* 141–154.

Campbell, D. T., & Fiske, D. W. (1959). Convergent and discriminant validation by the multitrait-multimethod matrix. *Psychological Bulletin, 56,* 81–105.

Campbell, S. B. (1989). Developmental perspectives in child psychopathology. In M. Hersen & T. Ollendick (Eds.), *Handbook of child psychopathology* (2nd ed., pp. 5–28). New York: Plenum Press.

Cannell, J., Hudson, J. I., & Pope, H. G., Jr. (2001). Standards for informed consent in recovered memory therapy. *Journal of the American Academy of Psychiatry and the Law, 29,* 138–147.

Canter, M. B., Bennett, B. E., Jones, S. E., & Nagy, T. F. (1994). *Ethics for psychologists: A commentary on the APA ethics code.* Washington, DC: American Psychological Association.

Cantor, D. W. (1996, November). Lowering the standard of care. *APA Monitor, 2.*

Cantor, N. L. (1998). Making advance directives meaningful. *Psychology, Public Policy, and Law, 4,* 629–652.

Cantwell, D. P. (1983). Depression in childhood: Clinical picture and diagnosis criteria. In D. P. Cantwell & G. A. Carlson (Eds.), *Affective disorders in childhood and adolescence* (pp. 3–18). New York: Spectrum.

Caplan, G. (1964). *Principles of preventive psychiatry.* New York: Basic Books.

Carere-Comes, T. (2001). Commentary on Boharts "The client is the most important common factor." *Journal of Psychotherapy Integration, 11,* 263–267.

Carmagnani, A., & Carmagnani, E. F. (1999). Biofeedback: Present state and future possibilities. *International Journal of Mental Health, 28,* 83–86.

Carroll, J. B. (1993). *Human cognitive abilities: A survey of factor-analytic studies.* Cambridge, England: University of Cambridge Press.

Carson, R. C. (1969). *Interaction concepts of personality.* Chicago: Aldine.

Carson, R. C. (1991). Dilemmas in the pathway of the DSM-IV. *Journal of Abnormal Psychology, 100,* 302–307.

Carter, C. S., Perlstein, W., Ganguli, R., Brar, J., Mintun, M., & Cohen, J. (1998). Functional hypofrontality and working memory dysfunction in schizophrenia. *American Journal of Psychiatry, 155,* 1285–1287.

Caruso, J. C., & Jacob-Timm, S. (2001). Confirmatory factor analysis of the Kaufman Adolescent and Adult Intelligence Test with young adolescents. *Assessment, 8,* 11–17.

Casey, R. J., & Berman, J. S. (1985). The outcome of psychotherapy with children. *Psychological Bulletin, 98,* 388–400.

Caspi, A., Henry, B., McGee, R. O., Moffitt, T. E., & Silva, P. A. (1995). Temperamental origins of child and adolescent behavior problems: From age 3 to age 15. *Child Development, 66,* 55–68.

Caspi, A., & Silva, P. A. (1995). Temperamental qualities at age 3 predict personality traits in young adulthood: Longitudinal evidence from a birth cohort. *Child Development, 66,* 486–498.

Cassel, E. (2000). Behavioral science research leads to Department of Justice Guidelines for eyewitness evidence. *Virginia Lawyer, 48,* 35–38.

Cassel, E., & Bernstein, D. A. (2001). *Criminal Behavior.* Boston: Allyn & Bacon.

Cates, J. A. (1999). The art of assessment in psychology: Ethics, expertise, and validity. *Journal of Clinical Psychology, 55,* 31–42.

Cattell, R. B., Eber, H. W., & Tatusoka, M. M. (1970). *Handbook for the Sixteen Personality Factor Questionnaire.* Champaign, IL: Institute for Personality and Ability Testing.

Cattell, R. B., Eber, H. W., & Tatusoka, M. M. (1992). *Handbook for the Sixteen Personality Factor Questionnaire (16PF).* Champaign, IL: Institute for Personality and Ability Testing.

Cautela, J. R. (1966). Treatment of compulsive behavior by covert sensitization. *Psychological Record, 86,* 33–41.

Cautela, J. R., & Kastenbaum, R. A. (1967). A reinforcement survey schedule for use in therapy, training, and research. *Psychological Reports, 20,* 1115–1130.

Cecero, J. J., Fenton, L. R., Frankforter, T. L., Nich, C., & Carroll, K. M. (2001). Focus on therapeutic alliance: The psychometric properties of six measures across three treatments. *Psychotherapy: Theory, Research, Practice, Training, 38,* 1–11.

Ceci, S. J., & Bruck, M. (1993). Suggestibility of the child witness: A historical review and synthesis. *Psychological Bulletin, 113,* 403–439.

Ceci, S. J., & Bruck, M. (1995). *Jeopardy in the courtroom: A scientific analysis of children's testimony.* Washington, DC: American Psychological Association.

Centers for Disease Control (2001a). About cardiovascular disease. Retrieved December 3, 2001 from http://www.cdc.gov/nccdphp/cvd/aboutcardio.htm.

Centers for Disease Control (2001b). Basic statistics—Cumulative AIDS Cases. Retrieved December 3, 2001 from http://www.cdc.gov/hiv/stats/cumulati.htm.

Centers for Disease Control (2001c). Basic statistics—International Statistics. Retrieved December 3, 2001 from http://www.cdc.gov/hiv/stats/cumulati.htm.

Chamberlin, J. (2000). Help is here for interpreting guidelines. *Monitor on Psychology, 31.* Retrieved December 22, 2001 from http://www.apa.org.monitor/oct00/guidelines.html.

Chambless, D. L. (1990). Spacing of exposure sessions in the treatment of agoraphobia and simple phobia. *Behavior Therapy, 21,* 217–229.

Chambless, D. L. (1995). Training in and dissemination of empirically-validated psychological treatments: Report and recommendations. *The Clinical Psychologist, 48,* 3–23.

Chambless, D. L., Babich, K., Crits-Christoph, P., Frank, E., Gilson, M., Montgomery, R., Rich, R., Steinberg, J., & Weinberger, J. (1995). Training in and dissemination of empirically-validated psychological treatments: Report and recommendations. *The Clinical Psychologist, 48,* 3–23.

Chambless, D. L., Baker, M., Baucom, D. H., Beutler, L. E., Calhoun, K. S., et al. (1998). Update on empirically validated therapies, II. *Clinical Psychologist, 51,* 3–16.

Chambless, D. L., & Hollon, S. D. (1998). Defining empirically supported therapies. *Journal of Consulting and Clinical Psychology, 66,* 7–18.

Chambless, D. L., & Ollendick, T. H. (2001). Empirically supported psychological treatments. *Annual Review of Psychology, 52,* 685–716.

Chambless, D. L., Sanderson, W. C., Shoham, V., Bennet-Johnson, S., Pope, K. S., et al. (1996). An update on empirically validated therapies. *Clinical Psychologist, 49,* 5–18.

Chan, D. W., & Lee, H. B. (1995). Patterns of psychological test use in Hong Kong in 1993. *Professional Psychology: Research and Practice, 26,* 292–297.

Chandler, M. (1973). Egocentrism and antisocial behavior: The assessment and training of social perspective-taking skills. *Developmental Psychology, 9,* 326–332.

Chapman, L. J., & Chapman, J. P. (1967). The genesis of popular but erroneous psychodiagnostic observations. *Journal of Abnormal Psychology, 72,* 193–204.

Chenneville, T. (2000). HIV, confidentiality, and duty to protect: A decision-making model. *Professional Psychology: Research and Practice, 31,* 661–670.

Cherry, D. K., Messenger, L. C., Jacoby, A. M. (2000). An examination of training model outcomes in clinical psychology programs. *Professional Psychology: Research & Practice, 31,* 562–568.

Chesler, P. (1972). *Women and madness*. New York: Doubleday.

Chess, S., & Thomas, A. (1986). *Temperament in clinical practice*. New York: Guilford Press.

Christensen, A., & Heavey, C. L. (1999). Interventions for couples. *Annual Review of Psychology, 50,* 165–190.

Christensen, A., Margolin, G., & Sullaway, M. (1992). Interparental agreement on child behavior problems. *Psychological Assessment, 4,* 419–425.

Christiansen, B. C., Smith, G. T., Roehling, P. V., & Goldman, M. S. (1989). Using alcohol expectancies to predict adolescent drinking behavior after one year. *Journal of Consulting and Clinical Psychology, 57,* 93–99.

Cicchetti, D., Toth, S. L., & Lynch, M. (1995). Bowlby's dream comes full circle: The application of attachment theory to risk and psychopathology. In T. H. Ollendick & R. J. Prinz (Eds.), *Advances in clinical child psychology* (pp. 1–75). New York: Plenum.

Ciminero, A. R., Calhoun, K. S., & Adams, H. E. (1986). *Handbook of behavioral assessment* (2nd ed.). New York: John Wiley.

Clark, B. J., & Abeles, N. (1994). Ethical issues and dilemmas in the mental health organization. *Administration and Policy in Mental Health, 22,* 7–17.

Clarke, G. N., Hawkins, W., Murphy, M., Sheeber, L. B., Lewinsohn, P. M., & Seeley, J. R. (1995). Targeted prevention of unipolar depressive disorder in an at-risk sample of high school adolescents: A randomized trial of a group cognitive intervention. *Journal of the American Academy of Child and Adolescent Psychiatry, 34,* 312–321.

Clarke-Kudless, D. (1996). Bringing psychology to the table—issues facing the American Psychological Association as psychology approaches the millenium: A conversation with Dorothy W. Cantor. *Professional Psychology: Research and Practice, 27,* 252–258.

Clingempeel, W. G., & Reppucci, N. D. (1982). Joint custody after divorce: Major issues and goals for research. *Psychological Bulletin, 91,* 102–127.

Cohen, B. B., & Vinson, D. C. (1995). Retrospective self-report of alcohol consumption: Test-retest reliability by telephone. *Alcoholism: Clinical and Experimental Research, 19,* 1156–1161.

Cohen, H. L. (1968). Educational therapy: The design of learning environments. *Research in Psychotherapy, 3,* 21–58.

Cohen, J., & Servan-Schreiber, D. (1992). Context, cortex, and dopamine: A Connectionist approach to behavior and biology in schizophrenia. *Psychological Review, 99,* 45–77.

Cohen, J. B., & Reed, D. (1985). Type A behavior and coronary heart disease among Japanese men in Hawaii. *Journal of Behavioral Medicine, 8,* 343–352.

Cohen, R. J., Swerdlik, M. E., & Smith, D. K. (1992). *Psychological testing and measurement*. Mountain View, CA: Mayfield.

Cohen, S., Mermelstein, R., Kamarck, T., & Hoberman, H. (1985). Measuring the functional components of social support. In I. G. Sarason & B. R. Sarason (Eds.), *Social support: Theory, research, and application* (pp. 73–94). The Hague: Nijhoff.

Cohen, S., & Rabin, B. S. (1998). Psychological stress, immunity, and cancer. *Journal of the National Cancer Institute, 90,* 3–4.

Cohen, S., Tyrrell, D. A., & Smith, A. P. (1991). Psychological stress in humans and susceptibility to the common cold. *New England Journal of Medicine, 325,* 606–612.

Cohen, S., & Wills, T. A. (1985). Stress, social support, and the buffering hypothesis. *Psychological Bulletin, 98,* 310–357.

Cohn, L. (1995). Risk-perception: Differences between adolescents and adults. *Health Psychology, 14,* 217.

Coie, J. D., Watt, N. F., West, S. G., Hawkins, J. D., Asarnow, J. R., Markman, H. J., Ramey, S. L., Shure, M. B., & Long, B. (1993). The science of prevention: A conceptual framework and some directions for a national research program. *American Psychologist, 48,* 1013-1022.

Collins, R. L., Parks, G. A., & Marlatt, G. A. (1985). Social determinants of alcohol consumption: The effects of social interactions and model status on the self-administration of alcohol. *Journal of Consulting and Clinical Psychology, 53,* 189-200.

Colmen, J. G., Kaplan, S. J., & Boulger, J. R. (1964, August). *Selection and selecting research in the Peace Corps.* (Peace Corps Research Note No. 7).

Comer, J. P. (1987). New Haven's school-community connection. *Educational Leadership, 44,* 13-16.

Conduct Problems Prevention Research Group. (1992). A developmental and clinical model for the prevention of conduct disorder: The FAST Track Program. *Development and Psychopathology, 4,* 509-527.

Conduct Problems Prevention Research Group. (2000). Merging universal and indicated prevention programs: The FAST Track model. *Addictive Behaviors, 25,* 913-927.

Cone, J. D. (1988). Psychometric considerations and the multiple models of behavioral assessment. In A. S. Bellack & M. Hersen (Eds.), *Behavioral assessment: A practical handbook* (3rd ed., pp. 42-66). New York: Pergamon Press.

Cone, J. D. (2000). *Evaluating Outcomes: Empirical tools for effective practice.* Washington, DC: American Psychological Association.

Cone, J. D., & Foster, S. L. (1982). Direct observation in clinical psychology. In P. C. Kendall & J. N. Butcher (Eds.), *Handbook of research methods in clinical psychology* (pp. 311-354). New York: John Wiley.

Congressional Record-Senate (1999). Deinstitutionalization of the mentally ill. 106th Congress, 1st session, 145 Cong Rec. S. 8295, vol. 145, No. 97.

Conners, C. K. (1989). *Conners rating scales.* North Tonawanda, NY: Multi-Health Systems.

Conte, H. R., Plutchik, R., Wild, K., & Karasau, T. B. (1986). Combined psychotherapy and pharmacotherapy for depression: A systematic analysis of evidence. *Archives of General Psychiatry, 43,* 471-479.

Cook, T. D., & Campbell, D. T. (1991). Quasi experimentation. In M. D. Dunnette & L. M. Hough (Eds.), *Handbook of industrial and organizational psychology,* vol. 1 (2nd ed., pp. 491-576). Washington, DC: Consulting Psychologists.

Coontz, P. D., Lidz, C. W., & Mulvey, E. P. (1994). Gender and the assessment of dangerousness in the psychiatric emergency room. *International Journal of Law and Psychiatry, 17,* 369-376.

Corcoran, K., & Fischer, J. (2000). *Measures for clinical practice: A sourcebook.* New York: The Free Press.

Corey, G. (1999). *Theory and practice of group counseling.* Pacific Grove, CA: Wadsworth.

Cormier, W. H., & Cormier, L. S. (1991). *Interviewing strategies for helpers: Fundamental skills and cognitive behavioral interventions* (3rd ed.). Pacific Grove, CA: Brooks/Cole.

Cornblatt, B., & Erlenmeyer-Kimling, L. E. (1985). Global attentional deviance in children at risk for schizophrenia: Specificity and predictive validity. *Journal of Abnormal Psychology, 94,* 470-486.

Corsini, R. J., & Wedding, D. (2000). *Current psychotherapies* (6th ed.). Itasca, IL: Peacock Publishers, Inc.

Costa, P., & McCrae, R. (1985). *NEO-Personality Inventory manual*. Odessa, FL: Psychological Assessment Resources.

Costa, P. T., & McCrae, R. R. (1992a). *Manual for the Revised NEO Personality Inventory (NEO-PIR) and the NEO Five-Factor Inventory (BEO-FFI)*. Odessa, FL: Psychological Assessment Resources.

Costa, P. T., & McCrae, R. R. (1992b). Normal personality inventories in clinical assessment: General requirements and potential for using the NEO Personality Inventory. *Psychological Assessment, 4*, 5-13.

Couch, R. D. (1995). Four steps for conducting a pregroup screening interview. *Journal for Specialists in Group Work, 20*, 18-25.

Covner, B. J. (1942). Studies in phonographic recordings. I. The use of phonographic recordings in counseling practice and research. *Journal of Consulting Psychology, 6*, 105-113.

Cowen, C. A., Lazenby, H. C., Martin, A. B., McDonnell, P. A., et al. (2001). National health expenditures, 1999. *Health Care Financing Review, 22*, 77-106.

Cowen, E. L. (Ed.). (1982). Research in primary prevention in mental health. *American Journal of Community Psychology, 10*, 239-367.

Coyne, J. C. (1976). Toward an interactional description of depression. *Psychiatry, 39*, 28-39.

Coyne, J. C., & Racioppo, M. W. (2000). Never the twain shall meet? Closing the gap between coping research and clinical intervention research. *American Psychologist, 55*, 655-664.

Craig, R. J. (1993). *Psychological assessment with the Millon clinical multiaxial inventory (II): An interpretive guide*. Odessa, FL: Psychological Assessment Resources.

Cramer, P. (2000). Defense mechanisms in psychology today: Further processes for adaptation. *American Psychologist, 55*, 637-646.

Crews, F. (1996). The verdict on Freud. *Psychological Science, 7*, 63-68.

Crick, N. R., & Dodge, K. A. (1994). A review and reformulation of social-information-processing mechanisms in children's social adjustment. *Psychological Bulletin, 115*, 74-101.

Crits-Cristoph, P., Frank, E., Chambless, D. L., & Karp, J. F. (1995). Training in empirically validated treatments: What are clinical psychology students learning? *Professional Psychology: Research and Practice, 26*, 514-522.

Crits-Christoph, P., & Mintz, J. (1991). Implications of therapist effects for the design and analysis of comparative studies of psychotherapy. *Journal of Consulting and Clinical Psychology, 59*, 20-26.

Cronbach, L. J. (1946). Response sets and test validity. *Educational and Psychological Measurement, 6*, 475-494.

Cronbach, L. J. (1960). *Essentials of psychological testing* (2nd ed.). New York: Harper & Row.

Cronbach, L. J., & Glesser, G. C. (1964). *Psychological tests and personnel decisions*. Urbana, IL: University of Illinois Press.

Cronbach, L. J. (1970). *Essentials of psychological testing* (3rd ed.). New York: Harper & Row.

Cronbach, L. J., Gleser, G. C., Nanda, H., & Rajaratnam, N. (1972). *The dependability of behavioral measurements*. New York: John Wiley.

Cronbach, L. J., & Meehl, P. E. (1955). Construct validity in psychology tests. *Psychological Bulletin, 52*, 281-302.

Crosbie-Burnett, M. (1991). Impact of joint versus sole custody and quality of co-parental relationship on adjustment of adolescents in remarried families. *Behavioral Sciences and the Law, 9*, 439–449.

Crumbaugh, J. C. (1968). Cross-validation of the Purpose in Life test based on Frankl's concepts. *Journal of Individual Psychology, 24*, 74–81.

Cullen, E. A., & Newman, R. (1997). In pursuit of prescription privileges. *Professional Psychology: Research and Practice, 28*, 101–106.

Cummings, N. A. (1995). Unconscious fiscal convenience. *Psychotherapy in Private Practice, 14*, 23–28.

Cunningham, C. E., Siegel, L. S., & Offord, D. R. (1985). A developmental dose-response analysis of the effects of methylphenidate on the peer interactions of Attention Deficit Disordered boys. *Journal of Child Psychology and Psychiatry, 26*, 955–971.

Dahlstrom, W. G. (1992). The growth in acceptance of the MMPI. *Professional Psychology: Research and Practice, 23*, 345–348.

Dahlstrom, W. G., Lachar, D., & Dahlstrom, L. E. (1986). *MMPI patterns of American minorities.* Minneapolis: University of Minnesota Press.

Dahlstrom, W. G., Welsh, G. S., & Dahlstrom, L. E. (1972). *An MMPI handbook: Vol. 1. Clinical interpretation* (rev. ed.). Minneapolis: University of Minnesota Press.

Dahlstrom, W. G., Welsh, G. S., & Dahlstrom, L. E. (1975). *An MMPI handbook: Vol. 2. Research applications.* Minneapolis: University of Minnesota Press.

Dalton, J. H., Elias, M. J., & Wandersman, A. (2000). *Community Psychology: Linking Individuals and Communities.* Pacific Grove, CA: Wadsworth.

Dana, R. H., & Leech, S. (1974). Existential assessment. *Journal of Personality Assessment, 38*, 428–435.

Dangel, R. F., & Polster, R. A. (Eds.). (1984). *Parent training.* New York: Guilford Press.

Davanloo, H. L. (1994). *Basic principles and techniques in short-term dynamic psychotherapy.* Northdale, NJ: Jason Aronson, Inc.

Davidson, W. S., Redner, R., Blakely, C., Mitchell, C. M., & Emshoff, J. G. (1987). Diversion of juvenile offenders: An experimental comparison. *Journal of Consulting and Clinical Psychology, 55*, 68–75.

Davis, D. L., Davis, H. L., & Davis, T. L. (1999). The further perils of psychotherapy practice: Ohio expands the duty to warn. *American Journal of Forensic Psychology, 17*, 25–39.

Davis, K. L., Kahn, R. S., Ko, G., & Davidson, M. (1991). Dopamine in schizophrenia: A review and reconceptualization. *American Journal of Psychiatry, 148*, 1474–1486.

Davison, G. C. (1998). Being bolder with the Boulder model: The challenge of education and training in empirically supported treatments. *Journal of Consulting & Clinical Psychology, 66*, 163–167.

Dawe, H. C. (1934). An analysis of two-hundred quarrels of pre-school children. *Child Development, 5*, 139–157.

Dawes, R. M. (1986). Representative thinking in clinical judgment. *Clinical Psychology Review, 6*, 425–442.

Dawes, R. M. (1992). *Psychology and psychotherapy: The myth of professional expertise.* New York: Free Press.

Dawes, R. M. (1994). *House of cards.* New York: The Free Press.

Dawes, R. M., Faust, D., & Meehl, P. E. (1989). Clinical versus actuarial judgment. *Science, 243*, 1668–1674.

del Carmen, R., & Huffman, L. (1996). Epilogue: Bridging the gap between research on attachment and psychopathology. *Journal of Consulting and Clinical Psychology, 64,* 291–294.

DeLeon, P. H., Wedding, D., Wakefield, M. K., & VandenBos, G. R. (1992). Medicaid policy: Psychology's overlooked agenda. *Professional Psychology: Research and Practice, 23,* 96–107.

DeNelsky, G. Y. (1996). The case against prescription privileges for psychologists. *American Psychologist, 51,* 207–212.

Dennis, W. (1948). *Readings in the history of psychology.* New York: Appleton-Century-Crofts.

Depression Guideline Panel. (1993). *Depression in primary care: Vol. 2. Treatment of major depression* (Clinical practice guideline, No. 5; AHCPR Publication No. 93–0551). Rockville, MD: U.S. Department of Health and Human Services, Public Health Service, Agency for Health Care Policy and Research.

Derksen, J. J., Hummelen, J. W., & Bouwens, P. J. (1994). Interrater reliability of the structural interview. *Journal of Personality Disorders, 8,* 131–139.

DeRubeis, R. J., & Crits-Christoph, P. (1998). Empirically supported individual and group psychological treatments for adult mental disorders. *Journal of Consulting & Clinical Psychology, 66,* 37–52.

DeSantis, B. W., & Walker, C. E. (1991). Contemporary clinical psychology. In C. E. Walker (Ed.), *Clinical psychology: Historical and research foundations* (pp. 513–535). New York: Plenum Press.

Diener, C. I., & Dweck, C. S. (1978). An analysis of learned helplessness: Continuous changes in performance, strategy, and achievement cognitions following failure. *Journal of Personality and Social Psychology, 36,* 451–462.

Diener, M. B., & Milich, R. (1997). The effects of positive feedback on the social interactions of boys with ADHD: A test of the self-protective hypothesis. *Journal of Clinical Child Psychology, 26,* 256–265.

DiLalla, D. L., & Gottesman, I. I. (1995). Normal personality characteristics in identical twins discordant for schizophrenia. *Journal of Abnormal Psychology, 104,* 490–499.

Dilk, M. N., & Bond, G. R. (1996). Meta-analytic evaluation of skills training research for individuals with severe mental illness. *Journal of Consulting and Clinical Psychology, 64,* 1137–1146.

Dimatteo, M. R., & Taranta, A. (1976). Nonverbal communication and physician-patient rapport: An empirical study. *Professional Psychology, 10,* 540–547.

DiNardo, P. A., Moras, K., Barlow, D. H., Rapee, R. M., et al. (1993). Reliability of DSM-III-R anxiety disorder categories: Using the Anxiety Disorders Interview Schedule-Revised (ADIS-R). *Archives of General Psychiatry, 50,* 251–256.

Dipboye, R. L., Stramler, C. S., & Fontenelle, G. A. (1984). The effects of the application on recall of information from the interview. *Academy of Management Journal, 27,* 561–575.

Division 17 Counseling Psychology. (2001). What is a Counseling Psychologist? Retrieved September 17, 2001 from http://www.div17.org/whatis.html.

Dodge, K. A., McClaskey, C. L., & Feldman, E. (1985). Situational approach to the assessment of social competence in children. *Journal of Consulting and Clinical Psychology, 53,* 344–353.

Dohrenwend, B. S. (1978). Social stress and community psychology. *American Journal of Community Psychology, 6,* 1–14.

Dornelas, E. A. (2001) Introduction: Integrating health psychology into clinical practice. *Journal of Clinical Psychology/In Session, 57,* 1261–1262.

Douglas, J., & Olshaker, M. (1995). *Mind hunter: Inside the FBI's elite serial crime unit.* New York: Scribner's.

Douglas, V. I. (1972). Stop, look and listen: The problem of sustained attention and impulse control in hyperactive and normal children. *Canadian Journal of Behavioral Science, 4,* 259–282.

Drotor, D. (1999). Psychological interventions for children with chronic physical illness and their families: Toward integration of research and practice. In S.W. Russ & T.H. Ollendick (Eds.), *Handbook of psychotherapies with children and families* (pp. 447–461). New York: Plenum.

DuBois, P. H. (1970). *A history of psychological testing.* Boston: Allyn & Bacon.

Duncan, B. (2001). The future of psychotherapy. *Psychotherapy Networker,* July/August, 24–33/52.

Duncan, B., & Miller, S. D. (2000). The client's theory of change: Consulting the client in the integrative process. *Journal of Psychotherapy Integration, 10,* 169–187.

Durlak, J. (1979). Comparative effectiveness of paraprofessional and professional helpers. *Psychological Bulletin, 86,* 80–92.

Durlak, J. A. (1981) Evaluating comparative studies of paraprofessional and professional helpers: A reply to Nietzel and Fisher. *Psychological Bulletin, 89,* 566–569.

Dush, D. M., Hirt, M. L., & Schroeder, H. E. (1989). Self-statement modification in the treatment of child behavior disorders. A meta-analysis. *Psychological Bulletin, 106,* 97–106.

Eagle, M. (1984). *Recent developments in psychoanalysis: A critical evaluation.* New York: McGraw-Hill.

Eaker, E. D., Abbott, R. D., Kannel, W. B. (1989). Frequency of uncomplicated angina pectoris in Type A compared with Type B persons (the Framingham study). *American Journal of Cardiology, 63,* 1042–1045.

Ebert, B. W. (1987). Guide to conducting a psychological autopsy. *Professional Psychology: Research and Practice, 18,* 52–56.

Edelbrock, C., Costello, A. J., Duncan, M. K., Kalas, R., & Conover, N. C. (1985). Age differences in the reliability of the psychiatric interview of the child. *Child Development, 56,* 265–275.

Edelstein, B. A., & Eisler, R. M. (1976). Effects of modeling and modeling with instructions and feedback on the behavioral components of social skills. *Behavior Therapy, 7,* 382–389.

Edelstein, B. A., & Michelson, L. (Eds.). (1986). *Handbook of prevention.* New York & London: Plenum Press.

Edwards, A. L. (1957). *The social desirability variable in personality assessment and research.* New York: Dryden.

Ehmann, T. S., Higgs, E., Smith, G. N., Au, T., Altman, S., Llyod, D., & Honer, W. G. (1995). Routinue assessment of patient progress: A multiformat, change-sensitive nurses instrument for assessing psychotic inpatients. *Comprehensive Psychiatry, 36,* 289–295.

Einhorn, H. J., & Hogarth, R. M. (1978). Confidence in judgment: Persistence of the illusion of validity. *Psychological Review, 85,* 395–416.

Elkin, I. (1994). The NIMH treatment of depression collaborative research program: Where we began and where we are. In A. E. Bergin & S. L. Garfield (Eds.), *Handbook of psychotherapy and behavior change* (4th ed., pp. 114–139). New York: John Wiley.

Elkin, I., Gibbons, R. D., Shea, M. T., & Sotsky, S. M. (1995). Initial severity and different treatment outcomes in the National Institute of Mental Health Treatment of Depression Collaborative Research Program. *Journal of Clinical and Consulting Psychology, 63,* 841–847.

Elkin, I., Gibbons, R. D., Shea, M. T., Sotsky, M. M., Watkins, J. T., & Pilkonis, P. A. (1995). Initial severity and differential treatment outcome in the National Institute of Mental Health Treatment of Depression Collaborative Research Program. *Journal of Consulting and Clinical Psychology, 63,* 841–847.

Elkin, I., Shea, M. T., Watkins, J. T., Imber, S. D., Sotsky, S. M., Collins, J. F., Glass, D. R., Pilkonis, P. A., Leber, W. R., Docherty, J. P., Fiester, S. J., & Parloff, M. B. (1989). National Institute of Mental Health Treatment of Depression Collaborative Research Program. General effectiveness of treatments. *Archives of General Psychiatry, 46,* 971–982.

Ellis, A. (1962). *Reason and emotion in psychotherapy.* New York: Lyle Stuart.

Ellis, A. (1973). Rational-emotive therapy. In R. Corsini (Ed.), *Current psychotherapies* (pp. 167–206). Itasca, IL: F. E. Peacock.

Ellis, A. (1993). Changing rational-emotive therapy (RET) to rational-emotive behavior therapy (REBT). *The Behavior Therapist, 16,* 257–258.

Ellis, A. (1995). Rational emotive behavior therapy. In R. J. Corsini & D. Wedding (Eds.), *Current psychotherapies* (5th ed., pp. 162–196). Itasca, IL: Peacock Publishers, Inc.

Ellis, A. (2001). Reasons why rational emotive behavior therapy is relatively neglected in the professional and scientific literatures. *Journal of Rational-Emotive and Cognitive Behavior Therapy, 19,* 67–74.

Ellis, A., & Dryden, W. (1987). *The practice of rational-emotive therapy.* New York: Springer.

Ellis, A., & Grieger, R. (Eds.). (1977). *Handbook of rational-emotive therapy.* New York: Springer.

Emery, R. E. (1982). Interparental conflict and the children of discord and divorce. *Psychological Bulletin, 92,* 310–330.

Emery, R. E., Matthews, S. G., & Kitzmann, K. M. (1994). Child custody mediation and litigation: Parents' satisfaction and functioning one year after settlement. *Journal of Consulting and Clinical Psychology, 62,* 124–129.

Emery, R. E., Matthews, S. G., & Wyer, M. M. (1991). Child custody medication and litigation: Further evidence on the differing views of mothers and fathers. *Journal of Consulting and Clinical Psychology, 59,* 410–418.

Emmelkamp, P. M. G., & Felten, M. (1985). The process of exposure in vivo: Cognitive and physiological changes during treatment of acrophobia. *Behaviour Research and Therapy, 23,* 219–224.

Endicott, J., & Spitzer, R. L. (1978). A diagnostic interview: The schedule for affective disorders and schizophrenia. *Archives of General Psychiatry, 35,* 837–844.

Englemann, S. (1974). The effectiveness of direct verbal instruction on IQ performance and achievement in reading and arithmetic. In R. Ulrich, T. Stachnik, & J. Mabry (Eds.), *Control of human behavior* (vol. 3, pp. 69–84). Glenview, IL: Scott, Foresman.

Ennis, B. J., & Litwack, T. R. (1974). Psychiatry and the presumption of expertise: Flipping coins in the courtroom. *California Law Review, 62,* 693–752.

Epstein, S. (1994). Integration of the cognitive and the psychodynamic unconscious. *American Psychologist, 49,* 709–724.

Erikson, E. H. (1946). *Ego development and historical change. The psychoanalytic study of the child* (vol. 2, pp. 359–396). New York: International Universities Press.

Erickson, P. I., & Kaplan, C. P. (2000). Maximizing qualitative responses about smoking in structured interviews. *Qualitative Health Research, 10,* 829–840.

Erikson, E. H. (1959). Identity and the life cycle. *Psychological Issues, Monograph 1.* New York: International Universities Press.

Erikson, E. H. (1963). *Childhood and society* (rev. ed.). New York: W. W. Norton.

Ernst, N. D., & Harlan, W. R. (1991). Obesity and cardiovascular disease in minority populations: Executive summary. Conference highlights, conclusions, and recommendations. *American Journal of Clinical Nutrition, 53,* 1507S–1511S.

Ernst, E. (2000). The role of complementary and alternative medicine. *British Medical Journal, 321,* 1133–1135.

Erwin, E. (1999). Constructivist epistemologies and therapies. *British Journal of Guidance and Counseling, 27,* 353–365.

Eslinger, P. J., & Damasio, A. R. (1985). Severe disturbance of higher cognition after bilateral frontal lobe ablation: Patient EVR. *Neurology, 35,* 1731–1741.

Esterson, A. (1993). *Seductive mirage: An exploration of the work of Sigmund Freud.* Chicago: Open Court.

Evans, G. D., & Murphy, M. J. (1997). The practicality of predoctoral prescription training for psychologists: A survey of directors of clinical training. *Professional Psychology: Research and Practice, 28,* 113–117.

Evans, M. D., Hollon, S. D., DeRubeis, R. J., Piasecki, J. M., Grove, W. M., Garvey, M. J., & Tauson, V. B. (1992). Differential relapse following cognitive therapy and pharmacotherapy for depression. *Archives of General Psychiatry, 49,* 802–808.

Exner, J. E. (1974). *The Rorschach: A comprehensive system* (vol. 1). New York: Grune & Stratton.

Exner, J. E. (1976). Projective techniques. In I. B. Weiner (Ed.), *Clinical methods in psychology* (pp. 61–121). New York: John Wiley.

Exner, J. E. (1986). *The Rorschach: A comprehensive system, Vol. 1: Basic foundations* (2nd ed.). New York: John Wiley.

Exner, J. E. (1993). *The Rorschach: A comprehensive system: Vol. 1. Basic foundations* (3rd ed.). New York: Wiley.

Exner, J. E. (1996). A comment on "the comprehensive system for the Rorschach: a critical examination." *Psychological Science, 7,* 11–13.

Eysenck, H. J. (1952). The effects of psychotherapy: An evaluation. *Journal of Consulting Psychology, 16,* 319–324.

Eysenck, H. J. (1966). *The effects of psychotherapy.* New York: International Science Press.

Eysenck, H. J. (1978). An exercise in mega-silliness. *American Psychologist, 33,* 517.

Eysenck, H. J. (1982). Neobehavioristic (S-R) theory. In G. T. Wilson & C. M. Franks (Eds.), *Contemporary behavior therapy: Conceptual and empirical foundations* (pp. 205–276). New York: Guilford Press.

Eysenck, H. J., & Eysenck, S. B. G. (1975). *Manual for Eysenck Personality Questionnaire.* San Diego, CA: Educational and Individual Testing Service.

Fagan, T. K. (1996). Witmer's contribution to school psychological services. *American Psychologist, 51,* 241–243.

Fairbairn, W. R. D. (1952). *Psychoanalytic studies of the personality.* London: Tavistock Publications/Routledge & Kegan Paul.

Fairweather, G. W. (1980). *New directions for mental health services: The Fairweather lodge: A twenty-five year retrospective.* San Francisco: Jossey-Bass.

Fairweather, G. W., Sanders, D. H., & Tornatzky, L. G. (1974). *Creating change in mental health organizations*. New York: Pergamon Press.

Fallon, T., & Schwab-Stone, M. (1994). Determinants of reliability in psychiatric surveys of children aged 6-12. *Journal of Child Psychology and Psychiatry and Allied Disciplines, 35,* 1391-1408.

Fancher, R. E. (1973). *Psychoanalytic psychology: The development of Freud's thought.* New York: W. W. Norton.

Farrington, D. P. (1991). Childhood aggression and adult violence: Early precursors and later-life outcomes. In D. J. Pepler & K. H. Rubin (Eds.), *The development of childhood aggression* (pp. 5-29). Hillsdale, NJ: Erlbaum.

Faust, D., & Ziskin, J. (1988). The expert witness in psychology and psychiatry. *Science, 242,* 31-35.

Fawzy, F. I., Cousins, N., Fawzy, N. W., Kemeny, M. E., Elashoff, R., & Morton, D. (1990). A structured psychiatric intervention for cancer patients: I. Changes over time in methods of coping and affective disturbance. *Archives of General Psychiatry, 47,* 720-725.

Fawzy, F. I., Fawzy, N. W., Arndt, L. A., & Pasnau, R. O. (1995). Critical review of psychosocial interventions in cancer care. *Archives of General Psychiatry, 52,* 100-113.

Fawzy, F. I., Fawzy, N. W., Hyun, C. S., Guthrie, D., Fahey, J. L., & Morton, D. (1993). Malignant melanoma: Effect of an early structured psychiatric intervention, coping and affective state on recurrence and survival 6 years later. *Archives of General Psychiatry, 50,* 681-689.

Feinstein, R. E., & Feinstein, M. S. (2001). Psychotherapy for health and lifestyle change. *Journal of Clinical Psychology/In Session, 57,* 1263-1275.

Feist, J., & Feist, G. (2001). *Theories of personality* (5th ed.). New York: McGraw-Hill.

Feldman-Summers, S., & Jones, G. (1984). Psychological impacts of sexual contact between therapists and other health care professionals and their clients. *Journal of Consulting and Clinical Psychology, 52,* 1054-1061.

Felner, R. D., Farber, S. S., & Primavera, J. (1983). Transitions and stressful life events: A model for primary prevention. In R. D. Felner, L. A. Jason, J. N. Moritsugu, & S. S. Farber (Eds.), *Preventive psychology: Theory, research, and prevention* (pp. 191-215). New York: Pergamon Press.

Feltham, C. (2000). What are counselling and psychotherapy? In C. Feltham & I. Horton (Eds.), *Handbook of counselling and psychotherapy*. London: Sage.

Felthous, A. R., & Kachingian, C. (2001). To warn and to control: Two distinct legal obligations or variations of a single duty to protect? *Behavioral Sciences and the Law, 19,* 355-373.

Fernandez-Ballesteros, R., & Staats, A. W. (1992). Paradigmatic behavioral assessment, treatments, and evaluation: Answering the crisis in behavioral assessment. *Advances in Behavior Research and Therapy, 14,* 1-27.

Ferro, T., Klein, D. N., Norden, K. A., Donaldson, S. K., et al. (1995). Development and reliability of the Family History Interview for Personality Disorders. *Journal of Personality Disorders, 9,* 169-177.

Field, T. M. (1998). Massage therapy effects. *American Psychologist, 53,* 1270-1281.

Fincham, F. D., & Beach, S. R. H. (1999). Conflict in marriage: Implications for working with couples. *Annual Review of Psychology, 50,* 47-77.

Fine R. (1971). *The healing of the mind: The technique of psychoanalytic psychotherapy*. New York: David McKay.

Fine, S., & Glasser, P. H. (1996). *The first helping interview: Engaging the client and building trust.* Thousand Oaks, CA: Sage.

Finger, M. S., & Ones, D. S. (1999). Psychometric equivalence of the computer and booklet forms of the MMPI: A meta-analysis. *Psychological Assessment, 11,* 58–66.

Finkelhor, D., & Browne, A. (1988). Assessing the long-term impact of child sexual abuse: A review and conceptualization. In L. Walker (Ed.), *Handbook on sexual abuse in children* (pp. 55–71). New York: Springer.

First, M. B., Gibbon, M., Spitzer, R. L., Williams, J. B. W., & Benjamin, L. (1997). *The Structured Clinical Interview for DSM-IV Axis II Personality Disorders (SCID-II).* Washington, DC: American Psychiatric Press.

Fischer, C. T. (1985). *Individualizing psychological assessment.* Monterey, CA: Brooks/Cole.

Fischer, C. T. (1989). A life-centered approach to psychodiagnostics: Attending to lifeworld, ambiguity, and possibility. *Person-Centered Review, 4,* 163–170.

Fischer, C. T. (2001). Psychological assessment: From objectification back to the life world. In B. D. Slife, R. N. Williams, & S. H. Barlow (Eds.), *Critical issues in psychotherapy* (pp. 29–44). Thousand Oaks, CA: Sage.

Fisher, C. T., & Fisher, W. F. (1983). Phenomenological-existential psychotherapy. In M. Hersen, A. E. Kazdin, & A. S. Bellack (Eds.), *The clinical psychology handbook* (pp. 489–505). New York: Pergamon Press.

Fishman, D. B. (1999). *The case for pragmatic psychology.* New York: New York University Press.

Finn, S. E. (1996). *Manual for using the MMPI-2 for a therapeutic intervention.* Minneapolis: University of Minnesota Press.

Fleisig, W. E. (1993). The development of the Illustrated Fear Survey Schedule (IFSS) and an examination of its reliability and validity with children with mild mental retardation. *Dissertation Abstracts International, 54,* 1719.

Fleming, I., Baum, A., Davidson, L. M., Rectanus, E., & McArdle, S. (1987). Chronic stress as a factor in psychologic reactivity to challenge. *Health Psychology, 6,* 221–238.

Fletcher-Jantzen, E., Strickland, T. L., & Reynolds, C. (Eds). (2000). *Handbook of Cross-Cultural Neuropsychology.* New York: Kluver Academic/Plenum Publishers.

Foa, E. B., Riggs, D., Dancu, C., & Rothbaum, R. (1993). Reliability and validity of a brief instrument for assessing post-traumatic stress disorder. *Journal of Traumatic Stress, 6,* 459–473.

Folkman, S., & Lazarus, R. S. (1980). An analysis of coping in a middle-aged community sample. *Journal of Health and Social Behavior, 21,* 219–239.

Folkman, S., & Lazarus, R. S. (1988). *Manual for the ways of coping questionnaire.* Palo Alto, CA: Consulting Psychologists Press.

Follette, W. C. (1996). Introduction to the special section on the development of theoretically coherent alternatives to the DSM system. *Journal of Consulting and Clinical Psychology, 64,* 1117–1119.

Follette, W. C., & Houts, A. C. (1996). Models of scientific progress and the role of theory in taxonomy development: A case study of the DSM. *Journal of Consulting and Clinical Psychology, 64,* 1120–1132.

Follette, W. C., Naugle, A. E., & Callaghan, G. M. (1996). A radical behavioral understanding of the therapeutic relationship in effecting change. *Behavior Therapy, 27,* 623–642.

Folstein, M. F., Maiberger, P., & McHugh, P. R. (1977). Mood disorders as a specific complication of stroke. *Journal of Neurology, Neurosurgery & Psychiatry, 40,* 1018–1020.

Ford, M., & Widiger, T. (1989). Sex bias in the diagnosis of histrionic and antisocial personality disorders. *Journal of Consulting and Clinical Psychology, 57,* 301–305.

Forehand, R., Lautenschlager, G. J., Faust, J., & Graziano, W. G. (1986). Parent perceptions and parent-child interactions in clinic-referred children: A preliminary investigation of the effects of maternal depressive moods. *Behaviour Research and Therapy, 24,* 73–76.

Forehand, R., & McMahon, R. J. (1981). *Helping the noncompliant child: A clinician's guide to parent training.* New York: Guilford Press.

Foster, G. D., & Kendall, P. C. (1994). The realistic treatment of obesity: Changing the scales of success. *Clinical Psychology Review, 14,* 701–736.

Foster, S. L., Bell-Dolan, D. J., & Burge, D. A. (1988). Behavioral observation. In A. S. Bellack & M. Hersen (Eds.), *Behavioral assessment: A practical handbook* (3rd ed., pp. 119–160). New York: Pergamon Press.

Fowler, R. D. (1985). Landmarks in computer-assisted psychological assessment. *Journal of Consulting and Clinical Psychology, 53,* 748–759.

Fowles, D. C. (1992). Schizophrenia: Diathesis-stress revisited. *Annual Review of Psychology, 43,* 303–336.

Fox, R. (1994). Training professional psychologists for the twenty-first century. *American Psychologist, 49,* 855–867.

Fox, R. E. (1995). The rape of psychotherapy. *Professional Psychology: Research and Practice, 26,* 147–155.

Foy, D. W., Nunn, L. B., & Rychtarik, R. G. (1984). Broad-spectrum behavioral treatment for chronic alcoholics: Effects of training controlled drinking skills. *Journal of Consulting and Clinical Psychology, 52,* 218–230.

Frances, A. J., Pincus, H. A., & Widiger, T. A. (1996). DSM-IV and international communication in psychiatric diagnosis. In Y. Honda, M. Kastrup, & J. E. Mezzich (Eds.), *Psychiatric diagnosis: A world perspective.* New York: Springer.

Frank, J. D. (1957). Some determinants, manifestations, and effects of cohesiveness in therapy groups. *International Journal of Group Psychotherapy, 7,* 53–63.

Frank, L. K. (1939). Projective methods for the study of personality. *Journal of Psychology, 8,* 343–389.

Frankl, V. (1963). *Man's search for meaning.* New York: Washington Square Press.

Frankl, V. (1965). *The doctor and the soul.* New York: Knopf.

Frankl, V. (1967). *Psychotherapy and existentialism: Selected papers on logotherapy.* New York: Washington Square Press.

Franks, C. M. (1964). *Conditioning techniques in clinical practice and research.* New York: Springer.

Fraser, J. S. (1996). All that glitters is not always gold: Medical offset effects and managed behavioral health care. *Professional Psychology: Research and Practice, 27,* 335–344.

Fredrickson, B. L. (2001). The role of positive emotions in positive psychology: The broaden-and-build theory of positive emotions. *American Psychologist, 56,* 218–226.

Freeman, A., Simon, K. M., Beutler, L. E., & Arkowitz, H. (1989). *Comprehensive handbook of cognitive therapy.* New York: Plenum Press.

Freud, A. (1946). *The ego and mechanisms of defense.* New York: International Universities Press.

Freud, A., & Burlingham, D. T. (1943). *War and children.* London: Medical War Books.

Freud, S. (1900). *The interpretation of dreams* (Avon Edition, 1965). New York: Avon Books.

Freud, S. (1901). *The psychopathology of everyday life*. New York: Macmillan.

Freud, S. (1904). On psychotherapy. Lecture delivered before the College of Physicians in Vienna. Reprinted in S. Freud, *Therapy and technique*. New York: Collier Books, 1963.

Freud, S. (1905). *Jokes and their relation to the unconscious*. In the Standard edition of the complete psychological works of Sigmund Freud (Vol. 8). London: Hogarth Press, 1953–1964.

Freud, S. (1912). *Recommendations for physicians on the psychoanalytic method of treatment*. Zentralblatt, DS. II. Reprinted in S. Freud, *Therapy and technique*. New York: Collier Books, 1963.

Freud, S. (1949). *An outline of psychoanalysis*. (J. Strachey, trans.). New York: W. W. Norton.

Freud, S. (1953–1964). *The standard edition of the complete psychological works of Sigmund Freud* (24 vols.). London: Hogarth Press.

Freund, K., & Watson, R. J. (1991). Assessment of the sensitivity and specificity of a phallometric test: An update of phallometric diagnosis of pediophilia. *Psychological Assessment, 2,* 254–260.

Friedman, M., & Rosenman, R. H. (1974). *Type A behavior and your heart*. New York: Knopf.

Friedman, M., & Thoresen, C. (1986). Alteration of Type A behavior and its effect on cardiac recurrences in post-myocardial infarction patients: Summary results of the Recurrent Coronary Prevention Project. *American Heart Journal, 112,* 653–665.

Fruzzetti, A. E., & Jacobson, N. S. (1991). Marital and family therapy. In M. Hersen, A. E. Kazdin, & A. Bellack (Eds.), *The clinical psychology handbook* (2nd ed.) New York: Pergamon Press.

Funder, D. (2001). *The personality puzzle* (2nd ed.). New York: W. W. Norton.

Furman, W. (1980). Promoting appropriate social behavior: A developmental perspective. In B. Lahey & A. Kazdin (Eds.), *Advances in clinical child psychology* (Vol. 3, pp. 1–41). New York: Plenum Press.

Furnham, A. (2000). Thinking about intelligence. *Psychologist, 13,* 510–515.

Gabbard, G. O. (2000). *Psychodynamic psychiatry in clinical practice*. Washington, DC: American Psychiatric Press.

Gaddy, C. D., Charlot-Swilley, D., Nelson, P. D., & Reich, J. (1995). Selected outcomes of accredited programs. *Professional Psychology: Research and Practice, 26,* 507–513.

Gaines, L. K., & Falkenberg, S. (1998). An evaluation of the written selection test: Effectiveness and alternatives. *Journal of Criminal Justice, 26,* 175–183.

Gainotti, G. (1972). Emotional behavior and hemispheric side of lesion. *Cortex, 8,* 41–55.

Galanter, M. (1988). Zealous self-help groups as adjuncts to psychiatric treatment: A study of Recovery, Inc. *American Journal of Psychiatry, 145,* 1248–1253.

Gallagher-Thompson, D., Hanley-Peterson, P., & Thompson, L. W. (1990). Maintenance of gains versus relapse following brief psychotherapy for depression. *Journal of Consulting & Clinical Psychology, 58,* 371–374.

Galton, F. (1883). *Inquiries into the human faculty and its development*. London: Macmillan.

Garb, H. N. (1984). The incremental validity of information used in personality assessment. *Clinical Psychology Review, 4,* 641–656.

Garb, H. N. (1989). Clinical judgment, clinical training, and professional experience. *Psychological Bulletin, 105,* 387–396.

Garb, H. N. (1992). The trained psychologist as expert witness. *Clinical Psychology Review, 12,* 451–468.

Garb, H. N. (1995). Sex bias and the diagnosis of borderline personality disorder. *Professional Psychology: Research and Practice, 26,* 526.

Garb, H. N. (1996). The representativeness and past-behavior heuristics in clinical judgment. *Professional Psychology: Theory and Practice, 27,* 272-277.

Garb, H. N. (2000). Computers will become increasingly important for psychological assessment: Not that there's anything wrong with that! *Psychological Assessment, 12,* 31-39.

Garb, H. N., & Lutz, C. (2001). Cognitive complexity and the validity of clinicians' judgments. *Assessment, 8,* 111-115.

Garb, H. N., & Schramke, C. J. (1996). Judgment research and neuropsychological assessment: A narrative review and meta-analysis. *Psychological Bulletin, 120,* 140-153.

Garber, J. (1984). Classification of childhood psychopathology: A developmental perspective. *Child Development, 55,* 30-48.

Garcia, J., McGowan, B., & Green, K. (1972). Biological constraints on conditioning. In A. H. Block & W. F. Prokasky (Eds.), *Classical conditioning* (pp. 3-27). New York: Appleton-Century-Crofts.

Gardiner, R. A. (1971). *Therapeutic communication with children: The mutual story-telling technique.* New York: Jason Aronson.

Gardner, H., Brownell, H. H., Wapner, W., & Michelow, D. (1983). Missing the point: The role of the right hemisphere in the processing of complex linguistic materials. In E. Perecman (Ed.), *Cognitive processing in the right hemisphere* (pp. 169-191). New York: Academic Press.

Gardner, W., Lidz, C. W., Mulvey, E. P., & Shaw, E. C. (1996). Clinical versus actuarial predictions of violence in patients with mental illnesses. *Journal of Consulting and Clinical Psychology, 64,* 602-609.

Garfield, S. L. (1965). Historical introduction. In B. B. Wolman (Ed.), *Handbook of clinical psychology* (pp. 125-140). New York: McGraw-Hill.

Garfield, S. L. (1974). *Clinical psychology: The study of personality and behavior.* Chicago: Aldine.

Garfield, S. L. (1994). Research on client variables in psychotherapy. In A. Bergin and S. Garfield (Eds.), *Handbook of psychotherapy and behavior change* (4th ed., pp. 190-228). New York: Wiley.

Garfield, S. L. (1996). Some problems associated with "validated" forms of psychotherapy. *Clinical Psychology: Science and Practice, 3,* 218-229.

Garfield, S. (2000). The Rorschach test in clinical diagnosis—A brief commentary. *Journal of Clinical Psychology, 56,* 431-434.

Garfield, S. L., & Bergin, A. E. (1994). Introduction and historical overview. In A. E. Bergin & S. L. Garfield (Eds.), *Handbook of psychotherapy and behavior change* (pp. 3-22). New York: Wiley & Sons.

Garfield, S. L., & Kurtz, R. (1976). Clinical psychologists in the 1970s. *American Psychologist, 31,* 1-9.

Garmezy, N. (1978). Never mind the psychologists: Is it good for the children? *Clinical Psychologist, 31,* 1-6.

Garmezy, N. (1983). Stressors of childhood. In N. Garmezy and M. Rutter (Eds.), *Stress, coping, & development in children* (pp. 43-84). New York: McGraw-Hill.

Garry, M. & Polaschek, D. L. L. (2000). Imagination and memory. *Current Directions in Psychological Science, 9,* 6-10.

Gatz, M., Fiske, A., Fox, L. S., Kaskie, B., Kasl-Godley, J. E., et al. (1998). Empirically validated psychological treatments for older adults. *Journal of Mental Health Aging, 41,* 9-46.

Gazzaniga, M. S., Fendrich, R., and Wessinger, C. M. (1994). Blindsight reconsidered. *Current Directions in Psychological Science, 3,* 93-95.

Geer, J. H. (1965). The development of a scale to measure fear. *Behaviour Research and Therapy, 3,* 45-53.

Gelfand, D. M., & Peterson, L. (1985). *Child development and psychopathology*. Beverly Hills, CA: Sage.

Gelles, R. J., & Straus, M. A. (1988). *Intimate violence*. New York: Simon & Schuster.

Gergen, K. J. (1985). The social constructionist movement in modern psychology. *American Psychologist, 40,* 266-275.

Gergen, K. J. (2001). Psychological science in a postmodern context. *American Psychologist, 56,* 803-813.

Getka, E. J., & Glass, C. R. (1992). Behavioral and cognitive-behavioral approaches to the reduction of dental anxiety. *Behavior Therapy, 23,* 433-448.

Giblin, P. (1986). Research and assessment in marriage and family enrichment: A meta-analysis study. *Journal of Psychotherapy and the Family, 2,* 79-96.

Gittelman, R. (1980). The role of tests for differential diagnosis in child psychiatry. *Journal of the American Academy of Child Psychiatry, 19,* 413-438.

Gittelman-Klein, R. (1986). Questioning the clinical usefulness of projective psychological tests for children. *Developmental and Behavioral Pediatrics, 7,* 378-382.

Givelber, D. J., Bowers, W. J., & Blitch, C. L. (1984). Tarasoff, myth and reality: An empirical study of private law reaction. *Wisconsin Law Review,* 443-497.

Gladwell, M. (2001, December 17). Examined life: What Stanley H. Kaplan taught us about the S.A.T. *The New Yorker,* 86-92.

Glaser, R., & Bond, L. (1981). Introduction to the special issue: Testing: Concepts, policy, practice, and research. *American Psychologist, 36,* 997-1000.

Glasgow, R. E., & Terborg, J. R. (1988). Occupational health promotion programs to reduce cardiovascular risk. *Journal of Consulting and Clinical Psychology, 56,* 365-373.

Glenmullen, J. (2000). *Prozac backlash: Overcoming the dangers of Prozac, Zoloft, Praxil, and other antidepressants with safe, effective alternatives*. New York: Touchstone Books/Simon and Schuster.

Glosoff, H. L., Herlihy, B., & Spence, E. B. (2000). Privileged communication in the counselor-client relationship. *Journal of Counseling & Development, 78,* 454-462.

Godard, S. L., Bloom, J. D., Williams, M. H., & Faulkner, L. R. (1986). The right to refuse treatment in Oregon: A two-year statewide experience. *Behavioral Sciences and the Law, 4,* 293-304.

Goffman, E. (1961). *Asylums*. Garden City, NY: Doubleday.

Goins, M. K., Strauss, G. D., & Martin, R. (1995). A change measure for psychodynamic psychotherapy outcome research. *Journal of Psychotherapy Practice and Research, 4,* 319-328.

Goldberg, L. R. (1959). The effectiveness of clinicians' judgments: The diagnosis of organic brain damage from the Bender-Gestalt test. *Journal of Consulting Psychology, 23,* 25-33.

Goldberg, L. R. (1968). Simple models or simple processes? Some research on clinical judgments. *American Psychologist, 23,* 483-496.

Golden, C. J. (1981). A standardized version of Luria's neuropsychological tests: A quantitative and qualitative approach to neuropsychological evaluation. In S. B. Filskov & T. J. Boll (Eds.), *Handbook of clinical neuropsychology* (pp. 608–642). New York: John Wiley.

Golden, C. J., Purisch, A. D., & Hammeke, T. A. (1978). Diagnostic validity of a standardized neuropsychological battery derived from Luria's neuropsychological tests. *Journal of Consulting and Clinical Psychology, 1982,* 50, 40–48.

Golden, C. J., Purisch, A. D., & Hammeke, T. A. (1985). *Luria-Nebraska Neuropsychological Battery: Forms I and II Manual.* Los Angeles: Western Psychological Services.

Goldenberg, H. (1973). *Contemporary clinical psychology.* Monterey, CA: Brooks/Cole.

Goldfried, M. R. (1980). Toward the delineation of therapeutic change principles. *American Psychologist, 35,* 991–999.

Goldfried, M. R. (1995). Toward a common language for case formulation. *Journal of Psychotherapy Integration, 5,* 221–244.

Goldfried, M. R., & Sprafkin, J. N. (1974). *Behavioral personality assessment.* Morristown, NJ: General Learning Press.

Goldfried, M. R., Stricker, G., & Weiner, I. B. (1971). *Rorschach handbook of clinical and research applications.* Englewood Cliffs, NJ: Prentice-Hall.

Goldfried, M. R., & Wolfe, B. E. (1996). Psychotherapy practice and research: Repairing a strained alliance. *American Psychologist, 51,* 1007–1016.

Goldfried, M. R., & Wolfe, B. E. (1998). Toward a more clinically valid approach to therapy research. *Journal of Consulting and Clinical Psychology, 66,* 143–150.

Golding, S. L., & Rorer, L. G. (1972). Illusory correlation and subjective judgment. *Journal of Abnormal Psychology, 80,* 249–260.

Goldsmith, J. B., & McFall, R. M. (1975). Development and evaluation of an interpersonal skill-training program for psychiatric inpatients. *Journal of Abnormal Psychology, 84,* 51–58.

Goldstein, A. J. (1973). Behavior therapy. In R. Corsini (Ed.), *Current psychotherapies* (pp. 207–249). Itaska, IL: F. E. Peacock.

Goldstein, A. P., & McGinnis, E. (1997). *Skillstreaming the adolescent: New strategies and perspectives for teaching prosocial skills.* Champaign, IL: Research Press.

Goldstein, G., & Hersen, M. (Eds.). (1990). *Handbook of psychological assessment.* New York: Pergamon Press.

Goodenough, F. L. (1931). Children's drawings. In C. Murchison (Ed.), *A handbook of child psychology* (pp. 480–514). Worcester, MA: University Press.

Goodenough, F. L. (1949). *Mental testing.* New York: Rinehart.

Goodman, S. H., Lahey, B. B., Fielding, B., Dulcan, M., Narrow, W., & Regier, D. (1997). Representativeness of clinical samples of youth with mental disorders: A preliminary population-based study. *Journal of Abnormal Psychology,* 3–14.

Goodwin, P. J., Leszcz, M., Ennis, M., Koopmans, J., Vincent, L., Guther, H., et al. (2001). The effect of group psychosocial support on survival in metastatic breast cancer. *The New England Journal of Medicine, 345,* 1719–1726.

Gottesman, I. I. (1991). *Schizophrenia genesis.* New York: W. H. Freeman.

Gottesman, I. I., & Shields, J. (1982). *Schizophrenia: The epigenetic puzzle.* Cambridge: Cambridge University Press.

Gottfredson, G. D., & Holland, J. L. (1989). *Dictionary of Holland occupational codes.* Odessa, FL: Psychological Assessment Resources.

Gottfredson, L. S. (1994). The science and politics of race-norming. *American Psychologist, 49,* 955-963.

Gottlieb, B. H., & Peters, L. (1991). A national demographic portrait of mutual aid group participants in Canada. *American Journal of Community Psychology, 19,* 651-666.

Gottman, J. M., & Levenson, R. W. (1992). Marital processes predictive of later dissolution: Behavior, physiology, and health. *Journal of Personality and Social Psychology, 63,* 221-233.

Gottman, J. M., Markman, H. J., & Notarius, C. (1977). The topography of marital conflict: A sequential analysis of verbal and nonverbal behavior. *Journal of Marriage and the Family, 39,* 461-477.

Gottman, J. M., & Roy, A. K. (1990). *Sequential analysis: A guide for behavioral researchers.* New York: Cambridge University Press.

Gough, H. (1987). *California Psychological Inventory: Administrator's guide.* Palo Alto, CA: Consulting Psychologists Press.

Graham, F. K., & Kendall, B. S. (1960). Memory-for-designs test: Revised general manual. *Perceptual and Motor Skills, 11,* 147-188.

Graham, J. R. (1990). *MMPI-2: Assessing personality and psychopathology.* New York: Oxford University Press.

Graham, S. R., & Fox, R. E. (1991). Postdoctoral education for professional practice. *American Psychologist, 46,* 1033-1035.

Grant, B. F., Harford, T. C., Dawson, D. D., Chou, P. S., et al. (1995). The Alcohol Use Disorder and Associated Disabilities Interview Schedule (AUDADIS): Reliability of alcohol and drug modules in a general population sample. *Drug and Alcohol Dependence, 39,* 37-44.

Grantham, R. J. (1973). Effects of counselor sex, race, and language style on black students in initial interviews. *Journal of Counseling Psychology, 20,* 553-559.

Greenberg, L. (1986). Change process research. *Journal of Consulting and Clinical Psychology, 54,* 4-9.

Greenberg, L. S., Elliot, R. K., & Lietaer, G. (1994). Research on experiential psychotherapies. In A. E. Bergin & S. L. Garfield (Eds.), *Handbook of psychotherapy and behavior change* (pp. 509-512). New York: John Wiley.

Greenberg, L. S., & Johnson, S. M. (1988). *Emotionally focused couples therapy.* New York: Guilford.

Greenberg, L. S., & Safran, J. D. (1989). Emotion in psychotherapy. *American Psychologist, 44,* 19-29.

Greenberg, M. T., Speltz, M. L., & DeKlyen, M. (1993). The role of attachment in the early development of disruptive behavior problems. *Development and Psychopathology, 5,* 191-214.

Greenwood, C. R., Carta, J. J., Kamps, D., Terry, B., & Delquadri, J. (1994). Development and validation of standard classroom observation systems for school practitioners: Ecobehavioral assessment systems software. *Exceptional Children, 61,* 197-210.

Greenwood, C. R., Walker, H. M., Todd, N. M., & Hops, H. (1979). Selecting a cost-effective screening measure for the assessment of preschool social withdrawal. *Journal of Applied Behavior Analysis, 12,* 639-652.

Griest, D. L., Forehand, R., Rogers, T., Breiner, J., Furey, W., & Williams, C. A. (1982). Effect of parent enhancement therapy on the treatment outcome and generalization of a parent training program. *Behaviour Research and Therapy, 20,* 429-436.

Griest, D. L., Wells, K. C., & Forehand, R. (1979). An examination of predictors of maternal perceptions of maladjustment in clinic-referred children. *Journal of Abnormal Psychology, 88,* 277-281.

Grisso, T. (1986). *Evaluating competencies: Forensic assessments and instruments.* New York: Plenum.

Grisso, T. (1997). The competence of adolescents as trial defendants. *Psychology, Public Policy, and Law, 3* (1), 3-32.

Grisso, T., & Appelbaum, P. S. (1995). The MacArthur Treatment Competence Study. III: Abilities of patients to consent to psychiatric and medical treatments. *Law and Human Behavior, 19,* 149-174.

Grissom, R. J., (1996). The magical number 7 plus or minus 2: Meta-analysis of the probability of superior outcome in comparisons involving therapy, placebo, and control. *Journal of Consulting and Clinical Psychology, 64,* 973-982.

Gross, M. L. (1962). *The brain watchers.* New York: Random House.

Gross, S. J. (1978). The myth of professional licensing. *American Psychologist, 33,* 1009-1016.

Grossarth, M. R., Eysenck, H. J., & Boyle, G. J. (1995). Method of test administration as a factor in test validity: The use of a personality questionnaire in the prediction of cancer and coronary heart disease. *Behaviour Research and Therapy, 33,* 705-710.

Groth-Marnat, G., & Edkins, G. (1996). Professional psychologists in general health care settings: A review of the financial efficacy of direct treatment interventions. *Professional Psychology: Research and Practice, 27,* 161-174.

Groth-Marnat, G. (1999). *Handbook of psychological assessment.* New York: John Wiley & Sons.

Groth-Marnat, G. (2000). Visions of clinical assessment: Then, now, and a brief history of the future. *Journal of Clinical Psychology, 56,* 349-366.

Grove, H. (1987). The reliability of psychiatric diagnosis. In C. G. Last & M. Hersen (Eds.), *Issues in diagnostic research* (pp. 99-117). New York: Plenum Press.

Grove, W. M., Zald, D. H., Lebow, B. S., Snitz, B. E., & Nelson, C. (2000). Clinical versus mechanical prediction: A meta-analysis. *Psychological Assessment, 12,* 19-30.

Grube, B. S., Bilder, R. M., Goldman, R. S. (1998). Meta-analysis of symptom factors in schizophrenia. *Schizophrenia Research, 25,* 113-120.

Grundy, S. M. (1999). Primary prevention of coronary heart disease: Integrating risk assessment with interventions. *Circulation, 100,* 988-998.

Grych, J. H., & Fincham, F. D. (1992). Interventions for children of divorce: Toward greater integration of research and action. *Psychological Bulletin, 111,* 434-454.

Guerney, B. G. (Ed.). (1969). *Psychotherapeutic agents: New roles of nonprofessionals, parents, and teachers.* New York: Holt, Rinehart & Winston.

Gullone, E., & King, N. J. (1992). Psychometric evaluation of a revised fear survey schedule for children and adolescents. *Journal of Child Psychology and Psychiatry and Allied Disciplines, 33,* 987-998.

Guntrip, H. (1973). *Psychoanalytic theory, therapy, and the self.* New York: Basic Books.

Gur, R. E. (1978). Left hemisphere dysfunction and left hemisphere overactivation in schizophrenia. *Journal of Abnormal Psychology, 87,* 225-238.

Gur, R. E., Cowell, P. E., Latshaw, A., Turetsky, B. I., Grossman, R. I., Arnold, S. E., et al. (2000). Reduced dorsal and orbital prefrontal gray matter volumes in schizophrenia. *Archives of General Psychiatry, 57,* 761-768.

Gurman, A. S., Kniskern, D. P., & Pinsof, W. M. (1986). Research on marital and family therapies. In S. L. Garfield & A. E. Bergin (Eds.), *Handbook of psychotherapy and behavior change* (3rd ed., pp. 565-624). New York: John Wiley.

Hacker, A. (1997). The medicine in our future. *New York Review of Books,* June 12, 26-31.

Hahlweg, K., Revenstorf, D., & Schindler, L. (1984). Effects of behavioral marital therapy on couples' communication and problem-solving skills. *Journal of Consulting and Clinical Psychology, 52,* 553-566.

Halgren, E., Raij, T., Marinkovic, K., Jousmaki, V., & Hari, R. (2000). Cognitive response profile of the human fusiform face area as determined by MEG. *Cerebral Cortex, 10,* 69-81.

Hall, G. C. N. (1990). Prediction of sexual aggression. *Clinical Psychology Review, 10,* 229-245.

Halleck, S. L. (1969). Community psychiatry: Some troubling questions. In L. M. Roberts, S. L. Halleck, & M. B. Loeb (Eds.), *Community psychiatry* (pp. 58-71). Garden City, NY: Doubleday, Anchor Books.

Halpern, E. (2001). Family psychology from an Israeli perspective. *American Psychologist, 56,* 58-64.

Halweg, K., & Markman, H. J. (1988). Effectiveness of behavioral marital therapy: Empirical status of behavioral techniques in preventing and alleviating marital distress. *Journal of Consulting and Clinical Psychology, 56,* 440-447.

Hammond, K. R., & Allen, J. M. (1953). *Writing clinical reports.* Englewood Cliffs, NJ: Prentice-Hall.

Handbook of Licensing and Certification Requirements for Psychologists in the U.S. and Canada. (2001). Washington, DC: Association of State and Provincial Psychology Boards.

Handler, L. (1974). Psychotherapy, assessment, and clinical research: Parallels and similarities. In A. I. Rabin (Ed.), *Clinical psychology: Issues of the seventies* (pp. 49-62). East Lansing: Michigan State University Press.

Hansen, J. C. (1984). Interest inventories. In G. Goldstein & M. Hersen (Eds.), *Handbook of psychological assessment* (pp. 157-177). New York: Pergamon Press.

Hansen, J. C., & Campbell, D. P. (1985). *Manual for the SVIB-SCII* (4th ed.). Palo Alto, CA: Consulting Psychologists Press.

Hansen, N. D., & Goldberg, S. G. (1999). Navigating the nuances: A matrix for considerations for ethical-legal dilemmas. *Professional Psychology: Research and Practice, 30,* 495-503.

Harbeck, C., Peterson, L., & Starr, L. (1992). Previously abused child victims' response to a sexual abuse prevention program: A matter of measures. *Behavior Therapy, 23,* 375-388.

Harbin, T. J. (1989). The relationship between the Type A behavior pattern and physiological responsivity: A quantitative review. *Psychophysiology, 26,* 110-119.

Hare, R. D. (1980). A research scale for the assessment of psychopathy in criminal populations. *Personality and Individual Differences, 1,* 111-119.

Hare, R. D. (1991). *Manual for the revised Psychopathy Checklist.* Toronto: Multi-Health Systems.

Harlow, H. F., & Zimmerman, R. (1959). Affectional responses in the infant monkey. *Science, 130,* 421-432.

Harris, F. C., & Lahey, B. B. (1982). Recording system bias in direct observational methodology: A review. *Clinical Psychology Review, 2,* 539-556.

Harris, M. J., Milich, R., Johnston, E. M., & Hoover, D. W. (1990). Effects of expectancies on children's social interactions. *Journal of Experimental Social Psychology, 26,* 1-12.

Harris, V. W., & Sherman, J. A. (1973). Effects of peer tutoring and consequences on the math performance of elementary classroom students. *Journal of Applied Behavior Analysis, 6,* 587–598.

Harrison, P. J. (1999). The neuropathology of schizophrenia: a critical review of the data and their interpretation. *Brain, 122,* 593–624.

Harrison, R. (1965). Thematic apperceptive methods. In B. B. Wolman (Ed.), *Handbook of clinical psychology* (pp. 562–620). New York: McGraw-Hill.

Harrower, M. R. (1965). Clinical psychologists at work. In B. B. Wolman (Ed.), *Handbook of clinical psychology* (pp. 1443–1458). New York: McGraw-Hill.

Hart, S. N., & Brassard, M. R. (1987). A major threat to children's mental health: Psychological maltreatment. *American Psychologist, 42,* 160–165.

Hartmann, H. (1939). Psychoanalysis and the concept of health. *International Journal of Psychoanalysis, 20,* 308–321.

Hartmann, H. (1958). *Ego psychology and the problem of adaptation.* New York: International Universities Press.

Hartup, W. W., & Stevens, N. (1997). Friendships and adaptation in the life course. *Psychological Bulletin, 121,* 355–370.

Hasemann, D., Nietzel, M. T., & Golding, J. (1996). Clinicians' beliefs about reprocessed memory: Effects of tough and tender-mindedness. Paper presented at the annual meeting of the American Psychological Society. San Francisco.

Haspel, K. C., Jorgenson, L. M., Wincze, J. P., & Parsons, J. P. (1997). Legislative intervention regarding therapist sexual misconduct: An overview. *Professional Psychology: Research and Practice, 28,* 63–72.

Hatala, R., & Case, S. M. (2000). Examining the influence of gender on medical students' decision making. *Journal of Women's Health & Gender-Based Medicine, 9,* 617–623.

Hathaway, S. R. (1958). A study of human behavior: The clinical psychologist. *American Psychologist, 13,* 255–265.

Hathaway, S. R., & McKinley, J. C. (1967). *The Minnesota Multiphasic Personality Inventory Manual.* New York: Psychological Corporation.

Hattie, J. A., Sharpley, C. F., & Rogers, H. J. (1984). Comparative effectiveness of professional and paraprofessional helpers. *Psychological Bulletin, 95,* 534–541.

Hauggard, J. J., & Reppucci, N. D. (1988). *The sexual abuse of children.* San Francisco: Jossey-Bass.

Hawley, D. R., Bailey, C. E., & Pennick, K. A. (2000). A content analysis of research in family therapy journals. *Journal of Marital and Family Therapy, 26,* 9–16.

Hayes, S. C. (1983). The role of the individual case in the production and consumption of clinical knowledge. In M. Hersen, A. E. Kazdin, & A. S. Bellack (Eds.), *The clinical psychology handbook* (pp. 181–195). New York: Pergamon Press.

Hayes, S. C. (1996). AABT and AAAPP sponsor national planning conference on practice guidelines. *The Behavior Therapist, 19,* 170.

Hayes, S. C., Follette, V. M., Dawes, R. M., & Grady, K. E. (Eds.). (1995). *Scientific standards of psychological practice: Issues and recommendations.* Reno, NV: Context Press.

Hayes, S. C., & Heiby, E. (1996). Psychology's drug problem: Do we need a fix or should we just say no? *American Psychologist, 51,* 198–206.

Haynes, R. B. (1982). Improving patient compliance: An empirical view. In R. B. Stuart (Ed.), *Adherence, compliance, and generalization in behavioral medicine* (pp. 56–78). New York: Brunner/Mazel.

Haynes, S. G., Feinleib, M., & Kannel, W. B. (1980). The relationship of psychosocial factors to coronary heart disease in the Framingham study: III. Eight-year incidence of coronary heart disease. *American Journal of Epidemiology, 111,* 37–58.

Haynes, S. N. (1990). Behavioral assessment of adults. In G. Goldstein & M. Hersen (Eds.), *Handbook of psychological assessment* (2nd ed., pp. 423–463). New York: Pergamon Press.

Haynes, S. N. (1993). Treatment implications of psychological assessment. *Psychological Assessment, 5,* 251–253.

Haynes, S. N., & Horn, W. F. (1982). Reactivity in behavioral assessment: A review. *Behavioral Assessment, 4,* 369–385.

Haynes, S. N., & O'Brien, W. O. (2000). *Principles of behavioral assessment: A functional approach to psychological assessment.* New York: Plenum/Kluwer Press.

Haynes, S. N., & Uchigakiuchi, P. (1993). Incorporating personality trait measures into behavioral assessment: Nuts in a fruitcake or raisins in a mai tai? *Behavior Modification, 17,* 72–92.

Hayvren, M., & Hymel, S. (1984). Ethical issues in sociometric testing: Impact of sociometric measures on interaction behavior. *Developmental Psychology, 20,* 844–849.

Haywood, T. W., Grossman, L. S., & Cavanaugh, J. L. (1990). Subjective versus objective measurements of deviant sexual arousal in clinical evaluations of alleged child molesters. *Psychological Assessment, 2,* 269–275.

Hazelrigg, M. D., Cooper, H. M., & Boudin, C. M. (1987). Evaluating the effectiveness of family therapies: An integrative review and analysis. *Psychological Bulletin, 101,* 428–442.

Heal, L. W., & Sigelman, C. K. (1995). Response biases in interviews of individuals with limited mental ability. *Journal of Intellectual Disability Research, 39,* 331–340.

Hedges, L. V., & Olkin, L. (1982). Analyses, reanalyses, and meta-analysis. *Contemporary Education Review, 1,* 157–165.

Heidegger, M. (1968). *Being and time* (J. Macquarrie & E. Robinson, Trans.). New York: Harper & Row. (Original work published 1927)

Heilbrun, K., & Collins, S. (1995). Evaluations of trial competency and mental state at time of offense: Report characteristics. *Professional Psychology: Research & Practice, 26,* 61–67.

Heine, S., Lehman, D., Markus, H., & Kitayama, S. (1999). Is there a universal need for positive regard? *Psychological Review, 106,* 766–794.

Helfer, R. E., & Kempe, C. H. (Eds.). (1968). *The battered child.* Chicago: University of Chicago Press.

Helgeson, V. S., Cohen, S., & Fritz, H. (1998). Social ties and the onset and progression of cancer. In J. Holland (Ed.), *Psycho-oncology.* New York: Oxford University Press.

Heller, K. (1996). Coming of age of prevention science. *American Psychologist, 51,* 1123–1127.

Heller, W. (1990). The neuropsychology of emotion: Developmental patterns and implications for psychopathology. In N. L. Stein, B. L. Leventhal, & T. Trabasso (Eds.), *Psychological and biological approaches to emotion* (pp. 167–211). Hillsdale, NJ: Lawrence Erlbaum Associates.

Heller, W., & Nitschke, J. B. (1997). Regional brain activity in emotion: A framework for understanding cognition in depression. *Cognition and Emotion, 11,* 637–661.

Henry, W. E. (1956). *The analysis of fantasy: The thematic apperception technique in the story of personality.* New York: John Wiley.

Henry, W. P., Strupp, H. H., Butler, S. F., Schacht, T. E., & Binder, J. L. (1993). Effects of training in time-limited dynamic psychotherapy: Changes in therapist behavior. *Journal of Consulting and Clinical Psychology, 61,* 434–440.

Herbert, T. B., & Cohen, S. (1993). Stress and immunity in humans: A meta-analytic review. *Psychosomatic Medicine, 55,* 364–379.

Hergenhahn, B. R. (1994). *An introduction to theories of personality* (4th ed.). Englewood Cliffs, NJ: Prentice Hall.

Herink, R. (Ed.). (1980). *The psychotherapy handbook: The A to Z guide to more than 250 different therapies in use today.* New York: New American Library.

Herrnstein, R. J., & Murray, C. (1994). *The bell curve: Intelligence and class structure in American life.* New York: Free Press.

Hersch, P. D., & Alexander, R. W. (1990). MMPI profile patterns of emotional disability claimants. *Journal of Clinical Psychology, 46,* 795–799.

Herz, M. I., & Melville, C. (1980). Relapse in schizophrenia. *American Journal of Psychiatry, 137,* 801–805.

Hess, A. K. (1999). Defining forensic psychology. In A. K. Hess & I. B. Weiner (Eds.), *The Handbook of forensic psychology* (2nd ed., pp. 24–47). New York: John Wiley & Sons.

Hess, A. K., & Weiner, I. B. (Eds.). (1999). *Handbook of forensic psychology* (2nd ed). New York: John Wiley and Sons.

Hetherington, E. M. (1989). Coping with family transition: Winners, losers, and survivors. *Child Development, 60,* 1–14.

Hetherington, E. M., & Arasteh, J. D. (Eds.). (1988). *Impact of divorce, single parenting, and stepparenting on children.* Hillsdale, NJ: Lawrence Erlbaum Associates.

Hetherington, E. M., Bridges, M., & Insabella, G. M. (1998). What matters? What does not? Five perspectives on the association between marital transitions and children's adjustment. *American Psychologist, 53,* 167–184.

Hetherington, E. M., Stanley-Hagan, M., & Anderson, E. R. (1989). Marital transitions: A child's perspective. *American Psychologist, 44,* 303–312.

Heubeck, B. (2000). Cross-cultural generalizability of CBCL syndromes across three continents: From the USA and Holland to Australia. *Journal of Abnormal Child Psychology, 28,* 439–450.

Hickling, F. W., McKenzie, K., Mullen, R., & Murray, R. (1999). A Jamacian psychiatrist evaluates diagnoses at a London psychiatric hospital. *British Journal of Psychiatry, 175,* 283–285.

Hile, M. G., & Adkins, R. E. (1997). Do substance abuse and mental health clients prefer automated assessments? *Behavior Research Methods, Instruments, and Computers, 29,* 146–150.

Himelein, M. J., & Putnam, E. A. (2001). Work activities of academic clinical psychologists: Do they practice what they teach? *Professional Psychology: Research and Practice, 5,* 537–542.

Hinshaw, S. P. (1992). Externalizing behavior problems and academic achievement in childhood and adolescence: Causal relationships and underlying mechanisms. *Psychological Bulletin, 111,* 127–158.

Hodgson, R. J., & Rachman, S. (1977). Obsessional-compulsive complaints. *Behaviour Research and Therapy, 15,* 389–395.

Hoelscher, T. J., Lichstein, K. L., & Rosenthal, T. L. (1986). Home relaxation practice in hypertension treatment: Objective assessment and compliance induction. *Journal of Consulting and Clinical Psychology, 54,* 217–221.

Hoffman, B. (1964). *The tyranny of testing.* New York: MacMillan.

Hoffman, I. Z. (1998). *Ritual and spontaniety in the psychoanalytic process: A dialectical-constructivist view.* Hillsdale, NJ: Analytic Press.

Hoffman, P. J. (1960). The paramorphic representation of clinical judgment. *Psychological Bulletin, 57,* 116–131.

Hogan, D. B. (1983). The effectiveness of licensing: History, evidence, and recommendations. *Law and Human Behavior, 7,* 117–138.

Holder, H. D., & Blose, J. D. (1987). Changes in health care costs and utilization associated with mental health treatment. *Hospital and Community Psychiatry, 38,* 1070–1075.

Holland, D. (1998). The cost-effective delivery of rehabilitation psychology services: The responsible utilization of paraprofessionals. *Rehabilitation Psychology, 43,* 232–245.

Holland, J. L. (1994). *The self-directed search.* Odessa, FL: Psychological Assessment Resources.

Holland, J. L. (1996). Exploring careers with a typology. *American Psychologist, 51,* 397–406.

Holland, J. L., & Gottfredson, G. D. (1994). *Career attitudes and strategies inventory: An inventory for understanding adult careers.* Odessa, FL: Psychological Assessment Resources.

Hollon, S. D. (1993). Review of psychosocial treatments for mood disorders. In D. D. Dunner (Ed.), *Current psychiatric therapy* (pp. 240–246). Philadelphia, PA: W. B. Saunders Co.

Hollon, S. D., & Beck, A. T. (1994). Cognitive and cognitive-behavioral therapies. In A. E. Bergin & S. L. Garfield (Eds.), *Handbook of psychotherapy and behavior change* (pp. 428–466). New York: Wiley & Sons.

Holmes, M. R., Hansen, D. J., & St. Lawrence, J. S. (1984). Conversational skills training with aftercare patients in the community: Social validation and generalization. *Behavior Therapy, 15,* 84–100.

Holt, R. R. (1958). Formal aspects of the TAT: A neglected resource. *Journal of Projective Techniques, 22,* 163–172.

Holt, R. R. (1978). *Methods in clinical psychology: Projective assessment* (Vol. 1). New York: Plenum Press.

Holt, R. R., & Luborsky, L. (1958). *Personality patterns of psychiatrists: A study of methods for selecting residents* (Vol. 1). New York: Basic Books.

Holtzman, W. H., Thorpe, J. W., Swartz, J. D., & Herron, E. W. (1961). *Inkblot perception and personality: Holtzman Inkblot Technique.* Austin: University of Texas Press.

Homant, R., & Kennedy, D. B. (1998). Psychological aspects of crime scene profiling. *Criminal Justice and Behavior, 25,* 319–343.

Hooley, J. M. (1985). Expressed emotion: A review of the critical literature. *Clinical Psychology Review, 5,* 119–139.

Horowitz, L. M., Rosenberg, S. E., Baer, B. A., Ureno, G., & Villasenor, V. S. (1988). The Inventory of Interpersonal Problems: Psychometric properties and clinical applications. *Journal of Consulting and Clinical Psychology, 56,* 885–892.

Horowitz, L. M., & Vitkus, J. (1986). The interpersonal basis of psychiatric symptoms. *Clinical Psychology Review, 6,* 443–469.

Hovarth, A. O. (2000). The therapeutic relationship: From transference to alliance. *Journal of Clinical Psychology/In Session: Psychotherapy in Practice, 56,* 163–173.

Hovarth, A. O., & Greenberg, L. S. (1989). Development and validation of the Working Alliance Inventory. *Journal of Counseling Psychology, 36,* 223-233.

Hovarth, A. O , & Symonds, B. D. (1991). Relation between working alliance and outcome in psychotherapy: A meta-analysis. *Journal of Counseling Psychology, 38,* 139-149.

House, J. S., Robbins, C., & Metzner, H. L. (1982). The association of social relationships and activities with mortality: Prospective evidence from the Tecumseh Community Health Study. *American Journal of Epidemiology, 116,* 123-140.

Howard, K. I., Lueger, R. J., Maling, M. S., & Martinovich, Z. (1993). A phase model of psychotherapy outcome: Causal mediation of change. *Journal of Consulting and Clinical Psychology, 61,* 678-685.

Howard, K. I., Moras, K., Brill, P. L., Martinovich, Z., & Lutz, W. (1996). Evaluation of psychotherapy: Efficacy, effectiveness, and patient progress. *American Psychologist, 51,* 1059-1064.

Hughes, C. F., Uhlmann, C., & Pennebaker, J. W. (1994). The body's response to processing emotional trauma: Linking verbal text to autonomic activity. *Journal of Personality, 62,* 565-585.

Hughes, R., Jr. (1996). The effects of divorce on children. Retrieved December 13, 2001 from http://www.hec.ohio-state.edu/famlife/divorce/index.htm.

Hull, C. L. (1943). *Principles of behavior.* New York: Appleton.

Humphrey, L. L., Apple, R. F., & Kirschenbaum, D. S. (1986). Differentiating bulimic-anorexic from normal families using interpersonal and behavioral observational systems. *Journal of Consulting and Clinical Psychology, 54,* 190-195.

Humphreys, K. (1996). Clinical psychologists as psychotherapists: History, future, and alternatives. *American Psychologist, 51,* 190-197.

Humphreys, L. G. (1988). Trends in levels of academic achievement of blacks and other minorities. *Intelligence, 12,* 231-260.

Hunt, W. A., & Jones, N. F. (1962). The experimental investigation of clinical judgment. In A. J. Bachrach (Ed.), *Experimental foundations of clinical psychology* (pp. 26-51). New York: Basic Books.

Hunter, R. H. (1995). Benefits of competency-based treatment programs. *American Psychologist, 50,* 509-513.

Huppert, J. D., Bufka, L. F., Barlow, D. H., Gorman, J, M., Shea, M. K., & Woods, S. W. (2001). Therapist, therapist variables, and cognitive-behavioral therapy outcome in a multicenter trial for panic disorder. *Journal of Consulting & Clinical Psychology, 69,* 747-755.

Husserl, E. (1969). *Ideas: General introduction to pure phenomenology.* New York: Humanities Press. (Original work published 1913)

Hutt, C., & Hutt, S. J. (1968). Stereotypy, arousal and autism. *Human Development, 11,* 277-286.

Ialongo, N., Edelsohn, G., Wertheimer-Larsson, L., Crockett, L., & Kellam, S. (1994). The significance of self-reported anxious symptoms in the first grade. *Journal of Abnormal Child Psychology, 22,* 441-455.

Impara, J. C., & Plake, B. S. (Eds.). (2001). *The fourteenth mental measurements yearbook.* Lincoln, NE: The Buros Institute of Mental Measurements.

Individuals with Disabilities Education Act (Public Law 105-17, 1997).

Inskipp, F. (2000). Generic skills. In C. Feltham & I. Horton (Eds.), *Handbook of counselling and psychotherapy.* London: Sage Publications.

Institute of Personality Assessment and Research. (1970). *Annual report: 1969-1970.* Berkeley: University of California.

Inui, T., Yourtee, E., & Williamson, J. (1976). Improved outcomes in hypertension after physician tutorials. *Annuals of Internal Medicine, 84,* 646–651.

Isenhart, C. E., & Silversmith, D. J. (1996). MMPI-2 response styles: Generalization to alcoholism assessment. *Psychology of Addictive Behaviors, 10,* 115–123.

Jackson, D. N. (1984). *Personality Research Form manual.* Port Huron, MI: Research Psychologists Press.

Jackson, D. N., & Messick, S. (1958). Content and style in personality assessment. *Psychological Bulletin, 55,* 243–252.

Jackson, D. N., & Messick, S. (1961). Acquiescence and desirability as response determinants on the MMPI. *Educational and Psychological Measurement, 21,* 771–790.

Jacobs, M. K., & Goodman, G. (1989). Psychology and self-help groups: Predictions on a partnership. *American Psychologist, 44,* 536–545.

Jacobson, N. S. (1991). Behavioral versus insight-oriented marital therapy: Labels can be misleading. *Journal of Consulting and Clinical Psychology, 59,* 142–145.

Jacobson, N. S., & Christensen, A. (1996). Studying the effectiveness of psychotherapy: How well can clinical trials do the job? *American Psychologist, 51,* 1031–1039.

Jacobson, N. S., Dobson, D. S., Truax, P. A., Addis, M. E., Koerner, K., et al. (1996). A component analysis of cognitive-behavioral treatment for depression. *Journal of Consulting and Clinical Psychology, 64,* 295–304.

Jacobson, N. S., Holtzworth-Monroe, A., & Schmaling, K. B. (1989). Marital therapy and spouse involvement in the treatment of depression, agoraphobia, and alcoholism. *Journal of Consulting and Clinical Psychology, 57,* 5–10.

Jacobson, N. S., Schmaling, K. B., & Holtzworth-Munroe, A. (1987). Component analysis of behavioral marital therapy: 2-year follow-up and prediction of relapse. *Journal of Marital and Family Therapy, 13,* 187–195.

Jacoby, L. L., & Kelley, C. M. (1987). Unconscious influences of memory for a prior event. *Personality and Social Psychology Bulletin, 13,* 314–336.

James, J. W., & Haley, W. E. (1995). Age and health bias in practicing clinical psychologists. *Psychology & Aging, 10,* 610–616.

Jang, D. P., Ku, J. H., Shin, M. B., Choi, Y. H., Kim, S. I. I. (2000). Objective validation of the effectiveness of virtual reality psychotherapy. *CyberPsychology and Behavior, 3,* 369–374.

Jason, L. A., McMahon, S. D., Salina, D., Hedeker, D., Stockton, M., Dunson, K., & Kimball, P. (1995). Asssessing a smoking cessation intervention involving groups, incentives, and self-help manuals. *Behavior Therapy, 26,* 393–408.

Jeffery, R. W. (1988). Dietary risk factors and their modification in cardiovascular disease. *Journal of Consulting and Clinical Psychology, 56,* 350–357.

Jennings, L., & Skovholt, T. M. (1999). The cognitive, emotional, and relational characteristics of master therapists. *Journal of Counseling Psychology, 46,* 3–11.

Jensen, M. P., Turner, J. A., Romano, J. M., & Karoly, P. (1991). Coping with chronic pain: A critical review of the literature. *Pain, 47,* 249–283.

Jensen, P. S., Kettle, L., Roper, R. S., Sloan, M. T., Dulcan, M. K., Hoven, C., Bird, H. R., Bauermeister, J. J., & Payne, J. D. (1999). Are stimulants overprescribed? Treatment of ADHD in four U.S. communities. *Journal of the American Academy of Child and Adolescent Psychiatry, 38,* 797–804.

Johansson, C. B. (1982). *Manual for Career Assessment Inventory* (2nd ed.). Minneapolis: National Computer Systems.

Johnsen, B. H., & Hugdahl, K. (1990). Fear questionnaires for simple phobias: Psychometric evaluations for a Norwegian sample. *Scandinavian Journal of Psychology, 31,* 42–48.

Johnson, J. H., Rasbury, W. G., & Siegel, L. J. (1986). *Approaches to child treatment: Introduction to theory, research, and practice.* New York: Pergamon Press.

Johnson, M. K., & Raye, C. L. (1998). False memories and confabulation. *Trends in Cognitive Sciences, 2,* 137–145.

Johnson, S. L., & Jacob, T. (1997). Marital interactions of depressed men and women. *Journal of Consulting and Clinical Psychology, 65,* 15–23.

Johnston, C., & Freeman, W. S. (1997). Attributions for child behavior in parents of children without behavior disorders and children with attention deficit hyperactivity disorder. *Journal of Consulting and Clinical Psychology, 65,* 636–645.

Johnstone, B., et al. (1995). Psychology in health care: Future directions. *Professional Psychology: Research and Practice, 26,* 341–365.

Jones, B. P., & Butters, N. (1983). Neuropsychological assessment. In M. Hersen, A. E. Kazdin, & A. S. Bellack (Eds.), *The clinical psychology handbook* (pp. 377–396). New York: Pergamon Press.

Jones, E. E. (1996). Introduction to the special section on attachment and psychopathology: Part I. *Journal of Consulting and Clinical Psychology, 64,* 5–7.

Jones, E. E., Cumming, J. D., & Horowitz, M. J. (1988). Another look at the nonspecific hypothesis of therapeutic effectiveness. *Journal of Consulting and Clinical Psychology, 56,* 48–55.

Jones, M. C. (1924a). The elimination of children's fears. *Journal of Experimental Psychology, 7,* 382–390.

Jones, M. C. (1924b). A laboratory study of fear: The case of Peter. *Pedagogical Seminary and Journal of Genetic Psychology, 31,* 308–315.

Jones, N. T., Menditto, A. A., Geeson, L. R., Larson, E., & Sadewhite, L. (2001). Teaching social-learning procedures to paraprofessionals working with individuals with severe mental illness in a maximum-security forensic hospital. *Behavioral Interventions, 16,* 167–179.

Jones, W. H., Adams, J. A., Monroe, P. R., & Berry, J. O. (1995). A psychometric exploration of marital satisfaction and commitment. *Journal of Social Behavior and Personality, 10,* 923–932.

Jouriles, E. N., & Farris, A. M. (1992). Effects of marital conflict on subsequent parent-child interactions. *Behavior Therapy, 23,* 355–374.

Jouriles, E. N., & O'Leary, K. D. (1985). Interspousal reliability of reports of marital violence. *Journal of Consulting and Clinical Psychology, 53,* 419–421.

Journal of Clinical Child Psychology (1998). Special issue: Empirically supported psychological interventions for children, *27,* 138–226.

Kagan, J. (1989). Temperamental contributions to social behavior. *American Psychologist, 44,* 668–674.

Kahn, E. (1985). Heinz Kohut and Carl Rogers: A timely comparison. *American Psychologist, 40,* 893–904.

Kahn, J. H., Achter, J. A., & Shambaugh, E. J. (2001). Client distress disclosure, characteristics at intake, and outcomes in brief counseling. *Journal of Counseling Psychology, 48,* 203–211.

Kahneman, D., & Tversky, A. (1979). Intuitive prediction: Biases and corrective procedures. *TIMS Studies in the Management Sciences, 12,* 313–327.

Kaiser, W., & Priebe, S. (1999). The impact of the interviewer-interviewee relationship on subjective quality of life ratings in schizophrenia patients. *International Journal of Social Psychiatry, 45,* 292-301.

Kalichma, S. C., Cherry, C. & Browne-Sperling, F. (1999). Effectiveness of a video-based motivational skills-building HIV risk-reduction intervention for inner-city African American men. *Journal of Consulting and Clinical Psychology, 67,* 959-966.

Kalichman, S. C., Rompa, D., & Coley, B. (1996). Experimental component analysis of a behavioral HIV-AIDS prevention for inner-city women. *Journal of Consulting and Clinical Psychology, 64,* 687-693.

Kalichman, S. C., Rompa, D., Cage, M., DiFonzo, K., Simpson, D. Austin, J., et al. (2001). Effectiveness of an intervention to reduce HIV transmission risks in HIV-positive people. *American Journal of Preventive Medicine, 21,* 84-92.

Kameguchi, K., & Murphy-Shigematsu, S. (2001). Family psychology and family therapy in Japan. *American Psychologist, 56,* 65-70.

Kamphaus, R. W., & Frick, P. J. (1996). *Clinical assessment of child and adolescent personality and behavior.* Boston: Allyn and Bacon.

Kane, E. W., & Macauley, L. J. (1993). Interviewer gender and gender attitudes. *Public Opinion Quarterly, 57,* 1-28.

Kanfer, F. H., & Gaelick, L. (1986). Self-management methods. In F. H. Kanfer & A. P. Goldstein (Eds.), *Helping people change: A textbook of methods* (3rd ed., pp. 283-345). New York: Pergamon Press.

Kanfer, F. H., & McBrearty, J. F. (1962). Minimal social reinforcement and interview content. *Journal of Clinical Psychology, 18,* 210-215.

Kanfer, F. H., & Saslow, G. (1969). Behavioral diagnosis. In C. M. Franks (Ed.), *Behavior therapy: Appraisal and status* (pp. 210-215). New York: McGraw-Hill.

Kanner, A. D., Coyne, J. C., Schaefer, C., & Lazarus, R. S. (1981). Comparison of two modes of stress measurement: Daily hassles and uplifts versus major life events. *Journal of Behavioral Medicine, 14,* 1-39.

Kanner, L. (1943). Autistic disturbances of affective contact. *Nervous Child, 2,* 217-250.

Kaplan, A. (1964). *The conduct of inquiry.* San Francisco: Chander.

Kaplan, E. (1990). The process approach to neuropsychological assessment of psychiatric patients. *Journal of Neuropsychiatry and Clinical Neurosciences, 2,* 72-87.

Kaplan, M. (1983). A woman's view of DSM-III. *American Psychologist, 38,* 786-792.

Kaplan, R. M., & Saccuzzo, D. P. (1993). *Psychological testing* (3rd ed.). Pacific Grove, CA: Brooks/Cole.

Kaslow, N. J., Rehm, L. P., & Siegel, A. W. (1984). Social and cognitive correlates of depression in children: A developmental perspective. *Journal of Abnormal Child Psychology, 12,* 605-620.

Kaslow, N. J., & Rehm, L. P. (1985). Conceptualization, assessment, and treatment of depression in children. In P. H. Bornstein & A. E. Kazdin (Eds.), *Handbook of clinical behavior therapy with children* (pp. 599-657). Homewood, IL: Dorsey Press.

Kaslow, N. J., & Thompson, M. P. (1998). Applying the criteria for empirically supported treatments to studies of psychosocial interventions for child and adolescent depression. *Journal of Clinical Child Psychology, 27,* 146-155.

Katanoda, K., Yoshikawa, K., & Sugishita, M. (2000). Neural substrates for the recognition of newly learned faces: A functional MRI study. *Neuropsychologia, 38,* 1616-1625.

Kaufman, A. S. (1994). *Intelligent testing with the WISC-III.* New York: John Wiley.

Kaufman, A. S., & Harrison, P. L. (1991). Individual intellectual assessment. In C. E. Walker (Ed.), *Clinical psychology: Historical and research foundations* (pp. 91–120). New York: Plenum Press.

Kaufman, A. S., & Kaufman, N. L. (1983). *KABC: Kaufman Assessment Battery for Children.* Circle Pines, MN: American Guidance Service.

Kaufman, A. S., & Kaufman, N. L. (1985). *Kaufman Test of Educational Achievement.* Circle Pines, MN: American Guidance Service.

Kaufman, A. S., & Kaufman, N. L. (1991). *Manual for the Kaufman Brief Intelligence Test (K-BIT).* Circle Pines, MN: American Guidance Service.

Kaufman, A. S., & Kaufman, N. L. (1993). *Manual for the Kaufman Adolescent and Adult Intelligence Test (KAIT).* Circle Pines, MN: American Guidance Service.

Kaufman, J., & Zigler, E. (1987). Do abused children become abusive parents? *American Journal of Orthopsychiatry, 57,* 186–192.

Kazantzis, N., & Deane, F. P. (1999). Psychologists' use of homework assignments in clinical practice. *Professional Psychology: Research and Practice, 30,* 581–585.

Kazdin, A. E. (1972). Response cost: The removal of conditioned reinforcers for therapeutic change. *Behavior Therapy, 3,* 533–546.

Kazdin, A. E. (1974). Self-monitoring and behavior change. In M. J. Mahoney & C. E. Thoresen (Eds.), *Self-control: Power to the person* (pp. 218–246). Monterey, CA: Brooks/Cole.

Kazdin, A. E. (1982a). *Single-case research designs: Methods for clinical and applied settings.* New York: Oxford University Press.

Kazdin, A. E. (1982b). Single-case experimental designs. In P. C. Kendall & J. N. Butcher (Eds.), *Handbook of research methods in clinical psychology* (pp. 461–490). New York: John Wiley.

Kazdin, A. E. (1989). Developmental psychopathology: Current research, issues, and directions. *American Psychologist, 44,* 180–187.

Kazdin, A. E. (1993). Evaluation in clinical practice: Clinically sensitive and systematic methods of treatment delivery. *Behavior Therapy, 24,* 11–45.

Kazdin, A. E. (1994). Methodology, design, and evaluation in psychotherapy research. In A. E. Bergin & S. L. Garfield (Eds.), *Handbook of psychotherapy and behavior change* (pp. 19–71). New York: Wiley & Sons.

Kazdin, A. E. (1997). A model for developing effective treatments: Progression and interplay of theory, research, and practice. *Journal of Clinical Child Psychology, 26,* 114–129.

Kazdin, A. E., Bass, D., Siegel, T., & Thomas, C. (1989). Cognitive-behavioral therapy and relationship therapy in the treatment of children referred for antisocial behavior. *Journal of Consulting and Clinical Psychology, 57,* 522–535.

Kazdin, A. E., Esveldt-Dawson, K., French, N. H., & Unis, A. S. (1987). Problem-solving skills training and relationship therapy in the treatment of antisocial child behavior. *Journal of Consulting and Clinical Psychology, 55,* 76–85.

Kazdin, A. E., Esveldt-Dawson, K., & Matson, J. L. (1983). The effects of instructional set on social skills performance among psychiatric inpatient children. *Behavior Therapy, 14,* 413–423.

Kazdin, A. E., Matson, J. L., & Esveldt-Dawson, K. (1984). The relationship of role-play assessment of children's social skills to multiple measures of social competence. *Behaviour Research and Therapy, 22,* 129–140.

Kazdin, A. E., Esveldt-Dawson, K., Sherick, R. B., & Colbus, D. (1985). Assessment of overt behavior and childhood depression among psychiatrically disturbed children. *Journal of Consulting and Clinical Psychology, 53,* 201–210.

Kazdin, A. E., & Wilson, G. T. (1978). *Evaluation of behavior therapy: Issues, evidence and research strategies.* Cambridge, MA: Ballinger.

Keijsers, G. P. J., Schaap, C. P. D. R., & Hoogduin, C. A. L. (2000). The impact of interpersonal patient and therapist behavior on outcome in cognitive-behavioral therapy: A review of empirical studies. *Behavior Modification, 24,* 264–297.

Keilin, W. G. (2000). Internship selection in 1999: Was the Association of Psychology Postdoctoral and Internship Centers' Match a success? *Professional Psychology: Research and Practice, 3,* 281–287.

Keilin, W. G., & Bloom, L. J. (1986). Child custody evaluation practices: A survey of experienced professionals. *Professional Psychology: Research and Practice, 17,* 338–346.

Keiser, R. E., & Prather, E. N. (1990). What is the TAT: A review of ten years of research. *Journal of Personality Assessment, 55,* 800–803.

Keith-Spiegel, P. C., & Koocher, G. (1985). *Ethics in psychology: Professional standards and cases.* New York: Random House.

Kellam, S. G., Rebok, G. W., Ialongo, N., & Mayer, L. S. (1994). The course and malleability of aggressive behavior from early first grade into middle school: Results of a developmental epidemiology-based preventive trial. *Journal of Child Psychology & Psychiatry & Allied Disciplines, 35,* 259–281.

Kelley, J. E., Lumley, M. A., & Leisen, J. C. C. (1997). Health effects of emotional disclosure in rheumatoid arthritis patients. *Health Psychology, 16,* 331–340.

Kelly, E. L. (1961). Clinical psychology—1960: A report of survey findings. *Newsletter, Division of Clinical Psychology of APA, 14,* 1–11.

Kelly, E. L., & Fiske, D. W. (1951). *The prediction of performance in clinical psychology.* Ann Arbor: University of Michigan Press.

Kelly, G. A. (1955). *The psychology of personal constructs.* New York: W. W. Norton.

Kelly, G. A. (1958). The theory and technique of assessment. *Annual Review of Psychology, 9,* 323–352.

Kelly, G. A. (1964). Personal construct theory as a line of inference. *Journal of Psychology, 1,* 80–93.

Kelly, J. A., & Murphy, D. A. (1992). Psychological interventions with AIDS and HIV: Prevention and treatment. *Journal of Consulting and Clinical Psychology, 60,* 576–585.

Kelly, J. A., St. Lawrence, J. S., Hood, H. V., & Brashfield, T. L. (1989). Behavioral intervention to reduce AIDS risk activities. *Journal of Consulting and Clinical Psychology, 57,* 60–67.

Kelly, J. B. (1991). Parent interaction after divorce: Comparison of medicated and adversarial divorce processes. *Behavioral Sciences and the Law, 9,* 387–398.

Kempler, W. (1973). Gestalt therapy. In R. Corsini (Ed.), *Current psychotherapies* (pp. 251–286). Itasca, IL: F. E. Peacock.

Kendall, P. C. (1984). Behavioral assessment and methodology. In G. T. Wilson, C. M. Franks, K. D. Brownell, & P. C. Kendall (Eds.), *Annual review of behavior therapy* (Vol. 9, pp. 123–163). New York: Guilford Press.

Kendall, P. C. (1994). Treating anxiety disorders in children: Results of a randomized clinical trial. *Journal of Consulting and Clinical Psychology, 62,* 100–110.

Kendall, P.C. (2000). *Child and adolescent therapy: Cognitive behavioral procedures* (2nd ed.). New York: Guilford.

Kendall, P. C., & Braswell, L. (1985). *Cognitive behavioral modification with impulsive children*. New York: Guilford Press.

Kendall, P. C., Butcher, J. N., & Holmbeck, G. N. (1999). *Handbook of research methods in clinical psychology* (2nd ed.). New York: Wiley and Sons, Inc.

Kendall, P. C., & Chambless, D. L. (Eds.). (1998). Empirically supported psychological therapies. *Journal of Consulting and Clinical Psychology, 66,* 3–167.

Kendall, P. C., Marrs-Garcia, A., Nath, S. R., & Sheldrick, R. C. (1999). Normative comparisons for the evaluation of clinical significance. *Journal of Consulting & Clinical Psychology, 67,* 285–299.

Kendall, P. C., & Panichelli-Mindel, S. M. (1995). Cognitive-behavioral treatments. *Journal of Abnormal Child Psychology, 23,* 107–124.

Kendall, P. C., & Sheldrick, R. C. (2000). Normative data for normative comparisons. *Journal of Consulting and Clinical Psychology, 68,* 767–773.

Kendall-Tackett, K. A., Williams, L. M., & Finkelhor, D. (1993). Impact of sexual abuse on children: A review and synthesis of recent empirical studies. *Psychological Bulletin, 113,* 164–180.

Kendler, K. S., & Roy, M. A. (1995). Validity of a diagnosis of lifetime major depression obtained by personal interview versus family history. *American Journal of Psychiatry, 152,* 1608–1614.

Kent, R. N., & Foster, S. L. (1977). Direct observational procedures: Methodological issues in naturalistic settings. In A. R. Ciminero, K. S. Calhoun, & H. E. Adams (Eds.), *Handbook of behavioral assessment* (pp. 279–328). New York: John Wiley.

Kern, J. M. (1982). The comparative external and concurrent validity of three role-plays for assessing heterosocial performance. *Behavior Therapy, 13,* 666–680.

Kern, J. M., Cavell, T. A., & Beck, B. (1985). Predicting differential reactions to males' versus females' assertions, emphatic-assertions, and non-assertions. *Behavior Therapy, 16,* 63–75.

Kernberg, O. (1976). *Object relations, theory and clinical psychoanalysis*. New York: Jason Aronson.

Kerr, M. E., & Bowen, M. (1988). *Family evaluations: An approach based on Bowen theory*. New York: W. W. Norton.

Kessler, R. C., Price, R. H., & Wortman, C. B. (1985). Social factors in psychopathology: Stress, social support, and coping processes. *Annual Review of Psychology, 36,* 531–572.

Kety, S. S., Wender, P. H., Jacobsen, B., Ingraham, L. J., Jansson, L., Faber, B., & Kinney, D. K. (1994). Mental illness in the biological and adoptive relatives of schizophrenic adoptees. *Archives of General Psychiatry, 51,* 442–455.

Kiecolt-Glaser, J. K., & Glaser, R. (1992). Psychoneuroimmunology: Can psychological interventions modulate immunity? *Journal of Consulting and Clinical Psychology, 60,* 569–575.

Kiesler, C. A. (1985). Psychology and public policy. In E. M. Altmaier & M. E. Meyer (Eds.), *Applied specialization in psychology* (pp. 375–390). New York: Springer.

Kiesler, C. A. (2000). The next wave of change for psychology and mental health services in the health care revolution. *American Psychologist, 55,* 481–487.

Kiesler, C. A., & Sibulkin, A. E. (1987). *Mental hospitalization: Myths and facts about a national crisis*. Beverly Hills, CA: Sage.

Kiesler, D. J. (1983). The 1982 Interpersonal Circle: A taxonomy for complementarity in human transactions. *Psychological Review, 90,* 185–214.

Kiesler, D. J. (1986a). The 1982 interpersonal circle: An analysis of DSM-III personality disorders. In T. Millon & G. L. Klerman (Eds.), *Contemporary directions in psychopathology: Towards the DSM-IV* (pp. 571–597). New York: Guilford Press.

Kiesler, D. J. (1986b). Interpersonal methods of diagnosis and treatment. In J. O. Cavenar, Jr. (Ed.), *Psychiatry* (vol. 1, pp. 1–23). Philadelphia: Lippincott.

Kiesler, D. J. (1987a). *Check List of Psychotherapy Transactions-Revised (CLOPT-R) and Check List of Interpersonal Transactions-Revised (CLOIT).* Richmond: Virginia Commonwealth University.

Kiesler, D. J. (1987b). *Research manual for the Impact Message Inventory.* Palo Alto, CA: Consulting Psychologists Press.

Kiesler, D. J. (1996). *Contemporary interpersonal theory and research: Personality, psychopathology, and psychotherapy.* New York: Wiley.

Kiesler, D. J. (2001). Therapist countertransference: In search of common themes and empirical referents. *Journal of Clinical Psychology/In Session: Psychotherapy in Practice, 57,* 1053–1063.

Kiesler, D. J., & Van Denburg, T. F. (1993). Therapeutic impact disclosure: A last taboo in psychoanalytic theory and practice. *Clinical Psychology and Psychotherapy, 1,* 3–13.

Kimble, G. A. (1989). Psychology from the standpoint of a generalist. *American Psychologist, 44,* 491–499.

Kimura, D. (1961). Cerebral dominance and the perception of verbal stimuli. *Canadian Journal of Psychology, 15,* 166–171.

Kimura, D. (1966). Dual functional asymmetry of the brain in visual perception. *Neuropsychologia, 4,* 275–285.

Kimura, D. (1967). Functional asymmetry of the brain in dichotic listening. *Cortex, 3,* 163–178.

Kirchner, E. P., & Draguns, J. G. (1979). Assertion and aggression in adult offenders. *Behavior Therapy, 10,* 452–471.

Kissen, D. M., & Eysenck, H. J. (1962). Personality in male lung cancer patients. *Journal of Psychosomatic Research, 6,* 123–127.

Klein, M. (1975). *The writings of Melanie Klein* (Vol. III). London: Hogarth Press.

Klein, R. A. (1999). Treating fear of flying with virtual reality exposure therapy. In L. VanderCreek & T. L. Jackson (Eds.), *Innovations in clinical practice: A sourcebook, Vol. 17.* Sarasota, FL: Professional Resources Press.

Klein, R. H. (1983). Group treatment approaches. In M. Hersen, A. E. Kazdin, & A. S. Bellack (Eds.), *The clinical psychology handbook* (pp. 593–610). New York: Pergamon Press.

Kleinknecht, R. A., & Bernstein, D. A. (1978). Assessment of dental fear. *Behavior Therapy, 9,* 626–634.

Kleinmuntz, B. (1963). MMPI decision rules for the identification of college maladjustment: A digital computer approach. *Psychological Monographs, 77* (14, Whole No. 477).

Kleinmuntz, B. (1969). Personality test interpretation by computer and clinician. In J. N. Butcher (Ed.), *MMPI: Research developments and clinical applications* (pp. 97–104). New York: John Wiley.

Kleinmuntz, B. (1984). The scientific study of clinical judgment in psychology and medicine. *Clinical Psychology Review, 4,* 111–126.

Klerman, G. L., Weissman, M. M., Rounsaville, B. J., & Chevron, E. S. (1984). *Interpersonal psychotherapy of depression*. New York: Basic Books.

Klopfer, B., & Kelley, D. M. (1937). The techniques of the Rorschach performance. *Rorschach Research Exchange, 2,* 1-14.

Klopfer, W. G. (1960). *The psychological report*. New York: Grune & Stratton.

Klopfer, W. G. (1983). Writing psychological reports. In C. E. Walker (Ed.), *The handbook of clinical psychology* (Vol. 1, pp. 501-527). Homewood, IL: Dow Jones-Irwin.

Knapp, R. (1976). *Handbook for the Personal Orientation Inventory*. San Diego, CA: Edits Publishers.

Knox, S., Goldberg, J. L., Woodhouse, S. S., & Hill, C. E. (1999). Clients' internal representations of their therapists. *Journal of Counseling Psychology, 46,* 244-256.

Koffka, K. (1935). *Principles of Gestalt psychology*. New York: Harcourt, Brace.

Kohlenberg, R. J., & Tsai, M. (1991). *Functional analytic psychotherapy: Creating intense and curative therapeutic relationships*. New York: Plenum Press.

Kohler, W. (1925). *The mentality of apes*. New York: Harcourt, Brace.

Kohout, J., & Wicherski, M. (1999). 1997 Doctoral employment survey. Retrieved December 9, 2001 from http://research.apa.rg/des97contents.html.

Kohout, J., Wicherski, M., & Pion, G. (1991). *1988-89 characteristics of graduate departments of psychology*. Washington, DC: American Psychological Association.

Kohut, H. (1971). *The analysis of self*. New York: International Universities Press.

Kohut, H. (1977). *The restoration of the self*. New York: International Universities Press.

Kohut, H. (1983). Selected problems of self-psychological theory. In J. D. Lichtenberg & S. Kaplan (Eds.), *Reflections on self psychology* (pp. 387-416). Hillsdale, NJ: Lawrence Erlbaum Associates.

Kokotovic, A. M., & Tracey, T. J. (1987). Premature termination at a university counseling center. *Journal of Counseling Psychology, 34,* 80-82.

Kolb, B., & Whishaw, I. Q. (1990). *Fundamentals of neuropsychology* (3rd ed.). New York: Freeman.

Kolotkin, R. H. (1980). Situation specificity in the assessment of assertion: Considerations for the measurement of training and transfer. *Behavior Therapy, 11,* 651-661.

Komiti, A. A., Jackson, H. J., Judd, F. K., Cockram, A. M., Kyrios, M., Yeatman, R., et al. (2001). A comparison of the Composite International Diagnostic Interview (CIDI-Auto) with clinical assessment in diagnosing mood and anxiety disorders. *Australian & New Zealand Journal of Psychiatry, 35,* 224-232.

Koocher, G. P., Goodman, G. S., White, C. S., Friedrich, W. N., Sivan, A. B., & Reynolds, C. R. (1995). Psychological science and the use of anatomically detailed dolls in child sexual-abuse assessments. *Psychological Bulletin, 118,* 199-222.

Koocher, G. P., & Keith-Spiegel, P. (1998). *Ethics in psychology: Professional standards and cases*. New York: Oxford University Press.

Koppitz, E. M. (1968). *Psychological evaluation of children's human figure drawings*. New York: Grune & Stratton.

Kopta, S. M., Howard, K. I., Lowry, J. L., & Beutler, L. E. (1991). Patterns of symptomatic recovery in psychotherapy. *Journal of Consulting and Clinical Psychology, 62,* 1009-1016.

Kopta, S. M., Lueger, R. J., Saunders, S. M., & Howard, K. I. (1999). Individual psychotherapy outcome and process research: Challenges leading to greater turmoil or a positive transition? *Annual Review of Psychology, 50,* 441-469.

Korchin, S. J. (1976). *Modern clinical psychology: Principles of intervention in the clinic and community*. New York: Basic Books.

Korman, M. (1974). National conference on levels and patterns of professional training in psychology: The major themes. *American Psychologist, 29,* 441–449.

Korman, M. (Ed.). (1976). *Levels and patterns of professional training in psychology.* Washington, DC: American Psychological Association.

Korsch, B. M., & Negrete, V. F. (1972). Doctor-patient communication. *Scientific American, 227,* 66–74.

Koslow, F. W. (Ed.). (1996). *Handbook of relational diagnosis and dysfunctional family patterns.* New York: Wiley.

Koslow, F. W. (2001). Families and family psychology at the millennium: Intersecting crossroads. *American Psychologist, 56,* 37–46.

Koss, M. P., & Shiang, J. (1994). Research on brief psychotherapy. In A. E. Bergin & S. L. Garfield (Eds.), *Handbook of psychotherapy and behavior change* (pp. 664–700). New York: Wiley & Sons.

Kovacs, M. (1992). *The children's depression inventory (CDI).* North Tonawanda, NY: Multi-Health Systems.

Kraemer, H. C., & Thiemann, S. (1989). A strategy to use soft data effectively in randomized controlled clinical trials. *Journal of Consulting and Clinical Psychology, 57,* 148–154.

Krantz, D. S., & Manuck, S. B. (1984). Acute psychophysiologic reactivity and risk of cardiovascular disease—a review and methodologic critique. *Psychological Bulletin, 96,* 435–464.

Krasner, L., & Ullmann, L. P. (Eds.). (1965). *Research in behavior modification: New developments and implications.* New York: Holt, Rinehart & Winston.

Kratochwill, T. R., Mott, S. E., & Dodson, C. L. (1984). Case study and single-case research in clinical and applied psychology. In A. S. Bellack & M. Hersen (Eds.), *Research methods in clinical psychology* (pp. 55–99). New York: Pergamon Press.

Krol, N., DeBruyn, E., & van den Bercken, J. (1995). Intuitive and empirical prototypes in childhood psychopathology. *Psychological Assessment, 7,* 533–537.

Krull, C. D., & Pierce, W. D. (1995). IQ testing in America: A victim of its own success. *Alberta Journal of Educational Research, 41,* 349–354.

Krupnick, J. L., Sotsky, S. M., Simmens, S., Moyer, I., Elkin, I., et al. (1996). The role of the therapeutic alliance in psychotherapy and pharmacotherapy outcome: Findings in the NIMH Treatment of Depression Collaborative Research Program. *Journal of Consulting and Clinical Psychology, 64,* 532–539.

Kubiszyn, T. W., Meyer, G. J., Finn, S. E., Eyde, L .D., Kay, G. G., Moreland, K. L., et al. (2000). Empirical support for psychological assessment in clinical health care settings. *Professional Psychology: Research and Practice, 31,* 119–130.

Kuncel, N. R., Hezlett, S. A., & Ones, D. S. (2001). A comprehensive meta-analysis of the predictive validity of the Graduate Record Examinations: Implications for graduate student selection and performance. *Psychological Bulletin, 127,* 162–181.

Kwon, P., & Lemon, K. E. (2000). Attributional style and defense mechanisms: A synthesis of cognitive and psychodynamic factors in depression. *Journal of Clinical Psychology, 56,* 723–735.

Kyle, T. M. & Williams, S. (2000). Results of the 1998–1999 APA survey of graduate departments of psychology. Retrieved December 11, 2001 from http://research.apa.org.

L'Abate, L. (1969). Introduction. In L. L'Abate (Ed.), *Models of clinical psychology. Research paper number 22*. Atlanta: Georgia State College.

LaFond, J. Q. (1998). The costs of enacting a sexual predator law. *Psychology, Public Policy, and Law, 4* (1/2), 468–504.

La Greca, A. M. (1990). Issues and perspectives on the child assessment process. In A. M. La Greca (Ed.), *Through the eyes of the child* (pp. 3–17). Boston, MA: Allyn & Bacon.

La Greca, A. M., Dandes, S. K., Wick, P., Shaw, K., & Stone, W. L. (1988). Development of the Social Anxiety Scale for Children: Reliability and concurrent validity. *Journal of Clinical Child Psychology, 17,* 84–91.

Lam, J. N. & Steketee, G. S. (2001). Reducing obsessions and compulsions through behavior therapy. *Psychoanalytic Inquiry, 21,* 157–182.

Lamb, H. R., & Zusman, J. (1981). Primary prevention in perspective. *American Journal of Psychiatry, 9,* 1–26.

Lambert, D. (1985). *Political and economic determinants of mental health regulations.* Unpublished doctoral dissertation, Brandeis University.

Lambert, M. J. (1992). Psychotherapy outcome research: Implications for integrative and eclectic therapies. In J. C. Norcross & M. R. Goldfried (Eds.), *Handbook of psychotherapy integration* (pp. 94–129). New York: Basic Books.

Lambert, M. J. (2001). Psychotherapy outcome and quality improvement: Introduction to the special section on patient-focused research. *Journal of Consulting and Clinical Psychology, 69,* 147–149.

Lambert, M. J., & Bergin, A. E. (1994). The effectiveness of psychotherapy. In A. E. Bergin & S. L. Garfield (Eds.), *Handbook of psychotherapy and behavior change* (pp. 143–189). New York: John Wiley & Sons, Inc.

Lambert, M. J., Shapiro, D. A., & Bergin, A. E. (1986). The effectiveness of psychotherapy. In S. L. Garfield & A. E. Bergin (Eds.), *Handbook of psychotherapy and behavior change* (3rd ed., pp. 157–211). New York: John Wiley & Sons, Inc.

Lambert, N. M. (1981). Psychological evidence in Larry P. v. Wilson Riles: An evaluation by a witness for the defense. *American Psychologist, 36,* 937–952.

Lambert, N. M., Cox, H. W., & Hartsough, C. S. (1970). The observability of intellectual functioning of first graders. *Psychology in the Schools,* 74–85.

Landau, S., & Milich, R. (1990). Assessment of children's social status and peer relations. In A. M. La Greca (Ed.), *Through the eyes of the child* (pp. 259–291). Boston: Allyn & Bacon.

Landman, J. T., & Dawes, R. (1982). Experimental outcome: Smith and Glass' conclusions stand up under scrutiny. *American Psychologist, 37,* 504–516.

Landrine, H., & Klonoff, E. (1992). Culture and health-related schemas: A review and proposal for interdisciplinary integration. *Health Psychology, 11,* 267–276.

Lang, P. J., & Lazovik, A. D. (1963). Experimental desensitization of a phobia. *Journal of Abnormal and Social Psychology, 66,* 519–525.

Lang, P. J. (1995). The emotion probe: Studies of motivation and attention. *American Psychologist, 50,* 372–385.

Langer, E. (1975). The illusion of control. *Journal of Personality and Social Psychology, 32,* 311–328.

Lanyon, B. P., & Lanyon, R. I. (1980). *Incomplete sentences task: Manual.* Chicago: Stoelting.

Laosa, L. M. (1996). Intelligence testing and social policy. *Journal of Applied Developmental Psychology, 17,* 155–173.

LaPerriere, A. R., Antoni, M. H., Schneiderman, N., Ironoson, G., Klimas, N., Caralis, P., & Fletcher, M. A. (1990). Exercise intervention attenuates emotional distress and natural killer cell decrements following notification of positive serologic status for HIV-1. *Biofeedback and Self-Regulation, 15,* 229-242.

LaPiere, R. T. (1934). Attitudes vs. actions. *Social Forces, 13,* 230-237.

Last, C. G., & Francis, G. (1988). School phobia. In B. B. Lahey & A. E. Kazdin (Eds.), *Advances in clinical child psychology* (Vol. 11, pp. 193-222). New York: Plenum Press.

Last, C. G., Hansen, C., & Franco, N. (1998). Cognitive-behavioral treatment of school phobia. *Journal of the American Academy of Child and Adolescent Psychiatry, 37,* 404-411.

Laurent, J., Swerdlik, M., Ryburn, M. (1992). Review of validity research on the Stanford-Binet Intelligence Scale: Fourth Edition. *Psychological Assessment, 4,* 102-112.

Lawlis, G. F. (1971). Response styles of a patient population on the Fear Survey Schedule. *Behaviour Research and Therapy, 9,* 95-102.

Lazarus, A. A. (1995). Multimodal therapy. In R. J. Corsini & D. Wedding (Eds.), *Current psychotherapies* (5th ed., pp. 322-355). Itasca, IL: Peacock Publishers, Inc.

Lazarus, R. S. (1993). From psychological stress to the emotions: A history of changing outlooks. *Annual Review of Psychology, 44,* 1-21.

Lazarus, R. S. (1998). *Fifty years of research and theory of R. S. Lazarus: An analysis of historical and perennial issues.* Mahwah, NJ: Erlbaum.

Lazarus, R. S., & Folkman, S. (1984). *Stress, appraisal, and coping.* New York: Springer.

Leary, T. (1957). *Interpersonal diagnosis of personality. A functional theory and methodology for personality evaluation.* New York: Ronald Press.

Lefkowitz, M. M., & Burton, N. (1978). Childhood depression: A critique of the concept. *Psychological Bulletin, 85,* 716-726.

Lennard, H. L., & Bernstein, A. (1960). *The anatomy of psychotherapy: Systems of communication and expectation.* New York: Columbia University Press.

Lerman, C., Caporaso, N., Main, D., Audrain, J., Boyd, N. R., & Bowman, E. D. (1998). Depression and self-medication with nicotine: The modifying influence of the dopamine D4 receptor gene. *Health Psychology, 17,* 56-62.

Levin, H. S., Eisenberg, H. M., & Benton, A. L. (Eds). (1991). *Frontal Lobe Function and Dysfunction.* New York: Oxford University Press.

Levison, H., & Strupp, H. H. (1999). Recommendations for the future of training in brief dynamic psychotherapy. *Journal of Clinical Psychology, 55,* 385-391.

Levy, L. H. (1963). *Psychological interpretation.* New York: Holt, Rinehart & Winston.

Lewinsohn, P. M., & Shaffer, M. (1971). Use of home observations as an integral part of the treatment of depression: Preliminary report and case studies. *Journal of Consulting and Clinical Psychology, 37,* 87-94.

Lewis, G. (1991). Observer bias in the assessment of anxiety and depression. *Social Psychiatry and Psychiatric Epidemiology, 26,* 265-272.

Lewis, G., Pelosi, A. J., Araya, R., & Dunn, G. (1992). Measuring psychiatric disorder in the community: A standardized assessment for use by lay interviewers. *Psychological Medicine, 22,* 465-486.

Ley, P., Bradshaw, P. W., Eaves, D. E., & Walker, C. M. (1973). A method for increasing patient recall of information presented to them. *Psychological Medicine, 3,* 217-220.

Lezak, M. D. (1995). *Neuropsychological assessment* (3rd ed.). New York: Oxford University Press.

Libet, J. M., & Lewinsohn, P. M. (1973). Concept of social skill with special reference to the behavior of depressed persons. *Journal of Consulting and Clinical Psychology, 40,* 304-312.

Lidz, R. W., & Lidz, T. (1949). The family environment of schizophrenic patients. *American Journal of Psychiatry, 106,* 332–345.

Lilienfeld, S. O., Wood, J. M., & Garb, H. N. (2000). The scientific status of projective techniques. *Psychological Science in the Public Interest, 1,* 27–66.

Lindner, R. (1954). *The fifty minute hour.* New York: Rinehart.

Lindsley, O. R., Skinner, B. F., & Solomon, H. C. (1953). *Study of psychotic behavior.* Studies in Behavior Therapy, Harvard Medical School, Department of Psychiatry, Metropolitan State Hospital, Waltham, MA, Office of Naval Research Contract N5-ori-07662, Status Report I, 1 June 1953–31 December 1953.

Lindzey, G. (1952). The thematic apperception test: Interpretive assumptions and related empirical evidence. *Psychological Bulletin, 49,* 1–25.

Lindzey, G. (1961). *Projective techniques and cross-cultural research.* New York: Appleton-Century-Crofts.

Linehan, M. M. (1993). *Cognitive-behavioral treatment of borderline personality disorder.* New York: Guilford Press.

Linehan, M. M., & Kehrer, C. A. (1993). Borderline personality disorder. In D. H. Barlow (Ed.), *Clinical handbook of psychological disorders* (pp. 396–441). New York: Guilford Press.

Linehan, M. M., & Nielsen, S. L. (1983). Social desirability: Its relevance to the measurement of hopelessness and suicidal behavior. *Journal of Consulting and Clinical Psychology, 51,* 141–143.

Lipsey, M. W., & Wilson, D. B. (1993). The efficacy of psychological, educational, and behavioral treatment: Confirmation from meta-analysis. *American Psychologist, 48,* 1181–1209.

Liss, M. B., & McKinley-Pace, M. J. (1999). Best interests of the child: New twists on an old theme. In R. Roesch, S. D. Hart, & J. R. Ogloff (Eds.), *Psychology and the law: The state of the discipline* (pp. 339–372). New York: Kluwer Academic/Plenum.

Little, K. B., & Shneidman, E. S. (1959). Congruences among interpretations of psychological test and amnestic data. *Psychological Monographs, 73* (Whole No. 476).

Lochman, J. E. (1992). Cognitive-behavioral intervention with aggressive boys: Three-year follow-up and preventive effects. *Journal of Consulting and Clinical Psychology, 60,* 426–432.

Loftus, E. (1993). The reality of repressed memories. *American Psychologist, 48,* 518–537.

Loftus, E. F. (1993). Psychologists in the eyewitness world. *American Psychologist, 48,* 550–552.

Loftus, E. F., & Polage, D. C. (1999). Repressed memories: When are they real? How are they false? *Psychiatric Clinics of North America, 22,* 61–70.

Lonigan, C. J., Elbert, J. C., & Johnson, S. B. (1998). Empirically supported psychosocial interventions for children: An overview. *Journal of Clinical Child Psychology, 27,* 138–145.

Lopez, S. R. (1989). Patient variable biases in clinical judgment: Conceptual overview and methodological considerations. *Psychological Bulletin, 106,* 184–203.

Lopez, S. R., Smith, A., & Wolkenstein, B. H. (1993). Gender bias in clinical judgment: An assessment of the analogue method's transparency and social desirability. *Sex Roles, 28,* 35–45.

Lopez, S. R., & Guarnaccia, P. J. (2000). Cultural psychopathology: Uncovering the social world of mental illness. *Annual Review of Psychology, 51,* 571–598.

Loranger, A. W. (1992). Are current self-report and interview measures adequate for epidemiological studies of personality disorders? *Journal of Personality Disorders, 6,* 313–325.

Loranger, A. W. (1999). *International Personality Disorder Examination (IPDE) Manual.* Odessa, FL: Psychological Assessment Resources.

Lorch, E. P., Milich, R., Sanchez, R. P., van den Broek, P., Baer, S., Hooks, K., Hartung, C., & Welsh, R. (2000). Comprehension of televised stories in boys with attention deficit hyperactivity disorder and nonreferred boys. *Journal of Abnormal Psychology, 109,* 321–330.

Lorr, M., McNair, D. M., & Klett, C. J. (1966). *Inpatient Multidimensional Psychiatric Scale.* Palo Alto, CA: Consulting Psychologists Press.

Lovaas, I. (1987). Behavioral treatment and normal educational and intellectual functioning in young autistic children. *Journal of Consulting and Clinical Psychology, 55,* 3–9.

Lubin, B., Larsen, R. M., Matarazzo, J. D., & Seever, M. (1985). Psychological test usage patterns in five professional settings. *American Psychologist, 40,* 857–861.

Luborsky, L. (1976). Helping alliances in psychotherapy. In J. Cleghhorn (Ed.), *Successful psychotherapy* (pp. 92–16). New York: Brunner/Mazel.

Luborsky, L. (1989). *Who will benefit from psychotherapy?* New York: Basic Books.

Luborsky, L., McLellan, A. T., Diguer, L., Woody, G., & Seligman, D. A. (1997). The psychotherapist matters: Comparison of outcomes across twenty-two therapists and seven patient samples. *Clinical Psychology: Science and Practice, 1,* 53–65.

Luborsky, L., Singer, B., & Luborsky, L. (1975). Comparative studies of psychotherapies: Is it true that "Everyone has won and all must have prizes"? *Archives of General Psychiatry, 32,* 995–1008.

Lunt, I. (1999). The professionalization of psychology in Europe. *European Psychologist, 4,* 240–247.

Lynam, D. R., Milich, R., Zimmerman, R., Novak, S. P., Logan, T. K., Martin, C., Leukefeld, C. & Clayton, R. (1999). Project DARE: No effects at ten-year follow-up. *Journal of Consulting and Clinical Psychology, 67,* 590–593.

Lyness, S. A. (1993). Predictors of differences between Type A and B individuals in heart rate and blood pressure reactivity. *Psychological Bulletin, 114,* 266–295.

Lyon, G. R., & Cutting, L. E. (1998). Learning disabilities. In E. J. Mash & R. J. Barkley (Eds.), *Treatment of childhood disorders* (2nd ed., pp. 468–498). New York: Guilford.

Lyons, H. A. (1971). Psychiatric sequelae of the Belfast riots. *British Journal of Psychiatry, 118,* 265–273.

Lyons-Ruth, K. (1996). Attachment relationships among children with aggressive behavior problems: The role of disorganized early attachment patterns. *Journal of Consulting and Clinical Psychology, 64,* 64–73.

MacDonald, G. (1996). Inferences in therapy: Processes and hazards. *Professional Psychology: Research and Practice, 27,* 600–603.

Machado, P. P. P., Beutler, L. E., Greenberg, L. S. (1999). Emotion recognition in psychotherapy: Impact of therapist level of experience and emotional awareness. *Journal of Clinical Psychology, 55,* 39–57.

Machover, K. (1949). *Personality projection in the drawing of the human figure.* Springfield, IL: Charles C. Thomas.

MacLennan, R. N. (1992). *Personality research form (PRF): Annotated research bibliography.* Port Hudson, MI: Sigma Assessment Systems, Inc.

MacMillan, M. (1991). *Freud evaluated: The completed arc.* Amsterdam: North-Holland.

MacPhillamy, D. J., & Lewinsohn, P. M. (1976). *Manual for the Pleasant Events Schedule.* Eugene, OR: Authors.

Magaret, A. (1952). Clinical methods: Psychodiagnostics. *Annual Review of Psychology, 3,* 283–320.

Magrab, P., & Papadopoulou, Z. L. (1977). The effect of a token economy on dietary compliance for children on hemodialysis. *Journal of Applied Behavioral Analysis, 10,* 573-578.

Mahler, M. S., Pine, F., & Bergman, A. (1975). *The psychological birth of the human infant.* New York: Basic Books.

Mahrer, A. R., & Nadler, W. P. (1986). Good moments in psychotherapy: A preliminary review, a list, and some promising research avenues. *Journal of Consulting and Clinical Psychology, 54,* 10-15.

Mahrer, A. R. (Ed.). (1970). *New approaches to personality classification.* New York: Columbia University Press.

Maier, S. F., & Watkins, L. R. (1998). Cytokines for psychologists: Implications of bidirectional immune-to-brain communication for understanding behavior, mood, and cognition. *Psychological Review, 105,* 83-107.

Maier, S. F., Watkins, L. R., & Fleshner, M. (1994). Psychoneuroimmunology: The interface between behavior, brain, and immunity. *American Psychologist, 49,* 1004-1017.

Main, M. (1996). Introduction to the special section on attachment and psychopathology: 2. Overview of the field of attachment. *Journal of Consulting and Clinical Psychology, 64,* 237-243.

Maine, M. (2001). Altering women's relationships with food: A relational, developmental approach. *Journal of Clinical Psychology/In Session, 57,* 101-110.

Maisto, S. A., & Maisto, C. A. (1983). Institutional measures of treatment outcome. In M. J. Lambert, E. R. Christensen, & S. S. DeJulio (Eds.), *The assessment of psychotherapy outcome* (pp. 603-625). New York: John Wiley.

Malarkey, W. B., Kiecolt-Glaser, J. K., Pearl, D., & Glaser, R. (1994). Hostile behavior during marital conflict alters pituitary and adrenal hormones. *Psychosomatic Medicine, 56,* 41-51.

Malgady, R. G. (1996). The question of cultural bias in assessment and diagnosis of ethnic minority clients: Let's reject the null hypothesis. *Professional Psychology: Research and Practice, 27,* 73-77.

Malmo, R. B., Shagass, C., & Davis, F. H. (1950). Symptom specificity and bodily reactions during psychiatric interviews. *Psychosomatic Medicine, 12,* 362-376.

Maloney, M. P., & Ward, M. P. (1976). *Psychological assessment: A conceptual approach.* New York: Oxford University Press.

Manning, W. G., Wells, K. B., & Benjamin, B. (1986). Use of outpatient mental health care: Trial of a prepaid group practice versus fee-for-service (Technical Report R-3277-NIMH). Santa Monica, CA: Rand Corporation.

Manuck, S. B., Kaplan, J. R., Adams, M. R., & Clarkson, T. B. (1988). Effects of stress and the sympathetic nervous system on coronary artery atheroslerosis in the cynomolgus macaque. *American Heart Journal, 116,* 328-333.

Manuck, S. B., Kaplan, J. R., & Clarkson, T. B. (1983). Behaviorally induced heart rate reactivity and atherosclerosis in cynomolgus monkeys. *Psychosomatic Medicine, 49,* 95-108.

Marcus, D. R., Lyons, P. M., & Guyton, M. R. (2000). Studying perceptions of juror influence in vivo: A social relations analysis. *Law and Human Behavior, 24,* 173-186.

Margolin, G., Mitchell, J., & Jacobson, N. (1988). Assessment of marital dysfunction. In A. S. Bellack & M. Hersen (Eds.), *Behavioral assessment: A practical handbook* (3rd ed., pp. 441-489). New York: Pergamon Press.

Markowitz, J., Kocsis, M., Fishman, B., Spielman, L, Jacobsberg, L., & Francis, A. (1998). Treatment of depressive symptoms in Human Immunodeficiency Virus–positive patients. *Archives of General Psychiatry, 55,* 452–457.

Marlatt, G. A., & Gordon, J. R. (Eds.). (1985). *Relapse prevention maintenance strategies in the treatment of addictive behaviors.* New York: Guilford Press.

Marmar, C., Gaston, L., Gallagher, D., & Thompson, L. W. (1989). Alliance and outcome in late-life depression. *Journal of Nervous and Mental Disease, 177,* 464–472.

Martell, R. F., & Willis, C. E. (1993). Effects of observers' performance expectations on behavior ratings of work groups: Memory or response bias? *Organizational Behavior and Human Decision Processes, 56,* 91–109.

Martin, D. J., Garske, J. P., Davis, K. M. (2000). Relation of the therapeutic alliance with outcome and other variables: A meta-analytic review. *Journal of Consulting and Clinical Psychology, 68,* 438–450.

Martin, R. P. (1988). *Assessment of personality and behavior problems: Infancy through adolescence.* New York: Guilford Press.

Marx, J. A., Gyorky, Z. K., Royalty, G. M., & Stern, T. E. (1992). Use of self-help books in psychotherapy. *Professional Psychology: Research and Practice, 23,* 300–305.

Mash, E. J. (1989). Treatment of child and family disturbance: A behavioral systems perspective. In E. J. Mash & R. A. Barkley (Eds.), *Treatment of childhood disorders* (pp. 3–36). New York: Guilford.

Mash, E. J., & Barkley, A. (1986). Assessment of family interaction with the Response-Class Matrix. In R. J. Prinz (Ed.), *Advances in behavioral assessment of children and families* (Vol. 2, pp. 29–67). Greenwich, CT: JAI Press.

Mash, E. J., & Dozois, D. J. A. (1996). Child psychopathology: A developmental-systems perspective. In E. J. Mash & R. A. Barkley (Eds.), *Child psychopathology* (pp. 3–60). New York: Guilford.

Mash, E. J., & McElwee, J. D. (1974). Situational effects on observer accuracy: Behavior predictability, prior experience, and complexity of coding categories. *Child Development, 45,* 367–377.

Mash, E. J., & Foster, S. L. (2001). Exporting analogue behavioral observation from research to clinical practice: Useful or cost-defective? *Psychological Assessment, 13,* 86–98.

Mash, E. J., & Terdal, L. G. (Eds.). (1988). *Behavioral assessment of childhood disorders* (2nd ed.). New York: Guilford Press.

Mash, E. J., & Wolfe, D. A. (2002). *Abnormal child psychology.* Belmount, CA: Wadsworth.

Masling, J. M. (1992). Assessment and the therapeutic narrative. *Journal of Training and Practice in Professional Psychology, 6,* 53–58.

Maslow, A. H. (1954). *Motivation and personality.* New York: Harper.

Maslow, A. H. (1962). *Toward a psychology of being.* Princeton, NJ: D. Van Nostrand.

Maslow, A. H. (1968). *Toward a psychology of being* (2nd ed.). New York: Van Nostrand Reinhold.

Maslow, A. H. (1971). *The farther reaches of human nature.* New York: Viking Press.

Masten, A. S. (2001). Ordinary magic: Resilience processes in development. *American Psychologist, 56,* 227–238.

Masterpasqua, F. (1989). A competence paradigm for psychological practice. *American Psychologist, 44,* 1366–1371.

Masters, J. C., Burish, T. G., Hollon, S. D., & Rimm, D. C. (1987). *Behavior therapy: Techniques and empirical findings* (3rd ed.). San Diego, CA: Harcourt, Brace, Jovanovich.

Masur, F. T. (1981). Adherence to health care regimens. In C. K. Prokop & L. A. Bradley (Eds.), *Medical psychology: Contributions to behavioral medicine* (pp. 442–470). New York: Academic Press.

Matarazzo, J. D. (1965). The interview. In B. B. Wolman (Ed.), *Handbook of clinical psychology* (pp. 403–450). New York: McGraw-Hill.

Matarazzo, J. D. (1986). Computerized clinical psychological test interpretations: Unvalidated plus all mean and no sigma. *American Psychologist, 41,* 14–24.

Matarazzo, J. D. (1987). There is only one psychology, no specialties, but many applications. *American Psychologist, 42,* 893–903.

Matarazzo, J. D. (1992). Psychological testing and assessment in the 21st century. *American Psychologist, 47,* 1007–1018.

Matarazzo, J. D., & Carmody, T. P. (1983). Health psychology. In M. Hersen, A. J. Kazdin, & A. S. Bellack (Eds.), *The clinical psychology handbook* (pp. 657–682). New York: Pergamon Press.

Matarazzo, J. D, Weins, A. N., Matarzzo, R. G., & Saslow, G. (1968). Speech and silence behavior in clinical psychotherapy and its laboratory correlates. In J. M. Shlien, H. F. Hunt, J. D. Matarazzo, & C. Savage (Eds.), *Research in psychotherapy*. Washington, DC: American Psychological Association.

Matarazzo, J. D., Weitman, M., Saslow, G., & Wiens, A. N. (1963). Interviewer influence on durations of interviewee speech. *Journal of Verbal Learning and Verbal Behavior, 1,* 451–458.

Matthews, K. A. (1982). Psychological perspectives on the Type A behavior pattern. *Psychological Bulletin, 91,* 293–323.

Matthews, K. A. (1988). Coronary heart disease and Type A behavior: Update on and alternative to the Booth-Kewley and Friedman (1987) quantitative review. *Psychological Bulletin, 104,* 373–380.

May, R. (1969). *Love and will*. New York: W. W. Norton.

May, R., Angel, E., & Ellenberger, H. F. (Eds.). (1958). *Existence: A new dimension in psychiatry and psychology*. New York: Basic Books.

May, W. T., & Belsky, J. (1992). Response to "Prescription privileges: Psychology's next frontier?" or the siren call: Should psychologists medicate? *American Psychologist, 47,* 427.

Mayberg, H. S. (1997). Limbic-cortical dysregulation: A proposed model of depression. *Journal of Neuropsychiatry and Clinical Neurosciences, 9,* 471–481.

Mayne, T. J., Norcross, J. C., & Sayette, M. A. (1994). Admission requirements, acceptance rates, and financial assistance in clinical psychology programs: Diversity across the practice-research continuum. *American Psychologist, 49,* 806–811.

McArthur, D. S., & Roberts, G. E. (1982). *Roberts Apperception Test for Children: Manual*. Los Angeles: Western Psychological Services.

McCarthy, R. (1998, August). Behavioral health: Don't ignore, integrate. *Business and Health,* 51.

McCartney, K., Harris, M. J., & Bernieri, F. (1990). Growing up and growing apart: A developmental meta-analysis of twin studies. *Psychological Bulletin, 107,* 226–237.

McCoy, S. A. (1976). Clinical judgments of normal childhood behavior. *Journal of Consulting and Clinical Psychology, 44,* 710–714.

McCrae, R. R., & Costa, P. T. (1983). Social desirability scales: More substance than style. *Journal of Consulting and Clinical Psychology, 51,* 882–888.

McDermut, W., Miller, I. W., & Brown, R. A. (2001). The efficacy of group psychotherapy for depression: A meta-analysis and review of empirical research. *Clinical Psychology: Science and Practice, 8,* 98-116.

McFall, R. M. (1991). Manifesto for a science of clinical psychology. *The Clinical Psychologist, 44,* 75-88.

McFall, R. M., & Lillesand, D. B. (1971). Behavior rehearsal with modeling and coaching in assertion training. *Journal of Abnormal Psychology, 77,* 313-323.

McGlashan, T. H., & Hoffman, R. E. (2000). Schizophrenia as a disorder of reduced synaptic connectivity. *Archives of General Psychiatry, 57,* 637-648.

McGlynn, F. D., Moore, P. M., Lawyer, S., & Karg, R. (1999). Relaxation training inhibits fear and arousal during in vivo exposure to phobia-cue stimuli. *Journal of Behavior Therapy and Experimental Psychiatry, 30,* 155-168.

McGoldrick, M., Giordano, J., & Pearce, J. K. (Eds.). (1996). *Ethnicity and family therapy* (2nd ed.). New York: The Guilford Press.

McGue, M. (1992). When assessing twin concordance, use the probandwise not the pairwise rate. *Schizophrenia Bulletin, 18,* 171-176.

McGuiness, J. (2000). Therapeutic climate. In C. Feltham and I. Horton (Eds.), *Handbook of counselling and psychotherapy.* London: Sage Publications.

McGuire, T. G. (1989). Outpatient benefits for mental health services in Medicare: Alignment with the private sector. *American Psychologist, 44,* 818-824.

McInnis-Dittrich, K. (1996). Violence prevention: An ecological adaptation of systematic training for effective parenting. *Family Sociology, 77,* 414-422.

McIntyre, T. J., Bornstein, P. H., Isaacs, C. D., Woody, D. J., Bornstein, M. T., Clucas, T. J., & Long, G. (1983). Naturalistic observation of conduct-disordered children: An archival analysis. *Behavior Therapy, 14,* 375-385.

McKay, S., & Golden, C. J. (1979). Empirical derivation of neuropsychological scales for the lateralization of brain damage using the Luria-Nebraska Neuropsychological Battery. *Clinical Neuropsychology, 1,* 1-5.

McLean, P. D., Whittal, M. L., Thordarson, D. S., Taylor, S., Söchting, I., Koch, W. J., et al. (2001). Cognitive versus behavioral therapy in the group treatment of obsessive-compulsive disorder. *Journal of Consulting and Clinical Psychology, 69,* 205-214.

McLemore, C. W., & Benjamin, L. S. (1979). Whatever happened to interpersonal diagnosis: A psychosocial alternative to DSM-III. *American Psychologist, 34,* 17-34.

McMahon, R. J., & Wells, K. C. (1998). Conduct problems. In E. J. Mash & R. A. Barkley (Eds.), *Treatment of childhood disorders* (2nd ed., pp. 111-207). New York: Guilford.

McNally, R. J., Clancy, S. A., & Schacter, D. L. (2001). Directed forgetting of trauma cues in adults reporting repressed or recovered memories of childhood sexual abuse. *Journal of Abnormal Psychology, 110,* 151-156.

McNally, R. J., Clancy, S. A., Schacter, D. L., & Pittman, R. K. (2000). Cognitive processing of trauma cues in adults reporting repressed, recovered, or continuous memories of childhood sexual abuse. *Journal of Abnormal Psychology, 109,* 355-359.

McQuaid, J. R., Granholm, E., McClure, F. S., Roepke, S., Pedrelli, P., Patterson, T. L., et al. (2000). Development of an integrated cognitive-behavioral and social skills training intervention for older patients with schizophrenia. *Journal of Psychotherapy Practice and Research, 9,* 149-156.

McReynolds, P. (1975). Historical antecedents of personality assessment. In P. McReynolds (Ed.), *Advances in psychological assessment* (Vol. 3, pp. 477-532). San Francisco: Jossey-Bass.

McReynolds, P. (1987). Lightner Witmer: Little-known founder of clinical psychology. *American Psychologist, 42,* 849-858.

McWilliams, N. (1999). *Psychoanalytic case formulation.* New York: Guilford Press.

Mead, M. (1928). *Coming of age in Samoa.* New York: Morrow.

Meador, B. D., & Rogers, C. R. (1973). Client-centered therapy. In R. Corsini (Ed.), *Current psychotherapies* (pp. 119-165). Itasca, IL: F. E. Peacock.

Meehl, P. E. (1954). *Clinical versus statistical prediction.* Minneapolis: University of Minnesota Press.

Meehl, P. E. (1956). Wanted—A good cookbook. *American Psychologist, 11,* 263-272.

Meehl, P. E. (1957). When shall we use our heads instead of the formula? *Journal of Consulting Psychology, 4,* 268-273.

Meehl, P. E. (1960). The cognitive activity of the clinician. *American Psychologist, 15,* 19-27.

Meehl, P. E. (1965). Seer over sign: The first good example. *Journal of Experimental Research in Personality, 1,* 27-32.

Meehl, P. E. (1986). What social scientists don't understand. In D. Fiske & R. A. Shweder (Eds.), *Metatheory in social science* (pp. 315-339). Chicago, IL: The University of Chicago Press.

Meichenbaum, D. H. (1971). Examination of model characteristics in reducing avoidance behavior. *Journal of Personality and Social Psychology, 17,* 298-307.

Meichenbaum, D. H., & Goodman, J. (1971). Training impulsive children to talk to themselves: A means of developing self-control. *Journal of Abnormal Psychology, 77,* 115-126.

Melby, J. N., Conger, R. D., Ge, X. J., & Warner, T. D. (1995). The use of structural equation modeling in assessing the quality of marital observations. *Journal of Family Psychology, 9,* 280-293.

Mellon, M. W., & McGrath, M. L. (2000). Empirically supported treatments in pediatric psychology: Nocturnal enuresis. *Journal of Pediatric Psychology, 25,* 193-214.

Melton, A. W. (Ed.). (1947). *Apparatus tests.* Washington, DC: Government Printing Office.

Melton, G. B., Petrila, J., Poythress, N. G., & Slobogin, C. (1987). *Psychological evaluations for the courts.* New York: Guilford Press.

Melton, G. B., Petrila, J., Poythress, N. G., & Slobogin, C. (1997). *Psychological evaluations for the courts* (2nd ed.). New York: Guilford Press.

Meltzoff, J., & Kornreich, M. (1970). *Research in psychotherapy.* New York: Atherton Press.

Menninger, K. (1958). *The theory of psychoanalytic technique.* New York: Basic Books.

Mercatoris, M., & Craighead, W. E. (1974). The effects of non-participant observation on teacher and pupil classroom behavior. *Journal of Educational Psychology, 66,* 512-519.

Mermelstein, R., Lichtenstein, E., & McIntyre, K. (1983). Partner support and relapse in smoking-cessation programs. *Journal of Consulting and Clinical Psychology, 51,* 331-337.

Messer, S. B. (2001). Empirically supported treatments: What's a neobehaviorist to do? In B. D. Slife, R. N. Williams, & S. H. Barlow (Eds.), *Critical issues in psychotherapy.* Thousand Oaks, CA: Sage.

Messer, S. B., & Winokur, M. (1980). Some limits to the integration of psychoanalytic and behavior therapy. *American Psychologist, 35,* 818-827.

Messick, S. (1995). Validity of psychological assessment: Validation of inferences from persons' responses and performances as scientific inquiry into score meaning. *American Psychologist, 50,* 741-749.

Meyer, A. J., Nash, J. D., McAlister, A. L., Maccoby, N., & Farquhar, J. W. (1980). Skills training in cardiovascular education campaign. *Journal of Consulting and Clinical Psychology, 48,* 129–142.

Meyer, G. J., Finn, S. E., Eyde, L. D., Kay, G. G., Moreland, K. L., Dies, R. R., et al. (2001). Psychological testing and psychological assessment: A review of evidence and issues. *American Psychologist, 56,* 128–165.

Meyer-Lindenberg, A., Poline, J-B., Kohn, P. D., Holt, J. L., Egan, M. F., Weinberger, D. R., & Berman, K F. (2001). Evidence for abnormal cortical functional connectivity during working memory in schizophrenia. *American Journal of Psychiatry, 158,* 1809–1817.

Meyers, J. (1975). Consultee centered consultation with a teacher as a technique in behavior management. *American Journal of Community Psychology, 3,* 111–122.

Milan, M. A., Chin, C. E., & Nguyen, Q. X. (1999). Practicing psychology in correctional settings: Assessment, treatment, and substance abuse programs. In A. K. Hess and I. B. Weiner (Eds.), *The handbook of forensic psychology* (2nd ed., pp. 580–602). New York: John Wiley & Sons.

Milan, M. A., Montgomery, R. W., & Rogers, E. G. (1994). Theoretical orientation revolution in clinical psychology: Fact or fiction? *Professional Psychology: Research and Practice, 25,* 398–402.

Milich, R., & Fitzgerald, G. (1985). Validation of inattention/overactivity and aggression ratings with classroom observations. *Journal of Consulting and Clinical Psychology, 53,* 139–140.

Milich, R., & Kramer, J. (1984). Reflections on impulsivity: An empirical investigation of impulsivity as a construct. In K. D. Gadow (Ed.), *Advances in learning and behavioral disabilities: A research annual* (Vol. 3, pp. 57–94). Greenwich, CT: JAI Press.

Milich, R., Loney, J., & Landau, S. (1982). Independent dimensions of hyperactivity and aggression: Validation with playroom observation data. *Journal of Abnormal Psychology, 91,* 183–198.

Milich, R., Widiger, T. A., & Landau, S. (1987). Differential diagnosis of attention deficit and conduct disorders using conditional probabilities. *Journal of Consulting and Clinical Psychology, 55,* 762–767.

Miller, B. (2000, April 11). Day releases sought for Hinckley. *The Washington Post,* B6.

Miller, G. E., & Cohen, S. (2001). Psychological interventions and the immune system: A meta-analytic review and critique. *Health Psychology, 20,* 47–63.

Miller, I. J. (1996a). Time-limited brief therapy has gone too far: The result is invisible rationing. *Professional Psychology: Research and Practice, 27,* 567–576.

Miller, I. J. (1996b). Managed care is harmful to outpatient mental health services: A call for accountability. *Professional Psychology: Research and Practice, 27,* 349–363.

Miller, J. O., & Gross, S. J. (1973). Curvilinear trends in outcome research. *Journal of Consulting Psychology, 41,* 242–244.

Miller, K. M. (1991). Use of psychological assessment and training in testing techniques in the UK. *Evaluacion Psicologica, 7,* 85–97.

Miller, S. B., Freise, M., Dolgoy, L., Sita, A., Lavoie, K., et al. (1998). Hostility, sodium consumption, and cardiovascular response to interpersonal stress. *Psychosomatic Medicine, 60,* 71–77.

Miller, T. Q., Turner, C. W., Tindale, R. S., Posavac, E. J., & Dugoni, B. L. (1991). Reasons for the trend toward null findings in research on Type A behavior. *Psychological Bulletin, 110,* 469–485.

Miller, W. R., & DiPilato, M. (1983). Treatment of nightmares via relaxation and desensitization: A controlled evaluation. *Journal of Consulting and Clinical Psychology, 51,* 870–877.

Millon, T. (1981). *Disorders of personality: DSM-III, Axis II*. New York: John Wiley.

Millon, T. (1991). Classification in psychopathology: Rationale, alternatives, and standards. *Journal of Abnormal Psychology, 100,* 245–261.

Millon, T., & Klerman, G. L. (Eds.). (1986). *Contemporary directions in psychopathology: Toward the DSM-IV*. New York: Guilford Press.

Millon, J., Millon, C., & Davis, R. (1997). *Millon Clinical Multiaxial Inventory: III (MCMI-III) manual* (3rd ed.). Minneapolis, MN: National Computer Systems.

Milne, D., Claydon, T., Blackburn, I., James, I., Sheikh, A. (2001). Rationale for a new measure of competence in therapy. *Behavioral and Cognitive Psychotherapy, 29,* 21–33.

Milner, B. (1974). Hemispheric specialization: Scope and limits. In F. O. Schmitt & F. G. Worden (Eds.), *The neurosciences: Third study program* (pp. 75–89). Cambridge, MA: MIT Press.

Milner, D. A., & Rugg, M. D. (1992). *The neuropsychology of consciousness*. San Diego, CA: Academic Press, Inc.

Mineka, S., Watson, D., & Clark, L. A. (1998). Comorbidity of anxiety and unipolar mood disorders. *Annual Review of Psychology, 49,* 377–412.

Minuchin, S. (1974). *Families and family therapy*. Cambridge, MA: Harvard University Press.

Mischel, W. (1968). *Personality and assessment*. New York: John Wiley.

Mischel, W. (1971). *Introduction to personality*. New York: Holt, Rinehart & Winston.

Mischel, W. (1984). Convergences and challenges in the search for consistency. *American Psychologist, 39,* 351–364.

Mischel, W. (1986). *Introduction to personality* (4th ed.). New York: Holt, Rinehart & Winston.

Mischel, W. (1993). *Introduction to personality*. New York: Harcourt Brace.

Monahan, J. (1988). Risk assessment of violence among the mentally disordered: Generating useful knowledge. *International Journal of Law and Psychiatry, 11,* 249.

Monahan, J., & Steadman, H. J. (Eds.). (1994). Violence and mental disorder: Developments in risk assessment. Chicago, IL: The University of Chicago Press.

Monahan, J., & Walker, L. (1990). *Social sciences in law: Cases and materials* (2nd ed.). Westbury, NY: Foundation Press.

Monahan, J., & Walker, L. (2002). *Social science in law: Cases and materials* (5th ed.). New York: Foundation Press.

Moncher, F. J., & Prinz, R. J. (1991). Treatment fidelity in outcome studies. *Clinical Psychology Review, 11,* 247–266.

Montgomery, L. M., Cupit, B. E., & Wimberley, T. K. (1999). Complaints, malpractice, and risk management: Professional issues and personal experiences. *Professional Psychology: Research and Practice, 30,* 359–366.

Moos, R., Schaefer, J., Andrassy, J., & Moos, B. (2001). Outpatient mental health care, self-help groups, and patients' one-year treatment outcomes. *Journal of Clinical Psychology, 57,* 273–287.

Moreno, J. (1946). *Psychodrama* (vol. 1). New York: Beacon House.

Morgan, B. L., & Korschgen, A. J. (2001). *Majoring in psych? Career options for psychology undergraduates* (2nd ed.). Boston: Allyn and Bacon.

Morgan, C., & Murray, H. A. (1935). A method for investigating phantasies: The thematic apperception test. *Archives of Neurology and Psychiatry, 34,* 289–306.

Morgan D. L., & Morgan R. K. (2001). Single-participant design: Bringing science to managed care. *American Psychologist, 56,* 119–127.

Morganstern, K. P. (1988). Behavioral interviewing. In A. S. Bellack & M. Hersen (Eds.), *Behavioral assessment: A practical handbook* (3rd ed., pp. 86–108). New York: Pergamon Press.

Morganstern, K. P., & Tevlin, H. E. (1981). Behavioral interviewing. In M. Hersen & A. S. Bellack (Eds.), *Behavioral assessment: A practical handbook* (2nd ed., pp. 71–100). New York: Pergamon Press.

Morrison, C. S., McCusker, J., Stoddard, A. M., & Bigelow, C. (1995). The validity of behavioral data reported by injection drug users on a clinical risk assessment. *International Journal of the Addictions, 30,* 889–899.

Morse, S. J. (1978). Law and mental health professionals: The limits of expertise. *Professional Psychology, 9,* 389–399.

Morton, A. (1995). The enigma of non-attendance: A study of clients who do not turn up for their first appointment. *Therapeutic Communities: International Journal for Therapeutic and Supportive Organizations, 16,* 117–133.

Moscarelli, M., & Capri, S. (1992). The cost of schizophrenia: Editors' introduction. *Schizophrenia Bulletin, 17,* 367–369.

Mrazek, P. J., & Haggerty, R. J. (Eds.). (1994). *Reducing risks for mental disorders: Frontiers for preventive intervention research.* Washington, DC: National Academy Press.

MRFIT (Multiple Risk Factors Intervention Trial Research Group). (1982). Multiple risk factor intervention trial: Risk factor changes and mortality results. *Journal of the American Medical Association, 248,* 1465–1477.

Mukherjee, D., Heller, W., & Alper, J. S. (2001). Social and Institutional Factors in Adjustment to Traumatic Brain Injury. *Rehabilitation Psychology, 46,* 82–99.

Mulvey, E. P., & Cauffman, E. (2001). The inherent limits of predicting school violence. *American Psychologist, 56,* 797–802.

Munroe, R. (1955). *Schools of psychoanalytic thought.* New York: Dryden Press.

Murray, B. (1996, February). Psychology remains top college major. *The APA Monitor, 1,* 42.

Murray, H. A. (1938). *Explorations in personality.* Fair Lawn, NJ: Oxford University Press.

Murray, H. A. (1943). *Thematic Apperception Test.* Cambridge, MA: Harvard University Press.

Mussen, P. H., & Scodel, A. (1955). The effects of sexual stimulation under varying conditions on TAT sexual responsiveness. *Journal of Consulting Psychology, 19,* 90.

Myers, D. G. (2000). The funds, friends, and faith of happy people. *American Psychologist, 55,* 56–67.

Myers, I. B., & Briggs, K. C. (1943). *The Myers-Briggs type indicator.* Palo Alto, CA: Consulting Psychologists Press.

Myklebust, H. R. (1975). Nonverbal learning disabilities: Assessment and intervention. In H. R. Myklebust (Ed.), *Progress in learning disabilities* (vol. 3, pp. 85–121). New York: Grune & Stratton.

Nathan, P. E. (1987). DSM-III-R and the behavior therapist. *Behavior Therapy, 10,* 203–205.

Nathan, P. E., & Groman, J. M. (Eds.). (1998). *A guide to treatments that work.* New York: Oxford University Press.

Nathan, P. E., & Langenbucher, J. W. (1999). Psychopathology: Description and classification. *Annual Review of Psychology, 50,* 79–107.

Nathan, P. E., Stuart, S. P., & Dolan, S. L. (2000). Research on psychotherapy efficacy and effectiveness: Between Scylla and Charybdis? *Psychological Bulletin, 126,* 964–981.

National Association of Social Workers. (2001). About NASW: NASW fact sheet. Retrieved September 17, 2001 from http://www.naswdc.org/about/naswfact.htm.

National Center for Education Statistics. (2000). Digest of Education Statistics, 1999. Retrieved December 13, 2001 from http://nces.ed.gov/pubs2000/Digest99/d99t298.htm.

National Institute of Justice. (1999). *Eyewitness Evidence: A Guide for Law Enforcement.* Washington, DC: U.S. Department of Justice.

Neimeyer, R., & Raskin, J. D. (Eds.). (2000). *Constructions of disorder: Meaning-making frameworks for psychotherapy.* Washington, DC: American Psychological Association.

Neisser, U., Boodoo, G., Bouchard, T. J., Boykin, A. W., Brody, N., Ceci, S. J., et al. (1996). Intelligence: Knowns and unknowns. *American Psychologist, 51,* 77-101.

Nelson, R. O. (1977). Assessment and therapeutic functions of self-monitoring. In M. Hersen, R. M. Eisler, & P. M. Miller (Eds.), *Progress in behavior modification* (pp. 264-308). New York: Academic Press.

Nelson, R. O., Hayes, S. C., Felton, J. L., & Jarrett, R. B. (1985). A comparison of data produced by different behavioral assessment techniques with implications for models of social-skills adequacy. *Behaviour Research and Therapy, 23,* 1-12.

Neukrug, E. S., & Williams, G. T. (1993). Counseling counselors: A survey of values. *Counseling and Values, 38,* 51-62.

Newman, D. L., Moffitt, T. E., Caspi, A., Magdol, L., Silva, P. A., & Stanton, W. R. (1996). Psychiatric disorder in a birth cohort of young adults: Prevalence, comorbidity, clinical significance, and new case incidence from ages 11 to 21. *Journal of Consulting and Clinical Psychology, 64,* 552-562.

Newman, F. L., & Tejeda, M. J. (1996). The need for research that is designed to support decisions in the delivery of mental health services. *American Psychologist, 51,* 1040-1049.

Nicholson, R. A. (1999). Forensic assessment. In R. Roesch, S. D. Hart, & J. R. Ogloff (Eds.), *Psychology and law: The state of the discipline* (pp. 122-173). New York: Kluwer Academic/Plenum.

Nicholson, R. A., & Berman, J. S. (1983). Is follow-up necessary in evaluating psychotherapy? *Psychological Bulletin, 93,* 261-278.

Nicholson, R. A., Briggs, S. R., & Robertson, H. C. (1988). Instruments for assessing competency to stand trial: How do they work? *Professional Psychology: Research and Practice, 19,* 383-394.

Nicholson, R. A., & Kugler, K. E. (1991). Competent and incompetent criminal defendants: A quantitive review of comparative research. *Psychological Bulletin, 109,* 355-370.

Nickelson, D. W. (1995). The future of professional psychology in a changing health care marketplace: A conversation with Russ Newman. *Professional Psychology: Research and Practice, 26,* 366-370.

NIDA Research Report—Prescription Drugs: Abuse and Addiction: NIH Publication No. 01-4881, Printed April, 2001 (Author).

Nietzel, M. T., & Bernstein, D. A. (1976). The effects of instructionally mediated demand upon the behavioral assessment of assertiveness. *Journal of Consulting and Clinical Psychology, 44,* 500.

Nietzel, M. T., Bernstein, D. A., & Russell, R. L. (1988). Assessment of anxiety and fear. In A. S. Bellack & M. Hersen (Eds.), *Behavioral assessment: A practical handbook* (3rd ed., pp. 280-312). New York: Pergamon Press.

Nietzel, M. T., & Fisher, S. G. (1981). Effectiveness of professional and paraprofessional helpers: A reply to Durlak. *Psychological Bulletin, 89,* 555-565.

Nietzel, M. T., Guthrie, P. R., & Susman, D. T. (1991). Utilization of community and social support services. In F. H. Kanfer & A. P. Goldstein (Eds.), *Helping people change* (4th ed., pp. 396–421). New York: Pergamon Press.

Nietzel, M. T., Speltz, M. L., McCauley, E. A., & Bernstein, D. A. (1998). *Abnormal Psychology.* Boston: Allyn & Bacon.

Nietzel, M. T., Winett, R. A., MacDonald, M. L., & Davidson, W. S. (1977). *Behavioral approaches to community psychology.* New York: Pergamon Press.

NIMH Committee on Prevention Research. (1995). *A plan for prevention research for the National Institute of Mental Health (A report to the National Advisory Mental Health Council).* Washington, DC: NIMH.

NIMH Prevention Research Steering Committee. (1994). *The prevention of mental disorders: A national research agenda.* Washington, DC: NIMH.

Norcross, J. C. (2000). Here comes the self-help revolution in mental health. *Psychotherapy: Theory, Research, Practice, and Training, 37,* 370–377.

Norcross, J. C. (2001). Introduction: In search of the meaning and utility of countertransference. *Journal of Clinical Psychology/ In Session: Psychotherapy in Practice, 57,* 981–982.

Norcross, J. C., Gallagher, K. M., & Prochaska, J. O. (1997). Clinical psychologists in the 1990s. *The Clinical Psychologist, 50,* 4–9.

Norcross, J. C., Hanych, J. M., & Terranova, R. D. (1996). Graduate study in psychology: 1992–1993. *American Psychologist, 51,* 631–643.

Norcross, J. C., Karg, R. S., & Prochaska, J. O. (1997). Clinical psychologists in the 1990s: Part I. *Clinical Psychologist, 50,* 4–9.

Norcross, J. C., & Prochaska, J. O. (1983). Psychotherapists in independent practice: Some findings and issues. *Professional Psychology: Research and Practice, 14,* 869–881.

Norcross, J. C., Prochaska, J. O., & Gallagher, K. M. (1989a). Clinical psychologists in the 1980s: I. Demographics, affiliations, and satisfactions. *The Clinical Psychologist, 42,* 29–39.

Norcross, J. C., Prochaska, J. O., & Gallagher, K. M. (1989b). Clinical psychologists in the 1980s: II. Theory, research, and practice. *The Clinical Psychologist, 42,* 45–53.

Norcross, J. C., Santrock, J. W., Campbell, L. F., & Smith, T. P. (2000). *Authoritative guide to self-help resources in mental health.* New York: Guilford.

Norcross, J. C., Sayette, M. A., Mayne, T. J., Karg, R. S., & Turkson, M. A. (1998). Selecting a doctoral program in professional psychology: Some comparisons among PhD counseling, PhD Clinical, and PsyD Clinical psychology programs. *Professional Psychology: Research and Practice, 6,* 609–614.

Norton, P. J., & Hope, D. A. (2001). Analogue observational methods in assessment of social functioning in adults. *Psychological Assessment, 13,* 86–98.

Nunes, E. V., Frank, K. A., & Kornfeld, S. D. (1987). Psychologic treatment for Type A behavior pattern and for coronary heart disease: A meta-analysis of the literature. *Psychosomatic Medicine, 48,* 159–173.

Obrist, P. (1981). *Cardiovascular psychophysiology: A perspective.* New York: Plenum Press.

Obrzut, J. E. (1988). Deficient lateralization in learning-disabled children: Developmental lag or abnormal cerebral organization? In D. L. Molfese & S. J. Segalowitz (Eds.), *Brain lateralization in children: Developmental implications.* New York: Guilford Press.

O'Connor, M., Sales, B. D., & Shuman, D. (1996). Mental health professional expertise in the courtroom. In B. D. Sales & D. W. Shuman (Eds.), *Law, mental health, and mental disorder.* Pacific Grove, CA: Brooks/Cole.

Office of Program Consultation and Accreditation, American Psychological Association. (1996). *Guidelines and principles for accreditation of programs in professional psychology/Accreditation operating procedures*. Washington D.C.: Author.

Office of Strategic Services Assessment Staff. (1948). *Assessment of men*. New York: Rinehart.

Ogden, J. (1996). *Health Psychology: A textbook*. Philadelphia: Open University Press.

Ogloff, J. R. P., & Otto, R. (1993). Psychological autopsy: Clinical and legal perspectives. *Saint Louis University Law Journal, 37*, 607-646.

Olbrisch, M. E. (1977). Psychotherapeutic interventions in physical health: Effectiveness and economic efficiency. *American Psychologist, 32*, 761-777.

O'Leary, K. D., & Becker, W. C. (1967). Behavior modification of an adjustment class: A token reinforcement program. *Exceptional Children, 33*, 637-642.

Olfson, M. (1990). Assertive community treatment: An evaluation of the experimental evidence. *Hospital and Community Psychiatry, 41*, 634-641.

Olfson, M., Marcus, S. C., & Pincus, H. A. (1999). Trends in office-based psychiatric practice. *American Journal of Psychiatry, 156*, 451-457.

Olfson, M., & Pincus, H. A. (1994). Outpatient psychotherapy in the United States: I. Volume, costs, and user characteristics. *American Journal of Psychiatry, 151*, 1281-1288.

Olfson, M., Pincus, H., & Sabshin, M. (1994). Pharmacotherapy in outpatient psychiatric practice. *American Journal of Psychiatry, 151*, 580-585.

Olive, H. (1972). Psychoanalysts' opinions of psychologists' reports: 1952 and 1970. *Journal of Clinical Psychology, 28*, 50-54.

Ollendick, T. H. (1996). Violence in youth: Where do we go from here? Behavior therapy's response. *Behavior Therapy, 27*, 485-514.

Ollendick, T. H., & Greene, R. (1990). Behavioral assessment of children. In G. Goldstein & M. Hersen (Eds.), *Handbook of psychological assessment* (2nd ed., pp. 403-422). New York: Pergamon Press.

Ollendick, T. H., & King, N. J. (1998). Empirically supported treatments for children with phobic and anxiety disorders. *Journal of Clinical Child Psychology, 27*, 156-167.

Olweus, D. (1995). Bullying or peer abuse at school: Facts and intervention. *Current Directions in Psychological Science, 4*, 196-200.

O'Neil, E. (2000). Psychology and the American health professional community in transition. *Professional Psychology: Research and Practice, 3*, 264-265.

O'Neill, P., & Trickett, E. J. (1982). *Community consultation*. San Francisco: Jossey-Bass.

Orlinsky, D. E., Grawe, K., & Parks, B. K. (1994). Process and outcome in psychotherapy—Noch Einmal. In A. E. Bergin & S. L. Garfield (Eds.), *Handbook of psychotherapy and behavior change* (4th ed, pp. 270-276). New York: John Wiley.

Orlinsky, D. E., & Howard, K. I. (1986). Process and outcome in psychotherapy. In S. L. Garfield & A. E. Bergin (Eds.), *Handbook of psychotherapy and behavior change* (3rd ed., pp. 311-381). New York: John Wiley.

Orne, M. T. (1962). On the social psychology of the psychological experiment: With particular reference to demand characteristics and their implications. *American Psychologist, 17*, 776-783.

Ossip-Klein, D. J., Martin, J. E., Lomax, B. D., Prue, D. M., & Davis, C. J. (1983). Assessment of smoking topography generalization across laboratory, clinical, and naturalistic settings. *Addictive Behaviors, 8*, 11-17.

O'Sullivan, J. J., & Quevillon, R. P. (1992). 40 years later: Is the Boulder model still alive? *American Psychologist, 47,* 67-70.

Othmer, E. M., & Othmer, S. C. (2002). *The clinical interview using DSM-IV-TR: Fundamentals.* Washington, DC: The American Psychiatric Association.

Owen, H. M. (2001). Pharmacological aversion treatment of alcohol dependence. I. Production and prediction of conditioned alcohol aversion. *American Journal of Drug and Alcohol Abuse, 27,* 561-585.

Owens, P. (1997). Mental health: Understanding work disability. *Health Insurance Underwriter, 45,* 12-15.

Ownsworth, T. L., McFarland, K., & Young, R. M. (2000). Development and standardization of the Self-Regulation Skills Interview (SRSI): A new clinical assessment tool for acquired brain injury. *Clinical Neuropsychologist, 14,* 76-92.

Pallak, M. S., Cummings, N. A., Dorken, H., & Henke, C. J. (1995). Effect of mental health treatment of medical costs. *Mind/Body Medicine, 1,* 7-11.

Parker, J. G., & Asher, S. R. (1987). Peer relations and later personal adjustment: Are low-accepted children at risk? *Psychological Bulletin, 102,* 357-389.

Parker, K. C. H., Hanson, R. K., & Hunsley, J. (1988). MMPI, Rorschach, and WAIS: A meta-analytic comparison of reliability, stability, and validity. *Psychological Bulletin, 103,* 367-373.

Parnas, J., Cannon, T., Jacobsen, B., Schulsinger, H., Schulsinger, F., & Mednick, S. (1993). Lifetime DSM-III-R diagnostic outcomes in the offspring of schizophrenic mothers. *Archives of General Psychiatry, 50,* 707-714.

Pate, W. E., II. (2001). Analyses of data from graduate study in psychology: 1999-2000. Retrieved December 12, 2001 from APA Research office, http://research.apa.org/grad00contents.html.

Patricelli, R. E., & Lee, F. C. (1996). Employer-based innovations in behavioral health benefits. *Professional Psychology: Research and Practice, 27,* 325-334.

Patterson, C. H. (1989). Foundations for a systematic eclectic psychotherapy. *Psythotherapy, 26,* 427-435.

Patterson, D. R., Everett, J. J., Burns, G. L., & Marvin, J. A. (1992). Hypnosis for the treatment of burn pain. *Journal of Consulting and Clinical Psychology, 60,* 713-717.

Patterson, G. R. (1975). *Families.* Champaign, IL: Research Press.

Patterson, G. R. (1976). The aggressive child: Victim and architect of a coercive system. In L. A. Hamerlynck, L. C. Handy, & E. J. Mash (Eds.), *Behavior modification and families: Theory and research* (Vol. 1, pp. 267-316). New York: Brunner/Mazel.

Patterson, G. R. (1982). *Coercive family process.* Eugene, OR: Castalia.

Patterson, G. R., & Forgatch, M. (1987). *Parents and adolescents: Living together.* Eugene, OR: Castalia.

Patterson, G. R., Ray, R. S., Shaw, D. A., & Cobb, J. A. (1969). *Manual for coding of family interactions* (Document NO. 01234). Available from ASIS/NAPS, c/o Microfiche Publications, 305 East 46th St., New York, NY 10017.

Paul, G. L. (1966). *Insight versus desensitization in psychotherapy: An experiment in anxiety reduction.* Stanford, CA: Stanford University Press.

Paul, G. L. (1969a). Behavior modification research: Design and tactics. In C. M. Franks (Ed.), *Behavior therapy: Appraisal and status* (pp. 29-62). New York: McGraw-Hill.

Paul, G. L. (1969b). Outcome of systematic desensitization II. In C. M. Franks (Ed.), *Behavior therapy: Appraisal and status* (pp. 63-159). New York: McGraw-Hill.

Paul, G. L., & Lentz, R. J. (1977). *Psychosocial treatment of chronic mental patients: Milieu versus social-learning programs.* Cambridge, MA: Harvard University Press.

Paul, G. L., & Licht, M. H. (1987). *The time-sample behavioral checklist: Observational assessment instrumentation for service and research.* Champaign, IL: Research Press.

Pavlov, I. P. (1927). *Conditioned reflexes.* New York: Oxford University Press.

Peck, C. P., & Ash, E. (1964). Training in the Veterans Administration. In L. Blank & H. P. David (Eds.), *Sourcebook for training in clinical psychology* (pp. 61–81). New York: Springer.

Pedersen, P., & Ivey, A. E. (1993). Culture-centered counseling and interviewing skills: A practical guide. Westport, CT: Praeger.

Pedro-Carroll, J. L., & Cowen, E. L. (1985). The children of divorce intervention program: An investigation of the efficacy of a school-based prevention program. *Journal of Consulting and Clinical Psychology, 53,* 603–611.

Pelham, W. E., Lang, A. R., Atkeson, B., Murphy, D. A., Gnagy, E. M., Greiner, A. R., Vode-Hamilton, M., & Greenslade, K. E. (1997). Effects of deviant child behavior on parental distress and alcohol consumption in laboratory interactions. *Journal of Abnormal Child Psychology, 25,* 413–424.

Pelham, W. E., McBurnett, K., Harper, G. W., Milich, R., Murphy, D. A., Clinton, J., & Thiele, C. (1990). Methylphenidate and baseball playing in ADHD children: Who's on first? *Journal of Consulting and Clinical Psychology, 58,* 130–133.

Pelham, W. E., & Murphy, H. A. (1986). Attention deficit and conduct disorders. In M. Hersen (Ed.), *Pharmacological and behavioral treatments: An integrative approach* (pp. 108–148). New York: John Wiley.

Pelham, W. E., Murphy, D. A., Vannatta, K., Milich, R., Licht, B. G., Gnagy, E. M., Greenslade, K. E., Grenier, A. R., & Vodde-Hamilton, M. (1992). Methylphenidate and attributions in boys with attention-deficit hyperactivity disorder. *Journal of Consulting and Clinical Psychology, 60,* 282–292.

Pelham, W. E., Wheeler, T., & Chronis, A. (1998). Empirically supported psychosocial treatments for attention deficit hyperactivity disorder. *Journal of Clinical Child Psychology, 27,* 190–205.

Pennebacker, J. W. (1995). *Emotion, disclosure, and health.* Washington, DC: American Psychological Association.

Perls, F. S. (1947). *Ego, hunger and aggression: A revision of Freud's theory and method.* New York: Random House.

Perls, F. S. (1969). *Gestalt therapy verbatim.* Lafayette, CA: Real People Press.

Perls, F. S. (1970). Four lectures. In J. Fagan & I. L. Shepherd (Eds.), *Gestalt therapy now* (pp. 14–38). Palo Alto, CA: Science and Behavior Books.

Perry, C. L., Klepp, K., & Shultz, J. M. (1988). Primary prevention of cardiovascular disease: Community-wide strategies for youth. *Journal of Consulting and Clinical Psychology, 56,* 358–364.

Perry, D. G., Hodges, E. V. E., & Egan, S. K. (2001). Determinants of chronic victimization by peers: A review and a new model of family influence. In J. Juvonen and S. H. Graham (Eds.), *Peer harassment: The plight of the vulnerable and victimized* (pp. 73–104). New York: Guilford Press.

Persons, J. B. (1991). Psychotherapy outcome studies do not accurately represent current models of psychotherapy: A proposed remedy. *American Psychologist, 46,* 99–106.

Peters, L., Clark, D., & Carroll, F. (1998). Are computerized interviews equivalent to human interviews? CIDI-Auto versus CIDI in anxiety and depressive disorders. *Psychological Medicine, 28,* 893–901.

Peterson, C. (2000). The future of optimism. *American Psychologist, 55,* 44–55.

Peterson, C., & Villanova, P. (1988). An Expanded Attributional Style Questionnaire. *Journal of Abnormal Psychology, 97,* 87–89.

Peterson, D. R. (1968). *The clinical style of social behavior.* New York: Appleton-Century-Crofts.

Peterson, D. R. (1985). Twenty years of practitioner training in psychology. *American Psychologist, 40,* 441–451.

Peterson, D. R. (2000). Scientist-practitioner or scientific practitioner? *American Psychologist, 55,* 252–253.

Peterson, D. R., & Baron, A. (1975). Status of the University of Illinois doctor of psychology program, 1974. *Professional Psychology, 6,* 88–95.

Petraitis, J., Flay, B. R., & Miller, T. Q. (1995). Reviewing theories of adolescent substance use: Organizing pieces in the puzzle. *Psychological Bulletin, 117,* 67–86.

Pettijohn, T. F. (1991). *The encyclopedic dictionary of psychology* (4th ed.). Guilford, CT: Dushkin.

Phelps, R., Eisman, E. J., & Kohout, J. (1998). Psychological practice and managed care: Results of the CAPP practitioner survey. *Professional Psychology: Research and Practice, 29,* 31–36. Online version retrieved December 13, 2001 from http://www.apa.org/practice/cappsurvey.html.

Piaget, J. (1947). *The psychology of intelligence.* London: Kegan Paul.

Piaget, J. (1962). *Play, dreams, and imitation in childhood.* New York: W. W. Norton.

Piane, G. (2000). Contingency contracting and systematic desensitization for heroin addicts in methadone maintenance programs. *Journal of Psychoactive Drugs, 32,* 311–319.

Pilkonis, P. A., Heape, C. L., Proietti, J. M., Clark, S. W., et al. (1995). The reliability and validity of two structured interviews for personality disorders. *Archives of General Psychiatry, 52,* 1025–1033.

Pimental, P. A., Stout, C. E., Hoover, M. C., & Kamen, G. B. (1997). Changing psychologists' opinions about prescriptive authority: A little information goes a long way. *Professional Psychology: Research and Practice, 28,* 123–127.

Pion, G., Kohout, J., & Wicherski, M. (2000). "Rightsizing" the workforce through training reductions: A good idea? *Professional Psychology: Research & Practice, 31,* 266–271.

Piotrowski, C., & Keller, J. W. (1984). Psychodiagnostic testing in APA-approved clinical psychology programs. *Professional Psychology: Research and Practice, 15,* 450–456.

Piotrowski, C., & Keller, J. W. (1989). Psychodiagnostic testing in out-patient mental health facilities: A national study. *Professional Psychology: Research and Practice, 20,* 423–425.

Piotrowski, C., & Keller, J. W. (1992). Psychological testing in applied settings: A literature review. *Journal of Training and Practice in Professional Psychology, 6,* 74–82.

Piotrowski, Z. (1972). Psychological testing of intelligence and personality. In A. M. Freedman & H. I. Kaplan (Eds.), *Diagnosing mental illness: Evaluation in psychiatry and psychology* (pp. 41–85). New York: Atheneum.

Pirozollo, F. J., & Rayner, K. (1977). Hemispheric specialization in reading and word recognition. *Brain and Language, 4,* 248–261.

Pittenger, R. E., Hockett, C. F., & Danehy, J. J. (1960). The first five minutes: A sample of microscopic interview analyses. Ithaca, NY: Paul Martineau.

Plante, T. G., Goldfarb, L. P., & Wadley, V. (1993). Are stress and coping associated with aptitude and achievement testing performance among children?: A preliminary investigation. *Journal of School Psychology, 31,* 259–266.

Plomin, R., & Crabbe, J. C. (2000). DNA. *Psychological Bulletin, 126,* 806–828.

Plous, S., & Zimbardo, P. G. (1986). Attributional biases among clinicians: A comparison of psychoanalysts and behavior therapists. *Journal of Consulting and Clinical Psychology, 54,* 568–570.

Pollock, K. M. (2001). Exercise in treating depression: Broadening the psychotherapist's role. *Journal of Clinical Psychology/In Session, 57,* 1289–1300.

Polster, E., & Polster, M. (1973). *Gestalt therapy integrated: Contours of theory and practice.* New York: Brunner/Mazel.

Pomeranz, D. M., & Goldfried, M. R. (1970). An intake report outline for behavior modification. *Psychological Reports, 26,* 447–450.

Pope, B., Nudler, S., Vonkorff, M. R., & McGhee, J. P. (1974). The experienced professional interviewer versus the complete novice. *Journal of Consulting and Clinical Psychology, 42,* 68–69.

Pope, K. S. (1998). Pseudoscience, cross-examination, and scientific evidence in the recovered memory controversy. *Psychology, Public Policy, and Law, 4,* 1160–1181.

Pope, K. S., Butcher, J. N., & Seelen, J. (1993). *The MMPI, MMPI-2, and MMPI in court.* Washington, DC: American Psychological Association.

Pope, K. S., & Tabachnick, B. G. (1994). Therapists as patients: A national survey of psychologists' experiences, problems, and beliefs. *Professional Psychology: Research and Practice, 25,* 247–258.

Pope, K. S., & Vasquez, M. J. T. (1991). *Ethics in psychotherapy and counseling: A practical guide for psychologists.* San Francisco, CA: Jossey-Bass.

Pope, K. S., & Vetter, V. A. (1992). Ethical dilemmas encountered by members of the American Psychological Association: A national survey. *American Psychologist, 47,* 397–411.

Porter, B. (1983). Mind hunters. *Psychology Today, 17,* 44–52.

Porter, E. H., Jr. (1943). The development and evaluation of a measure of counseling interview procedures. *Educational and Psychological Measurement, 3,* 105–126.

Porter, S., Birt, A. R., Yuille, J. C., & Lehman, D. R. (2000). Negotiating false memories: Interviewer and rememberer characteristics relate to memory distortion. *Psychological Science, 11,* 507–510.

Post, C. G. (1963). *An introduction to the law.* Englewood Cliffs, NJ: Prentice Hall.

Potts, M. K., Burnam, M. A., & Wells, K. B. (1991). Gender differences in depression detection: A comparison of clinician diagnosis and standardized assessment. *Psychological Assessment, 3,* 609–615.

Powell, T. J. (1987). *Self-help organizations and professional practice.* Silver Springs, MD: National Association of Social Workers.

Poythress, N., Hoge, S. K., Bonnie, R. J., Monahan, J., & Eisenberg, M. (2001). *The MacArthur Adjudicative Competence Study: Executive Summary.* Retrieved December 6, 2001 from http://www.macarthur.virginia.edu/adjudicate.html#N_2_.

Price, R. H., Cowen, E. L., Lorion, R. L., & Ramos-McKay, J. (1988). *Fourteen ounces of prevention: A casebook for practitioners.* Washington, DC: American Psychological Association.

Prigerson, H. G., Shear, M. K., Jacobs, S. C., Reynolds, C. F., Maciejewski, P. K., et al. (1999). Consensus criteria for traumatic grief: A preliminary test. *British Journal of Psychiatry, 55,* 75–81.

Prochaska, J. O., & DiClemente, C. C. (1984). *The transtheoretical approach: Crossing traditional boundaries of therapy*. Homewood, IL: Dow Jones-Irwin.

Prochaska, J. O., DiClemente, C. C., & Norcross, J. C. (1992). Stages of change in the modification of problem behaviors. In M. Hersen, R. M Eisler, & P. M. Miller (Eds.), *Progress in behavior modification* (pp. 184–218). Newbury Park, CA: Sage.

Prochaska, J. O., & Norcross, J. C. (1994). *Systems of psychotherapy: A transtheoretical analysis* (3rd ed.). Pacific Grove, CA: Brooks/Cole.

Prochaska, J. O., & Norcross, J. C. (1999). *Systems of psychotherapy* (4th ed.). Pacific Grove, CA: Brooks/Cole.

Prochaska, J. O., Velicer, W. F., Rossi, J. S., Goldstein, M. G., et al. (1994). Stages of change and decisional balance for 12 problem behaviors. *Health Psychology, 13,* 39–43.

Purdy, J. E., Reinehr, R. C., & Swartz, J. D. (1989). Graduate admissions criteria of leading psychology departments. *American Psychologist, 44,* 960–961.

Puttalaz, M., & Gottman, J. (1983). Social relationship problems in children. In B. B. Lahey & A. E. Kazdin (Eds.), *Advances in clinical child psychology* (Vol. 6, pp. 1–39). New York: Plenum Press.

Quality Assurance Project. (1985). Treatment outlines for the management of anxiety states. *Australian and New Zealand Journal of Psychiatry, 19,* 138–151.

Quay, H. (1986). A critical analysis of DSM-III as a taxonomy of psychopathology in childhood and adolescence. In T. Millon & G. L. Klerman (Eds.), *Contemporary directions in psychopathology: Toward the DSM-IV* (pp. 151–165). New York: Guilford Press.

Rabinowitz, J. (1993). Diagnostic reasoning and reliability: A review of the literature and a model of decision-making. *Journal of Mind and Behavior, 14,* 297–315.

Rachman, S. J., & Wilson, G. T. (1980). *The effects of psychological therapy*. Oxford: Pergamon Press.

Ragland, D. R., & Brand, R. J. (1988). Type A behavior and mortality from coronary heart disease. *New England Journal of Medicine, 318,* 65–69.

Raimy, V. C. (1950). *Training in clinical psychology*. New York: Prentice-Hall.

Ramirez, S. Z., & Kratchowill, T. R. (1990). Development of the Fear Survey for Children With and Without Mental Retardation. *Behavioral Assessment, 12,* 457–470.

Rapaport, D. (1951). *Organization and pathology of thought*. New York: Columbia University Press.

Rapaport, D., Gill, M. M., & Schafer, R. (1945). *Diagnostic psychological testing* (Vol. 1). Chicago: Yearbook.

Rappaport, J. (1977). *Community psychology: Values, research and action*. New York: Holt, Rinehart & Winston.

Rappaport, J. (1981). In praise of paradox: A social policy of empowerment over prevention. *American Journal of Community Psychology, 9,* 1–25.

Rappaport, J. (1987). Terms of empowerment/exemplars of prevention: Toward a theory for community psychology. *American Journal of Community Psychology, 15,* 121–148.

Rappaport, J., Seidman, E., Toro, P., McFadden, L., Reischel, T., Roberts, L., Salem, D., & Zimmerman, M. (1985). Collaborative research with a mutual help organization. *Social Policy, 15,* 12–24.

Raquepaw, J. M., & Miller, R. S. (1989). Psychotherapist burnout: A componential analysis. *Professional Psychology: Research and Practice, 20,* 33–36.

Rasmussen, T., & Milner, B. (1975). Clinical and surgical studies of the cerebral speech areas in man. In K. J. Zulch, O. Creutzfeldt, & G. C. Galbraith (Eds.), *Cerebral localization*. Berlin & New York: Springer-Verlag.

Redd, W. H., Jacobsen, P. B., Die-Trill, M., Dermatis, H., McEvoy, M., & Holland, J. C. (1987). Cognitive/attentional distraction in the control of conditioned nausea in pediatric cancer patients receiving chemotherapy. *Journal of Consulting and Clinical Psychology, 55,* 391–395.

Reed, G. M., Kemeny, M. E., Taylor, S. E., Wang, H. Y. J., & Visscher, B. R. (1994). "Realistic acceptance" as a predictor of decreased survival of gay men with AIDS. *Health Psychology, 13,* 299–307.

Reed, G. M., Levant, R. F., Stout, C. E., Murphy, M. J., & Phelps, R. (2001). Psychology in the current mental health marketplace. *Professional Psychology: Research and Practice, 1,* 65–70.

Reed, J. E. (1996). Fixed vs. flexible neuropsychological test batteries under the Daubert Standard for the admissibility of scientific evidence. *Behavioral Sciences and the Law, 14,* 315–322.

Reed, S. D., Katkin, E. S., & Goldband, S. (1986). Biofeedback and behavioral medicine. In F. H. Kanfer & A. P. Goldstein (Eds.), *Helping people change: A textbook of methods* (3rd ed., pp. 381–436). New York: Pergamon Press.

Rehm, L. P., Kornblith, S. J., O'Hara, M. W., Lamparski, D. J., Romano, J. M., & Volkin, J. I. (1981). An evaluation of major components in a self-control therapy program for depression. *Behavior Modification, 5,* 459–489.

Reich, W., Cottler, L., McCallum, K., & Corwin, D. (1995). Computerized interviews as a method of assessing psychopathology in children. *Comprehensive Psychiatry, 36,* 40–45.

Reik, T. (1948). *Listening with the third ear.* New York: Farrar, Straus & Giroux.

Rein, L. (2001, December 19). Crime panel assails Virginia insanity policy. *The Washington Post,* B1, B4.

Reisman, J. M. (1976). *A history of clinical psychology.* New York: Irvington.

Reiss, D., & Price, R. H. (1996). National research agenda for prevention research: The National Institute of Mental Health Report. *American Psychologist, 51,* 1109–1115.

Reitan, R. M. (1955). Certain differential effects of left and right cerebral lesions in human adults. *Journal of Comparative and Physiological Psychology, 48,* 474–477.

Reitan, R. M. (1964). Psychological deficits resulting from cerebral lesions in man. In J. M. Warren & K. Akert (Eds.), *The frontal granular cortex and behavior.* New York: McGraw-Hill.

Reitan, R. M., & Davison, L. A. (Eds.). (1974). *Clinical neuropsychology: Current status and applications.* Washington, DC: V. H. Winston.

Reitan, R. M., & Wolfson, D. (1993). *The Halstead-Reitan Neuropsychological Test Battery: Theory and clinical interpretation.* Tucson, AZ: Neuropsychology Press.

Renshaw, P. D., & Asher, S. R. (1983). Children's goals and strategies for social interaction. *Merrill-Palmer Quarterly, 29,* 353–375.

Report of the Ethics Committee, 2000. (2000). *American Psychologist, 56,* 680–688.

Repp, A. C., & Horner, R. H. (2000). *Functional analysis of problem behavior: From effective assessment to effective support.* Belmont, CA: Wadsworth.

Reppucci, N. D., Wollard, J. L., & Fried, C. S. (1999). Social, community, and preventive interventions. *Annual Review of Psychology, 50,* 387–418.

Reschly, D. J. (1984). Aptitude tests. In G. Goldstein & M. Hersen (Eds.), *Handbook of psychological assessment* (pp. 132–156). New York: Pergamon Press.

Reschly, D. J. (1990). Aptitude tests in educational classification and placement. In G. Goldstein & M. Hersen (Eds.), *Handbook of psychological assessment* (pp. 148-172). New York: Pergamon Press.

Resnick, J. H. (1991). Finally, a definition of clinical psychology: A message from the President, Division 12. *The Clinical Psychologist, 44,* 3-11.

Resnick, R. J. (1985). The case against the Blues: The Virginia challenge. *American Psychologist, 40,* 975-983.

Resnick, R. J. (1997). A brief history of practice—expanded. *American Psychologist, 52,* 463-468.

Ressler, R. K., & Shachtman, T. (1992). *Whoever fights monsters.* New York: St. Martin's Press.

Reynolds, C. R., Kamphaus, R. W., & Rosenthal, B. L. (1988). Factor analysis of the Stanfort-Binet Fourth Edition for age 2 years through 23 years. *Measurement and Evaluation in Counseling and Development, 21,* 52-63.

Rholes, W. S., Blackwell, J., Jordan, C., & Walters, C. (1980). A developmental study of learned helplessness. *Developmental Psychology, 16,* 616-624.

Rice, M. E. (1997). Violent offender research and implications for the criminal justice system. *American Psychologist, 52,* 414-423.

Rice, S. A. (1929). Contagious bias in the interview: A methodological note. *American Journal of Sociology, 35,* 420-423.

Rich, B. A. (1998). Personhood, patienthood, and clinical practice: Reassessing advance directives. *Psychology, Public Policy, and Law, 4,* 610-628.

Richey, C. R. (1994). Proposals to eliminate the prejudicial effect of the use of the word "expert" under the federal rules of evidence in civil and criminal jury trials. *Federal Rules Decisions, 154,* 537-562.

Richters, J. E. (1992). Depressed mothers as informants about their children: A critical review of the evidence for distortion. *Psychological Bulletin, 112,* 485-499.

Rickert, V., & Jay, S. (1995). The concompliant adolescent. In S. Parker and B. Zuckerman (Eds.), *Behavioral and developmental pediatrics* (pp. 219-222). Boston: Little, Brown & Company.

Roberts, C. F., Sargent, E. L., & Chan, A. S. (1993). Verdict selection processes in insanity cases: Juror construals and the effects of guilty but mental ill instructions. *Law and Human Behavior, 17,* 261-275.

Roberts, H. (1996, December). Test community responds to new statement of rights. *APA Monitor, 26.*

Robertson, G. J., & Eyde, L. D. (1993). Improving test use in the United States: The development of an interdisciplinary casebook. *European Journal of Psychological Assessment, 9,* 137-146.

Robiner, W. N., & Crew, D. P. (2000). Rightsizing the workforce of psychologists in health care: Trends from licensing boards, training programs, and managed care. *Professional Psychology: Research and Practice, 31,* 245-263.

Robins, L. N. (1995). How to choose among riches: Selecting a diagnostic instrument. *International Journal of Methods in Psychiatric Research, 5,* 103-109.

Robins, L. N., Helzer, J. E., Croughan, J. L., Williams, J. B. W., & Ratcliff, R. L. (1981). *The NIMH Diagnostic Interview Schedule: Version III.* Washington, DC: Public Health Service. (HSS) ADM-T-42-3 (5/81, 8/81).

Robins, L. N., & Regier, D. A. (1991). *Psychiatric disorders in America: The epidemiological catchment area study.* New York: The Free Press.

Robins, L. N., Cottler, L., Bucholz, K., & Compton, W. (1995). *Diagnostic Interview Schedule, Version IV.* St. Louis: Washington School of Medicine.

Robins, R. W., Gosling, S. D., & Craik, K. H. (1999). An empirical analysis of trends in psychology. *American Psychologist, 54,* 117–128.

Robinson, L. A., Berman, J. S., & Neimeyer, R. A. (1990). Psychotherapy for the treatment of depression: A comprehensive review of controlled outcome research. *Psychological Bulletin, 108,* 30–49.

Rock, D. L., Bransford, J. D., Maisto, S. A., & Morey, L. (1987). The study of clinical judgment: An ecological approach. *Clinical Psychology Review, 7,* 645–661.

Rodgers, D. D. (1987). Computer-aided interviewing overcomes first impressions. *Personnel Journal, 66,* 148–152.

Rodin, J., & Salovey, P. (1989). Health psychology. *Annual Review of Psychology, 40,* 533–580.

Rodriguez, R., Nietzel, M. T., & Berzins, J. I. (1980). Sex role orientation and assertiveness among female college students. *Behavior Therapy, 11,* 353–366.

Rodriguez, H., & Arnold, C. (1998). Children & divorce: A snapshot. Retrieved December 13, 2001 from http://www.clasp.org/pubs/familyformation/divfinal.htm.

Roe, A., Gustad, J. W., Moore, B. V., Ross, S., & Skodak, M. (Eds.). (1959). *Graduate education in psychology.* Washington, DC: American Psychological Association.

Roesch, R., & Golding, S. L. (1980). *Competency to stand trial.* Urbana, IL: University of Illinois Press.

Rogers, C. R. (1942). *Counseling and psychotherapy.* Boston: Houghton Mifflin.

Rogers, C. R. (1951). *Client-centered therapy.* Boston: Houghton Mifflin.

Rogers, C. R. (1954). *Psychotherapy and personality change.* Chicago: University of Chicago Press.

Rogers, C. R. (1959). A theory of therapy, personality, and interpersonal relationships as developed in the client-centered framework. In S. Koch (Ed.), *Psychology: A study of a science: Vol. III. Formulations of the person and the social context* (pp. 184–256). New York: McGraw-Hill.

Rogers, C. R. (1961). *On becoming a person.* Boston: Houghton Mifflin.

Rogers, C. R. (1970). *Carl Rogers on encounter groups.* New York: Harper & Row.

Rogers, R. (1995). *Diagnostic and structured interviewing: A handbook for psychologists.* Odessa, FL: Psychological Assessment Resources, Inc.

Rogers, R. (2001). *Handbook of structured clinical interviewing* (2nd ed.). New York: Guilford.

Rogers, R., Gillis, J. R., Dickens, S. E., & Bagby, R. M. (1991). Standardized assessment of malingering: Validation of the Structured Interview of Reported Symptoms. *Psychological Assessment, 3,* 89–96.

Rogers, R., Ustad, K. L., & Salekin, R. T. (1998). Convergent validity of the Personality Assessment Inventory: A study of emergency referrals in a correctional setting. *Assessment, 5,* 3–12.

Rohde, D. (1999, November 7). Juror and courts assailed in subway-killing mistrial. *The New York Times,* 32.

Rorschach, H. (1921/1942). *Psycho-diagnosis: A diagnostic test based on perception.* (P. Lemkau & B. Kronenburg, Trans.). Berne: Huber.

Rose, S. D., & LeCroy, C. W. (1991). Group methods. In F. H. Kanfer & A. P. Goldstein (Eds.), *Helping people change* (4th ed., pp. 422–453). New York: Pergamon Press.

Rosen, R. C., & Kopel, S. A. (1977). Penile plethysmography and biofeedback in the treatment of a transvestite-exhibitionist. *Journal of Consulting and Clinical Psychology, 45,* 908–916.

Rosenhan, D. L. (1973). On being sane in insane places. *Science, 179,* 250–258.

Rosenman, R. H. (1978). The interview method of assessment of the coronary-prone behavior pattern. In T. M. Dembroski, S. M. Weiss, J. L. Shields, S. G. Haynes, & M. Feinleib (Eds.), *Coronary-prone behavior* (pp. 55–69). New York: Springer-Verlag.

Rosenman, R. H., Brand, R. J., Jenkins, D. D., Friedman, M., Straus, R., & Wurm, M. (1975). Coronary heart disease in the Western Collaborative Group Study: Final follow-up experience after 8 years. *Journal of the American Medical Association, 233,* 872–877.

Rosenstock, I. M. (1974). Historical origins of the health belief model. *Health Education Monographs, 2,* 328–335.

Rosenthal, D. (1970). *Genetic theory and abnormal behavior.* New York: McGraw-Hill.

Rosenthal, M. J. (1989). Toward selective and improved performance on the mental status examination. *Acta Psychiatica Scandinavica, 80,* 207–215.

Rosenthal, R. (1966). *Experimenter effects in behavioral research.* New York: Appleton-Century-Crofts.

Rosenthal, R. (1983). Assessing the statistical and social importance of the effects of psychotherapy. *Journal of Consulting and Clinical Psychology, 51,* 4–13.

Rosenthal, R., & Rubin, D. B. (1978). Interpersonal expectancy effects: The first 345 studies. *Behavioral and Brain Sciences, 3,* 377–386.

Rosenthal, T. L., & Steffek, B. D. (1991). Modeling methods. In F. H. Kanfer & A. P. Goldstein (Eds.), *Helping people change* (4th ed., pp. 70–121). New York: Pergamon Press.

Rosenzweig, S. (1949). Apperceptive norms for the Thematic Apperception Test. I. The problem of norms in projective methods. *Journal of Personality, 17,* 475–482.

Rosenzweig, S. (1977). *Manual for the Children's Form of the Rosenzweig Picture-Frustration (P-F) Study.* St. Louis: Rana House.

Ross, D. M., & Ross, S. A. (1982). *Hyperactivity: Current issues, research, and theory* (2nd ed.). New York: John Wiley.

Ross, M. W., Stowe, A., Wodak, A., & Gold, J. (1995). Reliability of interview responses of injecting drug users. *Journal of Addictive Diseases, 14,* 1–2.

Roth, A., & Fonagy, P. (1995). *Research on the efficacy and effectiveness of the psychotherapies. Report to the Department of Health.* London: National Health Services.

Roth, A. D., & Fonagy, P. (1996). *What works for whom? A critical review of psychotherapy research.* New York: Guilford.

Roth, M., Tym, E., Montjoy, G. Q., Huppert, F. A., Hendrie, H., Verma, S., & Goddard, R. (1986). CAMDEX: A standardized instrument for the diagnosis of mental disorders in the elderly with special reference to the early detection of dementia. *British Journal of Psychiatry, 149,* 698–709.

Rothbaum, B. O., Hodges, L. F., Alarcon, R., Ready, D., Sharhar, F., et al. (1999). Virtual reality exposure therapy for PTSD Vietnam veterans: A case study. *Journal of Traumatic Stress, 12,* 263–271.

Rothbaum, B. O., Hodges, L. F., Kooper, R., & Opdyke, D. (1995). Effectiveness of computer-generated virtual reality graded exposure in treatment of agoraphobia. *American Journal of Psychiatry, 152,* 626–628.

Rothbaum, B. O., Hodges, L., Smith, S., Lee, J. H., & Price, L. (2000). A controlled study of virtual reality exposure therapy for the fear of flying. *Journal of Consulting and Clinical Psychology, 68,* 1020–1026.

Rothbaum, R., Weisz, J., Pott, M., Miyake, K., & Morelli, G. (2000). Attachment and culture: Security in the United States and Japan. *American Psychologist, 55,* 1093–1104.

Rothman, A. J. (2000). Toward a theory-based analysis of behavioral medicine. *Health Psychology, 19,* 64–69.

Rotter, J. B., & Rafferty, J. E. (1950). *The Rotter Incomplete Sentences Test.* New York: Psychological Corporation.

Round, A. P. (1999). Teaching clinical reasoning—A preliminary controlled study. *Medical Education, 33,* 480–483.

Rourke, B. P. (1989). *Nonverbal learning disabilities: The syndrome and the model.* New York: Guilford Press.

Routh, D. K. (1994). *Clinical psychology since 1917: Science, practice, and organization.* New York: Plenum.

Routh, D. K. (1996). Lightner Witmer and the first 100 years of clinical psychology. *American Psychologist, 51,* 244–247.

Rubin, R., Holm, S., Friberg, L., Videbech, P., Andersen, H. S., Bendsen, B. B., Stromso, N., Larsen, J. K., Lassen, N. A., & Hemmingsen, R. (1991). Altered modulation of prefrontal and subcortical brain activity in newly diagnosed schizophrenia and schizophreniform disorder: A regional cerebral blood flow study. *Archives of General Psychiatry, 48,* 987–995.

Rubinstein, E. (1948). Childhood mental disease in American: A review of the literature before 1900. *American Journal of Orthopsychiatry, 18,* 314–321.

Ruble, D. N., & Rholes, W. S. (1981). The development of children's perceptions and attributions about their social world. In J. H. Harvey, W. Ickes, & R. F. Kidd (Eds.), *New directions in attribution research* (Vol. 3, pp. 1–36). Hillsdale, NJ: Lawrence Erlbaum Associates.

Ruegg, R. G., Ekstrom, D. E., Dwight, L., & Golden, R. N. (1990). Introduction of a standardized report form improves the quality of mental status examination reports by psychiatric residents. *Academic Psychiatry, 14,* 157–163.

Rugh, J. D., Gable, R. S., & Lemke, R. R. (1986). Instrumentation for behavioral assessment. In A. R. Ciminero, C. S. Calhoun, & H. E. Adams (Eds.), *Handbook of behavioral assessment* (2nd ed., pp. 79–108). New York: John Wiley.

Rumsey, J. M., & Ernst, M. (2000). Functional neuroimaging of autistic disorders. *Mental Retardation and Developmental Disabilities Research Review, 6,* 171–179.

Ruscio, J. (2000). The role of complex thought in clinical prediction: Social accountability and the need for cognition. *Journal of Consulting and Clinical Psychology, 68,* 145–154.

Rutter, M., Maugham, B., Mortimore, P., Ouston, J., & Smith, A. (1979). *Fifteen thousand hours: Secondary schools and their effects on children.* London: Open Books; Cambridge, MA: Harvard University Press.

Rutter, M., & Shaffer, D. (1980). DSM-III. A step forward or a step backward in terms of the classification of child psychiatric disorders. *Journal of the American Academy of Child Psychiatry, 19,* 371–394.

Rutter, M., & Sroufe, L. A. (2001). Developmental psychopathology: Concepts and challenges. *Development and Psychopathology, 12,* 265–296.

Rutter, M. I. (1997). Nature-nurture integration: The example of antisocial behavior. *American Psychologist, 52,* 390–398.

Ryan, J. J., Paolo, A. M., & Smith, A. J. (1992). Wechsler Adult Intelligence Scale—Revised intersubtest scatter in brain-damaged patients: A comparison with the standardization sample. *Psychological Assessment, 4,* 63–66.

Rychtarik, R. G., Tarnowski, K. J., & St. Lawrence, J. S. (1989). Impact of social desirability response sets on the self-report of marital adjustment in alcoholics. *Journal of Studies in Alcohol, 50,* 24-29.

Sackett, P. R., & Wilk, S. L. (1994). Within-group norming and other forms of score adjustment in preemployment testing. *American Psychologist, 49,* 929-954.

Sacks, O. (1985). *The man who mistook his wife for a hat.* New York: Summit Books.

Sacks, O. (1990). *A leg to stand on.* New York: Summit Books.

Safer, D. J., & Krager, J. M. (1994). The increased use of stimulant medication for hyperactive/inattentive students in secondary schools. *Pediatrics, 94,* 462-464.

Safer, D. L., Telch, C. F., & Agras, W. (2001). Dialectical behavior therapy for bulimia nervosa. *American Journal of Psychiatry, 158,* 632-634.

Safran, J. D., Segal, Z. V., Vallis, M. T., & Shaw, B. F. (1993). Assessing patient suitability for short-term cognitive therapy with an interpersonal focus. *Cognitive Therapy and Research, 17,* 23-38.

Saklofske, D. H., Hildebrand, D. K., & Gorsuch, R. L. (2000). Replication of the factor structure of the Wechsler Adult Intelligence Scale—Third Edition with a Canadian sample. *Psychological Assessment, 12,* 436-439.

Sales, B. D., & Hafemeister, T. (1984). Empiricism and legal policy on the insanity defense. In L. A. Teplin (Ed.), *Mental health and criminal justice* (pp. 253-278). Newbury Park, CA: Sage.

Sales, B. D., & Shuman, D. W. (1996). *Law, mental health, and mental disorder.* Pacific Grove, CA: Brooks/Cole.

Salokangas, R. K. R., Honkonen, T., & Stengard, E. (1998). Community psychiatry and deinstitutionalization in Finland: Some results of the DSP project. *Psychiatriki, 9,* 49-58.

Salovey, P., & Singer, J. A. (1991). Cognitive behavior modification. In F. H. Kanfer & A. P. Goldstein (Eds.), *Helping people change* (4th ed., pp. 361-395). New York: Pergamon Press.

Salovey, P., Rothman, A. J., Detweiler, J. B., & Steward, W. T. (2000). Emotional states and physical health. *American Psychologist, 55,* 110-121.

Salzer, M. S., Rappaport, J., & Segre, L. (2001). Mental health professionals' support of self-help groups. *Journal of Community & Applied Social Psychology, 11,* 1-10.

Sammons, M. T., Gorny, S. W., Zinner, E. S., & Allen, R. P. (2000). Prescriptive authority for psychologists: A consensus of support. *Professional Psychology: Research and Practice, 31,* 604-609.

Samuda, R. J. (1975). *Psychological testing of American minorities: Issues and consequences.* New York: Dodd, Mead.

Sanders, M. R., & Dadds, M. R. (1992). Children's and parents' cognitions about family interactions: An evaluation of video-mediated recall and thought listing procedures in assessment of conduct-disordered children. *Journal of Clinical Child Psychology, 21,* 371-379.

Sandler, I., Wolchik, S., Braver, S., & Fogas, B. (1991). Stability and quality of life events and psychological symptomatology in children of divorce. *American Journal of Community Psychology, 19,* 501-520.

Sandler, J., & Steele, H. V. (1991). Aversion methods. In F. H. Kanfer & A. P. Goldstein (Eds.), *Helping people change* (4th ed., pp. 202-247). New York: Pergamon Press.

Sanford, F. H. (1951). Annual report of the executive secretary. *American Psychologist, 6,* 664-670.

Santostefano, S. (1962). Performance testing of personality. *Merrill-Palmer Quarterly, 8,* 83-97.

Sarason, S. B. (1974). *The psychological sense of community: Prospects for community psychology*. San Francisco: Jossey-Bass.

Sarason, I. G., Johnson, J. H., & Siegel, J. M. (1978). Assessing the impact of life changes: Development of the life experiences survey. *Journal of Consulting and Clinical Psychology, 46,* 932–946.

Sarbin, T. R. (1997). On the futility of psychiatric diagnostic manuals (DSMs) and the return of personal agency. *Applied Prevention Psychology, 6,* 233–243.

Sarbin, T. R., Taft, R., & Bailey, D. E. (1960). *Clinical inference and cognitive theory*. New York: Holt, Rinehart & Winston.

Sartorius, N., Kaelber, C. T., Cooper, J. E., Roper, M. T., et al. (1996). Progress toward achieving a common language in psychiatry: Results from the field trial of the clinical guidelines accompanying the WHO classification of mental and behavioral disorders in ICD-10. *Archives of General Psychiatry, 50,* 115–124.

Satir, V. (1967). *Conjoint family therapy* (rev. ed.). Palo Alto, CA: Science and Behavior Books.

Satterfield, J. H., Hoppe, C. M., & Schell, A. M. (1982). A prospective study of delinquency in 110 adolescent boys with attention deficit disorder and 88 normal adolescent boys. *American Journal of Psychiatry, 139,* 795–798.

Sattler, J. M. (1988). *Assessment of children's intelligence and special abilities* (3rd ed.). Boston: Allyn & Bacon.

Sattler, J. M. (2001). *Assessment of children: Behavioral and clinical applications* (4th ed.). San Diego: Jerome M. Sattler.

Satz, P., & Fletcher, J. M. (1981). Emergent trends in neuropsychology: An overview. *Journal of Consulting and Clinical Psychology, 49,* 851–865.

Saunders, S. M., Howard, K. I., & Orlinsky, D. E. (1989). The Therapeutic Bond Scales: Psychometric characteristics and relationship to treatment effectiveness. *Psychological Assessment, 1,* 323–330.

Sawyer, J. (1966). Measurement and prediction, clinical and statistical. *Psychological Bulletin, 66,* 178–200.

Saylor, C. F., Finch, A. J., Baskin, C. H., Furey, W., & Kelly, M. M. (1984). Construct validity for measures of childhood depression: Application of multitrait-multimethod methodology. *Journal of Consulting and Clinical Psychology, 52,* 977–985.

Saywitz, K. (1990). The child as witness: Experimental and clinical considerations. In A. La Greca (Ed.), *Through the eyes of the child: Obtaining self-reports from children and adolescents* (pp. 329–367). Boston: Allyn & Bacon.

Saywitz, K. J., & Snyder, L. (1996). Narrative elaboration: Test of a new procedure for interviewing children. *Journal of Consulting and Clinical Psychology, 64,* 1347–1357.

Schaefer, H. H., & Martin, P. L. (1975). *Behavior therapy* (2nd ed.). New York: McGraw-Hill.

Scheidlinger, S. (2000). The group psychotherapy movement at the millennium: Some historical perspectives. *International Journal of Group Psychotherapy, 50,* 315–339.

Schmidt, H. O., & Fonda, C. P. (1956). The reliability of psychiatric diagnosis: A new look. *Journal of Abnormal and Social Psychology, 52,* 262–267.

Schneider, S. F. (1991). No fluoride in our future. *Professional Psychology: Research and Practice, 22,* 456–460.

Schneider, S. L. (2001). In search of realistic optimism: Meaning, knowledge, and warm fuzziness. *American Psychologist, 56,* 250–263.

Schneiderman, N., Antoni, M. H., Saab, P. G., & Ironson, G. (2001). Health psychology: Psychosocial and biobehavioral aspects of chronic disease management. *Annual Review of Psychology, 52,* 555–580.

Schradle, S. B., & Dougher, M. J. (1985). Social support as a mediator of stress. Theoretical and empirical issues. *Clinical Psychology Review, 5,* 641–662.

Schretlen, D., Wilkins, S. S., Van Gorp, W. G., & Bobholz, J. H. (1992). Cross-validation of a psychological test battery to detect faked insanity. *Psychological Assessment, 4,* 77–83.

Schulte, D., Kunzel, R., Pepping, G., & Schulte-Bahrenberg, T. (1992). Tailor-made versus standardized therapy of phobic patients. *Advances in Behavior Research and Therapy, 14,* 67–92.

Schultz, D. P., & Schultz, S. E. (2001). *Theories of personality.* Pacific Grove, CA: Brooks/Cole.

Schwab-Stone, M., Fallon, T., & Briggs, M. (1994). Reliability of diagnostic reporting for children aged 6–11 years: A test-retest study of the Diagnostic Interview Schedule for Children—Revised. *American Journal of Psychiatry, 151,* 1048–1054.

Schweinhart, L. J., Barnes, H. V., & Weikhart, D. P. (1993). *Significant benefits. The High/Scope Perry School Study through age 27.* Ypsilanti, MI: High/Scope Press.

Schweinhart, L. J., McNair, S., Barnes, H., & Larner, M. (1993). Observing young children in action to assess their development: The High/Scope Child Observation Record study. *Educational and Psychological Measurement, 53,* 445–455.

Scoville, W. B., & Milner, B. (1957). Loss of recent memory after bilateral hippocampal lesions. *The Journal of Neurology, Neurosurgery, & Psychiatry, 20,* 11–21.

Sechrest, L. (1992). The past future of clinical psychology: A reflection on Woodworth (1937). *Journal of Consulting and Clinical Psychology, 60,* 18–23.

Sechrest, L. B. (1963). Incremental validity: A recommendation. *Educational and Psychological Measurement, 23,* 153–158.

Sechrest, L. B., McKnight, P., & McKnight, K. (1996). Calibration of measures for psychotherapy outcome studies. *American Psychologist, 51,* 1065–1071.

Sedlacek, K., & Taub, E. Biofeedback treatment of Raynaud's disease. (1996). *Professional Psychology: Research and Practice, 27,* 548–553.

Sedlak, A. J., & Broadhurst, D. D. (1996). *Executive summary of the third national incidence study of child abuse and neglect.* Washington, DC: U.S. Department of Health and Human Services.

Seeman, J. A. (1949). A study of the process of nondirective therapy. *Journal of Consulting Psychology, 13,* 157–168.

Segal, D. L., Hersen, M., & Van Hasselt, V. B. (1994). Reliability of the Structured Clinical Interview for DSM-III-R: An evaluative review. *Comprehensive Psychiatry, 35,* 316–327.

Seidman, E., Allen, L., Aber, J. L., Mitchell, C., & Feinman, J. (1994). The impact of school transitions in early adolescence on the self-system and perceived social context of poor urban youth. *Child Development, 65,* 507–522.

Seligman, M. E. P. (1995). The effectiveness of psychotherapy: The Consumer Reports study. *American Psychologist, 50,* 965–974.

Seligman, M. E. P., Abramson, L. Y., Semmel, A., & von Baeyer, C. (1979). Depressive attributional style. *Journal of Abnormal Psychology, 88,* 242–247.

Seligman, M. E. P., & Csikszentmihali, M. (2000). Positive psychology: An introduction. *American Psychologist, 55,* 5–14.

Seligman, M. E. P., Peterson, C., Kaslow, N. J., Tanenbaum, R. L., Alloy, L. B., & Abramson, L. Y. (1984). Explanatory style and depressive symptoms among school children. *Journal of Abnormal Psychology, 93,* 235-238.

Selye, H. (1956). *The stress of life.* New York: McGraw-Hill.

Serketich, W. J., & Dumas, J. E. (1996). The effectiveness of behavioral parent training to modify antisocial behavior in children: A meta-analysis. *Behavior Therapy, 27,* 171-186.

Sexton, T. L., & Whiston, S. C. (1994). The status of the counseling relationship: An empirical review, theoretical implications, and research directions. *The Counseling Psychologist, 22,* 6-78.

Shadish, W. R. (2002). Revisiting field experiments: Field notes for the future. *Psychological Methods, 7,* 3-18.

Shadish, W. R., Montgomery, L. M., Wilson, P. W., Wilson, M. R., Bright, I., & Okwumabua, T. (1993). Effects of family and marital psychotherapies: A meta-analysis. *Journal of Consulting and Clinical Psychology, 61,* 992-1002.

Shadish, W. R., Navarro, A. M., Matt, G. E., & Phillips, G. (2000). The effects of psychological therapies under clinically representative conditions: A meta-analysis. *Psychological Bulletin, 126,* 512-529.

Shaffer, D., Schwab-Stone, M., Fisher, P., Cohen, P., et al. (1993). The diagnostic interview schedule for children—Revised version (DISC-R): I. Preparation, field testing, interrater reliability, and acceptability. *Journal of the American Academy of Child and Adolescent Psychiatry, 32,* 643-650.

Shaffer, G. W., & Lazarus, R. S. (1952). *Fundamental concepts in clinical psychology.* New York: McGraw-Hill.

Shakow, D. (1942). The training of the clinical psychologist. *Journal of Consulting Psychology, 6,* 277-288.

Shakow, D. (1948). Clinical psychology: An evaluation. In L. G. Lowrey & V. Sloane (Eds.), *Orthopsychiatry, 1923-1948: Retrospect and prospect* (pp. 231-247). New York: American Orthopsychiatric Association.

Shakow, D. (1965). Seventeen years later: Clinical psychology in the light of the 1947 CTCP report. *American Psychologist, 20,* 353-362.

Shakow, D. (1968). Clinical psychology. In D. L. Sills (Ed.), *International encyclopedia of the social sciences* (pp. 513-518). London: Collier Macmillan.

Shakow, D. (1978). Clinical psychology seen some 50 years later. *American Psychologist, 33,* 148-158.

Shannon, D., & Weaver, W. (1949). *The mathematical theory of communication.* Urbana: University of Illinois Press.

Shapiro, A. E., & Wiggins, J. G. (1994). A PsyD degree for every practitioner: Truth in labeling. *American Psychologist, 49,* 207-210.

Shapiro, A. K. (1971). Placebo effects in medicine, psychotherapy, and psychoanalysis. In A. E. Bergin & S. L. Garfield (Eds.), *Handbook of psychotherapy and behavior change: An empirical analysis* (pp. 439-473). New York: John Wiley.

Shapiro, D. A., Firth-Cozens, J., & Stiles, W. B. (1998). The question of therapists' differential effectiveness: A Sheffield Psychotherapy Project addendum. *British Journal of Psychiatry, 154,* 383-385.

Shapiro, D. A., & Shapiro, D. (1982). Meta-analysis of comparative therapy outcome research: A critical appraisal. *Behavioral Psychotherapy, 10,* 4-25.

Sharpley, C. F., & Pain, M. D. (1988). Psychological test use in Australia. *Australian Psychologist, 23,* 361–369.

Shaw, B. V., Elkin, I., Yamaguchi, J., Olmsted, M., Vallis, T. M., et al. (1999). Therapist competence ratings in relation to clinical outcome in cognitive therapy of depression. *Journal of Consulting and Clinical Psychology, 67,* 837–846.

Shaw, D. L., Martz, D. M., Lancaster, C. J., & Sade, R. M. (1995). Influence of medical school applicants' demographic and cognitive characteristics on interviewers' ratings of noncognitive traits. *Academic Medicine, 70,* 532–536.

Shaywitz, S., & Shaywitz, B. (1999). Cognitive and neurobiologic influences in reading and in dyslexia. *Developmental Neuropsychology, 16,* 383–384.

Shea, S. C. (1998). *Psychiatric interviewing: The art of understanding* (2nd. ed.). Philadelphia: Saunders.

Sheel, K. R. (2000). The empirical basis of dialectical behavior therapy: Summary, critique, and implications. *Clinical Psychology: Science and Practice, 7,* 68–86.

Sheldon, K. M., & King, L. (2001). Why positive psychology is necessary. *American Psychologist, 56,* 216–217.

Shemberg, K. M., & Leventhal, D. B. (1981). Attitudes of internship directors toward preinternship training and clinical training models. *Professional Psychology, 12,* 639–646.

Shepherd, M., Oppenheim, B., & Mitchell, S. (1971). *Childhood behavior and mental health.* London: University of London Press.

Shepherd, M. D., Shoenberg, M., Slavich, S., Wituk, S., Warren, M., & Meissen, G. (1999). Continuum of professional involvement in self-help groups. *Journal of Community Psychology, 27,* 39–53.

Sheridan, E. P., Matarazzo, J. D., & Nelson, P. D. (1995). Accreditation of psychology's graduate professional education and training programs. *Professional Psychology: Research and Practice, 26,* 386–392.

Shiffman, S., Hickcox, M., Paty, J. A., Gnys, M., Kassel, J. D., & Richards, T. J. (1996). Progression from a smoking lapse to relapse: Prediction from abstinence violation effects, nicotine dependence, and lapse characteristics. *Journal of Consulting & Clinical Psychology, 64,* 993–1002.

Shipley, K. G., & Wood, J. M. (1996). *The elements of interviewing.* San Diego: Singular Publishing.

Shoham-Salomon, V. (1985). Are schizophrenics' behaviors schizophrenic? What medically versus psychosocially oriented therapists attribute to schizophrenic persons. *Journal of Abnormal Psychology, 94,* 443–453.

Shostrom, E. L. (1968). *Personal orientation inventory: An inventory for the measurement of self-actualization.* San Diego, CA: Educational and Industrial Testing Service.

Shuman, D. W., & Sales, B. D. (1999). The impact of *Daubert* and its progeny on the admissibility of behavioral and social science evidence. *Psychology, Public Policy, and Law, 5,* 3–15.

Siassi, I. (1984). Psychiatric interviews and mental status examinations. In G. Goldstein & M. Hersen (Eds.), *Handbook of psychological assessment* (pp. 259–275). New York: Pergamon Press.

Sigmundsson, T., Suckling, J., Maier, M., Bullmore, E., Greenwood, K., Ron, M., & Toone, B. (2001). Structural abnormalities in frontal, temporal, and limbic regions and interconnecting white matter tracts in schizophrenic patients with prominent negative symptoms. *The American Journal of Psychiatry, 158,* 234–243.

Silver, E., Cirincione, C., & Steadman, H. J. (1994). Demythologizing inaccurate perceptions of the insanity defense. *Law and Human Behavior, 18,* 63–70.

Silverman, L. H., & Weinberger, J. (1985). Mommy and I are one: Implications for psychotherapy. *American Psychologist, 40,* 1296–1308.

Silverman, W. H. (1996). Cookbooks, manuals, and paint-by-number psychotherapy in the 90s. *Psychotherapy, 33,* 207–215.

Simon, R. (2001). Psychotherapy soothsayer. *Psychotherapy Networker,* July/Aug, 34–39/62.

Simpson, J. A., & Rholes, W. S. (2000). Caregiving, attachment theory, and the connection theoretical orientation. *Psychological Inquiry, 11,* 114–117.

Sinacore-Guinn, G. A. (1995). The diagnostic window: Culture- and gender-sensitive diagnosis and training. *Counselor Education and Supervision, 35,* 18–31.

Singer, M., & Eder, G. S. (1989). Effects of ethnicity, accent, and job status on selection decisions. *International Journal of Psychology, 24,* 13–34.

Siqueland, L., Crits-Christoph, P., Barber, J. P., Butler, S. F., Thase, M., et al. (2000). The role of therapist characteristics in training effects in cognitive, supportive-expressive, and drug counseling therapies for cocaine dependence. *Journal of Psychotherapy Practice and Research, 9,* 123–130.

Skinner, B. F. (1953). *Science and human behavior.* New York: Macmillan.

Skinner, B. F. (1971). *Beyond freedom and dignity.* New York: Knopf.

Sleator, E. K., & Ullmann, R. K. (1981). Can the physician diagnose hyperactivity in the office? *Pediatrics, 67,* 13–17.

Sleek, S. (1996, April). Ensuring accuracy in clinical decisions. *APA Monitor.*

Sleek, S. (1998, February). Jury tuned out the science in the Nichols trial. *APA Monitor,* 2.

Slife, B. D., & Reber, J. S. (2001). Eclecticism in psychotherapy: Is it really the best substitute for traditional theories? In B. D. Slife, R. N. Williams, & S. H. Barlow (Eds.), *Critical issues in psychotherapy* (pp. 213–234). Thousand Oaks, CA: Sage.

Slipp, S. (Ed.). (1981). *Curative factors in psychodynamic therapy.* New York: McGraw-Hill.

Slobogin, C. (1985). The guilty but mentally ill verdict: An idea whose time should not have come. *George Washington Law Review, 53,* 494–527.

Small, R. F., & Barnhill, L. R. (Eds.). (1998). *Practicing in the new mental health marketplace: Ethical, legal, and moral issues.* Washington, DC: American Psychological Association.

Smallwood, J., Irvine, E., Coulter, F., & Connery, H. (2001). Psychometric evaluation of a short observational tool for small scale research projects in dementia. *International Journal of Geriatric Psychiatry, 16,* 288–292.

Smith, D., & Dumont, F. (1995). A cautionary study: Unwarranted interpretations of the Draw-A-Person test. *Professional Psychology: Research and Practice, 26,* 298–303.

Smith, M. L., & Glass, G. V. (1977). Meta-analysis of psychotherapy outcome studies. *American Psychologist, 32,* 752–777.

Smith, M. L., Glass, G. V., & Miller, T. I. (1980). *The benefits of psychotherapy.* Baltimore, MD: Johns Hopkins University Press.

Smith, S. (1989). Mental health expert witnesses: Of science and crystal balls. *Behavioral Sciences and the Law, 7,* 145–180.

Smith, S. R. (1996). Malpractice liability of mental health professionals and institutions. In B. D. Sales & D. W. Shuman (Eds.), *Law, mental health, and mental disorder* (pp. 76–98). Pacific Grove, CA: Brooks/Cole.

Snepp, F. P., & Peterson, D. R. (1988). Evaluative comparison of Psy.D. and Ph.D. students by clinical internship supervisors. *Professional Psychology: Research and Practice, 19,* 180–183.

Snyder, D. K. (1981). *Marital Satisfaction Inventory: Manual.* Los Angeles: Western Psychological Services.

Snyder, D. K., Lachar, D., & Wills, R. M. (1988). Computer-based interpretation of the Marital Satisfaction Inventory: Use in treatment planning. *Journal of Marital and Family Therapy, 14,* 397–409.

Snyder, D. K., & Wills, R. M. (1989). Behavioral versus insight-oriented marital therapy: Effects on individual and interspousal functioning. *Journal of Consulting and Clinical Psychology, 57,* 39–46.

Snyder, D. K., Wills, R. M., & Grady-Fletcher, A. (1991). Long-term effectiveness of behavioral versus insight-oriented marital therapy: A 4-year follow-up study. *Journal of Consulting and Clinical Psychology, 59,* 138–141.

Snyder, W. V. (1945). An investigation of the nature of nondirective psychotherapy. *Journal of General Psychology, 33,* 193–232.

Snyder, W. V. (Ed.). (1953). *Group report of a program of research in psychotherapy.* State College: Department of Psychology, Pennsylvania State University.

Sobell, L. C., Toneatto, T., & Sobell, M. B. (1994). Behavioral assessment and treatment planning for alcohol, tobacco, and other drug problems: Current status with an emphasis on clinical applications. *Behavior Therapy, 25,* 533–580.

Society of Clinical Psychology (Division 12). (2001). *Society of Clinical Psychology homepage.* Retrieved December 20, 2001 from http://www.apa.org/divisions/div12/homepage.shtml.

Soldz, S., Budman, S., Demby, A., & Jerry, J. (1993). Representation of personality disorders in circumplex and five-factor space: Explorations with a clinical sample. *Psychological Assessment, 5,* 41–52.

Somerfield, M. R., & McCrea, R. R. (2000). Stress and coping research: Methodological challenges, theoretical advances, and clinical applications. *American Psychologist, 55,* 620–624.

Somers-Flanagan, J., & Somers-Flanagan, R. (1995). Intake interviewing with suicidal patients: A systematic approach. *Professional Psychology: Research and Practice, 26,* 41–47.

Spanos, N. (1994). Multiple identity enactments and multiple personality disorder. *Psychological Bulletin, 116,* 143–165.

Spanos, N. P. (1978). Witchcraft in histories of psychiatry: A critical analysis and an alternative conceptualization. *Psychological Bulletin, 85,* 417–439.

Sparr, L. (1995). Post-traumatic stress disorder. *Neurologic Clinics, 13,* 413–429.

Spence, S. H., Donovan, C., Brechman-Toussaint, M. (2000). The treatment of childhood social phobia: The effectiveness of a social skills training-based, cognitive-behavioral intervention, with and without parental involvement. *Journal of Child Psychology and Psychiatry and Allied Disciplines, 41,* 713–726.

Sperry, R. (1968). Hemisphere deconnection and unity in conscious awareness. *American Psychologist, 23,* 723–733.

Sperry, R. W. (1961). Cerebral organization and behavior. *Science, 133,* 1749–1757.

Sperry, R. W. (1974). Lateral specialization in the surgically separated hemispheres. In F. O. Schmitt & F. G. Worden (Eds.), *The neurosciences: Third study program* (pp. 5–20). Cambridge, MA: MIT Press.

Sperry, R. W. (1982). Some effects of disconnecting the cerebral hemispheres. *Science, 217,* 1223–1226.

Spiegel, T. A., Wadden, T. A., & Foster, G. D. (1991). Objective measurement of eating rate during behavioral treatment of obesity. *Behavior Therapy, 22,* 61–68.

Spiegler, M. D., & Guevremont, D. C. (1993). *Contemporary behavior therapy* (2nd ed.) Pacific Grove, CA: Brooks/Cole.

Spielberger, C. D., Gorsuch, R. L., Lushene, R., Vagg, P. R., & Jacobs, G. A. (1983). *Manual for the State-Trait Anxiety Inventory.* Palo Alto, CA: Consulting Psychologists Press.

Spiers, P. A. (1980). Have they come to praise Luria or to bury him? The Luria-Nebraska controversy. *Journal of Consulting and Clinical Psychology, 49,* 331–341.

Spirito, A. (Ed.). (1999). Empirically supported treatments in pediatric psychology. *Journal of Pediatric Psychology, 24,* 87–174.

Spitz, R. (1946). Anaclitic depression. *Psychoanalytic Study of the Child, 1,* 113–117.

Spitzer, R. L., Williams, J. B. W., Gibbon, M., & First, M. B. (1990). *Structured clinical interview for DSM-III-R (SCID).* Washington, D.C.: American Psychiatric Press.

Spivack, G., & Shure, M. B. (1974). *Social adjustment of young children: A cognitive approach to solving real-life problems.* San Francisco: Jossey-Bass.

Sroufe, L. A. (1985). Attachment classification from the perspective of infant-caregiver relationships and infant temperament. *Child Development, 56,* 1–14.

St. Lawrence, J. S., Brasfield, T. L., Jefferson, K. W., Alleyne, E., & O'Bannon, R. E., III (1995). Cognitive-behavioral intervention to reduce African American adolescents' risk for HIV infection. *Journal of Consulting & Clinical Psychology, 63,* 221–237.

Staats, A. W. (1991). Unified positivism and unification psychology: Fad or new field? *American Psychologist, 46,* 899–912.

Stahl, P. M. (1994). *Conducting child custody evaluations: A comprehensive guide.* Thousand Oaks, CA: Sage.

Stapp, J., & Fulcher, R. (1983). The employment of APA members: 1982. *American Psychologist, 38,* 1330–1352.

Starkstein, S. E., & Robinson, R. G. (1988). Lateralized emotional response following stroke. In M. Kinsbourne (Ed.), *Cerebral hemisphere function in depression.* Washington, DC: American Psychiatric Press.

Steadman, H. J. (1979). *Beating a rap? Defendants found incompetent to stand trial.* Chicago: University of Chicago Press.

Steadman, H. J. (1993). *Reforming the insanity defense: An evaluation of pre- and post-Hinckley reforms.* New York: Guilford.

Steenbarger, B. N. (1994). Duration and outcome in therapy: An integrative review. *Professional Psychology: Research and Practice, 25,* 111–119.

Stein, D. M., & Lambert, M. J. (1984). On the relationship between therapist experience and psychotherapy outcome. *Clinical Psychology Review, 4,* 127–142.

Stein, D. M., & Lambert, M. J. (1995). Graduate training in psychotherapy: Are therapy outcomes enhanced? *Journal of Consulting and Clinical Psychology, 63,* 182–196.

Stein, R. E. K., Bauman, L. J., & Ireys, H. T. (1991). Who enrolls in prevention trials? Discordance in perception of risk by professionals and participants. *American Journal of Community Psychology, 19,* 603–618.

Steiner, J. L., Tebes, J. K., Sledge, W. H., & Walker, M. L. (1995). A comparison of the Structured Clinical Interview for DSM-III-R and clinical diagnoses. *Journal of Nervous and Mental Disease, 183,* 365–369.

Sternberg, R. J., & Detterman, D. K. (Eds.). (1986). *What is intelligence? Contemporary viewpoints on its nature and definition.* Norwood, NJ: Ablex.

Stevens, M. R., & Reilly, R. R. (1980). MMPI short forms: A literature review. *Journal of Personality Assessment, 44,* 368–376.

Stewart, D. J., & Patterson, M. L. (1973). Eliciting effects of verbal and nonverbal cues on projective test responses. *Journal of Consulting and Clinical Psychology, 41,* 74–77.

Stiles, W. A., Shapiro, D. A., & Elliot, R. (1986). "Are all psychotherapies equivalent?" *American Psychologist, 41,* 165–180.

Stokols, D. (1992). Establishing and maintaining healthy environments: Toward a social ecology of health promotion. *American Psychologist, 47,* 6–22.

Stolle, D. P., Wexler, D. B., & Winick, B. J. (Eds.). (2000). *Practicing Therapeutic Jurisprudence.* Durham: Carolina Academic Press.

Stolorow, R. D. (1993). An intersubjective view of the therapeutic process. *Bulletin of the Menninger Clinic, 57,* 450–458.

Stone, A. A., & Neale, J. M. (1984). New measures of daily coping: Developments and preliminary results. *Journal of Personality and Social Psychology, 46,* 892–906.

Stone, A. R., Frank, J. D., Nash, E. H., & Imber, S. D. (1961). An intensive five-year follow-up study of treated psychiatric outpatients. *Journal of Nervous and Mental Disease, 133,* 410–422.

Storm, J., Graham, J. R. (2000). Detection of coached general malingering on the MMPI-2. *Psychological Assessment, 12,* 158–165.

Street, E. (2000). Family and systematic therapy. In C. Feltham and I Horton (Eds.), *Handbook of counseling and psychotherapy* (pp. 617–623). Thousand Oaks, CA: Sage.

Stricker, G. (1992). The relationship of research to clinical practice. *American Psychologist, 47,* 543–549.

Stricker, G. (2000). The scientist-practitioner model: Gandhi was right again. *American Psychologist, 55,* 253–254.

Stricker, G., & Trierweiler, S. (1995). The local clinical scientist: A bridge between science and practice. *American Psychologist, 50,* 995–1002.

Strickland, B. R. (1985). Over the Boulder(s) and through the Vail. *The Clinical Psychologist, 39,* 52–56.

Strickland, G., Abrahamson, D. J., Bologna, N. C., Hollon, S. D., Robinson, E. A., & Reed, G. M. (1999). Treatment guidelines: The good, the bad, and the ugly. *Psychotherapy, 36,* 69–79.

Strohmer, D. C., & Shivy, V. A. (1994). Bias in counselor hypothesis testing: Testing the robustness of counselor confirmatory bias. *Journal of Counseling and Development, 73,* 191–197.

Strother, C. R. (1956). *Psychology and mental health.* Washington, DC: American Psychological Association.

Stroul, B. (1993). *Psychiatric crisis response systems: A descriptive study.* Rockville, MD: Substance Abuse and Mental Health Services Administration.

Strupp, H. H. (1960). *Psychotherapists in action: Explorations of the therapist's contribution to the treatment process.* New York: Grune & Stratton.

Strupp, H. H. (1989). Psychotherapy: Can the practitioner learn from the researcher? *American Psychologist, 44,* 717–724.

Strupp, H. H. (2001). Implications of the empirically supported treatment movement for psycho-analysis. *Psychoanalytic Dialogues, 11,* 605–619.

Strupp, H. H., & Blinder, J. L. (1984). *Psychotherapy in a new key: A guide to time-limited dynamic psychotherapy.* New York: Basic Books.

Strupp, H. H., & Hadley, S. W. (1977). A tripartite model of mental health and therapeutic outcomes. *American Psychologist, 32,* 187–196.

Strupp, H. H., & Hadley, S. W. (1979). Specific vs. nonspecific factors in psychotherapy. *Archives of General Psychiatry, 36,* 1125–1137.

Stuart, R. B. (1971). Behavioral contracting within the families of delinquents. *Journal of Behavior Therapy and Experimental Psychiatry, 2,* 1–11.

Stumphauzer, J. S. (1986). *Helping delinquents change: A treatment manual of social learning approaches.* New York: Haworth Press.

Suarez-Balcazar, Y., Durlak, J., & Smith, C. (1994). Multicultural training practices in community psychology programs. *American Journal of Community Psychology, 22,* 785–798.

Sue, D. W., & Sue, D. (1999). *Counseling the culturally different* (3rd ed). New York: Wiley and Sons.

Sue, S., Fujino, D. C., Hu, L. T., Takeuchi, D. T., et al. (1991). Community mental health services for ethnic minority groups: A test of the cultural responsiveness hypothesis. *Journal of Consulting and Clinical Psychology, 59,* 533–540.

Suh, C. S., Strupp, H. H., & O'Malley, S. S. (1986). The Vanderbilt process measures: The Psychotherapy Process Scale (VPPS) and the Negative Indicators Scale (VNIS). In L. Greenberg and W. Pinsof (Eds.), *The psychotherapeutic process: A research handbook* (pp. 285–323). New York: Guilford Press.

Sullivan, H. S. (1953). *The interpersonal theory of psychiatry.* New York: W. W. Norton.

Sullivan, H. S. (1954). *The psychiatric interview.* New York: W. W. Norton.

Sulloway, F. J. (1996). *Born to rebel: Birth order, family dynamics, and creative lives.* New York: Pantheon Books.

Suls, J., & Wang, C. K. (1993). The relationship between trait hostility and cardiovascular reactivity: A quantitative review and analysis. *Psychophysiology, 30,* 1–12.

Sulzer, E. (1965). Behavior modifications in adult psychiatric patients. In L. P. Ullmann & L. Krasner (Eds.), *Case studies in behavior modification* (pp. 196–200). New York: Holt, Rinehart & Winston.

Summit, R. (1983). The child sexual abuse accommodation syndrome. *Child Abuse and Neglect, 7,* 177–193.

Sundberg, N. D. (1977). *Assessment of persons.* Englewood Cliffs, NJ: Prentice-Hall.

Sundberg, N. D., Tyler, L. E., & Taplin, J. R. (1973). *Clinical psychology: Expanding horizons* (2nd ed.). Englewood Cliffs, NJ: Prentice-Hall.

Super, J. T. (1999). Forensic psychology and law enforcement. In A. K. Hess and I. B. Weiner (Eds.), *The handbook of forensic psychology* (2nd ed., pp. 409–439). New York: John Wiley & Sons.

Susser, E., & Lin, S. (1992). Schizophrenia after prenatal exposure to the Dutch hunger winter of 1944–1945. *Archives of General Psychiatry, 49,* 983–988.

Svartberg, M. (1999). Therapist competence: Its temporal course, temporal stability, and determinants in short-term anxiety-provoking psychotherapy. *Journal of Clinical Psychology, 55,* 1313–1319.

Swain, M. A., & Steckel, S. B. (1981). Influencing adherence among hypertensives. *Research Nursing and Health, 4,* 213–218.

Swanson, J. M., McBurnett, K., Christian, D. L., & Wigal, T. (1995). Stimulant medications and the treatment of children with ADHD. In T. H. Ollendick & R. J. Prinz (Eds.), *Advances in clinical child psychology* (Vol. 17, pp. 265–322). New York: Plenum.

Sweet, A. A. (1984). The therapeutic relationship in behavior therapy. *Clinical Psychology Review, 4,* 253–272.

Szapocznik, J., Kurtines, W., Santisteban, D. A., & Rio, A. T. (1990). Interplay of advances between theory, research, and application in treatment interventions aimed at behavior problem children and adolescents. *Journal of Consulting and Clinical Psychology, 58,* 696–703.

Szapocznik, J., Kurtines, W. M., Foote, F., Perez-Vidal, A., & Hervis, O. (1986). Conjoint versus one-person family therapy: Further evidence for the effectiveness of conducting family therapy through one person with drug-abusing adolescents. *Journal of Consulting and Clinical Psychology, 54,* 395–397.

Szasz, T. S. (1960). The myth of mental illness. *American Psychologist, 15,* 113–118.

Tallent, N. (1976). *Psychological report writing.* Englewood Cliffs, NJ: Prentice-Hall.

Tallent, N. (1992). *The practice of psychological assessment.* Englewood Cliffs, NJ: Prentice-Hall.

Tallent, N., & Reiss, W. J. (1959). Multidisciplinary views on the preparation of written psychological reports. *Journal of Clinical Psychology, 15,* 444–446.

Taplin, P. S., & Reid, J. B. (1973). Effects of instructional set and experimenter influence on observer reliability. *Child Development, 44,* 547–554.

Tarrier, N., Kiney, C., McCarthy, E., Humphreys, L., Wittkowski, A., & Morris, J. (2000). Two-year follow-up of cognitive-behavioral and supportive counseling in treatment of persistent symptoms in chronic schizophrenia. *Journal of Consulting and Clinical Psychology, 68,* 917–922.

Task Force on Pediatric Aids, American Psychology Association. (1989). Pediatric AIDS and human immunodeficiency virus infection. *American Psychologist, 44,* 258–264.

Task Force on Promotion and Dissemination of Psychological Procedures (1995). Training in and dissemination of empirically validated psychological treatments: Report and recommendations. *Clinical Psychologist, 48,* 3–23.

Taube, C. A., Goldman, H. H., Burns, B. J., & Kessler, L. G. (1988). High users of outpatient mental health services: I. Definition and characteristics. *American Journal of Psychiatry, 145,* 19–24.

Taylor, S. E. (1995). *Health psychology.* New York: McGraw-Hill.

Taylor, S. E. (1999). *Health psychology* (4th ed.) New York: McGraw-Hill.

Taylor, S. E., Kemeny, M. E., Reed, G. M., Bower, J. E., & Gruenewald, T. L. (2000). Psychological resources, positive illusions, and health. *American Psychologist, 55,* 99–109.

Tellegen, A. (1982). Brief manual for the Multidimensional Personality Questionnaire. Unpublished manuscript, University of Minnesota.

Tellegen, A., & Ben-Porath, Y. S. (1992). The new uniform T scores for the MMPI-2: Rationale, derivation, and appraisal. *Psychological Assessment, 4,* 145–155.

Tellegen, A., Lykken, D. T., Bouchard, T. J., Jr., Wilcox, K. J., Segal, N. L., & Rich, S. (1988). Personality similarity in twins reared apart and reared together. *Journal of Personality and Social Psychology, 54,* 1031–1039.

Temerlin, M. K. (1968). Suggestion effects in psychiatric diagnosis. *Journal of Nervous and Mental Disease, 147,* 349–353.

Tennen, H., Affleck, G., Armeli, S., & Carney, M. A. (2000). A daily process approach to coping. *American Psychologist, 55,* 626–636.

Testa, M., & Collins, R. L. (1997). Alcohol and risky sexual behavior: Event-based analyses among a sample of high-risk women. *Psychology of Addictive Behaviors, 11,* 190–201.

Thelen, M. H., Farmer, J., Wonderlich, S., & Smith, M. (1991). A revision of the Bulimia Test: The BULIT-R. *Psychological Assessment, 3,* 119–124.

Thelen, M. H., Mintz, L. B., & Boman, J. S. (1996). The bulimia test—revised: Validation with DSM-IV criteria for bulimia nervosa. *Psychological Assessment, 8,* 219–221.

Thelen, M. H., & Rodriguez, M. D. (1987). Attitudes of academic and applied clinical psychologists toward training issues: 1969–1984. *American Psychologist, 42,* 412–415.

Thoits, P. A. (1986). Social support as coping assistance. *Journal of Consulting and Clinical Psychology, 54,* 416–423.

Thomas, A., & Chess, S. (1977). *Temperament and development.* New York: Brunner/Mazel.

Thomas, A., Chess, S., & Birch, H. G. (1968). *Temperament and behavior disorders in children.* New York: New York University Press.

Thomas, E. J. (1973). Bias of therapist influence in behavioral assessment. *Journal of Behavior Therapy and Experimental Psychiatry, 4,* 107–111.

Thompson, L. W., Gallagher, E., Steinmetz, S., Breckenridge, J. (1987). Comparative effectiveness of psychotherapies for depressed elders. *Journal of Consulting and Clinical Psychology, 55,* 385–390.

Thoresen, C. E., & Powell, L. H. (1992). Type A behavior pattern: New perspectives on theory, assessment, and intervention. *Journal of Consulting and Clinical Psychology, 60,* 595–604.

Thorndike, R. L., Hagen, E. P., & Sattler, J. M. (1986). *What is intelligence? Contemporary viewpoints on its nature and definition.* Chicago: Riverside.

Thorne, F. C. (1972). Clinical judgment. In R. H. Woody & J. D. Woody (Eds.), *Clinical assessment in counseling and psychotherapy* (pp. 30–85). Englewood Cliffs, NJ: Prentice-Hall.

Tisdelle, D. A., & St. Lawrence, J. S. (1988). Adolescent interpersonal problem-solving skill training: Social validation and generalization. *Behavior Therapy, 19,* 171–182.

Todd, L. K. (1996). A computer-assisted expert system for clinical diagnosis of eating disorders: A potential learning tool for practitioners. *Professional Psychology: Research and Practice, 27,* 184–187.

Tomlinson, S. M., & Cheatham, H. E. (1989). Effects of counselor intake judgments on service to Black students using a university counseling center. *Counseling Psychology Quarterly, 2,* 105–111.

Tomlinson-Clarke, S., & Camilli, G. (1995). An exploratory study of counselor judgments in multi-cultural research. *Journal of Multicultural Counseling and Development, 23,* 237–245.

Tomlinson-Clarke, S., & Cheatham, H. E. (1993). Counselor and client ethnicity an counselor intake judgments. *Journal of Counseling Psychology, 40,* 267–270.

Torey, E. F., & Zdanowicz, M. T. (1999, July 9). Deinstitutionalization hasn't worked. *The Washington Post,* A29.

Tremblay, R. E., Pagani-Kurtz, L., Masse, L. C., Vitaro, F., & Pihl, R. O. (1995). A bimodal preventive intervention for disruptive Kindergarten boys: Its impact through mid-adolescence. *Journal of Consulting and Clinical Psychology, 63,* 560–568.

Tryon, G. S. (1990). Session depth and smoothness in relation to the concept of engagement in counseling. *Journal of Counseling Psychology, 37,* 248–253.

Tucker, N. (2001, December 11). High court passes on Capitol suspect. *The Washington Post,* B1.

Turk, D. C., & Rudy, T. E. (1990). Pain. In A. S. Bellack, M. Hersen, & A. E. Kazdin (Eds.), *International handbook of behavior modification and therapy* (2nd ed., pp. 399–413). New York: Plenum Press.

Turner, J. B., Kessler, R. C., & House, J. S. (1991). Factors facilitating adjustment to unemployment: Implications for intervention. *American Journal of Community Psychology, 19,* 521–542.

Turner, S. M., Beidel, D. C., Dancu, C. V., & Stanley, M. A. (1989). An empirically derived inventory to measure social fears and anxiety: The Social Phobia and Anxiety Inventory. *Psychological Assessment: Journal of Consulting and Clinical Psychology, 1,* 35–40.

Tutin, J. (1993). The persistence of initial beliefs in clinical judgment. *Journal of Social and Clinical Psychology, 12,* 319–335.

Tversky, A., & Kahneman, D. (1974). Judgment under uncertainty: Heuristics and biases. *Science, 185,* 1124–1131.

Twentyman, C. T., Rohrbeck, C. H., & Amish, P. (1984). A cognitive-behavioral model of child abuse. In Sanders (Ed.), *Violent individuals and families: A practitioner's handbook* (pp. 86–111). Springfield, IL: Charles C. Thomas.

Tyrka, A. R., Cannon, T., Haslam, N., Mednick, S., Schulsinger, F., Schulsinger, H., & Parnas, J. (1995). The latent structure of schizotypy: I. Premorbid indicators of a taxon of individuals at risk for schizophrenia spectrum disorders. *Journal of Abnormal Psychology, 104,* 173–183.

Uchino, B. N., Cacioppo, J. T. & Kiecolt-Glaser, J. K. (1996). The relationship between social support and physiological processes: A review with emphasis on underlying mechanisms and implications for health. *Psychological Bulletin, 119,* 488–531.

Ullmann, L. P., & Krasner, L. (Eds.). (1965). *Case studies in behavior modification.* New York: Holt, Rinehart & Winston.

Ullmann, L. P., & Krasner, L. (1975). *A psychological approach to abnormal behavior.* Englewood Cliffs, NJ: Prentice-Hall.

Unutzer, J., Klap, R., Strum, R., Young, A. S., Marmon, T., Shatkin, J., & Wells, K. B. (2000). Mental disorders and the use of alternative medicine: Results from a national survey. *American Journal of Psychiatry, 157,* 1851–1857.

U.S. Department of Education. (1995). *Integrated postsecondary education data system (IPEDS) "completion" survey.* Washington, DC: National Center for Education Statistics.

U.S. Public Health Service. (2000). *Report on the Surgeon General's Conference on Children's Mental Health: A National Action Agenda.* Washington, DC: Author.

U.S. Surgeon General. (1999). *Mental health: A report of the surgeon general.* Rockville, MD: U.S. Department of Health and Human Services.

Ustad, K. L., Rogers, R., Sewell, K. W., Guarnaccia, C. A. (1996). Restoration of competency to stand trial: Assessment with the Georgia Court Competency Test and the Competency Screening Test. *Law and Human Behavior, 20,* 131–146.

Vaillant, G. E. (1977). *Adaptation to life.* Boston, MA: Little, Brown.

Vaillant, G. E. (1984). The disadvantages of DSM-II outweigh its advantages. *American Journal of Psychiatry, 141,* 542–545.

Vaillant, G. E. (1994). Behavioral medicine over the life span. In S. J. Blumenthal, K. Mathews, & S. M. Weiss (Eds.), *New research frontiers in behavioral medicine: Proceedings of the National Conference.* Washington, DC: National Institute of Health.

Vaillant, G. E. (2000). Adaptive mental mechanisms: Their role in a positive psychology. *American Psychologist, 55,* 89–98.

Vallis, T. M., & Howes, J. L. (1995). The field of clinical psychology: Arriving at a definition. *Canadian Psychology, 37,* 120–127.

van Dam-Baggen, R., & Kraaimaat, F. (2000). Group social skills training or cognitive group therapy as the clinical treatment of choice or generalized phobia? *Journal of Anxiety Disorders, 14,* 437–451.

Van Denburg, T. F., & Kiesler, D. J. (1996). An interpersonal communication perspective on resistance in psychotherapy. *In Session: Psychotherapy in Practice, 2,* 55–66.

Van Ijzendoorn, M. H., Juffer, F., & Duyvesteyn, M. G. C. (1995). Breaking the intergenerational cycle of insecure attachment: A review of the effects of attachment-based interventions on maternal sensitivity and infant security. *Journal of Child Psychology and Psychiatry, 36,* 225–248.

VandenBos, G. R. (1993). U.S. mental health policy: Proactive evolution in the midst of health care reform. *American Psychologist, 48,* 283–290.

VandenBos, G. R., DeLeon, P. H., & Belar, C. D. (1991). How many psychological practitioners are needed? It's too early to know. *Professional Psychology: Research and Practice, 22,* 441–448.

VandenBos, G. R., & Stapp, J. (1983). Service providers in psychology: Results of the 1982 APA human resources survey. *American Psychologist, 38,* 1330–1352.

VanderBos, G. R., & Williams, S. (2000). Is psychologist's involvement in the prescribing of psychotropic medication really a new activity? *Professional Psychology: Research and Practice, 31,* 615–618.

Vane, J. R. (1981). The Thematic Apperception Test: A review. *Clinical Psychology Review, 1,* 319–336.

Vane, J. R., & Motta, R. W. (1990). Group intelligence tests. In G. Goldstein & M. Hersen (Eds.), *Handbook of psychological assessment* (pp. 102–119). New York: Pergamon Press.

Vassend, O., Eskild, A., & Halvorsen, R. (1997). Negative affectivity, coping, immune status, and disease progression in HIV-infected individuals. *Psychological Health, 12,* 375–388.

Vega, A., Jr., & Parsons, O. A. (1967). Cross validation of the Halstead-Reitan tests for brain damage. *Journal of Consulting and Clinical Psychology, 31,* 619–623.

Vermande, M. M., van den Bercken, J. H., & De Bruyn, E. E. (1996). Effects of diagnostic classification systems on clinical hypothesis generation. *Journal of Psychopathology and Behavioral Assessment, 18,* 49–70.

Viken, R. J., & McFall, R. M. (1994). Paradox lost: Implications of contemporary reinforcement theory for behavior therapy. *Current Directions in Psychological Science, 3,* 121–125.

von Bertalanffy, L. (1968). *General systems theory.* New York: Braziller.

Wachtel, P. (1977). *Psychoanalysis and behavior therapy.* New York: Basic Books.

Wada, J., & Rasmussen, T. (1960). Intracarotid injection of sodium amytal for the lateralization of cerebral speech dominance. *Journal of Neurosurgery, 17,* 266–282.

Waehler, C. A., Kalodner, C. R., Wampold, B. E., & Lichtenberg, J. W. (2000). Empirically supported treatments (ESTs) in perspective: Implications for Counseling Psychology Training. *The Counseling Psychologist, 28,* 657–671.

Wahler, R. G. (1980). The insular mother: Her problems in parent-child treatment. *Journal of Applied Behavior Analysis, 13,* 27–42.

Wakefield, H., & Underwager, R. (1992). Recovered memories of alleged sexual abuse: Lawsuits against parents. *Behavioral Sciences and the Law, 10,* 483–507.

Wakefield, J. C. (1997). Diagnosing DSM-IV—Part I: DSM-IV and the concept of disorder. *Behavioral Research and Therapy, 35,* 633–649.

Walcott, D. M. (2000). Repressed memory still lacks scientific reliability. *Journal of the American Academy of Psychiatry and the Law, 28,* 243–244.

Walker, C. E., Hedberg, A., Clement, P. W., & Wright, L. (1981). *Clinical procedures for behavior therapy.* Englewood Cliffs, NJ: Prentice-Hall.

Walker, E. F., Grimes, K. E., Davis, D. M., & Smith, A. J. (1993). Childhood precursors of schizophrenia: Facial expressions of emotion. *American Journal of Psychiatry, 150,* 1654–1660.

Walker, H. M., Colvin, G., & Ramsey, E. (1995). *Antisocial behavior in school: Strategies and best practices.* Pacific Grove: Brooks/Cole.

Wallace, C. J. (1993). Psychiatric rehabilitation. *Psychopharmacology Bulletin, 29,* 537–548.

Wallace, C. J., Liberman, R. P., Mackain, S. J., Blackwell, G., & Eckman, T. A. (1992). Effectiveness and replicability of modules for teaching social and instrumental skills to the severely mentally ill. *American Journal of Psychiatry, 149,* 654–658.

Wallen, R. W. (1956). *Clinical psychology: The study of persons.* New York: McGraw-Hill.

Wallerstein, J., Corbin, S. B., & Lewis, J. M. (1988). Children of divorce: A ten-year study. In E. M. Hetherington & J. Arasteh (Eds.), *Impact of divorce, single-parenting and stepparenting on children* (pp. 198–214). Hillsdale, NJ: Lawrence Erlbaum Associates.

Walsh, B. W., & Betz, N. E. (2001). *Tests and assessment* (4th ed.). Upper Saddle River, NJ: Prentice Hall.

Walsh, K. (1987). *Neuropsychology: A clinical approach* (2nd ed.). Edinburgh: Churchill Livingstone.

Wampold, B. E. (2001). *The great psychotherapy debate: Models, methods, and findings.* Mahwah, NJ: Erlbaum.

Wampold, B. E., Ahn, H., & Coleman, H. L. K. (2001). Medical model as metaphor: Old habits die hard. *Journal of Counseling Psychology, 48,* 263–273.

Wampold, B. E., Mondin, G. W., Moody, M., Stich, F., Benson, K., et al. (1997). A meta-analysis of outcome studies comparing bona fide psychotherapies: Empirically "all must have prizes." *Psychological Bulletin, 122,* 203–215.

Ward, J. C., & Naster, B. J. (1991). Reliability of an observational system used to monitor behavior in a mental health residential treatment unit. *Journal of Mental Health Administration, 18,* 64–68.

Ward, T. (1999). Method, judgement, and clinical reasoning. *Behaviour Change, 16,* 4–9.

Watkins, L. E., Jr., Campbell, V. L., Nieberding, K., & Hallmark, R. (1995). Contemporary practice of psychological assessment by clinical psychologists. *Professional Psychology: Research and Practice, 26,* 54–60.

Watley, D. J. (1968). Feedback training and improvement of clinical forecasting. *Journal of Counseling Psychology, 15,* 167–171.

Watson, D., & Friend, R. (1969). Measurement of social-evaluative anxiety. *Journal of Consulting and Clinical Psychology, 33,* 448–457.

Watson, J. B. (1924). *Behaviorism.* New York: W. W. Norton.

Watson, J. B. (1930). *Behaviorism* (rev. ed.). New York: W. W. Norton.

Watson, J. B., & Rayner, R. (1920). Conditioned emotional reactions. *Journal of Experimental Psychology, 3,* 1–14.

Watson, R. I. (1951). *The clinical method in psychology.* New York: Harper.

Watson, R. I. (1953). Measuring the effectiveness of psychotherapy: Problems for investigators. *Journal of Clinical Psychology, 8,* 60–64.

Wearden, A. J., Tarrier, N., Barrowclough, C., Zastowny, T. R., & Rahill, A. A. (2000). A review of expressed emotion research in health care. *Clinical Psychology Review, 20,* 633–666.

Webb, E., Campbell, D. T., Schwartz, R. D., & Sechrest, L. B. (1966). *Unobtrusive measures: Nonreactive research in the social sciences.* Chicago: Rand-McNally.

Webber, D. W. (1999). *AIDS and the law: 1999 cumulative supplement* (3rd ed.). New York: Panel.

Webster, C. (1996). Hispanic and Anglo interviewer and respondent ethnicity and gender: The impact on survey response quality. *Journal of Marketing Research, 33,* 62–72.

Webster-Stratton, C. (1988). Mothers' and fathers' perceptions of child deviance: Roles of parent and child behaviors and parent adjustment. *Journal of Consulting and Clinical Psychology, 56,* 909–915.

Wechsler, D. (1967). *Manual for the WPPSI.* New York: Psychological Corporation.

Wechsler, D. (1981). *Wechsler Adult Intelligence Scale—Revised.* New York: Psychological Corporation.

Wechsler, D. (1991). *WISC-III: Manual.* San Antonio, TX: Psychological Corporation.

Wechsler, D. (1997). *Manual for the Wechsler Adult Intelligence Scale-III.* New York: Psychological Corporation.

Weick, K. E. (1968). Systematic observational methods. In G. Lindzey & E. Aronson (Eds.), *Handbook of social psychology* (Vol. 2, 2nd ed., pp. 357–451). Reading, MA: Addison-Wesley.

Weiner, I. (2000). Using the Rorschach properly in practice and in research. *Journal of Clinical Psychology, 56,* 435–438.

Weiss, B., Catron, T., Harris, V., & Phung, T. M. (1999). The effectiveness of child psychotherapy. *Journal of Consulting and Clinical Psychology, 67,* 82–94.

Weiss, G., & Hechtman, L. T. (1993). *Hyperactive children grow up* (2nd ed.). New York: Guilford Press.

Weiss, R. D., Najavits, L. M., Muenz, L. R., & Hufford, C. (1995). Twelve-month test-retest reliability of the Structured Clinical Interview for DSM-III-R Personality Disorders in cocaine-dependent patients. *Comprehensive Psychiatry, 36,* 384–389.

Weissman, H. N. (1985). Psycholegal standards and the role of psychological assessment in personal injury litigation. *Behavioral Sciences and the Law, 3,* 135–148.

Weissman, H. N. (1991). Child custody evaluations: Fair and unfair professional practices. *Behavioral Sciences and the Law, 9,* 469–476.

Weissman, M. M., & Markowitz, J. C. (1994). Interpersonal psychotherapy: Current status. *Archives of General Psychiatry, 51,* 599–606.

Weissmark, M. S., & Giacomo, D. A. (1998). *Doing psychotherapy effectively.* Chicago, IL: University of Chicago Press.

Weisz, J. R. (July, 2001). Two traditions in psychotherapy with children and adolescents: The state of the evidence. Paper presented at the second biennial Niagara Conference on Evidence-based Treatments for childhood and adolescent mental health problems. Niagara-on-the-Lake.

Weisz, J. R., Donenberg, G. R., Han, S. S., & Weiss, B. (1995). Bridging the gap between laboratory and clinic in child and adoelscent psychotherapy. *Journal of Consulting and Clinical Psychology, 63,* 688–701.

Weisz, J. R., Weiss, B., Alicke, M. D., & Klotz, M. L. (1987). Effectiveness of psychotherapy with children and adolescents: A meta-analysis for clinicians. *Journal of Consulting and Clinical Psychology, 55,* 542–549.

Weisz, J. R., Weiss, B., & Donnenberg, G. R. (1992). The lab versus the clinic: Effects of child and adolescent psychotherapy. *American Psychologist, 47,* 1578–1585.

Wenar, C. (1994). *Developmental psychopathology: From infancy through adolescence* (3rd ed.). New York: McGraw-Hill.

Wernick, R. (1956). *They've got your number.* New York: W. W. Norton.

West, M., Bondy, E., & Hutchinson, S. (1991). Interviewing institutionalized elders: Threats to validity. *Journal of Nursing Scholarship, 23,* 171–176.

Westen, D., & Morrison, K. (2001). A multidimensional meta-analysis of treatments for depression, panic, and generalized anxiety disorder: An empirical examination of the status of empirically supported therapies. *Journal of Consulting and Clinical Psychology, 69,* 875–899.

Wettstein, R. M. (1999). Emerich v Philadelphia Center for Human Development: The new duty to warn in Pennsylvania. *Journal of the American Academy of Psychiatry and the Law, 27,* 309–313.

Wexler, B. E., & Cicchetti, D. V. (1992). The outpatient treatment of depression: Implications of outcome research for clinical practice. *Journal of Nervous and Mental Diseases, 180,* 277–286.

Whitehead, W. E. (1992). Behavioral medicine approaches to gastrointestinal disorders. *Journal of Consulting and Clinical Psychology, 60,* 605–612.

Whalen, C. K., Henker, B., & Dotemoto, S. (1980). Methylphenidate and hyperactivity: Effects on teacher behaviors. *Science, 208,* 1280–1282.

Wickrama, K., Conger, R. D., & Lorenz, F. O. (1995). Work, marriage, lifestyle, and changes in men's physical health. *Journal of Behavioral Medicine, 18,* 97–112.

Wicks-Nelson, R., & Israel, A. C. (1991). *Behavior disorders of childhood* (2nd ed.). Englewood Cliffs, NJ: Prentice Hall.

Widiger, T. A., & Frances, A. (1985). The DSM-III personality disorders: Perspectives from psychology. *Archives of General Psychiatry, 42,* 615–623.

Widiger, T. A., Frances, A. J., Pincus, H. A., Davis, W. W., & First, M. B. (1991). Toward an empirical classification for the DSM-IV. *Journal of Abnormal Psychology, 100,* 280–288.

Widiger, T. A., & Sankis, L. M. (2000). Adult psychopathology: Issues and controversies. *Annual Review of Psychology, 51,* 377–404.

Wiggins, J. G. (1994). Would you want your child to be a psychologist? *American Psychologist, 49,* 485–492.

Wiggins, J. S. (1973). *Personality and prediction: Principles of personality assessment.* Reading, MA: Addison-Wesley.

Wiggins, J. S. (1981). Clinical and statistical prediction: Where are we and where do we go from here? *Clinical Psychology Review, 1,* 3–18.

Wiggins, J. S. (1982). Circumplex models of interpersonal behavior in clinical psychology. In P. C. Kendall & J. N. Butcher (Eds.), *Handbook of research methods in clinical psychology* (pp. 183–221). New York: John Wiley.

Wiggins, J. S., & Pincus, A. L. (1989). Conceptions of personality disorders and dimensions of personality. *Psychological Assessment: A Journal of Consulting and Clinical Psychology, 1,* 305–316.

Wilkinson, G. S. (1993). *WRAT-3: Wide range achievement test administration manual.* Wilmington, DE: Wide Range, Inc.

Williams, C. (1988). The relationship of ethnic group membership on levels of responding skills to Black and White clients. *College Student Journal, 22,* 401–403.

Williams, C. L., Arnold, C. B., & Wynder, E. L. (1977). Primary prevention of chronic disease beginning in childhood: The Know Your Body Program: Design of study. *Preventive Medicine, 6,* 344-357.

Williams, C. L., & Heikes, E. J. (1993). The importance of researcher's gender in the in-depth interview: Evidence from two case studies of male nurses. *Gender and Society, 7,* 280-291.

Williams, J. M., Voelker, S., & Ricciardi, P. W. (1995). Predictive validity of the K-ABC for exceptional preschoolers. *Psychology in the Schools, 32,* 178-185.

Williams, L. (1994). Recall of childhood trauma: A prospective study of women's memories of child sexual abuse. *Journal of Consulting and Clinical Psychology, 62,* 1167-1176.

Willams, R. B. (2001). Hostility and heart disease. *Advances in Mind-Body Medicine, 17,* 52-55.

Williams, R. B., Jr., & Barefoot, J. C. (1988). Coronary-prone behavior: The emerging role of the hostility complex. In B. K. Houston & C. R. Snyder (Eds.), *Type A behavior pattern: Research, theory and intervention* (pp. 189-211). New York: John Wiley and Sons.

Williams, S., Kohout, J. L., & Wicherski, M. (2000). Salary changes among independent psychologists by gender and experience. *Psychiatric Services, 51,* 1111.

Williams, S., Wicherski, M., & Kohout, J. L. (2000). Salaries in Psychology: 1999. Retrieved December 13, 2001 from http://research.apa.org/99salaries.html.

Williams, T. R. (1967). *Field methods in the study of culture.* New York: Holt, Rinehart, & Winston.

Wills, R. M., Faitler, S. L., & Snyder, D. K. (1987). Distinctiveness of behavioral versus insight-oriented marital therapy: An empirical analysis. *Journal of Consulting and Clinical Psychology, 55,* 685-690.

Wilson, G. T. (1985). Limitations of meta-analysis in the evaluation of the effects of psychological therapy. *Clinical Psychology Review, 5,* 35-47.

Wilson, G. T. (1995). Behavior therapy. In R. J. Corsini & D. Wedding (Eds.), *Current psychotherapies* (5th ed., pp. 197-228). Itasca, IL: Peacock Publishers, Inc.

Wilson, G. T., & Rachman, S. J. (1983). Meta-analysis and the evaluation of psychotherapy outcome: Limitations and liabilities. *Journal of Consulting and Clinical Psychology, 51,* 54-64.

Wilson, J. J., & Gil, K. M. (1996). The efficacy of psychological and pharmacological interventions for the treatment of chronic disease-related and non-disease-related pain. *Clinical Psychology Review, 16,* 573-579.

Winnicott, D. W. (1965). *The maturational processes and the facilitating environment.* New York: International Universities Press.

Wittchen, H. U. (1994). Reliability and validity studies of the WHO-Composite International Diagnostic Interview (CIDI): A critical review. *Journal of Psychiatric Research, 28,* 57-84.

Wittchen, H. U., Kessler, R. C., Zhao, S., & Abelson, J. (1995). Reliability and clinical validity of UM-CIDI DSM-III-R generalized anxiety disorder. *Journal of Psychiatric Research, 29,* 95-110.

Wolfe, D. A. (1987). *Child abuse: Implications for child development and psychopathology.* Newbury Park, CA: Sage.

Wolpe, J. (1958). *Psychotherapy by reciprocal inhibition.* Stanford, CA: Stanford University Press.

Wolpe, J. (1982). *The practice of behavior therapy* (3rd ed.). New York: Pergamon Press.

Wolpe, J., & Lang, P. J. (1969). *Fear Survey Schedule.* San Diego, CA: Educational and Industrial Testing Service.

Wolpe, J., & Lazarus, A. A. (1966). *Behavior therapy techniques: A guide to the treatment of neuroses.* New York: Pergamon Press.

Wong, B. Y. L. (1986). Problems and issues in the definition of learning disabilities. In J. K. Torgesen & B. Y. L. Wong (Eds.), *Psychological and educational perspectives on learning disabilities* (pp. 3–26). New York: Academic Press.

Wood, J. M., Lilenfeld, S., Garb, H., & Nezworski, M. (2000). The Rorschach Test in clinical diagnoses: A critical review with a backward look at Garfield (1947). *Journal of Clinical Psychology, 56,* 395–430.

Wood, J. M., Nezworski, M. T., & Stejskal, W. J. (1996). The comprehensive system for the Rorschach: A critical examination. *Psychological Science, 7,* 3–10.

Wood, L. F., & Jacobson, N. S. (1985). Marital distress. In D. Barlow (Ed.), *Clinical handbook of psychological disorders* (pp. 344–416). New York: Guilford Press.

Woodcock, R., & Johnson, M. (1977). *Woodcock-Johnson Psycho-educational Battery.* Allen, TX: DLM/Teaching Resources.

Woodcock, R. W., & Johnson, M. B. (1989). *Woodcock-Johnson Psycho-educational Battery— Revised.* Allen, TX: DLM/Teaching Resources.

Woodworth, R. S. (1920). *Personal data sheet.* Chicago: Stoelting.

World Health Organization (1994). *Schedules for clinical assessment in neuropsychiatry: Manual.* Geneva: WHO.

World Health Organization—Alcohol, Drug, and Mental Health Administration. (1997). *The composite International Diagnostic Interview (Version 1, 12 month).* Geneva: Author.

Wortman, C. B., & Lehman, D. R. (1985). Reactions to victims of life crises: Support attempts that fail. In I. G. Sarason & B. R. Sarason (Eds.), *Social support: Theory, research, and applications* (pp. 463–489). Dordrecht, The Netherlands: Martinus Nijhoff.

Wrightsman, L., Nietzel, M. T., & Fortune, W. (1998). *Psychology and the legal system* (4th ed.). Pacific Grove, CA: Brooks/Cole.

Wrightsman, L. S. (2001). *Forensic Psychology.* Belmont, CA: Wadsworth/Thomson.

Wrightsman, L. S., Nietzel, M., Fortune, W., & Greene, E. (2002). *Psychology and the legal system* (5th ed.). Pacific Grove, CA: Brooks/Cole.

Wulfert, E., Greenway, D. E., & Dougher, M. J. (1996). A logical functional analysis of reinforcement-based disorders: Alcoholism and pedophilia. *Journal of Consulting and Clinical Psychology, 64,* 1140–1151.

Wyatt, F. (1968). What is clinical psychology? In A. Z. Guiora & M. A. Brandwin (Eds.), *Perspectives in clinical psychology* (pp. 222–238). Princeton, NJ: D. Van Nostrand.

Yalom, I. D. (1995). *The theory and practice of group psychotherapy* (4th ed.). New York: Basic Books.

Ying, Y. (1989). Nonresponse on the Center for Epidemiological Studies depression scale in Chinese Americans. *International Journal of Social Psychiatry, 35,* 156–163.

Yoav, G. (2000). The weighting of pathological and non-pathological information in clinical judgment. *Acta Psychologica, 104,* 87–101.

Yoken, C., & Berman, J. S. (1987). Third-party payment and the outcome of psychotherapy. *Journal of Consulting and Clinical Psychology, 55,* 571–576.

Yoshikawa, H. (1994). Prevention as cumulative protection: Effects of early family support and education on chronic delinquency and its risks. *Psychological Bulletin, 115,* 28–54.

Yoshimasu, K., et al. (2001). Relation of type A behavior pattern and job-related psychosocial factors to nonfatal myocardial infarction: A case-control study of Japanese male workers and women. *Psychosomatic Medicine, 63,* 797–804.

Young, L. D. (1992). Psychological factors in rheumatoid arthritis. *Journal of Consulting and Clinical Psychology, 60,* 619-627.

Yutrzenka, B. A. (1995). Making a case for training in ethnic and cultural diversity in increasing treatment efficacy. *Journal of Consulting and Clinical Psychology, 63,* 197-206.

Zabow, T., & Cohen, A. (1993). South African psychiatrists' criteria for predicting dangerousness. *Medicine & Law, 12,* 417-430.

Zametkin, A. J., Ernst, M., & Silver, R. (1998). Laboratory and diagnostic testing in child and adolescent psychiatry: A review of the past 10 years. *Journal of the American Academy of Child and Adolescent Psychiatry, 37,* 464-472.

Zanarini, M. C., Skodol, A. E., Bender, D., Dolan, R., & Sanislow, C., et al. (2000). The collaborative longitudinal personality disorders study: Reliability of axis I and II diagnoses. *Journal of Personality Disorders, 14,* 291-299.

Zax, M., & Specter, G. A. (1974). *An introduction to community psychology.* New York: John Wiley.

Zeanah, C. H. (1996). Beyond insecurity: A reconceptualization of attachment disorders of infancy. *Journal of Consulting and Clinical Psychology, 64,* 42-51.

Zetin, M., & Glenn, T. (1999). Development of a computerized psychatric diagnostic interview for use by mental health and primary care clinicians. *CyberPsychology and Behavior, 2,* 223-233.

Zigler, E., Taussig, C., & Black, K. (1992). Early childhood intervention: A promising preventative for juvenile delinquency. *American Psychologist, 47,* 997-1006.

Zilboorg, G., & Henry, G. W. (1941). *A history of medical psychology.* New York: W. W. Norton.

Zimet, C. N., & Throne, F. M. (1965). Preconference materials. Conference on the Professional Preparation of Clinical Psychologists. Washington, DC: American Psychological Association.

Zimmerman, M. (1983). Methodological issues in the assessment of life events: A review of issues and research. *Clinical Psychology Review, 3,* 339-370.

Ziskin, J., & Faust, D. (1988). *Coping with psychiatric and psychological testimony* (4th ed., Vols. 1-3). Marina del Rey, CA: Law & Psychology Press.

Zlotnick, C., Elkin, I., & Shea, T. M. (1998). Does the gender of a patient or the gender of a therapist affect the treatment of patients with major depression? *Journal of Consulting and Clinical Psychology, 66,* 655-659.

Zook, A., II, & Walton, J. M. (1989). Theoretical orientations and work settings of clinical and counseling psychologists: A current perspective. *Professional Psychology: Research and Practice, 20,* 23-31.

Zuardi, A. W., Loureiro, S. R., & Rodrigues, C. R. C. (1995). Reliability, validity, and factorial dimensions of the Interactive Observation Scale for Psychiatric Inpatients. *Acta Psychiatrica Scandinavica, 91,* 247-251.

Zubin, J. (1969). The role of models in clinical psychology. In L. L'Abate (Ed.), *Models of clinical psychology* (pp. 5-12). Atlanta: Georgia State College.

Zubin, J., & Spring, B. (1977). Vulnerability—A new view of schizophrenia. *Journal of Abnormal Psychology, 86,* 103-126.

Zuckerman, M., & Lubin, B. (1965). *Manual for the multiple affect adjective checklist.* San Diego, CA: Educational and Industrial Testing Service.

Zytowski, D. G. (1985). *Kuder Occupational Interest Survey manual supplement.* Chicago: Science Research Associates.

Author Index

Subject Index

Table X Significant Dates and Events in the History of Clinical Psychology

1879 Wilhelm Wundt establishes first formal psychology laboratory at the University of Leipzig.

1885 Sir Francis Galton establishes first mental testing center at the South Kensington Museum, London.

1890 James McKeen Cattell coins term *mental test.*

1892 American Psychological Association (APA) founded.

1895 Breuer and Freud publish *Studies in Hysteria.*

1896 Lightner Witmer founds first psychological clinic, University of Pennsylvania.

1905 Binet-Simon intelligence scale published in France.

1907 Witmer founds first clinical journal, *The Psychological Clinic.*

1908 First clinical internship offered at Vineland Training School.

1909 William Healy founds first child-guidance center, the Juvenile Psychopathic Institute, Chicago. Freud lectures at Clark University.

1910 Goddard's English translation of the 1908 revision of the Binet-Simon intelligence scale published.

1912 J.B. Watson publishes *Psychology as a Behaviorist Views It.*

1916 Terman's Stanford-Binet intelligence test published.

1917 Clinicians break away from APA to form American Association of Clincal Psychology (AACP).

1919 AACP rejoins APA as its clinical section.

1920 Watson and Rayner demonstrate that a child's fear can be learned.

1921 James McKeen Cattell forms Psychological Corporation.

1924 David Levy introduces Rorschach Inkblot Test to America. Mary Cover Jones employs learning principles to remove children's fears.

1931 Clinical section of APA appoints committee on training standards.

1935 Thematic Apperception Test (TAT) published.

1937 Clinical section of APA breaks away to form American Association for Applied Psychology (AAAP).

1938 First Buros *Mental Measurement Yearbook* published.

1939 Wechsler-Bellevue Intelligence Test published.

1942 Carl Rogers publishes *Counseling and Psychotherapy,* outlining an alternative to psychodynamic therapy.

1943 Minnesota Multiphasic Personality Inventory (MMPI) published.

1945 AAAP rejoins APA.
Journal of Clinical Psychology published.
Connecticut State Board of Examiners in Psychology issues first certificate to practice psychology.

1946 Veterans Administration and National Institute of Mental Health begin support for training of clinical psychologists.

1947 American Board of Examiners in Professional Psychology organized.
APA begins to evaluate graduate programs in clinical psychology.
Shakow Report recommends clinical training standards to APA.
Certification Committee of Canadian Psychological Association recommends standards for clinical psychologists in Canada.

1949 Colorado conference on training in clinical psychology convenes, recommends "Boulder Model."
Sixteen P–F personality test pulished.

1950 APA publishes first standards for approved internships in clinical psychology.

1952 American Psychiatric Association's *Diagnostic and Statistical Manual (DSM–I)* published.

1953 APA *Ethical Standards for Psychologists* published.

1955 Wechsler Adult Intelligence Test published.

1956 Stanford Training Conference.

1958 Miami Training Conference.
Clinical Division of APA holds NIMH-sponsored conference about research on psychotherapy.